IN ARDUIS AUDAX

HELEN & MICHAEL
OPPENHEIMER

CHARLES I

From the portrait by Van Dyck at Windsor Castle. Reproduced by gracious permission of
His Majesty the King.

(For a notice of this picture, see Appendix I.)

CHARLES I
AND THE
COURT OF ROME

A STUDY IN 17TH CENTURY DIPLOMACY

BY

GORDON ALBION

DOCTEUR EN SCIENCES HISTORIQUES (LOUVAIN)

WITH A FOREWORD

BY

David Mathew, M. A., Litt. D.

LONDON

BURNS OATES & WASHBOURNE LTD.

PUBLISHERS TO THE HOLY SEE

1935

TO

MY MOTHER AND MY FATHER

CONTENTS

ILLUSTRATIONS

FOREWORD

The relations, semi-official but very public, between King Charles I and Pope Urban VIII form a singular interlude in a period of otherwise incessant hostilities between the English Crown and the Papacy. The wordy conflict between James I and Cardinal Bellarmine had, perhaps, hardly prepared the cultivated circles in England for that uneasy amity between the Courts which was to develop in the years before the Civil Wars. The genesis of that association had lain in the desire of the old King for an equal marriage for his heir, and the Lutheran princesses could hardly be considered as brides suitable for the throne of Britain, very conscious of her place as a great power. An alliance with Spain or France thus became desirable and contact with Rome and the whole question of dispensatious and religious arrangements and promises arose inevitably in the marriage train of a Catholic princess.

Dr Albion's researches have dealt principally with such effects as the contact of Charles I with Rome resulting from, and conditioned by, his marriage. The letters in the Barberini Archives throw light upon the actions of the papal agents and the impression produced upon them by life in England. Clearly as such a man as George Con could see the Catholic minded circles about the Court, his despatches only serve to indicate the confused spectacle of English life as seen by a foreigner. On the question of the royal marriage, for instance, the attitude of Court and Parliament was very different, a result, in part, of the varying ease with which the courtiers and the country gentlemen adjusted their outlook to a changed political situation. Throughout all the negotiations with Rome of various degrees of seriousness, we find the background of that English prosperous opinion in town or country which was to support the Parliament in the Civil Wars ; strongly anti-Catholic, insular, suspicious of foreigners, with a conservative aversion to all taxation except the Recusancy Fines, and increasingly distrustful of the facile words of the dilettante and art-loving King. Throughout the negotiations with Rome this current of hostility and suspicion in England was always present. On this matter King Charles's point of view was clear. The sacramental Anglicanism in which he had been brought up satisfied him completely; but the assurance of his religious standpoint assisted him to show a cool and dignified forbearance towards the adherents of the Old Religion. A certain moral fastidiousness, which his father lacked, perhaps led him to refrain from interfering in the concerns of gentlemen. The custom of taking minors of rank from their Catholic guardians and handing them over to the Archbishop of Canterbury now ceased. At the same time the King was anxious that his personal attendants should frequent the Anglican communion, and he was inclined to show favour to such Catholics as had conformed to the Established Church. Beyond this he did not go.

The position of the Queen was important on account of King Charles's devotion to her, which developed after the early stormy period of their married life. The Van Dyck portraits enable us so easily to picture Henrietta Maria, slight and very graceful with her delicate features, the dark vivacious eyes, the chestnut hair. Her petulance and gaiety are cleary shown in the early paintings. She was quick-thinking and imprudent, indiscreet in her confidences, devoted to the play, childish at times yet half-sophisticated, always preferring London to the country. It is no wonder that she was never popular in England. Her religion was sincere, in some ways perhaps a little superficial; her outlook and thought wholly French, and for the first eight years of her reign her spoken English was very poor. She was comprehensible and, in fact, attractive to the Court gallants, but infinitely remote from the Catholic squires in the country who, nevertheless, gave to her and to King Charles so undeviating a loyalty. And if remote from the Catholics, she had still less in common with the Protestant country gentry of the shires.

Meanwhile the years of peace in which the negotiations with Rome were placed brought advantages to the Old Religion. The King's passivity and the Queen's zeal were the occasion, although not the cause, of a slow movement towards the Church. The half-submerged Catholic tendencies of certain families now cleared. Thus the Lord Treasurer Portland, who was practically the chief minister from 1628 until his death in 1635, declared himself a Catholic in his last illness. Lord Cottington and the Secretary of State, Windebank, were also numbered among an inner circle of Catholic sympathisers: both *died in communion with the see of Rome. There were wide ramifications of this outlook among the courtiers and their dependents. It was a curiously, even ominously peaceful time into which such adherents of the Old Religion as Inigo Jones and the playwright Philip Massinger and Sir John Beaumont the poet had survived.*

These slight Catholic increases, the Queen's favour, the convert courtiers like Walter Montagu, Her Majesty's chapels and, subsequently the establishment of the papal agent's public oratory, all helped to mislead Roman opinion. The King's interest in theological questions and readiness for the polite forms of disputation encouraged delusive hopes; while the desire on the King's part for the recovery of the Palatinate for his nephew lent tenacity to the English side of the negotiations. It is clear that the political motives were appreciated at the Roman Court, but it was the religious situation in England which remained essentially obscure. It would seem also that Laud's position was misunderstood. The light fell upon the Court circle and its courteous and sometimes frivolous approach to Catholicism. It was only a small segment of English life which stood revealed in this fitful light before the breaking of the storm.

David Mathew.

AUTHOR'S FOREWORD

The study now submitted to the University of Louvain for the *Doctorat en Sciences historiques* makes no endeavour to deal with the inner history of the Catholic Church in England under the second Stuart King : that is a subject already in the hands of its historian. The task attempted here, at once wider and more restricted, is an attempt to estimate the value to be placed upon the personal relations between Charles I and the Papacy and, in particular, to discover the measure of reality behind Rome's hopes of the King's — even of the kingdom's — conversion. The problem was neither easily nor directly to be solved, — there were too many extraneous interests, too many mixed motives involved for that. Religion, as Mr Churchill has aptly remarked in his *Marlborough*, played as large a part in the life of the 17th century as sport does now. One might add that its international ramifications were as tortuous and as dangerous.

The various contacts between the Stuart King and the Holy See were found to be of the deepest concern to Spain and France and the German Protestants and, in studying them, one soon found oneself entangled in a network of diplomacy that stretched across Europe.

The Spanish Marriage Treaty had to be examined again for several reasons : it gave Charles his first view of Catholicism at close quarters ; it provided the first opportunity for an attempt at his conversion ; it was his first experience of what he always criticized in the Catholic powers — their using the Pope for their own ends. In this connection, the well-known story has been supplemented from Arezio's exact study of the part Rome was forced to play in support of Spanish duplicity. [1] Also, greater

---

[1] L. Arezio, *L'azione diplomatica del Vaticano nella questione del matrimonio spagnuolo di Carlo Stuart, Principe di Galles*, p. 38 : " Egli (*i.e.* Gard-

emphasis has been given to the views of the Spanish Friars, Francisco de Jesús and Boverius, as regards the treaty itself and the attempt to convert the Prince.

In the negotiations for the French match Charles had again to deal with a Catholic power and indirectly with the Holy See ; the reactions of the latter have been studied from unpublished sources, while Goll is relied upon for some amplifications of Gardiner. [1]

In Chapter III the effect of Charles's broken promises on the Pope has been noted, as well as the latter's attempt to solve a double problem by urging France and Spain to join forces in punishing the English King. For this, recourse was had to the despatches of the Nuncio Spada in the Barberini Library, whose unending sources for the diplomatic history of the time enabled valuable sidelights to be thrown on the religious situation in England, as well as on its effect abroad, by the comments of diplomats in the employ of the Holy See of such experience as Padre Giacinto da Casale and Padre Alessandro d'Ales, besides the official notes it was the duty of the Nuncios of Brussels and Paris to forward to Rome. [2]

---

iner) non conosceva affatto i documenti che io ho sott' occhio, e stando a quelli de' quali s'avvalse, non poteva certamente mettere in chiaro gl' intrighi, cui era fatto segno il Principe Carlo da parte de' suoi ospiti, più che dalla Corte pontificia."

[1] J. GOLL, *Die französische Heirat : Frankreich und England*, 1624 *und* 1625, p. 1 : " Gardiner wollte und konnte auf Manches nicht eingehen was doch der Mittheilung werth zu sein scheint ; in einigen Punkten, glaube ich bringt meine Erzählung wesentliche Ergänzungen. So über das letzte Stadium der Unterhandlung, wo wir erfahren, durch welche Zugeständnisse die französische Regierung die päpstliche Dispensation erkauft hat."

[2] One of the first acts of the Congregation of Propaganda, created on March 8, 1622, was to divide the heretic countries between the various Nuncios. England was placed under the observation of the Nuncio at Brussels (*Arch. Propag., Acta*, vol. I, ff. 3 seq. : March, 1622), but the Secretaries of State continued to regard English affairs as the province of the Paris Nuncio, for as early as Jan. 15, 1582, Gregory XIII had, at the request of Cardinal Allen, placed the religious interests of England under the charge of the Nuncio of France. This ordinary jurisdiction of the Paris Nuncio over England was confirmed seven years before the erection of Propaganda by a decree of the Holy Office (*Arch. Propag., Anglia*, vol. I, f. 275 : July 23, 1615). Cf. A. LEMAN, *Recueil des instructions générales aux nonces ordinaires de France de* 1634, p. 45, note ; C. R. FISH, *Guide to the Materials for American History in the Roman and other Archives*, pp. 119-121.

For the more direct dealings of Charles with the Holy See and the efforts made in the middle years of his reign to produce a settlement of the English Catholic question and to sound the possibilities of reunion, the Public Record Office transcripts of the despatches of the Roman agents have been fully explored, but a copyist's remark at the end of a volume of George Con's letters [1] indicated the need for returning to the originals in Rome, where again additional commentary was at hand among the Chigi MSS., and in the Diary written by Panzani in England (a valuable document whose illegibility has hitherto deterred the transcriber) and in the Propaganda Archives, an endless source of information provided by innumerable private correspondents among the English clergy, secular and regular, all of them anxious to enlighten Rome on the complex situation in England.

The part the Palatinate problem played throughout Charles's dealings with Rome, while it appears constantly in the background, has not been given greater prominence owing to the absence of the despatches of Sir William Hamilton, the Queen's Resident in Rome. He had had instructions to write to Windebank, but it seems likely that his letters were lost either in the confusion, of the Secretary's sudden departure for France or later by Charles, who had probably taken possession of them, — his usual practice with the papers of his retiring Secretaries. [2]

The final attempt by Rome to induce Charles to become a Catholic leads one naturally to the efforts of the Holy See to win support for, and encourage directly, the Irish revolt. Here this study must be left to dovetail into the able account of Rinuccini's mission to Ireland in 1645 recently published by a friend and contemporary of the author at the History Schools of Louvain, the Reverend Michael J. Hynes. [3]

It will be seen that the writer's original interest in the personal attitude of Charles I towards the Catholic Church resolved itself, willy-nilly, into an excursion among the somewhat arid paths of

[1] " There are many more letters of Con in this volume which were not allowed to be copied."

[2] S. C. LOMAS, *Trans. Royal Hist. Soc.* (New Series, vol. XII), pp. 97-132 : *The State Papers of the Early Stuarts.*

[3] M. J. HYNES, *The Mission of Rinuccini, Nuncio Extraordinary ot Ireland,* 1645-1649, Louvain, 1932.

diplomatic, almost legal, discussion of formulas, conditions and concessions, pros and cons. The result is often, one fears, the necessarily actionless presentation of interminable argument with little decided upon in the end.

That so much was said and so little concluded is expressive of the uncertain, anxious calm of those interim years that culminated in the confusion of the Civil Wars, and will explain why, for this study as a whole as well as for individual chapters dealing with a specific subject of discussion, the rounded ending has perforce and, one ventures to think, preferably given way to the " falling close. "

The author wishes to express his gratitude to Dr Amigo, Bishop of Southwark, for allowing him the opportunity of making this study, and for his constant kindness and interest.

For an introduction to the Vatican Library and Archives and for continual assistance in his work there, the author offers his sincere thanks to Monsignori Giovanni Mercati and Tisserant, Prefect and Pro-prefect of the Library, Mgr Angelo Mercati, Prefect of the Archives, Mgr Pelzer, *Scrittore* of the Library, Mgr Hebbelynck, former Rector of Louvain and now at work on the Vatican Oriental MSS., Mgr Vaes, Secretary of the *Institut historique belge de Rome*, and to the Prefect of the Propaganda Archives. Also to the Reverend Ivor Daniel for his kind assistance and to Dr A. O. Meyer, Professor of the University of Munich, for general advice on a subject akin to his own. The author's special thanks are due to those who have helped him in the more immediate preparation of this book for presentation as a Doctorate thesis : to his Louvain professors, Monsieur van der Essen, Senior History Professor, Canon De Meyer, professor of Church History and Canon Van Cauwenbergh, the University Librarian. For the unstinted kindness and care of Professor De Meyer's direction during the whole period of his studies the author will be forever grateful. Lastly, a deep debt of gratitude is due to the Reverend David Mathew, M.A., Litt. D., Chaplain to the Catholics of the University of London, for kindly reading through the MS., for many helpful suggestions and, in particular, for the most apt and pleasing foreword with which he introduces this book.

BIBLIOGRAPHY

A. ARCHIVAL SOURCES   (i) Unprinted
                                     (ii) Printed

B. LITERARY SOURCES   Contemporary Works
                                     Memoirs
                                     Pamphlets, etc.

C. NON-CONTEMPORANEOUS and MODERN WORKS

Archival Sources. — (i) Unprinted.

1. — LONDON: BRITISH MUSEUM

SLOANE MSS. (*Index to the Sloane MSS. in the British Museum* by EDWARD J. L. SCOTT, London, 1904.)

Nᵒˢ 1470, ff. 37-53 b : Passages concerning the contribution of Roman Catholics towards his Northern Journey (1639).

1467, f. 144 : The Pope's Cabinet Council discabinetted (1640).

3299, f. 177 : Family of Barberini : account of their sudden flight from Rome, temp. Innoc. X.

STOWE MSS.

Nᵒˢ 96, ff. 296-303 ; 305-306 : Instructions from Rome on the Spanish Marriage.

132, ff. 219-274 : Bassompierre's Instructions.

145, ff. 23, 286 : French Marriage Articles.

492, f. 112 : Fr Philip before the Commons.

96, ff. 46-84 ; 125-130 : Characters of Urban VIII and his nephews.

2. — LONDON: PUBLIC RECORD OFFICE

ROMAN TRANSCRIPTS (referred to in text as *P.R.O. Rom. Trans.*)

Trans. 9, Nᵒ 16 : *Discurso sobre el Casamiento que se trata entre el Principe de Gales y la Serenissima Infanta de España del Conde Don Antonio Xerley Dirigido. Al Señor Duque Conde de Olivares des Consejo d'Estado y Guerra de su Magestad su Sumillier de Corps y Cavaller 30 Mayor.*

Trans. 9, Nᵒ 17 : Panzani Correspondence, 1634-1636.

Trans. 9, Nᵒˢ 18-20 : Rossetti Correspondence, 1639-1641 (3 vols), 1641-1644 (3 vols).

Trans. 9, Nᵒ 124 : Con Correspondence, 1636, etc. (V. General Series).

Trans. 9, Nᵒ 91 : General Series, 1626-1636.

Trans. 9, Nᵒ 92 : *Idem*, 1637-1643.

Trans. 9, Nᵒˢ 126-129 : Barberini Miscellanea, temp. Car. I.

Trans.10, Nᵒ 10 : Barberini's replies to Panzani.

3. — LONDON : SOUTHWARK DIOCESAN ARCHIVES

Gradwell MSS. (*i.e.* Roman Transcripts made by Bishop Grad-well, Rector of the English College, Rome, for Lingard, who subsequently gave them to Canon Tierney of Southwark.)

4. — ROME : PROPAGANDA ARCHIVES

SCRITTURE ANTICHE : Vols 84, 100, 101, 132, 133, 137, etc. *passim.*

5. — VATICAN ARCHIVES

EPISTOLAE AD PRINCIPES, vols XXXVII-LV.
NUNZIATURA DI FRANCIA, vols 66 and 89.
FONDO BOLOGNETTI, 108.
   Nº 8 : French Relation of the State of Catholicism in England.
   Nº 9 : Similar relation by Alessandro Bichi, Bishop of Carpen-tras, Nuncio at Paris, Sept. 28, 1632.
INSTRUMENTA MISCELLANEA.
   Nº 6635 : Autographs of Charles I to Innocent X and Card. Spada.

6. — VATICAN LIBRARY

CODICES BARBERINI LATINI (referred to in text as *B.L.*)
   5188, ff. 321-346. On the Spanish Marriage.
   5335, carte 123-129 : On the French Marriage.
   6016 : P. Giacinto di Casale al Card. Francesco Barberini, Jan.-Nov. 1624.
   6139 : Same to same, Brussels, 1623-1624.
   6183 : Minutes of Instructions to Giacinto on affairs of the Palatinate.
   6259 : Barberini to Claude Néri (*i. e.* Toby Mathew), July 20, 1624 (f. 29 : on English Affairs).
   6469 : Carlo Moroni (Bibliotecario della Barberini), Lettere a diversi, e principalmente al Card. Fr. Barberini dal 1641 al 1661.
   6792 : Giacinto Despatches, 1613-1623.
   6793 : *Idem,* 1624-1625.
   7048 : Padre Alessandro d'Ales, Cappuccino (*alias* Francesco Rota), Lettere quasi tutte al Card. Fr. Barberini : July 31, 1624 - Jan. 11, 1629 (ff. 58-64 : concerning England).

8059 : Nuncio Spada to Card. Francesco Barberini, May 1, 1624 - Nov. 11, 1626.

8060-8065 : Cardinal Secretary of State to Spada, May 16, 1624 - Dec. 28, 1626 (8065 con diversi allegati intorno agli affari di Spagna e d'Inghilterra).

8515 : Original autographs of James I, Charles I, Edward Conway, Henrietta Maria, etc.

8593, ff. 59-74 : Letters of Fra Diego de la Fuente to Urban VIII and Card. Fr. Barberini, Oct. 20, 1612 - July 27, 1624.

8616 : Various documents concerning English affairs temp. Caroli I.

8618, ff. 156-159 : Tobia Mathei. Lettera ò informazione (on Span. Marr.) dal 15 Aprile 1617, scritta da Bruxelles.

8619-8620 : Documents chiefly concerning the affairs of the English Catholics.

8622 : Lettere di Tommaso Courtneo (Coll. Ingl. Roma), 1640-1663.

8623, ff. 45, 47-48 : Geo. Musket to Card. Fr. Barberini, Feb. 10 and Apr. 9, 1642 de rege et regina Angliae aliisque rebus).

8625 : Instruzione originale data dal Card. Fr. Barberini a Tommaso Camerario mandato da Roma in Inghilterra per portare la statua del Re Carlo I, etc.

8632 : Minutes of Letters from Urban VIII and Card. Fr. Barberini to Henrietta Maria, Marie de' Medici, Fr Philip, etc.

8656 : Lettere e minuti di lettere... del Card. Fr. Barberini... al Card. di Bagno, e risposte di questi, con alcuni allegati al sudd(etto) Barberini sopra il modo di remediare alle dissensioni tra il clero secolare e regolare e di migliorare lo stato dei Cattolici in Inghilterra e lettere di altri personaggi, cioè, del Conte Angus, di Roberto Douglas, e del Conte Sterlin sopra lo stesso negozio, dal 5 Gen. 1633 al 22 Febr. 1634.

8666 : Patrick Con, dal 22 Giugno 1648 al 26 Agosto 1650.

CODICES CHIGIANI

Nº d'Ordini 2662 : Minuti di Lettere e di cifre scritte da Gregorio Panzani in Londra il 1636 al Cardinal Barberini e di altri circa i Cattolici di quei regni. (Al principio è una scheda illustrata scritta da Alessandro VII che dà notizie dell' autore.)

N° d'Ordini 2879 (cc. 175-198) : Scrittura data dal S^r d'Igby (*i.e.* Sir Kenelm Digby) residente d'Inghilterra presso Innoc. X, 1648.

N° d'Ordini 3007 (cc. 1-22) : Instruzioni a Mons. Maffeo Barberini, arcivescovo di Nazaret, destinato nunzio in Francia.

CODICES URBINATI LATINI

861, ff. 360-67 : *Discorso sopra il matrimonio trattato fra il principe d'Inghilterra e la Principessa di Toscana l'anno 1612.*

Archival Sources. — (ii) Printed.

1. — COLLECTIONS OF OFFICIAL DOCUMENTS

Bullarium Ordinis Capuccinorum, vol. III, Rome, 1740.

Calendar of Clarendon State Papers, Oxford, 1872, 3 vols.

Calendar of State Papers relating to English Affairs, principally at Rome in the Vatican Archives and Library, London, 1916.

Calendar of State Papers, Domestic Series :

Charles I (1625-1649), vols I-XXII, London, 1858-1893.

Calendar of State Papers belonging to His Majesty the King preserved at Windsor Castle, vol. VII (*Historical MSS. Commission*), London, 1923.

Catalogue of Engraved British Portraits in the British Museum, London, 1908-1925, 6 vols with supplements and indexes.

Catalogue of Prints and Drawings in the British Museum, Division I. — *Satires*, vol. I, 1320-1689, London, 1870.

Catholic Record Society, vol. I, *Miscellanea*, London, 1905 :

N° 5. V. *Papers concerning Catholics during the reign of K. Charles I* : A. *Relations of a brawl between the King's officers and the servants of the French Ambr., concerning the Catholics who resorted to Mass at Durham House,* 1626. With contemporary plan.

N° 6 : *The Notebook of John Southcote, D. D.,* 1628-1636, edited with permission of the Bishop of Southwark by the Rev. J. H. POLLEN, S. J., from the original in the Diocesan Archives.

Vol. XXXIII. *Memorials of Father Augustine Baker and other documents relating to the English Benedictines*, ed. DOM JUSTIN MCCANN, O.S.B. and DOM HUGH CONNOLLY, O.S.B., London, 1933.

Clarendon State Papers, Oxford, 1767-1786, 3 vols.

FISH, C.R.

Guide to the Materials for American History in Roman and other Archives (*Carnegie Institution* 128), Washington, 1911.

HARDWICKE, PHILIP YORKE, EARL OF

Miscellaneous State Papers (1510-1726), London, 1778, 2 vols.

NALSON, J.

An Impartial Collection of the Great Affairs of State, 1639-1649, London, 1682, 2 vols.

RUSHWORTH, JOHN

Historical Collections (1618-1649), London, 1659 ; new ed., 8 vols, 1721.

RYMER, THOS

Foedera, vols XIX-XX, London, 1732.

THURLOE, J.

Collection of State Papers (1638-1666), London, 1742, 7 vols in folio.

2. — CONTEMPORARY CORRESPONDENCE, PRIVATE DIARIES ETC., SINCE PUBLISHED.

ARMANNI, VINCENZO

Lettere politiche dal 1624 al 1644, pubbl. dal DOTT. GIUSEPPE MAZZATINTI (*Archivio storico italiano*, seria 4a, vol. XII-XVIII), Firenze, 1883.

CHARLES I

Charles I in 1646 : Letters of Charles I to Queen Henrietta Maria, ed. JOHN BRUCE (*Camden Society*, Nº 63), London, 1856.

The Works of King Charles I (Letters, Speeches, etc.), Aberdeen, 1766, 2 vols.

The Papers which passed at Newcastle betwixt his Sacred Majestie and Mr Al Henderson : Concerning the Change of Church Government. Anno Dom. 1646, London, 1649.

DENIS, PAUL

Nouvelles de Rome, précédées de listes de tous les fonction-

naires de la Cour de Rome (Documents pour servir à l'his-toire religieuse des XVIIe *et* XVIIIe *siècles*), Paris, 1913.

D'EWES, SIR SIMONDS

> *The Journal of Sir Simonds D'Ewes from the beginning of the Long Parliament to the opening of the trial of the Earl of Strafford,* ed. WALLACE NOTESTEIN, London and New Haven, 1923.

HENDERSON A. (v. *supra*, CHARLES I.)

HENRIETTA MARIA

> *Letters of Henrietta Maria, including private correspondence with Charles I,* ed. M. A. E. GREEN, London, 1857.

LAUD, WILLIAM

> *Diary* (Wharton's translation with notes by DR BLISS), *Works,* vol. III (*Library of Anglo-Catholic Theology* 136), Oxford, 1853.

LEMAN, AUGUSTE

> *Recueil des instructions générales aux nonces ordinaires de France de 1624 à 1634,* publ. par A. LEMAN, Paris, 1920.

MAZARIN

> *Lettres du Cardinal Mazarin pendant son ministère,* publ. par A. CHÉRUEL (*Coll. de Documents inédits sur l'histoire de France publiée par les soins du ministère de l'instruction publique*), Paris, 1879.

RICHELIEU

> *Lettres, Instructions diplomatiques et Papiers d'État du Cardinal de Richelieu,* publ. par M. AVENEL, Paris, 1856.

ROUS, JOHN

> *Diary of John Rous, incumbent of Santon Downham, Suffolk from 1625 to 1642,* ed. M. A. EVERETT GREEN (*Camden Society,* N⁰ 66), London, 1836.

B. Literary Sources

Memoirs, Contemporary, Works Pamphlets, etc.

ANON.

> *Advis donné au Roy sur l'Estat present des affaires de Rome sous Urbain VIII,* S. L., S. D.
>
> *An Appeale to every impartiall, iudicious and Godly Reader,*

— *whether the Presbyterie or Prelacie be the better Church-Government, etc.,* London, 1641.

The Bishop of London, His Legacy ; Or certaine Motives of D. King, late Bishop of London, for his change of Religion, and dying in the Catholike and Roman Church. Penned by himselfe, and delivered over to a friend, in his own lifetyme. With a Conclusion to his Brethren, the L. L. Bishops of England. Perm. Super., N. P., 1622 ; *idem,* 1624. (Attributed by Protestant writers to GEORGE MUSKET *vere* FISHER.)

The Bishop's Potion : or A Dialogue between The Bishop of Canterbury and his phisitian, wherein He desireth the Doctor to have a care of his Bodie and to preserve from him being let blood in the neck, when the signe is in Taurus, London, 1641.

A Coppy of 1.*The letter sent by the Queenes Majestie concerning the collection of the Recusants Money for the Scottish war, Apr.* 17, 1639.

2. *The Letters sent by Sir Kenelme Digby and M*ʳ *Mount-ague concerning the Contribution.*

3. *The letter sent by those assembled in London to every shire.*

4. *The names of the Collectors in each County in England and Wales*

AND 5. *The Message sent from the Queenes Majestie to the house of Commons by Master Comptroller the* 5. *of Febr.* 1639, London, 1641.

The Equallity of the Ministery plainly described, both by Scriptures, Fathers and Councils, layd open to this present Parliament to stop the mouthes of all fayne-sayers whatsoever by D. F., Minister, N. P., 1641.

The First and Large Petition of the City of London and of other Inhabitants thereabouts : for a reformation in Church-government, as also for the abolishment of Episcopacy, N. P., 1641.

A Great Conspiracy of the Papists against the worthy Members of both Houses of Parliament. And also against the City of London and generally the whole Kingdome. Discovered by divers wicked and bloody letters, which by God's providence came to light, and was read in the House of Commons the 10. and 11. January 1641, London, 1641.

The Lamentable Complaints of Nick Froth the Tapster, and Rulerost the Cooke. Concerning the restraints lately set forth against drinking, potting, and piping on the Sabbath Day, and against selling meate, N. P., 1641.

A Modest Advertisement concerning the present Controversie about Church Government etc., London, 1641.

The Passionate Remonstrance made by his Holinesse in the Conclave at Rome upon the late proceedings, and great Covenant of Scotland, etc., Edinburgh, 1641.

The Petition of the Prelates briefly examined, N. P., 1641.

The Pope's Brief : or Rome's inquiry after the death of their Catholiques here in England during these times of warre... with a catalogue of the vicars generall and archdeacons, London, 1643.

The Pope's Nuntioes or the negotiation of Seignior Panzani, Seignior Con, 1634-1636, London, 1643.

The Protestants' Plea for Papists and Priests, N. P., 1621.

The Popes Proclamation : together with the Lawes and Ordinances established by him and his Shavelings, concerning his adherents and rights which hee claimeth in England. whereunto is added six articles exhibited against Cheapside Crosse, whereby it stands guilty of high Treason, and ought to be beheaded, N. P., 1641.

A True Relation of the French Embassage with the confutation of some points of Father Phillips his letter, N. P., 1641.

A True Relation of some passages at Madrid in the year 1623, *with a discoverye of the ways which the Papish* (sic) *Bishop used to bring poperie into this nation,* London, 1655.

BALDINUCCI, F.

Filippo Baldinucci's Vita des Gio. Lorenzo Bernini mit Uebersetzung und Kommentar von ALOIS RIEGL, Wien, 1912.

BASSOMPIERRE, F. DE

Journal de ma vie : Mémoires du Maréchal de Bassompierre, 1e *édit. publ. pour la Société de l'histoire de France,* Paris, 1875, 4 vols.

Négociation du Maréchal de Bassompierre envoyé en Angleterre, Cologne, 1668.

BAYLIE, THOS

Certamen Religiosum, or a conference between His Late Majestie Charles King of England, and Henry late Marquess and Earl of Worcester, concerning religion, at his Majesties being at Raglan Castle, 1646, London, 1649.

BELLARMINE

Apologia Roberti S.R.E. Cardinalis Bellarmini pro responsione sua ad librum Iacobi Magnae Britanniae Regis, cuius titulus est Triplici nodo triplex cuneus, in qua Apologia refellitur Praefatio Monitoria Regis eiusdem. Accessit seorsim eadem ipsa responsio, quae sub nomine Matthaei Torti anno superiore prodierit, Coloniae Agrippinae,1610.

BOVERIUS (or BOËRO), FRAY ZACHARIAS BOVERIO DE SALUZO

Orthodoxa consultatio de ratione verae fidei et religionis amplectendae, ad ser. Carolum Stuartum, Walliae principem, Jacobi, Magnae Britanniae regis filium : ac regni successorem iuratum : in suo in Hispanias adventu, Madrid, c. 1623, 4º ; edition used here, Coloniae Agrippinae,1626,12mo.

BRISTOL

The Earl of Bristol's Defence of his negociations in Spain, ed. S. R. GARDINER (*Camden Miscellany*, Nº 6 ; *Camden Society*, Old Series, Nº 104), London, 1871.

CHARLES I

Eikon Basilike or *The King's Book*, ed. E. ALMACK (King's Classics), London, 1904.

CLARENDON, EDWARD HYDE, EARL OF

History of the Rebellion, ed. Oxford, 1888, 6 vols.

CON, GEORGE

Assertionum Catholicarum libri tres, Romae, 1629.

Georgii Conaei, de Duplici statu religionis apud Scotos libri duo, Romae, 1628.

DAVENPORT, CHRISTOPHER (*i.e.* FRANCISCUS A SANCTA CLARA)

Articles of the Anglican Church paraphrastically considered and explained, ed. by FREDERICK GEORGE LEE, London, 1 865.

Deus, Natura, Gratia, Lugduni, 1634.

D'EWES, SIR SIMONDS

Autobiography and Correspondence during the reigns of James I and Charles I, ed. J. O. HOLLIWELL, London, 1845, 2 vols.

DIGBY, SIR KENELM
>Conference with a Lady about Choice of Religion, Paris, 1638.
>Private Memoirs, London, 1728.

FANTOZZI PARMA, DOMENICO
>Diario del viaggio fatto in Inghilterra nel 1639 dal Nunzio
>Pontificio Rossetti, pubbl. dal PROF. GIUSEPPE FER-
>RARO, Bologna, 1885.

FRANCISCO DE JESÚS (referred to in text as F.J.)
>El hecho de los tratados del Matrimonio pretendido por el
>Principe de Gales con la serenissima Infante de España
>Maria, tomado desde sus principios para mayor demostra-
>ción de la verdad, y ajustado con los papeles originales
>donde consta por el maestro F. Francesco de Jesús, predi-
>cador del rey nuestro Señor. Narrative of the Spanish
>Treaty, ed. and trans. by S. R. GARDINER (Camden Society,
>London, 1869.

FULLER, THOMAS
>Church History of Britain... to the year 1648, London, 1655.

GAMACHES, CYPRIEN DE
>Mémoires de la mission des Capucins de la province de Paris,
>près de la reine d'Angleterre, depuis l'année 1630 jusqu'à
>1669 (Bibliothèque Franciscaine), Paris, 1881.

HOWARD, WILLIAM
>A Patterne of Christian Loyaltie, whereby any prudent man
>may clearly perceive in what manner the New Oath of
>Allegiance, and every clause thereof, may, in a true and
>Catholique Sense, without danger of Perjury, be taken by
>Roman-Catholikes... Collected out of authours, who have
>handled, the whole matter more largely. By WILLIAM
>HOWARD, an English Catholike, London, 1634.

KING, HENRY
>A Sermon preached at Paul's Crosse the 25 of November
>1621 upon occasion of that false and scandalous Report
>(lately printed) touching the supposed Apostasie of the
>right Reverend Father in God, John King, late lord bishop
>of London, by Henry King his eldest son. Whereunto is
>annexed the Examination and Answere of Thomas Preston,
>P. taken before my Lords Grace of Canterbury touching this
>scandall, London, 1621.

Lilly, William

> *Several Observations on the life and death of King Charles I.*
> Published for the first time in July 1651 in Select Tracts,
> ed. Fr. Maseres, London, 1815.

Ludlow, E.

> *Memoirs* (1625-1672), London, 1751.

Mason, R.

> *Certamen seraphicum provinciae Angliae pro sancta Dei ec-*
> *clesia in quo breviter declaratur, quomodo FF. Minores*
> *Angli calamo et sanguine pro fide Christi sanctaque eius*
> *ecclesia certarunt,* Duaci, 1649 ; Quaracchi, 1885.

Mercure François, Le, ou la suite de l'histoire de la paix, 1605-1640,
Paris, 1611-1648, 25 vols.

More, H.

> *Historia provinciae anglicanae Soc. Iesu* (1580-1635), Audo-
> mari, 1660.

Motteville, Madame de

> *Memoir by Madame de Motteville on the life of Henrietta Ma-*
> *ria (Camden Miscellany,* vol. VIII ; *Camden Society,* New
> Series, vol. XXXI), London, 1880.

Preston, O. S. B., Dom Thomas (Roland) (*alias* Roger Widdrington). See also under Henry King.

> *A Theologicall Disputation concerning the Oath of Alleg-*
> *iance, dedicated to the most Holy Father, Pope Paul the*
> *Fifth,* n. p., 1613.

> *Rogeri Widdringtoni Catholici Angli ad Sanctissimum Domi-*
> *num Paulum Quintum, Pontificem Max. humillima Sup-*
> *plicatio,* Albionopoli, 1616.

> *Last Reioynder to Mr Thomas Fitz-Herbert's Reply concern-*
> *ing the Oath of Allegiance, and the Pope's power to*
> *depose Princes,* n. p., 1619. (Reprinted 1633.)

> *Strena Catholica seu explicatio breuis et dilucida novi Fideli-*
> *tatis Iuramenti,* Augustae, 1620.

> *A New-Yeares Gift for English Catholikes, or a brief and*
> *cleare Explication of the New Oath of Allegiancee,* n. p.,
> 1620.

> *A Copy of the Decree wherein two books of Roger Widd-*
> *rington, an English Cathotholick* (sic) *are condemned*
> *and the Author commanded to purge himselfe,* n. p., 1614.

*A Copy of the Purgation which the same Roger Widdrington
sent to his Holiness Pope Paul the Fifth*, N. P., 1614.

PRYNNE, WILLIAM

Hidden Workes of Darkness brought to light, etc., London, 1645.

Romes Master-Peece, etc., London, 1643.

Mr. Prinn's Charge against the King, London, 1648.

A new discovery of some Romish emissaries... etc. London, 1656.

*The popish royal favourite, or a full discovery of his majesties
extraordinary favours to*... *Papists*, etc., London, 1643.

Canterbury's Doom, London, 1646.

Breviate of the Life of William Laud (v. LAUD's *Works*, vol.
III, p. 259).

*An exact chronological Vindication of our British King's
Supreme Jurisdiction with in their realms*, N.P., 1666-1668,
3 vols.

PYM, JOHN

*The reasons of the House of Commons to stay the Queenes going
into Holland. Delivered to the Lords, at a Conference the 14.
of July*, 1641, N. P., N. D.

RICHELIEU

*Mémoires du Cardinal de Richelieu sur le règne de Louis XIII
depuis 1610 jusqu'à 1638* (*Collection complète des mémoires relatifs à l'histoire de France*, sér. 2, tom. XXI bis-
XXX), Paris, 1823.

ROBERTS, LEWES

The Merchants Mappe of Commerce, London, 1638, 3 pt.

SATEREN, GEORGE

*A Treatise against Images and Pictures in Churches. And an
Answer to those who object that the times are changed*,
London, 1641.

SENAULT, JEAN-FRANÇOIS

*Oraison funèbre de Henriette-Marie de France, reine de la
Grande-Bretagne, prononcée dans l'église de Notre-Dame
de Paris le 25 novembre par le R. P. J.-P. Senault, prêtre
et supérieur de la congrégation de l'Oratoire de Jésus*,
Paris, 1670.

SIRI, VITTORIO

Memorie recondite, etc., Lione, 1679.

SUAREZ, FRANCISCO

Defensio Fidei Catholicae et Apostolicae adversus Anglicanae

sectae errores, cum responsione ad Apologiam pro iura-
mento fidelitatis et Praefationem Serenissimi Iacobi An-
gliae, Regis Conimbricae, 1613.

TILLIÈRES, COMTE DE

Mémoires inédits du Comte Leveneur de Tillières et de
Carrouges, Ambassadeur en Angleterre, sur la Cour de
*Charles I*ᵉʳ *et son mariage avec Henriette de France, re-*
cueillis etc. par M. C. HIPPEAU, Paris, 1862.

WALKER, H.

A Remarkable Revelation of the Wandrings of the Church of
England in Idolatry, Superstition, and Ceremonies, from
*the 1*ˢᵗ *motion through each particular station to the*
*1*ˢᵗ *great period. In parallel with the Children of Israel*
in the Desert from Rameses to Mount Sinai, N. P., 1641.

WIDDRINGTON, ROGER (v. *supra* PRESTON).

WOOD, ANTHONY à

Athenae Oxonienses, London, 1721.

C. Non-contemporaneous and Modern Works.

ADAMS, W.H.D.

The White King; or Charles the First, and the men and
women, life and manners, literature and art in the first
half of the 17th century, London, 1889.

Allgemeines Lexikon der bildenden Künstler, hrsg. von ULRICH
THIEME u. s. w., Leipzig, 1907, — 18 vols — .

AREZIO, L.

L'azione diplomatica del Vaticano nella questione del matri-
monio Spagnuolo di Carlo Stuart, Principe di Galles,
Anno 1623, Palermo, 1896.

BAILLON, CHARLES DE

Henriette-Marie de France, reine d'Angleterre, Paris, 1877.

BELL, HENRY

Archbishop Laud and Priestly Government, London, 1905.

BELLESHEIM, A.

Geschichte der katholischen Kirche in Irland, Mainz, 1890, 3 vols.

History of the Catholic Church in Scotland. English trans. by
DAVID HUNTER-BLAIR, 1889, Edinburgh, 1887-1890, 4 vols.

BELLOC, HILAIRE

Charles I, London, 1933.

Cromwell, London, 1934.

Richelieu, London, 1930.

BERINGTON, J.

   The Memoirs of Gregorio Panzani, Birmingham, 1792.

BIGHAM, HON. CLIVE

   The chief ministers of England (920-1720), London, 1923.

BIRCH, T.

   The Court and Times of Charles I illustrated by authentic and confidential letters etc., London, 1848, 2 vols.

BIRT, Dom H. N.

   Obit Book of the English Benedictines from 1600 to 1912, Edinburgh, 1913.

BLIGH, E. W.

   Sir Kenelm Digby and his Venetia, London, 1932.

BLISS, W.

   The religious belief of Anne of Denmark (*English Historical Review*, vol. IV, pp. 110 seq.).

BLUNDELL, M.

   Cavalier... Letters of William Blundell, 1620-1698, ed. by MARGARET BLUNDELL, London, 1934.

BRADY, W. MASIERE

   Annals of the Catholic Hierarchy in England and Scotland (1585-1876), Rome and London, 1877.

BROOKES, JOSHUA

   A Vindication of Charles I, London, 1934.

Bryan's Dictionary of Painters and Engravers, ed. G. C. WILLIAMSON, London, 1905, 5 vols.

BURTON, EDWIN H.

   London Streets and Catholic Memories, London, 1925.

BUTLER, CHAS

   Historical Memoirs of the English Catholics, London, 1822. 5 vols.

Cambridge Modern History, The, Vol. IV : *The Thirty Years' War*, Cambridge, 1906.

CAPPELLETTI, GIUSEPPE

   Chiese d'Italia, Venezia, 1844-1870, 21 vols.

CARDELLA, LORENZO

   Memorie storiche de' Cardinali delle Santa Romana Chiesa, Roma, 1792-1797.

CHASLES, V. E. PHILARÊTE

   Charles Ier, sa cour, son peuple et son parlement, Paris, 1844.

CHAVREBIÈRE, COISSAC DE
>   *Histoire des Stuarts*, Paris, 1930.

COLLIER, J.
>   *Ecclesiastical History of Great Britain*, London, 1846.

Complete Peerage (The) of England, Scotland, Ireland, GreatBritain and the United Kingdom, etc., ed. by G. E. C., VICARY GIBBS, DOUBLEDAY, HOWARD DE WALDEN, London, 1910 —, 8vols —.

COPPI, A.
>   *Discorso sul Consiglio e Senato di Roma*, Roma, 1848.

CUST, LIONEL
>   *Notes on some of the royal collections* (*Burlington Magazine*, vol. XIV, Oct. 1908 - Mar. 1909, pp. 337-340).

CUTHBERT, FR O.S.F.C.
>   *The Capuchins, a contribution to the history of the Counter-Reformation*, London, 1928.

D'ALTON, E. A.
>   *History of Ireland*, London, 1911.

DEDOUVRES, LOUIS
>   *Le Père Joseph de Paris, capucin. L'Éminence grise*, Paris, 1932, 2 vols.

Dictionnaire de théologie catholique, Paris, 1903 —, 11 vols —.

Dictionary of National Biography, London, 1908-1909, 22 vols. and supplement.

D'ISRAELI, I.
>   *Commentaries on the Life and Reign of Charles I, King of England*, London, 1828-1830, 4 vols.

DODD-TIERNEY
>   *Dodd's Church History of England from the commencement of the 16th century to the Revolution of 1688, with notes additions and a continuation by the* Rev. M. A. TIERNEY, F.S.A., London, 1839-43, 5 vols.

ENGELS, P.H.
>   *Dissertatio historico-juridica politica inauguralis de causis conversionis rerum Angliae regnante Carolo I°*, Lugduni Batavorum, 1836.

EVANS, F.M.G. (later Mrs HIGHAM, *q.v.*)
>   *The Principal Secretary of State* : *A Survey of the office from 1558 to 1680* (*Manchester Univ. Press, Historical Series*, N° 43), London and Manchester, 1923.

FAGNEZ, GUSTAVE
    Le Père Joseph et Richelieu, 1577-1638, Paris, 1894, 2 vols.

FLICHE, AUGUSTIN
    La réforme grégorienne (*Spicilegium sacrum Lovaniense*, vols VI
        and IX), Louvain, 1922-1926.

FOLEY, HENRY
    Records of the English province of the S. J., London, 1882,
        7 vols.

FORBES-LEITH, S.J., W.
    *Memoirs of Scottish Catholics during the 17th and 18th cen-
        turies*, London, 1909, 2 vols.

FULLERTON, LADY GEORGIANA
    Life of Elizabeth, Lady Falkland, London, 1883.

GALBREATH, D.L.
    Papal Heraldry, Cambridge, 1930.

GARDINER, S. R.
    Prince Charles and the Spanish Marriage, 1617-1623, London,
        1869, 2 vols. (This is noted apart from the *History*, as this
        particular edition has been used.)
    History of England, 1603-1643, London, 1884 ; new impression,
        1904-1929, 10 vols.
    History of the Great Civil War,1642-1649, London, 1893, 4 vols.

GARDINER S.R. and MULLINGER, J. B.
    Introduction to the Study of English History, London, 1881.

GASQUET, AIDAN
    History of the Ven. English College, Rome, London, 1920.
    *Fr Leander Jones, Abbot of Cismar, first President-General
        of the present Anglo-Benedictine Congregation* (*Downside
        Review*, vol. IV, 1885, pp. 35-43).

GILLOW, J.
    Bibliographical Dictionary of English Catholics, London and
        New York, N. D., 5 vols.

GODFREY, ELIZABETH
    Home Life under the Stuarts, London, 1925.

GOLL, J.
    Die französische Heirat ; *Frankreich und England*, 1624 *und*
        1625, Prag, 1876.

GUILDAY, PETER
    The English Catholic Refugees on the Continent, 1559-1795,
        London, 1914.

GUIZOT, F.
> *Un projet de mariage royal,* Paris, 1863. (Reprinted from the
> *Revue des Deux Mondes.*)

HARTING, J. H.
> *Catholic London Missions from the Reformation to the year*
> 1850, London, 1903.

HAY, M. V.
> *The Blairs Papers,* London, 1929.

HEIMBUCHER, MAX
> *Die Orden und Kongregationen der katholischen Kirche,*
> Paderborn, 3rd ed., 1934, 2 vols.

HERVEY, M.F.S.
> *The Life, Correspondence and Collections of Thomas Howard*
> *Earl of Arundel,* Cambridge, 1921.

HIGHAM, F. M. G. (v. *supra* EVANS, F.M.G.)
> *Charles I,* London, 1932.

HOOK, WALTER FARQUHAR
> *Lives of the Archbishops of Canterbury from St Augustine to*
> *Juxon,* London, 1879, 12 vols.

HOUSSAYE, M.
> *Le Cardinal de Bérulle et le cardinal de Richelieu,* Paris,
> 1875. (This is the third volume of a trilogy on Bérulle,
> the other vols being :— *M. de Bérulle et les Carmélites de*
> *France* (1576-1611) ; *Le P. de Bérulle et l'Oratoire de*
> *Jésus* (1611-1625). The third vol. contains the index to
> the whole work.)

HUGHES, PHILIP
> *The Conversion of Charles I (The Clergy Review,* vol. VIII,
> Aug. 1934, pp. 113-125).

HUGHES, S.J., THOMAS
> *History of the Society of Jesus in North America, colonial and*
> *federal,* London, 1907.

HYNES, M. J.
> *The Mission of Rinuccini, Nuncio Extraordinary to Ire-*
> *land, 1645-1649 (Recueil des travaux publiés par les mem-*
> *bres des Conférences d'Histoire et de Philologie,* 2e série,
> 24e fascicule), Louvain, 1932.

INGOLD, A.M.P. - BATTEREL, LOUIS
> *Mémoires domestiques pour servir à l'histoire de l'Oratoire,*
> Paris, 1902-1905.

INGRAM, J. DUNBAR
> *England and Rome, a history of the relations between the Papacy and the English State and Church*, London, 1892.

JESSE, J. H.
> *Memoirs of the Court of England during the reign of the Stuarts*, London, 1857, 3 vols.

JOHN, EVAN
> *King Charles I*, London, 1933.

LEE, SIDNEY, L.
> *The Life of Lord Herbert of Cherbury*, London, 1886.

LEMAN, AUGUSTE
> *Urbain VIII et la rivalité de la France et de la maison d'Autriche, de 1631 à 1365*, Paris, 1920.

LE NEVE, JOHN
> *Fasti Ecclesiae Anglicanae* etc. corrected and continued by T. D. HARDY, Oxford, 1854, 3 vols.

Life of Archbishop Laud by a Romish Recusant (i.e. T. G. LONGUE-VILLE), London, 1894.

LINGARD, John
> *History of England*, London and Manchester, 1855-1868, 6th edit., 10 vols.

Life of Sir Kenelm Digby by One of his descendants (i.e. T. G. LONGUEVILLE), London, 1896.

LOMAS, MRS S.C.
> *The State Papers of the Early Stuarts and the Interregnum (Transactions of the Royal Historical Society*, vol. XVI, 1902, in *New Series*, 1884-1906).

MATHEW, ARNOLD HARRIS
> *The Life of Sir Tobie Mathew*, London, 1907.

MEYER, A.O.
> *Charles I and Rome (American Historical Review*, vol. XIX, 1913, pp. 13-26).

> *Clemens VIII. und Jakob I. von England*, Rom, 1904.

> *England and the Catholic Church under Queen Elizabeth*, authorized translation by the Rev. J. R. McKee, London, 1916.

> *Der Toleranzgedanke im England der Stuarts* (Sonderabdruck aus der *Historischen Zeitschrift*, Band CVIII, Heft 2), München und Berlin, 1912.

MEYER, ALBERT DE
> *Les premières controverses jansénistes en France,* 1640-1649
> (*Université de Louvain. Thèses de la Faculté de théologie,*
> 2ᵉ sér. vol. IX), Louvain, 1919.

MONTAGUE, F. C.
> *The History of England from the accession of James I to the
> Restoration,* 1603-1660 (*Political Hist. of England,* vol.
> VII), London, 1907.

MORERI, LOUIS
> *Le grand dictionnaire historique,* Paris, 1759, 10 vols in folio.

MORONI, GAETANO
> *Dizionario di erudizione storico-ecclesiastica,* Venezia, 1840-
> 1879, 103 vols.

PAGLIUCCHI, PIO
> *I Castellani del Castello Sant' Angelo,* Roma, 1906-1928, 2 vols.

PASTOR L.
> *Geschichte der Päpste.* Band XIII : *Gregor XV. und Urban
> VIII.,* 1621-1644, Freiburg, i. Br., 1928.

PIERCE, H. K.
> *Some Pro-Romans of the Past* (*The Bulletin of the Confratern-
> ity of Unity,* Number CIII, 1929, pp. 6-8), London and
> Boston.

PLOWDEN, CHARLES
> *Remarks on a Book entitled " Memoirs of Gregorio Panzani ",*
> Liége, 1794.

RANKE, L. VON
> *History of the Popes* (Bohn's edition), Eng. transl. by MRS
> FOSTER, London, 1907.

ROCCO DA CESINALE, F.
> *Storia delle Missioni dei Cappuccini,* Parigi, 1867-1873, 3 vols.

RODOCANACHI, EMMANUEL
> *Le Château Saint-Ange,* Paris, 1909.

ROMISH RECUSANT, A. (*i.e.* T. G. LONGUEVILLE)
> *A Life of Archbishop Laud,* London, 1894.

SCHAEFFER, EMIL
> *Van Dyck. Des Meisters Gemälde in 537 Abbildungen* hrsgeg.
> von EMIL SCHAEFFER, (*Klassiker d. Kunst.* vol. XIII),
> Stuttgart und Leipzig, 1909.

Scots Peerage (The) founded on Wood's edition of SIR ROBERT

Douglas's *Peerage of Scotland...*, ed. by Sir James Balfour
Paul, Edinburgh, 1904-14, 9 vols.

Simmonds, Rev. L. F.
What do English Divines say? (Oxford Movement Centenary Tractates, VI), London, 1933.

Skelton, Sir John
Charles I, London and Paris, 1898, 1 vol. in-4º.

Spillmann, S.J., J.
Geschichte der Katholikenverfolgung in England, 1535-1681, Freiburg i. Br., 1905, 2 vols.

Stebbing, G.
The Church in England, London, 1921.

Stevenson, G. S.
Charles I in captivity, London, 1927.

Strickland, Agnes.
Lives of the Queens of England, London, 1905, 16 vols.

Strocchi, Andreas
Seria Cronologica storico-critica de' vescovi Faentini, Faenza, 1841.

Taunton, E. L.
History of the Jesuits in England, 1580-1883, London, 1901.

Townshend, Dorothea
The Life and Letters of Endymion Porter, London, 1897.

Vaes, Maurice
Le séjour d'Antoine Van Dyck en Italie, mi-nov. 1621 - automne 1627 (Extrait du *Bulletin de l'Institut historique belge de Rome* 4e fasc.), Rome, 1924.

Ward A. W.
James VI and the Papacy (Scottish Historical Review, vol. II, 1905, pp. 249 seq.).

Wassenhoven, Louis van
Ottavio Mirto Frangipani, nuntius van Vlaanderen en de Engelsche Katholieken, 1596-1606 (*Uitgave van het Vlaamsch Historisch Boekenfonds*, nº 1), Baasrode, 1925.

Waterworth, W.
England and Rome: or the History of the Religious connection between England and the Holy See, London, 1854.

GENERAL INTRODUCTION

§ 1. — NEW ORIENTATION OF EUROPE

With the dawn of the 17th century the political and religious questions that for the last two generations had involved the nations of Europe in religious wars and persecutions were still to be faced, but with the passing of the protagonists they had largely lost their piquancy, for William of Orange, Philip II, Elizabeth, were gone. Henry IV alone remained to pursue a wide European policy and, immediately on James I's accession to the throne, he sent the Duc de Sully as his Ambassador Extraordinary with proposals for an alliance against Spain and a double marriage between the Dauphin and Princess Elizabeth, and between the Prince of Wales and Elizabeth of France.

At the same time James found the other powers of Europe anxious for alliance with him, ministers arriving from Venice, Denmark, the United Provinces and the Archduke Albert, regent of the Catholic Low Countries. Envoys even came from Spain, the arch-enemy of Elizabethan England, and the peace that James concluded with Philip III was possibly the greatest benefit of his reign. But the new King aimed at something more, — a close family alliance with one of the great powers, France or Spain. This would necessarily mean a Catholic marriage for his son, and perhaps force him to adopt a new policy towards his own Papist subjects but, in his opinion, the added prestige his own dynasty would glean from kinship with the Bourbons or the Habsburgs would be eminently worth a few concessions in the matter of religion.

Rome was the first to realize the possibilities of relief for the English Catholics which James's dynastic ambitions offered, and ordered Mgr Maffeo Barberini, who went to Paris as Nuncio in 1604, to maintain the friendliest relations with the English Ambassador to France. The sojourn of Mgr Barberini in Paris is of the highest significance, for it gave him that close contact with, and interest in, the politico-religious situation in England which enabled him to serve on the congregation of Cardinals appointed in 1623 to deliberate on the Spanish Marriage Treaty and later when he became Pope Urban VIII coloured his whole outlook regarding a *rapprochement* between England and the Holy See. [1]

Pope Paul V was meanwhile hoping to consolidate the various peace treaties that had been made by bringing France and Spain together. He succeeded only after the death of Henry IV, when in 1615, during the regency of Marie de' Medici, Bourbons and Habsburgs were united by the marriage of Louis XIII with the Infanta Anne of Austria, and that of Philip III with Elizabeth of France, the two princesses being literally exchanged on the Franco-Spanish frontier at Handaya on the Bidassoa.

§ 2. — THE THIRTY YEARS' WAR

While peace treaties seemed the order of the day in the rest of Europe, forces were gathering in Austria and Germany for the forthcoming clash of dynasties and creeds. In 1608 a Union of German Protestant Princes was formed, a challenge accepted in the following year by the creation of the Catholic League. With Duke Maximilian I of Bavaria at the head of the League, and Frederick V, the Elector Palatine, as champion of Protestantism, the two branches of the Wittelsbachs were sundered.

When in 1618 the Elector Palatine allied himself with the Bohemian rebels against the Emperor, war was inevitable. In the following year the Elector made easy settlement impossible by his

---

(1) *Bibl.Vat., Cod. Chigi*, Q. 1. 16, ff. 17-18 : *Instructions to Maffeo Barberini* : " Le cose d'Inghilterra, dopo la morte della pseuda Regina, et assontione del Rè di Scotia al Regno, hanno mutato faccia, massime con la pace seguita trà il Rè di Spagna, et il med^{mo} Rè con la q^{ale} hà sempre N. S^{re} sperato et spera di far qualche cosa à benefitio della Relig^{ne} Catt^{ca} in quel regno... Il med^{mo} Rè d'Inghilterra tiene un Ambass^{re} in Parigi con il quale il S. Card^{le} del Bufalo, suo Predecessore, haveva qualche amicitia. V. S. la continuerà et trattarà seco sempre con dolcezza et benignità istillando di continuo nell' animo suo la buona volontà di S. B^{ne} verso il suo Rè." Such a beginning, it was foreseen, might one day lead to a direct diplomatic *rapprochement* : " Si apprivà la strada di trattar tal volta seco, et potrebbe venirle fatto d'introdurre tal negotiatione, che fusse poi molta sua gloria di havere incominciato, et buttato semi per riunire quel Rè et Regno con la S^{tà} Sede che sarebbe il maggior frutto, che ella potesse cavare dalle sue fatiche."

illegal acceptance of the Bohemian crown, yet after the Battle of the White Hill this Calvinist monarchy seemed crushed and, with the accession of Ferdinand II to the Imperial title, the Catholic cause was temporarily triumphant.

It was an awkward situation for the King of England, for in 1613 he had married his colourful daughter, Elizabeth, " *th' eclipse and glory of her kind,* " to the impetuous Palatine. The match proved highly popular, and the temper of the country inclined towards war on behalf of Frederick ; but to this James was opposed temperamentally. He was also deeply involved in negotiations for a marriage alliance with the Spanish royal family, Habsburgs as was the Emperor, and Spain had to some extent enforced his neutrality by a flattering appeal to adjudicate on the legality of Frederick's action.

In 1621 Paul V died, and was succeeded by Gregory XV who, with his nephew the Cardinal Secretary Ludovisi, was anxious to press on the Catholic revival in Germany which the initial victory of the League had promised, and fully supported the Emperor and Duke Maximilian, as Paul V had done, with financial as well as diplomatic aid. In February, 1623, the Pope conferred on the Duke of Bavaria, the Electoral dignity of which Frederick, James's son-in-law, had been deprived. Spain protested, fearful of the effect on opinion in England, with whom she was now in close negotiation for the marriage. The French, on the other hand, were pleased, seeing in the move a diminution of the power of the Habsburgs with no material strengthening of the Protestant side : it was their own policy.

At the moment when the new Elector and the Catholic League found themselves opposed by a powerful coalition including Denmark, Sweden, Venice, France, — all working for the restoration of the Palatine,—the world was taken completely by surprise, for the Prince of Wales, the Palatine's brother-in-law, went seeking a wife in Madrid. A close alliance between Protestant England and Catholic Spain seemed more than likely.

Little less surprising was the success of Gregory XV's policy in bringing France and Spain to agree to sequestrate the Valtelline Forts into Papal hands till a settlement was made. This important valley, one of the gates of Italy joining the Lombard Plains to the Tyrol, with its population of 80,000 ardent Catholics had been for over 200 years under the suzerainty of the Graubünden, a federation of three Leagues, half-Protestant, half-Catholic, with zealots in both camps. Religious friction was the result, and in this North Italian valley, not sixty miles long, became concentrated as in a microcosm the religious struggle that was dividing the world outside into two great groups, — the adherents of the Reformed Church, comprising England, the United Provinces and the Princes of the German Protestant Union ; the Catholic Church, upheld solidly by Spain and Austria, the two branches of the Habsburgs. " We find Europe," says Ranke, " divided into two worlds which at every point encompass, restrict, assail, and repel each other." When these too irreconcilable elements joined issue, Richelieu was pleased to throw Catholic France in the balance on the side of the Protestants : a policy that altered the whole course of the history of modern Europe.

The possession of the Valtelline Valley, highly important as a connecting link between francophil Venice, the anti-Spanish Graub ndners, and the Protestant Princes of Germany, engaged the attention of Spain, Savoy (for the moment pro-French), Milan, Venice, Austria and France, and became one of the dominating features of the early part of the Thirty Years' War. The security of the passes was equally vital for the Austro-Spanish combination and in 1620 the Duke of Feria occupied them with Spanish troops. The Marshal de Bassompierre was thereupon sent to Madrid to negotiate a treaty for the restoration of the Valley to its *status quo*. Strangely enough, the Pope's influence was thrown in on the side of the French who had frightened him with the prospect of the complete domination of the Spaniards in Italy, half of which they already ruled. Although the Treaty of Madrid of April 26, 1621, decreeing the restoration of the Valtelline to the Bund, fell through, an arrangement was come to in 1622/3 by which Spain agreed to evacuate the Forts and deliver the sequestrated district into Papal hands for four months on condition that all the forts were razed. It was the fulfilment of the cherished policy of Ludovisi, the Cardinal Nephew.

On August 6, 1623, the forces of Christian of Brunswick were annihilated by Tilly at Stadtlohn, and the Catholic revival had reached its highest point. The previous month Gregory XV had died, and with the election of Maffeo Barberini as Urban VIII there succeeded one of the few Cardinals who had opposed Ludovisi's Valtelline policy owing to the heavy toll it took of the

Papal Exchequer. While Spain desired a continuance of the Papal occupation of the Valley, Richelieu took advantage of Urban's hesitation and in November, 1624, attacked and drove out the Papal troops. Following a long period of negotiation in which Francesco Barberini, the Cardinal Secretary, went as Legate to Madrid and Paris, Spain and France concluded on March 5, 1626, the Treaty of Monzon allowing only the Catholic faith in the Valtelline, giving the Pope command of the Forts and making him arbiter of all religious questions. The two countries were to guarantee the Treaty.

With the Valtelline problem temporarily solved, the Holy See was involved in another exhausting dispute, — the Mantuan succession, a small matter in itself, but made deliberately of European significance, much as Serajevo was in 1914, by the eagerness of the powers to use it as a match to set Europe alight. On December 26, 1627, Vincent II, Duke of Mantua, died with no near male relative, leaving his duchy to Charles, Duc de Nevers, a Frenchman by education and sympathy, who at once took possession of his legacy. Spain objected to having a French prince ruling in an Italy she desired to dominate, and at once supported other claimants, in particular the Duke of Savoy, brother-in-law to Louis XIII. Meanwhile the Emperor sequestrated the Duchy ; but Spanish and Savoyard troops, taking advantage of Richelieu's preoccupation with the Huguenots, occupied all Montferrat save Fort Casale, but once La Rochelle was relieved the Cardinal despatched reinforcements to Casale and seized Susa. In 1629 he had not only made peace with England, but had formed a League with Venice, Mantua and Savoy for the defence of Italy. The Catholic star was waning, and 1630 saw the end of the Protestant collapse that had begun at White Hill a decade before, The struggle in Germany was still to drag on for another 18 years, a war of attrition, with the Protestant forces gradually gaining the ascendant.

The deciding factor had been the accession to power in 1624 of Richelieu with one all-absorbing aim, — to secure the downfall of the House of Austria, and set France secure in the hegemony of Europe by means of Protestant alliances. It was a policy in which the Roman Cardinal consistantly sacrificed the higher interests of the Church to the political ambitions of his country. He had driven the Papal troops from the Valtelline (Urban had hardly expected that), he had thwarted Spain's ambition in Mantua, and for the restoration of the Palatinate (occupied by Spanish troops) on which it seemed German, perhaps European Protestantism must stand or fall, he supported Christian IV of Denmark and the freebooter Mansfeld with money and men. Added to this he allied Catholic France with Protestant Holland and England. This last he counted one of his greatest strokes, for, in stepping in when the Spanish Marriage Treaty had failed, he strengthened himself at Spain's expense and used an outside hope of relief for the English Catholics to nullify the Pope's resentment over his Valtelline offence. At the same time he used this alliance with a Protestant power as a gesture towards the Huguenots, yet all the while hoped to get ships from England to use against them. Though he had no intention of embroiling France in the war for the restoration of Charles's brother-in-law, he saw to it that the war that was weakening Austria was kept alive, holding up the alliance with England as a constant threat. Everywhere, by pressure and threat without commitment, he employed the highest diplomatic skill in the pursuit of his aims.

It will be seen how far the Prince Palatine's interference in the Bohemian revolt against the Emperor now extended. The quarrels of the Alpine Grey Leagues, the petty war of the Mantuan succession, the military ambition of the Scandinavians, the re-awakened struggle of the United Provinces against Spain, the perennial rivalry of France and Spain in Italy — all were swept into a European conflict that had begun as a war of creeds and was developing into one of dynasties. " All the wars that are on foot in Europe," wrote Gustavus Adolphus in 1628, " have been fused together and become a single war."

England alone had kept aloof when everything invited armed participation, interests both of kinship and creed, even of *amour propre*, for she still stood nominally at the head of the Protestant nations of the North; but both James and Charles were opposed to war as such and hoped to attain their ends by diplomacy, yet neither had the cunning, the statesmanship, the forcefulness of a Richelieu for the task. In the early days of the war James had lost his chance. He might have prevailed with the Emperor for the good of Europe to give a fair hearing to Bohemian claims. In fact, his efforts were made on entirely unrealistic lines. During the Spanish Marriage Treaty he tried

half-heartedly to persuade the Spanish Habsburgs to the fratric-
idal course of arming against the Emperor for the restoration of the
Protestant Palatine. Vacillating, he then declared that he would
only support Frederick's claim to the Bohemian crown if there
were an *electio legitima*; yet he renewed his alliance with the
Protestant Union and allowed troops for the Protestants to be
levied in England.

Charles pursued a similar tortuous course. The offensive and
defensive alliance with France that was to have been an adjunct
of the French match was left vague, and the help for the Palatine
that should have been insisted upon was reduced by Richelieu
to the smallest of subsidies for Mansfeld. Charles had failed to
obtain support for his sister either from Spain or from France,
but he was not to abandon the cause of the Palatine and soon
turned as a last resort to the most unlikely source of assistance
for a Protestant prince — the Holy See.

§ 3. — THE STATE OF CATHOLICISM IN ENGLAND

Meanwhile, the affairs of the English Catholics presented a
sad spectacle. At the accession of James I, whose splendid
Catholic christening by Bishop Beaton was still recalled, and who
was remembered as the son of that devoted champion of the Faith,
Mary, Queen of Scots, the hopes of the English Catholics had
flown high, only to be doomed to disappointment all the more
embittered when the Gunpowder Plot, that deplorable folly of
a political faction, placed the whole Catholic body under a new
Penal Code (1606) that only served to intensify the severe
enactments of Elizabeth.

No longer would the King be satisfied with two-thirds of the
personal and all the real estate of a Papist refusing to attend the
State Church. Henceforth he required all to take an Oath of Allegiance to himself. At first sight this appeared a stroke of genuine
statesmanship, offering loyal Papists an opportunity of dissociating
themselves from the treason of plotters against the State. In fact,
the framing of the Oath seemed nothing more than an attempt to
sow discord among the Catholics by asking them to swear as
"impious, heretical and damnable" the doctrine of the Pope's power
of deposing princes. Probably the vast majority of English
Catholics felt little sympathy for such a doctrine but to be obliged

to use such strong terms in an oath that bound his conscience was too much to ask of the simpler type of Catholic, as determined in his loyalty to the Pope as to the King, and only offered a tortuous way of escape to the casuist, seeking at all costs a practical compromise. The Oath was soon condemned by Paul V, but Archpriest Blackwell refused to publish the Brief and himself took the Oath. He was deposed in 1608.

Under the rule of Archpriests Birkhead (1608-1614) and Harrison (1614-1621) efforts were made to procure a more normal government for the English Catholics, and it was thought that the prestige of a bishop would do much to restore unity and peace. It had just the contrary effect. In 1623 Dr William Bishop was consecrated titular bishop of Chalcedon and, though personally wellliked, created opposition by claiming the jurisdiction of an Ordinary, erecting a chapter of 24 Canons headed by a Dean and dividing the country into archdeaconries.

Dr Bishop died in 1624 and was succeeded by Dr Richard Smith with the same title. The new Bishop, less personally sympathetic, made the same claim to the powers of an Ordinary under the decree of Trent, and had to bear the full brunt of the hostility of the regular clergy who maintained he had only the limited faculties of a Vicar Apostolic. The heat of the dispute brought the presence of the Papist bishop in England to the notice of the Government, and two decrees were issued for his arrest in December 1628 and in March 1629. Finding the Pope had little sympathy with his case, Dr Smith retired to France and offered Rome his resignation, which was accepted.

§ 4. — RAPPROCHEMENT BETWEEN THE COURTS OF ENGLAND AND ROME.

So negative a step was no solution of the dissensions of the English Catholics among whom the factions for and against the Oath had now become more deeply embittered by the quarrels of the secular and regular clergy on the expediency of episcopal government in the present state of the country. The case called for immediate inquiry from Rome and, on appeal to the Pope, an agent was sent to England to deal with the matter, which he did with some success.

With the dissolution of Parliament in 1629 and the beginning of more than a decade of personal rule by the King, the anti-Catholic elements in England had no voice in the government. The same year brought peace with France and with the settlement of the Queen's personal religious requirements, and her influence over the King increased. The moment seemed ripe for an exchange of courtesies between the Pope and his godchild, which might open the way to still closer relations between England and Rome. To this Charles was amenable. While sharing the ingrained prejudice of the Englishman against the Papal system, he cavilled at few of the dogmas taught by the Church and, in his own attitude towards reform in the Establishment, showed himself sympathetic to doctrines and practices that to the Puritan were but Popery thinly-disguised.

To the Roman agents, accustomed to the frigid Calvinism of the *Eglise réformée* and the frankly political Lutheranism of the German princes, Anglicanism came as a surprise, while the presence on the episcopal bench of such men as Montague and Goodman, and in the government of crypto-Catholics such as Windebank and Cottington, led to enthusiastic talk of Reunion, the more so as conversions became fashionable when the growing influence of the Queen and the King's natural clemency tended to make the practice of the Faith less dangerously heroic while still leaving in it a spice of adventure.

Charles looked upon the exchange of courtesies as a harmless means to his political ends. He was ready to talk religion non-committally with the Roman agents if in doing so he could impress upon them, and upon the Pope through them, his tolerant attitude towards the English Catholics in the practice of their Faith. In this way he hoped to induce the Pope to make it possible for the Catholics to take the Oath of Allegiance as it stood, or with small concessions on his side. He hoped, too, to persuade the Pope to intervene in the German war and support the restoration of his sister and her sons to the Palatinate, — as unrealistic a policy as that of his father in asking Spain to take up arms against the Emperor. The international complications of the Thirty Years' War have been touched upon. Diplomatically the Pope was more deeply involved than anyone, trying with small success to hold the balance between France and Spain, and still support the Emperor and the Catholic League without antagonizing Richelieu. His half-hearted financial support of the League, in such contrast with Gregory XV's policy,

was deeply resented in Madrid and Vienna, where it was regarded
with some truth as playing indirectly into the hands of the French.
It must be pleaded for Urban that with Catholics and Protestants fighting side by side in the same army, with Catholic generals
enlisting Protestant officers and men, the German war was no longer
the religious issue it had been in the early days.   That the conflict
had become a purely political one seemed clearer than ever when
Richelieu found the Spaniards, who made such a show of religious
zeal, secretly supporting the Huguenots in France.

However unwilling Pope Urban was to undertake further obligations in his efforts for peace merely at the request of the non-
Catholic Charles, he must have found the *rapprochement* with
England and the encouraging reports of the Agents a pleasing
interlude among the ever-growing complications of his diplomatic
policy, and an offset to the discouraging rise of Gallicanism in
France.   Whether this interlude ever offered solid hope of winning
either Charles or England to the Church the reader must judge
for himself.

CHAPTER I

THE SPANISH MARRIAGE TREATY

Part I

Rapprochement

Paz con Inglatierra y con todo el mondo guerra [1]

On his accession to the throne of Elizabeth in 1603, James I lost no time in ending the wearisome war with Spain, and the truce was confirmed in August of the following year by a treaty that gave a grateful peace to the two countries. [2]

In pursuance of her new foreign policy Spain was anxious to consolidate the friendship by a marriage alliance, and one of the peace envoys, the Count of Villa Mediana, was given secret instructions to propose a match between the Infanta Anna and Henry, Prince of Wales. But the conditions were most explicit : the young Prince must become a Catholic and be brought up under the eye of his Catholic Majesty in Madrid, for the very good reason that, there being at the moment no Prince of the Asturias, the husband of Anna might one day wear the crown matrimonial of Spain. [3]

---

[1] Contemporary slogan, cf. *The Earl of Bristol's Defence,* ed. S. R. GARDINER, *Camden Miscellany,* vol. VI (Old Series, vol. CIV), p. 6.

[2] F. GUIZOT, *Un projet de mariage royal,* pp. 24 seq.

[3] S. R. GARDINER, *Prince Charles and the Spanish Marriage* (hereinafter called *G.P.C.*), vol. I, pp. 6-7 ; FRANCISCO DE JESÚS, *El hecho de los tratados del Matrimonio,* etc., *Narrative of the Spanish Marriage Treaty,* ed. and trans. by S. R. GARDINER (hereinafter called *F. J.*), pp. 103 [1] seq. : " que sus proprios vasallos no consenterán que la Ser^{ma} Infanta se casase con Principe de diferente religión contra la costumbre antiqua de aquella corona, por la qual conviene que este puncto quede llano antes que se trate de alguno otro."

And again : " sin consentir por ningun caso la crianca del Principe fuera de Hispaña."

Such conditions were so clearly unacceptable that it is doubtful if Villa Mediana ever put them forward ; at all events, the project, though in the minds of both parties, was not seriously discussed until 1611, when a formal offer came from James. By this time the Infanta Anna was promised to Louis XIII, the new King of France, but the English King was told that her younger sister Maria was at the Prince of Wales's disposal, could the religious question be arranged. When James found that this meant his son's conversion, he broke off negotiations and turning to France asked the hand of the Princess Christine, first for Prince Henry and, when he died suddenly in 1612, for his only remaining son, Charles. [1]

At the same time the King of England strengthened his Protestant connections by marrying his only daughter Elizabeth to Frederick, the Elector Palatine, and it looked for the moment as if James were going to revive his predecessor's policy by placing himself at the head of the anti-Spanish party in Europe. The flames of war-hate are not quickly quenched, and in England there were still enough smouldering embers to be kindled by the popular German Protestant match into a cry for war. To this James was strongly opposed, while Spain, lacking in leaders, men and money, was perforce pacific and hurriedly sent an Ambassador to smooth over an ugly situation. [2]

Don Diego Sarmiento de Acuña, [3] who arrived in London in 1613,was to sway the foreign policies of his own country and England for the next 10 years ; the more so, as he came with certain deep-rooted convictions on matters vitally connected with his mission. One was of the priceless value of alliance with Spain ; another, of the patent truth of the Catholic Faith, which none but fool or knave could deny ; the third, a corollary of this, was that English Protestantism rested on no deeper foundation than the whim of the sovereign, who once won over to Rome could carry the country with him. The official change of religion under Henry, Mary and Eliza-

---

[1] *G.P.C.*, vol. I, pp. 6-7 ; *F. J.*, pp. 105-106 [3].

[2] *G.P.C.*, vol. I, pp. 7-8.

[3] Later Count of Gondomar, Spanish Ambassador to England 1613-1622. Chief negotiator of the Spanish marriage treaty, to complete which he returned to Spain in 1622. He was loathed by the London populace but his gaiety and wit made him popular at Court. He obtained a great ascendancy over the mind of James I.

beth showed that the dictum *cujus regio, ejus religio,* so applicable to the German princelings, had already been realized three times in England and could be applied again. " Everything here depends on the King's will, " the Spaniard wrote in 1617. " This I have told him to his face in speaking about this matter, and that he has nothing to fear, as he has sufficient authority in England to introduce the sect of the Turks and Moors if he pleases. " [1]

In James's friendly relations with the heretics on the Continent Sarmiento saw the nucleus of a Protestant *bloc* powerful enough to threaten the Catholicism of Southern Europe ; but if once England were to cease her support of these allies, the Dutch rebels would yield again to Spain, the Huguenots become powerless against their king, the German princes capitulate to the Emperor. Conversely, the cause of Catholicism was the cause of legitimate monarchy.

Therefore, the English King must first of all be brought to relax the Penal Laws against his Catholic subjects. The country would then soon return to the Faith, elect a Catholic Commons, while James, to save his crown, would declare his own conversion. Chimerical as was the Spaniard's dream, it had a certain foundation in fact. Four times a day the Spanish Embassy chapel was crowded. Converts were numerous, and many eyes in England were turned towards Rome. Sarmiento considered England still a quarter Catholic, with another fourth ready to rally to the side in power. [2]

No longer was Spain able to attempt, as Philip II had done, the regaining of England to the Faith by arms, but the new Ambassador set himself to arrive at the same end through a marriage alliance. It was a reversion to the traditional rôle of the Habsburgs :

" *Bella gerunt alii, tu felix Austria, nube ;*
Nam quae Mars aliis, dat tibi regna Venus. "

[1] *G.P.C.,* vol. I, pp. 9-10 ; *F. J.,* p. 135 : Gondomar to Philip III, July 2/12, 1617.

[2] *Ibid.,* p. 23. The figures from Sarmiento's dispatches are worth reproducing here :

Recusants	300,000
Catholics attending Protestant worship	600,000
Atheists	900,000
Puritans	600,000
Other Protestants	1,200,000
	3,600,000

The task was a delicate one. King James's Scottish favourites and the moderate English Protestants inclined to an alliance with France. The Spaniard sought other friends at Court, — the Queen, Anne of Denmark, promised to help him even to the conversion of her son; of greater value was the friendship of the favourite Somerset. [1] Then in June 1614 an unexpected blow was struck for him by the King's sudden dissolution of Parliament after a stormy debate on alliance with France. James was needy, and the Commons had been niggardly over a grant, so Sarmiento seized the opportunity of assuring the King that concessions to his Catholic subjects groaning under the Penal Laws would win for his son Charles a Spanish bride with a dowry large enough to make him independent of Parliament. [2]

At the same time Philip III impressed upon his ambassador that in this matter he placed himself in the hands of the Pope, and to the latter wrote to say that in seeking alliance with England his motives were of the purest, — the service of God and the Faith. [3] Gratified at the Catholic King's sentiments, Paul V urged him to press for Prince Charles's conversion, without hope of which he could not grant a dispensation. He then enumerated the objections to a mixed marriage, — the danger to the Infanta's faith, still more to the children's, the danger to the marriage bond itself from the English law of divorce, and so on. To justify the facing of such risks, the strongest security must be obtained. Private religious freedom for the Infanta would be small safeguard to her, and of no use to the English Catholics; even tacit liberty of conscience would not prevent the Infanta's perversion, and would be of doubtful advantage to the Catholics, as the King could interpret it as he liked. The only genuine benefit for the Catholics was open toleration, the only real security for the Infanta was the conversion of the Prince. [4]

To Philip's mind there was no gainsaying the argument, and he demanded Charles's conversion. Sarmiento had never considered this as necessary to the realization of his dreams, and pointed out

[1] *G.P.C.*, vol. I, pp. 13 seq.

[2] *Ibid.*, pp. 20-21.

[3] *F.J.*, p. 113 [6].

[4] A. BELLESHEIM, *History of the Catholic Church in Scotland*, vol. III, App. XIII, pp. 481 seq. — Cod. Borghes., IV, 143, Cart. 45 : Autograph of Paul V.

the danger both to James and to his son. Even open toleration would mean repeal of the Penal Laws, an impossibility without consent of Parliament. The most the King was able and willing to do was to connive at the breach of the law by releasing priests from prison and remitting fines.

At this point negotiations might have ended had facts been faced, but each party had much to gain by an alliance and each hoped to talk the other into concession. A Junta of Spanish theologians was now appointed to consider the case for the match. Kept in ignorance of the Pope's discouraging reply, excited at the prospect of England's conversion, they voted in favour of a marriage, provided the Pope would grant a dispensation. Not only did they deem it unwise to demand the Prince's conversion, they even considered James's offer not to enforce the laws against the Catholics better than an open toleration extended to all sects.

Marriage articles were then drawn up and submitted to the new Ambassador Extraordinary now in Madrid. Sir John Digby [1] found fault with nearly every one of them and long refused to submit them to James. At last, in March 1615, he did so. The King's comment was that he intended his grandchildren to be brought up in his own religion, which he believed in as firmly as the King of Spain did in his; however, if they liked to turn Catholic later he would not on that account see them debarred from the succession. James added that he would allow the Infanta a private chapel, but not a public church. Complete remission of the Penal Laws he would look to later. [2]

All Sarmiento could see in the King's holding-back was jealousy of the influence Charles would acquire as the son-in-law of the King of Spain; he might become a Catholic, and depose his father. [3] As James once remarked drily to the Ambassador, he had no intention of emulating Charles V in abdicating and retiring to a monastery.

---

[1] Sir John Digby, later Earl of Bristol, Ambassador Extraordinary to Spain three times between 1611-1624. Returned to England in Jan. 1624, after the failure of the Spanish marriage treaty, and was impeached by Buckingham (Cf. *The Earl of Bristol's Defence*, p. v, note 1). He supported Charles in the Civil War and died an exile in Paris 1653.

[2] *G.P.C.*, vol. I, pp. 29 seq.

[3] *F. J.*, App. p. 293 : Sarmiento to Philip III, May 20/30, 1615 : " Teme que si su hijo se casa con hija de V. Mag^d, se hará luego Catholico y le prenderá, y se le alzará con el Reyno."

With Philip asking too much and James fearful of committing himself to concession, little progress could be made, and the deadlock seemed complete when in March, 1616, Digby returned home to say that Spain would not move save at the orders of the Pope, who would certainly demand relief for the English Catholics. [1] James, on the other hand, would discuss nothing till he knew whether the Pope was certain to grant a dispensation. Reluctantly Philip appealed to the Pope for some satisfaction on the point, but Paul V only repeated his answer of two years before, — the Prince's conversion and freedom for the Faith were to be insisted upon. [2]

Early in 1617 the Spanish theologians met to reconsider the situation in the light of Digby's and Sarmiento's despatches and the recent reply of the Pope. They now demanded to see toleration in practice for three years before the Infanta set out for England : the suggestion of Fray Francisco de Jesús, the King's preacher. [3] This man and Fray Antonio de Sotomayor were then asked to draw up all requirements concerning religion, copies of which were ordered to be sent to England. [4]

The negotiations, hitherto tentative, James was now ready to open formally, and on March 2, 1617, he called a meeting of the Privy Council to ensure its support, declaring he had been assured that alliance with Spain would mean neither a break with his Protestant allies, nor the conversion of his son, nor the toleration of Popery or of anything else abhorrent to an Englishman. The Council thereupon voted that Digby be sent as Ambassador Extraordinary with fullest powers to negotiate the mariage treaty. [5]

He was, in fact, empowered to accept any condition, even as to religion, provided the King knew to what his word was pledged.

---

[1] F. J., p. 126 [36], note.

[2] G.P.C., vol. I, pp. 35-36 ; F.J., pp. 125 seq., 218, note (1) : " que se effectuara este matrimonio en caso que le Principe de Gales se reduzca á la religion catholica, y se permita en aquel Reyno el uso y exercicio della."

[3] A Carmelite friar in possession of all official documents of the Marriage Treaty from which he drew up his Narrative used extensively here. Gardiner says of him : " His substantial accuracy wherever I have been able to compare his statements with the original papers from Simancas gives me confidence in his unsupported assertions." (G.P.C., Preface, p. VIII.)

[4] F. J., p. 132 [16].

[5] It appears from Digby's Secret Instructions as if James really thought he could escape with so little. (Cf. G.P.C., vol. I, p. 66 ; F. J., p. 134.)

James told him that if all went well with the match, he would deal with his Catholic subjects to the satisfaction of the King of Spain, but that he could not declare his intention openly beforehand for fear of compromising himself. Sarmiento, whose triumphant diplomacy now won him the title Count of Gondomar, had this in confidence from Digby, but warned his master not to trust the word of the English King without guarantees. [1]

In preparation for Digby's coming, Philip now ordered his theologians to draw up a final draft of articles, some concessions to be demanded as necessary, others to be asked for if occasion offered. The necessary concessions were fourteen in number, covering the religious freedom of the Infanta, the Catholic upbringing of the children, and the suspension of the Penal Laws with a view to ultimate repeal. They were ready by September 15, having been prepared by Fray Luis de Aliaga, the King's Confessor, who alone was to treat with Digby. [2]

The two met on December 17, and a bout of diplomatic fencing began. Formidably armed though he was, Aliaga let the Englishman open with three questions, — how far Spain would go in the matter of religion; whether Philip would agree to a dowry of two million crowns; whether he would apply for the dispensation as soon as the religious difficulties were settled. [3] Before answering, Aliaga asked for a statement as to liberty of conscience, but Digby hedged, declaring it outside his competence and a matter for Parliament; all he could discuss was the Infanta's household. The Spaniard could see this did not augur well for his fourteen articles, and wishing Digby to go away with a good impression, he held them back, contenting himself with a non-committal discussion of the Ambassador's three questions. Digby left delighted. [4]

---

[1] *F. J.*, p. 135 : Instructions to Sir J. Digby, April 4, 1617, *Cal. S. P.*, Spain. — *G.P.C.*, vol. I, p. 69 ; *F.J.*, p. 135 [17].

[2] *G.P.C.*, vol. I, p. 109 ; *F. J.*, App. V : " Conveniencias precisas con que se podrá tratar del matrimonio" and " Condiciones que se an de pedir por via de conveniencia." The latter were so exorbitant as to be rejected from the outset by the Spanish Government ; they included the Prince's conversion, repeal of the Penal Laws with liberty of conscience for the Catholics, a number of public Catholic churches in England, Scotland and Ireland, and Catholic chairs in Dogma, Canon Law and Scripture at the English Universities.

[3] *F.J.*, pp. 137-138 [18-19].

[4] *G.P.C.*, vol. I, p. 110.

Opinion in Madrid held this show of difficulty in conceding liberty of conscience a sheer pretence. The Spaniards noted, however, that Digby had given no outright refusal but appeared to be holding the threat of Parliament over them, much as they played off the Pope against James. This opinion was confirmed when Digby hinted that the best way of securing religious freedom for the English Catholics was for the Infanta to come and win the favour for them. [1]

The point was a real stumbling-block. In May, 1618, Digby left for London to discuss the matter before Gondomar sailed for Madrid. The Spaniard made one more attempt to persuade James, but the King, powerless to repeal the Laws, could only repeat his promise to relax their enforcement. So in July Gondomar took ship for Spain, while Digby, whose zeal was now rewarded with the Earldom of Bristol, stayed on in London. [2]

The two parties were clearly at cross-purposes, and again the negotiations might conveniently have lapsed, when the outbreak of what proved to be the Thirty Years' War put a pr mium on England's friendship. Not only did France suggest an alliance, offering the hand of the young princess, Henrietta Maria, but Spain came forward with the suggestion that the King of England should arbitrate in the German war. James's vanity was flattered and he was engaged in examining the legality of the Bohemian revolt when suddenly the whole problem of the war and of England's relations with Spain became infinitely more complex. In August 1619, James's son-in-law, the Elector Palatine, by accepting the crown of Bohemia, placed himself in open rebellion towards his Emperor, to whose fortunes Spain, as a collateral branch of the Habsburgs, was necessarily tied. [3]

Meanwhile, back in Madrid, Gondomar was meeting Aliaga twice weekly to discuss English affairs. While the Ambassador explained the baneful anti-Spanish influences surrounding King James, which he had tried to counteract, he showed he was still convinced that England, once allied to Spain, would return to the Faith. The two Spaniards therefore decided that the marriage treaty must be pressed forward, of prime necessity being a clear statement by the

[1] *F.J.*, pp. 142-143 ; p. 140, note 6.
[2] *Ibid.*, p. 145 [22] ; pp. 147-149 [23-24] ; *G.P.C.*, vol. I, pp. 111-112.
[3] *G.P.C.*, vol. II, pp. 268 seq.

English King as to his granting liberty of conscience to his Catholic subjects. [1] To grapple decisively with this problem, Gondomar was now ordered back to London by personal letter from Philip III.

" The principal point to be achieved, " the King 'wrote, " and without which this marriage cannot be concluded, is that of liberty of conscience, which the King of England has to grant generally in all his Kingdoms, both to natives and to foreigners... It is well you should understand this marriage is not to be effected unless the King of England grants liberty of conscience and gives sufficient security that he will execute what is agreed upon here." [2]

It was high time Gondomar returned to re-assert his former ascendancy over James, for the King had neither the moral courage nor the statesmanship necessary to cope with the greatest crisis of his time. Fearful of offending the Emperor and Spain, he could still only look upon the difficulties of his daughter and her rash husband with the anxiety of a father, and, while posing as impartial, allowed contributions to be raised in England for the defence of the Palatinate. Gondomar soon gave voice to Spain's displeasure, and James could only protest weakly that he desired no alliance but that of his Catholic Majesty. He then sent a letter to the Princes of the Protestant Union, declining English aid. [3]

In May, 1620, the Spanish Ambassador wrote home to say he was discussing the Marriage Treaty almost daily with the King and his son, — Bristol (i.e. Digby) and the Earl of Buckingham [4] completing the quorum. Charles seemed eager for the match, while to assist matters Buckingham promised to see that the activities of the pursuivants were checked. But Gondomar felt there was no trusting James, who in 1618 had broken a similar promise : until this promise was kept as a guarantee for the rest of the treaty, the Infanta could never become the Prince's bride. At the same time, the Ambassador showed the King that a dowry of two million crowns — four times more than the Catholic Louis had received

[1] F.J., pp. 149 seq. [24-25].

[2] Ibid., pp. 150-151 [25-26].

[3] G.P.C., vol. I, pp. 313 seq. ; F.J., p. 321, App. VII.

[4] George Villiers, the young country squire who succeeded Somerset as the King's favourite, soon had honours showered upon him. He became Earl (1617) and Marquis (1618) of Buckingham ; Lord High Admi ral (1619) ; Duke of Buckingham (1623). In 1626 he had to answer impeachment charges. In 1627 he led the attack on La Rochelle. He was assassinated the following year.

with the Infanta's elder sister — would fully recompense him for the fines he would lose in granting relief to the Catholics. James was effusive in expressing his desire to treat the Catholics on an equality with his other subjects, but Gondomar, mistrustful of the change in the King, told his Government to demand two guarantees of this promise, — first, the approval of Parliament; secondly, the detention of the Infanta in Spain for a year, while the English Catholics were seen to be enjoying their freedom. [1]

James's timid vacillation was seen as soon as he put pen to paper. In a letter to Philip written at this time he did not even mention liberty of conscience, and formulated no plan for the suspension of the Penal Laws, beyond saying he would remit the death penalty but was not competent to repeal the rest of the laws, yet legally the latter stood on the same footing as the capital charge, and in the opinion of the Spaniards could be remitted equally well with it. [2]

This letter was dated April 27, 1620 (o.s.). Philip waited till September before replying in two letters to Gondomar, one meant for James telling him his letter was under consideration ; the other, for Gondomar alone, stipulated liberty of conscience for the English Catholics as a *sine qua non* of the marriage. [3] The reason given for not putting this in the letter to James was fear that too blunt a statement of what would ultimately be required might break off the negotiations altogether. Typical examples, these three letters, of the circumlocutory diplomacy of the two Courts, asking for less, hoping for more, in the belief that by waiting long enough they would get it.

Replying to his King in October, Gondomar was able to say James had graciously agreed to order that no Catholic be molested for his religion. " What can a good King do more than this? " he blandly asked. A little later he confirmed this act of goodwill by refusing Parliament's demand for an increase in the laws against recusancy. Nevertheless, Gondomar avowed that he was now of the opinion that there should be not only a promise of liberty of conscience, but also fair hope of the prince's conversion before the match was made. [4]

---

[1] *F.J.*, pp. 153 [26] seq.

[2] *Ibid.*, pp. 157 seq. The letter is quoted *verbatim*, p. [28].

[3] *Ibid.*, pp. 321-323, App. VIII.

[4] *Ibid.*, p. 160 [31] : " juzgando según el estado presente de las cosas vuelve

The Spanish Council of State met in December to consider the King of England's letter of the previous April. They at once remarked how impossible it was to wring from him a clear-cut promise of liberty of conscience, and thought he was trying to shift on to Spain the responsibility for the next step. They advised Philip to accept the challenge and force the hand of the English King by asking the Pope to grant a dispensation for the marriage of the Infanta and the Prince on the condition that it would not be used till the English Catholics had been granted their religious freedom. The speedy completion of the treaty would then rest on the shoulders of the English. [1]

The King of Spain thereupon wrote to King James that he was sending Padre Diego de la Fuente to Rome for this purpose, but when he arrived in the New Year, 1621, Paul V was dead and, when Philip soon followed him to the grave, there was a further delay till Padre Diego's mission was confirmed by the new King. [2] By that time (May) George Gage, a Catholic Court messenger whom James often used, had arrived in Rome, ostensibly with a petition for the dispensation from the English Catholics, but in reality acting on the King's behalf. He was told bluntly by the new Pope, Gregory XV, that the King of England would be required to do much more than he was doing at present. The agent took this to mean that promises of liberty of conscience and the conversion of the Prince would be necessary. [3]

Pope Gregory wrote in August, 1621, to tell the new King Philip IV

---

de nuevo á apretar mas que este casamiento no puede ni debe hacerse sin libertad de consciencia muy asentada y asegurada, y probabiles esperanzas de la reducion de aquel Principe".

G.P.C., vol. I, pp. 402 seq. James told the ambassador about this time that he was ready to acknowledge the Pope as head of Christendom in matters spiritual and to allow appeals to Rome from the English bishops, if His Holiness would refrain from meddling in temporal jurisdiction and the deposition of Kings. Gondomar's somewhat ambiguous comment was that nothing was impossible with God.

[1] *F.J.*, pp. 160-161 [31].

[2] *Ibid.*, pp. 162 seq. [32-33].

[3] *Ibid.*, pp. 164 seq. [33-4] ; 168-169 [36]. Six months later John Bennett and another priest brought a similar petition from the English clergy, but it seems that they too were secret agents of the King, their passports being endorsed " specialibus ex causis Majestatis suae negotia concernentibus".

of the congregation of Cardinals he had appointed to consider the conditions on which a dispensation might be granted. [1] Their Eminences soon arrived at two conclusions : first, that the articles prepared hitherto had been concerned mainly with the Infanta, making small provision for the English Catholics ; secondly, that the King of England must offer genuine guarantees to back his promises. In both these statements, they were hinting at liberty of conscience, but refrained from demanding it openly as they thought the concession would make a better impression coming freely from the King than as a condition laid down by Rome. [2]

George Gage was only told this some time later (July, 1622) by Cardinal Bandini, who took the opportunity of making an appeal for the conversion of the King of England himself. So skilled a controversialist, he told Gage, could not but admit the claims of the Holy See. If human respect held him back, there was the example of the great Henry IV of France ; if fear of the Puritans, the remedy was adroit statesmanship. As a Catholic, James would have the whole-hearted support of his Catholic subjects at home, and of the Catholic powers abroad, including the special favour of the Pope. Even if conversion were too great a step to take himself, the King could at least promise to assist that of his son. [3]

All this Gage was to tell James on behalf of the Cardinals and present him with a copy of the amended articles. The Agent did so and was well received by both the King and Charles. Certain now of Rome's attitude, James inexcusably delayed his reply to the Cardinals, [4] yet wrote straightway to Bristol, now back in Madrid, complaining of their amendments. He could go no farther, he declared, than his 1620 promise to remit penalties and see that no Catholic suffered death for his faith. If the Spanish would not accept this within two months, the negotiations were to be at an end. [5]

Bristol at once presented a memorandum to Philip IV pointing

---

[1] *F. J.*, pp. 166 seq.   They were Cardinals Bandini, Mellini, Sacrati and the Cardinal of Santa Susanna.

[2] *Ibid.*, pp. 166 seq. [34-36].

[3] *F. J.*, pp. 173 seq. [38-40] ; *G.P.C.*, vol. II, p. 238.

[4] *F. J.*, p. 182 [42].   It took Gage from Oct. 22 / Nov. 1, 1622 till Jan. 31/ Feb. 10, 1623 to reach Rome.

[5] *G.P.C.*, vol. II, p. 239.

out that it was five years since the first draft of articles, and that when the King's father had applied for the dispensation in December, 1620, King James had regarded the religious question as settled. Now the Cardinals had confronted him with impossible demands. He was therefore anxious to know the King of Spain's intentions, as Prince Charles had waited six years for a wife, and must marry at once. Six weeks later a second memorandum followed, couched in still stronger terms, maintaining that they were not a stage farther than the generalities of six or seven years before. [1]

This energetic *démarche* of the English Ambassador stirred Philip into sending James a conciliatory letter, promising to apply to Rome for the dispensation and suggesting that in the meantime the temporal conditions of the match might be arranged. [2]

The State Junta now met to deliberate on Bristol's representations and the English King's criticism of the Cardinal's amendments. Olivares, the King's chief minister, [3] suggested that the match should be dropped altogether, owing to the impossibility of obtaining the right concessions and the Infanta's protest thereat. (She had declared she would enter a nunnery of barefooted Carmelites rather than marry under such conditions.) This startling proposal the Junta rejected, drafting a reply to James wherein they asked that if the Pope's idea of toleration, *viz.* a public church in every town, could not be conceded, at least the Catholics might be allowed to worship freely in the privacy of their homes. [4] In the meantime, they would try to get the dispensation by the following April (1623) ; the marriage would then be celebrated within 40 days of its arrival, and three weeks later the Infanta could take ship for England.

Bristol seemed satisfied with this, and though the Pope had mis-

---

[1] *F.J.*, pp. 178-179 [41-43] ; pp.187-188 [46]. Admitting this, Fray Francisco excuses Spain on the score of politeness, while blaming the ambiguous and general phrases of James, such as : " he would do his best," etc.

[2] *Ibid.*, p. 190 [47].

[3] Gaspar Guzman, Count-Duke of Olivares, favourite of Philip IV who abandoned the entire management of public affairs to him, though the title of minister was still held by Bernard de Zuñiga, Olivares' uncle, who held office under Philip III. Olivares held unbounded authority for 22 years. His aims were constantly thwarted by Richelieu, and he was dismissed in 1643.

[4] *F.J.*, pp. 190-192 [47-48] ; *G.P.C.*, vol II, pp. 277, 280.

givings, he again put the matter before the Cardinals for a decision. [1] So matters stood when all calculations were upset by the momentous news that the Prince of Wales proposed to come in person to Madrid.

[1] *F. J.*, p. 183, note (a) ; p. 198 [51]. This time they included Cardinal Maffeo Barberini, who later as Urban VIII was to be in such close relationship with Charles. He was already *au courant* with English affairs, having been Nuncio in Paris and Protector of Scotland.

Part II

Fiasco in Spain

> *Archie, the Court Fool, hearing from King James of the Prince's journey :"I must change caps with your Majesty."*
> *" Why?" asked the King.*
> *" Why? - Who sent the Prince to Spain?"*
> *" But supposing the Prince should come safely back again?"*
> *" Why, in that case, I will take my cap from my head and and send it to the King of Spain."* [1]

It is difficult to decide on whom to father the idea that the heir to the English throne should cross half a continent, practically unguarded, in search of a bride. Addressing Parliament years later, Charles claimed the plan as his own. [2] He was certainly tired of the long-drawn-out negotiations and eager for marriage, but Buckingham was the moving spirit in the final effort to get the King to consent, while Gondomar, who was intrigued by the idea, thinking Spanish Catholic atmosphere would help to convert the Prince, may have done much to stress the sensation the Prince would create. As early as May 1622, the Prince had asked his advice on the plan, and later in the year Endymion Porter, in Madrid on business connected with the Marriage Treaty, had sounded Spanish opinion on the projected visit. [3]

James, obsessed with fear of dying before the succession was safe, was ready to consent to what he at first believed to be nothing more startling than that Charles and Buckingham, the Lord High Admiral, should go with the fleet to fetch home the Infanta. It was only shortly before they started that James was told they were to make the journey incogniti with no more than two attendants ;

---

[1] Cf. W. H. D. ADAMS, *The White King*, vol. I, p. 39.
[2] P. CHASLES, *Charles Ier*, p. 22 : Speech to both Houses, 1632.
[3] *F.J.*, pp. 196 seq. [50-51] ; *G.P.C.*, vol. II, pp. 269 ; 282.

but the old King's timid opposition was quickly overridden by the blustering assurances of Buckingham. [1]

Charles, whose boyhood and youth had been overshadowed by his more colourful brother, as well as by his own physical disability and natural timidity, saw nothing but romantic adventure in a daring ride across France, a triumphal reception in Madrid, followed by a wooing worthy of the days of chivalry. The dashing Buckingham was as enthusiastic, so the two friends set out in February, 1623, disguised by false beards and the names Tom and John Smith. They were accompanied only by Sir Francis Cottington and Endymion Porter.

In Paris, still incogniti, they witnessed a Court Ball, and dazzled by the beauty of Anne of Austria, were the keener to reach Madrid to see her sister. [2] Spurred on by a message from the English Ambassador in Paris, who realized the risk they ran in France, they knocked at Bristol's door in Madrid on the evening of March 7. [3]

Overjoyed at the news, Gondomar at once informed Olivares, who heard it with mixed feelings. If Charles had come to declare his conversion, all would be well, but the visit placed a heavy responsibility upon the Spanish minister, with the prospect of disgrace should the alliance now fall through. Philip, delighted at the thought that Charles would soon become a Catholic, resolved that the Prince's presence would not make him yield one jot on the articles touching religion, nor run counter to the wishes of the Pope. [4]

News of Charles's arrival had different effects on the two capitals. London was irritated that the heir to the throne should throw himself in the arms of the Papists. They would assassinate him or, worse still, damn his soul by drawing him into their accursed net. The prince had made his person the centre of intrigue between Rome and Madrid, they had him in their hands, they could dictate their terms. Besides, England, as head of the Protestant nations of

---

[1] *G.P.C.*, vol. II, pp. 256 ; 298-299.

[2] *G.P.C.*, vol. II, p. 302 ; CHASLES, *op. cit.*, p. 25. Charles had later to appeal to a dimly-lit gallery to explain how he missed Madame de France who was dancing there that night and who, two years after, became his bride.

[3] S. L. LEE, *The Life of Lord Herbert of Cherbury*, pp. 238 seq.

[4] *G.P.C.*, vol. II, pp. 305 seq. ; *F.J.*, App. X.

the North, sensed the ridicule to which she was exposed by so rash a step. [1]

Madrid, on the contrary, went mad with joy. At the moment when Spain seemed in decline God had chosen her as the instrument to bring England back to the Faith. A certain affinity between Charles and the Spaniards made him popular. His gravity, his melancholy dignified bearing, his conventionalism, touched a chord in the soul of the grandiose people for whom Cervantes had written *Don Quixote*. So the townsfolk of Madrid took him to their hearts, and the streets rang with the shrill soprano of the *manolas* and the guttural accents of the *arrieros* repeating for the hundredth time the latest ditty of the popular song-writer, Lope de Vega :

> " Carlos Estuardo soy
> Que, siendo amor mi guia,
> Al cielo d'España voy
> Por ver mi estrella Maria. " [2]

On the second day after the Prince's arrival, when his carriage and the King's had met apparently by chance in the thronged streets — a little by-play satisfying to Spanish etiquette, — Charles and Philip met with much ceremony at the Prado, the Court being decked out in all its former splendour. Here the Prince presented letters from James, who recalled in a happy phrase that, drawn by the fame of the Infanta, Charles was emulating his father, grandfather and great-grandfather in seeking his bride abroad. [3]

The King now ordered the formation of a Junta, under the presidency of Olivares, to deal with all questions touching the Marriager Treaty, and they immediately arranged a public service in thanksgiving to God for inspiring the Prince's journey, and asking His further guidance. Why he had come none knew but all had

---

[1] CHASLES, *op. cit.*, pp. 26-27.

[2] *Ibid.*, p. 27 ; *G.P.C.*, vol. II, p. 314.
> " Charles Stuart I am
> Whom love has guided afar ;
> To the heaven of Spain I came,
> To see Maria, my star."

[3] *F. J.*, p. [56]. James had journeyed to Denmark to fetch Anne ; Darnley had conducted Mary Stuart from France, while James V had done the like for Marie de Vendôme, though he had soon changed his mind and married Madeleine de France, daughter of Francis I.

hopes. Charged with sounding Buckingham and Cottington, Gondomar told them that the Spanish people looked for some signal service to the Church as a result. [1]

What else than his desire to become a Catholic before the marriage could have induced the Prince of Wales to undertake so compromising a step as a visit to Madrid almost alone? Even Bristol thought this, and after a few days, as Charles made no sign, he broached the subject. Charles answered sharply that he would do nothing so base as to barter his religion for a bride. Apologizing, the Ambassador advised the Prince to make the matter clear at once. If he wished to become a Catholic and announced the fact, he would gain all at a blow. If he had no such intention, yet gave the impression that he had, the Spaniards would make no effort to obtain the dispensation for the marriage. [2]

Bristol was right. With the Prince in their hands, Philip IV and Olivares were prepared to stake all on his conversion (with its corollary — England on the Catholic side, or at least neutral, in the German war) and were anxious that the Pope should not grant the dispensation for a mixed marriage, involving a treaty of mutual concessions that neither Spain nor England were prepared to fulfil.

Therefore, although Olivares promised Buckingham to apply for the document immediately (it will be remembered that the Junta had told Bristol in December, 1622, that they would have it by the following April), he at the same time secretly instructed his envoy, the Duke of Pastrana, to block the granting of the dispensation the moment it was known that the Prince was not prepared to be converted. There was to be a Catholic marriage or none at all. [3]

Unfortunately for Olivares, the Madrid Nuncio, Mgr de' Massimi had written to Rome on March 20 (N. S.) of Charles's arrival three days before. This letter reached Rome about a fortnight later (not five days, as Gardiner maintains). The spontaneity of the Prince's visit at once sent hopes high, — his conversion or some signal favour to the English Catholics must result from it, — and made Gregory XV all the more disposed to grant the

[1] *F.J.*, p. 203.

[2] *Ibid.*, pp. 207-206 ; *G.P.C.*, vol. II, p. 312.

[3] *G.P.C.*, vol. II, pp. 329-330 ; L. AREZIO, *op. cit.*, p. 30. In all probability none knew of Pastrana's mission save Philip and Olivares.

dispensation that his predecessor, an acute canonist, had held back
on the score of insufficient security. [1]

The Cardinals, in whose hands the Pope had placed the matter,
had questioned both Padre de la Fuente and George Gage, and now
advised Gregory that he could and should grant the dispensation,
lest a refusal spoil all hope of the Prince's conversion and bring yet
worse calamities on the heads of the English Catholics. [2]

So the Brief of Dispensation was despatched on April 12, when
Pastrana had scarce set out on his obstructive mission. Under the
same date the list of still further amended marriage articles was sent
to the Nuncio with detailed instructions not to hand over the
dispensation to Philip until he had taken an oath to the Holy See to
guarantee that the English King and Prince and their posterity
would fulfil the articles. In other words his Catholic Majesty
was to bind himself in honour to obtain proper security from
England given in a promise legally drawn up, a copy of which
the Nuncio was to send to Rome.

The Cardinals had complained that none but the last of the articles
submitted to them had dealt with the relief of the English Catholics,
though this was the *causa motiva* of the dispensation. It was realized
that the present power of the Puritans and their hatred of Catholics
made public toleration a practical impossibility ; but the King of
England should at least allow the Catholics to practise their Faith
unmolested in their homes, and order a complete cessation of persecution : this much must be insisted upon once and for all. [3] Time
and again the King had promised this to Gondomar and others
without result. His hand must now be forced by a flat refusal
to allow the Infanta to set foot in England till it was seen over

---

[1] AREZIO, *op. cit.*, pp. 32-33.

[2] *Ibid.*, pp. 71-76 : Ludovisi to de' Massimi, April 12, 1623 : *Instruttioni
à V. S. Mon^re de' Massimi, Vescovo di Bertinoro, Nuntio di N. S^re ne' Regni di
Spagna, per trattare con la M^{tà} del Rè Cat^{co} sopra la dispensa del Matrimonio
di sua sorella col Principe d'Inghilterra :* " ... siamo unitamente venuti in parere,
che S. Sta possa, e debba concederla, .. non meno per le moltiplicate speranze
del bene, che per fuggir l'imminente male, che sopra i Cattolici Inglesi ande-
rebbe à cadere, se la dimandata dispensa si negasse.."

[3] *Ibid.*, pp. 74 seq : "... non potendosi in questi tempi per la potenza, e l'odio
implacabile de' Puritani verso il nome Cat^{co} sperar di ottenere in quel Regno la
libertà di conscienza, non sarebbe per hora di leggier momento, se le persecutioni
e molestie contro i cattolici del tutto cessassero."

a period of time that his promises had taken effect and that the Catholics were left in peace. [1]

In this way the Pope, while showing the greatest goodwill in granting the dispensation, was taking a firm stand on James's fulfilling his side of the bargain, and incidentally was forestalling any attempt on the part of Spain or England at making a scapegoat of the Holy See, should the negotiations eventually fall through. [2]

It is of the utmost importance to note that the dispensation and these instructions were despatched on April 12, hastened, if not actually occasioned, by the receipt in Rome (about April 4-7) of de' Massimi's letter of March 20 announcing Charles's arrival in Madrid. Meanwhile the Nuncio had heard of Philip's and Olivares's reluctance that the dispensation be granted, and of Pastrana's mission. He had hinted at this as far back as January, but Rome knew nothing for certain of the Spanish change of policy till the Nuncio wrote to this effect on April 1. This letter arrived in Rome on April 18, causing considerable consternation.

Replying post-haste the same day, the Cardinal Secretary pointed out to the Nuncio that it was impossible to recall the dispensation, now nearly a week on its way ; besides, both La Fuente and George Gage knew of its despatch. The only solution was to contrive to drag out the negotiations, making all chance of agreement seem hopeless by inserting conditions of which nothing had been said hitherto. This distateful task Cardinal Ludovisi was now reluctantly compelled to undertake. [3]

First he warned the Nuncio no longer to follow his instructions of the 12th to keep the dispensation a secret, since its sending was known and could not be denied. Difficulties, however, could be created over the conditions of its delivery, as these were not known. [4]

---

[1] *Ibid.* : " .. Mille volte per le speranze del matrimonio è stata data intentione dal Rè Inglese agli Ambasciatori del Cattolico di voler rimettere le pene e liberare i poveri afflitti dalle perpetue persecutioni ; .. nondimeno non vede seguirne altro effetto, che di parole ... Propongono dunque [i. e. the Spanish ministers whose suggestions were now incorporated in the Nuncio's Instructions]... che S. Mᵗᵃ non lasci in maniera niuna andare l'Infanta in Inghilterra, se non si vede del tutto eseguire quello che si puo fare in sua assenza delle cose promesse."

[2] *Ibid.*

[3] *Ibid.*, pp. 38-39 ; 77.

[4] *Ibid.*, p. 78 : Ludovisi to de' Massimi, April 10, 1623 : " Ma ch'ella possa, et debba far tutte le difficoltà che si stimeranno convenevoli intorno alle condit-

The Cardinal now added new conditions in this letter of the 18th, *which he pre-dated the 12th,* as if it had been sent under the same cover with the Brief of Dispensation and the original Instructions. [1] In the latter, it will be recalled, only cessation of persecution had been demanded from the English King ; in fact, the Cardinal had gone out of his way to admit that the time was not ripe for asking full religious freedom. Now, in this falsely dated letter, complete liberty of conscience for the English Catholics was asked for as a necessary condition of the dispensation, on the pretext that in the Articles submitted to Rome the concessions made were restricted to the Infanta, while those concerning the Catholics were secret and tacit, leaving a loophole through which the King of England could escape his obligations. Public practice of the Faith must therefore be allowed and confirmed by Parliament and the Privy Council. [2] At the same time the wish was clearly expressed that the marriage should not take place at all without the Prince's conversion, [3] which was now to be urged as greater security for the Infanta, and to forestall any future use of the English law of divorce. [4]

ione, le quali à niuno si son communicate, e si è fatto à posta, perche da lei se cerchi d'avantaggiare, quanto più si potrà ; *onde havrà V.S. il modo di tirare alla lunga il negotio* à compiacimento di S. Mᵗᵃ, e di avanzarsi conforme al nostro desiderio à beneficio della religione Cattolica."

[1] *Ibid.* : " Et à questo fine perche non le manchi alcuna cosa da mostrare, *le invio l'aggiunte lettere ostensibili, fatte sotto l'istessa data delli 12,* nelle quali si richiede per condizione la publica libertà di coscienza, e di più si desidera ardentemente la conversione del Principe."

[2] *Ibid.,* p. 76 : Ludovisi to de' Massimi, April 12 (really 18), 1623 : " ... Dunque sarebbe necessario, che à tutti li medesimi Cattolici suoi sudditi il Rè concedesse il libero e publico esercitio della religione Cattolica Romana, e la publica libertà di coscienza e che la concessione sua fosse e dal consiglio e dal Parlamento approvata." Yet in the original Instructions of the 12th, Ludovisi had said :" habbiamo creduto che sia più da desiderane che da sperare." (*Ibid.,* pp. 36, 76.)

[3] *Ibid.,* p. 76 : Ludovisi to de' Massimi, April 12 (really 18),1623 :".... senza la quale S. Sᵗᵃ non vorrebbe che se fosse possibile il matrimonio in niuna maniera si facesse."

[4] *Ibid.,* pp. 37-38. Arezio has based his study on a Codex now at Palermo entitled *Ludovisi, Lettere originali.* In this the process of falsifying the date of the 2nd Instruction from the 18th to the 12th can be followed. Gardiner, using a translation of a copy of the latter obtained by Cottington and *not knowing it had been pre-dated,* concluded that Rome's new conditions were decided, not

On April 19 (the day after Rome's new pre-dated conditions had been sent off) a courtesy letter from Charles arrived, thanking the Pope for the dispensation he had heard was on its way. George Gage, though he had not brought the letter, presented it to the Pope, at the same time complaining on the Prince's behalf of the Madrid Nuncio's aloofness towards him. The Holy Father explained that this attitude was a strictly correct one for his representative to adopt towards a heretic : the Prince would receive every honour once he became a Catholic.

The same day the Pope's nephew wrote to de' Massimi, ordering public prayers in all the Churches of Spain to win for the Prince the supernatural gift of Faith. Under the same date the Cardinal urged the same end in letters to Charles himself, Philip IV, Buckingham, the Patriarch of the Indies, the Grand Inquisitor and the King's Confessor. [1]

This attempt to convert the Prince the Spaniards were already making. Charles had soon realized their hopes : there could be no firm friendship without union in religion, they had hinted. But as he wrote to his father only ten days after his arrival in Madrid, his conscience bade him put such a possibility quite out of mind. [2] Had Charles been as frank with his hosts, he might have saved himself much humiliation.

---

as a result of the Nuncio's letter of April 1 telling of Spain's reluctance for the dispensation, but as a consequence of the news of Charles's arrival in Madrid, which the Nuncio announced in his letter of March 20, reaching Rome between April 4-7. (Cf. *G.P.C.*, vol. II, p. 327 note.) Gardiner's mistake is due to the fact of his translation not being identical with the original Ludovisi wrote. This is clear from certain particular differences, e. g. *à propos* of urging on Charles's conversion, the Cardinals suggest the Spanish ladies should lend their persuasions, — a point Gardiner would certainly have made had he known it. Therefore Arezio says of the English historian : "Egli non conosceva affato i documenti che io ho sott' occhio, e stando à quelli de' quali s'avvalse, non poteva certamente mettere in chiaro gl'intrighi, cui era fatta segno il Principe Carlo da parte de' suoi ospiti, più che dalla Corte pontificia." (*Ibid.*, p. 38.)

[1] AREZIO, *op. cit.*, pp. 42-43, 79-80 : Ludovisi to de' Massimi, April 19, 1623, where these letters are mentioned. On the point of prayer the Cardinal writes : " V. S. procurerà che si facciano orationi non solo costi, mà per tutta Spagna, massimamente da tanti religiosi divotissimi, che vi si trovano, che noi di quà operemo l'istesso. Et il Sig.re Iddio le conceda per ció la sua santa gratia. "

[2] *G.P.C.*, vol. II, p. 314, quoting Prince and Buckingham to James, March 17/27, 1623.

To bring the matter to a head, Philip ordered Olivares to intimate to Buckingham that the Prince should at least consent to hear the case for the Catholic Faith, having of his own free will come to its very gates. He might rest assured that no shadow of compulsion would be placed upon him. Buckingham brought a satisfactory answer from Charles, but asked that he might be questioned first, though in the utmost secrecy lest his countrymen should hear of it. [1]

Olivares agreed, and he, Buckingham and Fray Francisco de Jesús, the King's Preacher, met one evening in the royal apartments, the interpreter being one James Wadsworth, formerly a prominent Puritan, now a Catholic. All the chief points of controversy were gone through in a four hours' sitting. Buckingham had frequent recourse to a sheet of instructions he held in his hand, and it was clear to all that he had come purely out of politeness with no open mind. Still, Olivares arranged another meeting equally barren of results. [2]

Perseveringly, the Spaniards set to work on the Prince. On May 3 (N.S.) he met Philip in the royal apartments but, despite Charles's request for him to stay, the King soon went, as he refused to hear a word against the Faith. So the Prince was left with Olivares, Buckingham and the Fathers with whom he was to debate, Fray Antonio de Sotomayor, the King's Confessor, Fray Zacharias Boverio de Saluzo, a well-known Capuchin controversialist, and two Provincials of the same Order, Diego de Quiroga and Pedro de Barbastro.

The Fathers waited politely for the Prince to put a question on which they could enlarge, but Charles, saying there was no point of the Faith on which he was without information, preferred them to introduce a topic. Fray Zacharias quoted from St Luke,

---

[1] *G.P.C.*, vol. II, pp. 313. Buckingham's conduct had completely deceived the Spaniards. He made a point of not attending service at the English Embassy ; he would genuflect on entering a Catholic church. The Imperial Ambassador remarked that the Englishmen in Madrid " stellen sich sehr Catholisch."

[2] *F.J.*, pp. 209-210 [58] : "y viéndose conocidamente convencido en algunos quando ya le faltaban las réplicas generales de que venia advertido, sacaba un papel (que al parecer era instrucción de cómo se havia de haver) y buscaba en el si á caso havia alguno otro mejor socorro, y assí á mui pocos lanzes se hechó de ver que lo quo hacia era porque era complimiento, y que tenia su conversion pendiente de voluntad agena."

Chapter XXII, the words of Our Lord to St. Peter: " Simon, Simon, behold Satan hath desired to have you, that he may sift you as wheat ; but I have prayed for thee, that thy faith fail not : and thou, being once converted, confirm thy brethren. " This he applied to the Pope's position as Vicar of Christ and Head of the Church. Charles said the Father was forcing the text, and after asking him to repeat it twice in French, he voiced the same opinion in English to Buckingham, who thereupon showed his annoyance by pulling off his hat and jumping on it. [1]

Despite the failure of these conversations Charles told Fray Zacharias he would renounce his religion once convinced of its falsity, so Spanish hopes rose and Olivares was arranging another meeting when Buckingham objected that he had orders not to allow the Prince to discuss religion, though he had previously maintained the contrary. [2]

Fray Zacharias, whose fame as a controversialist as well as his fluency in French, which enabled him to deal directly with the Prince, had given him a leading part in the discussions,now published a book, dedicated to Charles, which, from its style and composition was possibly written from notes used in the talks, and perhaps represents an attempt to succeed in cold print, where the highly-charged atmosphere of a *viva voce* controversy had failed. [3]

Even after allowing for the high-sounding rhetoric of humanistic Latin, and the natural desire of the author to flatter as well as to argue the Prince into the Church, one can still read in Fr. Zachary's enthusiasm the far-reaching influence it was felt the conversion of the heir to the three kingdoms would have. [4]

[1] *F. J.*, p. 210 [58] : " para hacer grandes extremos de indignacion hasta arroxar el sombrero y pisarlo".

[2] *G.P.C.*, vol. II, p. 329.

[3] Boverius (Fray Zacharias Boverio de Saluzo), *Orthodoxa consultatio de ratione verae fidei et religionis amplectendae, ad Ser. Carolum Stuartum, Walliae principem, Jacobi, Magnae Britanniae regis filium : ac regni successorem iuratum : in suo in Hispanias adventu*. First published, Madrid July 1623 ; edition used here dated Coloniae Agrippinae, 1626. Cardinal Antonio Barberini had a further edition printed in Rome, 1635, at the moment of the Catholic revival in England.

[4] 5 *Apparatus* preparing the mind followed by 7 *Regulae* for finding the true Faith comprise the first part of the book ; the second part has 7 *Regulae* showing that the Church of Rome alone fulfils all these requirements. At each *Regula* the Prince is addressed in a high-sounding title stressing the hopes of his conversion.

Charles was urged above all to keep his mind open to candid inquiry, as true faith comes to the soul only with intellectual conviction. In his search for truth, hatred of Catholics and prejudice in favour of Protestantism must be equally absent from his mind, which should adopt towards all religion an attitude of methodic doubt. [1]

Having prepared the Prince's mind, Fray Zacharias proceeds to influence him with *ad hominem* arguments from history. Lutherans and Calvinists, Protestant and Puritan, wherever they had existed in England or Germany, had been the cause of internecine quarrels. They were a kingdom divided against itself, not even believing in the unity of the Church. [2] Let Charles use his judgment and see whither such religion led. Whence had it come? A hundred years before, Protestants had not existed; for centuries till Henry VIII the Catholic Faith had held sole sway in England, — this

Here are the most colourful :

> *Serenissime Carole, Christiani orbis Flos.*
> *Carole Princeps, future Catholicae Fidei Restitutor.*
> *Nobilissime Princeps, Britannici Regni expectatio.*
> *Serenissime Carole, spes Anglicanae Ecclesiae,* etc. etc.

Most curious of all, the *foelicissima auspicia* Fr Zachary sees in the anagram Charles's name made with that of Our Lord (*Op. cit.*, p. *2) :

> CHAROLUS STUARTUS
> CHRISTUS SALVATOR
>
> *Quis nouus hic Christus? Quibus hic Salvator ab oris*
> *Surgit? An ex Anglo nascitur orbe salus?*
> *Vnctio dat Christum Regalis, certa salutem*
> *Bisque dabit Christum mox renouanda Fides.*
> *Ast age, rumpe movas (Princeps) lege semina vitae ;*
> *Saluantem pariet te quoque parta salus.*
> *Gens antiqua, Dei soboles, rediuiua solantem.*
> *Te expectat, longo pondere pressagemens.*
> *Huc te fata vocant ; si quae aspera dogmata rumpas ;*
> *Tu Saluator eris, mox vbi Christus eris.*
> *Da palmas Christo : Christi foue semen et vt sis*
> *CHRISTUS SALVATOR, nomen vtrumque dabit.*

[1] *Op. cit.*, Apparatus 1us : Ut quoniam vera religioni tibi inquirenda est, antequam ad eam investigandam accedas, omnes prius religionem apud te suspectam habeas.... ac tandem omni, tum erga Catholicos odio, tum erga Protestantes amore prorsus exuto, teipsum liberum, ac medium inter utramque et Catholicorum et Protestantium religionem statuas ; per inde, ac si omni fide ac religione careres.

[2] *Op. cit.*, pp. 21-22 ; 103 seq.

alone must make the Prince think. [1] And what an example Catholic Kings had given to Catholic England! — Lucius, Edward, Ethelbert, Ethelwulf, all bowing to the authority of the Pope, even subjecting the realm to St. Peter in tribute paid till the time of Henry VIII, — that Henry who, as Luther's bitterest opponent, had shown that the bulk of the faithful held to the primacy of Rome, till hate and lust for power, not doctrinal doubts, had led even the Faith's Defender from his allegiance. [2]

So Charles was exhorted to mature reflection. Corruption had crept in among the bishops and clergy of England drawing them away from Rome, — let him not share their crime, but, purging his mind of hatred for the Holy See, dwell frankly on Our Lord's guarantee of the faith of Peter. [3]

It is just possible that arguments of such eloquence and point might have moved Charles, had he been free to meet Father Zachary, but the conferences were stopped, and the disgruntled Spaniards threw on to Buckingham the blame for hindering the Prince's conversion. [4]

The growing tension of the situation was not relieved by the decision of James to send out two chaplains to minister to the Prince. Armed with all the appurtenances of ceremonial, they were to devote themselves to the proper presentation of the Anglican liturgy, a service "decent and agreeable to the purity of the Prince's church, and yet as near Rome as can lawfully be done. " [5] They were to avoid all polemics in their sermons for it was James's fond belief that his chaplains would persuade the Spaniards not only that Anglicanism was poles apart from the teaching of Luther and Calvin, but that it was not much different from what they themselves practised. The poor men were never given a chance, Olivares

---

[1] *Op. cit.*, pp. 67-68.

[2] *Op. cit.*, pp. 183-184 ; 423 quoting HENRICUS VIII ANGLIAE REX, *in dissert. contr. Luther., art.* 2. *asser.* 7 : " Negare Lutherus non potest quia omnis ecclesia fidelium, sacrosanctam sedem Romanam, velut Matrem Primatemque recognoscat ac veneretur. "

[3] LUKE XXII, quoted above : *op. cit.*, p. 54.

[4] *G. P.C.*, vol. II, p. 328.

[5] *Ibid.*, pp.330-331 : James's Direction to the Prince's Chaplains, quoted here, gives a most informative inventory of paraphernalia for the chapel, as well as instructions for the conduct of the service.

intimating that any attempt to introduce them to Charles's apartments in the K ng's Palace would be resisted by force. [1]

James was annoyed, and justifiably so. " It is an ill preparation for giving the Infanta free exercise of her religion here to refusr it to my son there, since their religion is as odious to a numbee here as ours is there. " He therefore ordered Charles to hold the service at the Embassy and show both God and man that he was not ashamed of his religion. But despite Buckingham's persuasions only once did the Prince attend worship at Bristol's house, and even then against the Ambassador's wish. [2]

Once the grant of the dispensation was known, Olivares went to Buckingham to tell him that it now lay with the King of England to grant that complete liberty of conscience the Pope demanded for the English Catholics. This, said Buckingham, was impossible : it would only lead to disturbances in which the Catholics would suffer ; the most the King could do was to repeat his promise that the Catholics would not be molested while they practised their religion in the privacy of their own homes.

Olivares put this to the Nuncio who refused to yield an inch, pointing out that, if James showed now such fear of Parliament and of his subjects regarding concessions to the Catholics, there was little chance of his keeping his promises in the future. The Nuncio then suggested that the English Catholics should be secured by the grant of a stronghold on the lines of La Rochelle, till Buckingham showed the contrast between the bellicose Huguenots and the quiet retired lives of the English Papists. [3]

Representatives of both sides now held three conferences to discuss the Papal documents. The first meeting dealt with the form of oath to be taken by Philip ; in the second, Charles said he and his father were prepared to swear for themselves and their descendants to the suspension of the Penal Laws, and to get Parliament to confirm this within three years at the most. [4]

In the third and final meeting Charles raised objections to the

---

[1] *F.J.*, p. [59].

[2] *G.P.C.*, vol. II, p. 331 ; *F.J.*, p. 212.

[3] *G.P.C.*, vol. II, pp. 315-316.

[4] *F.J.*, p. 216 ; Guizot, *op. cit.*, p. 132. In excusing the rashness of this promise to his father, Charles said he and Buckingham held that as long as they did their best they would fulfil it, even though the effect did not follow.

Cardinals' amendments. Free entry to the Infanta's chapel for every Catholic was uncalled-for when private worship in their homes was allowed them ; he would tolerate their coming, but to grant it as of right would amount to that public toleration of Catholic worship to which his father was formally opposed. On the point of the children's education, the Prince said that his father was willing for them to stay under the care of the Infanta for three years more than he had formerly stipulated, *i.e.* till the age of ten ; farther he could not go, as it was the custom in England to take children away early from their mothers. [1]

The Council of State voted the Prince's replies inadequate as not differing in substance from former offers. Both the Pope and the King of Spain required greater safeguards, and the Prince was asked to save further delay by stating frankly the most he could concede. [2]

Charles's answer came in writing, and it was in the same vein as before — concessions to the Catholics must be gradual to avoid disturbance. On two minor points he yielded, however, for he would not allow the Infanta to be persuaded against her religion, but would himself be willing to listen at her request to expositions of Catholic doctrine. [3]

The Council of State now asked the Nuncio to its meetings to consider whether this answer was sufficient to justify the handing-over of the dispensation. The Nuncio was resolute : the document would not be valid till the Articles as sent from Rome were carried out exactly. This attitude he maintained in face of a midnight visit from Buckingham and Bristol. The Prince was told that nothing could be changed without leave from Rome. [4]

Olivares now offered Charles the alternative of applying to the Pope for further concessions or of asking his father to consent to the Articles as they stood. Charles asked Philip to appeal to His Holiness ; for the second alternative, he said, his presence in England was necessary, and he must leave at once. Philip urgently

---

[1] GUIZOT, *op. cit.*, p. 132, note 2.

[2] *F.J.*, pp. 217-218.

[3] *Ibid.*, pp. 228-229.

[4] *Ibid.*,pp. 229-230. In his interview with the Nuncio,Buckingham threatened. The only way to negotiate for this marriage, he said, was to keep the sword suspended over the heads of the English Catholics.

requested Charles to wait while messengers were sent to London and Rome. The Prince agreed, nominating Cottington to return to consult the King. Philip then ordered a new Junta of theologians to deliberate on the principal points laid before it. [1]

Prior to his talk with the Prince, Olivares had made two important pronouncements against the marriage. In a speech before the Council of State, he had argued cleverly to the conclusion that a marriage treaty was superfluous to induce what was clearly a practical necessity *viz.* an Anglo-Spanish alliance. Therefore, the sole aim of the treaty became the relief of the English Catholics, yet on this all-important point the King of England would give only general assurances of goodwill with no guarantee of fulfilment. If he refused practical concessions now when he had all to gain in granting them, what hope was there for the future when the Infanta would be held hostage against Spanish interference on an outbreak of persecution? As matters stood, the King of Spain was required by the Pope to bind himself in honour to enforce the grant of concessions that the English King believed harmful to him and evil in themselves. No solid friendship could be built on such a basis.

Nevertheless, Olivares concluded, if James or his son became Catholic, if toleration, confirmed by Privy Council and Parliament, became law, if Catholics were promoted to positions of confidence, or if the Infanta were kept in Spain until the English Catholics had enjoyed the concessions long enough to become independent of royal privilege, then he would willingly withdraw all he had said. [2]

The Spanish minister spoke to his King with equal frankness of the inadequacy of the purely verbal guarantees of the English, insufficient even if the King and his Catholic subjects had common interests ; yet the contrary was the case, for in engaging to favour them James was signing away his own political advantage, since he was encouraging within his realm a religion his conscience opposed. Therefore, his aim in making any promises at all must be either not to keep them, or else to gauge the strength of the English Catholics and then decide whether to grant them full

[1] *F.J.*, pp. 320-324. The Junta comprised 41 members, including Archbishops, Bishops, University Professors, Benedictines, Carmelites, Dominicans, Jesuits, Franciscans, Capuchins, Augustinians, etc. Fray Francisco was a member, but not Fray Zacharias.

[2] *F.J.*, pp. 221-228.

liberty or to bring in fresh measures of oppression, crushing them completely. Olivares said he considered James's intentions doubtful, but that were he to encounter any difficulty in keeping his promises, he would declare them impossible of fulfilment, and plead that nobody was bound to the impossible. The only safeguard was, therefore, to keep the Infanta in Spain while they watched the marriage concessions applied in practice. [1]

The folly of Charles's going to Spain can now be seen. Had he stayed at home, the marriage terms, discussed on their merits, would probably have been rejected. James's original idea had been to purchase Spain's support and the Infanta's huge dowry by granting her free exercise of her religion, and his Catholic subjects considerable relief. Complete liberty of conscience he would hardly have deigned to discuss, but that the presence of the Prince in Madrid gave the Spaniards so strong a vantage point in bargaining. [2]

Charles was willing enough to go on making promises lightly, if he could only get back to England quickly with his bride, and it was the suggestion that she should remain in Spain after the marriage that caused the breakdown of the negotiations. The Nuncio, on orders from Rome, had suggested this to the Spaniards, and the Junta of theologians saw in the plan their trump card to enforce full acceptance of the Articles. Rather than face a humiliating return without the Infanta, Charles now revoked his objections to the Articles approved by Rome. [3]

But the Theologians had still not had their say. They considered Philip would be justified in taking his oath to the Pope and consenting to the marriage, providing its consummation and the departure of the Infanta were delayed for a year. During this period the Articles would be put into practice in England. The Penal Laws would be suspended and private exercise of religion proclaimed by edict. James, Charles and the Privy Councillors would at once take an oath to carry this out, and within the year they must also show evidence of their efforts to obtain the confirmation of Parliament. When this was put before Charles, he again threatened to leave, but, reminded of his promise to stay, sent Cottington to London to consult with the King. [4]

[1] *F.J.*, pp. 218 seq.
[2] *G.P.C.*, vol. II, pp. 338-339.
[3] *Ibid.*, vol. II, pp. 340-341 ; *F.J.*, p. [60]. V. *supra* p. 23.
[4] *Ibid.*, vol. II, pp. 343-344 ; *F.J.*, pp. 235-236.

So great had been their disillusionment over the Prince's conversion that now, rather than risk a ' mixed ' marriage, the Spaniards seemed to be making conditions they hoped would be rejected. [1]

Charles was now engaged on two compositions. The first, which, contrary to general belief, he wrote unaided, was a reply to a hortatory letter from Gregory XV, itself an answer to the one from the Prince already mentioned. Though the Pope had written in April, the letter was not delivered by de' Massimi till June. [2] Charles wrote back immediately, assuring the Holy Father of his goodwill towards the Catholics and his desire for the union of Christendom. But before this letter reached Rome Gregory was dead, and it was left to the new Pope, Urban VIII to reply. [3]

The Prince now presented an elaborate reply to the Spanish theologians. In it he spoke very much as a theologian himself, arguing that to allow the marriage *ratum et non consummatum*, which the retention of the Infanta in Spain would mean, was to run a great risk, since Catholic theology held that the Pope could dispense from such a marriage, and had in fact done so. Charles therefore appealed to Philip to inquire whether there had been any minority vote among the theologians offering a simpler way out and, if so, to adopt it. [4]

Meeting a second time to consider the Prince's memorandum, the Junta decided against all further concession. The Council of State approved this resolution, which Olivares was asked to place before Charles. He did so, diplomatically reminding the Prince that he had come to Spain with two objects in mind, — to marry, and to marry quickly. As the latter appeared impossible, he ought not to abandon the first and principal end of his journey. Charles replied that he was not empowered to allow his bride to remain in Spain after the marriage ; he therefore considered himself free of all obligation under the treaty and at liberty to return home.

[1] *Ibid.*, vol. II, p. 342.

[2] BELLESHEIM, *op. cit.*, vol. III, App. XIV, pp. 484-486 : Gregory XV to Charles, April 20, 1623.

[3] J. RUSHWORTH, *Historical Collections*, vol. I, pp. 82-83 ; *G.P.C.*, vol. II, pp. 342-343. Urban's letters to James and Charles were both dated Oct. 15, 1623 (N. s.) by which time Charles was back in England (Cf. RUSHWORTH, *op. cit.*, vol. I, pp. 93 seq.).

[4] *F. J.*, p. 242. This, according to Fray Francisco, was to ask that on a purely religious question religion be left aside and only courtesy considered.

Buckingham expressed the same sentiments with less composure. [1]

It was now July and there seemed nothing left but for both sides to make the leave-taking as dignified as possible. Charles and Buckingham, accompanied by Aston and Bristol, waited on the King to bid farewell when, to the amazement even of the two Ambassadors, the Prince began to speak with great show of sincerity of his final resolve to accept all the Theologians' demands, and to give security for their execution. It was the decision of his father the King, and though the difficulties were great, alliance with Spain was worth the sacrifice. [2]

What had passed between Charles and Buckingham to produce within a week two resolutions so diametrically opposed? Towards the end of April, finding the negotiations held up by amendments to the Articles, Charles had applied to his father for *carte blanche* to promise in the King's name anything that might be asked. This James granted, increasingly anxious for his son's safety and the succession to the throne; it had been despatched on May 11, though the secret was closely guarded till the moment arrived for the Prince to make use of his powers. [3]

Bewildered though they were by this sudden *volte-face*, the Spaniards considered the decision irrevocable and the marriage a certainty. For four days the streets of Madrid were illuminated, and the Infanta appeared in public under the style Princess of England. [4]

Meanwhile, Cottington had reached England and told the King of the Spaniards' refusal to let the Infanta leave after the marriage. James's immediate reaction was the fear of a fond father that he would see his son no more; he would agree to any concession as long as Charles could be married quickly and come home, leaving the Infanta with her dowry to follow when she would. [5]

In August, Cottington was back in Madrid with a document certifying to the Oath the King and Privy Council had taken at Wanstead to fulfil all conditions touching religion and to grant the security asked for. This was still insufficient for the Spanish

[1] *F.J.*, pp. 242-245.
[2] *Ibid.*, pp. 246-247.
[3] *G.P.C.*, vol. II, pp. 348-349.
[4] *Ibid.*, vol. II, pp. 356-357.
[5] *Ibid.*, vol. II, pp. 350-352.

Theologians, and they asked the Prince to sign the Articles sent from Rome and the points agreed to by James. This Charles did with all solemnity, and Philip offered to have the marriage celebrated ten days after the arrival of the new Pope's confirmation of the dispensation. [1]

Charles's casual regard for his obligations can be seen in a letter he wrote at this time to his father, saying he would leave on August 29, and hoped to bring the Infanta with him, otherwise there would be no marriage. He continued to plague Olivares to allow the Infanta to leave, hoping to catch the Council of State in a yielding mood while they were still jubilant over the signing of the treaty. Buckingham tried all manner of argument, alleging the retention of the Infanta would affect James's health as well as the Prince's honour, and that the sooner she came to England and won the affection of her future subjects, the sooner would the whole Catholic question be settled. [2]

Declaring himself ready for yet more concessions, Charles begged Philip to reduce the period of the Infanta's stay to the remainder of the current year. But the Theologians to whom the King referred the point were adamant, and the most Philip would concede was permission for Charles to live with his wife if he stayed in Spain till Christmas. [3] To this there were obvious objections, — the Prince of Wales would be in Spain's power for a further six months, and if by that time the Infanta was likely to become a mother, there would be more delay, and another heir to the English throne would be in Spanish hands.

Charles, therefore, resolved to leave on August 30, without

[1] *F.J.*, pp. 247-248 ; *G.P.C.*, vol. II, pp. 357 seq. Gregory XV died July 8 ; his successor, Urban VIII was not elected till August 6.

[2] *G.P.C.*, vol. II, p. 385 seq.

[3] *F.J.*,pp.248-249 ; *G.P.C.*,vol.II, pp.394-395. Three events which at this time had a bad effect on Spanish opinion may have influenced the otherwise inopportune rebuff shown to Charles's request : (1) Cottington who, on falling ill, had been reconciled to the Church by La Fuente, lapsed again on recovery. (2) Another of Charles's servants, Walsingham, asked for a priest. An English Jesuit named Ballard, who came to minister to him, was insulted and struck by Sir Edmund Verney. When Walsingham died and was buried as a Protestant, the indignation of Philip and his Court forced Charles to order Verney to leave Madrid. (3) A Spanish translation of the Anglican catechism was found in Charles's room and taken to Philip. The Prince never made known the loss.

waiting even for the approbation of the new Pope, and having sworn to the Treaty signed conjointly with Philip on July 25, he presented farewell gifts to the Infanta and the Royal Family. [1]

Charles's eyes had by now been opened to that undercurrent of opposition to the marriage in which even the late King, Philip III, had been involved. In the heat of an argument with Buckingham, Olivares not only revealed his own attacks on the alliance, already noted, but showed the Englishman a letter in which Philip, following the death-bed wishes of his father, had ordered him to break off the match, — a revelation convicting the Spanish king and his chief ministers of gross deceit. [2]

Philip, and all Spain with him, was weary now of his guest's vacillation and for the first time took him at his word, telling the Prince that his presence in England would be the best guarantee of a speedy preparation for the Infanta's journey in the spring.

In expectation of the arrival of Urban VIII's approval, within ten days of which the marriage was to be celebrated, Charles made out a form of proxy in the names of Philip and the Infante Charles, and, in the presence of a notary and another witness, the document was handed to Bristol to be used at his orders. [3]

Officially all was in order for the due celebration of the marriage, but Charles was leaving embittered by the coldness of his treatment and mistrustful of Spanish intrigue. An as yet half-formed resolve to escape from the marriage at all costs was further crystallized by a talk on the Palatinate question that he had with Olivares prior to leaving. It was a subject that had been in the back of the minds of both parties throughout the negotiations and, with the lengthening-out of the German war, its settlement had become to both sides of more importance than the marriage alliance ; but here again each side mistook the measure of interest to the other. Olivares, who did not realize the depth of Charles's affection for his sister, the Palatine's wife, thought the Prince would prove as pliable in

[1] *F.J.*, pp. 251-253 : the Oath taken by Philip and Charles is quoted here. Buckingham and others were also required to swear to fulfil the Treaty in so far as it concerned them.

[2] *G.P.C.*, vol. II, pp. 405 seq. and note ; also *Ibid.*, vol. II, pp. 80 and 275, where the death-bed scene of Philip III is described.

[3] *G.P.C.*, vol. II, pp. 406 seq. ; *F.J.*, pp. 253-255.

the matter of her restoration as he had been over his Marriage Treaty. He therefore proposed that Elizabeth's son should marry the Emperor's daughter and be brought up a Catholic at Vienna.

Charles, who considered that his sister and her husband should be restored through Spanish influence as a concession to him in the Marriage Treaty, asked Olivares if Spain would give the Palatine and England armed aid in the event of the Emperor's opposing the restoration. To a Habsburg this was fratricide, and Olivares said so. " If you hold yourself to that, " replied the Prince, " there is an end of all ; for without this, you may not rely on either marriage or friendship. " [1]

Yet early in September Charles left Madrid, declaring to the Infanta that he would take the Catholics under his protection, and protesting to Philip by letter, even after he had left the coast of Spain, his intention of pursuing the Marriage Treaty. [2] That these were not sincere expressions of his feelings seems certain. Months of wearisome negotiation had worn out his patience ; the fire of his enthusiasm had been damped and his vanity wounded by the frigid decorum of Spanish etiquette, while the refusal of Olivares to render aid to the Palatine was a challenge to his honour. After all his irresolute yieldings in Madrid, he was returning home with his hands empty.

A violent outburst of bitter reproach would have been understandable in the circumstances, but Charles chose a less reputable

---

[1] *G.P.C.*, vol. II, pp. 398 seq. and 404.

[2] Arezio, *op. cit.*, p. 51 ; *F.J.*, pp. 256-7 : from Segovia, Sept. 3/13, Charles wrote : " I therefore declare to your Majesty that I will eradicate and efface everything which may impede or hinder the execution of these promises in the Kingdoms of the King my Lord and Father, and I trust and hope your Majesty will do the same," etc... These sentiments he repeated in letters from Olmedo (Sept. 5/15), Carrion (Sept. 8/18), Royston (Oct. 8/18), London (Nov. 6/16).

The day Charles left (Aug. 30/Sept. 9) he was asked to see a certain Madre Luisa (in all probability the daughter of the late Emperor Maximilian II, the Infanta Margarita, who was known to be a Carmelite in Madrid) for what was a final effort to win, by the prayers and persuasions of a saintly religious, what all the divines in Spain had failed so accomplish, *viz.* the Prince's conversion. This unsuccessful attempt was made at the instance of the Nuncio, who wrote to Madre Luisa " que V. Rᵃ procure con el más esquisito modo de encerrarse primero, y unirse con Dios, supplicándolo conceder áquel, lum[bre] que es necessario para la salud al dicho Principe. Plegue á Dios sea servido de oyrla." (Arezio, *op. cit.*, pp. 52 ; 87-88.)

way of revenge.   Letting his imagination play upon the Infanta's former threat to enter a convent rather than marry him, he magnified it into the possibility of her doing so even after her marriage.   To safeguard himself, as he alleged, he sent back to Madrid one Clarke, ostensibly on business for Buckingham, whose servant he was, in reality bearing a letter for Bristol with a command not to use the proxy for the marriage until both Philip and the Infanta had given satisfaction on the nunnery question.   The document was undated, and Clarke was told not to deliver it till the arrival of the Pope's confirmation of the dispensation, with the result that the marriage would suffer a further postponement while Bristol communicated with Charles in England. In the embarrassment of the Spaniards Charles would find his revenge.

As it happened, Bristol, suspicious of Clarke, forced the letter from him and at once sent off to James to try and forestall the affront his son was offering Spain.   He also wrote to Charles telling him that the Infanta, now demonstrative in her affection for him, ridiculed the idea of becoming a nun to avoid him. [1]

But the Prince, sailing from Santander, had arrived in London by October 6, to be greeted enthusiastically by a joyous crowd, relieved that Spanish domination and Papal aggression had both been warded off. [2]

While Charles and Buckingham told tales of insults suffered in Spain and laughed at their lucky escape, Bristol was left in a most delicate position.   His appeal to James had brought fresh conditions which, despite contracts signed and oaths sworn, made the marriage virtually impossible. The Papal Brief, delayed by Urban's illness, arrived in mid-November and confirmed the former Pope's dispens ation, which was formally handed over by the Nuncio five day- later (Nov. 19/29), after Philip had taken his oath.   Bristol was informed of it, and of the celebration of the marriage in ten dayss time.   To this he was forced to object, for James, completely' ignoring the Ambassador's warning against postponement, had blandly written to say it was his especial pleasure that the marriage should take place shortly after Christmas " that holy and joyful time best fitting so notable and blessed an action. " [3]   He then

[1] *G.P.C.*, vol. II, pp. 414-416.

[2] *Ibid.*, vol. II, p. 421.

[3] *Ibid.*, vol. II, pp. 425 seq. **James overlooked, or ignored, the fact that Charles's proxy expired at Christmas.**

went on to show the same inability as Charles to grasp the meaning of a contract binding in honour, as well as his incompetence in the complex field of European politics, by instructing Bristol in his next interview with the King of Spain to introduce the restoration of the Palatinate as a further condition of the marriage. In ordering this James appealed to an incautious remark Philip had made previously to Charles that he would give him *carte blanche* to demand what political favours he liked, if England would give way on the religious question.

So James, afraid of embroiling himself in the German war, was asking a Habsburg as a personal favour to fight against his own kin, not wishing in the alliance with Spain, he said righteously, to abandon his honour " nor at the same time we give joy to our only son, to give our only daughter a portion in tears." [1]

While flatly refusing to fight the Emperor, Philip was as anxious as James to have the Palatinate problem settled, otherwise, as Olivares said cynically, " they might give a daughter and have a war within three months." Yet, as Bristol hastened to tell James, for both to desire an agreement over the Palatinate was a different matter from making the marriage alliance dependent on that agreement. This was out the question, and he asked for power to use the proxy. [2]

James's reply (Nov. 13/23) was a wandering one : he was sorry about the expiry of the proxy and sent another available till March, before which date Bristol was to procure from Philip a declaration in writing of his determination to obtain the complete restitution of the Palatinate by mediation or, failing that, by arms. Unless he got satisfaction the Ambassador was to leave Spain within twenty days. [3]

Having all along insisted on the celebration of the marriage within ten days of the arrival of the Papal Brief, Philip would brook no postponement now, and as Bristol was forced to insist on this, he declared himself free of all obligation under the treaty. The Infanta ceased to be styled Princess of England.

---

[1] *G.P.C.*, vol. II, pp. 427 seq.

[2] *Ibid.*, vol. II, p. 432 ; *F. J.*, p. 267. Bristol's Instructions, Feb. 22, 1622, had ordered him " to insist upon the restoring of the Prince Palatine, but *not so as to annex it to the treaty of the match*, as that thereby the match should be hazarded."

[3] *G.P.C.*, vol. II, p. 436 seq.

On the day the marriage was to have taken place (Nov. 29/Dec. 9), the two English Ambassadors presented their petition for assistance in the Palatinate. Adopting a strong tone, Philip blamed the Prince Palatine for his own misfortunes, repeated the negative answer he had given Charles and pointed out that the linking of the marriage and the Palatinate quaestions was to change the contract substantially. He immediately instructed his Ambassadors in London to treat the two questions separately. [1]

Matters were at a deadlock, and to the Spaniards it was clear that Charles and Buckingham, now utterly hostile to the marriage, had forced James into making impossible demands and bringing about the break-down of the treaty. [2]

Even now (Dec. 30/Jan. 9, 1623/4), James professed not to see what Philip had to complain about, and said he never intended to make the restitution of the Palatinate a condition of the marriage, but rather a fruit and blessing thereof. [3] It was useless for James to continue to write like this. Officially the doors were still open, practically the Marriage Treaty was dead, the first decisive step being taken with the recall of Bristol, who had gone to Spain especially to conclude it. He returned under a cloud, accused by Charles of having offering to concur in his conversion. [4]

On arrival in London he found 22 articles of accusation ranged against him by Buckingham, and in the subsequent trial much underground intrigue was brought to light. Though little could be proved, the general opinion was that he had pressed the marriage too eagerly and trusted the Spanish ministers too much. [5] In the present temper of the people this was a crime to be condemned out of hand, and Buckingham, credited with breaking off the unwelcome alliance, was hailed as the Saviour of England.

[1] *G.P.C.*, vol. II, pp. 445 seq., *F.J.*, pp. 270-271.

[2] *F.J.*, 267 seq.

[3] *G.P.C.*, vol. II, p. 452.

[4] BRISTOL'S *Defence, op. cit.,* pp. 30-56, Article 5 ; Preface, p. xxx : Charles I to Bristol, Jan. 20, 1626 : " You will remember how at our first coming into Spaine, taking upon you to bee soe wise, as to foresee our intentions to chaunge our religion, you were soe farre from disswading us that you offered your service and secrecy to concurre in it, and in many other open conferences pressing to shew how convenient it was for us to bee a Romaine Catholick, it being impossible, in your opinion, to doe any greate action otherwise."

[5] BRISTOL'S *Defence*, Preface, p. xxvi : Kenelm Digby to Bristol, London, May 27, 1625.

CHAPTER II

THE FRENCH MATCH

" Richelieu a toujours compté le mariage d'Angleterre parmi les actes les plus importants de sa vie politique. " [1]

All England heaved a sigh of relief when the Prince landed safe and sound on English shores again after his rash venture into Spain. Personally he was none the worse for the exploit. He had seen something of the world and looked manlier with a beard. But it was generally voted that he had had a lucky escape from a compromising position and, at a thanksgiving service in St Paul's, a grateful congregation gave real meaning to the singing of Psalm CXIII, *" In exitu Israel de Aegypto. "* [2]

Already before negotiations with Spain were officially broken off, English public opinion had consigned the treaty to the dusty shelves of the archives, and the need of a bride for Charles being more pressing than ever with the failing health of the King, thoughts were turned towards France.

The French were not flattered by the thought that they and their princess were second choice; the less so, as several years before a hint by M. de Luynes, Louis XIII's favourite, as to the desirability of such an alliance had been received non-committally by the English Ambassador, Herbert. [3] Yet the latter's private opinion inclined towards a French rather than a Spanish alliance, and the following year, 1620, he wrote recommending the idea to James, saying the French had assured him they would see that the religious difficulties were easily overcome. [4]

---

[1] M. AVENEL, *Lettres etc. du Cardinal de Richelieu*, vol. II, p. 124, note 3.

[2] J. GOLL, *Die französische Heirat: Frankreich und England*, 1624 und 1625, Prag, 1876, p. 1.

[3] S. L. LEE, *op. cit.*, p. 350 : App. Corr.

[4] *Ibid.*, p. 236, note 1.

Even at the height of the Spanish negotiations, while the Prince was in Madrid, there had been a certain amount of backstairs diplomacy pressing for a French match. Towards the end of 1623 the Comte de Tillières,[1] French Ambassador in London, discovered that a Capuchin friar had been treating with Buckingham behind his back for nothing less than an alliance between France and England based on the marriage of Prince Charles with the young Henrietta Maria. The Ambassador also had reason to conclude that the friar's activities were not unknown to the French Queen-Mother, Marie de' Medici. He complained of this slight on his official position to Buckingham, who explained that the friar in question had tendered his services in Madrid and later had left for London *via* Paris. His work done, the unofficial diplomat was prudently disavowed by Marie de' Medici in a letter written at Richelieu's dictation to Tillières, who was told that the friar had never even spoken to the Queen-Mother, save perhaps on general topics. This the Ambassador retailed to Buckingham, who made as if to believe him. [2]

The favourite grew confidential after this episode and told Tillières that the Spanish Treaty was bound to fall through owing to the difficulty of agreement on the Palatinate question. He was therefore ready to send Lord Kensington to Paris to open the way for the French match. Tillières replied coolly enough that England ought first to break definitely with Spain. Buckingham answered that Parliament, when it met, would clear up the situation, and that meanwhile he would send Kensington over without a fixed mandate. Buckingham voiced similar sentiments in conversations

---

[1] Tanneguy Leveneur, Comte de Tillières. In 1609 he married Catherine, sister of the Maréchal de Bassompierre, whose fortunes he followed later. In 1619, appointed ambassador to England, he began the negotiations for the match. He and his wife remained with the new Queen. In domestic politics he opposed Richelieu, supporting Anne of Austria. He died in 1652.

[2] GOLL, *op. cit.*, pp. 2-3 ; AVENEL, *Lettres, Instructions diplomatiques et Papiers d'état du Cardinal de Richelieu*, vol. VII (1642 - supplément 1608-42 : Sommaire des Lettres), p. 938. Avenel says that the friar in question was an English Recollect named Robert Grey, often mentioned in Tillière's despatches. The Queen Mother's disavowal written about the middle of January, 1624, was worded as follows : "J'estonne de vostre credulité, je n'ay donné aucune charge au religieux, que vous me nommez, n'y à aucuns autres de traitter du mariage de ma fille en Angleterre."

subsequent to this one of January 9, 1624 (N.S.), urging that Tillières could do much to prepare the way in his dispatches. [1]

Louis's advisers approved the Ambassador's reserve and were at one with him in demanding that England should break formally with Spain, for, although Charles and Buckingham were quite determined to have no more to do with the Treaty, James, unable to make up his mind, scanned hopefully every fresh dispatch from Madrid. Besides, a special commission summoned to discuss the situation showed a majority in favour of further negotiation. [2]

On other points, however, Tillières and his government were out of sympathy. The Ambassador pointed out that the first consideration of the alliance must be to secure the Catholic religion in England. Unless Louis saw to this, not only would his sister's faith be endangered, but the support of the English Catholics would be lost to France and given once more to Spain. Tillières was shrewd enough to realize that, even if certain guarantees were offered by the English, France would be called upon to play a cat-and-mouse game to see they were carried out, and the result would be friction rather than friendship. Furthermore, even if the alliance continued a friendly one, Tillières had been long enough in England to know that the King's power rested on an understanding between himself and Parliament and, as a quarrel seemed by no means unlikely, France would be saddled with the support of a tottering throne. [3]

Again, while his government at home saw in the convocation of Parliament the surest means of forcing James to break with Spain, Tillières on the spot knew that an extreme Puritan element would be returned to Westminster and would clamour for nothing less than a Protestant marriage for the heir to the Throne. The consequence would see England at the head of a Protestant alliance, and a religious war involving France. The Ambassador was all for solving the Palatinate question through the peaceful mediation of France, and for inciting no one against Spain : Charles and

---

[1] GOLL, op. cit., pp. 3-4.

[2] Ibid., pp. 5-6.

[3] Tillières's prophetic insight was revealed 15 years later when the King, in a death-struggle with Parliament, appealed to France. Goll pays just tribute to the soundness of Tillières's judgment in his dispatches : " Tillières macht nach seinen Depeschen einen weit bedeutenderen Eindruck als nach seinen eigenen Memorien" (GOLL, op. cit., pp. 10-12, note 8).

Buckingham were hostile enough to make that unnecessary. [1]
Spain knew this and made one final bid to bring about Buckingham's
downfall. After the Infanta Isabella had been consulted in Brussels,
Padre de la Fuente was chosen for the task. He had been Gondomar's confessor in England, where he was popularly known as Padre
Maestro, and had acquired considerable influence over James.
In April, 1624, he handed the King a document in which Buckingham
was accused of a series of intrigues with the Puritans for the purpose
of annihilating the English Monarchy. The plan, it was alleged,
was to remove the King to the country, far from the seat of power,
where he would be kept a comparative prisoner while the Prince
of Wales took over the government.

In all probability the tale represented nothing more than the
wild flight of some Spanish imagination. Its effect was precisely
the contrary to that intended, — the favourite did not fall, but was
thrown more than ever into the arms of France. Yet the story
had not been lost on James, who told Tillières how displeased he
was at his son's fraternizing with the Puritans, whom he himself
disliked more than the Papists. [2]

Meanwhile, the moment was approaching when both sides must
make a stand for or against religious concessions. Already in
England a petition had been presented to the King asking that the
new marriage alliance should entail no favours to the Catholics,
and Prince Charles spoke in Parliament in favour of this attitude.
Tillières, on the other hand, expressed his indignation at the Penal
Laws and considered France might have to suspend dealings with
England altogether while they were being enforced. [3] But the suff-
erers, the English Catholics themselves, were resigned to expecting
smaller relief from the French than from the Spanish match, despite
Tillières's protests that Louis was as zealous a son of the Church as
the King of Spain. They feared a change of front in France and
they were right. Brienne suddenly forbade the negotiations to be
linked up for the time being with the interests of the English Cath-

[1] " Plus le Prince de Galles va en avant, plus il se déclare contre l'Espagne.
C'est en ce seul point que je l'ai vu perdre sa retenue et modestie " (Tillières
to Puissieux, Jan. 19, 1624, GOLL, op. cit., p. 11, note 13).

[2] GOLL, op. cit., pp. 7-8.

[3] Ibid., p. 14, note 25 : Tillières to Brienne, April 9, 1924. " elles [i.e. the
Penal Laws] nous pourroient nécessiter et par honneur et par conscience d'in-
terrompre tous traités avec l'Angleterre ".

olics [1]. He was rejecting Tillières's energetic attitude for a policy of procrastination, relying on the timidity of James to win concessions for the Catholics little by little without forcing anyone's hand. But this was not the way of the Ambassador, who protested to James against the new Penal Laws, and the King gave his word (which he kept) that they would not be enforced. This was in the beginning of June ; by the end of the month Tillières had been recalled. It is a wonder he had stayed so long, and the English justly interpreted the step as a sign that the French government wished to pursue the negotiations even if it meant making concessions. [2]

Rome was not slow to appreciate the change of attitude. Cardinal Barberini, the Secretary of State, was in close touch with Padre Giacinto, [3] the roving Capuchin diplomat, who had taken up a strategic position in Brussels (always a nerve-centre of European politics) where he was able to hear official Spanish news from the Infanta Isabella, and was equally well-placed between England France and Germany to gather all that was going on in the world of diplomacy. Early in the new year, 1624, he was able to give certain information of the break-down of the Anglo-Spanish treaty, [4] and of the overtures made to the French Ambassador. He immediately informed the Nuncio in Paris that he must be on the alert to keep the interests of the Catholics in the forefront from the first.

In addition, Giacinto was allowed to read the despatches of the Spanish Ambassador in London informing Philip of the *volte-face* in England. The news was despatched without ado to Rome, where it came as a hard blow to Pope Urban, whose dispensation had arrived in Madrid to be handed over without reserve or condition whatsoever. [5]

---

[1] *Ibid.*, p. 12-13.

[2] *Ibid.*, p. 19, note 46.

[3] Giacinto dei Conti Natta di Casale Monferrato, a powerful preacher and ascetic. From 1606 to 1626, he was employed by the Holy See in extensive diplomatic missions to Germany, Spain and the Catholic Low Countries (Cf. CUTHBERT, *The Capuchins*, vol. II, pp. 298-305).

[4] Bibl. Vat., *Codices Barberini Latini* (hereinafter called *B.L.*) 6793, f. 18 : Giacinto to Barberini, deciphered Feb. 1, 1624 : " ch'io so di certo e hô veduto co' li occhi miei. "

[5] *Ibid.*, ff. 19 seq. : Same to same.

Diplomatic circles in Brussels were amazed at Charles's and Buckingham's bitterness towards Spain, and the Prince's declared hostility towards the English Catholics. In April, when the Commons sent a petition to the Lords against the recusants, Charles went out of his way to swear that, in the event of his marriage to a Popish lady, she would have no privileges save for her household. It was evident, as it had been all along to the clear-sighted, that England would have none of the Infanta without the Palatinate. The Infanta Isabella said she was glad for her niece's sake, knowing all the difficulties she was escaping; but Giacinto was disgusted that the Spanish were showing so little fight. He considered Charles a heretic of the worst type, and had always mistrusted the optimism of his friends who had told him of the Prince's inclination towards Catholicism in Madrid. [1]

A definite step-forward on the tentative approaches made hitherto, and a decided blow to Spain was the arrival in Paris on February 25 (N. S.) of Lord Kensington to negotiate for the match. [2] Buckingham meant the visit to be "unofficial" but the Spanish Ambassador in Paris was immediately suspicious, and asked sarcastically if the Prince of Wales were to be allowed two wives. The Spaniards immediately tried to sabotage the negotiations by intrigue. Their attempt to ruin Buckingham having failed, they now brought pressure to bear on the Pope to refuse the dispensation, or at least to delay it indefinitely. At the same time a shower of pamphlets was let loose from the presses of Italy, Germany and Flanders, attacking the unnatural alliance between a Catholic monarch and Lutheran heretics. [3]

---

[1] GARDINER, History, vol. V, p. 222 ; B.L. 6793, f.20 : Giacinto to Barberini, Jan. 27, 1624 ; ibid., f. 33 : Giacinto Feb. 3, 1624, Brussels : ".. si dice ch' egl' era assai inclinato alla Cat^{ca}, ch'io no' lo credessi ; che no' era vero, anzi ch'egl'era un finiss^o Calvinista. " Other epithets he applies to Charles are " puritanissimo " and " pessimo heretico. " Giacinto also reported, with I know not how much truth, that at Christmas, 1623, Charles had given orders for all in his service to take the Calvinist bread with him, and that therefore any Catholics had to leave his service (B.L. 6139, f. 108 : Giacinto, Brussels, Feb. 3, 1624).

[2] The lynx-eyed Giacinto had news of the appointment three weeks before, and saw to it that Rome knew almost as soon as Kensington had reached Paris (B.L. 6139, f. 108 : Giacinto, Brussels, Feb. 3, 1624).

[3] Two pamphlets, in particular, caused a great sensation, as they were

The French countered by demanding an *official* appointment, if possible Lord Carlisle, who was known to be anti-Spanish. They had their way, and Carlisle came at the end of May with a numerous suite, he and Kensington receiving special faculties as Ambassadors Extraordinary to negotiate the marriage and an alliance between France and England. Sir Edward Herbert, the ordinary ambassador was recalled. [1]

With the first conference on June 10 (N.S.) direct negotiations for the match began, France being represented by La Vieuville, Aligre, Brienne and Richelieu. [2] The English Ambassador opened the proceedings by producing the draft of a match projected in 1613 between Charles and Henrietta's sister, Christine, in which toleration had been asked only for the bride and her household.

This was rejected by the French, who put forward now and in subsequent conferences a draft of 13 Articles modelled on the Spanish Treaty. For the Princess there was to be a private chapel and a public church, served by 20 priests and a bishop with the title of Grand Almoner and exclusive jurisdiction over the Princess's ecclesiastics. She was to be given the education of the children till they reached the age of twelve, and an oath had to be taken that her faith would not be disturbed.

The English reply was to refuse the public church and oppose the exclusively French character of the Princess's suite, clerical

---

condemned as libellous by the Sorbonne. They were by a German Jesuit named Keller (Cellarius) and entitled *Admonitio ad Ludovicum XIII* and *Mysteria Politica*. Cf. the curious account in *Le Mercure François*, vol. XI, p. 34.

[1] GARDINER, *op. cit.*, vol. V, p. 249 ; GOLL, *op. cit.*, pp. 20 seq. For faculties of Kensington and Carlisle, cf. RYMER's *Foedera*, vol. XVII, p. 599. James Hay, first Earl of Carlisle, had come from Scotland with James I, and was made a Gentleman-of-the Bedchamber. He married (1617) Lucy Percy, the Court beauty and wit, who betrayed Charles's plan to arrest the Five Members on Jan. 4, 1642. Carlisle served on various diplomatic missions in Germany and France. His lavish hospitality was notorious.

Henry Rich, son of the Earl of Warwick, created Baron Kensington (1623), Earl of Holland (1624). Later he was to enjoy the favour of Henrietta. During the Civil War he vacillated between King and Parliament and in 1648 was beheaded.

[2] The French feared Richelieu's participation might give offence, so Brienne wrote reassuringly to Tillières of the Cardinal, saying with exquisite irony " que quoiqu'ecclésiastique, il est né gentilhomme et François." GOLL, *op. cit.*, p. 22, note 7 : Brienne to Tillières, May 6, 1624.

and lay. But their chief objection concerned the last article which dealt with the future status of the English Catholics.[1] In this the King of England was to promise that, through the intercession of the French Princess, no Catholic in his Kingdoms would be molested for religion so long as he fulfilled his duty loyally to his King, nor would he be punished for the refusal of any oath incompatible with his conscience.[2]

Far-reaching as was this demand, the French considered that, in not asking for the repeal of the Penal Laws, they were requiring less than Spain had done and, as a further concession, they agreed to James's keeping this article secret, though it would have to be in writing ; it therefore appeared in the next draft of the Treaty as an *Article Secret*.[3] Furthermore, as James and his son had given their word to Parliament that they would make no treaty in favour of the English Catholics (a fact mentioned in Carlisle's and Kensington's instructions), the French subtly suggested that the promise could still be regarded as intact, since the toleration of

[1] For a comparison of the Spanish and French articles, cf. GOLL, *op. cit.*, pp. 22-23.

[2] A wide claim, embodying the remission of the Oath of Supremacy (an acknowledgment of the sovereign as sole ruler in spiritual as in temporal matters) and the Oath of Allegiance, introduced by James after the Gunpowder Plot and offensive to Catholics since it declared heretical the doctrine that a prince excommunicated by the Pope could be dethroned and even assassinated by his subjects.

[3] GOLL, *op. cit.*, p. 24, note 11 : Louis to Tillières, June 19, 1624 : " Article Secret qui sera mis hors du contract de Mariage : le Roy de la Grande Bretagne ayant égard à la prière de Madame, et pour témoigner l'affection qu'il lui porte, accorde aux Catholiques, ses sujets, la sureté de leur vie et de leurs biens sans qu'ils puissent être recherchés pour la profession de leur Religion Catholique lui rendans l'obéissance et la fidélité qu'ils lui doivent, à laquelle il ne sera point estimé manquer pour ne vouloir faire serment aucun ou action contraire à sa religion. "

The word *profession* instead of *exercice* roused the ire of the extremely pro-Spanish Toby Mathew, who wrote to Rome accusing Richeli eu of the change. *B.L.*, 8620, f. 60 : Claudio Néri [i.e. Toby Mathew] to Barberini, London, Oct. 14/24, 1624 : " Potrei far ricciar i capelli a V. S. Illma s'io le dicesi q^{llo} ch'io hò visto con li occhi miei, sotto la mano del Card^{le} Richieieu, il quale si diceva ch'il Rè d'Inghilterra non persequitarebbe li suoi vasalli Cat^{ci} per l'esercitio della loro Religione, il Card^{le} mutò la parola d'*essercitio* (*sic* !) in parola di professione, la quale ci servirà di poco, et il Rè non ne può haver difficultà nessuna di concederla. "

the Catholics would be the result of royal favour rather than of the treaty.

But the English Ambassadors objected that they had no competence in the matter and pressed for a purely oral promise. They might have held out on the point but La Vieuville assured them that, in asking for this secret promise in writing, he was simply satisfying the Pope so as to facilitate the grant of the dispensation. [1]

To persuade the King of this, La Vieuville asked Kensington to go back to James and suggest to him that, although he objected to any formal public engagement, he could surely sign a simple letter which the French would accept, provided the favours to the Catholics were put precisely enough.

It was a clever move to make the Englishman sponsor for the French plan, and La Vieuville needed only a letter of credence for Kensington to leave immediately : this he asked the Comte de Brienne to prepare. But La Vieuville had overreached himself. Brienne, Secretary of State and one of the Commissioners for the Treaty, drew back at so dangerous and unheard of a plan, which would make the Ambassador of England little less than the secret agent of the King of France. Suspecting La Vieuville of acting beyond his competence, he prepared what was merely a letter of courtesy to James, and joined forces with Richelieu to oust the minister from power by accusing him of breach of the King's confidence in treating with a foreign ambassador.

Simultaneously with the fall of La Vieuville came another vital change in French policy. Tillières had insisted throughout, even at the risk of the negotiations falling through, that the relief of the English Catholics should be a matter not for future discussion but of immediate concession. At this stage of the proceedings, the French were not prepared to back so imperious a demand, and Tillières had to give way to a more subtle diplomat, the Marquis d'Effiat. [2]

---

[1] GARDINER, op. cit., vol. V, p. 252, note 1, quotes La Vieuville's words : " Donnez-nous de faste pour contenter le Pape, et nous nous jetterons dans vos intérêts à corps perdus. "

[2] GOLL, op. cit., p. 23 seq. ; GARDINER, op. cit., vol. V, p. 250 seq. This seems to have been the real reason for Tillières's recall and not, as Gardiner alleges, because he was half-hearted in his diplomacy.

Antoine-Coiffier, Marquis d'Effiat (1581-1632), Maréchal de France, held

Arriving in London on July 3, the new Ambassador immediately interviewed a number of priests who told him plainly that England had little consideration for France and that the situation of the Catholics had been better during the negotiations with Spain. Effiat had instructions to make every effort to win over the English Catholics to lean on France, in order to counterbalance the fraternizing of the Huguenots with England. He was told, too, to try and obtain favours for the Catholics, everyone of which would make the Pope more inclined to grant the marriage dispensation.

Effiat soon found that the English Catholics, who had long learned to look to none but Spain for protection, were mistrustful of the French alliance, and he tried to persuade them that France in proceeding cautiously was only holding out for better conditions for them ; at the same time he hinted threateningly at what they might expect if, through their blind devotion to Spain, they forced France to give up her protection of them.

The Ambassador had his first audience at Windsor and straightway began working on the King in Gondomar-fashion, flattering the old man's conceit by listening to his hunting exploits, and showing an interest in his menagerie at Theobalds. Into these talks the astute Frenchman adroitly wedged a good word for the Catholics, and was thanked personally by them. Differing from his predecessor Tillières, Effiat did not consider Charles and Buckingham strongly hostile to the Catholics and thought it possible to win them over to agree to the suspension of the Penal Laws to which he was trying to urge James. Buckingham, however, was in emphatic opposition, holding that the King could not afford to quarrel with the nation on such a point, even at the price of the French alliance. Yet he declared, when he and Kensington were discussing the marriage articles with Effiat, that he would stake his reputation on the final success of the negotiations.

If the Ambassador failed for the moment on the major point, he enjoyed a minor success in the promise James gave to order Conway not indeed to suspend the laws but to submit every judgment to him before execution. Effiat was now in a position to ask the

office under Richelieu in the administration, the army and the embassies. Ambassador Extraordinary for the English marriage. After service at La Rochelle, he died when undertaking an important command in Alsace, 1631.

English Catholics to write and thank Louis for what he was doing for them, — a letter Richelieu was particularly anxious to be able to submit to the Pope. [1] He later asked them to write to the Pope, through the Nuncio in Paris, in testimony of their gratitude to the French King. [2] This was done by John Colleton, dean of the English Clergy, who informed Urban that, with the break-down of the Spanish Treaty a practical certainty, the English Catholics were placing all their hopes in France, through whom some relief had already been granted them. He concluded with the unanimous request of the English Catholics for the dispensation to be granted as soon as possible for fear of the fury of the Puritans. [3]

While Effiat was still engaged in conciliating the Catholics, Kensington was awaiting his orders to return to France. Late in July the Privy Council met at Theobalds and made two fresh concessions, — the Princess could have charge of her children till they were thirteen, and the number of her priests could be raised to 28. It was hoped that this would conciliate the French, and Kensington returned to Paris with the news that James was now ready to write the letter required promising to favour the Catholics. But the Ambassador brought the letter to Louis only to find the minister whose suggestion it was had been dismissed the day before (Aug. 3/13) and that the government of France was now in the hands of Richelieu.

When the English Ambassador reminded Louis of La Vieuville's promise with regard to the letter, the King disavowed his minister altogether, and in protest Carlisle and Kensington temporarily suspended negotiations. [4]

The problem at this stage was how the two parties could be brought to agree on the measure of relief to be granted to the English

---

[1] GOLL, op. cit., pp. 31 seq. ; 49-50. In this letter the English Catholics were bold enough to express doubt as to whether their Government would keep its promises. Toby Mathew, in his indictment of Richelieu cited above (v. supra, p. 56, note 3), accuses the Cardinal of being unwilling in the end to show this letter to the King as it spoke of the great persecution going on in England.

[2] AVENEL, op. cit., vol. II, p. 23 : Louis to Effiat, Aug. 13, 1624 ; p. 29, Aug. 25, 1624.

[3] B.L. 8619, f. 8 : Colleton to Urban, Sept. 1, 1624 : "Audire enim modo licet, Beatissime Pater, unam vocem, communia suspiria, vota et preces Catholicorum omnium ut hae nuptiae citissime peragantur."

[4] GOLL, op. cit., pp. 28 seq. ; GARDINER, op. cit., vol. V, pp. 254-255.

Catholics, — a relief which the French had all along demanded as the chief condition of the alliance. Though resolutely opposed to any public declaration of toleration, James was willing enough to meet the French demands if they would leave the matter to his own goodwill. For security's sake, the French statesman naturally asked for the point to be made an integral part of the marriage settlement, and the only concession they offered was that the article in question could be a secret one. La Vieuville's ill-fated compromise of embodying the promise in a letter outside the Treaty had suited James's style of diplomacy, but it had only offered the French statesman's rival a chance of getting rid of him, and the result was a deadlock.

The framing of a formula of toleration in a secret or public article inside or outside the treaty was for neither side an end in itself : it was consequential on the difference of interpretation each put upon the word toleration. For James and the English statesmen it meant something purely negative, that the Law would not be brought against Catholics practising a discreet Popery in the privacy of their homes, but it would by no means permit public worship. It was this interpretation that was contained in the letter Kensington took back with him to France on July 15 (o. s.). [1]

The initiative now lay with the French Government, who accordingly came forward with what was virtually a rehash of La Vieuville's original idea. They proposed that the *Article secret*, which they had demanded as an integral part of the Treaty, should now be separated from it and labelled *Écrit Particulier*. [2] This was to be a document signed by James, Charles, and a Secretary of State, and handed to Louis, promising to all Catholics, in virtue of the marriage, a greater freedom in the *secret* practice of their religion than they would have had from the Spanish Treaty, so that they need suffer no molestation in their persons or possessions, provided always that they used the privilege of private worship modestly and were otherwise loyal. Their loyalty they were to declare on oath. [3]

---

[1] GOLL, *op. cit.*, pp. 30-31, note 9.

[2] *Ibid.*, p. 34, note 7. It was chiefly a matter of words. James had disliked the term *Article*. *Écrit particulier* was a less official phrase, as Brienne told Effiat (Sept. 1, 1624, N.S.) : " pour Rome un peu plus d'une lettre, et beaucoup moins pour le Roi de la Grande Bretagne s'il le veut céler au Parlement. "

[3] GOLL, *op. cit.*, p. 35, note 8, gives the *Écrit particulier*. Emphasis is laid

When this document was submitted to the English Ambassadors, Carlisle voiced his disapproval but, with Richelieu stressing the fact that it was outside the main treaty and the need for satisfying the Pope, Kensington proved more amenable. So with one ambassador on his side, the Cardinal felt strong enough to insist on the *Écrit* to the rejection of fresh suggestions from James and Buckingham that arrived early in September. [1]

Meanwhile, Effiat had been told to win over Buckingham, and through him the King, to the new formula. The difficulty from the English point of view was that, although this *Écrit Particulier* conceded only the secret practice of their religion to the Catholics, the main articles of the Treaty demanded for the Princess a chapel to be open to all ; at first a public church had been asked for as well, but the deletion of the adjective, which the French conceded, meant nothing as long as the private chapel could be attended publicly by the King of England's Popish subjects, a fair example of the astute diplomacy of Richelieu and Effiat.

Buckingham made a half-hearted attempt to parry the subtle thrust by going back to the plan of a simple written statement that toleration would be granted at the King's good pleasure. He even threatened to break off negotiations rather than yield, but the French knew he could not afford to do this and, in fact, he immediately changed his tactics. At an audience Effiat had with the King early in September, Charles and Buckingham, who were present, argued hotly against the *Écrit particulier*, at the same time urging James to accept the other public articles. It

---

on *secrecy* of worship : " Il promettra à tous ses sujets catholiques romains... de jouir de plus de liberté et franchise en ce qui est de l'*exercice secret* de leur religion qu'ils n'eussent eu en vertu d'articles quelconques accordés par le traité de mariage fait avec l'Espagne : ne voulant pour cet effet que ses sujets catholiques puissent être inquiétés en leurs personnes et biens pour faire *secrètement* profession de leur religion pourvu... " etc. The whole formula and particularly the citation of the Council of Toledo on civil allegiance shows Richelieu's conception of the power of the State, and reflects, too, the position the French Government was driven to by having the Huguenots to deal with. (" Je dis avec les pères du concile de Tolède : si quelqu'un de nous enfreint par quelque conjuration ou dessein le sacrement de la foi qu'il a jurée... ou entreprend quelque chose contre l'autorité et l'État, qu'il soit anathème. ")

[1] GARDINER, *op. cit.*, vol. V, pp. 258 seq.

was evidently the favourite's plan to win over the King in easy stages, for within three weeks, backed by Charles, he had persuaded James to accept the *Écrit*. [1]

This was a long step forward, and the greatest difficulties were considered vanquished when on September 7 the English Ambassadors at St-Germain-en-Laye accepted a fresh draft of the *Écrit* in which neither confirmation by oath nor even the *secret* practice of religion was mentioned, the matter being left in the air-and, in consequence, open to difference of interpretation.

On September 26 Effiat was able to write home that the Privy Council had declared itself in favour of the *Écrit*, but at such a stage of the proceedings it was considered dangerous to face Parliament, which was therefore prorogued till the following February, when it was hoped to present the Commons with a *fait accompli* in the form of a winsome Princess of Wales and a promise of French aid in the recovery of the Palatinate. [2]

The aims of neither party to the alliance had ever been confined to the religious issues involved. France wanted help in the reconquest of the Valtelline ; she wished, too, to make impossible that Anglo-Spanish alliance that had loomed so threateningly on the horizon the year before. England's policy, particularly Conway's, was a similar anxiety to drive France against Spain and to form with her a defensive and offensive alliance for the restoration of the Prince Palatine. [3]

---

[1] GOLL, *op. cit.*, pp. 35 seq. GARDINER, *op. cit.*, vol. V, pp. 261 seq. Effiat wrote to Brienne, Sept. 11-12 : " aujourd'hui il [le roi] a été vaincu. " Gardiner is scathing in his indictment of Buckingham who showed Effiat the dispatches of the English Ambassadors " acting more as an agent of France than as an English minister " ; and of Charles " whose mind was always fertile in excuses for doing that which at the moment he wished to do. " James, isolated gave way after two days' argument and, under the impression that all was settled, created Kensington Earl of Holland.

[2] *Ibid.*, p. 38 ; GARDINER, *op. cit.*, vol. V, pp. 261 seq.

[3] The keen-eyed Giacinto, watching the political horizon from his diplomatic crow's-nest in Brussels, declared that the English thought more of restoring the Palatine than of securing a bride for the Prince : all they wanted with France was somebody to fight the Emperor for them. Of the French, the Capuchin was equally contemptuous : for security's sake they would justify an alliance with heretic, Turk or the Devil himself ! (*B.L.*, 6139, f. 156 : To Barberini, Brussels, June 29, 1624 : " Tengo opinione che l'Inglese cerchi più

A most important step towards this would be to secure from France at least financial support for Mansfeld, a free-booter of the Du Guesclin type, in his campaign against the German Catholic princes. Therefore at Secretary Conway's instigation the English Ambassadors, before signing the Marriage Articles now agreed upon, demanded a formal guarantee from France that she would subsidize Mansfeld for a period of six months, during which time she would also bind herself to further the restoration of the Palatinate by making no treaty or peace against this end. The promise was to be made by Louis through an Ambassador sent to England for this purpose but, when the matter was discussed at a conference at Richelieu's house on November 3, the French statesmen pressed for a less formal promise and won. They further forestalled the Ambassadors' attempts to bring the Marriage Articles into discussion again by producing Effiat's dispatches showing they had already been accepted in England.

Therefore, after leave had been given to Effiat to inform James *unofficially* that France would pay Mansfeld for six months, and allow troops levied for him in England to land on French soil, Richelieu once again requested Carlisle and Holland to sign the Treaty. This they did on November 20 (N. s.), at the same time promising that James would draw up the *Écrit Particulier* in the form agreed upon. [1]

The Treaty now needed only the ratification of the King of England and the grant of the Papal dispensation to become effective. James ratified on December 12 (o. s.), and he and Charles also signed their private agreement to grant greater relief to their Catholic subjects than they would have been given under the Spanish articles. The King's promise was countersigned by Conway as Secretary of State. [2]

tosto la restitutione del Palatino che la Sposa, e poiche gli rincresce di far la guerra, vorrebbe o che altri la facesse per lui, o che con l'autorità loro promovesse... In Francia corre questa Dottrina che sia lecito per difesa propria di collegarsi non solo con heretici e Turchi, mà col Demonio stesso. ")

[1] GOLL, *op. cit.*, pp. 42 ; 47-48. A further concession to England, interesting in the light of later events, was the provision that the Princess's lay suite could in time be replaced with Englishmen. For the 30 Articles signed on Nov. 10/20, 1624, cf. BELLESHEIM, vol. III, *op. cit.*, pp. 431 seq.

[2] *B.L.* 8615, f. 10 : Cambridge, Dec. 12, 1624 ; *ibid.*, f. 7 : Similar document signed by James and Conway, London, Dec. 20.

To ensure that the Treaty would be immediately acted on as regards the relief of the Catholics and to make provision for the efficacy of the *Écrit Particulier* in the event of James's death, de la Ville-aux-Clercs was now sent over to England as a second Ambassador Extraordinary. He too was told, as Effiat had been told before him, to make friends with the English Catholic leaders and to stress the fact that Louis's chief motive in allying himself with England was the amelioration of their state. [1]

On December 11 (o. s.) the two Ambassadors proceeded to Cambridge where the Court was. Within a fortnight orders had been given that the Penal Laws were no longer to be enforced against recusants ; soon afterwards the Lord Keeper was told to release all Catholics imprisoned for their religion. At the same time the Archbishops of Canterbury and York were ordered to stop all proceedings against Papists in their Ecclesiastical Courts. [2] In addition, the Lord Treasurer was ordered to repay all fines levied on recusants since the last Trinity Term, and an order was made out that future fines, instead of being paid directly into the Exchequer, were to be handed to two officials appointed for the task, who would immediately give them back : in this way the remission would be concealed. In consequence, up to Spring, 1625, sums amounting to something like £ 17,710 were handed back. Besides this financial relief a number of Jesuits and Seminary priests who had been condemned to death for high treason were pardoned, and for the future banishment was to replace the severer penalties. [3]

ROME AND THE DISPENSATION

Although the Pope was not officially petitioned for the dis-

---

[1] AVENEL, *op. cit.*, vol. II, p. 44 : *Inst. baillée à M. de la Ville-aux-Clercs, allant Amb. Extr. en Angleterre de la part du roi*, 27 nov. 1624 : " Le roi enjoint donc aux ambassadeurs qu'avec soin ils ménagent l'amitié des catholiques, et pour se gagner leurs chefs, ils n'y obmettent aucun soin cela en temps et lieu pouvant estre utile. "

[2] A copy of this letter dated Dec. 26, 1624 (o.s.), translated into French and authenticated by Conway was sent by James to Louis. It was sent on to Rome, probably by Richelieu in order to dispose the Pope to grant the dispensation, and now lies among the Barberini MSS. in the Vatican Library (*B.L.* 8615, f. 5).

[3] GARDINER, *op. cit.*, vol. V, pp. 269-280 ; GOLL, *op. cit.*, pp. 49-50.

pensation till the mission of Père de Bérulle [1] in August, 1624, he had been constantly kept informed of the state of the negotiations between France and England and had appointed a commitee of Cardinals, similar to that which functioned in the Spanish affair, to draw up instructions for Spada, the Nuncio, to act on while the English Ambassadors were in Paris. [2]

The Roman theologians, naturally enough, took the Spanish Marriage Articles as a model, there being two series of demands, *Conventiones* and *Conditiones necessariae*, authentic copies of which duly signed by the King of England and his son were to be obtained by the Nuncio before ever he handed over the dispensation. Spada was also told to ask Louis to guarantee to the Pope, on a par with the Spanish conditions, the fulfilment of the promises made by James and Charles.

The distinctive feature of the treaty agreed upon between Richelieu and the English Ambassadors was, as has been noted, the introduction of a document outside the main articles, in which the promise of concession to the English Catholics had been placed. The idea of this *Écrit Particulier* is to be found also in these instructions sent to Spada, where it was suggested that, besides the official articles, other conditions equally necessary, though perhaps

---

[1] Pierre de Bérulle (1575-1629), Cardinal and statesman, overcame great obstacles to establish the Carmelites in France ; he then founded the Congregation of the Oratory which, approved by Paul V in 1613 and favoured by Louis XIII and his mother, spread remarkably in face of opposition from the Jesuits. As a statesman de Bérulle concluded the Treaty of Monzon in 1626 besides obtaining the dispensation dealt with here. Rivalry with Richelieu forced him from Court after he had become Cardinal in 1627. He died suddenly while saying Mass, 1629.

[2] *Arch. Secr. Vat., Miscell. Arm.* III 5, ff. 37ª-39ª : *Difficoltà fatta da Urbano VIII sopra il modo di contraersi e concedersi la disp*ª *per il matr*º *tra la sorella del Rè di Francia et il figliolo del Rè d'Inghilterra eretico, et instruttioni diverse.* This document is followed in the same volume by a summary of the Spanish Articles signed in London, February 20, 1623, by James. They consist of nine short points, and Urban and his advisers evidently tried to reproduce them in the Spada Instructions, a point Goll seems to have missed.

Bernardino Spada (1594-1661), Archbishop of Damiata, had a most difficult *triennium* at Paris with the Valtelline question dividing France and Spain, the alliance and subsequent quarrel between England and France, and the latter's attitude towards the Huguenots and the German protestants. For his good work, the Nuncio was created cardinal in his second year of office.

they could not be put in as solemn or public a form as the others, should be promised and signed by both parties and by their Secretaries of State. The main concession in this document was that the Catholics were to enjoy greater liberty than they would have had under the Spanish Treaty. This suggestion of the Pope's was adopted by Louis and promised by James and Charles on December 12/22, 1624. Spada was also told to demand letters from Henrietta to James and Urban, promising that only Catholics would be charged with the care of her children : this also was complied with. [1]

The Nuncio Spada was given particular orders not to hand over the dispensation until he had received the originals or at least authentic copies of all these promises to be made by Louis, James and Charles.

Other points not stipulated explicitly, but which Louis was to promise to work for both before and after the marriage, were the baptism and confirmation of the children with full Catholic ritual, the immediate relief of the Catholics of all burdens borne in excess of other subjects, and the confirmation of the Articles by the Privy Council and, if possible, by Parliament.

This in substance was the instruction sent to Spada, and which had been drawn up by Urban's advisory committee and amplified by his personal wishes. [2]

As the Marriage Articles gradually took shape, Richelieu decided to apply to Rome for the dispensation. This was to be done through the French Ambassador in Rome, de Béthune, who would have the support of the experienced and trusted Père de Bérulle. The mission of the latter it was at first desired to keep secret, so that when he left Paris in August, it was ostensibly to make a pilgrimage to Loreto and then to Rome in time for the Holy Year, 1625. In reality he held important instructions petitioning for the dispensation, and a personal letter from Louis to Urban, in which the French King avowed that following the example of

---

[1] B.L., 8616, f. 11 : Autograph of Henrietta to Urban VIII, dated Paris, April 6, 1625 ; B.L. 8615, f. 16 : Similar letter to James, same date : " ... je ne feray aucune eslection pour nourrir, eslever et servir les enfans qui en pourront naistre, que de personnes catholiques." [N.B. The day on which this was written James died, Mar. 27/Apr. 6.]

[2] V. supra, p. 65, note 2.

his predecessors he would do nothing without the guidance of the Pope, which he knew would be for the greater good of Christendom and of the harassed English Catholics. [1]

The Oratorian's instructions, which bore the stamp of the hand of Père Joseph, Richelieu's close friend and adviser, [2] recalled the fact that the English had first been led to a knowledge of Christ through the good offices of a daughter of France, [3] and the hope was expressed that history would repeat itself and that through this dispensation there would be once more a Catholic Queen in England to lead that country back to the Church.

The Articles agreed upon between the English and French statesmen were then expounded one by one, and the document concluded with a plea that they would be sufficient for the dispensation. The obvious objection to them (which in fact Urban made) was that they offered less advantage to religion than Spain had demanded. This the French explained away by alleging first that Spain had negotiated merely to gain time and get possession of the Palatinate with no serious intention of bringing the match to a conclusion ; and secondly, that the Prince of Wales on his side had been ready to agree to anything, being only anxious to get away from Madrid and regain his liberty.

The King of France, the document concluded, much as he would have liked to press for the same advantages was in no position to do so when the King of England and his son were leaning more towards the Puritans, and when new laws had

[1] AVENEL, op. cit., vol. II, pp. 18-19 : Louis to Urban, August, 1624 : " .. Nous n'avons pas voulu y résoudre aucune chose sans en préalable avoir eu non seulement sa dispense, mais aussi ses advis... comme nous defférons entièrement aux sages conseils de Vostre Saincteté, nous espérons, et de sa prudence et de son zelle au bien public, qu'elle prendra..." etc., — noteworthy phrases in view of the later discussions in France as to the lawfulness of proceeding without the dispensation.

Spada had soon discovered the real purpose of Berulle's visit and forewarned the Pope (Ibid., p. 19, note 1).

[2] The phrase " con questa unione il Turco men' oserebbe d'intraprendre" betrays the hand of the Capuchin who had spent long years in the Orient, and had written on the Turkish problem. It was, besides, Père Joseph's official task to draw up instructions of this sort. The Comte de Brienne, however, in his Mémoires attributed the document at himself (Cf. L. DEDOUVRES, Le Père Joseph de Paris, capucin. L'Éminence grise, vol. II, p. 107, note 2).

[3] Bertha, daughter of the King of Paris, married Ethelbert, King of Kent and was instrumental in the coming and ultimate success of St Augustine.

already been enforced against the Catholics. For the latter there was nothing but ruin ahead if their hopes of the French Marriage were disappointed. [1]

Receiving Père de Bérulle and the Ambassador de Béthune in audience, Pope Urban immediately began to raise objections to certain points of the Treaty. He was afraid that James's promise not to ask the Catholics to take any oath against their conscience would only include the Oath of Allegiance formulated by himself, and that he would still enforce Elizabeth's Oath of Supremacy. To avoid such trickery, the Pope suggested that the King of England should never ask any oath of the Catholics not first approved by Rome.

Urban then went on to point out that the Spanish Articles had conceded a public church and, when the two Ambassadors said the difficulties were insuperable and they despaired of obtaining it, he discussed the question of attendance at the Princess's private chapel, it being his desire that any who wished to accompany the Princess there might do so. Bérulle and his companion pointed out that this might lead to riots, and alleged that the goodwill of the English King and his son had been sufficiently shown by their allowing the Princess to name anyone she liked to attend her. The Pope quickly pointed out the emptiness of the concession, for the Princess's choice was limited and, as it was not likely to reach Catholics of the lower classes, a great chance of helping them would therefore be lost. Nor would she be completely free in her choice of Catholics of quality, for she would constantly risk running counter to the wishes of the King and Charles, who would soon let it be known what Catholics they would prefer to see around her. At the very least the Princess would be forced into appearing partial to certain Catholics, and the rest would look on her with suspicion and mistrust instead of regarding her as their protectress.

The French Ambassador, de Béthune, tried to counter Pope Urban's objections by saying he had it from Paris that the Nuncio Spada had declared his Holiness very pleased with the negotiations that had taken place. Urban's answer to this was that just the

---

[1] Siri, *Memorie recondite*, vol. V, pp. 625 seq., where the Instructions of de Bérulle, dated July 31, 1624 (N.S.) are to be found.

POPE URBAN VIII
(From the Barberini Collection.)

opposite could be gathered from Spada's correspondence, for the Nuncio wrote that he had constantly objected when anything had been suggested to the disadvantage of religion or less than was given in the Spanish articles.

The following Monday Urban sent for de Bérulle and, before speaking of anything else, told him that nothing could be found in Spada's despatches that could have given the impression that the Nuncio had assented to all the negotiations going on in Paris, unless one took for assent a remark Spada had let fall that this century was fortunate in possessing a number of theologians who would agree to any opinion. Apart from this there was nothing to be encountered in Spada's correspondence but such words as " opposition" and " difficulties," which he had used as a mild reproof of a suggestion that the dispensation should not be asked for.

Despite the Pope's energetic defence of Spada, Bérulle pulled out a letter that Cardinal Richelieu had written to him, saying he had been told the very same thing about the Nuncio from one who had heard it from Spada's own lips.

As a result of these recriminations, Cardinal Barberini, the Secretary of State, wrote to warn Spada of what had happened, and to be non-committal over any further proposal made to him, while always stressing the Pope's good-will towards France.

When Père de Bérulle saw the Pope alone, Urban specified his objections to the marriage articles on four principal points, viz. the refusal of a public church, the choice of nurses for the children, the question of their education should perchance their mother die before they reached the age of 13, and the oath the English Privy Council should take to guarantee the fulfilment of the treaty.

Always harking back to the Spanish Articles, the Pope pointed out that in them a public church had been granted, not only for London but wherever the Infanta should happen to be staying, and that the free attendance of the English Catholics, the Prince of Wales had promised, would be winked at.

Again, the choice of nurses was to have been left entirely to the Infanta or to those deputed by her or, failing both, to the King of France.

Finally, under the Spanish Treaty, the Privy Councillors had taken an oath to observe it.

To all this, the Père de Bérulle replied that such conditions would now be impossible to obtain and that, when the King of England and his son promised them, the latter had been almost a prisoner in the hands of the Spaniards and was anxious at any price to get away. Here Urban quickly pointed out that when the dispensation was delivered, the Prince had already left Spain and that, although the treaty had been made while the Prince was in Spain, it was really concluded after his departure. Bérulle retorted that Charles could promise what he would, since he had no intention of keeping his word. The obvious answer to this, and the Pope made it, was to ask who was to assure France that the same thought was not still present in the minds of the English, seeing that a new Parliament had been convoked for November. Urban further asked de Bérulle if he knew that, during the negotiations with France, England had made overtures for the hand of the Duke of Saxony's daughter for the Prince of Wales, and that the Duke had replied that he would not marry his daughter to a Calvinist. Bérulle's only comment on this thrust was a shrug of the shoulders.

Urban concluded the audience by saying he had pointed out the major difficulties in the articles, and closer comparison with the Spanish articles only revealed others ; however, he would proceed to overcome them to the satisfaction of the King of France. The Pope then repeated an offer he had made before of appointing to deal with the matter two Italian, and therefore neutral, Cardinals, and one other in the confidence of France. [1]

The obtaining of the dispensation was evidently going to prove more difficult than Richelieu, for one, had anticipated. Even before Père de Bérulle arrived in Rome, rumour had reached Paris that Urban would not dispense on terms less than those obtained by Spain, whereat Richelieu had irritatedly observed that it was enough if the French King obtained conditions which safeguarded the faith of his sister and her household, and brought some relief to the English Catholics. Actually, the Cardinal insisted, matters were better than this, but in any case it was pointless to ponder on the concessions Spain had been granted ; the question to decide was, — were those obtained by France legitimate and sufficient? If they were, a refusal of the dispensation would force France to

---

[1] *Arch. Vat., Nunz. di Francia*, 59 : Francesco Barberini to Spada, Oct. 2, 1624 (N.S.), quoted BELLESHEIM, *op. cit.*, vol. III, pp. 488 seq. App. XVI.

an unpleasant issue certainly prejudicial to the Church. Richelieu ordered this point to be impressed upon the Pope, *viz.* the danger of refusing, as well as the good that would come from granting the dispensation. [1]

That the Pope's reluctance was forcing Richelieu into a threatening attitude may be seen again from a letter he wrote to de Bérulle three weeks later. Urging that there was no substantial difference between the French and the Spanish Articles, the Cardinal maintained that in fact the last French article, meaning presumably the *Écrit particulier*, allowed greater freedom to the English Catholics than the corresponding Spanish article. He therefore hinted that in the unbelievable event of refusal the Pope would have to face the protests of all Christendom. [2]

At the same time he sent de Bérulle the latest version of the Articles, and one more advantageous than that the Oratorian had taken with him six weeks before. Even Spada seemed satisfied, except that he wanted a free permit for Catholics to attend the Princess's chapel. Though this was not in the contract, Richelieu said confidently they could leave that to the zeal of the Princess, and he again stressed the importance of a prompt decision in the matter of the dispensation, as the French King had given the English Ambassadors to understand in June that three months would be ample time to obtain the document. [3]

On the very day Richelieu was writing so urgently for the dispensation, Padre Giacinto was equally vigorously opposing it; in a letter to Cardinal Barberini he gave it as his considered opinion that the English King's chief thought in the alliance with France was the restoration of his son-in-law, the Prince Palatine.

---

[1] AVENEL, *op. cit.*, vol. II, p. 28 : à M. d'Herbault à Rome, St. Germain, August 22, 1624. SIRI, *op. cit.*, vol. V, pp. 627-628.

[2] AVENEL, *op. cit.*, vol. VII, p. 550 : à M. de Bérulle (c. Sept. 12, 1624) : " Je ne croy pas que le pape puisse faire difficulté en cette affaire, et véritablement, s'il en faisoit, je croy que la chrestienté y trouveroit quelque chose à redire."

[3] Further evidence of Richelieu's underestimation of the difficulties attached to obtaining the dispensation. It explains the threatening tone he adopted towards the Pope. Cf. AVENEL, *op. cit.*, vol. VII, pp. 548-549, and note 2 : Richelieu to Bérulle, St-Germain-en-Laye, Sept. 12, 1624 : " J'estime du tout important au bien de l'église que sa Sainteté accorde cette dispense *promptement.*"

This would only incense Spain, while France herself would be
disillusioned at England's lack of interest in the re-capture of the
Valtelline, and the general result of the match would be further
disturbance of the peace of Europe. [1]

But Richelieu was pressing too strongly for Giacinto to have
much influence in stopping the dispensation. Again in November
the Cardinal sent a copy of the Articles to Rome, deprecating
any further delay. He also enclosed letters to himself from James
and Charles for the Pope's edification. [2]

Time was indeed an important factor for the French, and
mindful of the delays in the Spanish case, Père de Bérulle hoped
to obtain the dispensation *motu proprio* from the Pope, but Urban
insisted on the whole merits of the case being discussed by a
Congregation of Cardinals under the presidency of his nephew,
Francesco Barberini.

Acting on their advice, Urban granted the dispensation on December 1, 1624 (N.S.), and wrote to congratulate and encourage those
who had petitioned for it. [3] The grant was, however, made
subject to certain alterations in the Articles, which Bérulle in
writing home to Brienne, quite underestimated in describing as
merely verbal changes which would not affect the issue. This
was repeated to Buckingham in reporting to him the return of
Bérulle and the arrival of the dispensation in the hands of the
Nuncio. Certain unessential changes were demanded, he was told,
— a mere matter of translation, as Rome had demanded a Latin
draft of the Treaty. [4]

But the amendments Rome asked for went farther than that.
The future Queen was to have a church or chapel not only in London

---

[1] *B.L.* 6139, ff. 172-173 : Giacinto to Barberini, Sept. 12, 1624.

[2] AVENEL, *op. cit.*, vol. VII, pp. 554-555 : Richelieu to Bérulle, Paris, Nov.
26, 1624. The Cardinal was extremely proud that the King of England gave
him his full cardinalitial titles and showed him, as he said, more respect than
any other King.

[3] *Arch. Vat.*, *Epist ad Principes*, vol. XXXIX, Nos 114-118 : the Pope's
congratulatory briefs to Louis, Henrietta, Marie de' Medici, Anne of Austria
and the Duc d'Orléans, all under the one date, Dec. 28, 1624. *Ibid.*, No 109
is a brief to John Colleton, Dean of the English Clergy, expressing great hopes
of the dispensation (Dec. 23, 1624).

[4] These Latin Articles are to be found *Arch. Secr. Vat.*, *Miscell. Arm.*,
III 5, ff. 36 seq.

but wherever the Court happened to be, and the Article was so worded that free entry for all Catholics was expected, although not explicitly asked for. [1]

More important still, it was required that the *Écrit particulier* should be confirmed by a public declaration of the King, a stipulation which would destroy the whole nature of the document.

Finally, this Latin text of the Treaty was to be signed by both Kings and handed to the Pope or to his Nuncio in France.

The French raised no objection save to the second request, the *public* announcement of the *Écrit particulier* being refused point-blank. The other points they thought they could persuade the English Ambassadors were of small importance and could be conceded. But the latter would listen to no innovation and complained so bitterly in their dispatches that Buckingham, now enthusiastically pro-French, kept away from Court and left Effiat to bear the brunt of Charles's sour charge that France had outdone Spain in chicanery, that such deceit might have been expected all along, etc., etc. James refused even to receive the French Ambassador till Buckingham came to the rescue and arranged an audience for March. The King then began loudly with his complaints, but Effiat showed him a French translation of the Latin Articles in which they did not appear so strong. After a five-hours' audience, James consented to his replies being put down in writing, which was considered something of a triumph for the Ambassador.

A conference with the English Ambassadors in Paris was to have taken place a week later, but Holland, hitherto pliable, pleaded indisposition, while Carlisle demanded a favourable decision within three days under threat of departure. The French ministers hurried to the Nuncio, pleading that the Treaty was in danger, but Spada remained adamant. A new mission to Rome offered little hope even if there were time. The only solution was for the English to yield to the Papal amendments. Effiat was ordered to plead the case,

---

[1] GOLL, *op. cit.*, p. 59, note 7. The Latin Article was worded as follows : " habeat... ecclesiam sive sacellum capax et amplum *cum sufficientibus et commodis additibus,* non ad usum dumtaxat ejusdem Madamae ac ejus nobilioris familiae, verum etiam *familiae humilioris et infimae"* — the phrases italicized intimate that the chapel was to be open to all whom the Princess cared to invite, *i.e.* in practice any Catholic could come.

and pressure was placed on Buckingham to whom it was hinted that Gondomar was on his way back to England, and that the only way to counter Spanish intrigue was to push through the French match at all costs and so ensure that the new Queen would be on his side.

On March 20 (N.S.), Carlisle, in an interview with Richelieu and Schomberg, was told that France would ask Rome to give way on the amendments she had made, so that the dispensation could be used without delay. This, however, Carlisle did not want, and was given instead a formal written promise that the marriage would take place in thirty days' time.

To make so dangerously definite a promise, the French must have counted on James's giving way entirely at the persuasion of Buckingham and Effiat, but the King's illness now put an end to further negotiation. On March 27 (O.S.) James died, and Buckingham's power increased. He immediately put the new conditions of the Treaty before the Privy Council for their approval, silencing any voices raised against particular points. At the same time, on account of the King's death, the 30-day time-limit was extended by another month. Formal application for the delivery of the dispensation had again been made to Rome, [1] but at the same time Richelieu let it be known that, if the worst came to the worst, the marriage ceremony would be carried through without dispensation. [2]

Whether the threat was an earnest one or a bluff to force Rome to a panic decision is difficult to say. At all events, towards the end of March, the French statesmen held a conference that they took care Rome should hear about, in which the lawfulness of the marriage without dispensation was discussed. Cardinal Richelieu, the Comte de Schomberg and others were present, and two theologians were called. The statesmen appealed to the common practice in countries where heresy had a holding : in such places, any scandal given by doing without the dispensation would be passive scandal not conducive to sin and therefore no obstacle to the ceremony. The two theologians opposed this and ultimately

---

[1] Père Joseph arrived in Rome, March 14/24, for the General Chapter of his order and soon had an audience with Urban to whom he protested against the Latin Articles (DEDOUVRES, *op. cit.*, vol. II, p. 98).

[2] GOLL, *op. cit.*, pp. 58 seq.

won the others to their view that positive scandal would arise from the common sense notion people held that persons of different religion should not contract matrimony without dispensation; moreover, the scandal would be the greater seeing that recourse had already been had to Rome, and that the King of France had even committed himself so far as to say in writing that the marriage could not be contracted lawfully without a dispensation. This scandal, the theologians concluded, must be active, not passive, as it arose from something introduced against common custom and opinion, which the particular custom of France or of anywhere else where there was a mixture of Catholics and Protestants did not refute. Besides, in France the *curés* did not dare assist at mixed marriages without the licence of their bishops; if they did, they were punished. It could, therefore, be argued that the same *jus corrigendi* vested in the bishops *vis-à-vis* the people belonged to the Pope in regard to princes. With this argument the conference concluded after a resolution to dispatch another courier to Rome; if that failed, some other remedy would have to be sought in so vital an affair of state. [1]

Meanwhile, Louis had been doing all he could to satisfy the Pope's demands, and in March he signed the guarantee Urban had asked of Bérulle, *viz.* that the King of France would see that

[1] *B.L.* 8616, f. 15, senza titolo : a copy, April 14, 1625, [Spada ? (reporting Père Coton, one of the theologians) to Barberini ?].

The question whether a " mixed " marriage could take place licitly without a dispensation depended on contemporary custom in any particular country. Absence of danger to the faith of the Catholic party and of the children would have to be morally certain, but contemporary canonists were not decided on the form the guarantee should take. TANNER (fl. 1604) and GROBAT (1600-1679) held that no *explicit* promise was required, and all would have regarded the present custom of asking the non-Catholic party to sign the three promises as only one of many ways. However, granted there is no danger of perversion CASTROPALAO (*Opera moralia*, Pars V, tract. 28, disp. 4, punct. XI, 1st ed. 1647) holds that the obligation of asking for dispensation ceases; and consequently argues that even where there is danger of perversion the Pope may still allow the marriage by dispensation. He adds that in such places the solemn promise of a sovereign is sufficient guarantee (" equidem si inter magnos principes, si fidem dent juramento firmatam sufficiens securitas reputanda est "). In saying this he may well have had the marriage of Charles and Henrietta in mind.

England kept the promises made under the Treaty. [1] The young Henrietta thereupon wrote the letters required of her to the Pope and to James, but the latter was dead before his arrived. [2]

The dispensation was now handed over by the Nuncio and on May 11, 1625 (N.S.) the marriage was solemnized at the Great West Door of Notre Dame, the Duc de Chevreuse standing proxy for Charles, whose presence in France, it was privately hinted, was not desired. [3]

In fulfilment of his promises Charles immediately gave orders to Williams, the Lord Keeper, to carry out the provisions of the Treaty and stay the execution of the Penal Laws. To this purpose some 3,000 letters were sent out to the judges and bishops. However, many Catholics applying for remission of fines were told they would have to wait for relief till the Parliamentary session was over, as it would be unwise to risk the displeasure of the House. [4]

Meanwhile, Buckingham had crossed the Channel to fetch home the new King's bride and to enforce the fulfilment of that other part of the Treaty in danger of being forgotten, — the defensive and offensive alliance. The favourite failed to persuade France to support England in a declared war against Spain but Louis agreed to send money to the King of Denmark, and subsidize Mansfeld for another seven months. So Buckingham had to return to face Parliament with nothing more attractive than a pretty Papist Queen, and the explanation of his notorious conduct on the way home may well be that he sought a petty revenge for his failure to impress Louis and his ministers. At all events he outraged French opinion and offered insult to the King by making

---

[1] GOLL, op. cit., p. 62, note 18 : *Lettres patentes du Roy sur les articles latins dressez à Rome*, 21 mars 1625. Urban may well have been influenced in this demand by the advice of Sir Toby Mathew : " La miglior sicurtà et più facile da ottenere che si potesse negotiare con il Rè di Francia, sarebbe ch'il Papa premesse che d^{to} Rè facesse giuram^{to} à S. Santità di voler compire le conditioni in favor de' Cat^{ci} dal Rè d'Inghilterra" (*B.L.* 8620, f. 61 : Claudio Neri [*i.e.* Toby Mathew] to Barberini, Oct. 14/24, 1624).

[2] V. *supra*, p. 66, note 1.

[3] GARDINER, op. cit., vol. V, pp. 306, 325. Somewhat tardy congratulations were offered by the Pope to Henrietta and her brother, Louis XIII, in briefs dated Rome, Aug. 9, 1625 (*Arch. Vat.*, *Epist. ad Principes*, vol. XXXIX, N°s 388-389).

[4] GARDINER, op. cit., vol. V, pp. 326 seq.

love to Louis's neglected wife as the royal party halted at Amiens. [1]

This was not the only incident of interest that occurred in the town. After Mass attended by the three Queens, Marie de' Medici, Anne of Austria and Henrietta Maria, the last-named was presented with the Golden Rose by the Pope's representative. [2]

The arrival of the Papal messenger and the prolonged delay at Amiens due to the Queen Mother's indisposition gave rise to the wildest rumours in England, already worked up to a pitch of excitement at the prospect of welcoming the Popish Princess. It was whispered that the Pope's Legate had come to impose a 15 days' penance on Henrietta for marrying without a dispensation, and that she would have had to complete this before receiving absolution, had not Charles insisted on her coming, whereat she left at once with the Legate still at Amiens. [3]

Eventually the new Queen set sail for England and on June 12 a bright-eyed girl of fifteen landed at Dover, to be met by her twenty-four-year-old husband. The marriage was consummated at Canterbury, and four days later the King and Queen arrived in London. [4]

---

[1] *Ibid.*, pp. 331-332.

[2] *B.L.* 8616, f. 28 : Vincenzo Martinozzi to Barberini, Parigi, 19 Giugno, 1625. A little tactlessly the Papal Brief conferring the Rose speaks of England's new Queen as " inter spinas hebraicae iniquitatis flos de radice Jesse " (*Arch. Vat., Epistolae ad Principes*, vol. XXXIX, N° 305 : Urban to Henrietta, Rome, May 30, 1625).

[3] T. BIRCH, *Court and Times of Charles I*, vol. I, p. 32 : Rev. Joseph Mead to Sir Martin Stutteville, Christ College, June 18, 1625.

[4] GARDINER, *op. cit.*, vol. V, pp. 333-334.

CHAPTER III

BROKEN FAITH

" This affair of the French household which constituted a party of French politics and Roman Catholicism under the roof of the Sovereign was one of those intricate cases, where political expediency seems to violate all moral right." [1]

The early happiness of two such souls as Henrietta, a charming child, quickly responsive, vivacious with all the gaiety of Gaul, and Charles, heavy-witted, serious, with a premature gravity that had long been his, was doomed to disaster by the unnatural burden laid on them as champions of rival religions. Henrietta had entered upon her marriage with written promises to King James, to her brother, Louis, and to the Pope, her godfather, that she would make her own the cause of the harassed Catholics of her husband's realms. Her duty was drummed stilld eeper into her impressionable mind by her mother and her Confessor, P. de Bérulle ; [2] and the pressure was not relaxed by her suite, clerical and lay, who went with her to live among the heretics. Charles, too, to counteract the promises of his marriage contract, " made lightly when hope was young," was surrounded by counsellors advising him to play up to the petition of a Puritan Parliament for rigid reinforcement of the Penal Laws against Papists. For the present both were puppets with parts to play, stiffly self-conscious while others pulled the strings.

---

[1] I. D'ISRAELI, *Commentaries on the Life and Reign of Charles I, King of England*, vol. II, p. 230.

[2] Before Henrietta left France, Père de Bérulle wrote her in her mother's name some inspired advice on her duty as a Catholic and the daughter of St Louis : " Ayez soin de protéger envers le Roy vostre mary les pauvres catholiques affligés et soïes une Esther envers eux... Ne les oublies pas, ma fille et croyès que Dieu vous a envoïée en ce pays pour eux, car c'est son peuple, et son peuple souffrant depuis tant d'années ! " Cf. M. HOUSSAYE, *Le Cardinal de Bérulle et le Cardinal de Richelieu*, vol. III, pp. 4-8.

The first clash came when on August 14, 1625, the King and his Privy Council met to approve unanimously a proclamation for the banishment of Catholic priests.[1]   Unable to see he was in the wrong, Charles was incapable of understanding his wife's bitter resentment, nor could he flatter, threaten or cajole her into meek acceptance of the wifely rôle he looked for, — unquestioning obedience to his will.

Nevertheless, the King was quick to see that Henrietta's French suite were exploiting the quarrel to give the girl a grievance. To counter this he commanded her to receive as Ladies-of-the-Bed- chamber, the Duchess of Buckingham, the Countess of Denbigh and the Marchioness of Hamilton. The provision of the Marriage Treaty had been that future vacancies in the Queen's French Catholic Household might be filled by English Catholics ; the appointment of Protestants had never been considered but, if it did not contravene the letter of the law, it was an utter violation of its spirit. Henrietta rightly protested, stung by personal pique at the tactless choice of the wife, sister and niece of Buckingham, whose influence over her husband she so detested.

This first engagement was succeeded by a number of " scenes " whose pettiness only served to magnify the state of nervous tension in which the couple moved.

Charles's command to the loquacious Irish Catholic Lord to leave his prating and come to prayers, or get out of his sight is a sample of the King's unwonted testiness. It was generally voted that he would suffer no Papist to be of his household — a prophecy happily repeatedly disproved — nor would he allow any English Catholic to serve his wife and be present in her chapel. [2]

The Queen's chaplains were anxious that this chapel at St James's should be completed as soon as possible. The King's alleged answer, so unlike his normal self, but well enough in tune with his

[1] *Arch. Propaganda*, I *Anglia*, 347, f. 178 : *A Proclamation for recalling his Maiesties Subiects from the Seminaries beyond the Seas, and putting the Lawes against Iesuites and Popish Priests in execution*. Given at the Court at Woodstocke the foureteenth day of August, in the first yeare of his Maiesties Raigne of Great Britaine, France and Ireland.

[2] BIRCH, *op. cit.*, vol. I, pp. 20, 39 : Rev. Joseph Mead to Sir Martin Stuteville, London, May [June ?] 1625 ; Dr Meddus to Rev. Jos. Mead, London, July 1, 1625.

present mood, was that if the Queen's closet, where they were saying Mass, were not large enough, let them have it in the great chamber : and if the great chamber were not large enough, they might use the garden ; and if the garden would not serve their turn, then was the park the fittest place. [1]

But Henrietta was quite capable of playing Kate (" If I be waspish, best beware my sting ") to Charles's incongruous Petruchio, and when the latter ordered an English service to be held in the guard-room of her residence at Titchfield, the Queen and her ladies strolled up and down laughing and chatting during the sermon, while afterwards the French Gentlemen-in-waiting made the luckless preacher jump with fright by letting off a pistol behind a hedge where he was sitting. [2]

The Queen's protest against the violation of her Marriage Treaty was made known to her brother personally by Père de Bérulle and in writing, by several of her Gentlemen, the Duc de Chevreuse, the Marquis d'Effiat, M. de la Ville-aux-Clercs, and the Bishop of Mende, her Majesty's Almoner.

Louis and Richelieu made haste to send over the Sieur de Blainville as Ambassador — the post was vacant — with instructions to treat of the Anglo-French alliance, the grievances of the Queen and the relief of the English Catholics, the three points to be dealt with as an ensemble. Blainville was to point out that the English King had promised, if not revocation, at least non-execution of the Penal Laws, and that it was the Most Christian Kings's special desire that the promise be honoured in all fullness. The suggestion was to be made that the Archbishops and Bishops be asked not to worry out the Catholics merely to mulct them. [3]

---

[1] *Ibid.*, pp. 32-33 : Dr Meddus to Rev. Jos. Mead, London, June 24, 1625.

[2] GARDINER, *op. cit.*, vol. VI, p. 5.

[3] AVENEL, *op. cit.*, vol. II, pp. 124-136 : Blainville's first Instructions (not actually written by Richelieu but reflecting his ideas), Sept. 4, 1625 :" L'intérêt des Catholiques anglais est de grande conséquence pour sa Majesté qui désire avant tout qu'on lui tienne ce qu'on lui a promis... Bienque le roy de la Grande-Bretaigne n'ait promis que la surséance, et non la révocation des lois, toutefois il est obligé à la cessation de la persécution... Il faut donc se borner à demander que le roi ordonne aux archevêques et évêques de ne point faire faire de recher-ches." *Ibid.*, pp. 137-140 : Blainville's second Instructions, Sept. 17, 1625, — the same in substance as the foregoing, save that a special protest is made against Buckingham's anti-Catholic activities.

Charles resented this interference, and replied that he had only guaranteed his protection to the Catholics while they behaved with a moderation, of which he took upon himself to judge. He added the preposterous argument that neither he nor the French Government had taken seriously the *Article Secret,* which had been so much dust thrown in the eyes of the Pope. The make-up of his wife's household, a purely domestic affair, he refused to discuss with the Ambassador.

Williams, one of the few around the King courageous enough to suggest that his Majesty, having promised not to enforce the Laws against the Catholics, was unwise to break his word, now found himself relieved of the Great Seal. Buckingham thereupon secured as Lord Keeper, Coventry, a man hostile to all concessions to the Catholics, with the result that the August order for the banishment of priests was followed in November by the appointment of a Commission to see to the execution of the Penal Laws and to the payment of all fines to a special defence-of-the-realm fund. [1]

The English Catholics were nearing the zero-hour of the trials they suffered under Charles's personal rule. There had been so much talk of the benefits they would get, first from the Spanish, then from the French Match; their hopes had been so bolstered up by petition and promise that over-confidence now led them to neglect their customary caution, and brought them within the tightened ambit of the Law. On this score the French alliance was proving disastrous for the Catholics in the opinion of the Bishop of Mende. The Queen's Almoner did what he could to lighten the Catholics' burden, but found his episcopal office brought him under suspicion. [2]

The Bishop, who was considered the French King's agent to deal with the relief of the English Catholics, had withstood threat and flattery alike in their cause, and there were appeals to Rome

---

[1] GARDINER, *op. cit.,* vol. VI, pp. 27-29 ; 32-33.

[2] *B. L.* 8616, f. 34 : Mende to [Paris Nuncio?] N. D. [end of 1625 ?]: " Il est bien certain que l'alliance de France est la ruine des Catholiques en Angleterre, parcequilz ont negligé leurs précautions accoustumes sur la confiance quilz avoient en promesses faictes entre les deux couronnes... Je ne desespere point qu'on ne donne quelque soulagement a leurs peines : A mon instance on a adoucy lexecution de quelques loix, et en eusse tire beaucoup plus si on n'avoit croyance que Je m'en mesle plustost par office que par ordre."

when it was rumoured that he had asked to be recalled to France. [1]

The rest of the Queen's following were less of a help than a hindrance to the English Catholics. Originally, as Princess of Wales, Henrietta was to have had a suite of some 120, but the colony had swollen so considerably when she came as Queen that it was said to be more in the neighbourhood of 400. [2] With all the pride and elegance of France to uphold as well as the prestige of their Faith, they made no attempt to conceal their fine contempt for the rough-and-ready style of the English Court, and made themselves obnoxious in a hundred and one ways till by the end of the year (1625) Charles was driven to desperation and began to form plans to rid himself of the pest, attributing all his troubles to them rather than to his own neglect of the Marriage Contract. [3]

Charles soon received another shock for, when arranging for his own and his wife's coronation, he was surprised to hear Henrietta voicing her scruples at being present at a Protestant service. Unreasonably he blamed the new French Ambassador for stirring up trouble between himself and the Queen. Certainly Blainville, in his instructions of six months before, had been told to prepare the Queen to make a stand against joining in any heretical rites at the Coronation ceremony. It would have to be *outside* the Church, and she could accept no anointing, though there would be nothing against her receiving the crown from the lay peers, even if the Archbishop of Canterbury placed it on her head in the presence of the others. [4]

This unrealistic request made compromise impossible, but Charles still hoped to have his Queen by his side as an

---

[1] *B. L.* 8619, f. 62 : Claudio Neri [*i. e.* Toby Mathew] to Barberini, Dec. 13, 1625 : " Il Vescovo di Mandes è accreditato e creduto in quella corte, et hà commissione espressa e larga di trattar le cose de Cattolici Inglesi in questo... il quale non s'è voluto mai lasciar piegare, ò a lusinghe ò minaccie de' Protestanti maggiori di questa Corte ne per le buone ne per le brusche che gli hanno più volte rappresentato." Similar testimony, *ibid.*, f. 65 : Wm. Thomson, a Scot, to Barberini, Nov. 27, 1625. Also *B.L.* 8616, f. 31 : Tillières to [Paris Nuntio?] Hampton Court, Nov. 24, 1625.

[2] D'ISRAELI, *op. cit.*, vol. II, Chap. IX.

[3] GARDINER, *op. cit.*, vol. VI, p. 38.

[4] AVENEL, *op. cit.*, vol. II, pp. 124-136 : *Instruction baillée à M. de Blainville allant Ambr. Extr. en Angleterre,* Sept. 4, 1625.

interested spectator of the ceremonies, even if she played no formal part. He was doomed to disappointment, however, and on February 2, 1626 (N.S.) when the Coronation took place, the Queen's curtained chair was empty. [1] The most she would do was to watch the procession returning to Whitehall after the long ceremony. The King caught sight of her and with very good grace under the circumstances, saluted her, " en mettant les deux mains a sa couronne en la souslevant ung peu. " [2]

The pomp of Parliament's reopening was to follow four days later, and Charles, determined to show that he, and no Frenchman, was his wife's master, asked her to watch the scene from the Countess of Buckingham's balcony. Henrietta said she would, but when the moment came for crossing the street, imagined she saw rain and asked to be excused. Not all the exasperated arguments of Charles and Buckingham could convince her of the opposite till Blainville, who had from the first advised her not to be seen in the old Countess's company, counselled compliance. Straightway she allowed Buckingham to lead her across. The patent influence of the French Ambassador only irritated Charles the more and, determined on taming his shrew, he ordered his wife away from the window she was now occupying. She meekly complied. For three days Charles sulked, till Henrietta came to ask what was her offence. " You said it was raining when it wasn't, " was the answer. " I should never have thought that to be an offence, " the young Queen said sweetly, " but if you think so, I do too. " To Charles, so long on his dignity, this was irresistible : he took her in his arms and kissed her. [3]

By this time the King had had more than enough of Blainville, and demanded his recall. Resolving pettily on a parting insult, he gave orders in Council that the throng of English Catholics attending Mass at the French Embassy, Durham House, Strand, was not to be tolerated. As a result, on Sunday morning, February 26 (O.S.), a posse of constables was stationed in the Strand to catch the English Catholics coming out from Mass. The French attachés at the Embassy felt in honour bound to come to the

---

[1] GARDINER, op. cit., vol. VI, pp. 48-49.

[2] B. L. 8619, f. 70 : Extraict dune lettre escripte par ung Gentilhomme de la Royne d'Angleterre.

[3] GARDINER, op. cit., vol. VI, pp. 56-57.

rescue with their swords. The clatter soon brought out the neighbours to join in the fracas, and it needed all the prestige of the Bishop of Durham to prevent a serious riot. The Ambassador was indignant at this violation of the *jus gentium*. [1]

Charles and Henrietta were now nearly a year married and continued to bicker. The King had never made allowances for his child-wife's inevitable home-sickness, and was pained to see her gay and happy with her countrymen, while she kept her moods for him. Nor were there wanting wagging tongues to carry tales to the King of the tyranny her French priests exercised over his wife. A contemporary letter calls them " the most superstitious, turbulent and jesuitical priests that could be found in all France, very fit to make firebrands of sedition in a foreign state ". [2]

The Queen's visit to Tyburn Tree gave such scandalmongers excellent copy. The simple story was that she strolled through St James's Park and Hyde Park to the scene of so many martyrdoms, where she naturally prayed for guidance. In a week or two the version that reached the King's ears was that the Queen of England had led barefoot a pilgrimage to pray to dead traitors. Further embellishments were that her priests had " also made her to dabble in the dirt, on a foul morning, from Somerset House to St. James's, her luciferian confessor riding along by her in his coach." The Queen was also reported to have been made to spin, go barefoot, serve her own servants and so on. [3]

Whether or no he believed these tales, Charles was becoming restive under the strain of tittle-tattle from his own people and of petty annoyance from the Queen's. Seeing the departure of the French was becoming inevitable, treaty or no treaty, he scraped up a pretext to send Carleton on a special mission to France, and incidentally to drop a hint to Louis of what was coming. The envoy met with a cool reception. [4]

---

[1] GARDINER, *op. cit.*, vol. VI, pp. 70-71 ; *Catholic Record Society Publications*, vol. I, *Miscellanea*, V, A : *Relation of a Brawl between the King's officers and the servants of the French Ambassador, concerning the Catholics who resorted to Mass at Durham House*, 1626 (with contemporary plan, p. 96).

[2] BIRCH, *op. cit.*, vol. I, pp. 121-122 : Mr Pory to Rev. Jos. Mead, London, Saturday, July 1, 1626.

[3] *Ibid.*

[4] GARDINER, *op. cit.*, vol. VI, pp. 135-136.

The blow contemplated the winter before fell on the last day of July (1626), when Charles told his wife after dinner at Whitehal that her attendants must go. Henrietta flew into a paroxysm of rage [1] but her husband remained adamant, and the next day the French were told of their fate. They refused to go, but a week later a peremptory letter from the King to Buckingham decreed their expulsion. Charles had no wish to appear vindictive, however, and sugared the pill with gifts to the tune of £22, 602. [2]

At once explanations were offered : the French had given intolerable scandal in proclaiming the Jubilee Year (1625) in England, in meddling with the affairs of the English Catholics and in proselytizing. [3] A further accusation was that they had conspired with Blainville to bring about the downfall of the Duke, — a charge, they retorted, Buckingham himself had trumped up through pique at the Queen's rejection of his relatives in favour of her country-women. [4] Père de Sancy, the Queen's Confessor, even alleged that advantage was taken of secret intelligence from one of Buckingham's creatures in Paris of the intrigues rampant at the French Court to get rid of the Queen's attendants in the knowledge that no avenge of the insult could be sought. [5]

---

[1] According to Gardiner (*op. cit.*, vol. VI, p. 136) she flew to the window and dashed in the glass to call for the last time to her attendants... Charles dragged her back into the room with her hands bleeding from the energy with which she clung to the bars. Compare this with a contemporary account in Richelieu's *Mémoires* (in all probability written by Père Sancy, who had succeeded Père de Bérulle as Queen's Confessor and in addition was Charles's *bête-noire*) : ' Elle se jette en terre, lui embrasse les genoux, lui baise les pieds, lui demande pardon pour les siens qui l'ont offensé, lui fait souvenir des promesses portées par son contrat de mariage, et de ses serments dont Dieu est le vengeur, mais tout cela en vain." (*Mémoires*, vol. XVII, p. 176, cited AVENEL, *op. cit.*, vol. II, p. 245.)

[2] BIRCH, *op. cit.*, vol. I, p. 120, note 1.

[3] SIRI, *op. cit.*, vol. VI, p. 160.

[4] *B.L.* 8616, f. 35 : Mende to [?], N.D., but before the banishment. He speaks of the charge that " Blainville et le reste des françois se sont ingerez de faire des caballes dans l'estat à la ruyne du duc."

[5] INGOLD, *Mémoires domestiques pour servir à l'histoire de l'Oratoire*, vol. I, p. 194 : " P. de Sancy nous apprend dans un écrit imprimé... la nouvelle qu'un des confidents du duc de Buckingham apporta de Paris à Londres que les cartes étaient alors fort brouillées en France... qu'ainsi on pouvait renvoyer toute la maison de la reine sans crainte que la cour de France, si intriguée au dedans, fût en état de tirer justice de cet affront." — The Queen had petitioned

The whole affair was taken with very bad grace at the French Court, but Louis would make no official statement till he had the report of the Maréchal de Bassompierre, the Ambassador Extraordinary whom he now sent to investigate the matter. [1] The instructions Richelieu drew up for this mission recalled the sanctity of the Marriage Contract sworn upon the Gospels and enumerated the infringement thereof, *viz.* the Proclamation against the English Catholics, their being forbidden the Queen's Chapel, the deliberate delay in the construction of the new Chapel at St. James's, and the attempt to appoint Protestant Ladies-in-Waiting to the Queen. Besides these points, there were complaints over the management of the Queen's jointure (already the subject of a personal quarrel between husband and wife) and the seizure of French ships.

The line the Ambassador was told to take was a fair one : he was to listen to the King's complaints, and, while not blaming him personally, to be firm in demanding fulfilment of the Marriage Articles concerning the English Catholics and the household of the Queen. On the latter point he was to forestall any *argumentum ad hominem* against Louis, who had himself cashiered his wife's Spanish entourage, by stressing that Henrietta's freedom of conscience depended on her having Catholics around her, and that Charles had sworn upon the Gospels never to meddle with her conscience. [2]

the Pope for leave for herself and the English Catholics to gain the Jubilee Indulgence in England. For Urban's reply, cf. *Epist. ad Principes*, vol. XL, N⁰ 218 : Urban to Henrietta, Rome, Apr. 21, 1626.

[1] François de Bassompierre (1579-1646), Maréchal de France, saw service in Hungary against the Turks. A favourite at the Courts of Henry IV and Louis XIII, till Luynes's jealousy forced him to leave and accept an Embassy, first in Spain, then in Switzerland and finally in England. He served at La Rochelle. In 1631, having incurred the dislike of Richelieu, he was thrown into the Bastille, where he remained till the death of the Cardinal in 1643. Generally one reads only of the mission of de Bassompierre, who certainly did the work. Actually the Instructions were made out by Richelieu to both Bassompierre and Tillières ; they were brothers-in-law, and Madame Tillières, one of the Queen's Ladies, was named in the Instructions as expected to be of use. (AVENEL, *op. cit.*, vol. II, pp. 241-255 : *Instructions au Sieur de Bassompierre... et au Sieur Comte de Tillières... Sa Majesté les envoyant ses Ambrs extraordinaires vers le Roy de la Grande Bretagne...* Fait à Nantes 23 août 1626.)

[2] At Cambridge on Dec. 12, 1624 (o. s.), Charles had taken a separate oath not to interfere with his wife's beliefs. The original of this document, signed by Charles, is exposed in the *Sala Sistina* of the Vatican Museum. The

The Ambassador was empowered to make changes in the personnel of the Queen's suite, if the charges against them were substantiated ; he could also curtail the number if expense was complained of. Till this point was settled there could be no agreement between the two Kings, — this he was to insist on should Charles, to try him out, refuse concession. Strong emphasis was laid on the need for consoling the Queen in her isolation. Finally, the Ambassador was advised to use a little largesse where he deemed it expedient — full reimbursement was promised.

The Maréchal de Bassompierre saw the Nuncio, Spada, before leaving Paris and told him all the items of his instructions. He was cynically sure of success, too, saying that, if the English would not give way to the French, the French would to the English. [1]

The new Ambassador arrived in London on Sept. 29/Oct. 9, 1626, bringing (with some reluctance but at the express desire of the Queen Mother, Marie de' Medici) Henrietta's banished Confessor, Père de Sancy, who was to console the Queen and give the Ambassador an eye-witness account of much that had happened. His presence provided a pretext for the insult that Buckingham was determined to serve on the Ambassador in retaliation for the cold comfort Carleton had received in Paris. Bassompierre was met by an official request for the Oratorian to leave at once. He refused, saying that the man was his Confessor : he also contested the right of the King to pry into his entourage : rather than yield, he would go himself. More threats and stubborn refusals, till a compromise was reached on the understanding that Père de Sancy, if he stayed, must keep himself to himself and not be seen at Court. But, in spite of this, he contrived to see the Queen. [2]

Bassompierre showed himself a capable diplomat, firm but able to see the other side, while he was realist enough to admit that

glass case in which it formerly lay was completely smashed when that part of the Library crashed, Christmas 1931. By a rare chance this and other autographs of English royalties escaped destruction. This information was given me by an official on duty at the time.

[1] *Arch. Vat., Nunz. di Francia*, 66, ff. 148-151 : Spada to the Card. di S. Onofrio, Paris, Sept. 29, 1626. *B.L.* 8065, f. 146 : Spada to [Barberini ?], Sept. 11, 1626.

[2] *B.L.* 8065, f. 344 : Spada to [Card. Secretary]?, Oct. 23, 1626 ; INGOLD, *op. cit.*, vol. I, pp. 194-195 ; F. DE BASSOMPIERRE, *Journal de ma vie*, vol. III, p. 258.

the treaties of princes, especially marriage treaties, were never kept strictly despite all safeguards. [1] Nevertheless, he was not afraid to stand up to the King, and when Charles, after listening to his complaint for nearly two hours, said sarcastically that he was not fulfilling his mission and declaring war in his master's name, Bassompierre retorted coolly that he was not a Herald to proclaim war, but a Marshal of France to carry it out when declared. [2]

Eventually the Ambassador won over both Charles and Henrietta, making peace between them and giving the Queen sound paternal advice on adapting herself to her new life and surroundings, but poor Henrietta was still at white heat over the ignominy to which she had been subjected, and did not want to be told. [3]

Bassompierre soon discovered that his presence in England, implying as it did the interference of the French King, was not at all welcome, and that more was likely to be conceded by the Queen's personal plea directly, or through Buckingham, to her husband than by any diplomacy. When the Duke told him plainly that they had no intention of yielding to Louis's demands, Bassompierre's private opinion was that to remain longer in England was useless. [4]

He stayed on, however, and met the Commissioners appointed to defend the English case and treat with him for a settlement. [5]

---

[1] F. DE BASSOMPIERRE, *Négociation du Maréchal de Bassompierre envoyé en Angleterre*, p. 1.

[2] *Ibid.*, pp. 90 seq.

[3] F. DE BASSOMPIERRE, *Mémoires (Journal de ma Vie)*, vol. III, p. 260 ; *Negociation*, p. 283 : To the Bishop of Mende, London, Oct. 20, 1625 : " J'ay eu en suitte à combattre l'esprit de la Reyne qui estoit tellement animée de l'outrage qu'on luy avoit fait par l'esloignement de ses domestiques que je ne la pouvois en aucune façon remettre."

[4] BASSOMPIERRE, *Négociation*, pp. 119 seq. : " Ils tiennent une maxime de ne rien accorder ny à la Reyne, ny aux Catholiques, par l'intervention et entremise du Roy, offrant auxdits Catholiques meilleur traittement si la Reyne seule en prie son Mary, et promettant à la Reyne qu'elle obtiendra la plus grande partie de ce qu'elle desirera quand elle employera le Duc de Buckingham... il m'est désormais inutile de demeurer icy ; car le Duc mesme m'a dit franchement que le Roy ne se disposera jamais à contenter le Roy, mon maître, sur ce qu'il désire."

[5] They were Coventry (the Lord Keeper), the Earl of Marlborough (Lord Treasurer), the Earl of Manchester (Lord President of the Council), Buckingham, the Earls of Pembroke, Dorset, Carlisle and Holland, Lords Conway and Carl-

All the old grievances were resurrected : the Queen's bishop and priests were intriguers ; her lay attendants had lent their names to priests for the hire of houses, and had made the Queen's house a rendezvous for Jesuits and men on the run ; they had made her Majesty follow a monastic rule, and had sown in her mind a contempt for all that was English and a reluctance to do her husband's will.

The renewed persecution, it was claimed, did not violate the Marriage Treaty, as the promise concerning relief of the Papists was in the *Article Secret* set apart from the other Articles, and it had been agreed that infringement of this would not break the main Treaty. Then again, relief had only been promised while the Catholics used their privileges with moderation. [1]

In reply the Marshal flatly denied any such agreement as was claimed for the *Article Secret,* and said that the measures taken against the Catholics transgressed all the bounds of reason. Equally irrational were the steps taken against the French. In what had they done wrong? All the accusations were general, and unspecified charges proved nothing. [2]

Bassompierre found himself strongly opposed in the discussions by the anti-Catholic diplomat, Carlisle, who had played a leading part in arranging the King's marriage. It was he who persuaded the Commissioners to refuse ever to have a bishop as Queen's Almoner and to accept only eight priests, *not* regulars, who would be nominated by the King to ensure their being independent of the Pope. [3]

The Ambassador quickly disillusioned the Commissioners. None but an apostate priest, he told them, was independent of the Pope,

eton and Sir Richard Weston (Chancellor of the Exchequer). (Cf. *B.L.* 8065, f. 582 : List sent by Spada, Dec. 4, 1626.)

[1] BASSOMPIERRE, *Négociation*, pp. 166 seq. Cf. also *B. L.* 8065, ff. 574-582 : Spada Corr., Dec. 4, 1626 : *Responce de Messieurs les Commiss^res de sa Majesté de la grande Bretaigne à la proposition présentée par Monsieur le Mareschal de Bassompierre Ambassadeur extraordinaire du Roy très Chrestien.*

[2] *Ibid.,* pp. 182 seq. ; 194 : " Il faut dire où, quand, comment, quelles choses et quelles personnes les ont commises, autrement les accusations sont tenues frivoles et les accusateurs impertinents : il faut voir aussi si les crimes conviennent aux personnes, et s'ils en peuvent estre facilement convaincus. "

[3] Bassompierre's opinion of Carlisle : " qui est fort Puritain, et qui fait le subtil dans sa religion" (*Ibid.,* p. 221).

and for a Protestant prince to pretend to nominate priests was ridiculous. He then went on to point out what was apparently not appreciated, *viz.* the importance put upon the Queen's freedom of conscience, which would be more menaced by the subtleties of the heterodox priests the King would appoint, than if Turk or Jewish Rabbi were to argue with her. [1]

In response to the Marshal's demands the Commissioners made certain concessions and stipulations. After affirming that the King would certainly make no attempt on the Queen's conscience, they said that for this time they would allow a bishop and twelve priests provided they behaved themselves ; also, a French Chamberlain, a Secretary, a Doctor and two Ladies-of the Bedchamber (this last at the request of the Queen Mother). With the consent of her husband, the Queen could replace any of her attendants with French or English, as she pleased. In return the Ambassador was asked to bear witness to the efforts the King was making to win his wife's affections. [2]

In view of the high temper of the parties before the discussions began, these concessions were a feather in the Marshal's cap, but he waxed ironical at the patronizing tone of the English. Condescension, if any, should have come from the French ; and why the permission for a bishop and priests *for this time*, when the solemn promise in the contract had allowed them once and for all ? Again, all the demands must be conceded, not at the request of the Queen Mother, the King of France or anyone else, but in virtue of the articles of the Marriage Contract. On the last point, the Ambassador undertook to give a faithful account of Charles's fair treatment of his wife.

An agreement was eventually signed on November 16/26, providing for a Household of 46 (as against the original suite of some 104), including a bishop, who was to usurp no authority outside the Queen's household by ordaining or appointing priests. The twelve priests were to include neither Jesuit nor Oratorian, saving Fr Philip, who as her Majesty's confessor had survived the expulsion, and his companion, Fr Viette. Finally, none of the former domestics were to return except the Queen's physician. [3]

[1] BASSOMPIERRE, *Négociation*, pp. 211 seq.

[2] *Ibid.*, pp. 246 seq.

[3] *Ibid.*, pp. 56, 271. The Signatories were Bassompierre, Buckingham, Pembroke, Carlisle, Holland, Conway, Carleton and John Coke.

Bassompierre was now ready to return, only awaiting the new Ambassador, de Fontenay, and the birthday celebrations of the King and the Queen. [1] Before he left he was given letters for Louis and the two Queens, Anne of Austria and Marie de' Medici, all loud in praise of the Marshal's tact and discretion.   More valued as testimony to his skill were copies he brought of a letter sent to the Archbishop of Canterbury telling him to check the activity of the Pursuivants, and an order for the release of sixteen priests imprisoned in London, whom he was allowed to take with him out of the country. [2]

The difficulties the Ambassador had overcome were not the mere winning of concessions ; he had encountered opposition to his mission on all sides.   Charles was understandably obsessed with the idea that the French suite had been responsible for all the petty vexations that had upset the happiness of his first year of married life.   The English ladies who had stepped into their shoes were not inclined to make things easy for the Ambassador whose aim had been to see them displaced, while, unexpectedly, he found war with France was the wish not only of the Puritans but of the English Catholics, priests and laity alike.   Finally, the English Ambassadors had made negotiations more difficult by meddling in the French King's peace with the Rochellois. [3]

Although the general opinion in England was that he had had a successful mission, Bassompierre, knowing perhaps what awaited him at home, was sceptical of its effect. [4] He soon found Richelieu and de Bérulle indignant at his compromise and, as the Pope had urged the acceptance of nothing but an exact carrying-out of the original treaty, Louis,who had previously approved a less favourable scheme, now disavowed his Ambassador. [5] This was little less than a personal insult to the English, and Buckingham informed Richelieu that the King considered himself henceforth free of all obligation in regard to his wife's household. A further source of

[1] *Ibid.*, pp. 261, 266.

[2] *Ibid.*, pp. 274 seq.

[3] *Ibid.*, pp. 283.

[4] BIRCH, *op. cit.*, vol. I, p. 166 ; HOUSSAYE, *op. cit.*, vol. III, p. 188 : " Le fait d'un Ambassadeur," was the Marshal's remark, " est de porter et de re-porter des paroles, non pas des effets. "

[5] *B.L.* 8065, f. 540 : To Spada, Rome, Dec. 2, 1626.

friction, which arose after the expulsion of the French, was the capture of three Rouen ships by Lord Denbigh, who said he thought they were laden with Spanish merchandise and therefore fair booty, England being at war with Spain. When reprisals were taken, the English, who could play this game to perfection, decreed on December 13, 1626, the confiscation of all French ships and merchandise lying in English waters. The French were then told that they had been the first to seize ships unjustly, and must be the first to restore. [1] No wonder, then, that the New Year, 1627, seemed certain to plunge Charles and Louis into open warfare.

Meanwhile, before ever Bassompierre set out on his mission, the news of the English King's violation of his Marriage Contract by the expulsion of the French had caused great indignation in Rome, and the Secretary of Briefs to Princes was soon set to work sending out protests and appeals to the principal persons affected. Henrietta herself; Louis and the Duc d'Orléans, her brothers; Marie de' Medici, her mother; Philip of Spain, her brother-in-law; Richelieu, and the Spanish and French Ambassadors Extraordinary in England, — all received Briefs under the one date, September 21, 1626 (N. S.) in which Urban gave vent, in varying degrees of heat, to his indignation at the trials of the English Queen and at the insult offered Christendom by so flagrant a breach of contract. He had foreseen something of the sort and had warned Louis in the previous May. [2]

Whoever is to be credited, the Pope or his Secretary, with the style of these Briefs, it was most subtly tempered to the characters of the recipients. For Louis pure rhetoric was used, well calculated to impress his responsibility upon him : all Europe stood stupefied at Britain's inhuman conduct, and the faithful, burning with righteous indignation, were calling down the fire of Heaven on the enemies of Christ and mockers of his Most Christian Majesty. The Marriage Treaty, the *Jus Gentium*, the Laws of Humanity itself had been violated, while the Queen, his Majesty's sister, was being forced to live on unhappily widowed of her friends, hemmed in by heretics in a land worse than a prison. [3] Those

---

[1] GARDINER, *op. cit.*, vol. VI, pp. 142-148 ; 152.

[2] *Arch. Vat., Epistolae ad Principes*, vol. XL, Nos 409-417 (all are of the same date, Sept. 21, 1626) ; *B.L.* 8065, f. 164 : To Spada, Sept. 22, 1626.

[3] To the Duc d'Orléans the phrase was " inter satellites inferni " ! (*Epistolae ad Principes*, vol. XL, N° 412).

who thought to enjoy with impunity the fruits of so vile a crime surely knew little of the mind of the Most Christian King or of the spirit of the French. Tearful sympathy was of small worth in face of such infamy : men must be shown that the shafts of divine vengeance came not only from the clouds of heaven, but from angry princes whose power the Almighty sometimes willed to be the scourge of his wrath.

The Pope then described how, on receipt of the news, he had prayed that the English King, seeing the perfidy of his decision, would revoke it ; but now as the King flaunted his power, he prayed, and would always pray, the God of Revenge that the right arm of the Most Christian King, made strong for the task, might lay low those princes whom the voice neither of humanity nor of divine authority could bring to heel. All Christendom awaited the King's decision to right his sister's wrongs. [1]

A similar high-toned appeal was made to Philip IV to aid his sister-in-law. A shrewd thrust, calculated to catch the King on the raw, was a hint at the previous year's rash attempt by the English on Cadiz : the two most powerful of earthly Kings could scarcely let England vaunt such deeds unpunished. [2]

The letter to Richelieu was cleverer than either of the foregoing. Frankly admitting the issue was not so clear-cut but that human interest might obscure it, the Pope hinted at the undying triumph now offered by this opportunity for concerted action against England. It was a subtle appeal to all the Cardinal had in him, his ambition, his statesmanship, his long-sightedness. [3]

In each of these Briefs the recipient was referred to the Papal Nuncios in Paris or Madrid for an elaboration of the plans the Pope had in mind for a Franco-Spanish offensive alliance against England. This was not the first effort Urban had made to bring the two countries together. In an attempt to transform their opposing claims to the Valtelline Forts into an alliance, the Pope's nephew,

---

[1] *Ibid.*, Nos 409, 410 : Urban to Louis, Sept. 21, 1626.

[2] *Arch. Vat.*, *Epistolae ad Principes*, vol. XL, No 416 : Urban to Philip, Sept. 21, 1626.

[3] *Ibid.*, No 413 : Urban to Richelieu, same date : " Occasionem habes in manibus comparandi animae tuae spem coelestium triumphorum, et nomini tuo immortalitatem famae plaudentis."

Cardinal Francesco Barberini had gone as Legate in 1625 both to Paris and Madrid. [1]

Urban was also far-sighted enough to appreciate the possibility, which unhappily Richelieu's overweening nationalism made into a reality, of France and Spain, two Catholic powers, taking opposite sides in what would otherwise have remained a clear-cut issue between Catholic and Protestant princes, *viz.* the Thirty Years' War.

A pact negotiated by Olivares and the Comte de Fargis, French Ambassador to Spain, had been signed between the two countries at Monzon on March 5, 1626, [2] while in Paris the consolidation of the alliance was put in the hands of Père de Bérulle who, after leaving the English Court in November, 1625, and seeing his Oratorians follow him the following August, consistently opposed all compromise with Charles. On first hearing of the expulsion he went to consult the Spanish Ambassador in Paris, and they agreed that Spain should make it clear that she would exploit any hostility between England and France by uniting with the latter. [3]

The day following the despatch of the Papal Briefs a long instruction was sent to Spada ordering him to wait upon Louis, the Queen Mother and Richelieu and urge them to turn a deaf ear to the English King's attempts to justify himself. The Pope had already told de Béthune that the whole affair showed up the faithlessness of Calvinism to both God and man. It was no time to shut one's eyes to an attitude offering no hope in negotiation. The Most Christian King had been insulted in a matter touching his religion, his state and his family. His reputation was at stake to see the broken promises fulfilled; failing which, he should take away the crown which his brother-in-law of England wore unjustly as a heretic in the sight of God, and unworthily as a perjuror before men. [4]

[1] HOUSSAYE, *op cit.*, vol. III, p. 178; AVENEL, *op. cit.*, vol. II, p. 203, note 3.

[2] LEMAN, *Recueil des Instructions générales aux nonces ordinaires de France de 1624 à 1634*, p. 129, note 1.

[3] *B.L.* 8065, f. 146 : Spada to [Card. Secretary], Sept. 11, 1626 ; DEDOUVRES, *op. cit.*, vol. II, p. 107.

[4] *B.L.* 8065, f. 164 : To Spada, Sept. 22, 1626 : " Di q° fatto dice S. B. esser il tempo di fare l'espiatione coraggiosamente col farsi adempire q^ello che gli è stato promesso, ò torre al Cog^to q^ella corona che illegitimant^e porta come eretico app° Dio, et indegnam^te come mancatore della sua fede tra gli huomini."

The situation in Germany and the Turks' preoccupation with Persia left France free to strengthen herself at home, while the attitude of England offered an excellent opportunity for a unanimous decision with Spain to avenge outrages which both had suffered, and to join together in the service of God and the Faith. In such a cause they could sink their mutual jealousies.

To this end the Holy Father offered himself as mediator, stressing the fact of his Apostolic authority, which not only empowered him to proceed against the English King as an enemy of the Faith, but gave him a just and holy title to Ireland, as coming under the direct dominion of the Holy See, in view of which, the Pope added pointedly, France should be the last to encourage the Sorbonne in detracting from the power of Peter.

Neither of the two Crowns, pursued the Pope, could afford to have such false friends as the English, who, in the Marriage Treaty with Spain, had aimed at giving France cause for jealousy and had adopted a similar policy towards Spain in the French match. It was time, therefore, for the two to unite to tear off the mask from the face of God's enemies and show them that their arts had been discovered.

De Béthune listened attentively to all Urban said, but discreetly showed no cognizance of the Franco-Spanish plan that Spada had written to Rome about, so the task of advocating in the Pope's name the formation of a League against England fell wholly on the Nuncio, who had also to follow the comings and goings of the French statesman and Spanish Ambassador in Paris and forward to Rome all the information he could glean. [1]

Even before he received this despatch and the Briefs he was to deliver, the Nuncio, in an effort to strengthen the French alliance with Spain, had called on the Marqués de Mirabel, Spanish Ambassador in Paris, to remind him that while the two Crowns were talking of working together in perfect understanding against England, France was offering a subsidy of 60,000 francs to the Dutch, who were not only Protestant, and therefore pro-English, but rebels against Spain.

[1] Some idea of the intensity of diplomatic activity in Paris at this period, and the importance Rome attached to it, can be gathered from the volume of correspondence (the 635 ff. contained in *B.L.* 8065) that passed between Spada and the Cardinal Secretary of State merely between Aug. 4 and Dec. 28, 1626.

At this time the likelihood of Bassompierre's mission proving a success was a further obstacle to the League against England. Spada's personal opinion, however, was that the English were so foolishly proud that they would hardly agree to all that was asked. Louis would, therefore, be forced into an agreement with Spain.

Sounding the Spanish Ambassador as to the form this would take, Spada was told that Philip would scarcely entertain an attack on England, but might well approve of designs on Ireland, [1] while France would lend support by a simultaneous sally against the Isle of Wight. At the end of this interview, the Nuncio impressed upon Mirabel that his master, already at war with England, had all to gain by such an alliance. [2]

Spada now went to see Richelieu, the Queen-Mother and the King, to whom he outlined three points. First, a plan for burning all the men-of-war lying in the leading English harbours. Secondly, he pointed out that in a month or so (it was then the end of September) the English wine-fleet would be sailing all along the coast from Bordeaux to St-Malo : these ships could be taken for use as men-of-war or the transport of troops. Lastly, the Nuncio expounded the strategic advantages of capturing the Isle of Wight and the Channel Islands, — all badly guarded, and most useful bases. [3]

The Nuncio's peregrinations had not been unobserved, and rumour was in the air. One day late in September the Ambassador of Savoy came with a story of leagues the French were making with the Spaniards and the Pope, but Spada would not be drawn and parried the implied question. [4]

When Spada's new instructions and the Briefs of September 21 arrived in Paris nearly a month later, Père de Bérulle, who had been working with Mirabel to consolidate the Franco-Spanish alliance since before the expulsion of the French from England, came to ask the Nuncio to hold over the presentation of the Briefs, so as not to complicate his own negotiations which now only needed

---

[1] Père de Bérulle's way of putting the plan was that the sovereignty of Ireland should be acquired for the Holy See and a Viceroy established there. Spada erased the reference to Ireland when writing to Rome (*B. L.* 8065, f. 342 : Spada to [Card. Secretary], Oct. 23, 1626). V. App. III.

[2] *Ibid.*, f. 179-180 : Spada to [Cardinal Secretary] Sept. 29, 1626.

[3] *Ibid.*, f. 184 : Spada to [Cardinal Secretary], Sept. 29, 1626.

[4] *Ibid.*, f. 188 : Same to same, same date.

the consent of the Spaniards. He also asked that the matter might not be discussed in Rome with de Béthune or anybody else ; but it was, of course, too late. However, Spada agreed to delay the delivery of the Briefs till Spain's answer arrived. [1]

In sending Bassompierre to England, the French showed that they preferred not to risk an open rupture, if matters could be settled by diplomatic means. Nevertheless, in view of the proposed league against England, Richelieu had already appealed to the Pope (as he did again in the following year) for support, either financial or diplomatic. Urban was anxious that this request should not come to light, as he wished any subsequent action of his to be determined purely by popular demand and his regard for religion. [2]

On the mission of Bassompierre the Nuncio Spada was now told to advise that a Yes-or-No answer be brought back as soon as possible, otherwise long-drawn-out discussions would only make the Spanish suspicious and give the English time to prepare for an outbreak and perhaps again excite the rebels and malcontents of France. A further important charge on Spada was to compose the differences between Louis and his consort, lest Philip take offence and seek to avenge his sister. [3]

As de Bérulle was considered the chief power in the Franco-Spanish negotiations, Spada was told to enlighten him on Rome's wishes. The Oratorian answered that it would be much to the point if the Pope would ask to join the alliance against England, so that he might be fully acquainted with all that was afoot, maintain accord between Louis and Philip, and give some colour to the the Holy See's pretensions to Ireland ; all this would need to be managed with great delicacy, however, lest the Pope's good offices be discredited and private interest enter in.

De Bérulle admitted that all were not of his opinion, and that some considered it undesirable for the Pope to ask to enter the League or wish to direct it, as the attempt to christen war with religion would only damp the ardour of many now eager to avenge the outraged honour of France.

On the night of November 24 (N. s.), the long-awaited answer

---

[1] *Ibid.*, ff. 344-345 ; 370 ; 440 seq.: Spada to [Card. Secretary], Oct. 23 ; Nov. 10, 1626.

[2] *Ibid.*, f. 227 : To Spada, Oct. 5, 1626.

[3] *Ibid.*, f. 402 : To Spada, Rome, Nov. 3, 1626.

to de Bérulle's despatch arrived from Spain. It was disappointing ;
not opposed to the League, but neither so favourable as was
desired. The Spaniards sent no acceptance of the proposals made,
and showed no enthusiasm for the harbour facilities offered them
by the French, but they demanded a guarantee from the latter
regarding the Dutch. [1]

The fact of the matter was that neither Richelieu nor Olivares
trusted each other, the latter thinking that France was only using
Spain to frighten the English. De Bérulle tried to convince the
Spaniard of his country's good faith, saying that umbrage should
not be taken at Bassompierre's mission, as the English were morally
certain to refuse the French demands, and that the negotiation
would serve to expose England's guilt before all Europe, and thus
give France and Spain a breathing-space to prepare armaments. [2]

De Bérulle and Mirabel now met again for further discussion.
They continued to differ on the French attitude towards the Dutch,
but were in agreement on the general proposal to attack England.
Cardinal Richelieu had suggested the following July or August
for the manœuvres, but de Bérulle did not consider the preparation
of the French fleet far enough advanced. At this Spada said that
Spain might be induced to carry out the invasion without waiting
for the French, provided France in the meantime would pledge
herself to war and make the League known to the world.

De Bérulle, however, was cautious of commitments, saying such
a proposal would raise a host of difficulties. In the first place, it
would spoil all chance of their using the intervening months for
getting a fresh suite of Catholic attendants accepted for the English
Queen. Secondly, it would give a lead to all malcontents opposed
to an attack on England and an alliance with Spain. Thirdly, Louis
was in the midst of negotiations with the Huguenots and the
Rochellois, and would not relish rendering them more difficult or
breaking them off altogether.

On December 2 the Nuncio called on Mirabel who told him, à
propos of the Cadiz landing, which the Pope looked upon as a likely
pretext for reprisals, that the standard borne by the invaders had
been the Palatine's, not King Charles's, and so the King of Spain

---

[1] *Ibid.*, ff. 503, 508 : Spada to [Card. Secretary], Nov. 29, 1626.
[2] HOUSSAYE, *op. cit.*, vol. III, pp. 178 seq.

need not recognize the affront as offered by England. When Spada spoke of de Bérulle's readiness for an understanding, the Spanish Ambassador said that during the expedition against England Philip would want a guarantee from France that the Dutch would reduce their troops to a minimum.

The same afternoon the Nuncio went to see de Bérulle, who told him that Cardinal de la Cueva was still trying to dissuade Philip from attacking England. He added that he had even got wind that Spain and England had concluded a treaty. [1]

Despite the extreme caution that both France and Spain were using for fear of committing themselves, rumour soon ran wild of what was being discussed in Paris. Early in December de Bérulle was reported to have hinted darkly that Calais was not more than eight hours from Dover and that, if the Prince of Piedmont wanted a genuinely royal crown, he should fix his thoughts on Ireland, easiest of conquests with 10,000 foot. The Duke wrote from Savoy to say he had heard of a league being formed at the French Court between the Pope, the Kings of France and Spain and the Catholic Electors of Germany against the Huguenots on all sides; Catholic princes were being invited to join, and those who held back were to be excommunicated. He was not worrying about excommunication, the Duke added, but would join the League voluntarily for the propagation of the Faith and the stamping out of heresy, though he did not consider the present moment opportune for the Holy See, France or any of the others, unless they were thinking of putting the whole world under Spanish yoke. [2]

His agreement with de Bérulle having expired, Spada now presented the Papal Briefs of September 21, to the Queen Mother on December 11, to Louis four days later, appealing to the King to give the English a salutary lesson once and for all. Naturally Louis made only a general reply, but the disavowal a few weeks later of de Bassompierre's compromise with Charles seemed to indicate that France was preparing for an open rupture.

---

[1] *B.L.* 8065, ff. 562 seq. : Spada to [Card. Secretary], Dec. 4, 1626. The Frenchman may here be referring to notes that had passed between Mirabel and Carleton in Paris through the medium of a Portuguese merchant. These, however, concerned only the Palatinate and English aid given to the Dutch.

[2] *Ibid.*, f. 592 : Spada to [Card. Secretary], Paris, Dec. 18, 1626.

On April 20, 1627, Louis ratified the League defensive and offensive with Spain against England, which du Fargis, the French Ambassador to Spain, had signed at Madrid on March 20 under pressure from Olivares. It had been carried through with great secrecy, and the Nuncio could not worm out of either French or Spaniards a deed in writing of their anti-English alliance, although Richelieu, Mirabel and de Bérulle gave their word for it and had, in fact, done so some time back. France was now bound to fit out ten or twelve vessels and hold them ready in ports facing England for use according to her discretion, or as need should arise. Mirabel thought the Spanish Armada would be ready about the end of July or the beginning of August to embark against both England and Ireland with 50 ships. [1]

About the same date as the ratification Spada was replaced at Paris by Mgr del Bagno, who since 1621 had been Nuncio in Brussels, with a temporary break in 1625, when he had visited Paris to assist the Papal Legate, Barberini, as Nuncio Extraordinary. In his instructions, dated from Rome March 1, 1627, (N. S.), the new Nuncio was told to urge the French King to assert his rights in England by force of arms but, although he could offer his services as a go-between as Spada had done, he was not to engage the Holy See financially. As for the Franco-Spanish alliance del Bagno was told to spur on the parties to some enthusiasm in the hope that God might use the League to restore the Faith in England. At the moment (the pact had not been signed when these instructions were drawn up) the two Crowns were mutually mistrustful, each thinking the other was using the League as a threat to win better terms from England. It was for the Nuncio to soften these antipathies.

Despite a Spanish offer of men -of-war the French declared they could not have their fleet ready before May, 1628, and urged Spain to redeem her honour alone, but Olivares said the Spanish forces were inadequate for a royal attack on England, unless supported by twenty-five ships from France. [2]

---

[1] SIRI, *op. cit.*, vol. VI, pp. 257, 261 ; HOUSSAYE, *op. cit.*, vol. III, pp. 190-191.

[2] LEMAN, *op. cit.*, p. 145 seq. This, despite the fact that Siri says the French had 25 large men-of-war ready to move against the Isle of Wight in the summer of 1627.

In his first burst of indignation at the expulsion of Henrietta's entourage, Pope Urban had hinted at help he would give a Franco-Spanish League by censures and pronouncements against the English King, when the occasion seemed expedient and opportune. Temporal aid in the form of ships and money he had always refused. Now, the Pope was chary of any declaration whatsoever against Charles, at least until the League really took effect, as the irritation caused in England would react unfavourably on the English Catholics. The new Paris Nuncio was therefore to manifest the greatest goodwill on the part of the Pope, but to avoid committing either himself or his Holiness to any action. [1]

This was not at all to Richelieu's taste. The Cardinal wanted help, and that not merely spiritual. In the early autumn, after the proposed date for the expedition against England had come and gone, he and de Bérulle drew up a memorandum for de Béthune, their Ambassador in Rome, to present to the Pope. The Holy Father was told frankly that it was impossible for the King of France to defray the cost of a double expedition against La Rochelle and England without some extraordinary measure of assistance.

Now these two enterprises, Richelieu suggested artfully, were more in the interest of the Church than of the State : he therefore proposed asking the Pope to allow some alienation of Church property in France or, better still, a double tithe for two years. There had also been a proposal, though the Cardinal did not wish to be identified with it, that his Holiness might grant for France a Bull of Indulgence similar to the historic Spanish *Bula de la Cruzada.* By this the Holy Father, in view of the Most Christian King's resolve to resist the evil designs of the English, and the rebel heretics of France, would grant a plenary indulgence to all rendering personal aid to so holy an end. For those unable to go to this " Holy War" a contribution of 20 *sous* would win the same favour together with permission to eat eggs and cheese in Lent. [2]

---

[1] *Ibid.,* pp. 147-148.

[2] AVENEL, *op. cit.,* vol. II, pp. 626-627 : Richelieu to Béthune, Sept. 24, 1627 : " Il y en a qui estiment que Sa Sainteté pourroit aussy accorder une bulle pareille à celle qui est en Espagne pour la croisade, par laquelle, en considération de ce que le roy, contraint de s'opposer aux mauvais desseins des Anglois et hérétiques rebelles de France, s'est résolu de tesmoigner son zelle contre les uns et les autres, Sa Sainteté accorderoit plenière indulgence à tous ceux qui serviroient personnellement à un si saint dessein ; et ceux qui

The King of France felt assured, concluded Richelieu, that his Holiness would not wish to see France and Spain embarked on a war of aggression against England without being a party to it and making a considerable contribution.

The Cardinal was insistent on the importance of an immediate reply and told de Béthune to present the petition in that light. Urban's answer arrived about the time of the English defeat at Ré. He urged the French clergy to assist the King to the sum of a million gold francs (" un million d'or ") ; but gave no authorization for any alienation of Church property, and explicitly refused anything like the *Bula de la Cruzada* attached to which, the Pope added, there was much that was blameworthy. As for the League against England, Urban quickly disillusioned Richelieu, — he refused either to join or contribute towards it. [1]

The most the Pope would do was to signify his approval of successes that French arms might win,—which he did at the victory snatched by the French, when Buckingham, after a siege begun in July abandoned the Isle of Ré in October, 1627. [2] In the following year after Buckingham's death Urban ordered the fall of La Rochelle to be fêted in Rome by the illumination of the Castel Sant' Angelo. [3] The Papal Aggression threatened two years before literally went up in smoke, and the cause of Catholicism in England stood much the better for the Pope's discretion.

n'y pourroient aller auroient les mesmes grâces, en contribuant à la mesme fin vingt sols par teste, et en outre permission de manger du fromage et oeufs en caresme."

[1] AVENEL, *op. cit.*, vol. II, p. 628, note 4.

[2] *Arch. Vat., Epistolae ad Principes*, XLII, N° 139 : Urban VIII to Louis XIII, Rome, Dec. 3, 1627 : " Militat coelum pro religione, neque desunt trophaeo crucis fulmina actionis cum carbonibus desolantibus impietatem." The Pope then speaks of his prayer for the English King's right guidance, finally calling on Louis to exterminate heresy from England. Congratulatory briefs on the same victory were sent to Richelieu, Toiras the defender of Ré, and the Comte de Schomberg (*Ibid.*, N° 140-142, same date).

[3] E. RODOCANACHI, *Le Château Saint-Ange*, p. 205.

CHAPTER IV

RESPITE FOR THE PAPISTS

" As for the affair of these priests, Charles well knew that they were not of that class which had terrified his father as well as Elizabeth : they were not gunpowder traitors, poisoners of saddles, or rapier-men who were to fall on the beefeaters ; some were bookmen, who had engaged their inkstands in the cause which the monarch was so desirous to maintain. He knew them to be zealots, who at least suffered for conscience' sake ; many were condemned merely for having taken priests' orders, though living obscurely as the disguised dependents of some ancient Roman Catholic family. Could he, divesting himself of the true dignity of a sovereign, and of that intelligence which the office of sovereignty should include, run with the clamours of a party and the illusions of a people? Charles could not have imagined that the commonweal was to be preserved by a heca omb of miserable priests. Much we grant to the panic of those unhappy times, and more to the passions ; but can we entertain a doubt that the merciless persecutions of these priests was one of the stalking-horses of party?" [1]

As long as Charles waged war he had to go to Parliament for the wherewithal, and Parliament consistently asked for a *quid pro quo* in the form of enforcement of the Penal Laws. The Commons were always ready to cry *Wolf !* at their own shadows at a whisper of the word Papist, and had a fine opportunity for raising a scare when, a few days before they met in March, 1628, a handful of Jesuits were discovered and arrested in a house in Clerkenwell. No treasonable document came to light, but soon one appeared, a clear forgery, referring to designs on the Duke of Buckingham. In Parliament Sir John Coke spoke of the "pretended Parliament of Jesuits...

---

[1] D'ISRAELI, *op. cit.*, vol. I, pp. 192-193.

within a mile of this place," while complaints were made of the scandal the large attendance at the Queen's Chapel was giving, and how common it was to hear in conversation," Will you go to Mass?" or "Have you been to Mass at Somerset House?" [1]

There seemed no limit to the petty tyranny of Parliament, and with the King at war with his Catholic wife's brother, the early hopes raised by the the French match among the English Catholics seemed doomed to disappointment, till a succession of events brought them a period of unprecedented peace that was to last for over a decade.

With the defeat of the fleet at Ré, and the fall of La Rochelle the next year, following close on Buckingham's assassination, Charles had had his fill of foreign wars, while the trouble he had had with the Commons over Pym's *Petition of Right* and Eliot's resolutions against the taking of tonnage and poundage and the bringing in of Popery and Arminianism and innovations in religion had given him a surfeit of Parliament, too.

On March 2, 1629, after a scene of confusion consequent on Charles's order of adjournment, Parliament ceased for more than ten years to trouble either King or Catholics, while on the following April 24 the Treaty of Susa put an end to the quarrel with France. Both these events cleared the way to the re-formation of the Queen's Catholic household. Moreover, with the passing of Buckingham, Charles's closest friend, Henrietta stood alone in her husband's affection and, as warm hearted and impulsive in her love as she was shrewish when piqued, she now began to win the confidence of the lonely King in a way that was to influence him in all the happiest years of his life. [2] A seal was set on their new-found affection by the birth of a Prince of Wales in 1630. At such a moment Charles could deny his wife no favour, while she, eager to redeem her prestige as champion of the Catholics, exploited the King's tenderness by helping them in the practice of the Faith. [3]

---

[1] *Camden Miscellany*, vol. II (1854), Preface, p. 13 ; GARDINER, *op. cit.*, vol. VI, pp. 238-239.

[2] GARDINER, *op. cit.*, vol. VI, pp. 367 seq.

[3] Charles had shown the same sollicitude the previous year in his wife's first pregnancy (the child died soon after birth). Cf. *Arch. Prop.*, *Scritture Antiche* 131, f. 201 : *Avvisi da Brusselles con lettere di Mons. Nuntio de 24*

The Catholics had still one foremost danger to fear, — that the money no longer forthcoming in the absence of Parliamentary grants would be found at their expense. Already a commission had been set up in the North for the composition of fines : by direct collection, the pickings of the " middlemen," the informers, would, it was hoped, be saved to the Crown. [1] Then again, dark hints were already being whispered of the King's Popish tendencies, a charge that always caus ed him alarm, and it was feared that to give it the lie he would enforce the Penal Laws and so pacify the Puritans. [2]

It was therefore a happy turn of fortune for the Catholics when the death of Buckingham placed the reins of power in the hands of Lord Treasurer Weston,a man whose Catholic sympathies were well enough known, though he himself was one of a class all too common at this period, determined to die in the Faith but lacking the heroism involved in its daily pra ctice.

Weston kept up a regular correspondence with Père Joseph, Richelieu's lieutenant, [3] and the latter's influence had much to do with the choice of his fellow-Capuchins to replace de Bérulle's Oratorians, whom Charles had banished, all save two, in August, 1626. The choice of these Friars was a happy one. Henrietta had known them at the French Court, whither the presence of Père Joseph had drawn them ; Charles held the order in high esteem, having met them in Madrid, where Fray Zacharias had tried to convert him first viva voce and later in the book he dedicated to him.[4]

Febb., 1627 : " Di Londra danno avviso che 'l Rè per non dar disgusto alla Regina, la quale tuttavia si trova con certezza di gravidanza, hà prohibito ogni processo et esecutione contro Cattolici, ne contro il Vescovo Calcedonense si faceva altr' inquisitione."

[1] GARDINER, *op. cit.*, vol. VI, p. 238, note 2.

[2] *Arch. Prop.*, *Scritture Antiche* 347, f. 47 : *Avvisi cavati da lettere fresche di Londra*, 1629.

[3] Weston was in touch with Père Joseph through a Catholic named Forster living in Paris, who was used by the Capuchin as an intermediary in arranging a secret truce between France and England pending the peace of Fontainebleau. One of Weston's promises had been that " le roi de la Grande-Bretagne traitera si bien ses sujets catholics qu'ils n'auront jamais plus sujet de s'en plaindre." It was certainly kept. (Cf. AVENEL, *op. cit.*, vol. III, p. 505 ; DEDOUVRES, *op. cit.*, vol. II, p. 108 ; R. DA CESINALE, *Storia delle missioni dei Cappuccini*, vol. II, p. 432.)

[4] Cf. Chap. I, p. 33 seq. ; DEDOUVRES, *op. cit.*, vol. II, p. 108, note 7. Two

Lastly, the Pope would be pleased at the honour paid the order, of which his brother Antonio, the Cardinal di Sant'Onofrio, was so distinguished a member.

In Paris, after the death of Cardinal de Bérulle in October, 1629, had lessened the influence of the Oratory, Père Joseph pulled the necessary wires to induce Louis to send over Capuchins to serve his sister now that the way was clear.[1] All his natural sympathies attracted him to the new enterprise himself, but he was far too useful to Louis and Richelieu to be released for even a brief visit to the English mission.[2]

Instead, Père Léonard of Paris was given the leadership of the eight priests and two lay-brothers, who left Calais, on February 24, 1630 (N. S.), with the new French Ambassador, the Marquis de Fontenay-Mareuil, for the service of the Queen's Chapel.[3]

years later Fray Zacharias applied to Rome for leave to make a third attempt at Charles's conversion. Called in consultation by Propaganda, Père Léonard, the first superior of the Queen's Capuchins and a man fiercely jealous of his rights, strongly opposed the plan on 3 heads : 1. that the King was obstinately attached to his own form of Christianity. 2. that in view of the power of the English parliament it was more that the King's life was worth to turn Papist. 3. that Charles was unlikely to contemplate such a step while he had hopes of restoring his sister and nephews to the Palatinate with the aid of German Protestant princes. (*Arch. Propaganda, Scritture Antiche* (1633) 133, f. 27 : *Responsio ad propositionem utrum conveniens sit modo Reverendum Patrem Zachariam de Saluce praedicatorem Capucinum in Angliam mittere, Regis huius gentis procurandae conversionis gratia*). Propaganda over-ruled Père Léonard's objections, but it does not appear that the Spanish Capuchin ever took advantage of the permission to go to England. Cf. PHILIP HUGHES, *The Conversion of Charles I* in the *Clergy Review*, vol. VIII (Aug. 1934), pp. 115-117.

[1] DEDOUVRES, *op. cit.*, vol. II, p. 108, note 8 : " Le P. Joseph fit, par divers moyens, que le roi et la reine demandèrent des Capucins pour les servir en cette fonction ecclésiastique. "

[2] DEDOUVRES, *op. cit.*, vol. II, p. 109 and note 6, quoting del Bagno to Card. Secretary, Oct. 15, 1629 : " P. Giuseppe pensa d'andarvi ancor esso, dopo che vi siano introdotti, per veder occultamente come le cose passano. " He had been interested in England since 1597 when as Baron de Maffliers he had gone with a special embassy to the Court of Elizabeth. The following year he had met an English Capuchin in Paris, who had persuaded him to join the order. Then in 1625 the English mission, together with all the foreign missions of the Capuchins (Morocco, Canada, the East), had been placed under Père Joseph's direction (Cf. DEDOUVRES, *op. cit.*, vol. II, pp. 91, 105 ; FAGNIEZ, *op. cit.*, vol. I, p. 30).

[3] For their names, cf. the *Mémoires* (p. 10) of Père CYPRIEN DE GAMACHES,

Graciously received by their Majesties, the Capuchins were lodged in a house bought by the Queen and adjoining her palace, Somerset House. (Their predecessors had been at St. James's.) It had a large garden enclosed by a strong wall.

After a few weeks in the black cassocks and long coats they had travelled in, they donned their habits with the Queen's leave. Père Aimé of Beauvais preached the first sermon, drawing an analogy from the cure of the deaf mute to the case of the Queen who had so long been deprived of hearing the Gospel preached, though the Master of preachers, the Holy Ghost, had spoken to her heart. [1]

Great crowds soon flocked to the royal chapel as news of the services ran around town. Normally Masses were being said and Holy Communion distributed from 6 a. m. till noon, while the confessionals were thronged. On Sundays and Feastdays there was a Controversial Hour from 1 till 2, followed by Vespers and a Sermon, while Christian Doctrine was taught publicly in English and French on three different days each week. The Fathers also formed Confraternities of the Rosary and of the Third Order, of which the Queen became a member. Their ministry proved highly fruitful, particularly among Anglicans, and produced numerous conversions.

The King saw all and said nothing, — a silence accepted gratefully enough as a tacit approval. Left to himself, it seemed Charles was at last redeeming his marriage pledge, though in two points he still failed. On the birth of his son he sent word to the Queen's Capuchins not to put themselves to trouble over the baptism ; he wished to deal with the matter himself, he said, and would satisfy Louis on the point. So Prince Charles was christened by William Laud, Dean of the Chapel, his Grace of Canterbury being infirm. Neither Louis, one of the godparents, nor the Pope seem to have protested. [2]

---

himself one of the Fathers and later their superior. He wrote these recollections at the age of 74, but although handicapped by the fading memories of 40 years, asserts that " quoique c'en seroit je ne rapporterai rien dont je n'aie eu parfaite connaissance." An English translation forms half the second volume of BIRCH's *The Court and Times of Charles the First*, the footnotes betraying a complete lack of sympathy with the Capuchins' work in London.

[1] GAMACHES, *op. cit.*, pp. 15-17 ; DEDOUVRES, *op. cit.*, vol. II, p. 110 and note 2.

[2] *Ibid.*, pp. 24-25 ; 39-40 ; 85 seq. ; *Acta Regia*, p. 764.

The King also consistently refused to accept a bishop as head of his wife's entourage. Henrietta's former Almoner, the Bishop of Mende, Charles believed to have been the centre of the petty intrigue that had so annoyed him, — this and the trouble he had had over the English Catholics' own bishop, Dr Richard Smith of Chalcedon, made Charles obstinate in his refusal, so Mgr Barrault, Bishop of Bazas, whom Louis had appointed to accompany the Capuchins as his sister's Grand Almoner, stayed at home.

After four months' negotiation the French finally conceded the point, and a simple priest, the Abbé Duperron, nephew of the famous controversialist Cardinal of that name, was appointed to the post with the full approval of the Pope.[1] His moderation and good temper won him the favour of Protestants and Catholics alike, while Charles, always responsive to charm, delighted in his company. As a result, when in 1635 the See of Angoulême fell vacant, Louis unostentatiously nominated Duperron to it, Charles raising no objection, — a quietly triumphant *solvitur ambulando*.[2]

The Capuchins soon became one of the sights of Town. They were spoken of as strange folk, wearing outlandish clothes and practising austerities that gained many conversions and particularly intrigued the comfortable Londoner, who went to see the Friars as he would to see an Indian or a Muscovite or some savage from the other end of the earth.[3]

The foreign onlooker at these signs of the times, used to the frigid Calvinism of the continent, thought the Englishman would be easy to convert, seeing that as a result of the confusion of creeds in his country, he did not know just what he did believe. There was a quick and abundant harvest for a band of zealous labourers; no less needful was a competent superior to discipline and organize the missionaries.[4] The Catholics of England,

---

[1] *Arch. Vat., Epist. ad Principes*, vol. XLVI, Nº 94 : Urban to Duperron (*De eius in Britanniam profectione*), Rome, Jan. 10, 1632.

[2] GAMACHES, *op. cit.*, pp. 11-12 ; 20 ; ROCCO DA CESINALE, *op. cit.*, vol. II, pp. 428-429. *B.L.* 8616, f. 56 : Duperron writing from London to Rome in May, 1635, mentions his nomination and asks for the Bull of appointment. He was consecrated in France, 1636, and later translated to Evreux, formerly the see of his famous uncle.

[3] GAMACHES, *op. cit.*, pp. 30-31.

[4] *Arch. Vat., Fondo Bolognetti* 108, f. 47 *verso* : " è il popolo d'Inghilterra non difficile à ridursi alla vera Religione, sì perche viene così a tornare al suo

particularly of London, now enjoyed a quiet unknown since the break with Rome and, generally speaking, were left free in the practice of the Faith, provided they used the privilege unostentatiously.

For this they had chiefly the Queen to thank. She was devoted to her godfather, Pope Urban, and zealous in the use of her new-found influence with Charles to assist her fellow-Catholics.

The Abbé Duperron described the situation to the French Nuncio, Mgr Alessandro Bichi, on a visit to Paris during the summer of 1633. He had great hopes, he said, that this powerful influence of the Queen would win from Charles an official disavowal of persecution that would be something approaching liberty of conscience. In the absence of Parliament the King was the source of all such relief, and Duperron saw in him the kindest of natures, averse from violence and harbouring no hatred against the Catholics. In the opinion of many he would be easy of conversion, if the Archbishop of Canterbury and Lord Treasurer Weston would only take the lead.

Some such lead had indeed been given in the exclusive choice of divines of the Laudian school, moderate towards Rome and violently anti-Puritan, to fill the sees as they fell vacant. [1] Again, a Government comprising Weston, Windebank and Cottington, all crypto-Catholics, could not but be moderate, and their example secured the Catholics better treatment at the hand of lesser officers of the Crown [2].

In 1623 a Vicar Apostolic had been appointed for England in the person of William Bishop, who did much to reconcile Seculars and Regulars but died the following year, 1624. The consecration of Dr Richard Smith as his successor with the same title, Bishop of Chalcedon, bid fair to continue the same conciliatory policy. It was, therefore, unfortunate that the new Bishop's flair for organization and discipline (and both were badly needed on the

---

stato antico, sì perche quella confusione di varie Religioni, che vi si professano, hà postogli più in termine che non sanno ciò che credano. ''

[1] In 1628 between April and July such appointments had been made to Winchester, Durham, York, London, Ely and Chichester. Cf. GARDINER, op. cit., vol. VI, pp. 329-330.

[2] *Arch. Vat., Fondo Bolognetti* 108, ff. 44-51 : di Nancy dal vescovo di Carpentras, Nun° [i.e. Bichi reporting Duperron], Sept. 25, 1633.

English mission) should have caused him to overstep his powers as a titular bishop by arrogating to himself ordinary jurisdiction in maintaining a Chapter, Vicars, Archdeacons, Notaries and Registrars, while he involved himself in a bitter controversy which his predecessor had started with the Regulars by claiming that their faculties must come from him, otherwise their absolutions would be invalid.

This provocative claim was an irritant powerful enough to kindle an already highly inflammable situation into open schism. This Rome realized, and in a unusually long and strongly-worded Brief to the Bishop, to the Clergy, Secular and Regular, and to the whole English Catholic body, Pope Urban exhorted all to charity and peace, pointing out the scandal that was being offered to heretics and expressing his disappointment that these dissensions centring round the Bishop of Chalcedon should have succeeded so soon upon the unseemly controversy aroused by Archpriest Blackwell.

The Holy Father therefore forbade under pain of excommunication *ipso facto* all further participation in the quarrel, referring all that had been written on the subject to the Roman Inquisition. Finally, he confirmed the Regulars in the faculties they had enjoyed under Paul V and Gregory XV and exempted them from the necessity of applying to Bishop Smith. [1]

---

[1] *Arch. Vat., Epist. ad Principes* , vol. XLV, n° 141, ff. 112-116 : Urban to Bishop Richard Smith, the English Clergy, secular and regular, and to the whole Catholic people (*De Controversiis inter ipsos obortis quas S. S. per litteras has supprimit et sedat auct° Ap*ª) Rome, Apr. 3, 1631 : " ... Vobis autem universis sub poena excommunicationis latae sententiae praecipimus, ne ulterius litem super praedictis controversiis praeterquam apud Apostolicam sedem intentis, aut easdem quocumque modo urgeatis aut defendatis, aut quacumque ratione nutrire aut favere progrediamini. Jam vero cum ipsa etiam illustrium ingeniarum sapientia in praesenti rerum discrimine pro discordia militaverit, et non pauci tum typis descripti, tum manu exarati libri in lucem litigiosi prodierint, eos, qui Romam pervenerunt, diferri iussimus ad Cardinales Sanctae Inquisitionis Antistites." And on the question of faculties : " Ne autem ambigentis conscientiae fluctibus iactentur... declaramus confessiones a Regularibus Sacerdotibus hactenus auditas validas fuisse et in posterum fore. Cum enim eas au[c]toritate Apostolica exceperint excepturique sint, ordinaria facultas, vel ap[p]robatio eis nec fuit nec futura est necessaria. Porro autem singuli Missionarii suis facultatibus ac privilegiis utantur, eadem ratione quibus ante has controversias et temporibus foel. record. Gregorii XV et

The attention of the English Government had already been drawn to the fierceness of the quarrel and a decree of banishment had been issued against the Bishop in 1628. He lay in hiding and, as no attempt was made by the pursuivants to catch him, a further decree was passed in March, 1629, (not without accusations against the Bishop's opponents of treachery and collusion with the Government) and a prize of £100 was offered for his capture. The decree was never executed, however, for when the Papal Brief just cited showed him he could expect no support from Rome Dr Smith withdrew discreetly to France to pass his remaining years in the writing of controversy under the protection of Richelieu. [1]

The absence of the Bishop unfortunately did little to lessen the bickerings of Seculars and Regulars. Even while he was still in England the clergy had enjoyed an altogether unhealthy sense of freedom; [2] indeed, it would not be far wrong to say that the disputes and dissensions rife among the English Catholics, clergy and laity alike, on points of doctrine and discipline were but the symptoms of a disease that went far deeper.

The situation was fully revealed to Cardinal Barberini, Protector of England as well as Secretary of State, by Padre Alessandro, the secret emissary sent by Padre Giacinto to James in 1622/3. [3]

Pauli V gavisi sunt." Already 4 years before the danger of schism had been pointed out to Rome : *Arch. Prop.*, *Scritture Antiche* (1627) 129, ff. 355-356 : To the Cardinal Protector from the Vicars and Archdeacons of the English Chapter, Lond., 4 Cal. Maij 1627.

[1] For fuller notice of the work of both Bishop Bishop and Bishop Smith, cf W. M. BRADY, *Annals of the Catholic Hierarchy in England*, pp. 68-103.

[2] *Arch. Prop.*, *Scritture Antiche*, (1629) 131, f. 343 : Br. Simon Stock (Discalced Carmelite), London, Aug. 9, 1629 : " Et molti missionarii stanno quà come cavalli senza freno che no' cognoscano superiore alcuno."

[3] Padre Alessandro d'Ales or, more correctly, d'Alice Montferrato (a district between Piedmont, the Milanais and Genoa), figures in the history of the period chiefly as the lieutenant of his better-known countryman, Fra Giacinto, though his diplomatic travels, under the *alias* Francesco Rota, seem to have been as extensive. He went to London from Brussels twice in 1622/3 ; he thereafter appears in Paris (1625/6) Munich (1628), Bonn (1629), London (1630), Vienna and London (1632), Rome (1633). Munich and Vienna (1634). Some of his activities in London and Rome will be dealt with in the following Chapter. An attempt to obtain from the Capuchins at Assisi more personal details of this energetic diplomat elicited the reply " que ce P. Alexandre est encore enveloppé d'épaisses ténèbres."

The Capuchin had visited the country since, and stressed the need for immediate reform of disorders, abuses and discord among the English Catholics, which were a check to progress and a serious menace to all that had been built up with so much labour since England broke from Rome.

Though the Penal Laws remained the same, persecution was not the main stumbling-block. The former bitter priest-hunting had now mellowed into a dispassionate consideration of persecution as a business proposition chiefly levelled at the laity who, anxious to buy freedom from molestation, offered easy prey for the needy purse of pursuivant and common informer.

The priest was still liable to imprisonment, but this in itself held no terrors for him and often enough (with bad exceptions, especially in the provinces) was merely farcical. By payment of a " rent" for his cell, by dispensing a little largesse and giving some security for himself, the prisoner could go to and fro through London without contradiction. Even priests under sentence of death still went about London and into the country ; it made little difference that officially they were prisoners, in fact many took it rather as a grievance when they were set at liberty. [1]

This paradoxical state of affairs was the outcome of Charles's natural clemency. It was the outcome, too, of the easy-going nature of the country where there had never been that violent segregation of Catholic and heretic that the Continent had known, and where there existed a large class of nominal Protestants (a third of the population, Alessandro alleged) ready to return

---

[1] *B. L.* 7049, ff. 4 seq. : Alessandro to Barberini, Vienna, Jan. 7, 1633 (N.S.) : " La verità di tutto questo (*i.e.* the moderation of Charles and his ministers) si può in parte cavare dalla prigionia de Sacerdoti, la quale, parlando in general propriam^{te} è ridicola. Perche con pagare il Sacerdote un tanto, che sarà peraventura il fitto della stanza nella prigione, con mediocre favore, ò con dar di se stesso qualche sigurtà, resta con titolo di prigioniero talmente libero, che va dove vuole senza nessuna contradittione. E di questi molti se ne veggono per Londra ; e tali che condannati a morte vanno no' solo per Londra, mà per l'istesso paese ancora. Per questo crescendo tanto il numero de sacerdoti. E una gran parte venendo quivi con fine di stabilirvisi poco loro importa l'esser prigioniero. Ansi molti vi sono c'havrebbono per aggravio l'esser liberi." Contrast with this *A relation of A. B. when he offered to depose concerning the Catholic prisoners at York*, 1635, in FOLEY, *Records of the English Province of the Society of Jesus*, vol. V, pp. 765-766.

to their former Faith but for the fear of loss of goods, human respect or other interests.

These reasons, and the fact that life in England offered ease, plenty and a demoralizing freedom from restraint for those who sought such things, caused a large number of missionary priests to crowd across the Channel with no correspondingly good results. Incompetence, bad example and scandal were shown by many fit neither for the mission nor for the priesthood itself. Little zeal for souls was to be expected when the greater part of the immigrant missionaries came to England intent on settling down to a life of comfort, and preferring to retire to a leisurely apostolate in the households of the well-to-do rather than face possible poverty and persecution in the open.

The absolute dependence of the priest for bed, board and clothing on the well-to-do layman was fruitful of manifold abuses disastrous to the moral standards of both. The treatment that priests met with was generous, and the practice harmless in itself but, with the way open to emulation and self-seeking, it was at the bottom of all the discords among the clergy. [1]

Many of the laity were Catholic in name alone, showing scant respect for the Holy See and flagrantly flouting the Pope's pro-hibition of reading or writing on the current disputes : so pamphlets continued to be read and passed on, and discord increased.

Irregularities in marriages were numerous, — the result of the ignorance and self-interest of many priests. Compliance on the part of the confessor was so taken for granted that, when necessary questions were put, penitents went away with a grievance. In conversation and general behaviour, Catholics, clerical as well as lay, often stood out only to their disadvantage. Back-biting, treachery even, tippling in taverns and gaming — all were becoming associated with the name of Catholic and priest.

On the other side of the picture there were in England priests, secular and among the orders, who led saintly lives, and layfolk of solid piety and good example, who showed the utmost reverence for the Apostolic See and the Pope's authority. These men wanted the abuses stopped and first and foremost a check put upon the number of English, Scotch and Irish ordained, especially in the

---

[1] *Arch. Vat., Fondo Bolognetti*, 108, ff. 44-51 : Bichi reporting Duperron, Sept. 25, 1632.

lesser-known orders, for it had been found by experience that, when a man of one of these countries received the religious habit abroad, he moved heaven and earth to be sent back to his own land as a missionary, with the scandalous result that there were many vagrant religious about who acknowledged no superior. Young men came over full of self-conceit and curiosity, living with little self-control. Others were uneducated, badly grounded in Morals and worse in Dogma, so that converts were ill-instructed, and apostasies and other scandals the consequence. [1]

Padre Alessandro, who claimed to have seen all this with his own eyes, was of opinion that no missionary should be allowed to go to England till he had sworn on oath to observe and, as far as he could, to see observed the Sacred Canons of Trent. In addition, all religious should be placed under some superior, and the Orders should hold Congregations and Chapters.

Such suggestions, however, were only complementary to the one remedy that all disinterested parties were agreed in hoping the Pope would decide upon, *viz.* to maintain in England, as his representative, a man of experience and judgment who, backed by the authority of Rome, would be able to put the affairs of the missionaries in order.

Selection of the right man for the task was important. If the confidence of all parties was to be won, the choice had not to fall on Englishman, Irishman or Scot, not only because of the antipathy between these nations, but because a disinterested foreigner would work so much more fruitfully. Here again the pick was limited. Neither Frenchman nor Spaniard could be sent, as war between England and one or other nation was always imminent, besides which the English Catholics were already divided into factions looking to these two countries for support.

---

[1] *B. L.* 7049, ff. 4-7 : Alessandro to Barberini, Vienna, Jan. 7, 1633. This indictment of the clergy on the English Mission seems at first sight to contrast strongly with the report mentioned later (v. *infra* pp. 146 seq.) of Dom Leander who spoke of them as for the most part possessing " great learning in philosophy, in ethics and in theology, so that, if we look for erudition and edification, scarcely any Catholic Kingdom can display a more splendid priesthood." This eulogy by a witness not altogether disinterested is further tempered considerably by a recapitulation of the abuses Alessandro had noticed. The English Benedictine goes even farther than the Italian Capuchin in admitting the danger of open schism between the Seculars and Regulars (Cf. *Clarendon State Papers, loc. cit.*).

Process of elimination seemed to point to an Italian. There were positive arguments, too, as the Italians were generally liked in England and regarded as indifferent to party. An Italian would therefore be above suspicion, and could stimulate the Ambassadors of the Catholic princes to protect the Catholics and help on the Faith : this assistance was important as it was felt that they stood in some way responsible for the large number of priests in the country.

If this papal agent were not a permanent appointment to England, he could at least stay some time as a kind of Apostolic Visitor to observe the state of affairs at first-hand, and report to the Holy Father. This was all the more needful as it was a commonly-expressed opinion among English Catholics that their spiritual wants were neglected in Rome, which greatly lessened their regard for the Holy See.

Padre Alessandro's final advice was that, if the person sent were of episcopal rank, he would already be some way towards solving the quarrel over the Bishop question. [1]

Duperron, the Queen's Almoner, corroborated all the Capuchin's statements in an independent account of his own. He also noted that without a bishop the English Catholics felt themselves outside the normal government of the Church and deprived of many favours.

In view of this the Queen had had in mind to ask for the recall of Bishop Smith, but Duperron advised against so impolitic a step as needlessly antagonizing the regular clergy. He was emphatic, however, that the situation in England demanded personal inquiry from Rome ; and a visit of an envoy from the Pope would, he felt sure, not only gratify the Queen but be well received by Charles. [2]

---

[1] *B.L.* 7049, ff. 4-7 : Alessandro to Barberini, Vienna, Jan. 7, 1633. The Capuchin said he had himself heard laymen of quality voice the opinion (which they said they had from their confessors) that bishops were of no use in the Church and a hindrance to the salvation of souls.

[2] *Arch. Vat., Fondo Bolognetti*, 108, ff. 44-51 : Bichi reporting Duperron, Sept. 25, 1633.

CHAPTER V

STUDIED DIPLOMACY

" Se mai alcun' negotio m'ha tenuto perplesso, è il presente"[1]

When the Stuarts came to Whitehall a marked Scottish influence was soon felt at Court. The change was seen in Catholic circles, too, as James made free use of his compatriots in his dealings with the Holy See. [2]

The Scottish Catholics kept in close touch with Rome on their own account, sending constant appeals for the restoration of their hierarchy extinct since April, 1603. It was felt that missionary work was being hampered largely through lack of co-operation, and the Earl of Angus, in 1610 when in exile in Paris, and again in 1619, urged on the Paris Nuncio, who was later to become Urban VIII, the need for uniting disorganized groups of missionaries under a bishop.

More than twenty years later the political outlook for the Catholics had so far improved that the same nobleman determined on a more ambitious scheme, which would, he knew, enjoy the active co-operation of the Secretary of State for Scotland, [3] of the Queen and of her Confessor, Father Philip of Sanquhar (himself named by the Paris Nuncio as a likely bishop for Scotland) and the tacit consent of the King. This plan was to send to Rome a kinsman

---

[1] The Cardinal Secretary of State on the mission recounted in this Chapter v. p. 118, n. 1).

[2] M. V. HAY, *The Blairs Papers*, pp. 189-190; *B. L.* 8614, f. 80: Angus to Maffeo Barberini, London, Sept. 6, 1619.

[3] Sir William Alexander, Earl of Stirling (1567?-1640), conspicuous as scholar, courtier, statesman, colonizer, poet; 1621 granted Nova Scotia; 1626 till his death, Secretary of State for Scotland, showing consummate ability. On June 14, 1633, when Charles was crowned at Holyrood Palace, Alexander was made Earl of Stirling and Viscount Canada. He died insolvent Sept. 12, 1640.

of his, Sir Robert Douglas,[1] armed with credentials from the Queen, Father Philip, and Angus himself as representing the Catholic nobility. There Douglas was to tell Barberini, the Cardinal Secretary of State and Protector of England and Scotland, of the hopes placed in his patronage and to beg him to back with his authority and influence the plan Angus had in mind.[2] This was then to be laid before the Pope, whose interest in England and Scotland had not diminished since Angus had known him as Nuncio. The Earl told Urban he could have every confidence in Sir Robert Douglas whose loyalty to the faith was unshakeable.[3]

Early in October, 1633, Douglas arrived in Rome to find the city empty and the Papal Court still enjoying its *villeggiatura* at Albano. He succeeded, however, in placing before Barberini a confirmation of all that had been previously reported. The English Catholics, disrupted by the dissensions of the clergy over the disputed jurisdiction of the Bishop of Chalcedon, were becoming further demoralized through lack of clear guidance on such questions as the Oath of Allegiance. In their attitude towards marriage, especially, the conduct of some of the laity was scandalous, while many of their pastors were distinguished only by their slackness.

Politically, on the other hand, the Catholics were enjoying unprecedented peace. The earlier bickerings of the King and Queen had given way to complete understanding and a domestic bliss that yielded its happiest results in the clemency shown towards the Queen's co-religionists. Moreover, the King's interest in theology, but dislike for polemics, offered genuine hope of his conversion.

Now was the moment for the Holy Father to raise one of his Majesty's subjects to the Cardinalate, — an honour which at one stroke would draw the King nearer to the Church, pull the Catholics together and provide them with an arbiter for all their disputes. The scheme had the strong support of the Queen, who suggested an admirable candidate in George Con, a noble Scot in the personal household of the Cardinal Secretary of State.[4]

---

[1] This person is probably the 4th son of William, 9th Earl of Angus. He was born about 1560 and later obtained Glenbervie (Cf. BALFOUR PAUL, *The Scots Peerage*, s. v. *Angus*).

[2] *B.L.* 8656, f. 1 : Angus to Barberini, Chasteau Douglas, Jan. 5, 1633.

[3] *Ibid.*, f. 81 : Angus to Urban VIII, Chasteau Douglas, Jan. 5, 1633.

[4] *B.L.* 8615, f. 34 : Henrietta to Barberini, London, Apr. 2, 1633. " Mon

The possibilities opened up by such a plan found Barberini quite unprepared to meet them. [1] In his perplexity he wrote off at once to the man most competent to give him counsel, — Cardinal del Bagno, who after serving nine years in the Nunciatures of Brussels and Paris where it had been his duty to study the English situation closely, had now retired from Court intrigues to a leisurely administration of the miniature diocese of Cervia on the Adriatic. His likely influence as an adviser on England had been foreseen, as Douglas had brought him a letter from Stirling asking support of the plan. [2]

Barberini told his colleague he foresaw opposition from his uncle to the English Queen's proposal, as his Holiness objected to creating Cardinals at the instance of royalties, fearing to expose himself

---

cousin, ayant jugé a propos a raison des plusieurs affaires qui arrivent continuellement et pour la consolation et utilité des Catholiques de ce pais, que quelqu'un de ceste nation fut promeu par sa S^té a fin de pouvoir avec plus d'autorité subvenir aux particuliers, et soliciter le bien publique, iay escrit à sa S^té sur ce subiect, et luy ay recommandé la personne de Georgio Coneo gentilhomme escossois, des vertus et bonnes qualités du quel iay eu bonne relation." — A succinct biography of Con is to be seen in the inscription on his tomb in San Lorenzo in Damaso, Rome : *Georgio Conaeo Scoto Aberdonensi Patricii Domini de Achry ex antiqua Magdonaldi familia et Isabellae Comyn ex baronibus de Esselmont filio, qui inter conterraneos eloquentia et doctrina Duaci et Romae haustis librisque editis immortalitati se commendavit, prudentia vero et agendi dexteritate summorum principum ac praesertim Cardinalis Barberini, in cuius aula diu vixit cuiusque legationes Gallicanam Hispanicamque secutus est; benevolentiam promeruit quem Urbanus VIII Pontifex ingeniorum Maximus existimator quanti fecerit et ad Magnae Britanniae Reginam Henrichettam in Catholicorum solamen allegatione et ingenti in ipsius morte, quae ne in editiori loco positus clarius elucesceret, vetuerat moerore testatus est. Obiit die X ianuarii an. M.DC.XL. in aedibus Vicecancellarii qui amico funus amplissimum in hac basilica faciendum curavit et monumentum P. ΦΩΣ · ΕΝ · ΤΗ, · ΣΚΟΤΙΑ, · ΦΑΙΝΕΙ · ΚΑΙ · Η · ΣΚΟΤΙΑ, · ΑΥΤΟ · ΟΥ · ΚΑΤΕΛΑΒΕΝ.* The play on the word *ΣΚΟΤΙΑ* (Con was a Scot) should be noticed. Details of Con's life in England will be met with *passim* in the following chapters.

[1] *B. L.* 8656, f. 3 : Barberini to Bagno, Oct. 19, 1633 : " Se mai alcun' negotio m' hà tenuto perplesso è il presente."

[2] Gianfrancesco dei Conti Guidi del Bagno, Archbishop of Patras. He was Nuncio at Brussels 1621-1627, and at Paris 1627-1630 ; Nuncio Extraordinary to help the Legate, Barberini, in Paris, 1625 ; Cardinal *in petto*, 1627, promulgated 1629. In 1630 he retired to the See of Cervia and died in 1641, when considered a likely successor to Urban VIII.

to jealousy. Moreover, Henrietta was not a *crowned* queen (a fact looked on with disfavour in England, as Douglas admitted) and so her influence would naturally be less.

Again, the desire for a cardinal seemed to come from the Scots rather than from the English, and Barberini was not slow to see the possibility that the scheme might be merely the machinations of enemies seeking to embarrass him, as well as the Queen, in the event of a refusal. Besides, an end of such importance as the King's conversion should be induced by secret means rather than by the nomination of a cardinal, and in any case would merit someone more suitable than Con, who was always ill. The proposal that the Holy See should send a representative to England, Barberini added, had been in the air when Con first came to Italy ; Padre Alessandro d'Ales had been concerned in it and had even suggested candidates to Barberini, as also had the Nuncio in Paris.

Having explained the situation, Barberini put his trust entirely in del Bagno, at the same time warning him in dealing with Douglas not to attack the project in any way. His own inclination was to delay decision and in any case not to concede all that was asked at once ; they might, for instance, send George Con to England, alone or with a companion, as the representative of the Bishop of Chalcedon. [1]

At the time of receiving this letter Cardinal del Bagno was taking a cure for his gout at Ghiaggiolo and asked for time to sleep on so complex and delicate an affair. Assuring Barberini of his secrecy, he promised a detailed reply at the earliest opportunity. [2]

Four days later del Bagno forwarded an acute analysis of the proposals Douglas had made. He admitted that the raising of one of their own to the purple would be an inspiration to the English and Scottish Catholics in their struggle for the Faith ; at the same time the Cardinal did not see how such a move could be efficacious for the King's conversion,— on this point he suspected either deliberate deception or that Douglas and his sponsors were groundlessly credulous. On the other hand, while avoiding precipitate action of which they might later repent, they (the Pope and the Cardinals) must not lay Rome open to the reproach of

---

[1] *B.L.* 8656, ff. 4-5 : Barberini to Bagno, Oct. 19, 1633.

[2] *Ibid.*, f. 7 : Bagno to Barberini, Ghiaggiolo, Oct. 25, 1633 : " ... Materia assai delicata e intricata che ben ricerca dormirvi un poco sopra. "

prejudicing the negotiations by their incredulity. Douglas must therefore be assured that the importance of his mission was fully recognized and that every effort would be made to give him satisfaction. They, on their account, must use all moral diligence to discover the measure of reality behind the proposals, so as to enable them to adopt a definite policy and not be feeling their way in the dark.

The soundest way of setting to work, del Bagno continued, was to send a disinterested party to England to hear the Queen's views from her own lips, for little credit could be given to her letter which might easily have been drawn up by some French secretary without her having full knowledge of its contents. The extent of her influence over the King could also be seen at first hand, how far she used it in the interests of religion, and the amount of truth in his Majesty's supposed leanings towards the Faith. Then there was Laud's attitude to be diagnosed, for in religious affairs the King trusted him completely, and they must ascertain the amount of co-operation they might expect from Weston, the Lord Treasurer and King's favourite, for in the past his goodwill towards Catholics had proved barren of results.

An envoy sent to England should not talk freely of the Red Hat or of other honours, but should take steps to sound the Secretaries of State and those of the King's household who have his ear and with whom it is his habit to declare his sentiments more openly. If the Agent used his skill and discretion and kept within his mandate, the information obtained should enable the authorities in Rome to form a good idea of the situation in England and come to a decision on Douglas's proposals at some future date. The immediate advantage of sending a Papal representative to England would be to make Douglas go home to some extent satisfied and provide a means of paying official homage to the Queen (a course advised by the Paris Nuncio), and of settling the affairs of the missionaries. [1]

---

[1] In his original cipher (but omitted from the copy made, presumably, for Barberini's guidance — the two are placed next to each other in the Barberini MSS.) Cardinal del Bagno adds a paragraph on the choice of George Con for the Agency, pointing out that, though Con may not have been privy to the original plan, he knew all now and, being an interested party, *viz.* the Queen's candidate for the cardinalate, he would not be the right

Having advised the Cardinal Secretary on the means of meeting Douglas's proposals, del Bagno proceded to analyse the proposals themselves, which he reduced to three heads, *viz.* the misbehaviour of the missionaries, the hope of the King's conversion, and the suggestion that this end would be furthered, and English Catholicism preserved, by the creation of a national Cardinal as the Queen requested. [1]

Satisfaction could be given on the first point by the sending of an Agent. On the second, Douglas and Angus must be praised for their zeal and exhorted to perseverance, with a hint of something big being done if the King's conversion became a fact. The third point must be brought down from the clouds and Douglas told bluntly that the Pope had never considered the promotion of subjects of the King of England, since derisive attacks against the Holy See had been printed with impunity in London, and even with the royal licence. [2] There was, besides, the violation of the Marriage Pact and of the promise made to the Holy Father by the King of France to see it fulfilled ; which promise had been confirmed on oath by the King of England. Greatest sorrow of all to his Holiness was the cruel vexations to which the English Catholics were being put, — forced to join in the new religion under pain of severe fines, the wretched people, faced with confiscation of their goods, the break-up of their families and the driving of their daughters through poverty on to the streets, were turning away from the Faith, though latterly the evil had become less marked.

For these and like reasons, Douglas should be told, the idea of favouring the English had been repugnant to the Pope, but in view of the forceful arguments Douglas had brought and the hopes held out, he was prepared to consider the raising of a British subject to the purple, and would inform himself of the candidates

person to sound the opinions of his compatriots on the matter. If once Con's candidature were an accepted fact, however, he could be sent to England without scruple to win merit for his final promotion.

[1] In his original cipher, del Bagno adds a 4th point, *viz.* the candidature of Con. He says he is not clear whether this is mentioned in the Queen's letter or is the personal proposal of Douglas

[2] The original cipher adds that if such calumnies appeared in Rome against England they would be punished severely.

most likely to be of service to religion.[1] With these answers the Scot ought to go away satisfied.

Del Bagno thought it might be going too far for the Holy Father to pledge himself to nominate a national Cardinal, but on second thoughts he said such a promise would not tie him down to any precise time or person, so the Pope would retain full freedom of action and, when he did choose to act, the person promoted would be under all the greater obligation to the Holy Father the more unexpected his preferment. If the Pope allowed a nomination by the Queen of England, he would not only lose the credit of the promotion, but would be setting a bad precedent for other Queens.

Cardinal del Bagno added the final warning that the French might be at the back of the whole business, for he remembered Richelieu telling him once that the Pope ought to create more French Cardinals to put them on a par with the Spaniards. When he (del Bagno) had pointed out the difficulties, Richelieu had said, " Why not make the Bishop of Chalcedon, an Englishman, a Cardinal?" It was possible, therefore, that the French had been using someone to work on the Queen of England to make this petition and to obtain her husband's consent to it, as to something which would not concern him closely.

Thinking the matter over, however, Cardinal del Bagno discounted this posibility, as such a plan would not have escaped Père Joseph, who in his own interests would have baulked it. Besides, the French were most unlikely to have taken Padre Alessandro d'Ales into their confidence, yet the Capuchin had known all about Douglas's mission before ever the Scot crossed France and had written of it to del Bagno, with the exception of the nomination of Con, which he would doubtless also have mentioned had he known of it, as both he and del Bagno were friends of Con. Cardinal del Bagno, indeed, considered George Con one of the best friends he had at the Papal Court and praised him to Barberini as a man of the finest intellect and of excellent birth and qualities, which rendered him worthy of promotion once he had passed through the necessary stages of the diplomatic career.[2]

Before del Bagno had prepared his detailed reply to Barberini,

---

[1] The original cipher adds that in deference to the Queen special consideration would be given to the claims of Con.

[2] *B.L.* 8656, ff. 10-30 : Bagno to Barberini, Ghiaggiolo, Oct. 29, 1633.

Douglas and Padre Alessandro, awaiting an audience at Albano, had both written to him, — Alessandro at Douglas's request, to tell him of the hope of the King's conversion (to which end he asked his friend's influence in obtaining a Cardinal's Hat for England), and of Charles's wish for his wife to maintain, as he could not, a Resident in Rome, although the Queen personally did not favour the project. Douglas, who was growing impatient and wanted del Bagno's influence to get him his interview with the Pope, wrote to tell the Cardinal he had letters for him from England and to ask him to let Barberini know that he (Douglas) was in communication with him. [1]

These two letters del Bagno forwarded to Barberini, with the comment that he was beginning to think that the Queen of England was not applying herself to the good of religion : he knew what they thought about it in France. What they said about the King's conversion was quite possible, as he was a good-living man, and perhaps God was beginning to enlighten him. [2]

After a perusal of del Bagno's long memorandum Barberini replied explaining several points on which his colleague was not clear. The Queen of England had made express mention of George Con, though Douglas, in his audience with the Pope, did not intend doing so, wishing to leave his Holiness free.

The King, according to Douglas, desired a sincere understanding with the Holy See for a wholly spiritual end, that of conversion. The idea was backed by the strongest supporters of the Crown and if the English Catholics had not made the same suggestion it was because they were so disunited. Douglas was now asking for a trustworthy person with whom to talk matters over as soon as possible, which made Barberini wish his friend del Bagno were in Rome to deal with the Scot ; in any case, he said, they would have to be circumspect as it had already been whispered that the two Cardinals were too much hand-in-glove. [3]

Nearly two weeks later Barberini wrote again to say Douglas was pressing for an answer and threatening that unless it were favourable, the King would turn against the Catholics. This change of attitude

---

[1] *Ibid.*, ff. 32-33 : Alessandro to Bagno, Albano, Oct. 21 enclosing (f. 34) Douglas to Bagno, Albano, Oct. 19, 1633 ; f. 51 : Alessandro to Bagno, undated.

[2] *Ibid.*, f. 37 : Bagno to Barberini, Ghiaggiolo, Nov. 1, 1633.

[3] *Ibid.*, ff. 40, 48 : Barberini to Bagno, Rome, Nov. 5 and 12, 1633.

made Barberini less inclined to trust Douglas. He was afraid, too, though del Bagno reassured him, that the same thing might happen under Charles as under Elizabeth, who employed Catholics in her foreign diplomacy and at the same time persecuted them at home. However, he told del Bagno he had made up his mind to send a man to England through Mgr Bichi, the Paris Nuncio. [1]

The issue of Douglas's mission had been complicated by the introduction of the name of George Con, which stood in all the commendatory letters that come from England, though Rome realized no pressure was intended. It was a mistake ever to have mentioned him, and del Bagno was quick to point out the embarrassing position in which Con would find himself, for if his nomination had come solely from the Queen, it would be most unwelcome to the Pope; if on the other hand Con fell under suspicion of having procured his own nomination, it would ruin his chances. [2]

Douglas was clearly becoming restive, so Cardinal del Bagno wrote to urge him to patience, assuring him of his own devotion to the English Catholics and of the interest of the Pope and his nephew. Douglas would do well to subordinate all else to this fact. Negotiations were bound to be long drawn out; they were at any Court, and particularly in Rome, where the affairs of all Christendom were concentrated. His Holiness was obliged to weigh up his decision more carefully than any other sovereign, especially in affairs of such importance as Douglas's, which would be laid bare to the criticism of the whole world. It would be a mistake to rush matters, and Douglas should make up his mind to allow the time required to bring his mission to the desired conclusion. It would be a six months' affair, del Bagno told Barberini, whom he advised to appoint someone to go with Douglas to England or confer with him in Rome. [3]

Cardinal del Bagno had apologized to Douglas for not welcoming him on his arrival in Rome. Ill-health he gave as the reason, but it was something more that was keeping him away

---

[1] *Ibid.*, ff. 44, 48 : Barberini to Bagno, Nov. 12 and 16, 1633 ; f. 75 : Bagno to Barberini, Ghiaggiolo, Nov. 19, 1633.

[2] *Ibid.*, ff. 54-57 : Bagno to [Barberini?], Nov. 12, 1633.

[3] *Ibid.*, ff. 66-67 : no title, signature, or date, but probably from Bagno to Douglas, in answer to f. 68 : Douglas to Bagno, Nov. 4 ; ff. 54-57 : Bagno to [Barberini?], Nov. 12, 1633.

now. Douglas and Alessandro wanted him, and the Pope had given leave for him to come to Rome, but Barberini, while equally desirous of his friend's advice, was afraid his presence in Rome would cause the secret of the negotiations with England to leak out. He therefore judged it inadvisable for del Bagno and Douglas to meet either in Rome or elsewhere, and told Douglas he would himself keep in touch with the former Nuncio, in consulation with whom he would make his decision. Barberini added that he was quite favourable to an exchange of agents between Rome and London, and suggested Douglas could stay on to confer in Rome or that a competent person be sent to England for more information. But the Scotsman was unwilling to remain negotiating indefinitely in Rome and took umbrage at the idea of a Papal Agent going to investigate the truth of his statements. [1]

Padre Alessandro also seems to have spoken plainly to the Cardinal Secretary, saying he was edified at the sincerity shown but feared nothing would be done to give the Queen satisfaction : he would not answer for the consequences, should Douglas's mission prove fruitless. Barberini was irritated at this attempt to force his hand, and it needed all del Bagno's tact to excuse the Capuchin's familiarity and excess of zeal. [2]

Cardinal del Bagno had foreseen Douglas's objection and advised that the Agent be sent expressly to settle the missionnaries' quarrels and should not go at the bidding of the Paris Nuncio, Bichi, but under the immediate orders of the Pope, who would thus be able to give him fuller instructions.

Del Bagno said Douglas must be brought to see the reasonableness of this procedure ; it was a common practice of princes to reply to a request made through an ambassador by sending an ambassador in return. If this was to be done now, it did not mean that they doubted Douglas's word, but that they had to satisfy their consciences in a matter demanding so much discretion. The Pope would give him his final answer after the Agent's report.

Although he probably did not think Douglas was withholding

---

[1] *Ibid.*, ff. 72, 79 : Barberini to Bagno, Nov. 19, 26 ; f. 76 : Anon. to V. S. [Alessandro ? to Bagno ?], Rome, Nov. 12, 1633.

[2] *Ibid.*, f. 72 : Barberini to Bagno, Nov. 19 ; f. 75 : Bagno to Barberini, Nov. 19 ; f. 76 ; Anon. to V. S. [Alessandro ? to Bagno ?], Rome, Nov. 12, 1633.

the truth deliberately, Cardinal del Bagno suspected something more behind King Charles's desire for an understanding with Rome than the purely spiritual motives Douglas had alleged. The King, he thought, was angling for the Pope's support of his sister's and nephews' restoration to the Palatinate. It was the most urgent task the King had on hand and involved his prestige as well as his own flesh and blood. Del Bagno told Barberini it would be better for them not to show they realized this. [1]

Impatient for the audience he had been awaiting so long, Douglas now decided to put his petition into writing to be presented to the Pope.

Appealing to Urban's piety and zeal, the Scot stressed the bearing of his mission on the good of religion and the personal prestige of the Papacy. The long separation of England from Rome had done untold harm to souls, but now the King was offering to come to a sincere understanding with the Holy Father. Although his Majesty was aware that such a proposal had been made already within memory, [2] it had never met with the same support. Douglas said he could tell the Holy Father things that would amaze him and gladden his heart. He would realize then that his project was no trickery nor inspired by human interests, but aimed solely at the conversion of the King and his realms to the Papal obedience.

Although Douglas's letters of credence could not represent directly a King out of communion with the Holy See, his Majesty, in his regard for the Pope, had ordered to plead in his stead those closest to his person and crown, *viz.* the Queen, the principal Catholics of Scotland and the Scottish Secretary of State. The leading English Catholics would have done as much, had they been a united body and were there no fear of the secret leaking out. Even the Queen was not privy to the complete plan, so important was secrecy considered.

Her Majesty's main contribution was her petition, approved by her husband, for the creation of a Cardinal from among his Majesty's subjects, who, in close touch with the Holy See, would be the means of the King's safely and confidently representing his sentiments and aims to Pope.

---

[1] *Ibid.*, ff. 82-83 : Bagno to Barberini, Ghiagglolo, Nov. 22, 1633.
[2] During the Pontificate of Gregory XV (1621-1623), v. *infra*, pp. 136 seq.

Douglas again made it clear that if in the letters he brought express mention was made of George Con, a subject of the King and of noble blood, it was not that the Queen or the Scottish Catholics or the King had any intention of forcing a candidate on the Pope: on the contrary, Con's name, it was thought, would allay suspicion in the Holy Father's mind, for the man was far more the servant of his Holiness than a subject of the King, who wished to show every respect to the Pope and leave him entire liberty of choice.

As for various reasons, political and religious, it was important for the negotiations to be kept secret, Douglas declared his desire not to be seen frequently at the Papal Court. This, and his lack of fluency in Italian, made him petition the Holy Father to delegate someone with whom he might discuss his mission in all confidence. It was with this end in view that at the express command of the King he had brought commendatory letters from the Secretary of State to Cardinal del Bagno and Padre Alessandro d'Ales, the Capuchin, in whose prudence and integrity his Majesty had entire confidence. He had therefore communicated the whole matter to them in the hope that his Holiness would not only allow them to accept these letters, but would call Cardinal del Bagno to Rome for consultation or appoint some other person qualified to negotiate. The hopes of their Majesties and their Catholic subjects were in the Pope's hands. [1]

Cardinal del Bagno was clearly the key-figure of these negotations. At their inception Stirling, the Secretary of State for Scotland, had appealed to him to help Douglas, recalling the earlier contact the Cardinal had had as Nuncio with King James. [2] Barberini also looked wholly to his colleague for advice. This Douglas realized and, in the hope that the powerful influence of Cardinal del Bagno would be placed unreservedly on his side, the Scot sent him, through Padre Alessandro who had a cipher with the Cardinal, an annotated memorandum outlining the motives of his mission to Rome and repeating much of what he had said in his petition to the Pope.

In view of his disqualification from direct negotiation with the

---

[1] *B.L.* 8656, ff. 58-60 : Copy of Douglas's Petition to the Pope, no title no signature, no date.

[2] *Ibid.*, f. 86 : Stirling to Bagno, London, May 22, 1633.

Pope as a sovereign separated from Rome, the King had made Douglas his plenipotentiary (" hà dato ordine et autorità assoluta ") to arrange an *entente* between the Courts of England and Rome, as an offset to which his Majesty made two requests. First, that the Holy Father would deign to have him as a friend and favour him in all that concerned the peace and tranquility of his person and state. Secondly, for the stability of this understanding and to further their ends with greater convenience and security, the King was anxious for one of his subjects to be raised to the purple as soon as possible and, as George Con was well-known to his Holiness and at home in the Papal Court, his Majesty begged the Pope to take his name into consideration at the first promotion of Cardinals, as a person enjoying his Holiness's entire trust. [1]

Douglas accompanied his *status quaestionis* with lengthy explanations. If the Holy Father desired an *entente* with England and the conversion of her King, the raising of one of the King's subject to the purple was of paramount importance for all concerned, but chiefly for his Majesty himself. For, if at any moment he resolved to declare himself the Catholic he was believed to be at heart, he could not conveniently do so without manifest danger to his life and crown, unless the step were prepared for by a real understanding with the Holy See touching the present state of the religion which the King now professed, so that his Majesty's Catholic subjects would rally round him, if the need arose to pursue his pious intentions by force.

The *entente* and all connected with it could not be properly established save by an intermediary with the authority, ability and confidence to negotiate with the highly-placed persons concerned.

Now obviously in a matter so closely concerning his person and realm the King would never show complete trust save to one of his own subjects. The royal dignity and the fact that the negotiation was one of concession both demanded that it should be carried out on a basis of mutual generosity. Again, with such important business passing through the hands of a subject of so high a dignity and a priest, there would be no need of secrecy

---

[1] *Ibid.*, f. 94 : Douglas to Bagno, undated but enclosed with letter from Alessandro, Nov. 16, 1633.

and so a great deal of difficulty and delay would be avoided. Lastly, a King's subject in such a position would be able not only to further his Majesty's pious designs, but he could more easily check the opposition of ill-affected or interested parties which would be raised to discredit and thwart them.

A private person could clearly not accomplish all this. Experience had shown that even Catholic princes with Cardinals of their own in Rome were often hard put to it to free themselves from opposition to their just aims. It was all the more reasonable, therefore, to allow the intermediary for such an enterprise as this, which had and would always have its enemies, to be a subject and a Cardinal rather than a private person, exposed to a thousand mishaps, of small credit and less authority, or with other interests that would not only impede progress, but would cause the whole affair to become suspect and go up in smoke.

Surely the King's request was not unreasonable when Catholic princes, his inferiors in dignity, had asked for and obtained Red Hats for their subjects for reasons of less importance and not concerned with religion.

Also, the Queen needed to be consoled in her troubles, spurred on to greater effort for the Faith, and kept in touch with the Pope, — all of which activities, to be effective, must be the work of a person of rank. Again, were the King to die while his wife remained uncrowned, her Majesty's person and faith would be in extreme danger. Such perils could be foreseen and remedied through the prudence of a Cardinal enjoying the confidence and authority of his Holiness.

If this Cardinal were a Scot, it would be a greater gain for the Catholics, as the King's penchant for his compatriots was evident from his choice of ministers: even the Queen's Confessor was Scottish. The English Catholics particularly wanted Con, as there were divisions among them, and if a partisan of one of their own factions were chosen, it would only create greater discord. The Scottish Catholics were united and interrelated, so the King had more confidence in them. Already the confidant of all parties, George Con would hold yet greater prestige, enjoying as a Cardinal influence with the Pope and the confidence of the King. For these reasons and for his understanding of the genius and interests of the English, he would be the best qualified to remedy present disorders and to root out from England those dangerous doctrines

9

that belittled the Catholic Faith and the authority of the Pope.

It was most important for the Catholics that this *entente* between England and the Holy See should be begun and maintained by a Cardinal, otherwise it would fall through as it had before when attempts had been made without this foundation under other Pontificates, and a splendid opportunity of reconciling the realm would be missed, with the consequent loss of so many souls. When such chances are let slip, dissension and abuses grow, while false teaching secures a firm footing, and the evil becomes daily more complex and irremediable.

His Holiness himself stood to gain by having such a Cardinal immediately dependent upon him, who, being a foreigner and so aloof from certain private interests, would be of all the greater utility in this and other negotiations with princes.

Finally, there was every probability of the Holy Father, by these means, winning the merit of converting the King and his realm, — an end at which every Pope was bound to aim at all costs.

This negotiation was, therefore, of the utmost importance for the good not only of the particular persons concerned but of the Faith in general. Its genuineness and the quality of the participants demanded all sincerity, faith and candour that the right steps to be taken might not be despised nor shelved through irresolute procrastination.

Having stated his case with all the resource of an advocate, Douglas appealed to Cardinal del Bagno to envisage the tragedy of a refusal to meet the King's demands. His Majesty had exposed himself to some risk in sending an envoy to Rome ; he was willing for the Pope to send a confidential Agent to England to settle the differences of the English Catholics without let or hindrance ; in addition, he had ordered the Queen to maintain a Resident in Rome. In return, he was asking for a Red Hat, a thing often granted, though never in circumstances promising better results. What if this means of approaching the Faith were denied to his Majesty? The King, who knew his own needs best, judged it the best and safest way to ask as his confessor an intermediary between himself and the Holy See. If he found this way of settling his affairs closed, it would not be difficult to imagine the ideas that would be put into his head by bad counsellors, heretical Puritans hostile to the Catholic religion or interested princes out of sympathy with the Pope. How would it be possible to stay execution of the Penal Laws, the use of anti-Catholic Oaths and other abuses directed to the alienation of men's minds from the Apostolic See?

How would the Queen react to a refusal, seeing herself so little esteemed and her peace of mind among heretics considered of so little importance? Without doubt she would show no more zeal for the Catholic cause, to which end whispered persuasions would not be wanting.

What would the Catholics themselves do, seeing in circumstances so favourable everything turning towards their total ruin and extermination?

Doubtless, in the event of such refusal the whole negotiation would leak out, and King, Privy Council and Parliament would be constrained to repressive measures against any who had had a hand in it. Nor would they pay less dearly than with their lives.

Last of all, what would disinterested zealous onlookers in the world say, seeing so providential an opportunity neglected on the flimsiest of pretexts?

Douglas said he could never believe that such was the future, given the piety of Pope Urban, the zeal of his nephew and the support of del Bagno himself. Nevertheless, if for their sins the negotiations did fall through, it would be the cause of irremediable evil, even of despair, to the harassed Catholics of England. It would be a tale for all the world to talk of, for the enemies of public peace to mock at. Satan, with all the devils of Hell, would alone remain triumphant.

In conclusion, Douglas said it was to Cardinal del Bagno that the Catholics commended the whole affair. His Eminence could impart force to their arguments and persuade the Pope and the Cardinal Secretary to come to a generous decision without loss of time before some interested sovereign smelt out the whole affair. [1]

But so experienced a diplomat as del Bagno was not to be carried away by the eloquence of Douglas's special pleading. In writlng to Barberini a week or so later he gave a shrewd estimate of the situation. Anyone with the slightest knowledge of the King of England's nature and of those around him would never consider

---

[1] *B.L.* 8656, ff. 88-93 : Douglas to Bagno, undated but enclosed with letter to Alessandro, Rome, Nov. 16, 1633.

he was interested in having a Cardinal, a thing that did not enter into his calculations. A more likely explanation of this complicated business was that the King's most urgent interests were those of the County Palatine. He had the tenderest affection for his sister, who was cleverly (and tearfully) exploiting her troubles, — the exile of herself and her children, and so on. Her lamentations touched the King to the quick, both from the circumstance of relationship and because of the slight at his own prestige. After his marriage he had tried to urge France to take up the defence of the Palatinate. Meeting with no success, he had turned to Spain, making peace with that intent though nothing had been promised, but after various comings and goings of Ambassadors from himself to tho Emperor, from the Emperor to Brussels, from Brussels to Spain, he had seen he was being made a fool of and had desisted.

Cardinal del Bagno said he was persuaded that, with his sister still pressing him for help, the King was trying as a last resort to secure the intervention of the Pope with the Emperor and the Duke of Bavaria. In pursuance of this end he was suggesting an *entente* with the Holy See and asking for a Cardinal of his own realm to be created to show enthusiasm for the negotiations and perhaps with the idea of sending him later to Germany to complete them.

In giving this opinion the Cardinal did not exclude the possibility that this might be the providential beginning of the King's enlightenment, so that, if they let things take their course in the hope of reaping something greater, it could not but be pleasing to the Almighty, just as it would be blameworthy to show the King too little credit, — was not Clement VII now being found fault with for too harsh a treatment of Henry VIII?

Del Bagno therefore suggested that Barberini should come to some arrangement with Douglas for him or another to stay on in Rome as the Queen's Agent, while they for their part could safely send a man to England with the title of Dean of the Missions rather than that of Agent, as referring more to the service of religion. [1]

This reply of his friend gave the Cardinal Secretary something to think over. He agreed with it in substance, only pointing out

---

[1] *B.L.* 8656, ff. 98-99 : Bagno to Barberini, Ghiaggiolo, Nov. 26, 1633.

that when Douglas had first come to Italy the affairs of the Palatine had been in better shape, but now as the situation changed in Germany, he could also see a change in Douglas.

With his letter del Bagno had enclosed Douglas's long memorandum. Barberini, like del Bagno, was not deceived. The whole composition, its phraseology and impassioned eloquence smacked of Alessandro rather than of the dour Scot, and Barberini, much as he admired the former, suspected this collaboration the more as he knew of the intimacy between the Capuchin and George Con.

With this commingling of forces behind the scenes, the Cardinal Secretary felt it would be doubly difficult to shake off Douglas with a vague promise of a Red Hat, by taking the responsibility of the promise on himself, and so providing a means of escape for Urban later on. So tried a diplomat as Padre Alessandro would never suffer Douglas to be satisfied with this or with any of the suggestions del Bagno had made.

Moreover, if they were to pursue their plan of sounding the minds of the King and Queen on all this business, it would be fatal to send Douglas home disgruntled and mistrustful. Barberini therefore suggested a subtle move, — taking Con into their confidence. The latter would then be bound to deal discreetly with the negotiation, so as not to prejudice his own interests that were involved. In this way they could settle Douglas, for when he discovered that the Papal Agent going to England knew the whole secret of his mission, or that the Queen had shown her keenness to negotiate, he would be content to await results, suppressing any annoyance he might feel. If, on the other hand, it came out that the Queen was not eager and that there was nothing for the negotiation to feed upon, Douglas would have only his own rashness to blame, not the caution Rome had used.

On the question of the Red Biretta, Barberini was convinced, in spite of the Douglas-Alessandro memorandum, that it was a mere accessory to the King's main desire, which was the exchange of agents. He advised del Bagno to give away nothing in talking to Douglas, but to limit the discussion to the qualifications of some person to visit the English mission. Barberini agreed with his colleague that it would be an excellent idea to send a man to England, but the difficulty was in the choosing, especially as added to the secrecy and intricacy of the diplomacy necessary there was the question of hope of preferment for the Agent selected.

Mgr Bichi, the Paris Nuncio, had suggested sending Père Vigier, Provincial of the Somaschi Fathers and former superior of the Fathers of Christian doctrine at Lille.[1] Both Barberini and del Bagno approved of the choice, for Père Vigier appeared to have every qualification of piety, learning and that common-sense indispensable to the advantageous use of both. If he were sent by Bichi before the latter's return to Italy, Douglas would entertain no suspicions, while the Father could profess complete ignorance of Douglas's mission, saying he had gleaned all his information not from Rome but from the English Queen and others. If this man were not suitable, an envoy could be sent from Italy to receive verbal instructions from Bichi ; later, if he proved acceptable to the Queen, he could be given charge of the English Mission.

Barberini now advised del Bagno to reply in general fashion to the letter he had received from Stirling, and asked him for a copy. [2]

Cardinal del Bagno, having now completed his cure at Ghiaggiolo, was back in his diocese of Cervia.   On the very day Barberini was making the leisurely suggestions just outlined, del Bagno again wrote to him, urged to the task by the insistence of Douglas, who was growing more and more impatient of the repeated expressions of goodwill *et praeterea nihil*, which he was receiving from both their Eminences.

The Scot had as yet had no audience with the Pope and wrote

---

[1] The Somaschi (their official title approved by Pius V was *Clerici regulares S. Maioli Papiae Congregationis Somaschae*) were founded in 1532 by St Jerome Emilian for the education of orphans and the care of the sick and the poor. The name derives from Somasca, an out-of-the-way village between Milan and Bergamo, where St Jerome established his headquarters and wrote his first rule.

The *Prêtres séculiers de la doctrine chrétienne* or *Pères doctrinaires* were founded in 1597 by the Ven. César de Bus to combat Calvinism. Père Vigier, the second superior, applied to Paul V to allow the Fathers to take solemn vows. This the Pope would only grant on the condition that they amalgamated with some congregation already well-established. In 1616, therefore, Père Vigier's party joined with the Somaschi, while the rest led by Romillion, one of de Bus's first followers, linked up with the Oratorians. In 1647 Innocent X broke off the union with the Somaschi, while in 1659 Alexander VII confirmed their original simple vows. (Cf. M. HEIMBUCHER, *Die Orden und Kongregationen der katholischen Kirche*, 3rd ed., vol. II, pp. 111, 572.)

[2] *B.L.* 8656, ff. 102-105 : Barberini to Bagno, Dec. 7, 1633.

to del Bagno complaining loudly of this shelving of proposals so clear and void of difficulty. He again spoke of advantages to the Church in reunion and the propagation of the Faith, both causes jeopardized by this procrastination. For him to stay on in Rome under such conditions would be worse than useless.

Cardinal del Bagno replied soothingly, explaining away the delay as due to pressure of business at the Roman Curia arising from the Holy Father's indisposition, which had been the cause of great dislocation in the normal routine. He strongly advised Douglas not to prejudice his cause by too great a desire to rush it through. It was an important matter needing time to mature, and he promised to ask leave from Stirling for Douglas to stay on a little longer in Rome. [1]

Although he did not mention the point, del Bagno could see that Padre Alessandro was at the back of Douglas, giving expression in eloquent Italian to the Scot's impatience. He therefore begged Barberini to give the Capuchin full audience as soon as possible to allay his suspicions and prevent his persuading Douglas to hasty action. There was all the more need for giving him some satisfaction, as the promotion of Cardinals had recently been made. [2]

Having hurried off this letter of December 7, del Bagno now received Barberini's of the same date, which had crossed his in the post. He there read his friend's suggestion for Père Vigier, the Provincial of the Sommaschi. His comment was that he would not like to say how Douglas would take the sending of this man, — probably violently. He therefore suggested that, if Vigier were sent, Douglas should be told that his mission was to congratulate the Queen on her recent safe delivery [3] or to deal with the missionary problem, but that it had nothing to do with Douglas's own mission to Rome. This assurance could be given him by Alessandro or Con.

---

[1] *Ibid.*, f. 119 : Douglas to Bagno, Nov. 26 ; f. 120 : [Bagno? to Douglas?] [Dec. 7?] ; f. 123 : Dec. 7 del Bagno asks Barberini if he is to write to Stirling.

[2] *Ibid.*, ff. 118, 123 : Bagno to Barberini, Cervia, Dec. 7, 1633. This promotion of Cardinals, the 7th under Urban VIII, took place on Nov. 28, 1633. The names of eight Cardinals, together with two reserved since 1629, were promulgated, while one was reserved *in petto, viz.* Franciotti, promulgated March 30, 1637. (Cf. CARDELLA, *op. cit.*, vol. VI, p. 302.)

[3] The future James II was born at midnight on Oct. 14, 1633 (o.s.). A letter of congratulation was sent eventually. (Cf. *Arch. Vat., Epist. ad Principes,* vol. XLVIII, N° 47 : Urban to Henrietta, Rome, Dec. 31, 1633.)

To send Douglas away satisfied on the Cardinalate question del Bagno thought the Cardinal Secretary need have no qualms about expressing a general intention of creating an English Cardinal, providing no restrictions were made as to time or candidate. He could advise the Pope to this effect. In saying this del Bagno repeated his conviction that the King of England did not want a Cardinal and instanced Sterling's letter as sufficient proof of this.

Finally, del Bagno endorsed Barberini's view that they could put little confidence in Alessandro, nor did he think he could be won over by favour. He added that, if they could not get rid of Douglas in the way suggested, he could perhaps be persuaded to retire to France and continue negotiations from there. [1]

At the end of his letter of December 7, the Cardinal Secretary had asked the ex-Nuncio, in view of Douglas's plan of an exchange of agents, for particulars of a previous abortive correspondence between the Courts of England and Rome. Del Bagno looked up his notes on the subject and enclosed them in a postscript to his letter of the 15th.

It appears that in the time of Gregory XV (1621-1623) rumour came from England that King James, having laid aside his old mistrust of the Catholics consequent on the Gunpowder Plot, was showing signs of sympathy for the Faith. Del Bagno, Nuncio in Brussels at the time, was therefore told to find out the true intentions of the King. This he did by sounding William Trumbull, English Resident in Brussels, a man neither hostile to Catholicism nor a very subtle diplomat. [2] The Nuncio gave Trumbull to understand that once the King of England gained the goodwill of the Pope he could sleep secure as regards his Catholic subjects, for such was the Holy Father's authority over their consciences that at his command they would obey, serve and defend their sovereign to the shedding of their blood — always, of course, saving the integrity of their Faith — and in addition would help to worry

---

[1] *B.L.* 8656, ff. 124-125 : Bagno to Barberini, Cervia, Dec. 15, 1633.

[2] Originally attached to Sir Thomas Edmondes' embassy to the Archduke Albert, regent of the Catholic Low Countries, Trumbull succeeded Edmondes in 1609, remaining in Brussels till 1625, when England was again at war with Spain. Trumbull's correspondence forms a valuable source for the diplomatic history of the period.

out the plots of the Puritans. This goodwill of the Pope could be won by the King's showing kindness to the Catholics ; the fact of his asking his Nuncio to approach the English Resident was evidence enough of the Holy Father's attitude.

Trumbull referred all this in due course to James, who told him to confer with del Bagno secretly and thank him on the King's behalf. He was to tell the Nuncio that his Majesty had changed his opinion that the Popes favoured assassination and was now anxious for ways of *rapprochement* to be discussed.

Later, Trumbull persuaded the Nuncio to write to James, which he did, receiving a gracious reply from the King and from the Secretary who now was writing under the title of Earl of Stirling.

At this stage there arrived in Brussels from Germany Padre Giacinto da Casale, the Capuchin roving diplomat, with whom the Nuncios had strict orders to correspond. When Giacinto heard the tale of del Bagno's dealings with Trumbull, he looked on the whole thing as providential and of great promise, especially for the negotiations in Germany that were his own special field.

Del Bagno did not understand exactly how matters stood and decided to humour the Capuchin. He had little doubt that the Spaniards, who had a large party in their pay at King James's Court, would soon ferret out what was going on in Brussels and put a sinister interpretation upon it, for it was their business to keep James in a continual state of fear.

The Nuncio, in consequence, willingly yielded place to Giacinto, who sent over to England Padre Alessandro, till then unknown to del Bagno, with orders to treat of the affairs of the Prince Palatine and his sons. To enable the envoy to act with authority and to remove the ill opinion James had of Giacinto, the Nuncio made Alessandro see Trumbull first and then gave him letters of credence for the King and Secretary Stirling, which won him a warm welcome from both, James referring him to Stirling to talk over his mission.

After Alessandro returned to Brussels to report, Giacinto sent him a second time to England. The Nuncio was kept *au courant* with the negotiations, but the whole burden of them, the expense and the report to Rome rested on the shoulders of Giacinto who, on the death of Gregory XV in 1623, sent Alessandro to give an account of the whole affair to the present Pope, Urban VIII, while del Bagno also sent in a report of the part he had played.

Since that time, ten years before, Cardinal del Bagno admitted many details had escaped his memory, though he was quite emphatic in saying that this secret *entente* never came to anything, and that he had heard no more of it or of Secretary Stirling till three years previously (1630), when Padre Alessandro went to England a third time, sent by the Spaniards on the business of evading the restitution of the Palatinate. At that time the English Secretary had asked Alessandro to bring del Bagno into the discussions and had even given him a cipher for the Nuncio, but the latter, who had just completed his *triennium* in France, was able to reply that he was no longer in office. [1]

In the present business Cardinal Barberini was happy in having del Bagno as a buffer between himself and Douglas and Alessandro. The last named, realizing del Bagno's intervention was all-important if anything was to be done, launched a long letter at him from Rome on December 10. The Capuchin complained that he had to bear the full force of Douglas's indignation at the delay, at del Bagno's alleged lack of interest and at Barberini's distrust, after the Scot had hoped for frequent discussion with the Cardinal Secretary, to whom he could have explained all the implications of his mission and cleared up many doubts. After the interest the Pope and Barberini had professed in the negotiations, Douglas had hoped to deal with his Holiness as with a father.

Douglas considered, as he had told Barberini in writing, that all his travels and all his efforts were orientated to the King's conversion, and he would therefore have liked to have seen the same readiness and adaptability in the Cardinal Secretary; instead of which he was faced with two unpleasant facts. The first was this procrastination, for which he held the Jesuits responsible: they were trying to carry their contention that the King had not the slightest leaning towards the Catholic Faith, doing this through certain confidential friends of theirs with whom Barberini was in constant consultation.

The second reason for Douglas's pique was his suspicion that Rome wanted to send someone secretly to England to spy out the

[1] *B.L.* 8656, ff. 126-128 : Bagno to Barberini, Cervia, Dec. 15, 1633. For an account of P. Alessandro's mission to England, cf. P. DAVID DE PORTO-GRUARO, *Il P. Giacinto dei Conti Natta da Casale e la sua opera attraverso i dispacci degli ambasciatori veneti* (1621-1627), in *Archivio Veneto*, vol. V (1929), pp. 176-211.

ground, — a most pernicious procedure, he thought, and one that could not be carried through without violation of his secret. He was ready enough to follow del Bagno's advice and agree to a Papal envoy being sent to England, alone or with him, but he wanted the Cardinal Secretary to adopt no resolution without consulting him, otherwise all would be spoilt. It was essential for the person chosen to have the confidence of the King, lest he incur his Majesty's suspicion and jealousy, — this tendency to mistrust could be seen in the relations between Douglas himself and the Roman authorities.

The Scottish envoy was determined that he and no one else should declare so important a point as the King's attitude of mind. He would have to report, too, on how the Pope had regarded the letters sent from England for Cardinal del Bagno and Padre Alessandro, with which the negotiations had begun. His Majesty would be mightily offended (this was Alessandro reporting Douglas), if he saw the affair pass into other hands, seeing that Alessandro had so often had dealings with the English Court. If he were again sent to England, less suspicion would be given than by anyone else sent on one pretext or other with many points to treat of.

Alessandro himself (he swore to this in all conscience) was most averse to going again to England and was anxious that neither the Pope nor Barberini should entertain false notions of his ambitions. He thought that someone should go to congratulate the Queen on her safe delivery and to settle the disputes of the Seculars and Regulars. Douglas, while agreeing that the Pope and Barberini should pick the person they thought most suited to the task, would have liked Alessandro to have gone as well, but the Capuchin had dissuaded him from pressing this point on del Bagno and he was now himself writing to ask the latter to try and keep him out of the whole affair. [1]

It was clear what Alessandro really wanted (he subsequently changed his tune) so Cardinal del Bagno, also modifying his earlier view, wrote suggesting that Barberini should overlook his mistrust of Alessandro and consider sending him to England. Whatever his

---

[1] *B.L.* 8656, ff. 133-136 : Alessandro to Bagno, Dec. 10, enclosed with Bagno's letter to Barberini, Dec. 21, 1633.

defects he would do his best. Choice of him would go a long way towards allaying Spanish suspicion and jealousy of the mission, for he had formerly served both Spain and the Emperor. Whoever was sent with him could deal with the clerical controversies and tender the Pope's congratulations to the Queen. Best of all, choice of Alessandro would send Douglas away satisfied and would leave those in Rome no room for regret at not trying all possible means to meet the English demands. [1]

While del Bagno was sending the Cardinal Secretary this sound advice as to the most satisfactory means of disposing of Douglas without giving away too much, the Scot was growing even more impatient at what he termed " a clearly hostile want of confidence and a highly dangerous irresoluteness." [2] He complained that not the slightest satisfaction had been given him on the principal point of his mission, namely, the conversion of the King and his realm.

Another cause of irritation to Douglas was that the secret of his mission had leaked out in Rome. Somebody, taking him for a Frenchman, had retailed the whole affair to him with an amazing wealth of detail. [3] There was common talk of a lay gentleman having come to Rome to declare the King of Great Britain's intention of becoming a Catholic; and the Pope, it was said, was looking round for a learned man suitable to send to England to deal with the matter.

That these stories should be bandied about when the authorities seemed so off-hand with him irritated Douglas in the extreme. In six weeks he had been unable to make the slightest progress, he grumbled. The Papal audience, so frequently promised, had not been forthcoming. He had not even seen the Cardinal Secretary despite Alessandro's request for an audience for him. He was left to draw one of two conclusions, — either Rome had a clear aversion

---

[1] *Ibid.*, ff. 130-131 : Bagno to Barberini, Dec. 21, Card. del Bagno also enclosed, as his chief had requested, a draft of his reply, containing nothing but generalities and expressions of goodwill, to Stirling's letter. He explained to Barberini the length of this letter by saying the English would see in brevity only subtlety and double-meaning : " Hò havuto riguardo che quella natione difficilissima (*sic !*) se vi n'è altra in Europa suol pigliar per cupezza il poco dire. "

[2] *Ibid.*, f. 143 : Douglas to Bagno, Dec. 17 : " ...manifesta diffidenza, freddenza et pericolosissima irresolutione. "

[3] *Ibid.*, ff. 141-142 : Alessandro to Bagno, Rome, Dec. 17, 1633.

to the whole business or she distrusted him personally, since she was refusing to treat with him either directly or through an intermediary. And now he heard they were thinking of sending a man to England without saying a word to him ; if they had only treated confidentially with him, Douglas protested to del Bagno, they would have already discovered the genuine good faith of his mission. It was not his affair, he allowed, to decide whether a Papal envoy should be sent to England or not, although if the man were unknown and went without him, the effect would be disastrous. What he did object to was the fact that the whole business had been taken out of the hands of those officially concerned with it.

Douglas concluded his criticism by declaring that,with irresponsible persons spreading rumours and the authorities showing him no confidence, he could stay in Rome no longer. He would wait over the Christmas holidays, call on del Bagno at Cervia and go back to England with a clear conscience and but one consolation : they at least spoke well in Rome of the King's good dispositions. [1]

Probably both Douglas and Alessandro counted on del Bagno's forwarding their letters to the Cardinal Secretary. They were not the less outspoken for that, seeing their opportunity of saying through del Bagno what they could not tell Barberini to his face.

The Cardinal Secretary duly acknowledged del Bagno's advice and the letters he enclosed, but complained that pressure of business before the holidays, coupled with the demands the Christmas services made on his time, quite disabled him from dealing with the English affair till later. Another delay for Douglas. [2]

So overworked was the Cardinal Secretary of State that again after the Christmas holidays he wrote bemoaning his lack of time and frankly confessing that it was only on January 4 that he first read del Bagno's letters (with the enclosures referred to above) of December 7, 15, 21 and 28.

Realizing at last the urgency of Douglas's case, Barberini promised to give him an audience the following day, January 5. At the same time he dismissed his complaints at the secret of his mission being known as a figment of his and Alessandro's imagination, or else a mere trick to hurry matters along. [3]

---

[1] *Ibid.*, f. 143 : Douglas to Bagno, Dec. 17, 1633.
[2] *Ibid.*, f. 148 : Barberini to Bagno, Dec. 28, 1633.
[3] *Ibid.*, f. 150 : Barberini to Bagno, Jan. 4, 1634.

True to his word, or with but one day's difference, the Cardinal Secretary duly received Douglas and Alessandro on January 6, urging the Scot to stay on in Rome as the best means of reaching the goal of his negotiations. This Douglas refused to do. Barberini then explained that, much as the Pope would like to create an English Cardinal, he was unwilling to pledge himself ; for, were such an election attributed to the good offices of the English Queen, the Holy Father would have claims from all the other Queens to contend with. Douglas, after several answers, held his peace, while Barberini went on to ask him not to take it amiss that the November promotion of Cardinals had passed without consideration of the claims of England. He said that the negotiations would be greatly helped when del Bagno came to Rome and advised Douglas to call on the Cardinal at Cervia. [1]

Within three weeks Douglas saw Barberini a second time, adding to his other demands the request for a man to be sent to Germany. The Cardinal, seeing his chance of breaking the Douglas-Alessandro combination, packed the Capuchin off to Vienna despite his show of reluctance. The reason for Douglas's demand was left vague (presumably he wanted the Emperor approached on the Palatinate problem), so del Bagno advised the Cardinal Secretary to give Alessandro whatever instructions he thought best. As the Capuchin had already been on missions to Germany, Spain and England in the general interests of peace in Christendom, Barberini could go over the points of his previous negotiations with him and easily find a title, such as the Pacification of Germany, for his latest venture. A testimony of goodwill could be had from Castelrodrigo, the Spanish Ambassador in Rome, and part of the mission could be to Bavaria.

In this way, del Bagno pointed out, three people could be gratified, — Douglas, by the choice of an envoy at his wish and to his liking ; the King of Spain, for it would appear to be pursuing his former policy ; the Duke of Bavaria, by the confidence thus shown in him. [2]

---

[1] *Ibid.*, f. 153 : Same to same, Rome, Jan. 7, 1634.

[2] *Ibid.*, ff. 168-169 : Bagno to Barberini, Cervia, Feb. 4, 1634. Del Bagno adds the informative remark that although the negotiations of Friars did not always give complete satisfaction, their use was considerable, seeing the access they had to the zealous Emperor, and the confidence placed in them by Olivares and even more by Richelieu.

It was eventually decided to give negotiation in favour of the Palatine's children as the specific purpose of Alessandro's mission — an end bound up with the service of religion. Douglas seemed satisfied and with his usual impatience asked for his letters of dismissal, *viz.* the official reply to Stirling ; but Barberini had sent del Bagno's draft back to him for revision and Douglas was told he could collect it when he called at Cervia. [1]

Cardinal del Bagno was delightedly surprised at Douglas's apparent contentment and attributed it to Barberini's usual dexterity and affability, but the latter, though glad to get Douglas off his hands, soon realized that the Scot's readiness to leave did not mean he would go home pleased, and he asked del Bagno to reassure him. He also sent for Douglas again and promised that a Papal Agent would be sent to discover the true cause of dissension among the clergy and to find an adequate remedy. He also agreed to an exchange of Residents between the Pope and the Queen ; with this Douglas was especially pleased as it would go far towards making his Roman mission a success. [2]

Though there is no record of Douglas's having treated directly with the Pope, he submitted a questionnaire to which Urban obligingly added marginal answers, illuminating in their vagueness and explaining why Douglas went home somewhat disillusioned.

To the question " What had Catholics to hope for from the Pope in an outbreak of persecution ? " Urban answered that he would always champion their cause and had in fact already placed them under the care of his nephew. [3]

" What aid would be given to the Queen for the advancement of the Catholic Faith and the stabilization of her own position in the event of the King's death ? " No specific measures could be guaranteed, was the Pope's reply, seeing that no one could foretell the future state of the world.

Next, the Holy Father was petitioned to further the peaceful restitution of the Palatinate and to send a confidential agent to Germany in support the aims of the King of England. Urban's answer was to refer Douglas to his nephew ; he added that Cardinal del Bagno could be consulted. The result has already been seen.

Finally, the Pope was asked to allow Douglas to warn the King

[1] *Ibid.*, ff. 161-163 : Barberini to Bagno, Jan. 28, Feb. 1, 1634.

[2] *Ibid.*, ff. 171, 173-174 : Barberini to Bagno, Feb. 10, 11, 1634.

[3] Francesco Barberini had succeeded Cardinal Farnese in 1626 as Cardinal Protector of England and Scotland.

officially of the harm that could come to his kingdoms if the differences of the Catholic missionaries were left unsettled. This bold request Urban answered by saying that Douglas would do better to allude to the matter only in a general way, as the details of the problem seemed to touch the province of politics and were therefore outside the ambit of papal jurisdiction. The Pope thought, nevertheless, that Douglas could drop a hint that foreign sovereigns were maintaining two parties in England and using them to get news of all went on at Court. [1]

To this series of questions, Douglas added a number of points on which he asked leave to speak in the Pope's name on his return :

(1) that the King should in no way allow the Catholics to be harrassed by the Pursuivants, who served no useful purpose and only alienated Catholics from the Crown ;

(2) that his Majesty be pleased to remit the fines of the Catholics ;

(3) that his Majesty declare his mind on the question of his Catholic subjects having one or more bishops over them ;

(4) that his Majesty be pleased to send a Resident to the Papal Court in the Queen's name and to allow an agent of the Pope to reside in London under the protection of the Queen. In this way a number of difficulties could be settled.

Whether or no Douglas ever received a mandate to put these points to the King does not appear. Possibly, as the list was forwarded to Cardinal del Bagno, Barberini left it to the latter to discuss them with Douglas in a general way only. This rôle the ex-Nuncio could play to perfection, for the Scot was delighted with the welcome he received at Cervia on his way home. The Cardinal touched most kindly on all the points of his mission, handed him a letter for Stirling and gave him wise counsel and a warning as to how much he might legitimately hope for the future. [2]

Douglas and Stirling's son, Alexander, were royally entertained at Cervia and then sent off to Florence, whence they proceeded to England via Leghorn, Genoa and Marseilles. [3] Douglas stayed some time in Paris awaiting the mandate he had asked for, but nothing came and in July he crossed the Channel. [4]

---

[1] B.L. 8656, f. 175 : Enclosure A. in Barberini's letter to Bagno, Feb. 11, 1634. Cf. App. IV.

[2] Ibid., f. 186 : Douglas to Barberini, Cervia, no date (between Feb. 11-19). Cf. App. IV.

[3] Ibid., ff. 188-189 : Bagno to Barberini, Feb. 17, 1634.

[4] B.L. 8616, ff. 38, 39 : Douglas to Barberini, Paris, April 2, 22 July, 1634.

CHAPTER VI

INTERCHANGE OF COURTESIES

MARIA *laeto nomine, nomine*
Quod terra adorat quod celebrat polus:
Tu iunge concordes in aevum
PONTIFICIS CAROLIQUE *dextras.*

. . . .

Io MARIAE *cum* CAROLI ROSIS,
Spargantur astris aemula LILIA,
Laetis ubi VRBANI *susurris*
Mellificum satietur agmen. [1]

Although Sir Robert Douglas had not the satisfaction of knowing it, preliminary steps towards sending an envoy to England had been taken before he left Italy. On Sunday morning, February 5, 1634 (N. S.), the Cardinal Secretary sent for one Gregorio Panzani to tell him in the strictest confidence that he was thinking of sending him to England. [2]

About the time Panzani was being interviewed in Rome, Dom Leander a Sancto Martino, President-General of the English Benedictines and Prior of Douai, crossed the Channel with a royal permit and under orders from the Holy See to report on the situation of the Catholics in England. [3] He quickly compiled

---

[1] From *Faelicitas Ominata,* an Ode by a boy of 15, the nephew of George Fortescue (Cf. GILLOW, *op. cit.,* vol. II, p. 325). Panzani sent the poem in MS. to Cardinal Barberini (*B.L.* 8637, f. 1: Panzani to Barberini, May 7, 1635).

[2] Panzani was a priest of *Chiesa Nuova* (St Philip's Oratory), and on returning from England became Bishop of Mileto (1640-1661) (Cf. D. TACCONE-GALUCCI, *Cronotassi dei metropolitani, arcivescovi e vescovi della Calabria,* Tropea, 1902). There is also a short notice of Panzani by Alexander VII (Fabio Chigi) in the Vatican Library, MSS. *Chigi,* M. I. 23, f. 1.

[3] Leander, the name in religion of John Jones, *alias* Scudamore, or Skidmore, born c. 1575 in Llan Winach, Brecknockshire. He went to Merchant Taylors' and St John's College, Oxford, where he studied law, exhibiting a fascinating

statistics of the missionaries and sounded the Catholics in general and the Regulars in particular on the Bishop question, he himself naturally deprecating the appointment of a successor to the heartily disliked Bishop Smith, and suggesting another Archpriest. [1]

But Father Leander soon saw that the Oath of Allegiance was at the root of all the troubles of the Catholics, both among themselves and with the Government. Showing considerable courage, if less tact, he penned a number of strongly worded letters to Pope Urban, to the Cardinal Secretary and to Cardinal Bentivoglio, an ex-Nuncio of Brussels and Paris and a personal friend of his, urging a more tolerant attitude towards the Oath and advising that a check be put upon books by English Catholics extolling to excess the authority of Rome. The King was kindly disposed towards the Pope and Catholics in general, he wrote, but felt very strongly on the Oath question and, as he had declared that he demanded a purely civil allegiance without any interference with the Pope's spiritual jurisdiction, he could not understand Rome's steadfast opposition to the Oath. If it continued, Dom Leander hinted, the King's natural sympathy would be alienated and the Catholics fall under further penalties.

The Benedictine said he had taken counsel with several Catholic noblemen, moderate and prudent in their views, and all were of one mind, — that the Oath in the King's intention was quite

---

eloquence and subtle judgment. An interest in religious disputations bringing him under suspicion of being a Catholic at heart, his position was settled by a chance meeting with a Jesuit in disguise. Leaving Oxford to study theology with the Jesuits at Valladolid, he there joined the Benedictines of St Martin's. After a brilliant D. D. at Salamanca and specialized studies at various monasteries, he became in quick succession Novice-Master at Douai (1608), Vicar-General of the Spanish Benedictines in England (1612), first President General of the restored Anglo-Benedictine Congregation (1619-1621), Prior of Douai (1621-1625 ; 1629-1633), Abbot of Cismar (1629) ; Cathedral Prior of Canterburi (1633) and again President-General from 1633 till his death on Dec. 7, 1635, when he was buried in the Queen's new Chapel Royal at Somerset House, being *primitiae dormientium ibidem.* (Cf. H. N. BIRT, *Obit Book of the English Benedictines,* s.v. *John Jones* ; GILLOW, *op. cit.,* vol. III, pp. 660-666 ; F. A. GASQUET in *Downside Review,* vol. IV, pp. 35-43.)

[1] Leander's letters to Rome are to be found in *Clarendon State Papers,* vol. I, *passim.* They are treated with some fullness in CHARLES BUTLER's *Historical Memoirs of the English Catholics,* vol. II, pp. 316 seq., and by T. DUNBAR INGRAM, *England and Rome,* pp. 381 seq.

different from what Paul V had thought when he had condemned it, and that therefore the present Pope should revoke all decrees that had been issued against the Oath, especially seeing that the rejection by clergy, nobility and people of the Deposing Power was tolerated in France. The Englishman also suggested that the Pope should send Charles a friendly letter ; there was no reason why he should not, when he wrote to pagan princes in India and to the schismatic sovereigns of Abyssinia. Counsels of kindness were called for ; the wounds England had suffered in the wrench from Rome needed the touch of a gentle hand rather than the thunder of excommunications or the lightning of prohibitions.

Leander thereupon forwarded to Rome a specimen letter from the Pope to the English King, together with a minute analysis of the current Oaths, a new one of his own, and a memorandum on the points of dogmatic contact between Catholics and Anglicans. [1]

But the Benedictine's zeal had over-ridden his discretion. His suggestions met with a cool reception in Rome, his orthodoxy was even questioned, and he was careful never to leave the country again, the official Agent from Rome having in the meantime arrived in England. [2]

During the first part of Leander's negotiation in England Panzani stood awaiting further orders in Rome. On August 24, six months after he had been interviewed by Barberini, he had his farewell audience of Urban who spoke at some length of his hope of Charles's conversion, which would have taken place before, he thought, but for the King's fear of his nephews, the young Princes Palatine, acknowledged champions of Protestantism. [3]

---

[1] For all these documents, cf. *Clarendon State Papers*, vol. I, p. 129 : Leander to Cardinal Bentivoglio, July 12/22, 1634 ; p. 169 : to Urban VIII, Nov. 15/25, 1634 ; p. 180 : to Barberini, Dec. 8/18, 16/26, 17/27, 1634 (this last including his Oath formula). For a more detailed account of Leander's views on the Oath v. *infra*, Chap. XI. This *Instructions relating to the reconciliation of moderate Papists and Protestants* (*ibid.*, vol. I, pp. 207-208) are dealt with *infra*, Chap. VII.

[2] *Ibid.*, vol. I, p. 106 : *Leander's letter to Windebank craving protection*. In response to this Windebank begged Panzani in Feb., 1635, to obtain leave for Leander to remain a further six months in England on a pretext of arranging the exchange of agents between England and Rome (*P. R. O. Rom. Trans.* : Panzani to Barberini, Feb. 9, 1635). See also INGRAM, *op. cit.*, p. 389.

[3] *Arch. Vat., Nunz. d'Inghilterra* 3A (Panzani's Diary), ff. 3, 23-24. Frederick V,

Bearing letters of credence for Cardinals del Bagno and Bichi, for Father Robert Philip, and Douglas, the new Agent left Rome on August 28 for Ghiaggiolo, where Cardinal del Bagno was again taking a cure for his gout. On Tuesday, September 5, Panzani supped with the ex-Nuncio, who gave him some idea of the task ahead, — the difficulty of settling the disputes of the English Catholics to the satisfaction of all, the calumnies that would be levelled against him, and the danger of his name becoming linked with that of any of the foreign Ambassadors in London. The Cardinal was not optimistic of the conversion of the King, whom he regarded as lacking in learning, dull and not to be convinced by reason ; moveover, being extremely timorous, he was unlikely to take a step that politically would be highly hazardous for him. The Queen, who was ardently Catholic and strongly swayed by her Confessor, Father Philip, could of course do much, for Charles was devoted to her, but, added del Bagno cynically, she and her ladies were fully occupied with dancing and balls. He was equally sceptical of the genuineness of their Majesties' desire for an English Cardinal and said that the recommendations Douglas had brought gave the impression of having been written with some reluctance.

Returning to the same point the next day, del Bagno warned Panzani against the use of the term Protestant as the Archbishop of Canterbury was not hostile to Rome and, he had reason to think, had some pretentions to the purple. [1] Del Bagno then

---

Charles's brother-in-law had died Nov. 19, 1632, leaving three sons : Charles Louis, Maurice and Rupert, and one daughter Sophia, from whom the Hanoverian Georges descended.

[1] This remark of the well-informed and by no means credulous ex-Nuncio is interesting in view of the offer of a Red Hat made to Laud the previous year by some person who remains anonymous and is generally supposed to have acted without authority. The entries in Laud's *Diary* (*ed. cit.*, p. 219) are as follows :

" A.D. 1633, Aug. 4, Sunday, *News came to Court of the Lord Archbishop of Canterbury's death ; and the King resolved presently to give it to me.*

Aug. 4. *That very morning at Greenwich, there came one to me, seriously, and that avowed ability to perform it, and offered me to be a Cardinal*: *I went presently to the King, and acquainted him both with the thing and the person.*

Aug. 17, Saturday, *I had a serious offer made me again to be a Cardinal... I acquainted his Majesty with it. But my answer again was, that somewhat dwelt within me, which would not suffer that, till Rome were other than it is.*"

Various guesses have been made at the identity of the personage who

passed to the problem of the English Catholics. At the bottom of all their quarrels was private interest, — the Jesuits were too clever for the rest, so all were ranged against them. Still the Cardinal said he did not see how a bishop could be denied to the English clergy, and that for his part he would have appointed three. Lastly, he advised Panzani to make priests circulate through the country, as they were inclined to succumb to the comforts of life in London. On September 7, after adding some biographical notes on the personalities Panzani was likely to meet, del Bagno sent him on his way. [1]

The Agent arrived in London on December 15 (o.s.) to be met by Father Philip and the next day presented to the Queen, whom he thanked in the name of the Pope and his nephew for the cessation of persecution in England. He also handed her his credentials, saying he had come to find out her sentiments regarding the affairs of the English Catholics, whom his Holiness desired always to show a loyal obedience to the King. [2]

This the Queen retailed to Charles, who seemed pleased at Panzani's coming, only warning him to work quietly and avoid meddling in affairs of state, as he did not wish it to be thought that the Pope's envoy was accredited to him. [3]

Panzani's mission had been carefully confined to the task of uniting the Catholics, particulary the secular and regular clergy, acutely divided, first on the necessity or expediency of their having a bishop to rule them, then on the lawfulness of taking the Oath of Allegiance. Barberini told him to keep strictly aloof from

provoked this half-regretful refusal from Laud. Was it Père Gilles Chaissy, the Observant Friar who in the day of Laud's trials was so eager to convert him? Or Dom Leander, who always retained the friendship Laud had sworn him when the two had shared rooms in their undergraduate days at St John's, Oxford? This circumstance and the boldness of Leander's other proposals already mentioned point to him as the one most likely to have made the offer, yet it is doubtful if he was in England at the time, as it was only in the autumn of 1633 that he applied to Secretary Windebank for a royal warrant to return to the contry (Cf. *Clarendon S.P.,loc. cit.*). The offer was most probably made by some ecclesiastic in the Queen's entourage, possibly by Dom David Codner, *alias* Matthew Savage, at Leander's suggestion.

[1] *Arch. Vat., Nunziatura d'Inghilterra* 3A (Panzani's Diary), ff. 25 seq.

[2] *B.L.* 8632, No 2 : Barberini to Henrietta, — 1634. *P.R.O. Rom. Trans.* : Panzani to Barberini, Dec. 18/28, 1634.

[3] *Ibid.* : Panzani to Barberini, Dec. 24/Jan. 3, 1634-5.

discussing with non-Catholics likely concessions from Rome on the Oath and Reunion questions, a *Mare Magnum* wherein he might easily come to grief. [1]

Though Panzani was not officially accredited to the Queen's Court, he found a lodging in the heart of affairs by St Martin's-in-the-Fields and was soon taken up by men of standing, in particular by Mr Secretary Windebank. On all sides he heard it hinted how graceful a gesture it would be, in view of the Agent's reception in England, for the Pope to write to Charles, as father to son, thanking him for stopping the persecution of the Catholics. Barberini did not welcome the suggestion, which had already been pressed by Dom Leander to the point of importunity. The Cardinal insisted that if Urban wrote at all it would be to exhort the King to conversion but, as this was as yet unlikely, his Holiness would not risk being laughed at. As Panzani persisted in the request the Cardinal silenced him once and for all by saying there could be no correspondence with heretics. [2]

This intransigence did not hold for the Queen for several letters had already passed between Urban and his godchild. As Windebank grew more friendly with Panzani there was question of an exchange of agents between the Pope and Henrietta — a courtesy correspondance which would also keep Charles covertly in close relationship with the Holy See.

In answer to Panzani's query Windebank guaranteed that, if a Papal Agent were sent to England as " a step towards reunion," he would enjoy the privileges of other royal ambassadors and could maintain a public chapel. The Secretary was anxious, however, for this to be kept a close secret, as he said he had no orders to speak for the King and, although Panzani pointed out that a recommendation to Rome would mean little unless it could

---

[1] *Ibid.*: Barberini to Panzani, April 15/25, 1635. How far Panzani disobeyed this injunction, at least regarding the Reunion question, will be seen in the next Chapter. The limitations of Panzani's mandate are clearly set out in the Papal Brief introducing the Agent. Cf. *Arch. Vat.*, *Epist. ad Principes*, vol. XLIX, N° 127 : Urban to the English Clergy, Secular and Regular (*Ut dissidia inter ipsos tollantur, mittitur Gregorius Panzanus*), Castelgandolfo, Oct. 10, 1634.

[2] *Ibid.* : Panzani to Barberini, Dec. 24 /Jan. 3, 1634/5 ; Jan. 7/17, March 13/23 ; Barberini to Panzani, Feb. 18/28, March. 3/13, 18/28, 1635. *Calendar of State Papers, Domestic* (1635), p. 457.

QUEEN HENRIETTA MARIA
(From the Barberini Collection.)

be made with Windebank's authority as Secretary, the latter was adamant and referred the Agent to the Queen for a command to write. [1]

But Windebank's caution was only to safeguard himself, and he soon spoke to Charles of the project. The King was willing enough for his wife to have a Resident in Rome but he was fearful of a Puritan outcry if she openly received the Pope's man in London. The Secretary then waited on the Queen and, with her promise of help, he told Panzani he would try the King again and had hopes of winning him over.

Windebank seemed to know nothing of Douglas's mission, nor was it mentioned by the King and Queen, but Father Philip, discussing an exchange of agents with Panzani, told him the whole business had been arranged by Douglas and then postponed. [2]

The Cardinal Secretary raised no objection to Panzani's talking of a mutual correspondence with whomsoever he would, — indeed, to sound the genuineness of Douglas's proposals was part of his general mandate, but Barberini, suspicious that the King and his ministers were working purely for their own ends, wanted Panzani, without committing himself, to get them to specify their aims and, as a warranty of their friendly intentions, to suppress the Pursuivants. Father Philip should be asked to urge this on the Queen. [3]

In the meantime Lord Cottington had taken a hand in moving Charles to agree to the exchange of agents. In May, 1635, the King consented, insisting however on reserving to himself the nomination of the man to go to Rome. The Queen inclined to Douglas but Charles wanted to know if he were partial to the Jesuits and in the confidence of Windebank and Cottington. He also asked for the matter to be kept a dead secret, as he was not discussing it in Council. The Lord Treasurer was delighted to tell the Queen and Panzani of his success and asked the latter if he was likely to stay on as Papal Agent in London. If not, he advised the appointment of a layman, since either priest or friar would be partial to his own set. Neither Frenchman nor Spaniard must come, since neutrality and discretion were essential. [4]

[1] *Ibid.* : Panzani to Barberini, Feb. 20/Mar. 2, 1635.
[2] *Ibid.* : Panzani to Barberini, Mar. 20/30, Apr. 3/13, 1635.
[3] *Ibid.* : Barberini to Panzani, May 23, 1635.
[4] *Ibid.* : Panzani to Barberini, May 20/30, June 3/13, 1635.

After consultation with Father Philip, Panzani was able to add to the requirements Cottington had specified, — the Papal Agent must be a man of fine presence, noble, rich enough to keep a fine table and household (his servants must show a certain liberality with the shopkeepers), of exemplary life though of no strait-laced piety, and not too close a confidant of the Jesuits. Father Philip further suggested that, if he were a man destined for promotion to one of the major Nunciatures, it would add considerably to his influence and prestige.

He must know French well, as all the Court does, and remember to keep on the right side of the Queen, who, being young, likes perfumes, beautiful dresses and witty conversation. Likewise must he pay homage to all her Ladies, through whom much business had to be done at the English Court. Here Panzani was quick to add the warning that such attentions must never be open to wrong interpretation, as the English, with the irreproachable example of the King and Queen before them, took scandal at the slightest thing.

Father Philip told Panzani that all his Majesty's ministers were venal and that therefore the Papal Agent should be able to buy them over through the Queen. Jewels sent ostensibly for her Majesty could be passed on. In this way the King and Privy Council could be influenced to check pursuivant and common informer. This would amount to tacit liberty of conscience, which later he could persuade the King and the Archbishop of Canterbury to make express. In three years, predicted Father Philip enthusiastically, Parliament would revoke the Penal Laws, and the country return to its former Faith by uniting with the Holy See. [1]

At the same time Panzani wrote that Charles had consented to the appointment of Sir Robert Douglas as the Queen's first Roman Agent. Barberini had previously written to say that Douglas had made a good impression on his visit to Rome and he seemed agreeable to his coming again but, on learning that Sir Robert had charge of a company of Scots in a French regiment, the Cardinal was obliged to write that Douglas would be suspect of leanings towards France and was therefore *persona non grata*. This veto, fortunately, had no effect on the negotiations, as a little later news arrived of Douglas's death. [2]

---

[1] *Ibid.*, Panzani to Barberini, June 10/20, 17/27, 1635.
[2] *Ibid.*, Barberini to Panzani, July 5, Aug. 1, 1635.

The Cardinal Secretary saw the reasonableness of Cottington's stipulations concerning the Agent for England and said the same would apply *a fortiori* to the Queen's man sent to Rome, where he would be beset on all sides in the interests of the various sovereigns. When he read the list of qualities Panzani and Father Philip demanded, Barberini confessed that the man possessing them was a *rara avis* indeed and asked if, as Montagu wrote, George Con would be acceptable. [1]

Panzani said he thought so. Con seemed well qualified for the post and would like it, while the Queen's sponsorship of his advancement to the purple would spur him on to earn the honour. On the other hand the King was counting on Con to advise the Queen's agent in Rome. Besides, as a British subject in the papal diplomatic service, he would be owing a two-fold allegiance ; for this reason he would be better suited as a bishop for England, though, as this would necessitate his lying very low, it would be quite incompatible with the office of agent at Court. [2]

Panzani was more than satisfied with his preliminary success. Charles had told him great changes would be seen if the Pope sent a legate to England, and the Italian looked on the Agency as a real step towards reunion. He and Cottington gave themselves mutual encouragement by telling each other how the artificial barrier of prejudice was already breaking down. No longer was the Pope referred to as the Beast athirst for the blood of Englishmen, fiercely hostile to the nation, intractable, mean ; no longer in Rome was the English King called a tyrant, or the people, barbarous, cruel, untrustworthy. Lavishly praising the friendliness of Pope Urban and his nephew, Panzani waxed lyrical in his hope that the British Rose would one day offer honeyed pastures to the Bees of Urban ! [3]

---

[1] *Ibid., Trans.* 10, 10 : [Barberini] alla cifra di 30 Maggio, 1635. *Ibid.*, Barberini to Panzani, Aug. 1, 1635.

[2] *Ibid.* : Panzani to Barberini, Sept. 2/12, Oct. 21/31, 1635.

[3] *Ibid.* : Panzani to Barberini, July 1/11, July 29/Aug. 8, 1635 : " Dopo Dio si deve à S. Sta et à V. Emza chi con le loro lodevoli attioni hanno sparso tanto odore, che infino la Rosa Britannica cerca di parteciparne, desiderosa forse un giorno di dare soavissime pascole alle Api Urbane." — A pretty conceit, as Urban's family arms comprised three bees. It seems a pity that the poetry of the picture should be spoilt by the remark that the bees in the Barberini escutcheon embarked on their heraldic career as horse flies (Cf. D. L. GALBREATH, *Papal Heraldry*, p. 97).

In more practical vein Cardinal Barberini answered that the true road to reunion was for the King and his Ministers to examine the causes of England's break with the Holy See and see how trivial and contemptible they were, — no step could be taken till this was admitted. [1]

Panzani now tackled the task of finding a substitute for Douglas. Urging the Queen to action, he reminded her of her all-powerful influence over Cottington and Windebank as well as the King. With a personal agent in Rome she would be greater than the Empress, who had none. Panzani told her later that he expected her to emulate Bertha, who first brought Christianity to the English and was, like her, of Gallic blood. Greatly flattered, Henrietta promised every effort. [2]

The choice was considerably restricted during the summer owing to the absence from Court of the nobility and therefore of the most likely candidates for the new post. Expense was a consideration, and Barberini, as an incentive to a decision, offered to lodge the Agent with religious in Rome and to keep him *au courant* with all news not prejudicial to other princes. [3]

At length Panzani wrote to say Sir Arthur Brett, [4] a great favourite with Charles and Henrietta, was the most likely choice but, as he had been thrown from his horse at the end of September, and later laid low with fever, his appointment was indefinitely postponed. Panzani went to Hampton Court to see him and was impressed by his fine presence, — he had been a captain in the army. Brett was well versed in the current controversies of the English Catholics though, to the volatile Italian, he seemed a little tongue-tied.

By the middle of October Brett had recovered sufficiently to interview Charles, Cottington and Windebank, — the last-named telling him that, apart from his work for the Queen, the King

[1] *Ibid.* : Barberini to Panzani, Sept. 16/26, 1635.

[2] *Ibid.* : Panzani to Barberini, Aug. 26/Sept. 5, Oct. 21/31, 1635.

[3] *Ibid.* : Barberini to Panzani, Aug. 5/15, 1635.

[4] In 1623, a handsome young Gentleman-of-the-Bedchamber, Brett had been considered by his brother-in-law, Middlesex, then Lord Treasurer, as a possible rival to Buckingham for James's royal favour ; but the favourite was shrewd enough to make friends with him, having him knighted and packed off to the Continent for a year's travel (Cf. S. R. GARDINER, *History*, vol. V, p. 6).

wished to confide a secret negotiation to him under a special cipher. (It was the Palatinate problem, in Panzani's opinion.) George Con would be his adviser in Rome, though in addition he was to consult Cardinals del Bagno, Spada, and perhaps Bichi, — all ex-Nuncios who had had dealings with England. [1]

Early in November Brett was handed his Instructions by Charles who impressed two important facts upon him, — that in these times of differences in religion he was not to meddle in such matters, save on points of which he was specifically ordered to treat. Secondly, in all his dealings with Pope and Cardinals he was to style himself the Queen's servant only and not pretend to any mandate from the King, but even to go out of his way to disavow the latter's connection with his mission. " Nevertheless," Charles continued, " ...this must not slacken your diligence in any service that may concern us ; to the advancement whereof you are to have a special eye... which, that you may the better perform, you shall hold a strait intelligence with our Secretary Windebank."

The items of religion the Agent was expressly ordered to negotiate were first the project, now threatening to come up again, of appointing a Catholic Bishop for England. Charles flatly refused to tolerate a foreign jurisdiction rivalling that of the Church of England, — they would fight with each other, raise dissensions in both Church and State and perhaps prove the utter ruin of the Catholics.

Next there was the Oath question on which the King felt even more strongly. The Agent, after representing " unto them there the happy estate and condition of the Roman Catholick party here under our mild government," was to ask that the Catholics might be told to keep from faction and sedition, the best remedy for which was the settling of outstanding differences on the Oath of Allegiance.

The Agent was to press the Pope to consider the current formula more favourably and to revoke or suspend such briefs or censures as he had issued against the Oath and those that took it, seeing that " the only scope and intent is civil, and refers merely to govern-

[1] *P.R.O. Rom. Trans.* : Panzani to Barberini, Sept. 9/19 ; Oct. 7/17, 14/24, 1635.

ment, and was made to distinguish loyal and disloyal Roman Catholicks." Charles went on to insist: "We desire nothing more than to be assured of that fidelity of our subjects which is due to us by the laws of God and Man; and without which we can neither be sure of them, nor of the safety of our person nor state, but shall ever be in distrust and jealousy of them."

The Agent was therefore to plead for relief for those whose conscience bade them refuse the Oath, and for a gentle hand towards those who had seen their way to taking it. " Without satisfaction in this business of the Oath," the King concluded, " you must assure them there can be no good intelligence between us and that party. "

Then, giving way to that obsession he had inherited from his father, Charles said he wanted the Pope to check the daily increase of the English Jesuits who, " being for the most part practicall and overbusy in matters of state, may become dangerous, and yet, [Charles's natural self breaks in here] we are not willing but upon great necessity to use remedies which our laws do provide against them."

Then came the third point the King had so much at heart — the peace of Christendom and his sister's welfare: he coupled the two, seeing in the restoration of the Prince Palatine the solution of the German politico-religious war that was harrowing Europe. " As the Pope is a temporal Prince," he said, " we shall not be unwilling to join with him, as we do with other Catholick Roman Princes, in any thing that may conduce to the peace of Christendom and of the Church. " What the Agent was to suggest was that this end could be reached by the restoration of the Prince Palatine. " You must well observe how the Pope will entertain this notion, and his carriage and answer thereupon."

A final recommendation to Brett was to follow in his negotiations the advice and assistance of Dom Wilfrid Reade, Procurator of the Benedictines, " of good affection in our service — one whom you may trust. " [1]

Together with these instructions Brett received letters of

---

[1] *Clarendon State Papers*, vol. I, pp. 354-357, *Instructions for Captain Arthur Brett sent to Rome by our dearest Consort the Queen...*, Hampton Court, Oct. 28, 1635 (signed and dated by the King).

credence for the Pope, the Cardinal Secretary and the College of Cardinals, — this last on Barberini's advice. Then at the last moment the appointment met with sudden opposition from the Spanish London Agent and from Cottington and Windebank, — pro-Spanish both. The Secretary said Brett was quite unfitted for the art of diplomacy and would be laughed at in Rome. There were money difficulties, too, for Cottington, the Lord Treasurer, refused the Agent anything more than £500 as his annual stipend.[1]

At length Brett embarked but had not gone far before he again contracted a violent fever and, after suffering a great deal from storms at sea, he decided to return and go by land. The King, who wanted him to leave as soon as possible, gave him till Easter, 1636, to get fit, but by that time he was dead.[2]

Panzani now noted a curious change at Court, where the Roman Agency became a topic of open discussion, even the Puritans proposing candidates as they would were an ordinary embassy in question. The two most likely were William Habington, the poet of *Castara*, and Sir William Hamilton, both Catholics as Brett had been. Hamilton, favoured by the Queen, was eventually chosen by Charles and straightway set to work to gather information of the affairs of the English Catholics.[3]

In the meantime, for the post of Papal Agent in England Con had been temporarily dropped for a Conte Ambrogio di Carpegna, brother of the Cardinal of that name and *gentilhuomo* to Cardinal Barberini. The latter went so far as to send Panzani details of the household he was to keep up, but Walter Montagu, who was in Rome in the spring of 1636, argued strongly for Con, and Barberini decided after all to send him to England, though the Pope stipulated that Panzani should also stay on for a short time with him.[4]

---

[1] *P.R.O. Rom. Trans.*: Panzani to Barberini, Oct. 21/31; Nov. 11/21; Barberini to Panzani, Oct. 28/Nov. 7, 1635.

[2] *Ibid.*: Panzani to Barberini, Feb. 3/13, 10/20; Feb. 24/March 5; Mar. 23/Apr. 2; Mar. 30/Apr. 9, 1636. Brett died March 17 (o.s.) Cf. *John Southcott's Notebook, Catholic Record Society*, vol. I, p. 109.

[3] *Ibid.*: Panzani to Barberini, Mar. 30/Apr. 9; Apr. 13/23, May 4/14, 1636. Hamilton was a young man of 25, speaking Italian well. He was brother to the Earl of Abercorn, and related to the Marquis of Hamilton, the Duke of Lennox, and Charles himself. Hamilton was given the same Instructions as Brett. Cf. *B.L.* 8645, f. 28 : Con to Ferragalli, Aug. 8/18, 1636.

[4] *Ibid.*: Barberini to Panzani, Dec. 5, 1635; Feb. 14, Mar. 27; Apr. 10,

At the choice of two Scots, Hamilton and Con, for this important diplomatic venture, there were many murmurs among the English. Even Laud, the Archbishop, remarked to a Catholic, " Is it possible that among us Catholics (sic) there is not one fit to go to Rome?" That the Agency would meet with opposition from many English Catholics as well as Puritans, and possibly from all the Catholic Kings, Panzani had shamefacedly to admit. It soon became the talk of the Courts, particularly in Spain and Germany, and the general view seemed to be that the Puritans were only tolerating the reciprocal Agency as the restoration of the Calvinist Prince Palatine was one of the chief points to be treated. This irritated Cardinal Barberini and he insisted that at least the Holy Father's sole aim was the good of the Faith and the salvation of souls, — in particular that of the King of England. [1] It was, nevertheless, true as far as Charles was concerned that he had given Hamilton the same instructions as Brett and that they included a secret commission to negotiate a settlement of the Palatinate and the Oath questions on the King's behalf.

Leaving England in May, Hamilton arrived in Rome at the end of June, 1636, and was lodged at the Theatine convent of San Silvestro on Monte Cavallo. He was given a great welcome in Rome, and the return of England to union with the Holy See was spoken of high-spiritedly as a mere matter of days. In his first audience Hamilton talked eloquently of the Queen's piety and loyalty to the Holy See and then hinted at the King's hopes regarding the Palatinate. In reply Urban spoke of the dispensation he had granted for the marriage of Charles and Henrietta, and then referred to his time as Nuncie when he had been Protector of Scotland, declaring that at that time he would have got into touch with King James but for the Gunpowder Plot. [2]

When passing through Nice Hamilton had met George Con. The latter was on his way to London and, as the rumour of his approach ran around Town, the Spanish Resident declared half-mockingly

---

1636. Panzani to Barberini, Jan. 6/16, 1636. Father Philip was keen for Mazarin to be sent, as he thought he would be able to work on the young Prince Palatine who was in London, and a likely convert.

[1] *Ibid.* : Panzani to Barberini, May 18/28, May 31/June 10 (Barberini's marginal note) ; Barberini to Panzani, July 17, 1636.

[2] *Ibid.* : Barberini to Panzani, July 3, 17, 1636.

that the Papal Agent was coming in great pomp to receive the King into the Church. Panzani thought it wise to advise the Queen of this, that Charles might know whence the story came. Both were annoyed, but expressed their pleasure at Con's coming. Windebank, who heard the same tale, told Panzani he wished an Italian had been sent instead of Con as he would have met with less opposition. Panzani agreed. Already the Jesuits were being accused of discrediting the Agency, and of boasting that both Hamilton and Con were devoted to the Society. [1]

The Spanish Resident told Panzani bluntly that he disapproved of Con's coming. He would not say why, but asked what his mandate was. The general good of religion as opportunity offered, answered the Italian, and Hamilton had gone to Rome with the same aim. But the Spaniard was suspicious and said he would make further inquiries. The Agency would harm the cause of the Catholics, he declared, as the Spanish Ambassador, who hitherto had taken them under his wing, would not now be so eager and, since his influence was indubitably greater than the Papal Agent's was likely to be, the Catholics stood to lose. It was well known, he added cuttingly, that the Queen's name was only a cloak to shield the King's part in the Agency,— a strange rôle for the man who had broken his word to the Pope in his Marriage Contract. A little later the Spaniard was telling Con, who prudently paid him a courtesy visit, that he thoroughly approved of the Agency and would do all he could to help. [2]

George Con took ship at Dieppe on St Anne's Day, July 26, 1636, (N. S.), and was amused to find on landing at Rye next day that he was 10 days younger, for in England, where the Julian Calendar till held, it was only the 17th. After proceeding to London, he left immediately by river-boat for Windsor where the Court was. The Queen sent for him after Mass on Sunday, the 24th, and the Papal Agent presented his credentials and a jewelled cross from the Pope, which Henrietta delightedly fastened round her neck. Soon afterwards Charles came in and, giving his hand to Con in friendly fashion, spoke highly of him to the courtiers present. The Earls of Holland and Carnarvon, Lord Goring and others were

[1] *Ibid.* : Panzani to Barberini, June 7/17, June 21/July 1, 1636.
[2] *Ibid.* : Panzani to Barberini, Oct. 20/30, Oct. 27/Nov. 6, 1636.

there and as he left the Agent found himself besieged with invitations to supper.   He tactfully refused. [1]

The prestige of Con's position as the Pope's representative, the cordiality the King had shown him, together with his own courteous service of the Queen and ready wit, made him much sought after, and Panzani, accompanying him everywhere, bore generous witness to his popularity.   He soon found himself a guest at frequent banquets and, on an occasion when the Earl of Stirling proposed the health of Cardinal Barberini, Con, feeling as he afterwards admitted that in England he had more need of his head than of his stomach, asked leave to drink in small beer, a practice he continued. It was a neat gesture, showing he belonged to the country despite an absence of twenty-four years.

The courtiers, amazed at Charles's frank friendliness, were still in the dark as to the purpose of the Papal Agent's coming, and the King was content for them to remain so. With this Con was ready enough to comply and, when questioned by the inquisitive after an audience with Charles, he answered disarmingly that he had been discussing art with his Majesty, — which was the truth but not the whole truth, for both the King and Queen had shown the greatest eagerness to hear of Con's chances of promotion to the purple. [2]

Charles also referred to the Spanish *canard* about Con's coming to receive him into the Church.   In the Agent's opinion it was intended to raise discord between their Majesties and wreck the Agency. Charles agreed. " This is sheer malice, " he said, " but it shall cause no harm. " He thereafter made a point of picking Con out from among the courtiers and of praising the Pope and Barberini, while expressing his hopes for the peace and reunion of Christendom.

In implicit praise of his master the Papal Agent told Charles of Olivares's quarrel with the Madrid Nuncio some years before, when Urban had refused to join France and Spain in the League against England.   Con also spoke of Austrian jealousy at Urban's showing more interest in the King of England than in the heretic princes of Germany.   Charles acknowledged the Pope's friendliness

---

[1] *B.L.* 8639, ff. 21-22 : Con to Barberini, July 25/Aug. 4, 1636.

[2] *Ibid.*, ff. 26, 92 : Con to Barberini, Aug. 8/18, Sept. 14/24, 1636 ; *P.R.O. Rom. Trans.* : Panzani to Barberini, Sept. 16/26, Sept. 28/Oct. 8, Oct. 6/16, Oct. 20/30, 1636.

and further confessed that he also did not stand well with Spain and France, as he particularly resented Richelieu's insolence. This was equally displeasing to his Holiness, rejoined the Agent readily. [1]

Con went out of his way to keep on good terms with his fellow diplomats in London and, discussing the politics of Europe with them, was able to send Barberini a great deal of detailed news and advice that the Cardinal welcomed.

Both Olivares and Richelieu were astute enough to realize the significance of Con's position, enhanced by his quick friendship with the King and by his prospects, which then seemed rosy, of becoming a Cardinal. Olivares had known Con as a *gentilhuomo* in Barberini's train when he had visited Madrid as Legate, on which occasion he had asked the Scot to accept a present of 2,000 ducats. Now, in the spring of 1637, the Spanish Minister again proffered his patronage. Richelieu followed suit; showing the greatest concern in Con's career and in his and the Queen's work for the English Catholics, he actually offered him a million crowns if it would help him in any way! [2]

The Papal Agent continued to be lionized by the nobility, particularly by his own compatriots. There was hunting at the Earl of Northumberland's place at Ashby, when Con rode a horse the King had ridden and was afterwards presented with one of the two sets of antlers that formed the day's spoil. Then on to Oxford with the Marquis of Hamilton to see the Bodleian, — wonderful, he thought, but still a far cry from the Vatican Library. At Oxford Con and Panzani received an invitation from the Archbishop of Canterbury, through Duperron, the Queen's Almoner, to attend a banquet in honour of her Majesty at St John's, Laud's old College of which he had been president. They went to look over the Library, but would not attend the play given afterwards, as they did not wish to seem greedy of favour. [3]

In spite of this there were sneers that Con stood on the doorstep wherever he went waiting to be received as Apostolic Legate, but on Barberini's advice he took no notice and treated all the nobility

---

[1] *B.L.* 8639, f. 26 : Con to Barberini, Aug. 8/18, Sept. 14/24, 1636.

[2] *B.L.* 8640, ff. 239, 242, 263 : Con to Barberini, Apr. 7/17, Apr. 21/May 1, 1637.

[3] *B.L.* 8639, ff. 38 seq., 69 : Con to Barberini, Aug. 24/Sept. 3 ; Sept. 5/15, 1636.

with just that degree of familiarity they happened to have shown him at the Queen's Court, now yielding, now taking precedence.

In this way Con's tact and personality won for him invitations from the most unlikely people, — when Bishop Juxon of London asked him, it was the talk of the hour, the Queen herself would scarce believe it. Then the Puritan Earl of Holland invited him to his beautiful villa just beyond Hyde Park to meet the Marquis of Winchester and other Catholics. [1]

Following Panzani's advice Con did his best to ensure the support of the Ladies at Court, — a policy that brought from the foreign Ambassadors, not so successful perhaps, the remark that the Papal Agent evidently contemplated subjecting the whole realm through women. Con met this sarcasm with the ready reply that as his mission was to the Queen, not the King, he had necessarily more to do with the ladies than the men. In consequence Con was devotedly served during the whole of his stay in England by Lady Arundel; when mob-violence threatened in London, the Countess of Banbury offered him the seclusion of her country home; even the beautiful Lady Carlisle, Court intriguante-in-chief, spoke up in defence of the Agent and was suspected of Popery for her pains though, as Con drily remarked, the poor lady had no religion but her own complexion. [2]

On arriving in England the Papal Agent, tactfully refusing the lodging offered him by the Queen, had taken a London house of his own for a year at a rental of 300 crowns. Here he fitted up a chapel by knocking two rooms into one. For any priests who might come to say Mass, he kept an open breakfast table, and his cook was equally liberal to beggars, save after dark when there was fear of the plague-stricken stalking abroad. With these expenses, the upkeep of his horses and carriage, and the twelve mouths he had to feed daily, his outlay was considerable — twice the amount the Pope allowed him — and he often found himself pinched for ready cash, as the English bankers would only pay his drafts at three months' date. He therefore decided not to entertain

---

[1] *B.L.* 8640, ff. 329 ; 8643, ff. 112, 163 : Con to Barberini, May 19/29, 1637 ; Sept. 21/Oct. 1, Oct. 19/29, 1638.

[2] *B.L.* 8645, f. 216 : Con to Ferragalli, Oct. 6/16, 1637. *B.L.* 8642, f. 66 : Con to Barberini, Jan. 19/29, 1638 :"... Mà la povera Sig.ra non hà mai pensato ad altra Religione che à quella di abellirsi."

and, to avoid the crowds coming to visit his ever-open chapel he would leave at noon and stay away till midnight. [1]

The Pope's Chapel — Con had the Barberini arms erected as in the Roman Churches — now became the centre of the Catholic revival in London, and Père Cyprien de Gamaches bears willing witness to the crowds attending Mass there without let from early morn till noon. The success of the Chapel did not go unchallenged, for the Puritan Secretary of State, Coke, came sourly complaining of the ten or twelve Masses said daily in the Pope's Chapel (there were actually half that number, according to Con), and warning the King of letting his subjects slip from their obedience. Charles promised to look into the matter and, as Coke persisted, said abruptly he would speak to the Papal Agent, but Con heard nothing and was soon talking of enlarging his Chapel. [2]

The Oratory remained open to the public even when there was plague about or when the Ambassadors shut down and left town. On Saturdays and Vigils well-known priests came to hear confessions and as a result on Feast-days the Chapel was crowded out, — a typical example being the Feast of the Immaculate Conception, 1637, when Don Antonio, Con's Chaplain, said they spent more for Mass-wine and candles than one of the major churches of Rome. Hearing of the success of the Pope's Chapel, the Queen asked Con if his Holiness had hoped for as much. " For the conversion of England, " answered the Agent. " We must act then and not talk, " said Henrietta with a laugh. [3]

Writing in February, 1638, Con said he had never, through threats, had to postpone any service in his chapel ; on the contrary, the number of daily masses had increased to eight, and many came there not bold enough to seek the Sacraments elsewhere. It became a centre, too, for fashionable functions. In July, 1637, Viscount Montagu was married there to the Earl of Worcester's daughter,

[1] *B.L.* 8645, ff. 44, 99, 102, 104, 118, 143, 180, 285 : Con to Barberini, Oct. 13/23, 1636 ; Jan. 12/22, 19/29, Feb. 16/26, Mar. 30/Apr. 9, July 7/17, 1637 ; March 9/19, 1638.

[2] GAMACHES, *op. cit.*, pp. 63-64. — *B.L.* 8640, f. 177 : Con to Barberini, Mar. 2/12, 1637. *B.L.* 8645, f. 170 : Con to Ferragalli, June 24/July 4, 1637.

[3] *B.L.* 8640, f. 188 ; 8641, f. 130 : Con to Barberini, Mar. 9/19, Sept. 29/ Oct. 9, 1637. *B.L.* 8645, ff. 141, 250 : Same to same, Mar. 30/ Apr. 9, Dec. 8/18, 1637.

while in the following November the Queen went to the Chapel
for a Pontifical Requiem for the late Duke of Savoy, her brother-
in-law. The celebrant was Duperron, whose recent promotion
to the See of Angoulême was a genuine mark of the influence the
Queen and Con were exercising over Charles, formerly so adamant
in rejecting a bishop as head of his wife's household. No doubt
Duperron's own easy-going disposition had helped the King to
relent. [1]

With a Papal Agent in London and the Queen so solicitous for
their welfare, the English Catholics were enjoying not merely peace
but added prestige. Windebank, a man of petty views in Con's
opinion, was always worrying him to report all this to Rome.
The Agent's answer was that if he kept praising this-and-that
small favour of their Majesties, it would only throw into relief
the general state of hardship in which the Catholics lived. [2]

The Queen had certainly some claim to the gratitude of the
English Catholics. She had struggled against odds to have her
Marriage Contract fulfilled and now kept two chapels open for
the Catholics, the new one at Somerset House and that built
for the Infanta at St James's. To her credit must go the presence
of a Papal Agent in England, a thing not even envisaged at the
time of her marriage. Yet the English Catholics had never
recovered from the damping of their first high hopes of the French
Marriage and had soon sunk back into what had become a deep-
rooted tradition with them, — a leaning on Spain for protection.
" They would think little of Heaven itself, unless they got it at the
hands of Spain," was the Queen's caustic comment. [3]

Besides those questions of the general good of religion that he
treated of so freely with the King, the Agent made every effort
to relieve individual hardships brought to his notice. Two typical
cases of Charles's intervention at Con's request were for the return
of certain richly-worked Mass paraphernalia taken by one Newton,
a pursuivant, and again for an increase of income for a man who
had forgone a patrimony of 4,000 crowns to become a priest and was

[1] *B.L.* 8640, f. 230 : Con to Barberini, Apr. 28/May 8, 1637. *B.L.* 8641,
ff. 33, 215 : Same to same, July 14/14, Nov. 24/Dec. 4, 1637. *B.L.* 8642, ff. 85,
225 : Same to same, Feb. 2/12, Mar. 18/28, 1638.

[2] *B.L.* 8640, f. 201 : Con to Barberini, March 16/26, 1637.

[3] *Ibid.*, f. 92 : Same to same, Jan. 19/29 1637.

now being stinted by his brother. Trifling matters, Con admitted, but unheard of before. [1]

Again, on the question of fines the Papal Agent won the King's consent to five or six poor Catholics combining to buy a permit for composition under the Great Seal, so that as regards relief rich and poor might meet on a level. On this particular occasion, after the Agent had won several concessions, Charles asked him to come to Newmarket to hunt. Con excused himself as he had to return to Town for some medicine, though he admitted slyly to Barberini that the King's clemency had contributed more to his health than all the medicos in England could have done.

The Agent hoped to have the whole curse of the Pursuivants reviewed by a committee of impartial Privy Councillors, — the Earl of Arundel, Cottington, Windebank and others. Laud and the Earl of Manchester (Walter Montagu's father), who was Lord Privy Seal, he wanted if possible to exclude. Con's object was to deprive the Pursuivants of their authority and to have the Star Chamber entrusted with any order to be carried out against the Catholics. [2]

Charles granted Con the command he wanted and in the following July he succeeded in having the misdeeds of certain Pursuivants brought before Windebank and the Privy Seal, deputed for the task by the Privy Council; more significant still, priests were called as witnesses against them. [3]

Undoubtedly, the influence of the Pope's Agent, well supported by the Queen, was winning for the Catholics greater privileges than they had ever enjoyed before. Peter Fytton, Roman Agent to the English Clergy, was amazed at the change he saw in the spring of 1638 : he, a priest, was actually taken to kiss the king's hand by Lord Arundel, while the latter's wife declared that before the Agency she would not have dared invite a priest to her table for a million pounds. [4]

Unfortunately, many of the Catholics, not realizing that kissing

[1] *Ibid.*, f. 230 ; *B.L.* 8641, f. 6 : Con to Barberini, Mar. 30/Apr. 9 ; June 24/July 4, 1637.

[2] *B.L.* 8642, ff. 95-97 : Con to Barberini, Feb. 16/26, 1638.

[3] *B.L.* 8643, f. 20 : Con to Barberini, July 6/16, 1638.

[4] *B.L.* 8642, f. 240 : Same to same, June 1/11, 1638.

goes by favour, began taking their privileges for granted and by boasting of them kept Con on tenterhooks lest the Puritans should raise an outcry against the Papists, who were freer in their talk than ever they dared be. " Prudentiores sunt filii tenebrarum," was the Agent's exasperated comment. [1]

---

[1] *B.L.* 8643, f. 45 : Same to same, July 27/Aug. 6, 1638.

CHAPTER VII

REUNION DREAMS

" 1626/27 Mar. 8, Thursday, I came to London. The night following I dreamed that I was reconciled to the Church of Rome. This troubled me much ; and I wondered exceedingly, how it should happen... So being troubled at my dream, I said with myself that I should go immediately, and, confessing my fault, would beg pardon of the Church of England. Going with this resolution, a certain priest met me, and would have stopped me. But moved with indignation I went on my way. And while I wearied myself with these troublesome thoughts, I awoke.
Herein I felt such strong impressions, that I could scarce believe it to be a dream. " [1]

. . . .

" I hope ye reader will note my trouble at ye dream, as well as ye dream." [2]

Though it would be rash to maintain that reunion of the Churches of England and Rome even came within the ambit of practical politics, it is certain that in the middle years of Charles's reign both sides were stirred from that apathetic hostility in which each had become entrenched. With leading personalities of both camps in sympathy, points of contact rather than of opposition were stressed and, with many, reunion became the topic of the hour.

Dom Leander counselled this method of approach by drawing up for the guidance of the Holy See, which he considered ill-informed on the matter, a memorandum pointing out the difference between the Protestant Church of England, to which the King and the Bishops adhered, and the Puritans who on the Continent would be called Huguenots, Calvinists or Socinians.

---

[1] LAUD's *Diary*, p. 201.
[2] PRYNNE's *Breviate*, p. 10, l. 12, marginal note added by Laud.

Wh'le the Established Church undoubtedly differed from Rome on many points, the Benedictine laid special emphasis on the points of agreement, which included such important dogmas as the Trinity, the Incarnation and Godhead of Christ, Providence, Predestination, Justification, the necessity of good works, and the co-operation of freewill with grace.

Further, the Church of England was at one with Rome in subscribing to the first four General Councils and the three authentic Creeds of the Apostles, of Nicea and of St Athanasius. Both reverenced the Early Church and the unanimous consent of the Fathers, while the Church of England followed a liturgy taken from the Roman liturgy and admitted an essential difference between bishop, priest and deacon. [1]

The prime advocate for a *rapprochement* was Christopher Davenport, an Oxford convert ; he had joined the Franciscan Recollects at Douai as Franciscus a Sancta Clara, attaining a position of eminence among them as Superior and theologian. [2]

Returning to England as a Queen's Chaplain, he began advocating the cause he had at heart,— corporate reunion with Rome. He was in constant contact with Laud, Bishop Montague and Dr Cosin, and was convinced that he and his Anglican friends agreed more and differed less than was commonly thought.

In proof of this he published in 1634 a treatise on justification, *Deus, Natura, Gratia*, to which was soon subjoined a commentary on the *XXXIX Articles*, attempting to show article by article that the charter of the Establishment could be reconciled with the tenets of Rome, and that therefore there was nothing separating the two save an unnatural barrier of prejudice which goodwill and a realistic policy should be able to raise. [3]

[1] *Clarendon State Papers*, vol. I, pp. 207-209 : *Instructions relating to the reconciliation of moderate Papists and Protestants* (In Leander's hand).

[2] Christopher Davenport (1598-1680) was the son of John Davenport, alderman of Coventry. He went to Merton College, Oxford, 1613 ; in 1617, he joined the Franciscans at Ypres, transferring to the English Recollects at Douai, 1618 ; after graduating in divinity at Salamanca, he became chief lecturer in divinity, and guardian at Douai. On returning to England, he laboured for 50 years in the cause of conversion. At the Restoration he became chaplain to Catherine of Braganza. He was thrice Provincial of his Order.

[3] *Deus, Natura, Gratia, sive tractatus de praedestinatione, de meritis et peccatorum remissione, seu de justificatione et denique de Sanctorum invocatione. Ubi*

The *Deus, Natura, Gratia* consists of a series of problems, 37 in all, in which the author examines first the Catholic, then the Anglican view. Some questions are purely academic, *e. g.* N° 24, *An Deus de potentia absoluta potest hominem justificare non infudendo gratiam.* Others are more directly apologetical, *e. g.* N° 37, *de invocatione sanctorum*; N° 2, *de causis Praedestinationis*; N° 17, *de justificatione.* Yet the method is never polemical, and rather than attack his opponents Davenport tries to quote them in support of the Catholic view.

In his commentary on the *XXXIX Articles* the Franciscan quotes each article and, for explanation, either adds a note or refers back to some *Problema* of his main treatise, the *Deus, Natura, Gratia.* He then labels the article according to its bearing on Catholicism. The result is startling. As many as nineteen, together with parts of five others, he fully approves of as Catholic, and consonant with Scripture and the tradition of the Fathers and Councils. To nine others and two halves of articles he allows a favourable interpretation. The residue (six articles and three parts of articles) he admits require more skilful dialectic than his to make acceptable. [1]

To forestall criticism Davenport prefaced his book with testimonials of approval from a formidable array of Catholic theologians, which were authenticated by Dom David Codner, O. S. B. [2] The

ad trutinam Fidei Catholicae examinatur Confessio Anglicana et ad singula puncta, quid teneat, qualiter differat, excutitur... Accessit paraphrastica expositio reliquorum Articulorum Confessionis Anglicae (Lugduni, 1634). The latter portion has been edited and translated with an introduction and life of the author by Frederick George Lee, D.C.L. (London, 1865).

[1] The " Catholic" articles are N°ˢ 1-5, 7-8, 9 (first half), 10, 12, 15 (first half), 16-18, 19 (first half), 20 (first half), 23, 25 (half), 26, 27, 33, 34, 38, 39.

Favourable interpretation possible : N°ˢ 6, 9 (second half), 11, 13, 14, 20 (half), 24, 29, 30, 32, 35.

Needing more skilful dialectic : N°ˢ 15 (second half), 19 (second half), 21, 22, 25 (half), 28, 31, 36, 37.

[2] They are : Jacques Dreux, Doctor of the Sorbonne ; Thomas Blacklow, Professor of Sacred Theology ; William Thomson, S.T.D. ; Tho. P., S. Theol. Professor ; Gilles Chaissy, extra Mnr. Provinc. PP. Recol. Prov. S. Bernard. et olim tam in Italia quam Gallia S. Theol. Lector Generalis ; Fr John Gennings, Angliae Mnr. ; Peter Martin, Theol. prof. All contributed a word of praise for the book. — Father Codner signed himself : D. David, Monachus et Decanus Congregationis Casinensis, olim Romae Sereniss. D. N. Urbani Papae octavi Poenitentiarius, Notarius Apostolicus.

latter was staying at Court at the time and, under his courtier's *alias* of Matthew Savage, wrote to Mgr Francesco Ingoli, the Secretary of Propaganda, emphasizing the influence the book had had in softening hard hearts. Many had been drawn to consult the author to their great profit, and several of the nobility had come into the Church. On the other hand, it was a favourable sign that the extreme Protestants were condemning the book as against their faith. [1]

Dom David insists that he is merely drawing notice to facts and is neither defending nor condemning the book. His personal views he had voiced a few months before in a letter to Padre Alessandro in Rome, whole-heartedly supporting the work and deploring the calumnies of those who, without reading the book, said it had been prohibited in Paris and would soon be condemned in Rome, though its orthodoxy had been sworn to by the most learned and upright theologians. [2]

Among those who sought the condemnation of the book were many of Davenport's own Franciscan brethren. Some Catholics questioned the writer's policy and refused to allow that the Church of England retained all he claimed for it. Others commended its Christian tone and looked with great hope towards the future. The Puritans were contemptuous of it, while the Laudian School (Laud, Cosin, Skedlington and Pocklington) seemed unprepared to accept its line of argument or to admit its conclusions.

When Panzani arrived in London, he found the book the talk of the town, and soon heard from Windebank how pleased the King and his ministers were with the author's mild and unexag-

---

[1] *Arch. Prop.*, *Scritt. Ant.* 134, f. 220 : Selvaggio to Ingoli, London, Sept. 30, 1634.

[2] *Ibid.*, ff. 313-314 : D. David to Padre Alessandro, London, 5º Kal. Apr. 1634 : "... Caue autem aliud! Quid? Noui hic rumores, pessimi clamores, o[mn]ium iam auribus insonant, librum quendam, praelo nuper absolutum, nec dum tum in uulgus ho[m]i[n]um,et lucem editum, iam Parisijs proscriptum, ac Romae propediem et[iam] fore condemnandum. Deus bone! quam preceps Britannicu[m] ho[m]i[n]um genus! non legerunt, non viderunt hic illor[um] unus, qui linguas tanto aculeo tam odiosi in librum iam armaverint, et rumore nescio quo, certo an incerto tum eundem tanta cum infamia declamitant, ac si nihil preter infame facimus contineret..." And so on for two folio pages. Dom David is so eloquent in defence of the book and its author, that he forgets to mention the names of either, adding the information in a postscript.

gerated treatment of the Protestants. If the work were censured therefore, they would draw the conclusion that Rome wanted heretics positively flayed (" lacerati "), so Panzani was asked to stop the condemnation, which he promised to do. Charles thought Rome had been far too severe on it and told the Queen that Davenport and his supporters should print another book, which, if the Pope prohibited, he would take it as a singular injury, — he had in mind, it seems, an answer to Father Courtenay's work advocating the right of the people to depose their king. [1]

Panzani had also to foil the machinations of a certain Scotch Friar Metelano [Maitland ?] who had written to Rome that the King and Government actually wanted Davenport's book prohibited.

The ire of several members of the Government had been aroused by the reply of the Cardinal di Sant' Onofrio promising to deal with the matter, and the unhappy friar, fearing imprisonment, brought the letter to Panzani at whose request Windebank promised to take no further action. [2]

Panzani then appealed to Rome not to proceed against the *Deus, Natura, Gratia*. In reply the Cardinal Secretary told him to find out secretly whether the author was ready to correct its errors, and to exhort him to do so as soon as possible. If Davenport resolved on revising his work, Panzani was to advise him that he could do so better abroad under the Pope's protection. [3]

---

[1] *P.R.O. Rom. Trans.* : Panzani to Barberini, Apr. 10/20, 1635. The book Charles referred to may have been *A Discourse against the Oath of Allegiance* by Fr Edward Leedes *alias* Courtenay, S. J. (Cf. Chap. XI, p. 257, n. 2).

[2] *P.R.O. Rom. Trans.* : Panzani to Barberini, Jan. 16/26, 1635. This friar, a Minim of St Francis of Paula, had been in hot water some years before, when a number of Scots Catholics in London had petitioned the Paris Nuncio, del Bagno, for his recall on a charge of loitering about the Court, stirring up sedition. The evidence was conflicting. What seems certain is that he lived with the Queen's Doorkeeper, went off to say Mass and preach in private houses, and was very vain in dress, while his boastful talk was largely discredited. Lastly, he shared a vice that even then was only too common in these islands, —" è soggetto al tobacco, vitio commune in quelle parti." — To check this license the Nuncio recommended the friar's recall for a year. (*Arch. Prop., Scritt. Ant.* 132, ff. 55-56 : Bagno to Card. Ludovisi, Lyons, Aug. 29, 1630.)

[3] *Ibid.* : Barberini to Panzani, March 3/13, 1635. Later in the year Barberini served Davenport with a personal notice to quit the country (*Ibid.* : Same to same, May 27/June 6, 1635), but he pleaded infirmity and stayed in

This provocative book had sounded an entirely new note in
controversy and set all the Court discussing the pros and cons
of reunion with Rome. Lord Arundel (the son and father of martyrs
for the Faith, and himself a Catholic till he took the sacrament in
the Chapel Royal on Christmas Day, 1616) had a long talk on the
subject with Panzani on New Year's Day, 1635. The Earl said
he thought it would be easy to persuade the King to grant liberty
of conscience but for the thorny question of restitution of Church
property. He added that he would be willing to go as Ambassador
to Rome. [1]

A few weeks later a sermon was preached in the Chapel Royal
before Charles and his Court that amazed the listeners. The
preacher, one of Laud's closest friends, vehemently attacked the
authors of England's schism : like a tailor who cuts out a number
of garments and then finds himself unable to piece them together,
these people had cut about and torn apart so much that now they
were hard put to it to rejoin the bits. [2]

England (BERINGTON, op. cit., pp. 165-168). This book, though disapproved
of by Rome, was never placed formally on the *Index* even at a later date when
the hopes of reunion placed in Charles had long since faded. (The book is not
to be found in the *Index* of Alexander VII, 1665, consulted in the Vatican
Library.)

[1] *P.R.O. Rom. Trans.*: Panzani to Barberini, Jan. 6/16, 1635. The Earl's
offer was, perhaps, not altogether altruistic. The greatest art connoisseur and
collector of his time, he was interested less in diplomacy than in the Galleries
and Museums of Italy, to a quiet contemplation of which he eventually
retired from the turmoils of the Civil War. He died at Padua in 1646. For
a discussion of the Earl's religious views and the staunchness of his Catholic
relatives, v. pp. 113-118 of his *Life* by M. F. S. HERVEY.

[2] *Ibid.* : Same to same, Feb. 6/16, 1635 : " ... Che li autori dello scisma hanno
fatto come qual sartore, che taglia tanti vestiti che poi non li può cuscire,
così essi hanno tagliato tanto, e tanto disunito, che adesso sì stenta assai à
potere riunire."

In the same strain wrote Herbert Thorndike (1598-1672), a prominent
Caroline divine : " I am confident that no Church can separate from Rome but
must make themselves schismatic before God... I insist on such a principal as
may serve to reunite us with Rome, being well assured that we never can be
well united with ourselves otherwise, and that not only the Reformation, but
our Common Christianity will be lost in the divisions which will never have
an end otherwise." (H. K. PIERCE, in *The Bulletin of the Confraternity of
Unity*, Nos VIII-IX (1930), pp. 8 seq., quoting THORNDIKE's *Theological
Works*, Oxford, 1844-1846.)

The courtiers' wonderment increased when three days later Charles, discussing these first schismatics, declared he would give his own right hand that this schism had never been. " Take care, Sire, of what you are saying," one of them warned him. " I repeat, I would give this right hand," answered the King, and went on to speak with great affection of Pope Urban. These sentiments seemed a happy augury for the future, but there were some who put little trust in such demonstrations.

Panzani was not of these, and the slightest reaction against the dreary Calvinism of the Establishment he seized upon as a trend towards Rome. Gleefully he reported Laud's order for the City Churches to prefix *Saint* to the name of their Patron in sending in their weekly returns, and to sing the Psalms in future to the Gregorian tone. [1]

Cardinal Barberini's kindness towards English visitors to Rome was greatly appreciated and many hoped the Pope would follow suit. Certainly in England favour was being shown the Catholics, particularly by Windebank, who pocketed a present of 600 crowns from the Queen for all he had done for them. The Secretary, now at the peak of his power, had struck up a friendship with Panzani, whom he urged to go up to Oxford and Cambridge to confer with the Catholics there, promising him letters of introduction. [2]

[1] *P.R.O. Rom. Trans.* : Panzani to Barberini, Feb. 6/16, 1635. In his original despatch (*B.L.* 8633, ff. 183-184), Panzani encloses two return sheets, the first for the week ending Dec. 25, 1634, listing the churches in alphabetical order, — Albans, Wood Street, Alphege, Andrew Hubbard, Anne Black-Fryers, etc. In the second list (week ending Feb. 5, 1635) the prefix *Saint* occurs, *e. g.* St Bennet Fynck, St Botolph Billingsgate, St Faith's, etc. It is of interest to note in this list that at Westminster, though there were fewer Christenings (11 as against 13) considerable zeal was shown for the due application of the matter of the sacrament, for one luckless infant was drowned ! In the same returns the analysis of causes of death makes gruesome reading, *e.g.* flocks, flux, liver growne, rising of the lights, strangurie, suddenly, surfet, teeth, tissicke, wind, woolfe, wormes.

[2] *P.R.O. Rom. Trans.* : Panzani to Barberini, Feb. 20/Mar. 2, 1635. Mr Secretary Windebank, whose rise from a minor clerkship in 1632 was entirely due to Laud, had deserted his patron in 1635 over the new Soap Monopoly (the Jesuits were supposed to have financed the product which was sold on the London streets as *Popish Soap*) and had formed a triumvirate with Weston, Lord Treasurer and Earl of Portland, and Lord Cottington, Chancellor of the Exchequer. All were friends of Fr Leander, reunionists and pro-Spanish,

As has been seen, Windebank, eager to establish diplomatic relations with Rome, was prompted by Panzani to discuss the matter with the King, as the Queen, though good enough to set the ball rolling, was, he thought, too weak in answering her husband. The Secretary, whom Panzani hoped to convert, freely discussed the reunion problem. He told the Italian he had this greatly at heart, and would let him know for his guidance the concessions the English Church would demand, *viz.* Communion under both kinds, Mass and the Liturgy in E nglish, and leave for priests and bishops to marry. Father Philip, the Queen's Confessor, had, it seems, hinted to Windebank that the first two would be granted by Rome, but Panzani made no promises. Of the third demand he said he was surprised it was not clear to all that this came from the married clergy. Windebank said he disliked the idea very much, but that all were not of his opinion.

In the meantime, while their plans were maturing and they were feeling their way towards reunion, Panzani begged his friend to see his way to grant the Catholics at least their liberty of con-science. Windebank answered that this would be the easier to concede when the King saw his Catholic subjects were not refusing the Oath of Allegiance. To this Panzani could only answer that he had written to Rome and was expecting as favourable a reply as was possible

Meanwhile, alive to all that went on at Whitehall, Panzani was able to report another sermon with a Rome-ward trend, this time by a Bishop who, on the 1st Sunday in March, 1635, preached before the Court on the necessity for Sacramental Confession without which the Church's influence had never been maintained. It was the best-proved of all dogmas in the Scriptures, the preacher contended ; and he exhorted his hearers to put it into practice.

As usual the sermon was discussed over the dinner-table. The King spoke of the necessity of telling all the circumstances of sin in Confession. Someone objected to this, as from it must needs follow the injustice of taking away another's good name. Charles agreed immediately that one should not mention the names of

— and all died Catholics. (F.M.G. Evans, *The Principal Secretary of State,* p. 93.)

partners in sin and appealed to Father Philip for confirmation of the point. [1]

With the King expressing himself so orthodoxly Windebank was anxious for him to meet Panzani. The latter's official mission had mainly to do with the domestic affairs of the English Catholics, with the lesser task of scouting for signs of good will towards Rome at the English Court, and so the Papal Envoy had no claim to wait upon or be received by the King. If the two met, it could only be by adroit diplomacy. Windebank, therefore, went to the Queen and offered to serve her in the cause of union with Rome. He followed this up quickly by saying that King would have great pleasure in speaking with the person who had come from Rome, and asked her Majesty to suggest a meeting without, however, telling her husband that he (Windebank) had mentioned the matter. [2]

It was the high esteem shown by all save the Puritans for the personal qualities of Urban VIII that gave ground for hopes of a *rapprochement*. When Nuncio in Paris, he had been in constant touch with English affairs and his friendliness and kindly disposition were still remembered. Panzani heard the Pope praised on all sides as both benevolent and discreet, and great hopes were placed in his Pontificate. Rumours were already rife in Court circles of Rome's great desire for union with England and of the Holy Father's readiness to go as far as he could in concession, — to allow Mass in English, for example.

Father Philip thought this would be granted and that Rome would have to allow the Chalice to the laity as had been done eleswhere in the Church. On the point of the married clergy he thought a compromise could be effected if the present incumbents were allowed to retain their benefices on conversion, provided they arranged for a celibate priest to take over their sacred functions. [3]

---

[1] *Ibid.*: Panzani to Barberini, Feb. 27/Mar. 9 ; March. 6/16, 13/23, 1635.

[2] *Ibid.*: Panzani to Barberini, Feb. 20/Mar. 2, 1635.

[3] *Ibid.*: Panzani to Barberini, Mar. 12/23 ; Apr. 3/13 ; June 3/13, 1635.
Among the Barberini MSS., there is an anonymous document, undated but in all probability written about this time by Christopher Davenport and entitled *Monitum ad Anglos* : *Pax Christi, amici mei honoratissimi charissimique*. Seeking to minimize the obstacles to reunion with Rome, the writer cites St Thomas, Bellarmine and Fr Persons in pointing out that celibacy of the

The Queen's Confessor was optimistic at the signs of the times Every day, he told Panzani, saw favourable evidence of desire for reunion both in the King and in those who surrounded him, clergy and laity alike ; every day some proposal was put forward. Nevertheless, the situation was most difficult and complex owing to the severity of the laws against Catholics, with the result that those most desiring reunion were not eager to show it openly, — rather the contrary. The same fear was present in the King, timid by nature, and was doing a great deal of harm, as one could make no sound and prudent judgment of the King and his Council, seeing them so hesitant and changeable.

Moreover, Father Philip continued, there were rumours of war, which meant money and the summoning of Parliament, — a Parliament packed with Puritans bargaining for more persecution of the Papists. This prospect made even the moderate among bishops and clergy severe on the Catholics through fear. [1]

Endorsing this statement, Windebank declared to Panzani that were it not for private interests something would be done for the conversion of England. In reply the Italian was careful to state that although he held no special instructions for this important business, he could promise from his knowledge of the Holy See that, were his Majesty to unite with her, he would be allowed nomination to bishoprics and a concordat such as France and Germany had. Nobody would be able to say Rome was acting from self-interest. Windebank said this was an important point he was glad to hear, and would avail himself of it on occasion. He then revealed to Panzani that the lawyers were most hostile to reunion, as they were

---

clergy is only of ecclesiastical law. He then puts forward the amazing possib- ility of Henry VIII, " bis trigamus," becoming a priest by dispensation ! He also suggests that those returning to the Church could retain their ecclesiastical dignities, including the King his right of nomination. Reunion could therefore take place without any outward change of status in those concerned : " Hinc igitur perspicitis, quod si Regiae suae Maiestati placuerit, cumque vestris bonis desideriis steterit, reuniri poteritis cum Ecclesia Catholica absque ulla vel in statu ipso, vel in gubernatione Reipublicae mutatione, sed sola mutatione particularis ac specialis vestrae fidei in Catholicam atque Apostolicam, ad salutem animarum tum vestrarum, tum eorum qui sub vestro degunt onere." (*B.L.* 8620, ff. 29-30 : Anon. [Franciscus a Sancta Clara?] s. d. [1634-5-6?]).

[1] *Ibid.* : Panzani to Barberini, June 10/20, 1635.

possessed of the loot of the monasteries. [1] This need present no obstacle, the Italian pointed out, as in Queen Mary's reign Cardinal Pole had removed all censures and with them the possibility of any action being taken against the possessors of ecclesiastical property. [2]

For all Windebank's enthusiasm and his own optimism Panzani was acute enough to realize that the religious problem could never be settled without the co-operation of Laud, who was not only Primate of the English Church but possessed of a powerful influence with Charles, by nature irresolute and governed in such matters by the Archbishop. [3] But despite his reforms in the Church of England, because of them perhaps, Laud had not the slightest intention of capitulating to, or compromising with Rome. He had his own axe to grind, and the gibe of the old jingle that dubbed him " our English Pope" was more than an empty sneer, — it was a fair estimate of all the Archbishop's ambitions, which he had no inclination to sacrifice to make a Roman holiday.

Not knowing all that was in Laud's mind, Panzani hoped to treat with him directly or through another. In the meantime, he had others to talk with. He thought Cottington still more in favour of reunion than Windebank. Barberini, too, had a high opinion of the man and his sentiments. It seems Cottington had voiced the opinion that the King of England in union with Rome could win the regard of the Catholic princes and make himself arbiter of their disputes, seeing that the situation of his own realm put him outside the pale of their domestic interests. This view Panzani was ordered to persuade Cottington to urge upon Charles as a " holy and profitable resolution." [4]

Cottington evidently looked upon reunion of England with Rome as the key-move to the solution of the intolerable politico-religious schism into which continental Europe was split. Pope Urban was no different from his predecessors in experiencing the utmost difficulty in holding the balance between his Catholic

---

[1] An interesting point supporting from a different angle Mr Belloc's indictment of the lawyers who in this reign ranged themselves for the first time in a body against the Crown. (Cf. BELLOC, *Charles I*, pp. 128, 148, 192.)

[2] *P.R.O. Rom. Trans.* : Panzani to Barberini, Oct. 7/17, 1635. The Cardinal Secretary was particularly pleased with Panzani's replies on this occasion (*Ibid.* : Barberini to Panzani, Nov. 25, Dec. 5, 1635).

[3] *Ibid.* : Panzani to Barberini, Oct. 21/31, 1635.

[4] *P.R.O., Trans.* 10, 10 : Barberini to Panzani, alla 2ᵈᵃ cifra di 27 Apr., 1635.

Majesty and the Most Christian King, — the one looked upon him as a Frenchman, in the realm of the other he was taken for a Spaniard. So, as Cardinal Barberini recalled in a happy phrase, in looking to England for solace against the ingratitude of other sovereigns, Urban would only be wearing the mantle of Hildebrand. It, therefore, came as a shock to his Holiness to find that even in England he was regarded by some as pro-French, when a dispassionate judgment could not reveal him guilty of any favour either to France or to Spain that went against his conscience. [1]

At one with Cottington and Barberini in regarding a *rapprochement* between England and Rome as a warranty of peace in Christendom, Panzani told the English Lord Treasurer that exchange of diplomatic agents would be a definite step towards this end. He also suggested they would do well to examine the causes that placed Henry VIII in schism. But Cottington cut him short, saying with great emotion : " For the love of God do not let us dwell on our miseries. We have reflected on them so many times and know them well enough." Here he paused, and then added : " Would that it would enter the King's head that the Pope wishes him well, and that he is not despised in Rome." The Chancellor said this with some feeling, stressing, too, the notable change that could be seen in England ; previously, at any mention of Rome, people would turn away, now men were less bitter and spoke honourably of her. [2]

Panzani busied himself with finding out not only the general opinion of Rome, but also the attitude of the Church of England towards her teachings. He was told that many bishops and clergy prominent in learning, the two Archbishops and the Bishop of London among them, held all the dogmas of Rome except Transubstantiation, which they regarded as the invention of Innocent III and the Lateran Council. This was the real stumbling-block. The Pope they confessed to be Christ's Vicar and the Successor of St. Peter, without whom it was impossible to con-

---

[1] *P.R.O. Rom. Trans.* : Barberini to Panzani, 14/24 Oct., 1635. The Cardinal is referring to the famous letter written by Hildebrand to William the Conqueror in 1071 praising him for his respect for religion in a wicked and corrupt world. (For a French translation of this letter cf. A. FLICHE, *La réforme grégorienne*, vol. I, p. 364). Relationsbetween England and the Pope continued cordial, during the time that Gregory was having considerable trouble with France and Germany (*Ibid.*, vol. II, p. 127 and *passim*).

[2] *P.R.O. Rom. Trans.* : Panzani to Barberini, Oct. 21/31, 1635.

vene a Council or determine what was binding on the whole Church.

To demonstrate exactly how near each side was to the other suggestions were made for moderate men from both sides to hold certain ' conversations ' in France, it being considered that the opinions of the French were close to those held in England and, besides, the two crowns were kin. Another suggestion was that learned Spanish and French Theologians should be invited to England to talk matters over. [1]

All this time the Court sermons continued and, sure of their ground, the preachers waxed bolder in their statements. Calvin and Geneva had been the cause of much harm in England, said one clergyman in front of the King and the Prince Palatine, champion of Protestantism. The phrase was commented on ; it had been chosen deliberately, it was said, to open the eyes of the Palatine. It could never have been used had the speaker not been certain of offending neither the King nor the Archbishop. [2]

Certainly most moderate Protestants deplored the split the Reformation had cleft in Christendom, and it seemed this lingering regret might make common ground for negotiation. Alive to this, Barberini told Panzani to impress upon Windebank and everyone else, that Rome's only aim was to heal schism among Christians and bring all to the knowledge of the true Church. To reach this goal, so important for the salvation of her separated brethren, the Holy See was above all earthly interests : results would witness to it. Windebank or some other, said Barberini, should put this last point to the King, who should be brought to see that, reunited to the Church, his own royal authority would increase, as he would find the Holy See most liberal in matters of purely temporal interest.

All this Panzani was told to keep driving home till he kindled some spark of comprehension in those who ruled England. A further point that seemed in doubt and needed emphasis was the deep regard the Pope had for the King of England, an affection personal to Urban and not merely his official interest as Sovereign Pontiff. [3]

[1] *Ibid.* : Panzani to Barberini, Nov. 4/14, 1635 ; Mar. 23/Apr. 2, 1636.

[2] *Ibid.* : Same to same, Dec. 23/Jan. 2, 1635/36.

[3] *Ibid.* : Barberini to Panzani, Nov. 25/Dec. 5, 1635. The Cardinal lets his L atin ardour run into his pen in describing his uncle's love for Charles :

Moreover, Urban's interest was a family one ; years ago he had written beautiful verses on the death of the Queen of Scots, and now Barberini bore witness to the Pope's emotion whenever he spoke of the possibility of the conversion of Mary's grandson. [1]

While eager in the cause of reunion and generous in his expression of what was undoubtedly a genuine regard for Charles and his Queen, Cardinal Barberini was rightly chary of any attempt to talk away the Church's doctrine in conversations of the kind Panzani had referred to, and he told him to proceed with great circumspection.

No negotiations could be admitted in which there would be the slightest question of the truth of dogmas established even recently by the Church on the warranty of Scripture and the definitions of the Councils. As the Cardinal pointed out, it was not fitting for Catholics to call in question their articles of faith, or to open up fresh discussion on points determined after such mature consideration by the Universal Church in her Sacred Councils. But, if the tenets of the Catholic Faith were taken for granted, there would be no objection to the discussion of matters dependent on positive law and in the competence of the Sovereign Pontiff to concede.

Further to fend discussion off doctrines defined Barberini suggested that the causes of the present lack of unity could be gone into. For this the Anglicans' historical knowledge would serve them well, and they would see how disproportionate had been the gains to the sacrifices made, — an easier, more expeditious way of arriving at a practical resolution than any discussion of dogmatic truth. This advice the Cardinal Secretary thought important enough to be repeated later, adding that, if it were

---

" S. S^{tà} ama S. M^{tà} più che cosa alcuna di questo mondo, più che i miei nipoti che tutta la mia casa, più che qualsivoglia cosa ò casa a S. S^{tà} ò potente che si truovi."

[1] *Ibid.*, Same date. Urban's *Poemata*, written when he was Cardinal Maffeo Barberini, include the *De Nece Reginae Scotiae*. Published three or four times before he became Pope, they ran through edition after edition in Rome, Paris, Vienna, Bonn and Antwerp during his Pontificate. The best is perhaps that from the famous Plantin press ; the most interesting, as well as one of the finest, is the Clarendon Press edition of 1726, — 82 years after Urban's death, — a great tribute.

kept in mind, Pope Urban would consider any proposals made and try to give every satisfaction. [1]

Having clearly safeguarded the dogmatic standpoint of Rome in view of any conference, Barberini was only too eager to emphasize the eternal reward Almighty God would grant, the undying glory the world would concede to him who would win the King of England to the True Faith. No effort was to be spared, and the Cardinal gave due praise to Father Philip for urging the Queen to gain the goodwill of the Archbishop of Canterbury that his co-operation might be had in the cause of reunion, — co-operation that might have been won despite Laud's ambitions, had not the Puritans, by constant threats, forced the Archbishop to placate them by persecuting the Papists. As an Oxford preacher declared publicly, reunion with Rome would be an easy matter but for the hostility of the Puritans. [2]

With a view perhaps to formal discussions, Panzani now set himself the task of collecting information on the Anglican Bench of Bishops and particularly on their dispositions towards Rome. He thought this the more important as the King was not only governed by Laud (at the latter's suggestion the Bishop of Oxford had been appointed to the offices hitherto held by Cottington, who was now out of favour[3]) but he had great confidence in all the Bishops, whom he considered disinterested servants of the crown and not prone, as others were, to foreign influence. [4]

It was clearly important for the Holy See to know in which direction a body having such sway with the King was itself leaning. Panzani found one of the Bishops, Godfrey Goodman of Gloucester, notoriously " Roman." He said the office of the Roman Breviary and daily read the Martyrology, while in the House of Lords he took upon himself the defence of Catholics at every opportunity.

---

[1] *Ibid.* : Barberini to Panzani, Jan. 7/17 ; March 16/26, 1636.

[2] *Ibid.* : Panzani to Barberini, Feb. 10/20, 1636 ; March 16/26, 1636.

[3] This was a triumph for *Thorough* (Laud and Wentworth) over *Lady Mora* (Laud's name for the dilly-dallying of Cottington and Windebank). These two parties, or rather policies, contested the power between 1629-1640. Cf. F.M.G. EVANS, *The Principal Secretary of State*, p. 97.

[4] *P.R.O. Rom. Trans.* : Panzani to Barberini, April 20/30, 1636. It was no uncommon practice for statesmen to receive refreshers from a foreign power, and rumours were current at this time that both Cottington and Windebank had accepted bribes from Spain. (GARDINER, *History*, vol. VIII, p. 162.)

Panzani he greeted with a present, which the Italian declined, asking with all his native courtesy for the gift of the Bishop's soul. Goodman then asked that he might have an Italian priest to live quietly in his house, promising him the best of treatment. Though the Bishop did not specify the reason for this strange request, Panzani was of opinion that he wanted to be sure of daily Mass and consulted Davenport, an intimate friend of Goodman, for confirmation of this. He was dubious of the expediency of allowing a Mass-priest to live with a Protestant prelate and put the petition to Rome. Barberini, immediately suspicious that Davenport might be working on some scheme in his own interest, warned Panzani to be sure first that the request was not a fabrication of the Franciscan; apart from that, said the Cardinal, he would allow it, provided the Bishop intended to be reconciled to the Church at least *in foro conscientiae*. His continuing as a Protestant was an obstacle he alone could remove. [1]

Panzani now met Richard Montague, Bishop of Chichester, who by his writings had become a pioneer of that middle way between Rome and Geneva that was so characteristic of the Laudian school. [2]

---

[1] *P.R.O. Rom. Trans.*: Panzani to Barberini, Jan. 27/Feb. 6; Barberini to Panzani, March 16/26, May 25/June 4, 1636. Hamilton wrote from Rome in 1638 that Goodman had been converted in 1635/6 by one William Hanmer, *alias* John Challoner. In 1640, after a resolute refusal to subscribe to certain Canons drawn up by Laud to denounce Popish practices, Goodman's See was sequestrated by a Decree of deprivation *a beneficio et officio*. He died 1655/6 professing in his will to have died as he had lived " most constant in all the doctrines of God's holy and apostolic Church, whereof I do acknowledge the Church of Rome to be the Mother Church. And I do verily believe that no other church hath any salvation in it but only so far as it concurs with the faith of the Church of Rome." (Extract from his will, *D.N.B.*, vol. XX, p. 133.)

[2] In 1619 as rector of Stamford Rivers, Montague had found priests proselytizing in his parish — " Romish Rangers" he called them — and challenged them to debate. Meeting with no response, he drew up three propositions, promising to become a Papist if any one of them were refuted. They were :

   (1) that the present Roman Church is neither the Catholic Church nor a sound branch thereof.

   (2) that the present English Church *is* a sound member of the Catholic Church.

   (3) that none of the points maintained by Rome against the Church of England is the perpetual doctrine of the Catholic Church.

These provocative propositions elicited from Dr Matthew Kellison, the learned

He told Panzani he was ready at any time to kiss the feet of Peter and acknowledge the Pope as head of the Church. At the same time he professed himself completely satisfied of the validity of Anglican Orders ; as Bellarmine and others were of the opposite opinion, Panzani was bound to confess this to be a *petra scandali.* As a natural corollary of his contention, Montague thought the Pope ought to allow Catholics to frequent Protestant Churches, and Protestants to go to Mass.[1]

Montague was an historian of Primitive Christianity, professing to steer a middle course between the Magdeburg Centuriators, whom he considered too hostile to the Church, and Baronius, whom he classed as too partisan. Panzani here saw an excellent opportunity for a Catholic, *not* a Jesuit, eminent in learning and a good linguist, to strike up a correspondence friendship with Montague. After a study of the latter's historical method he could courteously point out his errors, leaving him bound in honour to correct them. Public correction and censure would, Panzani foresaw, be fatal, for the Bishop was a man of deep erudition and, dealing as he did with vital turning-points in the Church's history, could either do incredible harm or prove of immense assistance.[2]

Bishop Montague told Panzani that in his judgment only three of his colleagues on the Bench were Puritan in sentiment and hostile to the Catholics, *viz.* Durham, Salisbury and Exeter ; the rest showed great moderation. Though adding to the others the name of John Bowle, Bishop of Rochester, Panzani confirmed

President of the English College, Douai, a refutation in *A Gag for the New Gospel,* to which Montague replied with *A New Gagg for an old Goose,*maintaining that only eight of the 47 propositions Kellison attributed to the Church of England were, in fact, her true doctrine. For this he was delated by the Commons to his Archbishop (Abbott). Jostled by both Papist and Puritan Montague sought refuge in the royal protection, publishing *Appello Caesarem,* and all the efforts of Parliament failed to block his rapid rise to a Court Chaplaincy followed by the Bishopric of Chichester.

[1] *P.R.O. Rom. Trans.* : Panzani to Barberini, Mar. 23/Apr. 2, 1636.

[2] *Ibid.* : Same to same, Apr. 27/May 7, 1636. Montague's works to which Panzani refers are *Apparatus ad Origines Ecclesiasticas* (Oxford, 1635) and *De Originibus Ecclesiasticis* (London, 1636, 1640). A copy of the *Apparatus* was presented to Barberini by Sir William Hamilton, going to Rome as Queen's Agent, July, 1636.

Montagues's statement in a dossier he sent to Rome on the two Archbishops and twenty-five Bishops who composed the Anglican hierarchy. [1]

Eight bishops Panzani classifies as very moderate or well affected towards the Catholics, *viz.* London, Llandaff, Oxford, Bangor, Hereford, Norwich, Gloucester and Coventry. The last-named, Robert Wright of Coventry, he considers almost Catholic, while John Williams of Lincoln, the statesman of James's reign and always more of a politician than an ecclesiastic, he reports as considered by some to be a friend of the Jesuits. Sodor and Man had no seat in Parliament, so Panzani passed him by, while George Coke of Bristol lived too cautiously to allow his sentiments to be known. The rest of their Lordships are labelled " rather good, " " not bad, " or " fairly moderate. " [2]

A fuller report is sent in on the Archbishop of Canterbury, and Panzani's estimate of Laud's character and activities is a sound one. Wholly devoted to the service of the King, the Archbishop was working hard to increase the royal revenue. In ecclesiastical affairs he was absolute dictator and had the honour of the clergy much at heart. Regarded as Arminian, he approximated in dogmatic teaching to Catholicism, hence the many reforms he introduced both in England and in Scotland after his elevation to the Primacy. He was not hostile to the Church of Rome and many thought he had in mind reconciliation with her; others held the opposite. As Panzani shrewdly remarked, both were right for, while he affected in many ways to favour Catholic rites and appeared to entertain no hatred of Papists and their religion, from time to time he acted with Spartan severity against them, though this had been interpreted as inspired not by dislike but by prudence, the better to counter rumour and the grumblings of the Puritans. On one point he showed himself inexorable,— the exaction of the Oath of Allegiance from Catholics. [3]

[1] *Ibid.* For the complete list v. App. V.

[2] Panzani hoped that in the event of reunion many of the Bishops would secure themselves by reordination. As one among them had said to Father Leander some time before, " profecto non aestimaret pacem ecclesiae qui recusaret iterum ordinari." (*P.R.O. Rom. Trans.*: Panzani to Barberini, June 17/27, 1636.)

[3] One of the rumours Laud felt so damaging was that he had told his friend, the Duchess of Buckingham, not to become a Catholic as all England would soon be reconciled to Rome. Dr Leyburn, Agent to Bishop Smith and

It was Laud's reforming zeal in his own Church that deceived so many, friend and foe alike. His introduction of " Popish practices," though so far removed from the complete capitulation that reunion with the Holy See would presuppose, were nevertheless regarded as a step nearer Rome.

" He will be no Protestant, but a Christian,
And comes out Catholike the next edition." [1]

It was for this next edition that Catholic and Puritan were kept on the tip-toe of expectancy. It was looked for in every new reform, in every promotion of a moderate churchman, and its arrival seemed imminent when the Sacrament of Penance was preached publicly and clergymen were seen in the City Churches openly hearing confessions like Catholic priests. [2]

Bishop Montague hailed the signs of the times with enthusiasm. He told Panzani that each day saw them nearer reunion ; if he had been in England 10 years before, better still 20 or 30 years before, he would be of the same opinion, noticing the change in teaching and attitude. Montague added that he and all the Anglican clergy believed as much as the Gallican Church, and that, although in print there was still a certain aversion shown for Rome, this was merely a sop to public opinion. [3]

Cardinal Barberini was sceptical of this bland assertion. He was very pleased, he said, to hear that *all* the clergy of the Church of England believed as the Gallican Church did, but how was it that several of their Bishops were so decidedly Puritan? Barberini was quick to detect in the emphasis Montague laid on the Gallican Church the *arrière-pensée* that it was an autonomous branch of the Catholic Church, as he and his followers claimed the Anglican Church to be. The Cardinal therefore explained that in the Gallican Church there was no essential difference from the Church of Rome. With the so-called national churches the only variant was the name, and he cited the *African* and *Spanish* Churches as examples. The Anglican clergy, and especially Charles, the King,

---

Queen's Chaplain, vouched for this, but Panzani rejected it as at most **a** jest. (*P.R.O. Rom. Trans.* : Panzani to Barberini, Apr. 27/ May 7, 1636.)

[1] From *The Newe Churchman* (1635) (Rous's *Diary*, pp. 78-79).

[2] *P.R.O. Rom. Trans.* : Panzani to Barberini, May 4/14, 1636.

[3] *Ibid.* : Panzani to Barberini, May 11/21, 1636.

liked to talk of the *Gallican* Church, because of certain tendencies at the Sorbonne to regard, as they did, the doctrine of the deposition of kings as heretical; but the French Church did not differ from Rome on articles essential for salvation. Barberini then turned the argument on the Anglicans, so devoted to the Doctors of the Sorbonne, by recalling to every good Englishman that it was the famous University's interpretation of the Salic Law that had excluded an English King from the throne of France. [1]

It seems that in the mind of the Cardinal Secretary was a lurking suspicion that the fair signs of friendliness in England might be little more than a pose to political ends. Panzani dare not contradict his master flaty but urged in his optimism that Providence could make use of even this unpromising attitude; they should pray earnestly for this end. He assured the Cardinal that the common opinion in England was that, if Rome had proceeded in the past as she was doing now, matters would have been settled long ago; the kind words and actions of the present Pope, it was being said, avail more with princes than all manner of threats and excommunications.

Barberini himself as Cardinal Protector of England made a point of showing particular favour to Englishmen visiting Rome, and all to give pleasure to the King and further the cause of conversion. He was, therefore, painfully surprised to hear that Calvinists were increasing daily in number and power. Panzani was at pains to explain this away. The rumour must refer to Calvinists on the continent, he said, or, if Great Britain were meant, the increase could only be relatively to other heretics; the news may well have come from an interested party, for certain it was that the Catholics in England were daily growing stronger, — this the missionaries had vouched for to him. [2]

To prove his point and show the gradually changing attitude even in country folk, Panzani described how they flocked to see the Queen's Chapel when she held her Court in the country. Many were surprised, after the scandals they had heard preached about the Papists, to find nothing evil in the place. Others sighed that they could have no such beautiful things in their own Churches.

---

[1] *Ibid.*: Barberini to Panzani, July 3, 1636.
[2] *Ibid.*: Barberini to Panzani, May 12/22; Panzani to Barberini, June 21/ July 1, 1636.

A number of people stayed for Mass and Litanies. And all this near Northampton, a centre of Puritanism, where Panzani himself was staying, not at Court but with a non-Catholic lady, who not only gave him candles and wine for his Mass, but wanted to go to Confession! As someone remarked to him, these people were no heretics, but Christians badly catechized. [1]

Another curiosity Panzani noticed in England was the authority still claimed for former Papal decrees. The Dean of Westminster (John Williams, Bishop of Lincoln, whom Panzani notes as a friend of the Jesuits) maintained he had found some Papal Bulls that made the Abbey exempt from Canterbury's jurisdiction, — a claim which Laud refuted by saying that he had found other Bulls rescinding the former!

A further dispute over jurisdiction was taken before the King, the University of Cambridge resisting Laud's right of visitation on the score of a Papal Bull. This time the Archbishop settled the matter in a fashion more truly Protestant by saying that now the King held the authority of the Pope in England and had ordered him to visit the University as Primate. [2]

Then there was the new attitude towards polemics. A former Puritan College, founded in Chelsea 50 years before for the refutation of Catholic books, had long since exchanged its early activities for something infinitely less worthy in the social scale, and Catholics were trying to buy the building for use as a school, when someone suggested to the King that the least he could do would be to restore the place to its original purpose. Charles's answer was emphatic. " This I will not do," he said. "Too much time is spent on controversies which displease me.   I would rather study were devoted to reunion."   Father Philip was enthusiastic about this statement. " Is not this enough?" he asked Panzani. " Does not this show the King's goodwill?" These words of Charles, following Laud's orders that at Oxford the Fathers and Councils should be studied rather than controversy, were interpreted as showing a genuine desire for reunion on the part of both King and Archbishop. [3]

Panzani, now nearing the term of stay in England, was still

[1] *Ibid.* : Panzani to Barberini, Aug. 15/25, 1636.
[2] *Ibid.* : Panzani to Barberini, June 28/July 8, 1636.
[3] *Ibid.* : Panzani to Barberini, Sept. 20/30, 1636.

among the optimists chasing the rainbow of reunion. He had at least succeeded with Windebank in establishing diplomatic relations between the Courts of England and Rome ; it was now for George Con, the Pope's accredited Agent to the Queen, to take up the chase where Panzani had left it. Soon after Con's arrival the two were asked to dinner one evening by Hay, a Gentleman of the Queen's Household. Their host raised his glass to the success of the new Agency " whatever it is about." " What if I am treating of union with Rome?" Con asked. " I wish it success all the same," answered the Scotch Protestant, — a sign that Con's mission was regarded in Court circles as pregnant with possibilities. [1]

But the new Papal Agent was a Scot enjoying advantages of language, understanding and constant converse with all sundry, especially with the King, that Panzani had never had. His first talk on reunion with Windebank, the Italian's great friend, at once revealed what Panzani had never seen, — that the Secretary's head was full of some chimerical kind of reunion with the English and Roman Churches enjoying a certain parity of rights. Con gave Windebank clearly to understand that this could never be.

The Agent then turned to sound the King on the subject. Affinity of race and temperament gave Con something in common with Charles that he was able to exploit in his conversations with the King to whom he spoke freely of the possibilities of a Concordat with the Holy See. He assured his Majesty that he would still be at liberty to embrace many opinions that suited his taste,—always presupposing the King's complete union with Rome, as he had hurriedly to explain to an irate Cardinal Secretary. [2]

Later Con tried to find out what Laud thought of reunion. But the Archbishop would jump from a eulogy of the Early Church (to which he professed to adhere) to an attack on the Council of Trent, and it was difficult to discover what he wanted. The Papal Agent soon decided that Laud's ambition, coupled with timid

[1] *Ibid.* : Same to same, Sept. 6/16, 1636.

[2] *B.L.* 8640, f. 56 : Con to Barberini, Jan. 5/15, 1636. That Barberini was determined not to force the question of reunion in the slightest degree is evident in the severe snub he gave an enthusiastic Friar who, in opening the 1637 Lent sermons at the *Ara Coeli* in Rome, offered exaggerated hope of England's conversion in the near future (*B.L.* 8645, f. 130 : Ferragalli to Con, Mar. 25, 1637).

vacillation, was no groundwork for a great undertaking. [1] From this poor opinion of the Archbishop the Scot refused to budge. The Almighty would never make use of so inept an instrument, although, as he admitted drily, " Potens est Deus ex lapidibus suscitare semen Abrahae." [2]

In May, 1638, Christopher Davenport came to the Papal Agent with the MS. of his new book on the authority of bishops, saying that he had already shown it to several but did not wish to send it to press without informing him. Con at once reminded the Franciscan of the trouble his treatment of the *XXXIX Articles* had caused without the expected good results, and warned him that he had full faculties to censure any doctrine not generally accepted in the Church. Davenport offered to have the book censored by anyone but a Jesuit, and Con agreed that the canonical imprimatur of his religious superior in Flanders should be sought. [3]

The Papal Agent had no time for Davenport's methods of compromise and just before he left England had a straight talk with him on the subject, extracting a promise from the Franciscan that he would give his pen a rest from dangerous topics. [4]

The former interview with Davenport made Con express himself strongly to Windebank on the mistake Anglicans were making in thinking they could effect union with Rome through the medium of liberal-minded priests and semi-schismatics (the Agent never minced his words) ; such persons adopted broad opinions for no

[1] *Ibid.*, f. 346 : Same to same, May 26/June 5, 1637 : "Hò ben' procurato di far tastare il Cantuariense in ordine al levar lo Scisma, mà egli è molto vario nel suo discorso, hora mostrando di volere adherire alla dottrina delli primi 400 anni, hora lamentandosi del Concilio di Trento solam.te. La sua natura timida ambitiosa et incostante è puoco habile ad impresa grande."

[2] *B.L.* 8641, f. 34 : Same to same, July 7/17, 1637 : " Dica il Mondo quel che vuole del Cantuariense, io per mè lo ritruovo un' soggetto puoco atto à far cosa alcuna in ordine al servicio di Dio, il quale non vorrà forse servirsi d'un tale istrumento, mà vorrei bene ingannarmi ; e mi vò consolando con le parole : Potens est Deus ex lapidibus suscitare semen Abrahae."

[3] The book, which incurred the disapproval of the Jesuits, was ultimately published in Cologne as *Apologia Episcoporum, seu Sacri Magistratus Propugnatio* (Coloniae Agrippinae, 1640).

[4] *B.L.* 8644, f. 398 : Con to Barberini, Aug. 23/Sept. 2, 1639 : "Al P. Franco de Santa Clara hò parlato chiaro, rappresentando quanto si era ingannato nella sua pastata impresa. Egli m' hà promesso di non mettere più penna in carta in quella, ò simile materia."

other end than the enjoyment of a certain freedom and were true subjects neither of Rome nor of any other ecclesiastical authority in England. As such they were hostile to any attempt to help them and therefore to reunion itself.

Windebank listened to this tirade in patience, and agreed that it was impossible for such men to be good instruments of reunion; they obtained no credit with him or his friends, he protested rather inaccurately. [1]

If for many a stout Protestant reunion meant subjugation to the yoke of a foreign potentate, King Charles was ready enough to allow dependence on the Pope to be a lesser evil than dependence on the Puritans, but he had some hard things to say of Clement VIII, whose double-dealing with his father James had, he asserted, hindered the cause of reunion: St Gregory would never have acted thus. This gave Con a chance to harp on his favourite theme. He was sure, he said, that Pope Urban VIII yielded in sincerity to no Pontiff of the past and that, if his Majesty let slip the opportunity of reaching a satisfactory agreement with the Holy Father, the Popes of the future would think rather of imitating Clement than Urban. As the King expressed his regard for both Urban and his nephew, Con again begged him to seize his chance. His Holiness was an old man; his Majesty would not always have an Urban to deal with. [2]

But Charles could do nothing without Laud, and Laud, however highly he might conceive the unity of Christendom as an ideal, was a practical politician intent on pursuing his own reform in his own church. For this he had to face a charge of " romanizing" from the Puritans, an accusation the Archbishop tried to escape in somewhat cowardly fashion by renewed persecution of the Catholics. At the end of 1637 he had issued his Proclamation to prevent them " perverting" members of his own church. Two years later he called on the Bishops in Convocation to sign Canons framed to secure the settlement of the Catholics as respectable members of the Establishment. These " Proceedings against the Papists" Windebank and the Papal Agent tried in vain to stop the King from confirming. [3]

[1] *B.L.* 8642, f. 203 : Con to Barberini, May 4/14, 1638.
[2] *B.L.* 8643, f. 235 : Same to same, Dec. 7/17, 1638.
[3] *P.R.O.Rom. Trans.*, *Rossetti Corr.*, vol. I, f. 230 : Rossetti to Barberini, Jan. 15, 1640. For the 1637 Proclamation v. App. VI.

It had become a settled policy of the Puritans to play off Laud against the Papists, and their success at the game virtually destroyed even the chimera of reunion that had taken shape in the imaginations of so many. Windebank was of the few who still saw visions and dreamed dreams. His enthusiasm had been somewhat damped by Con's unsympathetic insistence on the facing of facts, but in Count Carlo Rossetti, who, as will be seen, came to England late in 1639 to replace the Scot, he found an imaginative optimism as out of touch with reality as Panzani's had been.

The King's affairs were in a bad way by that time and the Agent had orders to tender every sympathy from the Holy See, expressing regrets that no material help could be forthcoming to a King who was not a Catholic. After Rossetti had told Windebank this, he continued to discourse at length on the trouble the rebellious Puritans were making for the King. A disunited state could be neither happy nor safe, and there could be no unity without uniformity of religion. This was axiomatic and the conclusion following from it was that the ruler whose subjects were of one faith was stronger than he whose people were divided into sects hostile to every form of government. If his Majesty could be persuaded to become a Catholic, Anglicans and Catholics would form a *bloc* sufficient to check the Puritans who, if they were not repressed, would one day be powerful enough to imperil the very Throne of England. The spirit of Calvin was hostile to royal authority; it was becoming increasingly evident that the Puritans could not tolerate Kingship and would not rest satisfied till they introduced popular government in some form or other.

A holy resolve to unite with Rome, Rossetti argued, would heighten the prestige of the Crown. England would become arbitrator between France and Spain; the Catholic princes would rival each other for the hands of the royal children; heretic powers would see added cause to keep on friendly terms. Lastly, seeing that the royal revenue consisted chiefly of customs dues, the King's finances must improve through increased commerce brought by freedom of trade with Catholic Spain and Italy.

Nor need his Majesty fear his authority in church matters, bishoprics, benefices and the like, for an agreement could be arrived at conferring on him by Apostolic *Beneplacitum* the right of presentation.   With all this in his favour the King ought not to let fear of the consequences delay his taking the step. [1]

But Count Rossetti's eloquence was racing ahead of his reason. With revolution looming ahead Charles and Laud were not likely to precipitate matters by an act which, even   if it brought all the political advantages that Rossetti promised so airily, would mean a complete capitulation in the spiritual sphere which they had never at any time been prepared to make.   " For composition is impossible with such, who will not agree except all they sue for, and all the charges of their suite be to the utmost farthing awarded unto them. Our reconciliation with Rome is clogged with the same impossibilities: She may be *gone* to, but will never be *met with*, such her Pride or as (sic) Peevishness, not to stir a step to obviate any of a different Religion. Rome will never so far *un-Pope* itself, as to part with her pretended *Supremacy* and *Infallibility*, which cuts off all possibility of Protestants Treating with her." [2]

That master of the quaint conceit, Thomas Fuller, a Royalist Divine typical of his time, saw many things clearer than some of his more advanced brethren and voiced his view of the situation in terms none too gentle, but no Catholic will cavil at his con- clusions.

---

[1] *P.R.O. Rom. Trans.*, *Rossetti Corr.*, vol. I, ff. 327 seq. : Rossetti to Barberini, Aug. 10, 1640.

[2] T. FULLER, *Church History* (London, 1655, 1 in-fol.), Bk XI, p. 217.

CHAPTER VIII

CONVERTS AT COURT

" The danger from Rome was less serious than it seemed...
Fantastic speculators like Sir Kenelm Digby, witty intriguers
like Walter Montagu, brought no real strength to the cause
which they had espoused ; whilst the gay Court ladies, whose
life had hitherto been passed in a round of amusement, were
personally the better by submitting to a sterner discipline
than any which they had hitherto known." [1]

However slight a value some may place upon the type of convert
that turned to Rome in the first half of the 17th century, there
can be no doubting the fact. The reigns of James I and his son
saw a remarkable nostalgia for Rome among court circles and,
if the influx can scarcely be called a stream, it was certainly more
than a mere trickle, and increased in volume till it became a con-
tributory cause of the subsequent friction between King and
Parliament.

Whilst the realm had been in danger from Catholic Spain,
political necessity had identified patriotism with the rigid doctrines
of Calvin. But when James I had soon ended the tedious war,
Calvinism had lost much of its political significance, while at the
same time the King-Theologian's love of controversy, and dislike
of the extremists of both parties (James put Jesuit and Puritan
on a par and hated both) had further softened the bitter
hostility of former days. It was not that the official position of
England towards Rome had changed: the Penal Laws were still there,
and Parliament was continually clamouring for their execution ;
it was the personal attitude of both James and Charles that
favoured tolerance, and while this did not greatly help the poorer
Catholics of the provinces, it made a deal of difference to Catholics,

---

[1] S. R. GARDINER, *History*, vol. VIII, p. 243.

more especially luke-warm Catholics or would-be Catholics, who lived at or near the Court.

The changed attitude of the Court towards Rome and the type of Catholic to be found there are seen in the story of Charles's mother, Anne of Denmark. Part of her childhood had been spent at the Court of a Catholic princess, who made her go to Mass. Further, following her father Frederick II, a staunch Lutheran, she hated Calvinism and on coming to Scotland refused to have her children brought up in that heresy. Her first serious doubts as to her position came to her during those debates her husband loved — between Jesuits and Protestant divines. Under the influence of the Countess of Huntly and other Catholic noblewomen she began to consult Father Robert Abercrombie, S. J., who instructed and received her into the Church.[1] Seeing a change in her, James suspected the truth, and on her confessing, cautioned her to keep her conversion as secret as possible. To this end Father Abercrombie was appointed the Queen's falconer and went with her to England.[2]

She was in constant touch with Rome and actually acted as intermediary between James and the Pope,[3] but her life at the English Court was an enigma to the Catholics, and the manner of her death equally unsatisfactory. Whether she was ministered to by a priest is uncertain ; commonly known, however, is the answer she made to Archbishop Abbot who attended her at the end : " I renounce the mediations of all saints and my awen mereits, and [..] only rely upone my Saviour Chryst, who has redeemed my soul with his bloode. "[4] So Anne died as ambiguously as she had lived.

How widely the Queen's Catholicism was known and what

---

[1] I am not unaware of the differences of opinion as to the fact of Anne's conversion. The affirmative opinion was held by authoritative contemporaries. (Cf. G. CON, De duplici Statu, pp. 147-148 ; also W. BLISS, English Historical Review, vol. IV (1889), p. 110, quoting Paul V to the same effect.) Strongest argument of all, the complete change-over of that fine historian, A. W. WARD (Cf. James VI and the Papacy, in the Scottish Historical Review, vol. II (1905), pp. 249-252), consequent on the researches of Mr J. Stevenson, Dr Bellesheim and Fr Plenkers.

[2] CON, op. cit., pp. 147-148 ; English Historical Review, vol. III, pp. 795-798. A. W. Ward's review of Er Frederik II's Dalter Anna, Dronning af Storbritannien gaaet over til Katholicismen, by W. PLENKERS, Copenhagen, 1888.

[3] A. O. MEYER, Clemens VIII. und Jakob I. von England, passim.

[4] English Historical Review, loc. cit., citing from Abbotsford Miscellany an eye-witness account of Madam the Queen's death and Maner thereof.

nfluence it had is hard to gauge. What is certain is that a wave of conversions passed over the country remarkable enough to attract the attention of a sympathetic Spanish diplomat, who commented on the number of Anglican clergymen[1] seceding to Rome, with the consequent loss of their livings and a financial embarrassment which the kindly foreigner hoped to relieve, feeling sure it was only the haunting fear of destitution that was keeping many more from the Church. [1]

These conversions began to be talked about. Toby Mathew, Bacon's *alter ego* and the son of the Archbishop of York, had been received into the Church some years before by Father Persons, and ordained in Rome by Cardinal Bellarmine; rumour had it that he was also a member of the Society. Poor recommendations to James, one would think, yet Toby moved continually in Court circles, was employed by the King in the Spanish negotiations and knighted in 1623. [2]

But conversions and rumours of conversions did not stop at sons of bishops, — it began to be whispered that the lately deceased Bishop of London had become a Catholic on his deathbed. John King had been devoted to Charles and a great friend of the late Queen Anne, so many Catholics believed the story and it got into print, [3] gaining enough credence to provoke an indignant denial by the late Bishop's son, Henry King, in a sermon preached at Paul's Cross. He gave no reasons, but " a plaine, unglost deniall. They say it is so, I know it is not, in a iust case it is Rhetorik enough. " [4] It was not enough, however, to satisfy the anxiety

[1] *Arch. Prop., Scritture Antiche*, I, *Anglia* 347, f. 234 : Don Carlos Coloma to the Archbishop of Patras, London, March 30, 1623 : " En este Reyno se va convertiendo cadadia mucha gente a nuestra sancta fe, y agora entre otros, tenemos ocho ministros predicantes, que se han reconciliado con la Iglesia Católica, y asu exemplo es cierto que se reducirán otros muchos, si la ley de la necessidad no se lo impidiese, por haver de dexar y perder totalmente sus beneficios y provendas con que se sustentar ; y asi creo que Su Sant[d] no podria haver limosna may digna de su grandeza y oficio pastoral que embiar aquí a distribuir algún dinero por mano de V. S. I. entre los ministros convertidos y que se fueren convirtiendo, precediendo para ello suficientes informaciones."

[2] Laud, *op. cit.*, p. 230.

[3] Cf. *The Protestants' Plea for Priests and Papists* [Sept. 1621].

[4] *A Sermon preached at Paul's Crosse the 25 of November* 1621 *upon occasion of that false and scandalous Report (lately printed) touching the supposed Apostasie of the right Reverend Father in God, John King, late Lord Bishop of London, by*

of the Episcopal Bench to disprove so vital a defection from
their midst, and Thomas Preston, *alias* Roger Widdrington, the
Benedictine whose controversial activities are recorded in another
chapter, was summoned to appear before the Archbishop of
Canterbury on a charge of having received the late Bishop into the
Catholic Church.   Father Preston swore on oath that he had never
even seen his lordship, much less had he confessed him or ministered
to him ; nor did he know of any priest having done so, though
he knew the tale that was going round and had also heard that
Masses had been offered abroad for the repose of the Bishop's
soul. [1]

Despite these authoritative denials the story was used for
propaganda purposes by an anonymous Catholic who set out
what were likely to have been the late Bishop's motives for joining
the Church of Rome.   The writer made no attempt to have these
' motives ' accepted as authentic ; he was sure himself of the Bishop's
conversion, and equally sure he must have had reasons akin to
these, which might in their turn very easily become motives of
credibility for Bishop King's colleagues on the Bench. [2]

Defections to Rome become more frequent under Charles I,
especially after the Peace of Fontainebleau had provided once more
for the adequate service of the Queen's chapel. This was supplied by
the French Capuchins whom Père Joseph sent over. Their zeal,
helped in no small degree by their charm and moderation, brought
them a great number of converts (two or three a week) among the
nobility, particularly after the opening of the new Chapel at Somerset
House. The merely curious who became converted in turn brought

*Henry King his eldest son.   Whereunto is annexed the Examination and Answere
of Thomas Preston, P. taken before my Lords Grace of Canterbury touching this
scandall,* London, 1621.

[1] *Ibid.*

[2] *The Bishop of London his Legacy, or certaine motives of D. King, late
Bishop of London for his change of Religion, and dying in the Catholike, and
Roman Church with a conclusion to his Brethren, the L. L. Bishops of England.
Permissu Superiorum,* 1624. — This was attributed, by Protestant writers
at least, to George Fisher *alias* Musket (1580-1645) who had been educated and
converted by the priests imprisoned in the notorious Wisbeach Castle. He was
ordained at the English College, Rome (1606) and appointed a Canon by Bishop
William Bishop in 1623. He later (1641) became president of Douai College
(Cf. GILLOW, *op. cit.,* vol. V, pp. 144-146).

along their friends and relatives to the Chapel services, which, conducted with some elaboration, seemed the acme of colour, warmth and imagination in religion after the meagre fare offered by the Establishment, and the woeful barrenness of Calvinism. [1]

Anglican clergymen were frequently to be found at one or other of the London Chapels, and many eventually made their submission to Rome. Marie de' Medici, who during her stay in England maintained a public oratory, told the Papal Agent of three clergymen who came to the chapel and asked the meaning of the various Mass vestments. One became a Catholic, while the others continued to come and hear Mass with great devotion. [2]

The conversion of Edmund Price made a great impression at the time. He had passed from the service of Buckingham to become Dean of Lincoln, sub-Dean of Westminster and a King's Chaplain. In addition he was held in great esteem for his learning. At the age of 60 he was taken seriously ill and received into the Church by an English secular priest. He resisted all the efforts of his Protestant friends to " reconvert " him, remaining constant to his new profession of faith till his death a few weeks later. [3]

Such conversions were by no means all death-bed decisions. Dom David, the Benedictine, who was still passing as a gentleman of the Queen's household under the *alias* Matthew Savage, wrote to Rome in October, 1634, of a young ex-parson he had under instruction and of whom he had the greatest hopes. He intended sending him to study under the Jesuits in the Eternal City. [4]

Yet another remarkable clergyman convert was Stephen Gough who, after taking orders in the Established Church and proceeding Doctor of Divinity at Oxford, became chaplain to Laud. He was strongly attached to the King, and during the Revolution left for France with Father Philip, the Oratorian confessor of Henrietta Maria. He already had some doubts as to his position, and after attending a series of conferences by M. Faydeau, a doctor

---

[1] GAMACHES, *Mémoires*, p. 32.

[2] *P.R.O. Rom. Trans., Rossetti Corr.*, vol. I, f. 196 : Rossetti to Barberini, May 1, 1640.

[3] *Arch. Prop., Scritture Antiche* 150 (1632), f.318 : Ex litteris Londino scriptis a Vicario Epi Chalced. ad Petrum Fittonum Romae Agentem pro dicto Epo et Clero Anglicano, datis 30 Decem. [1632].

[4] *Ibid.*, 134 (1634), p. 225 : Selvaggio to Ingoli, London, Oct. 10, 1634.

of the Sorbonne, he became a Catholic in 1645, subsequently entering the French Oratory. [1]

Encouragement to would-be Papists did not come only from the Queen's household. The King, too, had surrounded himself with a number of weaker brethren such as Windebank, Weston, Cottington and Endymion Porter, all of whom were Catholics under the skin and contrived to die in the Faith ; there were also at Court a number of Charles's own countrymen, Catholics of the stauncher sort, Huntly, Angus, Argyle, Nithsdale, Abercorn, all of whom were daily pressing his Majesty for liberty to live openly in the practice of their religion. [2]

The number of Catholics who lived at or near the Court provoked scandalized comment in the Commons, a Mr Whitaker on June 5, 1628, pointing out the national peril : " There is a commonwealth of Papists, nobility, gentry, clergy and commonalty that serve the Duke [i. e. Buckingham] constantly. In Drury Lane, there are three families of Papists there residing for one of Protestants ; insomuch that it may well be called Little Rome. " [3]

It was this constant threat of criticism, voiced so vehemently by the Commons and later, in the absence of Parliament, penned so acrimoniously by Prynne and the pamphleteers, that made Charles extremely sensitive to any sign of " romanizing " at his court, however sympathetic his personal views may have been. Earlier in his reign and before his reconciliation with the Queen his attitude towards the Catholics had not yet softened and in November, 1626, he banished from Court Lady Falkland, wife of the Lord Deputy of Ireland and a recent convert, for going to Mass with the Queen. [4] This was the least acute of her sufferings which form an epic of Christian patience worthy of the Early Church. Personal conviction

[1] INGOLD, op. cit., vol. III, p. 169.

[2] FORBES-LEITH, op. cit., vol. I, p. 60.

[3] Parliamentary History, vol. II, p. 406 (1807).

[4] T.BIRCH, Court and Times of Charles 1, vol. I, p. 170 : To Mead, London, Nov. 17, 1626. Charles had already tried vainly to prevent her from seceding to Rome by sending her a defence by an Anglican Bishop of the King's own view, viz. that while admitting the truth of the Roman Church, one could still lawfully remain in the Church of England. The document was forwarded to Fr Leander at Douai who completely exposed the fallacious argument. (Cf. G. FULLERTON, Life of Elizabeth, Lady Falkland, p. 75 ; GILLOW, op. cit., vol. III, p. 666).

and a large amount of self-interest made Lord Falkland urge the King to enforce the Penal Laws against his recusant wife, and Charles, fearful of showing undue favour to converts, ordered the lady to remain in the custody of her mother, who, luckily for her perhaps, refused to give her shelter.

Exiled from her husband's house, passed over in her father's will, though an only child, she faced dire poverty in a miserable hovel in London, too proud and too careful of her husband's reputation to appeal to her Catholic friends for help.

Eventually her patience and fidelity won over her husband, who was arranging for her to return to him and actually supervising a chapel for her in his country house, when he met with a hunting accident at Theobalds. This, followed by clumsy surgery, cheated her of her material reward, and she had to rest content with a full reconciliation with her husband before he died.

Her youngest children, who had been taken from her at her conversion, were now placed in the charge of their eldest brother, Lucius, Lord Falkland, who caused his mother exquisite pain by appointing as their tutor the apostate Chillingworth, who, having returned to the Church of England, was now dabbling in Socinianism. But the children, four girls and two small boys, resisted all the persuasions of their Protestant mentor and relatives, and insisted that they were of their mother's faith. The latter, after several unsuccessful attempts, managed to get the children away from their unhappy surroundings and hid them in London. She was immediately charged by the Council with sending them out of the country, which at the moment she could safely deny. But Patrick and Placid soon left for the Continent and eventually became priests. [1]

The case of Lady Falkland was, among all the cases where Charles felt compelled officially to censure a convert, the one that had the saddest consequences for the victim. Later in his reign he had frequently to show his displeasure at some notable defection to Rome at the Court but, if such occurrences irritated him, it was more through his dislike of the gossip caused than because of any real anger at the step taken. Agreeing perfectly with nearly all Rome taught, he could never see the necessity of leaving the

[1] E. GODFREY, *Home Life under the Stuarts*, pp. 68-71, 194-196.

Church of England. He called himself a Catholic and considered it unnecessary to prefix an adjective to the title.

To Archbishop Laud, as was only natural, secession to Rome came as a keen blow, the more painful in several cases as his own personal friends were concerned. Already in the previous reign, the conversion of his friend the Countess of Buckingham, mother of the favourite, had led to his famous Conference with Fisher the Jesuit, who had received the lady into the Church. [1]

Then in March, 1636, to his great grief he received a letter from Sir Kenelm Digby giving his reasons for returning to Rome. Digby, son of the Sir Everard Digby executed for complicity in the Powder Plot, had been born and bred a Catholic, but in 1630 to the great scandal of his co-religionists, he took the Sacrament in the Chapel at Whitehall and professed the Anglicanism of the King. His motive was naturally put down to ambition, though it would, probably be truer to say that his desire for freedom of philosophic thought was the cause, and that for a time he succumbed to the perennial scare that Rome fetters Reason. In any case, by October, 1635, he had returned to the fold, convinced, after thrashing the matter out, that he could still retain his liberty within the Church. He told Laud he had for two years made every effort to come to a decision, consulting the authorities on both sides, from whom, however, the Archbishop, Digby's former tutor and one of his greatest friends, had much to his chagrin been omitted. [2]

About this time occurred what Charles always dreaded with these " society " conversions — one of them became a *cause célèbre* and the talk of the town. Frances Coke, daughter of the anti-Catholic Lord Chief Justice, had married Buckingham's brother, John Villiers, who after being received into the Church by Fr John Piercey, *alias* Fisher the Jesuit, had set his mother, the Countess of Buckingham, on the road to Rome. Raised to the peerage as

---

[1] *Life of Archbishop Laud*, pp. 76-77.

[2] E. BLIGH, *Sir Kenelm Digby and his Venetia*, pp. 165, 195 ; W. HOOK, *Lives of the Archbishops of Canterbury*, vol. VI (new series), pp. 274 seq. Laud's long and dignified reply to his friend occupied some eight pages of print. Another of Digby's biographers, T. G. Longueville, a Catholic, suggests Sir Kenelm's reversion to the Faith of his baptism may have been induced by " a keen eye to the main chance," as in Paris he had heard of Panzani's Reunion talks and of Con's coming. (Cf. *Life of Sir Kenelm Digby by One of his descendants*, p. 230.)

Viscount Purbeck, he soon became weak in his mind and was deserted by his wife for Robert Howard. The lady was cited for adultery before the Court of High Commission, fined £500 and condemned to do penance in a white sheet at the Savoy Chapel. To escape the ignominy she fled to the country, where she and Howard lived unmolested. Emboldened by time they made the mistake of going to live at Westminster, where their proximity to the Court so irritated Charles that he reproached Laud for neglect of duty in allowing such a scandal to the Church and the nation to continue. The Archbishop thereupon had Lady Purbeck rearrested and imprisoned in the Gatehouse, but she escaped a second time in man's clothes to Paris. There she met Sir Kenelm Digby who, fresh from the throes of conversion himself, urged her to become a Catholic, marshalling in a studied thesis all the arguments from tradition and the authority of the Church. [1]

Soon the disconcerting news reached London that the notorious lady had declared herself a Papist and, worse still, was moving heaven and earth to win the King's pardon and her return to Court. To this end she engaged their Majesties of France and the powerful Richelieu to intercede for her with Charles, and herself wrote a long letter to Henrietta, recounting the story of her life from childhood to conversion and begging her Majesty to plead for her. She also bombarded the Duchess of Buckingham and other Court ladies with letters, — all apparently on the advice of Digby, who himself wrote (Jan. 1637) in the same cause to Lord Conway and other friends of his among the Privy Councillors, proclaiming the virtues of the new convert. But her choice of Digby as adviser only irritated Charles, and did nothing to further her plan. All hope of return abandoned for the time, she decided to enter a Paris nunnery and, with her usual boldness, obtained the sponsorship of the Queen through the influence of no less a person than the Cardinal Secretary of State himself. [2]

---

[1] *Ibid.*, p. 199 ; *Life of Archbishop Laud*, pp. 360 seq. Digby published these talks with Lady Purbeck as a *Conference with a Lady about Choice of Religion* (Paris, 1638), a quaint 16mo of unusual cut. There exists a MS., not in Digby's hand, in which the argument is addressed to a man, though on p. 4 Digby says distinctly he is writing a summary of these talks.

[2] BIRCH, *op. cit.*, vol. II, p. 241 : Mr E. R. to Pickering, [London], April 13, 1636. *B.L.* 8632, N⁰ 15 : Barberini to Henrietta, Rome, June 19, 1636. She

The establishment of diplomatic relations between England and the Holy See, and the residence in London of three successive Papal Agents, Panzani, Con and Rossetti, not only made the practice of religion easier for the Catholics, but gave the more timid would-be converts and crypto-Catholics the courage of their convictions. Conversion became the order of the day, although it was generally admitted even by the most optimistic that the country as a whole would never become reconciled to Rome without the conversion of the King. [1] There was little hope of this while Charles argued, as he always did, that there was nothing to be gained in going over to Rome when he was a perfectly good Catholic in the Church of England, — as good a Catholic as any Roman, without the disadvantages of adhering to an obscurantist Papal system.

This view was shared by others who abhorred the rise of the Protestant tradition in the Established Church. Windebank, for example, when taxed by Panzani with not being a Catholic, answered very decidedly : " I tell you, if I did not believe I was a Catholic, I would not stay in the country." The Papal Agent suggested he should discuss the matter with some learned Catholic friend, but Windebank evaded the issue, insisting with a smile, " I am a Catholic, though not a Roman Catholic." In commenting on the incident to the Cardinal Secretary Panzani adds rather ruefully that in this smiling fashion are questions of such serious import passed off. [2]

Although Panzani was greatly interested in the conversion and reunion movements, his official task in England was first to settle the differences between the Catholic clergy, secular and regular, and secondly to prepare the way for a papal minister to be accredited to the Queen. As has been seen, when George Con arrived at the Queen's Court as Papal Agent, he immediately set up a public oratory in his lodgings. The Pope's Chapel, as it was called, not only

---

appears to have entered as a visitor only, not as postulant or novice, and soon left after refusing to obey the rules. She then lived in penury in Paris till returning to England, where she died in 1645. (Cf. *Life of Sir Kenelm Digby*, p. 236.)

[1] *P.R.O. Rom. Trans.* 9, 139, f. 133 : D. David to Barberini, Sept. 7/17, 1634.

[2] *Ibid.* : Panzani to Barberini, Aug. 5/15, 1635.

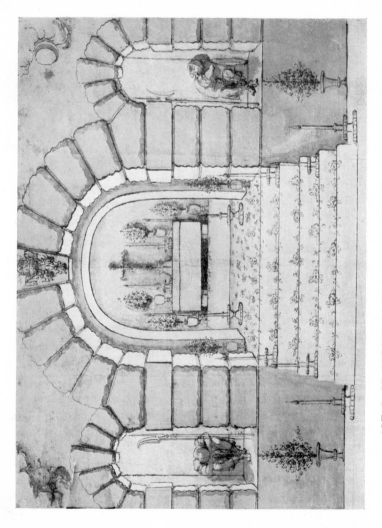

ALTAR OF REPOSE IN THE 'POPE'S CHAPEL,' LONDON, 1638

improved the facilities London Catholics enjoyed for the practice of their religion (all the houses near it were soon taken by Catholics [1]), but exercised, through the pleasing personality of the Agent, a considerable influence on a considerable number of the nobility favourable to Rome.

It was known in London that on his arrival George Con, though a Canon of San Lorenzo in Damaso, was not a priest, but it was the impression among many that he had been ordained since, — by Papal Brief was one ingenious suggestion, a thing quite possible to those who knew no better, the Agent said witheringly. Tales were also spread around that the King went to confession to him, and that he had reconciled the Countess of Arundel to the Church.

The latter, a god-daughter of Queen Elizabeth, became his faithful friend and helped him in seizing every opportunity of explaining the Faith. At Easter, 1638, Con and the Countess took the Earl of Bath and other Protestant friends to see the Good Friday sepulchre in the Papal Chapel and explained its significance. The Earl appeared impressed, saying politely he felt more devotion there than in any of his own churches. He asked, with a plaintiveness the Agent swallowed whole, why Protestants were deprived of such consolations. [2]

The *rapprochement* between the Court of England and Rome was greatly helped by the courtesy and kindness shown to English travellers by Cardinal Barberini, the Pope's nephew. Con offered to the Countess of Arundel the Cardinal's patronage for anyone she knew who would like to visit Rome, and a number of wealthy Englishmen and Scots, both Catholic and Protestant, took advantage of the offer for themselves or for their sons travelling for their education. The presence of Sir William Hamilton as Queen's Resident at the Papal Court made access to the Cardinal easy. In November, 1636, the sons of Mr Secretary Windebank came to pay their respects to the Pope's nephew; the following February he had visits from the sons of Bishop Montague, of the English Ambassador in Paris and of the late Prince Henry's tutor. Easter, 1637, brought the Earl of Erskine, and Messrs Alec and David

---

[1] *B.L.* 8644, f. 364 : Con to Barberini, July 26/Aug. 5, 1639.
[2] *B.L.* 8642, ff. 85, 157 : Con to Barberini, Feb. 2/12 ; Mar. 23/Apr. 2, 1638.

Carnegie, as well as two young English merchants, one of whom was a non-Catholic. [1]

All were welcomed by Cardinal Barberini who never failed to record these visits, which, he felt, gave him a chance of breaking down the old anti-papal prejudice. For this reason he even received visitors who did not wish to see the Pope, and was most amused by the Duke of Lennox's brother, who wanted to see him but not Pope Urban, as he had some Calvinists in his party, who, half-pagan themselves, he said, thought it idolatry to genuflect to the Pope! [2]

A Court conversion which caused considerable éclat at this time, both in London and Rome, was that of the witty Walter Montagu, son of the first Earl of Manchester, Lord Privy Seal. Young Montagu had earlier on been employed on diplomatic missions in Lorraine, which brought him into conflict with Richelieu and landed him in prison. The Cardinal summed him up contemptuously as a little fool only fit for entertaining the ladies! [3] The judgment seemed prophetic when Montagu began to acquire the Queen's favour and a reputation as a Court wit. His opportunity came when a play had to be written for the Queen. The Court Masques were famous, but old Ben Jonson, who wrote the verse, and Inigo Jones, who devised the weird and wonderful engines that worked the scenery, were bitter rivals, and a fierce quarrel over precedence led to the resignation of the playwright. Wat Montagu, called upon in an emergency, showed so great a facility for versifying that he quickly produced *The Shepherd's Paradise*, a pastoral lasting seven or eight hours, but as one of the chief uses of these masques was to give practice to the Queen in her English, her Majesty could hardly complain! [4]

The lively Montagu was not so frivolous as either Richelieu or Charles or even the Queen herself, who so enjoyed his wit, had thought.

---

[1] *B.L.* 8639, ff. 118-119 : Con to Barberini, Sept. 29/Oct. 9, 1636. *Ibid.*, f. 238 : Barberini to Con, Nov. 28, 1636. *B.L.* 8640, f. 116 : Same to same, Feb. 12, Apr. 12, 1637.

[2] *P.R.O. Rom. Trans.*, *Rossetti Corr.*, vol. III, f. 97 : Barberini to Rossetti, April 6, 1641.

[3] *B.L.* 8656, f. 83 : Bagno to Barberini, Nov. 22, 1633 : "Il cardinale di Richelieu mi soleva dire ch' era *un petit fou da trattener dame.*" The words were spoken to Card. del Bagno, Paris Nuncio at the time.

[4] D'ISRAELI, *op. cit.*, vol. III, pp. 153 seq.

At Easter, 1635, he was secretly received into the Church by Father Philip, and, although unwilling as yet to jeopardize his position by proclaiming his conversion, he kept away from Protestant churches and the communion table. This was brought to the notice of the Archbishop of Canterbury who reported it to the King. Charles at once spoke to Henrietta on the matter, telling her how sorry he was that Montagu should choose to ruin himself on the verge of a promising career. He said, however, that, although his custom was to banish such cases from Court, he would be satisfied if Montagu withdrew himself voluntarily for a time. The King hastened to soften the blow for his wife by adding that he had no desire to persecute the Catholics, but was bound to show some official sign of displeasure. [1] He would not have minded, he said, if Montagu had continued to take the sacrament. The Queen then sent for the new convert and told him of the King's decision, whereat Montagu resolved to retire to Paris and Rome for a year in the hope of returning later to the Queen's service.

The young courtier's conversion was not at first generally known, and Windebank, when discussing the reciprocal agency, tried to angle for how much Panzani knew by suggesting Montagu as Queen's Resident in Rome, adding with a sly smile that he had ambitions for the post. But the Italian was too astute to be drawn and answered that any good servant of the Queen would do, provided he were a Catholic; Montagu would, indeed, be an admirable choice, were he a Catholic. He would soon be a very fervent one (" si farebbe Cattolicissimo "), hinted the Secretary. " Please God both Montagu and all England with him will become Catholic, " murmured Panzani non-committally. [2]

At this point Montagu made public his conversion in a splendid letter to his father explaining his motives. The Earl of Manchester was a lawyer of extraordinary energy and a zealous Protestant extremely well read in divinity. Whether to answer his son or

---

[1] *P.R.O. Rom. Trans.* : Panzani to Barberini, Sept. 23/Oct. 3, 1635 :" ... dicendo che se bene non voleva persequitare li cattolici nondimeno in questi casi non poteva far di meno di non far qualche dimostratione."

[2] *Ibid.* : Same to same, Oct. 7/17, 1635. When sounded by Panzani, Montagu denied all pretensions to the agency. This Fr Philip confirmed, saying the new convert's journey to Rome was in order to become a priest of the Roman Oratory, Chiesa Nuova.

not, he drew up a comprehensive summary of the arguments in favour of Protestantism to meet the case put by Catholics, and was naturally angry at the step his son had taken. Charles, however, showed no further sign of displeasure beyond refusing to read Montagu's letter. English opinion as a whole was lenient, but the Scotch Puritans cursed him roundly. Cardinal Barberini, of course, was delighted at the reception of so distinguished a convert and wrote to congratulate him, placing his services at Montagu's disposal, [1] — an offer that was to cause the Cardinal some embarrassment when, a few years later, Montagu pressed so persistently his claims to a Red Hat.

Early in 1636 Montagu arrived in Rome with letters from the Queen. It was his first visit as a Catholic, and he lost no time in charming both Barberini and the Pope, who wrote in praise of him to Henrietta. [2]

By the end of the year he had returned to England without the King's consent, though he was seeking permission to frequent the Court again. Barberini supported him in this resolution, feeling his influence would be a real help to Con. The Queen, only too anxious to have him back, was afraid to broach the matter with her husband and, rather than embarrass her, Montagu was ready to spend the winter quietly studying somewhere in England, unless the King raised no objection to a return to Rome. [3]

Montagu's fiercely Protestant father was the real obstacle to his return to Court. Charles soon gave his consent, but the old Earl threatened to use his authority as a Privy Councillor to have his son arrested and brought under the Law if he ventured back. Meanwhile Con strained every nerve to smooth over the situation,

---

[1] *The Complete Peerage*, vol. VIII, pp. 365 seq.; *Hist. MSS. Commission*, 8th *Report*, Pt. II, p. 10. *P.R.O. Rom. Trans.*: Panzani to Barberini, Dec. 2/12, 1635. *B.L.* 8632, N⁰ 8 : Barberini to Montagu, Dec. 20, 1635.

[2] *B.L.* 8632, N⁰ 10 : Barberini to Henrietta, Rome, Feb. 14, 1636. *Ibid.*, N⁰ 12 : Urban to Henrietta, Rome, Feb. 26, 1636.

As evidence of a former visit to Rome, in Nov. 1633, Barberini refers to the projected visit of " il piccolo Montagù," who was too well liked by the Queen of England (*B.L.* 8656, f. 44 : Barberini to Bagno, Nov. 16, 1633). Also in the English Coll. Archives, *Liber Peregrinorum*, Jan. 3, 1634, the visit of one D. Gualterus Montacuto is recorded.

[3] *B.L.* 8632, N⁰ 18 : Barberini to Montagu, Rome, Nov. 14, 1636. *B.L.* 8639, f. 233 : Con to Barberini, Hampton, Nov. 17/27, 1636.

asking the Queen to intercede with Charles, and the Countess of Buckingham and the Earl of Holland to plead with Montagu's father. But his greatest stroke was to win for himself the old man's friendship and confidence, and make him reveal his genuine affection for his son. What had irritated the Earl, it appeared, was not so much the fact of his son's conversion, as his persistence in making it public and thus wounding his father's pride and prestige as a champion of Protestantism. Eventually Con told the Earl that his son was actually back in England and begged him not to interfere in any way; the old man agreed, though he would not see his son without the King's leave, which was of course readily given. Still, he flatly refused to have him under his roof for fear of slanderous tongues whereat Con said he had already invited Montagu to stay with him.

Con had given the invitation in the name of Cardinal Barberini, feeling sure the illustrious convert's unhoped-for return to Court would add great prestige to the Catholics and help the cause of religion. [1]

At length Montagu made his appearance at Court, was received with infinite kindness by the Queen and allowed to kiss the King's hand, though no word passed. Charles continued to maintain a studied chillness towards the convert courtier, until one day in the Queen's apartments he was discussing a point with George Con, the answer to which the Papal Agent pretended not to know, but said that Montagu certainly did. Before the King could intervene, Con had called Montagu from another part of the room and introduced him into the conversation. The ruse succeeded perfectly and Charles continued to chat familiarly with the new convert to the amazement of the courtiers and the delight of the Queen. Montagu was jubilant to have obtained, as he put it, by means of Rome (*i.e.* through the Pope's Agent) what the influence of all his friends, including the Queen, had failed to win for him. [2]

Montagu had apparently been ordained priest during his short stay in Rome and now, with the express approval of Cardinal Barberini, chose Con's Chapel as the centre of his ministry. The

---

[1] *Ibid.*, f. 280 : Con to Barberini, Hampton, Dec. 8/18, 1636. *B.L.* 8640, ff. 91, 146, 192, 239 : Same to same, Jan. 19/29 ; Feb. 16/26 ; Mar. 9/19 ; Apr. 7/17, 1637.

[2] *B.L.* 8640, f. 267 : Same to Same, London, April 21/May 1, 1637.

Papal Agent suggested that he would have plenty to do there, but his work had scarcely begun before it was cut short by a severe illness, during which Con attended him.[1] Montagu was back again towards the end of the year (1637) and, subsequent to Con's leaving London, played a great part in the Queen's efforts to obtain a Cardinal's Hat for England.

During the Revolution, he accompanied the Queen into exile, acting as her almoner, and in France became Abbot, sucessively, of Nanteuil and of St Martin's, Rouen. At this time he appeared, according to his contemporary Clarendon, " wholly restrained from all the vanity and levity of his former life and perfectly mortified to the pleasures of the world, which he enjoyed in a very great measure and excess, "[2]— a great tribute to the power of conversion in the ladies' man whom Richelieu had known.

The Court converts naturally received the greatest possible support from the Papal Agent, who wrote to Rome in terms of superlative praise of the apostolic activities, somewhat overbearing to modern ideas, of one who was, as Gardiner calls her, the soul of the proselytizing movement at the Court of Charles. The young and beautiful Olive Boteler enjoyed a privileged position both as the wife of Endymion Porter, Gentleman-of-the-Bedchamber to the King and one of his privileged companions on the Spanish journey, and as the cousin of the late Duke of Buckingham, many of whose finer qualities, his energy and impetuous, generous enthusiasm, she possessed herself and turned to good account in pursuit of the souls of her weaker relatives.

Olive's sister, Lady Newport, was, for the moment, as zealous a Puritan as she was a Catholic, and each sister in her own way was anxious for the soul of their father, Lord Boteler, who in the spring of 1637 lay dangerously ill. Losing no time Mrs Porter drove down to Woodhall and fetched the dying man to her house. She then sent for George Con who visited him daily and prepared him for a general confession. — a difficult task in England, as the Agent remarked drily. The old man was received into the Church before he died.[3]

---

[1] *Ibid.*, f. 248 : Con to Barberini, London, Apr. 14/24, 1637 ; f. 354 : Barberini to Con, Rome, June 8, 1637. *B.L.* 8641, f. 142 : Barberini to Con, Oct. 17, 1637. Barberini thanks Con as for a personal favour for visiting Montagu.

[2] ADAMS, *op. cit.*, vol. III, pp. 113-114.

[3] *B.L.* 8640, f. 226 : Con to Barberini, March 30/April 9, 1637 : "... hora

The energetic Mrs Porter, while still awaiting the final submission of her father, turned her attention to her brother-in-law. Hearing he lay dying in the house of a heretic relative three miles out of town, she hurried off in a carriage with a doctor and a priest, who reconciled the dying man and gave him the Last Sacraments. Then, lest he should lapse, Mrs Porter had him removed to London, where Con visited him. After some months he died, firm in his faith and grasping Con's rosary. The Papal Agent wrote proudly of this case to Cardinal Barberini, showing him that amid all the temptations of Court life there were people like Olive Porter capable of heroic action. [1]

Less completely successful was the case of Mary Feilding, Marchioness of Hamilton, Mrs Porter's cousin, who in the late summer of 1637 was laid up with a violent fever. The lady had been a Puritan of strong views till a few months before, when Con had visited her and talked with her. He now continued to send her messages through Mrs Porter, who also gave her Catholic books to read. Her father, the Earl of Denbigh, whom Con immediately black-listed as a timid Puritan ass, sent for the Bishop of Carlisle to provide an antidote. His lordship declared to the sick Marchioness he would give his soul for her. Olive Porter's riposte was characteristic: " Little will it help you, my sister, that the soul of that old man shall be with you in the Devil's House." The sequel is unsatisfactory. In October, 1637, Con wrote: " I visit her daily. God knows what will follow." The lady's conversion was never openly acknowledged. [2]

Such deeds, Con wrote indignantly to Barberini, could not long escape the venom of malicious tongues, and it was reported to the King that the wife of Mr Porter, his Gentleman-of-the-Bedchamber, was unsound on matters of religion and was bringing up her sons as Jesuits, — this last no doubt an attack on the Jesuit chaplain she kept in her house to serve her private Chapel. Charles was not likely to take action against his friends on the strength of such tales, and nothing further was heard of the accusations. It

---

[il Boteler] attende à far la confessione generale, che pare un duro negotio in questo paese." *Ibid.*, f. 290 : Same to same, Apr. 28/May 8, 1637.

[1] *Ibid.*, f. 242 : Con to Barberini, London, April 7/17, 1637. *B.L.* 8641, f. 112 : Same to same, Sept. 22/Oct. 2, 1637.

[2] D. TOWNSHEND, *The Life and Letters of Endymion Porter*, pp. 165-166.

14

was, however, deemed prudent that the Jesuit should disappear till the talk died down. As a further measure of prudence Con also advised the walling up of a private door connecting the Porters' house with that of their neighbours who were priests. [1]

Like his master and friend the King, Endymion Porter was an Anglican who did much for the Catholic cause. His early education in Spain as a page in the Olivares family, his several return visits to that Catholic country *par excellence* convinced him of the truth of the Faith, but he had not his wife's courage nor could he, with a wife and family, risk his position at Court as Montagu had done in declaring himself a Catholic. [2] Occupying a position necessitating close attendance on the King's person, he was obliged to accompany his Majesty to the Royal Chapel. Could he continue doing so, if he were to become a Catholic? George Con was consulted and put the case to Barberini who naturally asked for more specific details. First, did Porter intend to declare himself a Catholic publicly, or keep his conversion a secret? Secondly, had the King other Catholic servants who went with him to chapel? If so, how was it generally regarded by the Catholics? Thirdly, as the Brief of Paul V forbidding Catholics to enter heretical places of worship was known, were such servants of the King who attended Protestant service in the course of their duty generally regarded as transgressing the Brief? [3]

Con replied that Porter did not wish to make his conversion public, and therefore in his continuing to attend the King at service there would be no question of giving scandal. Cardinal Barberini had also mentioned the possibility of Porter's relapsing if he continued going to the Protestant Church. This Con ridiculed, saying that he would to God there were more religious who knew how to speak up for the Faith as Porter did. Con replied by implication to the other questions, asking Barberini to have the case thoroughly examined privately, as it was one that might occur often and a decision would therefore be useful as a precedent. It was the common opinion in England, he added, that there was

    [1] *B.L.* 8641, f. 203 : Con to Barberini, Nov. 17/27, 1637. *B.L.* 8642, f. 48 : Same to same, Jan. 12/22, 1638.

    [2] *P.R.O. Rom. Trans.* : Same to same, Dec. 8/18, 1636 : "... in sostanza egli [i.e. Porter] è d'intelletto cattco mà con la voluntà seguita il Rè."

    [3] *B.L.* 8641, f. 170 : Barberini to Con, Oct. 31, 1637.

no need for dispensation to frequent the churches of heretics, provided there was neither scandal given nor danger of perversion. Pleading the case, Con said the French Catholics did so without scruple, just as Catholics in Rome went occasionally out of curiosity to the Jewish Synagogue. He added persuasively that many Catholics went to listen to the lies of Protestant ministers simply in order to refute them. [1]

But Barberini, who never liked being driven to a categorical decision that might involve him in difficulties, contented himself with saying that his three questions would solve Porter's case and any others like it. He therefore left the matter to Con's discretion. [2]

Mrs Porter was as energetic in the defence of her religion as she was zealous in winning souls to it. She liked to thrash out the reason for everything and, after every argument on religion, contrived to introduce her opponent to the Papal Agent. On one occasion she brought along her glover, a violent devotee of Robert Browne, the ultra-Puritan who favoured a purely congregational system of Church government opposed to both Presbyterianism and Episcopacy. As the man came to the interview armed with his Bible, Con, an astute controversialist, accepted the challenge, pointing out several passages in the Scriptures that so upset the poor Brownist's equilibrium that he hurried off and soon after was reported to have gone mad!

Mrs Porter's cousin, the Marquis of Hamilton, made some reference in conversation to this case, but only elicited from the intransigent Olive the disconcerting reply: " Cousin Marquis, your whole heresy is madness; and I am afraid that if, after reflecting on your errors, you do not abandon them, you will go mad too." [3]

Her own example was as arresting as her fearless words and, when

[1] *Ibid.*, f. 238 : Con to Barberini, London, Dec. 8/18, 1637 : " ... molti vanno per osservare le bugie de' Ministri, e rifutarli."

[2] Endymion Porter was received much later but suffered for the Faith before he joined it. He was delated to Laud by Boswell, Ambassador to the Netherlands as being " most addicted to the Popish Religion" and a bitter enemy of the King. His wife's friendliness with Con was naturally interpreted as the means Porter used to reveal secrets to the Pope's Legate. As a reward for all this, there was a Red Hat awaiting his younger son ! (William PRYNNE, *Rome's Master-peece*, 1644, p. 23.)

[3] *B.L.* 8641, f. 16 : Con to Barberini, London, June 30/July 10, 1637.

she faced death in childbed, her piety and devotion were so exemplary, her faith in the relics to which she attributed her recovery so complete, that her mother and a sister-in-law asked to be put under instruction. The mother became a Catholic, and Con had the greatest hopes from her conversion, as her zeal in her former religion had given her a wide influence and she could be the means of saving many souls who would otherwise die without baptism. [1]

If the conversion and proselytizing activities of Olive Porter escaped official censure, the reception into the Church of her sister, Lady Newport, set all Town talking and became a matter of appeal from the Privy Council to the King. She was the wife of a well-known Puritan who had great influence at Court and was the brother of the Earl of Holland ; only a few months previously she had, as the champion of Puritanism, tried to baulk her sister in her efforts to secure the conversion of their father, Lord Boteler. Now, in October, 1637, came the rumour that she herself had decided to go over to Rome. The Queen's joy was tempered with fear of the consequences, especially for Mrs Porter who was bound to be blamed. The latter, however, was jubilant and said she was going to do all she could to urge her sister to the final step.

George Con had been giving Lady Newport instructions in the Catechism, and she now pronounced herself satisfied. After reminding her of all the difficulties she might have to face from the King and her husband, the Papal Agent suggested she should make her confession to one of the Queen's French Capuchins, to escape the gossip there would be among the English priests if she went to one of them. [2]

The Earl of Newport was so fierce in his opposition to his wife's becoming a Papist that he complained to the Archbishop of Canterbury and caused the matter to be debated at a meeting of the Privy Council. Laud was very free in his denunciation of the ever-increasing Roman party and the freedom allowed them at the Queen's Court ; in particular he criticized the attitude of Wat Montagu and Sir Toby Mathew, the latter of whom was supposed to

---

[1] *B.L.* 8642, f. 101 : Con to Barberini, London, Feb. 16/26, 1638.
[2] *B.L.* 8641, f. 165 : Con to Barberini, London, Oct. 20/30, 1637.

have had a hand in Lady Newport's conversion. [1] When the Queen heard of Laud's strictures, she made no attempt to hide her displeasure from him. But the Archbishop was not alone in his attitude. For once in a way Charles was thoroughly roused and followed Laud with such pointed criticism of Montagu and Sir Toby that they were frightened out of their wits and lay low for a time. [2]

The effect of the conversion on the Newports themselves was curious. Previously, the staunchly Puritan Countess had domineered over her husband as she pleased.   Now the position was reversed ; she became the model wife, only anxious to set her husband a good example to induce him to follow her, while he continually drew her into argument, plaguing her for the step she had taken, until eventually, at the instance of the Queen, Charles rebuked the Earl and made him promise to drop all further disputes. [3]

Despite her complete change of life Lady Newport could not escape the malicious calumnies that had attacked her sister, and it was not long before she came to Con in tears, complaining that stories were being bandied about that she was visiting men friends, when actually she was on her way to Mass [4].

But the Papal Agent could not always write of such valiant souls as Montagu, Olive Porter and Lady Newport, ready at all times to risk banishment and the idle slanders of wagging tongues for their new-found Faith. The Countess of Arundel, one of Con's

---

[1] A. H. MATHEW, The Life of Sir Tobie Mathew, p. 304 : Sir Wm. Calley to Rich. Harvey, Nov. 27, 1637 : " It is voysed abroad as if Sir Toby Mathew was questioned for converting my Lady of Newport."

[2] LAUD, Diary, p. 229 and note (a) ; STRAFFORD, Letters, vol. II, p. 125 : Viscount Conway to the Lord Deputy (no date) : " ... the King did use such words of Wat Montague and Sir Tobie Matthew that the fright made Wat keep his chamber longer than his sickness would have detained him ; and Don Tobiah was in such perplexity that I find he will make a very ill man to be a martyr, but now the dog doth again wag his tail."

[3] B.L. 8641, f. 211 : Con to Barberini, Dec. 1/11, 1637 : " ... questa Sig^ra prima d'esser Catt^ca strappazzava il marito ad ogni suo piacere, et hora gli fà ossequio esemplare, cosa che dovrebbe muovere lui et altri à far riflessione, quali siano gli effetti della nostra santa Religione."

[4] B.L. 8642, f. 17 : Con to Barberini, Dec. 29/Jan. 8, 1637/8. Such talk was common, writes Con, and gallantry in love was the boast of all but a few. As he put it caustically, the effects of heresy cannot be washed away with holy water.

staunchest supporters and as zealous as Mrs Porter in a quieter way, was doing her best to persuade her daughter-in-law, Elizabeth Stuart, sister of the Duke of Lennox and cousin to the King, to become a Catholic. The lady was willing enough but feared the consequences of publicity. After taking the utmost precautions to prevent the secret leaking out, she could not make up her mind to take the step, — one day she was keenness itself, the next day saw her indifferent. The chief effect of her chronic indecision was to alienate her husband, Henry Howard, from his mother, Lady Arundel, whom he blamed for it all. Another consequence was to make her quarrel with all her Catholic servants, — a fatal thing, Con told her, as nobody else could approach her. The mania for secrecy that afflicted her was a family complaint ; her sister Frances, Countess of Portland, had already become a Catholic, but the fact was closely guarded, not even the Queen knowing of her conversion. [1]

---

[1] *B.L.* 8642, f. 52 : Con to Barberini, Jan. 12/22, 1638. *B.L.* 8640, f. 197 : Same to same, Mar. 16/26, 1637. — The religious situation of the Lennox-d'Aubigny Stuarts was a complicated one. The third Duke Esme, an Anglican, married Catherine Clifton who seems to have been a Catholic. Their eldest son James, fourth Duke of Lennox (1637) and first of Richmond (1640) and Charles's most faithful friend remained an Anglican, and his three sisters Elizabeth, Frances and Anne seem to have been the same, since the conversion of the first two is spoken of here. Of the younger brothers, Henry, George, Ludovic and probably also Bernard (titular Earl of Lichfield) were allowed by James I to go at an early age to France to be brought up as Catholics by their grandmother, Catherine de Balzac, wife of the first Duke of Lennox. At Henry's christening at Whitehall in 1616, Charles had stood godfather, and in 1632 wrote to him personally to recall the brothers, promising preferment. The lad did not want to leave and wrote asking the Pope to intervene, as he said he feared for the faith of his younger brother Ludovic (*B.L.* 8620, f. 17 : Henry Stuart d'Aubigny to Urban VIII, Paris, May 28, 1632). He died soon after writing this letter. George, who had been at the Collège de Navarre, Paris, succeeded him in the family's French estates, as ninth Seigneur d'Aubigny. He obeyed the King's call, and returning to England married secretly the convert Catherine Howard, daughter of the Earl of Suffolk (cf. Chap.XI, p. 282, note 2). He died for the King at Edge Hill in 1642. Ludovic, who studied at Port-Royal des Champs, took orders and, as will be seen later (cf. Chap. XIII), was favoured by Charles for the purple. He became Almoner to the Dowager Queen Henrietta, returning to London with her for a short time after the Restoration, when he is said to have secretly performed the Catholic rites of Charles II's marriage with Catherine of Braganza. His long-

Yet despite the timidity of some converts and the honest caution of others, the case of Lady Newport had raised the alarm and the Archbishop of Canterbury caused a Royal Edict to be issued, forbidding, under the severest penalties of the law, any form of proselytism whatsoever. [1]

awaited Red Hat came to him almost simultaneously with death, Nov. 3, 1665. (Cf. JAMES BALFOUR-PAUL, *The Scottish Peerage*, in loco ; also COISSAC DE CHARREBIÈRE, *Histoire des Stuarts*, pp. 222 seq. For a genealogical table of the d'Aubigny Stuarts, v. *ibid.*, facing p. 40).

[1] *A Proclamation restraining the withdrawing His Majesties subjects from the Church of England, and giving scandall in resorting to Masses.* B.L. 8641. f. 146 : Con to Barberini, Dec. 20, 1637 The copy reached Rome, Jan. 8, 1638. A Latin version is to be found *Arch. Prop., Scritture Antiche* (137), 1638, f. 340 (V. App. VI, where this Proclamation is given in full).

CHAPTER IX

THREE-CORNERED CONTEST

*" He [i.e. Laud] wanted to fight the Pope with his own weapons
and was dubbed a papist for his trouble."* [1]

Laud, the Reformer, found himself sandwiched-in between
Puritan and Papist, and saw two ways of working his way free.
He could have steered his reform Rome-ward, intensifying into
a definite policy the King's natural aversion to persecuting
Catholics. He could have listened to the reunion enthusiasts
at Court, — Windebank, Cottington, Walter Montagu, Father
Leander, Father Philip, Panzani ; any encouragement he gave
them he knew would receive ample support among his colleagues
on the episcopal bench, Goodman of Gloucester, Richard
Montague of Chichester and Robert Wright of Coventry. The other
alternative was to pursue this purely autonomous reform within
the English Church, looking to the King and to none other for
support, and if the Puritans called him papist, he could give them
the lie by persecuting the Catholics.

The latter way was chosen and reunion remained a dream ; for
Laud, last of a great line of churchmen who had ruled England,
was the least theocratic of them all. With a flair for organization
and discipline, and an eye for the right ordering of things (there
was still much of the Oxford Don, the strict President of St John's,
left in him), his ambition led him to seek not union but uniformity, [2]
and a uniformity based on that great principle of the English
Reformation, the Royal Supremacy. The King was ruler by

---

[1] Evan John, *King Charles I*, p. 181.

[2] Laud has been brilliantly summed up as " un esprit myope qui voyait bien
les détails et se trompait sur l'ensemble" (Chasles, *op. cit.*, p. 120). For other
excellent estimates of his character, always provocative of the epigram, cf.
F. M. G. Higham, *Charles I*, pp. 123-124 ; J. Skelton, *Charles I*, p. 105 ;
Life of Archbishop Laud, op. cit., p. 478.

Divine Right, supreme in spiritual matters as in temporal, and Laud, the Archbishop, was there to see that he was obeyed.

The first obstacle to his campaign was the easy-going nature of the King himself. There were Penal Laws against recusants and infringement meant a fine to help replenish the empty coffers of the Treasury. Yet when the Archbishop cited Papists before his Ecclesiastical Court, he was exasperated to see them appear with orders under the Great Seal for composition of their fines, which they had bought for the low price of a crown. Laud complained of his Majesty's leniency at a Privy Council meeting, meaning at the same time to deal a blow at the Catholic Cottington, whom Charles had appointed one of the Commissioners for composition of fines. Cottington retorted tartly that no one was admitted to composition till the Church had done its worst against him.

In his craze for uniformity, Laud could not let anyone alone — an ecclesiastical mosquito, he has been called — and he even cited some Spaniards before his court for not receiving the communion at Easter. " We shall see what the Inquisition will do against the English in Spanish countries," was the Papal Agent's sinister comment. [1]

All knew the Archbishop was the declared enemy of the Puritans, and he was afraid, in view of the sympathies of many of his friends, that some would draw the false conclusion (as, in fact, Lord Arundel did in talking to Con) that he was not, therefore, opposed to Popery. One of his friends who had become a Catholic was asked by Laud, in rather a pained tone, why? The lady retorted : " My Lord it was because I ever hated a crowd." As Laud looked puzzled, she explained : " I perceived that your Lordship and many others are making for Rome as fast as you can, and therefore to prevent a press, I went before you. " [2] It was this complete misunderstanding of his aims that made him so over-anxious and intolerant. To specify his position, Laud again used the Council Chamber for a long speech against the Puritans, or, as he classed them, the Papist-Puritans (*i. e.* the Jesuits) and the Protestant Puritans. He closed his indictment with an appeal to the Privy Council for assistance in ruling the Anglican Church.

[1] *B.L.* 8640, ff. 205, 256 : Con to Barberini, Mar.23/April 2, April 14/24,1637.
[2] FULLER, *op. cit.*, Bk. XI, p. 217.

A further demonstration of the Archbishop's hostility to Popery
was the order made by the Privy Council for the destruction of all
articles of devotion connected with St Winifred's well, whither
Catholic and Protestant alike flocked in pilgrimage. It was a wonder
the pilgrimages themselves had not been stopped — even Charles
thought them superstitious — but they were not interfered with,
nor was the Council's order carried out. A Jesuit father came
to thank the Papal Agent for this and, although Con did not deny
having pulled the necessary wires, he refused to accept the Father's
thanks in case the order might yet be put through. [1]

Another move of Laud's to silence accusations of his being popishly
affected was the issue of a proclamation calling in a translation
of St Francis of Sales's *Introduction to a Devout Life*. It had been
brought for licence to Haywood, Laud's chaplain, who passed it
" expurged in several unorthodox passages. " When printed,
however, it was found to include these. The printer was apprehended,
the translator searched for, and all copies of the book seized and
publicly burnt. The demonstration did Laud little good, and
George Con's only comment was that the book deserved to be
burnt as the word Mass, among others, had been removed. [2]

Con had been some time in England and had not yet met Laud,
although the Archbishop spoke very politely of the Papal Agent,
only complaining that he was too partial to the Jesuits, and should
have expelled from England Fr Edward Knott, their Vice-Provincial,
who had written against the necessity of episcopacy. Windebank
carried this remark to Con, who replied that, if Laud would like
to treat with him or hear him justify his attitude towards the
Society of Jesus, he would be only too willing to do so, with
Windebank as intermediary, as he trusted him more than any of the
priests with whom the Archbishop had been dealing. He added
that he was in England at the orders of the Cardinal Secretary of
State and not for the purpose of expelling any Jesuit, unless
punished by the Pope. Laud maintained, however, that he knew
Con had had orders from Rome to send Father Knott away. This
implicit accusation met with the icy response that a Papal Agent

---

[1] *B.L.* 8640, ff. 131, 311 seq.: Con to Barberini, Feb. 2/12 ; May 5/15 ;
May 26/June 5, 1637.

[2] *Ibid.*, f. 287 : Con to Barberini, Apr. 28/May 8, 1637.

was answerable for his conduct only to the Pope and Cardinal Barberini.

Archbishop and Roman Agent continued to keep each other at a distance, for, as Laud explained to a party of friends that included Buckingham's widow, Lord Arundel and Windebank, — all sympathetic to Con, — he had to act with indifference towards the envoy from Rome, as he had no more wish to appear a Papist than a Puritan. But Con was not so sure of the Archbishop's impartiality and had suspicions, which later developed almost into a phobia, that Laud was undermining his influence with the King. [1]

One trait they had in common, — hatred of the Puritans, but far from suggesting a truce, this was the means of driving Laud against Con and his Catholics to placate the common enemy. The Puritans were at this time making themselves a nuisance to both Churchmen and Papists ; they excited the Pursuivants against the priests, and the people they stirred up against Laud's government in their lampoons attacking Romish innovations introduced in to the Establishment by the Bishops, — " the cringing and ducking to altars, the barking, roaring and grunting of choristers, and the silk-and-satin divines of Laud's church." At last the Archbishop was forced to take proceedings against their leaders, Prynne, Bastwick and Buxton, before the Court of High Commission. Already in 1633 the Puritan lawyer William Prynne, that tough courageous fighter with so soured an outlook on life, had been condemned before the same court for his scurrilous indictment of stage plays in *Histrio-mastrix*, a barely disguised attack on the Queen, whose love of the play was well known.

Now, in 1637, Prynne stood before the Star Chamber on a charge of libelling the hierarchy. Some twenty judges passed sentence on him, the penalties including the ear-cropping, nose-slitting and cheek-branding that were the common fate of the libeller. Laud was not among those who passed judgment ; instead, he took the opportunity of speaking for over two hours against the offensive writings, and in his own defence. [2] His conclusion to every argument was that he was far from introducing Popery into the Church and, against the charge that his changes were novelties, he appealed partly to the ancient practice of the Church of England,

[1] *Ibid.*, f. 337, 346 : Con to Barberini, May 19/29, May 26/June 5, 1637.
[2] *Life of Archbishop Laud*, pp. 201 sqq.

and partly to the written orders of the King, its Supreme Governor. He admitted holding that Bishops were *de jure divino* in the Church, but contended that his interpretation of the dogma was different from the Roman view.

Although at pains throughout to maintain his innocence of the charges brought against him in the Puritans' writings, Laud was most temperate in his discourse. After defending himself, he went on to show his accusers that the Catholic religion — meaning, presumably, his own — was no revolt against tradition, appealing to the glory of the Early Church, the Church of St Cyprian, for proof. It was the Roman, not the English Church that had changed since that time.

George Con, who had been listening to everything, protested to the Duchess of Buckingham (he knew it would reach Laud's ears) against this interpretation of history, yet he had nothing but praise for the eloquence of the Archbishop and his manner of expounding his argument. The Papal Agent had been an interested spectator of the whole proceedings, which lasted eight hours, having a seat in a box bought at some expense by Lady Arundel, who had hurried back to town to enable Con to be present. [1]

He also witnessed the punishment of the three Puritans. Four years before the hangman had been bribed to strike lightly, and making quick use of the surgeon's stitches Prynne had managed to save his ears. Now they were cropped off close and a deep S. L. was burnt into the cheek of the Seditious Libeller, who still had spirit enough to interpret the letters *Stigmata Laudis* — the Scars of Laud. The three condemned men were allowed to address the crowd—bad tactics of the Archbishop's, Con thought — and were loudly acclaimed by the people, who soaked their handkerchiefs in their blood, as they had done before when the Catholic Martyrs died. But the Puritans were not willing to allow fellowship in suffering to soften their feelings, and protested that the punishments due to the Papists were falling now on the Servants of God. [2]

As long as Laud was not directly goaded on by the Puritans or

---

[1] *B.L.* 8640, f. 382 : Con to Barberini, June 16/26, 1637. Laud had his speech printed, erasing, however, anything he had said in praise of the Church of Rome. *B.L.* 8641, f. 16 : Same to same, June 30/July 10, 1637.

[2] *B.L.* 8641, f. 25 : Same to same, July 7/17, 1637.

provoked by the Catholics, the latter enjoyed a certain tranquillity. The Justices of the Peace were constantly telling their over-ardent underlings not to molest the Papists, as they had the King's ear; while, according to Con, all his Majesty's higher officials were walking warily to avoid giving offence to the Queen, whose influence with her husband was held to be greater than ever.

But Laud also enjoyed the King's favour, and Lord Arundel warned Con that as long as he did so there was little hope for the Catholics. Unfortunately the latter were not alive to the delicacy of their position, and their indiscretions not only taxed the patience of Charles, who complained of them bitterly to Con, but they brought discredit on those who were trying to help them, as the Papal Agent was to discover more than once. [1]

It looked as if the fate of the Catholics would rest on the rivalry between Archbishop and Queen in competition to sway the King. To Laud Henrietta was not just a rival. She was a Catholic and the acknowledged champion of the Catholics. In consequence, pursuing his policy of showing his other foes, the Puritans, how good a Protestant he was, the Archbishop eschewed all but the barest civilities in dealing with the Queen. He may have thought his methods were carrying him too far for one day towards the end of October, 1637, he expressed a wish to go to her Majesty and ask pardon for his neglect, but he was frightened off his good resolution by bad news from Scotland, hotbed of hostility to episcopacy, and by the appearance of a lampoon accusing him of popery and of dealings with the Pope's Nuncio. At this the Archbishop hurried in a panic to Charles, begging his help to show people he was no Papist, and his protection against the violent anger of the Queen! "You will find my wife very reasonable," the King said calmly, and promised to speak to her.

Soon after this Laud renewed his anti-Catholic tirades at a Privy Council meeting, and gave the impression that there would

[1] *Ibid.*, ff. 78, 107, 111 : Same to same, Sept. 8/18, 15/25, Sept.22/Oct. 2. 1637. The Catholics were far too fond of squabbling among themselves, and then dragging their differences before the public Courts. This Con tried to prevent ; one of several cases he settled privately was a dispute between a Catholic gentleman and a priest over pious legacies which would have given a deal of scandal if taken before the Courts. (*Ibid.*, f.192 : Same to same, Nov. 10/20, 1637.)

be many more to follow.   The Archbishop's words carried weight :
the Councillors began talking of issuing edicts against the Queen's
and the Ambassadors' chapels.   They even ordered the usual
formula to be drawn up, and invited suggestions for bridling the
advance of Popery that was so disturbing to the Government.

As soon as he heard this, the Papal Agent reported it to the Queen,
saying that Laud's rash ardour was a danger not only to Catholicism
in England, but to her Majesty's own person. It took little of this
to set the spirited Henrietta aflame, and Con had to urge her to
temper her indignation and show her husband she had the good
of his realm at heart as much as Laud. The Agent then saw the
King and, as a result of his and the Queen's pleadings, Charles
promised that nothing would be done about his wife's chapel,
though measures would be taken to restrict the immense crowds
customary at the Chapels of those Ambassadors with whom he did
not wish his subjects to hold intercourse. On this point Charles
was unyielding, especially when he heard the Spanish Ambassador's
statement that he had taken a house in Town where he was going
to have a chapel larger than the Queen's and maintain it even when
he was not in residence, — a provocative boast. Con then begged
the King to do nothing to excite the Archbishop. Charles replied
impatiently, " These things are being done every year, and nobody
would speak of them if you did not pester my wife. "   Con protested
it was his duty to use every effort in the cause of religion, and
reminded the King of the goodwill he had expressed towards him
at other times. " I do not blame you, " answered Charles, " but
everything takes time. I am always the same. "

Laud, still fearful of happenings in Scotland, now urged a
Proclamation against the Catholics as an expedient to calm the
Presbyterians. This Con fought might and main with the help of the
Queen, Cottington and Windebank. It was a battle against odds,
but he hoped at least to have the proclamation deferred indefinitely.

The countering of the Archbishop's outbursts against the Catholics
kept Con continually at Court. This constant worry, together
with the unsatisfactory progress of his own promotion towards the
Cardinalate, began to take toll of his never robust health. A
further source of anxiety was the indiscretion of the Catholics who
could not keep from imprudent remarks that only served to incense
Laud.

The Archbishop continued to maintain a glacial deportment

towards the Papal Agent. When one of his friends among the
Queen's Ladies reproached him for his scant respect, he said he
had never spoken disrespectfully of Con and, far from wishing to
give offence, he would be only too willing to do the Pope's Agent
some service in anything that did not concern religion. When
Con heard this, he said the only service he wanted from the
Archbishop was some relief for the harassed Catholics. [1]

The distance that separated Con and Laud was no secret at
Court, and more than one attempt was made to bridge it.   On
the occasion of the French Ambassador Seneterre's leave-taking,
Summer 1637, the Papal Agent stood in his rightful place by the
Queen's throne, which was on the left of the King's, while Laud,
Juxon of London, the Lord Privy Seal and the rest of the Council
were gathered round Charles, with the Archbishop next to him as
of right. Now was the chance, with only a step between them,
someone whispered to Con, for him to go up to the Archbishop,
take his hand and come to a friendly understanding.   Con's answer
was grandiosely irrelevant. " His Holiness, " he said, " is standing
with his arms wide open to receive all into the bosom of the
Church. " [2]

This much must be said for Laud that his coolness to Con was
a deliberate policy of caution, and not the outcome of personal
spleen ; on the contrary, he praised the Papal Agent to his friend,
the Duchess of Buckingham, while justifying his not seeing Con
by explaining that his position as Archbishop precluded any
dealings with a servant of the Pope without exciting an uproar far
worse than the one seen in the Star Chamber. As it was, Con's
influence with the King had already placed a bit between the
teeth of the more violent Puritans and Privy Councillors. But
for that, Laud added with unusual silkiness, there was no one in
the world whose friendship and conversation he would have
preferred to George Con's. [3]

After such gracious words the Archbishop was hurt to hear
Con had been speaking against him, but malicious tongues had

---

[1] *Ibid.*, ff. 172 ; 214 : Con to Barberini, Nov. 3/13, Dec. 1/11, 1637.

[2] *Ibid.*, f. 22 : Same to Same, July 7/17, 1637.

[3] *Ibid.*, f. 41 : Same to same, July 21/31, 1637.   It is interesting how Laud
and Con would each talk of the other to the Duchess of Buckingham, knowing
the conversation would be carried across without delay.

been wagging, as they were bound to do at the slightest provocation ; all that had happened was that Con had protested on hearing Laud called a Catholic. [1]

In writing to Barberini, however, Con had already given his true estimate — a sound one — of Laud's character. " The Archbishop acts in such changing fashion, " he said, " that he gives the impression of a being politician rather than of any kind of churchman. " [2]

The Queen noticed how harassed the Papal Agent was becoming through having to contend with pin-pricks from Laud, the hostility of the Puritans and the foolishness of many of his own Faith. Henrietta spoke to her husband about him, and one evening after supper, drawing Con into a corner, Charles apologized for the troubles of the times, with the Puritans putting everything into confusion. It was a miracle, the King said, that their seditious pamphlets had made no direct onslaught on Con's coming to England and opening a chapel. For this escape Charles praised Con's diplomacy in acting as if he had come for nothing but to pay compliments to the Queen and talk pictures and sculpture with him. He then assured Con that Laud held him in great respect, and not only the Archbishop but all the Lords and Ladies of the Court as well. [3]

For many months now the idea of a Proclamation against the Catholics had been simmering in Laud's mind. It would check their growing arrogance, warn off would-be converts and, above all, placate the Puritans who thought the Church was drifting Rome-ward. The project was an open secret and near the end of November rumours were already rife that it had gone to press. The Queen heard it and to show her feelings, on walking over to speak to Cottington, she passed in front of the Archbishop, deliberately ignoring his Grace. [4] The studied snub may have stung Laud into action, for soon afterwards secret orders were given, without further discussion in Council, for the proclamation to be made. When Henrietta was told, she would hardly credit it

---

[1] *Ibid.*, f. 48 : Con to Barberini, July 27/Aug. 6, 1637.

[2] *B.L.* 8640, f. 263 : Same to same, Apr. 21/May, 1, 1637 : " Il Cantuariense è tanto vario nel suo procedere che da Occⁿᵉ di credere che egli sia huomo più tosto di stato, che di qualsivoglia religione."

[3] *Ibid.*, f. 61 : Con to Barberini, July 4/14, 1637.

[4] *B.L.* 8641, f. 222 : Con to Barberini, Nov. 24/Dec. 4, 1637.

but soon found from Charles that the matter was decided upon and there was no further remedy.

Con made a last bid for delay, telling the King he had orders from the Pope to obtain for him all possible obedience from the Catholics. He further assured Charles that by dealing generously with them he would put his Holiness under an obligation to prevent the Catholics taking part in any rising or disturbance against the Crown. Con then begged the King not to consent to further edicts against the Catholics. Charles answered that he was grateful for the Pope's good will, but his Holiness could hardly quarrel with him for wanting to ensure quiet for his kingdoms. " As long as the right means are used, no," said Con, " but it is not right to placate the Puritans by proclamations against the Catholics." The King's reply, which Con found hard to refute, was that comment had been caused by several Catholic christenings and marriages, celebrated by indiscreet persons as publicly as if they had been in Rome.

The two then argued spiritedly on the conditions of marriage, till Charles said, " I will not go against any of the conditions you put forward ; but, by your good leave, I desire to show I am of the religion I profess. I know the Pope would have me other than what I am, and I am obliged to him. You understand me well enough and, if you will, you will justify my action." Retorting that the Proclamation spoke for itself, Con said he questioned whether the good results the King hoped for would outweigh the scandal he would give by playing the rôle of persecutor. To this thrust Charles answered sharply that it would be scandal taken, not given ; the quiet that Catholics enjoyed through his clemency was common knowledge ; they should curb their insolence, remembering how the law stood and the abuse they were making of the royal favour. Con's riposte was that his Majesty should punish the guilty and not give the law further advantage against all.

The Papal Agent again reminded Charles of the affection Pope Urban and his nephew had for him ; greater, he added with a sudden show of feeling, than that the Archbishop bore him. The King answered with dignity that as regards the Proclamation, Laud was acting at the desire of the whole Council who judged it necessary.

The interview concluded on a conciliatory note, the King saying that the edict would be worded with such moderation that Con

15

would be satisfied when he saw it, and, indeed, the Queen told him
afterwards that her husband had promised to remove any phrase
to which she objected. [1]

At last, on December 20, 1637, the Proclamation was published
" restraining the withdrawing His Majesties subjects from the
Church of England, and giving scandall in resorting to Masses, "
all of which was contrary to the Law. Former Proclamations
and Orders in Council against popish practices were recalled and
declared to be still in force. The whole power of the Law was
threatened against all future celebrations in the rites of Rome and
especially against proselytism practised on members of the Established
Church. To enforce this measure His Majesty's officers would be
called to keep sterner watch and give stricter account than they
had done hitherto. [2]

So Laud had his way. For some time he had longed to brandish
the big stick, and it was singularly unfortunate for him that,
through the Queen's energetic intervention with the clement king,
he found himself waving not a rod of correction for the Catholics,
but a red rag in the faces of the Puritans. The Proclamation had
not enforced the Penal Laws, but simply reminded the Papists of
their existence in the Statute Book ; it made no attempt to justify
the Pursuivant or forbid the return of priests from abroad ; no
names were mentioned, nor was the frequenting of the Queen's and
the Ambassadors' Chapels forbidden, as Laud had originally
hoped. The Puritans were irritated and called it a bad joke,
seeing the Papists suffer no ill effects. In fact, as Con wrote
exultantly in the New Year, not a hair of any Catholic head had
been harmed over the Christmas holidays. [3]

Henrietta's Gallic wit flashed scathingly at the expense of Laud's
Proclamation. Three month's procrastination while a pretext was
sought for avoiding it (this was untrue — it was she and her friends
who fought for postponement) and then, instead of a threat to
the Catholics, it had turned out to be only a fatherly warning,
and unfortunately for the Archbishop it was looked upon as such
by the heretics !

Five days after its publication, large crowds flocked to Midnight

[1] *Ibid.*, f. 230 : Con to Barberini, Dec. 8/18, 1637.
[2] V. App. VI, where the Proclamation is found in full.
[3] *B.L.* 8642, ff. 46, 52 : Con to Barberini, Jan. 12/22, 1638.

Mass in the Queen's Chapel, and her Majesty's own tribune was filled with ladies, who all received Holy Communion with her. The Countess of Newport and other recent converts were there on their first public appearance as Catholics. The expediency of inviting them had been questioned, but Henrietta was insistent that all should come, — an unprecedented step for her. After Mass she sent for Con, saying triumphantly, " You see the effect of the Proclamation?" Her Majesty was satisfied that she had staged a complete reply to his Grace of Canterbury.

This much the Queen did to justify herself and maintain her own dignity and influence, but deep down she considered the English Catholics had asked for a reprimand. She told Con they were as pro-Spanish as they had always been since the days of Elizabeth, and unappreciative of her good offices ; also their criticisms were directed not only at her but at Con and the Pope himself for not supporting Spain. The Papal Agent did his best to calm the Queen, but had to admit to Cardinal Barberini that a large number of the Catholics showed little discretion and were swayed by passion to an extent it was scarcely possible to credit.

Charles apparently had foreseen the Proclamation would be still-born, for when next he saw Con he began laughing and asked him if he had been a man of his word. As the Agent bowed, but showing a somewhat mournful face, the King asked with delicate irony, " Which troubles you more, the Proclamation made in England, or the Promotion *not* made in Rome?" Con, embarrassed, murmured that his elevation to the purple did not disturb him in the least, as he was sure that once its useful purpose was seen, it would not be delayed a day. " I leave that thought to my wife," answered the King, still sarcastic. He went on to tell Con that he thought his influence was on the wane, as the negotiations for his Red Hat had been made public and, therefore, with the continued delay, his prestige was suffering. Charles then, counselled the Agent for the future to undertake no more conversions nor anything else that could cause him anxiety, as there was no lack of malicious tongues ready to do him harm. [1] Returning to the Proclamation, the King explained that he had himself removed several clauses harmful to the Catholics besides,

---

[1] *Ibid.*, ff. 14-16 ; Con to Barberini, Dec. 29/Jan. 8, 1637/8.

those to which the Queen had objected. He finally promised Con to stop Laud's taking advantage of the edict to give the Pursuivants a general mandate to harass the Catholics.

A paradoxical and altogether lamentable result of the Proclamation was to reveal the hostility to the Public Chapels shown by certain priests, who now noised it abroad that Con's Chapel was being watched by pursuivants, and that many had been arrested and imprisoned on leaving the Chapel of the Queen.

The Papal Agent attributed this malicious attitude to self-interest — at the root of all the troubles of the English Catholics — and to the preference of priests for going the round of private houses saying four or five Masses a day. The discovery of this opposition to the Chapels caused Con, who had at first thought the Government's Proclamation sheer madness, to change his mind and put it down to Laud's malice, — a subtle ruse to divide the Catholics among themselves. [1] A Machiavellian move, if it were true, though the disturbed state of Con's mind and health at this period probably made him attribute to Laud a Satanic cunning greater than the honest Archbishop possessed.

The excitement aroused by the Proclamation soon died down. The anxiety of awaiting it had given way to relief when it was seen to be so harmless, and by summer-time the Catholics had again given the King cause to complain to the Papal Agent of their insolence and swagger. Con spiritedly brought the same charge against Laud, and offered to deal with any complaint against the Catholics, if Charles would do the same with the Archbishop ! Patient as usual with his outspoken compatriot, the King passed this by, simply asking Con to restrict the crowds attending the Chapel of Don Alonso de Cárdenas, the Spanish Resident in London. When Con, still worked up, said it was his business in England to promote religion, not to check it, Charles reminded him threateningly that he could take the Catholics away from the Chapels by force if he liked. At this Con begged the King not to make himself minister to the passions of Laud, who, to ingratiate himself with the Puritans, did not hesitate to prejudice his Majesty's mind. He added pathetically that, since coming to England, he had not had a moment's peace for fear of what Laud might do. At this

[1] *Ibid.*, f. 35 : Con to Barberini, Jan. 5/15, 1638.

Con left. " He is a man of great goodness," Charles told the Queen, " but he wants everything his own way. " [1]

During the conversation, her Majesty, the Duchesse de Chevreuse and other Ladies had been giving the Archbishop very short shrift.

The English Catholics had traditionally looked to Spain for relief in their troubles, and Henrietta always felt, however hard she strove to help them (and this she had promised the Pope to do), that they were mistrustful of her influence, which must come largely through the support of her brother, Louis XIII.

It was to Laud's advantage to encourage this lack of confidence in the Catholics and to raise further discord in the enemy's camp. In pursuance of this policy he had used William Howard, a Catholic, to argue for the Oath of Allegiance against the general run of English Catholic opinion.

The Archbishop now found a further use for him. Howard came one day to his mother, the Countess of Arundel, Con's great friend and helper, asking her to persuade the Papal Agent that the best way of winning over Laud to look with favour on the Catholics was to urge the Queen to abandon France and dispose the King to an alliance with the House of Austria. But Con made short work of this subtle attack, pointing out the benefit the Catholics had always had from the Queen, while they had met with nothing but opposiiton from Laud. It would be foolish to offend her Majesty with such a suggestion, when she already had good reason for lamenting Catholic leanings towards the Habsburgs. Besides, he as Papal Agent had express orders from Rome not to meddle in any matter affecting France and Spain, towards whom the Pope desired to show the greatest impartiality. [2]

Concurrently with this underground strategy the Archbishop kept up a continued frontal attack, growing ever more violent in his pronouncements. In the Lord Chamberlain's opinion he was ruining King and kingdom by his ravings, now against the Puritans, now against the Papists. Con heartily endorsed this view, saying the Catholics could not be sure of an hour's peace, wondering what Laud would say or do next.

The Agent had always been fearless in defence of his own, and

[1] *Ibid.*, ff. 35, 38 : Con to Barberini, July 13/23, 1638 : " ... è grand 'uomo da bene, mà vorrebbe ogni cosa à modo suo."

[2] *B.L.* 8643, f. 88 : Con to Barberini, Aug. 31/Sept. 10, 1638.

he was solemnly warned by Cardinal Barberini to keep a sharp guard on his tongue lest any contemptuous phrase of his should involve himself and others in the Archbishop's anger. But Con had already lost his most effective means of letting Laud know his mind, for the Duchess of Buckingham, "Fond Kate," who could say what she liked to the Archbishop and was always ready to carry Con's comments across, had left for Ireland and married again. [1]

As Con's channel of criticism closed, it seemed Laud's outbursts increased, — though there were always varying versions of the Archbishop's latest utterance. Some said he had threatened before the Court of High Commission to stop Papists frequenting Signor Coneo's and the other Catholic Chapels. Another reported that he had said publicly, " We have here Signor Coneo. If he is Ambassador, Agent or Spy I know not, nor do I wish to know ; but I do know he is destroying what I am building up with so much trouble." Hearing this, Charles sent Windebank to the Papal Agent to dissociate himself with the report, while Laud protested he had said no such thing. In all probability, the report was a double-edged attack on Con and Laud by the Puritans, or even by some disgruntled Catholic.

In private, at least, Laud had spoken slightingly of Con's projected promotion to the purple and of the artifices of Rome ; but anything he said, or was supposed to have said, only served to increase the number of visitors who called to see not only Con's Chapel but the Agent himself. The Archbishop was annoyed to find the Papal Agent frequently visited by the nobility and higher Officers of the Crown. He had just cause for anger, as Con himself believed many of the Courtiers only came to see him to spite Laud. [2]

As exaggerated accounts of the hostility between Archbishop and Papal Agent had failed, a subtler attack was tried to make them both a laughing-stock to the Puritans. The rumour soon ran round that far from being enemies, Laud and Con were the greatest

---

[1] *B.L.* 8644, f. 118 : Barberini to Con, March 12, 1639.

B.L. 8643, f.244 : Con to Barberini, Dec.14/24, 1637. The Duchess's second husband was Randal Macdonnell, second Earl and Marquis of Antrim.

[2] *B.L.* 8644, ff. 66, 86, 101 : Con to Barberini, Feb. 1/11, 15/25 ; Feb. 22/ Mar. 4, 1639.

of friends; in fact, they played tennis together, but while the Pope's man was intent on the game, the Archbishop preferred shouting and marking down the points ! " This," said Con, with a curious insensibility that perhaps twenty years abroad, or his poor health, had bred in him, " is in conformity with the humour of the country." (L'humour anglais was evidently a curious phenomenon to the foreigner even 300 years ago.) Con added, with almost comic dignity, that he did his best to stop such tales, which could do nothing but harm![1]

Laud had been faring badly in his policy of keeping the twofold foe at bay. The Papists safely snapped their fingers at his Proclamation; the Puritan wags were making rare sport of him, — the latest story was that the Archbishop was in personal correspondence with the Pope. In a final effort to bring both birds to earth — refute the Catholic argument and convince the Puritan of his Protestantism — Laud reprinted his book against Fisher the Jesuit, written fifteen years before.

It misfired completely, Puritan and Catholic alike deriding it. Fisher had his answer ready at once, while Con thought it so easy to refute that many would be tempted to do so.[2] Someone so tempted actually alleged that " the sum of this book is to reconcile the Church of England with that of Rome."[3]

But someone had a good word for it — the antiquarian politician, Sir Edward Dering, who is reported to have said that Laud " had muzzled the Jesuit and would strike the Papists under the fifth rib, when he was dead and gone."[4]

---

[1] Ibid., f. 112 : Con to Barberini, March 1/11, 1639.

[2] B.L. 8644, ff. 101, 192, 246: Same to same, Feb. 22/Mar. 4; April 12/22 ; May 13/23, 1639. Ibid., f. 150 : Barberini to Con, April 2, 1639. Father Piercey, alias Fisher, brought his reply to Con, who in consultation with the Jesuit provincial and under Barberini's orders decided they must ponder carefully before printing it.

[3] Calendar of State Papers, 1641-1643, p. 53.

[4] J. COLLIER, Ecclesiastical History of Great Britain, vol.VIII, pp. 144-145. On the lasting value of the book Anglicans are at variance. Dean Hook gave it the first place in the theological literature of England. On the other hand, A. C. Benson, son of the Archbishop, calls it " a nearly unreadable folio... justly forgotten." Cf. Life of Archbishop Laud, pp. 77-78.

CHAPTER X

THE KING AND THE ROMAN AGENT

> " *Charles was quite satisfied to find in Con a well-informed
> and respectful man, ready to discuss politics or theology without
> acrimony by the hour, and to flatter him with assurances of the
> loyalty of his Catholic subjects, without forgetting to point to
> the sad contrast exhibited by the stiff-necked and contemptuous
> Puritan.*" [1]

Charles had been brought up on theology. A second son and
a weakling, he had never been trained for kingship and his brother
Henry's jest in popping the Archbishop of Canterbury's cap on the
boy's head with the promise that one day he would make him
Primate may well have expressed the mind of their father, the
King-Theologian. [2]

Though Providence placed sceptre instead of crozier in his
hand, Charles never gave up the interests of his youth and loved
nothing more than a theological argument. For this he found an
ideal *vis-à-vis* in George Con, an able, cultured controversialist,
and a fellow Scot. [3]

At Somerset House the King was treated informally as his
wife's guest, and nothing delighted him more than to stroll through
the corridors or the Queen's apartments, buttonhole the Papal
Agent and engage him in a discussion on dogma, art, or the political

---

[1] S. R. GARDINER, *History*, vol. VIII, p. 236.

[2] *Arch. Prop., Scritt. Originali* 297, f. 194 : Père Gilles Chaissy to the Cardinals of Propaganda, Oct. 28, 1653 : " Erat ab incunabulis a rege Jacobo patre
educatus in controversiis qui hunc praeficere ecclesiae Cantuariensi certo
statuerat apud se, si princeps Henricus primogenitus superstes fuisset."

[3] Con's work included one of Apologetic, — the *Assertionum Catholicarum
libri tres, in quibus ex solo scripto Dei verbo praecipua haeresum aetatis nostrae
dogmata refelluntur* [Romae, 1629], dedicated to Urban VIII, with prefaces
to the Catholic and to the Heretic Reader.

situation, to the amazement, sometimes to the irritation of the courtiers. But the Queen only smiled and refrained from interrupting the pair, in the hope that her husband would be drawn a little nearer to Rome and to concessions for the Catholics.

Con had made an impression straightway by telling the King that the Pope deplored the dependence of English Catholics on foreign princes and wanted their allegiance only as their Spiritual Father and Shepherd. [1]

But in argument the Agent yielded nothing, calling the King's co-religionists heretics, though Charles, referring to Papists, spoke always of Catholics or Roman Catholics. [2] The King could be contradicted, too, and seeing himself in the wrong would refrain from retort. [3]

He would not always wait to catch Con alone and was fond of introducing a topic at the supper-table with the Queen and her Confessor, as well as the Papal Agent, to argue with him. It was on an evening early in the New Year, 1637, that Charles began telling them of a procession he had been at in Spain. He noticed, he said, that when the people passed the Crucifix they made a deep reverence but, on coming to the Madonna, all went down on their knees. This was an abuse to pay more attention to Our Lady than to her Son. After Father Philip had made a studied reply, the Queen remarked that it was nothing new for the populace, used to favours at the hands of a favourite, to pay more respect apparently to the latter than to the sovereign himself, though knowing well enough he was only a subject. Then someone quoted a passage from St Bonaventure where he begs the Mother to give a *command* to her Son (*commander à son Fils*). The Queen chimed in quickly: "You have left out a syllable; it should be *recommend* (*recommander*)." As the conversation was in French, the correction was a happy one. [4]

---

[1] *B.L.* 8639, f. 147 : Barberini to Con, Oct. 12/22, 1636, where the Cardinal Secretary commends the tact of Con's remarks.

[2] *Ibid.*, f. 93 : Con to Barberini, Hampton, Sept. 24,1636 : " Il Rè in tutti li discorsi meco chiamava li Catt^cl ò Catt^cl semplicem^te ò Catt^cl Romani, benche io chiamassi li Protestanti heretici."

[3] *B.L.* 8640, f. 53 : Same to same, Hampton, Jan. 5/15, 1637 : "Spesso si parla di queste cose per passar il tempo et il Rè con m^to piacevolezza si lascia contradire, e quando vede d'haver torto tace modestissimamente."

[4] *Ibid.*

Charles said his personal belief was that Our Lady was greater than all but God. Con assured him that this was the mind of the Church, which was not to be judged by a few ignorant Spaniards; if he had only been to Rome he would have learnt the Church's practice better. The King took this in good part and they continued the conversation. Lady Arundel told Con afterwards that the Protestant Ladies-of-the-Household were gossiping about his talks with the King and would be glad to know him back in Rome again, as they were saying he was under the thumb of the Jesuits and the Spaniards. Worse things were being said about the Queen. [1]

His Spanish trip — Charles's one great adventure — was a favourite source of reminiscence; he recalled to Con the talks he had had in Madrid with the King's Confessor, remarking how little satisfaction he got from them. The two then discussed the Invocation of Saints, Purgatory, and the Infallibility of the Church. Con answered as best he could and then boldly implored his Majesty for the love of Our Lord to reflect upon the harm done to Christendom by schism from the Church of Rome. The King admitted it, but remarked upon the peace and tranquillity of his own realms. This Con daringly denied, pointing out the dissension at home, his Majesty's lack of prestige abroad, and the danger he ran, in the event of any neighbouring sovereign wishing him ill, of their exploiting religion for the purpose.

Seeing the King was listening good-humouredly, Con begged him to do away with this schism, so prejudicial to his reputation, and, as St Augustine held, a deadly sin. Charles said he would like to do so and was willing to perform any kind of bodily penance for that end, but he considered that the Church of Rome stood too haughty and resolute on certain points, on holding to the Council of Trent, for instance. Con explained that included in the Council were Canons which could not be changed and Decrees which could, namely, those dealing with the reform of morals and exhortations on matters not *de fide* in the Church. The expediency of putting such Decrees into force *hic et nunc* could be opened to fresh discussion.

Con concluded by appealing to the King to appoint some moderate persons, well-intentioned towards reunion, to confer with the

---

[1] *B.L.* 8642, ff. 34, 36 : Con to Barberini, Jan. 5/15, 1638.

Pope's representatives ; his Majesty would then be enlightened as to how benign a mother the Catholic Church was. Charles, with his hand on Con's shoulder, said. " It is not the moment yet : things are not favourable enough. We look to the future and say nothing. " [1]

Cardinal Barberini was delighted with the long report of this conversation which Con sent him in code — *La Cifra d'Oro*, he called it. He told the Agent to nail the King down to particular points on which he wanted the Catholic Church to give way : he would always find her a kind mother where concession was possible. His Majesty had himself said that not everyone was a Pope Urban and, as he must realize, the Pope could not live for ever ; now was the time to help matters along. [2]

On the question of schism, Con returned to the attack in a three hours' talk he had with the King on Christmas Eve, 1638. The argument started *à propos* of some Apostle Tapestries. They were alone at first, but soon all the Court came in and Con changed his method. He had made it a rule never to press the King with arguments when others were present. Instead, after letting Charles have his say, he would turn to the Queen and point out to *her* the advantages they Catholics had of being told by the Church that they must believe such-and-such a doctrine for such-and-such a reason. Con would then expound this reason and, by thus making the argument an impersonal one, he avoided giving offence. When the Queen was absent, he would begin his argument with some such cliché as "I thank God he has made me a member of a Church which teaches me this for such a reason," and so on as before.

On this occasion Con had, as usual, let fall the word heretics, and the King took him up. " Heretics is too cruel a word," he said, " when at most you can only call us schismatics. " Con replied that no private person was competent to pass judgment on points of doctrine : the Church had passed sentence, and every Catholic was bound to abide by it. Anyway, he added, St Augustine said schismatics were in a state of damnation no less than heretics. "But I do not acknowledge myself a schismatic, " said the King,

---

[1] *B.L.* 8640, ff. 184-5 : Con to Barberini, March 2/12, 1637 :" Il Rè mettendomi una mano in spallo, mi rispose : Non è ancora tempo ; le cose non sono disposte, bisogna veder più avanti, e non dir parola."

[2] *B.L.* 8619, f. 170 : Barberini to Con, May 4, 1637.

adding slyly, "I can easily show you a book by one of yours to which you would not subscribe." To this Con retorted that Catholics were bound to believe and subscribe to the teaching of the Catholic Church; they left the particularist spirit to the Puritans.

" You will not deny." the King insisted, " that you have bad and rascally men in your Church?" " True," said Con quickly, " and rather more than the good men in your Majesty's sect." So the argument finished with a laugh, and the Queen went home to Somerset House. [1]

A few weeks previous to this they had been celebrating the King's birthday, and the father of one of the Queen's French maids came into the conversation. The girl was sent for to ask what he was and, afraid their Majesties thought he was a Huguenot, said quickly, " By God's grace, my father is a Catholic." Charles burst out laughing and with an eye on Con said teasingly, "My dear, I also am a Catholic." " There is none more desirous of that than I," murmured the Agent. Here Marie de' Medici, the King's mother-in-law, spoke up : " It is necessary to be Catholic, Apostolic and Roman." This gave Charles his chance : "You Ladies will not understand me but *he* will, — est implicantia in adjecto. " Con bowed, delicately ironical : " Your Majesty will never want to play with that false logic," he said. [2]

Charles's intimacy with the Papal Agent was no backstairs affair conducted only in the privacy of his own or the Queen's apartments. He was sincere enough, imprudent enough perhaps, to allow his talks with Con to be noticed and commented on by the highest peers of the realm. When the Agent went to watch the ceremonies of the Knights of the Garter, the King, seeing him in the gallery, led him in person to the Queen's tribune, pointing out pictures and rare pieces on the way. As they were talking, word was brought that the Knights were awaiting his Majesty. Charles bade them have patience and went on talking to Con. Apropos of a picture they were looking at, the King said the Pope ought to do something about the fables written in the lives of the Saints. Con replied that his Holiness was doing all he could but that, if he were in a position to remedy all the disorders of Christendon, he would begin by wiping out the heresies afflicting the Church, since they were

---

[1] *B.L.* 8644, f. 9 : Con to Barberini, Dec. 28/Jan. 7, 1638/9.
[2] *B.L.* 8643, ff. 207, 210 : Same to same, Nov. 23/Dec. 3, 1638.

the source of all evils. " But," he added, with characteristic bluntness, "it is you kings who obstruct the doing of what is right. " Charles laughed and said : " You reason as if you were in Rome."

Other arguments followed on various matters and Lord Arundel afterwards told Con he had been roundly cursed by the Knights for delaying the start of their function. The Earl added that many of the Puritan Privy Councillors were furious with him, and considered the King committed so much sacrilege each time he took hold of Con's hand ! [1]

The Papal Agent was seeing the King daily and, in face of criticism at home and abroad, Charles showed him every confidence and affection, but to all Con's persuasive arguments only replied that, although he felt assured of the goodwill of the Pope and Cardinal Barberini, he would need to take his time as his Holiness was doing. Con must persuade Urban to meet him half way. "Sire, " said the Agent, " his Holiness would, if need be, come all the way to London to unite your Majesty to the Catholic Church." " I believe you but I do not mean that, " said Charles, ignoring the pun. "I would like him to give way on certain points that may ease the way." Con said the Pope would do all his conscience and honour allowed him, and reminded his Majesty of what the Spanish Ambassador had said in Rome, — that the Pope's nephew, at a moment when the Pope lay dying, had no other friendship than that of a heretic king. Charles called the Ambassador something unmentionable and added, "My friendship, while it is for good, shall never fail. Would that Pope Clement, God forgive him, had been as this Pope. I tell you this, — he treated my father unworthily, and it was that that kept him so hostile all his life. " Con did not appear to grasp the King's allusion, but said, " I am Pope Urban's servant, and his honesty and sincerity cannot be denied even by his enemies. " Without disputing this, Charles continued to talk of the good understanding there had been between Pope Clement and King James ; friendly couriers had been exchanged, while at the same time the Pope was pledging himself to exclude his father from the English throne. [2]

[1] *B.L.* 8640, ff. 174, 266, Con to Barberini, March 2/12, Apr. 21/May 1, 1637.
[2] This was not altogether true. The friendly relations referred to had been initiated by James through his Catholic wife, Anne of Denmark, to win the Pope's support of his claims to the English crown. (Cf. A. O. MEYER,

Charles then criticized the absence of any condemnation by the Popes of the Gunpowder Plot, an act so infamous that now the Jesuits themselves were trying to plant it on the Puritans. [1] "Believe me," the King continued, " Pope Urban — and I speak thus for the regard I bear him — would do well to show his horror of such undertakings and to declare the murder and deposition of princes a most odious doctrine. If I did not desire a *rapprochement*, I would not speak like this but would let things go from bad to worse. When you see the Pope, you must try and arrange matters. I will never go against what is reasonable and I assure you I trust you as much as any man alive." [2]

When Charles execrated the authors of the break with Rome, Con, reminding him of the Pope's goodwill and the advantages of reunion, suggested his Majesty should make the Archbishop of Canterbury take a new line and, since he wanted to establish a church, unite it to the true one ; when he had spoken against the Puritans in the Star Chamber, Laud had taken all his arguments from the Catholics. The King replied that Laud was not so mad as to undertake anything as difficult as union with Rome. Con nsisted that it would be easy, and offered himself as go-between.

Clemens VIII. und Jakob I. von England, p.36 ; L. Van Wassenhoven, *Ottavio Mirto Frangipani, Nuntius van Vlaanderen, en de Engelsche Katholieken*, p. 52 : " Jacobus, die geen zekerheid had dat hij Elisabeth zou opvolgen, zag dat de gunst van den paus hem hoogst noodig was.") Clement in reply always urged James's conversion. As Elizabeth's end drew near the Pope certainly instructed the English Catholics through the Brussels Nuncio Frangipani to support a Catholic candidate (Cf. Dodd-Tierney, *op. cit.*, vol. III, App. XIV), but as he would name no one, despite the Nuncio's appeal, he could not be said to be directly opposing James. Cf. Van Wassenhoven, *op. cit.*, p. 54 : " Hij [i.e. Clement] zag maar al te wel dat een open strijd met Jacobus nadeelig zou zijn voor de Katholieken... Het was dus goed te zien dat, indien er geen veranderingen kwamen, de Kroon van Engeland aan Jacobus van Schotland zou komen."

[1] Charles is again inaccurate. Paul V, as soon as he heard of the plot sent an agent to London assuring James of his detestation of the attempted violence, at the same time asking for better treatment for the Catholics. Cf. Gardiner, *History*, vol. II, p. 17.

[2] *B.L.* 8641, ff. 62-63 : Con to Barberini, Walton, Aug. 4/14, 1637 : " Sè io non desiderassi d'accostarmi, non parlerei cosí, mà lascerei correr le cose alla peggio. Voi quando sarete col Papa, procurarete di disporre le cose, et io non mi scosterò mai dalla ragione. Vi assicuro, che mi fido di voi quanto di huomo che viva."

To demonstrate his point, the Agent asked Charles what doctrines he believed outside the Scriptures. " The first four Councils and the three Creeds," answered the King. " Why these rather than the others?" pursued Con. The King hedged, asking his questioner if he believed the same. Con said yes, adding that the reasons that made him believe them urged him also to believe in Trent. At this point Charles sent for Windebank, and Con asked jokingly if he wanted the Secretary as witness to convict him under the recent Proclamation against proselytism. The King laughed and said, " The Statute will not hold for us. I want to ask the Secretary if he believes in Trent as well as in the Four General Councils." Windebank, evading the question, began to recount the intrigues at Trent, but Con reminded him that they were worse at the first four councils. Turning to the King, he asked him if he believed that the Church of God and the assistance of the Holy Ghost would ever fail. So the three began to argue, while the Queen, rehearsing a ballet with her Ladies in a near-by room, refrained from interrupting them for a whole hour. [1]

From the first Con had acquired among the courtiers a reputation for spirited defence of his Faith. As he told the King when they joked about it, although he had not come all the way to England to argue, he could not bear to hear ill said of the Catholic religion without at least a protest, even if reasoned defence failed him.

On Charles's behalf, Con had to delve into the finer points of controversy. St Augustine's teaching on Purgatory, and the opinions for and against a dispensation to marry one's brother's wife, were subjects he went into to the King's satisfaction. On another occasion they had a dispute about the Epistle of Pope Gregory to the Emperor Maurice rebuking John of Constantinople for usurping the title of Universal Bishop. Charles was as ready as the Papal Agent with quotations from the Fathers, particularly from St Gregory, but Con had the livelier wit. " I know," said the King, " that you people pretend the Fathers are all for you." Con replied that Catholics were in undisputed possession of the teaching of the Fathers : others did the pretending without having the reality. [2]

---

[1] *B.L.* 8642, f. 59 : Con to Barberini, Jan. 19/29, 1638.
[2] *B.L.* 8641, f. 218 : Con to Barberini, Nov. 24/Dec. 4, 1637. *B.L.* 8640,

A typical illustration of Con's position at Court was seen in November, 1637, when Charles was laid up with an injured thigh and unable to leave his sofa. Con came to pay him a short visit and found the Duke of Lennox, the Marquis of Hamilton and others attending his Majesty. Henrietta, having devotedly nursed her husband, was sent out for a breath of fresh air. The conversation then turned on Faith, Purgatory, Works of Supererogation, Indulgences, the Prohibition of Bad Books, the Council of Constance, St Bartholomew's Eve, the story of Fra Paolo Sarpi and so on, with the Papal Agent imperturbably facing a heavy battery of questions. " You people get excited and make blunders," said the King, " but he has answered me with all the phlegm in the world. "   Con then ran off to a belated supper and was soon back looking refreshed. Lennox turned quickly to Charles : " Your Majesty has made George change something, to be sure, — his shirt. " Con turned the joke neatly. " For your Majesty's sake, " he said, "I will change all that my honour and conscience allow. " [1]

Charles was interested in the cult of images. He had noticed the devotion in Spain and had read up the theology of it. Not well enough, perhaps, as he laid a wager with Father Philip on Bellarmine's opinion and lost. He held that the Church had changed her mind on the subject,but Con told him that on this, as on all other matters of faith determined by her, the Church's teaching had always been the same, though there may have been diversity of opinion among individuals. " Then why is the Church's practice not in conformity with her teaching ? " exclaimed the King, referring to the *cultus* paid to Father Garnet in Spain.   There was absolute agreement, Con contended, notwithstanding the scandals his Majesty had observed in Spain and which the Pope would remedy immediately they were brought to his notice. [2]

---

ff.194, 338 : Same to same, Mar. 9/19, May 19/29, 1637 : "Dopo varie citationi de' Padri, e particolarmente di S. Gregorio, il Rè me disse : Sò, che voi altri pretendete che li Padri faccino per Voi. Io risposi che noi eramo in possessione non controversa della dottrina de' Padri, mà che erano altri che pretendevano senza fondamento."

[1] *B.L.* 8641, f. 206 : Con to Barberini, Nov. 17/27, 1637.

[2] Father Garnet, the Jesuit Provincial executed for complicity in the Gunpowder Plot, was naturally regarded by Charles as a traitor, and it came as a shock to him on going to Spain, where the Jesuit was revered as a martyr,

Con then turned the argument on the King.   His Majesty knew well enough in England, where he acted both pope and king, how difficult it was to maintain uniformity between the deeds of the Protestants and their doctrines.   If only his Majesty would unite with the Pope, a remedy could be found for a thousand difficulties. Evasively, Charles made his favourite complaint against the Catholic Kings who, he said, gave the Pope nought but his titles, only obeying him where it was easy.   Con asked the King not to imagine that the Pope would demand more from him than from any other Power.   Charles laughed, saying, " When you are Pope, we shall be in accord. "   It would be no small matter, if he were ever a Cardinal, answered Con, but he would always strive to the shedding of his blood for his Majesty's well-being. [1]

Disloyalty to the Pope of princes Catholic in name was a point Charles harped on continually, not only to the Papal Agent but to the Ambassadors of the countries in question.   " You people call the Pope the Common Father, " he said to the Ambassador of Parma, " but you do not treat him as such. "   His own bearing towards the Pope and the Cardinal Secretary was irreproachable, his reverence for the Apostolic See being backed by personal admiration of the qualities and intellectual powers of Urban himself.

Here again his memories of Spain served him to show that the Spaniards thought as little of *obeying* the Pope as he, a non-Catholic, did, though he at least did honour to the person of the Pontiff. " The respect offered the Pope by your Catholic princes is a cere-

---

to find his picture in the Churches.   He had mentioned this to Panzani in 1635, strongly criticizing Roman methods of canonization.   Panzani promptly took the Decree on Beatification to Windebank, showing the care the Holy See used before conferring the honours of the Altar.   It pleased Windebank to be able to tell Charles that Father Garnet was not beatified. (*P.R.O. Rom. Trans.* : Panzani to Barberini, June 17/27, 1635.)

[1] *B.L.* 8640, ff. 15-16 : Con to Barberini, Hampton, Jan. 1, 1637. This was Con's actual reply as he sent it to Barberini, but Ferragalli, the Cardinal's Secretary who deciphered Con's letters, considered it wiser, in view of the tension over Con's preferment, to omit " non sarà puoco, sè io sarò Cardinale " and substitute " io rispose à S. Mᵗᵃ che meglio, e più facilmente lo sarà con Papa Urbano," — which is what Barberini actually read. Ferragalli begged Con not to take umbrage at what he had done purely in his interests (*B.L.* 8645, f. 105 : Ferragalli to Con, Feb. 12, 1637).

mony," Charles told Con, and went on to relate how Olivares had told Buckingham that the Pope dare not refuse the marriage dispensation when it was asked for by the King of Spain, as he was nothing but the King's chaplain. At this Con said he had no wish to argue about the past but, thank God, he served a Pope who time and again had known how to say " No" to France, Spain and the Emperor, when their demands were unreasonable. If the Pope had not acted thus, Christendom would be in a far worse state than was actually the case. [1]

Charles heartily acknowledged all Urban's virtues, but ventured to criticize his attitude when the rumour came through that the French were threatening to set up a patriarchate of their own. Con had had no news of it but remarked that the King should take it ill, for, if the French broke with Rome, they, would ingratiate themselves with the Pope's enemies, *viz.* the English and Scottish Puritans, who were his Majesty's enemies too. Charles answered that if the Pope would listen to reason everything could be settled easily. Con confessed that at this he made an unseemly gesture and laughed. In the same vein the King protested : " You always make out your own position to be beyond doubt." The Agent then asked whimsically whether the King thought him a scoundrel for looking on while his Majesty was being deceived or a madman for allowing himself to be deceived. Charles steered through the dilemma by saying that Con was being deceived unwittingly. These were Laud's arguments, who judged others by himself, said the Agent, but he would make it quite clear to his Majesty that, as far as the Holy Father was concerned, the negotiations were being conducted in all sincerity. [2]

The intimacy between King and Papal Agent had long been noticed, and not in silence, for the whisperings that wafted through the corridors of the Court soon reached Con's ears. He was told in confidence by a friendly Lady-of-the-Household, not a Catholic, that there were many murmurings at the King's lack of zeal for the Protestant religion, shown by his long talks with the Pope's envoy from which no good could come. Con at first treated the matter as a jest. He was accredited to the Queen, not to the

---

[1] *B.L.* 8641, ff. 137, 148 : Con to Barberini, Oct. 6/16, 13/23, 1637.
[2] *B.L.* 8643, f. 2 : Con to Barberini, June 22/July 2, 1638.

King, he said lightly, and his business was to deal with her Majesty and her Ladies, not to talk religion with the King. The latter's interest in pictures and sculpture was known to all and, if his Majesty and he chose to discuss the arts in public, it was that all might hear. Con was as evasive when he was asked, as often he was, what had been the topic of his talk with the King : he never remembered. [1]

Tongues wagged harder, however, when someone produced a copy of Con's controversial works [2] brought from Rome, and showed Charles a passage calling Elizabeth a bastard and labelling as impious the Oaths of Supremacy and Allegiance. The King made light of the matter and in no way relaxed his friendly attitude. He would discuss all the Scottish news with Con, asking his advice how to deal " with those countrymen of yours. " [3]

It was Con's habit when mention was made of the insubordinate Puritans to contrast the loyalty and long-suffering of the Catholics. At such moments the King had an unhappy knack of remembering something against the Jesuits. They were as pernicious as the Puritans, he alleged, and were trying to start a faction through their penitents, chiefly ladies. Con protested against this slander. The ladies he had had to deal with who were penitents of the Jesuits, he remarked drily, were far from trying to influence him in favour of the Society ; they seemed only too anxious to justify themselves for going to Jesuit Fathers rather than to others.

But when it came to obeying their sovereign, the King insisted, Puritan and Jesuit were of the same kidney. Again Con objected : the Jesuits were, if anything, too much in favour of monarchy. " Yes, for that of Spain, " retorted the King. The Papal Agent pointed out that those days were gone. Now the Spanish stayed in Spain, the French in France, and the English Catholics no longer held the key position they had had under

---

[1] *B.L.* 8640, f. 226 : Con to Barberini, Mar. 30/Apr. 9, 1637. *B.L.* 8644, f. 10 : Same to same, Dec. 28/Jan. 7, 1638/9.

[2] Presumably the *Assertionum Catholicarum* v. *supra*, p. 232, note 3. Con's only other printed works are *De Institutione Principis* (Regij, 1621), *De Duplici Statu Religionis apud Scotos* (Romae, 1628) ; *Vita Mariae Stuartae* (Romae, 1624) and a poem written for the wedding of Taddeo Barberini, Urban's nephew, with Anna Colonna (Romae, 1629).

[3] *B.L.* 8641, ff. 130, 151 : Con to Barberini, Sept. 29/Oct. 9 ; Oct. 13/22, 1637. *B.L.* 8642, f. 61, Same to same : Jan. 19/29, 1638.

Elizabeth when the Crown seemed in dispute. His Majesty, concluded Con, did the Catholics too much honour in thinking they could move princes to aught but their own interest. The solution was for his Majesty to reach a real understanding with the Pope and become a Catholic; then the Holy Father would see that all gave due obedience to the King. [1]

But nothing could change the ingrained prejudice Charles had inherited from his father. " If all agreed as we do, everything would go well, " he told Con, " but the Jesuits are as hostile to kings and bishops as the Puritans are. " [2]

Charles's view of the Society was not so utterly distorted that he would refuse to stand by even a Jesuit in the pure ministration of souls. For some time, Con had been working on the King to intervene and stop the nuisance of the Pursuivants. Charles knew well enough that these guardians of the peace were only too often grasping informers out to fill their own pockets and he showed every sympathy to the harassed Catholics, while forbidding Con to let this beknown lest they should indiscreetly vaunt the fact and cause a public outcry. The King preferred to step in *post factum* and prevent unjust punishment rather than check the Pursuivants altogether. [3]

Con now took up the case of a Jesuit priest who, while devotedly ministering to the plague-stricken, many of whom he reconciled to the Church, was arrested and charged with perverting his Majesty's liege-subjects. Laud was annoyed and said so at the Council table, while Windebank tactlessly added fuel to the flame by remarking that there was not a Catholic gentleman in the land who did not keep a priest in his house. Con hurried with the case to the King. Charles showed no displeasure at the priest's having ministered to Catholics, but said it was going too far to disturb nrotestants on their death-beds, making them die in despair Peither good Catholics nor good Protestants. [4]

The man was brought to trial, accused by a pursuivant of being a priest. " I am not worthy; would that I were, " was the

---

[1] *B.L.* 8641, f. 60, 137 : Con to Barberini, Walton, Aug. 4/14, Oct. 6/16, 1637.

[2] *B.L.* 8643, f. 77 : Same to same, Aug. 24/Sept. 3, 1638.

[3] *B.L.* 8640, f. 75 : Same to same, Hampton, Jan. 12/22, 1637.

[4] *Ibid.*, f. 205 : Same to same, Mar. 23/Apr. 2, 1637.

cool reply. But the pursuivant persisted : the man had confessed to his priesthood, and a secular priest had supplied the information that he was a Jesuit. A friendly judge told the jury they had two points to decide : had the man perverted the King's subjects? was he a priest? There was no evidence of the former, so they need consider only the second point. They did, and brought in their verdict : the man was a priest.

Con went straight to Queen about it but, finding her in bed with bronchitis, waited on the King. Charles asked why he had not been told before, so Con said he had waited for authentic information of the charge first, *viz.* that it was merely the man's priesthood and ministrations to the plague-stricken that were against him. His silence, added Con, had been to his chagrin interpreted as fear of risking his Majesty's frown. Charles told him not to worry ; he would remedy the rest.

Con begged the king to prevent similar happenings in the future by disbanding the Pursuivants. This the King said, he could not do, as they were the ministers of justice, but he wou'd punish them when at fault. Con asked him to begin with this rascal who had offered to release the Jesuit for £5, though he (Con) had opposed the payment, hoping once and for all to get rid of this pest plaguing his Majesty's subjects. The King told him to prove the fact and the pursuivant would receive exemplary punishment.

The next evening Con approached the King who led him out on to the balcony of the Queen's apartment. Charles said he had sent for the chief judge and told him not to proceed in that way in future. He added, " I have told Windebank that sentence is not to be carried out on your Jesuit. I assure you I do not want blood to be shed for the sake of religion. " So the death-sentence was commuted to imprisonment, but Con soon obtained the man's release.

The affair set many tongues wagging. It was whispered that the Jesuits had wanted the man impeached to prove that there was persecution in England, while Con was accused of letting the case go so far to show his influence with the King. [1]

---

[1] *B.L.* 8640, ff. 285-286 : Con to Barberini, April 28/May 8, 1637. *B.L.* 8641, f. 7 : Same to same, June 24/July 4, 1637.

The Jesuit provincial told Con that this was the first instance of a priest who had been condemned to death by a jury and had not served his sentence.   A little later the Agent secured the first release of a priest, also a Jesuit, for refusing the Oath.

There were not wanting priests, both secular and regular, who deplored all this, declaring Con's concern was the triumph of the Society. Proof of this, they said, was that the Jesuits spoke well of him and that, despite his knowing how much the King, Laud and the Government hated the Jesuits, the Papal Agent did nothing about it ! [1]

Even Charles taxed his friend on the point, and Con had to protest that he did no more for the Jesuits than he would for any Catholic.   He said he was sorry he had done all too little for the general reunion of the realm with the Holy See. At this the King apologized, and acknowledged himself satisfied with the Papal Agent. [2]

Con's privileged position with the King had not escaped the notice of the Powers, who were not above seeking his influence for an alliance with England, dangling before him as a bait the hope of relief for the Catholics. The Spanish Ambassador came to him with talk of an alliance between England and Spain for the recovery of the United Provinces, formerly a Spanish possession. Spain would support the English Catholics in their bid for relief, he said, and, in any case, it would be all for the good of religion to make the English and Dutch heretics cut one another's throats.

The Papal Agent put the whole matter before the King, deprecating the idea of war but stressing what the Ambassador had said in favour of the English Catholics. While satisfied that Con was doing his duty in seeking the advantage of the Catholics, Charles flatly refused to do anything for them at the instance of the Spaniards. " They care no more for them than for dogs, " he said, "except in so far as they think them good enough to maintain a party devoted to them in England. What I desire to do for the Catholics must come from me alone. I do not wish them to depend on anyone but the Pope and myself. "   This was

---

[1] *B.L.* 8640, f. 287 : Same to same, April 28/May 8, 1637. *B.L.* 8641, ff. 72, 82 : Same to same, Aug. 18/28 ; Aug. 25/Sept. 4, 1637.

[2] *B.L.* 8641, f. 60 : Same to same, Walton, Aug. 4/14, 1637.

entirely the mind of his Holiness, Con assured him. Charles then referred to Cardinal Richelieu in no friendly tone, adding, " If any of these priests of my wife happens to die, I want the new ones to depend on the Pope and not on Richelieu or anybody else. " [1]

In his talks with the King, Con always put up a spirited defence of the Catholics, especially against the common charge of political intrigue and disloyalty. The Gunpowder Plot must have been one of Charles's earliest memories. He realized, too, the Power the Pope had to absolve subjects from their allegiance; always in the back of his mind there was the haunting fear of a repetition of the excommunication that befell Elizabeth. What was the effect of excommunication, and what ought a priest to do if someone confessed a plot against the person of the King?

The Papal Agent pointed out that the real consequences of excommunication were neither assassination nor personal violence. He added that all princes were in the same position as the Pope himself in such matters. The Holy Father could do no more than detest such plots and forbid them under the direst threats. Charles agreed, but asked that, in order to shut the mouths of those who were maligning the Catholics with diabolical accusations, Con on his return should get the Pope to declare publicly his good-will towards England. He added that before Con left he would tell him candidly all that occurred to him for the stabilization of the good understanding between himself and the Pope, and told Con to remember what he had said so often : "At the price of my life I want us to be in agreement. " [2]

In the last months of Con's residence at Court, he saw less of the King, owing to the latter's Scottish excursion and also perhaps to a strained feeling due to the non-arrival of the hoped-for Red Hat. Nevertheless, the Papal Agent not only left the heretic King on the best of terms, but secured a warm welcome for his successor, Count Carlo Rossetti.

George Con's prudence and integrity had done much to make lasting the friendly feelings that his daily intercourse with their

[1] *B.L.* 8640, ff. 309-311 : Con to Barberini, May 5/15, 1637.
[2] *B.L.* 8640, f. 304 : Con to Barberini, May 5/15,1637 : " Ricordatevi di quello che vi significai altre volte, che io vorrei à prezzo di sangue che fossimo ben d'accordo."

Majesties had created. The confidence and familiarity he enjoyed from the King had never made him less fearlessly outspoken, nor prevented him from winning the friendship of a large part of the nobility despite a good deal of underground criticism inevitable at a Court. [1]

But the hopes entertained in Rome that this intercourse with Con would draw the King towards concession and perhaps conversion were wholly disappointed. The most conventional of kings, Charles was completely content with his sacramental Anglicanism and this the Agent had soon realized. " The King's conversion is more a matter to be desired than to be genuinely hoped-for, " he wrote shortly after arriving in England. Six months later he was still more emphatic : " All is in the hands of God, especially the King's heart. I do not say nor will I ever say he will become a Catholic. " [2]

[1] *B.L.* 8616, f. 75 : Fr Philip to Barberini, London, Sept. 9, 1639. After describing Rossetti's welcome and his opinion that the Agency was now firmly established, the Queen's Confessor continues : " Ad hoc contulit plurimum, Dei gratia cooperante, D. Georgij Conei prudentia agendo, et integritas vitae ; quibus adeó Regis et Reginae animum sibi conciliavit ut cum ipso ferè quotidie conversati sint in palatio familiariter et confidenter tamquam cum domestico suo, servando tamen decorem quod convenit ministro principis cui inservit. Ad Regis exemplum non solum aulici, sed et alii nobiles ipsum perhumaniter tractaverunt, quibus occasionibus solerter usus profuit multum quibusdam haereticis, et Catholicis mirificè innuit, ad quorum utilitatem promovendam omnem opem suam et operam continue impendit."

[2] *B.L.* 8639, f. 194 : Con to Barberini, Nov. 6/Oct. 27, 1636 : " Che fosse cosa da desiderare più che da sperare". *B.L.* 8640, f. 386 : Same to same, June 16/26, 1637 : " gli effetti sono in mano di Dio, particolarmente il cuore del Rè, il quale non dico, nè dirò mai, che sara Catt[co]. "

CHAPTER XI

ROYAL VIEWS ON ALLEGIANCE

> " *Peruse the Oath and you shall soon descry it,*
> *By all the Father Garnets that stand by it ;*
> *'Gainst which the Church of which I am a member,*
> *Shall keep another fifth day of November.*" [1]

The discovery of the Gunpowder Plot in 1605 awakened all the old fears for their loyalty that Catholics had been at pains to live down since the furore caused by the excommunication of Elizabeth and the absolving of her subjects from allegiance. But James and his Government had known well enough that the perpetrators of the plot received scant sympathy from the main body of Catholics, who would have welcomed a chance of officially dissociating themselves from disloyalty to the Crown.

It was therefore peculiarly bad statesmanship, only explainable by a misguided hatred of Popery, that this test of loyalty should have taken the form of a political oath to be tendered to all Catholic commoners, and containing a denial as heretical of the offensive doctrine that popes could depose kings. [2] As a result, a potential instrument of political unity became a channel for fresh persecution, for, while those who took the new Oath still incurred the ordinary penalties of recusancy, those who refused it were subject to all the terrors of a *Praemunire*. [3]

---

[1] *A Dialogue between Two Zealots, corcerning* ETC. *in the newe Oath.*, 1640, Rous's *Diary*, p. 101.

[2] For the text of the original Oath of Allegiance as passed by Parliament cf. DODD-TIERNEY, *op. cit.*, vol. V, App. XX, pp. CXVII-CXVIII.

For the early history of the Oath and its effects, cf. *ibid.*, vol. V, pp. 66-83. There is also an account in ETHELRED TAUNTON's *History of the Jesuits in England*, pp. 351-365.

[3] GARDINER, *History*, vol. I, p. 288. In virtue of a *Praemunire* pursuivants might at all times enter the abode of Catholics, and children seize the property of their parents ; in fact all life's amenities were denied to the proscribed Papist.

It was doubtless the deliberate policy of the Government to ignore the opportunity of winning over all Catholics to undisguised loyalty to the King by pursuing the more profitable policy of making the contentious phrase on the power of the Pope a means of striking discord in the ranks of the Papists. The stratagem certainly succeeded.

When the Governments's intention became known, Archpriest Blackwell called a meeting of five other priests at his house and declared his opinion that the new Oath could be taken. Against the Deposing Power he produced the ingenious argument that, as the Pope could not depose the King without harm resulting, he could not do so at all, and therefore the Catholics could safely swear he had not the power. Two of his hearers were convinced but three opposed him and, as these were followed by the greater part of English Catholic opinion, when the Archpriest's approval became known, he withdrew it.

The new Pope, Paul V, deeply versed in the law of the Church, lost no time in condemning the Oath by Brief dated September12/22, 1606, and the English Catholics found they could take it only under pain of mortal sin. Vainly they offered to accept another oath equally binding on their consciences but leaving Papal claims untouched. The Government remained adamant and the prisons soon filled with loyal subjects of the King, whose consciences forbade them to yield ; others escaped confinement only to find themselves a prey to the overbearing insolence of a brood of sycophants who blackmailed them for conscience' sake. Many Catholics followed Mr Blackwell's example and, on the ground of some informality in the Brief, took the Oath ; but a second Brief of August 13/23, 1607, settled the matter, and the Archpriest was deposed. [1]

In the years that followed, the lawfulness of the Oath was fiercely championed and attacked in a spirited pamphlet war typical of the time. When Blackwell was taken up by Bellarmine, King James himself stepped into the fray with his *Apologie for the Oath* [2] in reply to the Papal Briefs, and with a *Letter to Cardinal Bellarmine*. Also, in a *Letter to Christian Princes* James strenuously refuted the charge of being a persecutor. The answer Bellarmine

---

[1] GARDINER, *op. cit.*, vol. II, pp. 16, 20.

[2] London, 1609 ; it was immediately placed on the *Index* by decree dated July 23, 1609 (N.S.). Cf. *Elenchus librorum omnium...*, Romae, 1632.

wrote brought into the arena Dom Thomas Preston, O. S. B., thenceforward the champion of the Oath among the English Catholics. [1]

Father Thomas Preston, under the *alias* Roger Widdrington, wrote between 1616 and 1620 a number of pamphlets, attacking the Jesuits' intransigent attitude towards the Oath, [2] refuting the argument of Thomas Fitzherbert, Bellarmine and Lessius, and " discovering " the " divers cunning shifts of Cardinal Peron. " Nor did he spare his own Benedictine brethren who, he maintained, attacked him unreasonably for presenting a doctrine the Pope tolerated in France.

In support of his own view he cited *arrêts* of the Paris *parlement* condemning books of Bellarmine (Nov. 26, 1610) and of Suarez (June 27, 1614), and the decree against the doctrine of deposition promulgated in Paris, 1615.

The Benedictine analysed the Oath into eight parts, explaining each and basing his main defence of it on the celebrated *Protestation of Allegiance* made on January 31, 1602, before the Archbishop of Canterbury by thirteen priests who promised to fight for her Majesty, Queen Elizabeth, in the event of plot or invasion by any foreign Prelate, Prince or Potentate, and to defend her even in face of excommunication and censure. At the same time they asserted that by this they yielded no particle of their Christian duty to the supreme Spiritual Power of the Pope. This *Protestation*,

---

[1] BERINGTON, *op. cit.*, pp. 78-79. — Roland Preston born 1567, educated at Oxford, and at English College, Rome, for the secular priesthood ; June 16, 1592, professed a Benedictine at Monte Cassino ; 1602, sent on the English Mission, where in Norfolk he found Dom Sigebert Buckley, on whose authority he took steps to perpetuate the English Congregation of Benedictines. After undergoing many terms of imprisonment he died in the Clink (Cf. Dom H.N.BIRT, *Obit Book of the English Benedictines*, p.21).—For Bellarmine's views, v. *Apologia Roberti S.R.E. Cardinalis Bellarmini pro responsione sua ad librum Iacobi Magnae Britanniae Regis, cuius titulus est Triplici nodo triplex cuneus, in qua Apologia refellitur Praefatio Monitoria Regis eiusdem. Accessit seorsim eadem ipsa responsio, quae sub nomine Matthaei Torti anno superiore prodierit* (Coloniae Agrippinae, 1610). — For a full list of the protagonists for and against the Oath, cf. DODD-TIERNEY, *op. cit.*, vol. V, p. 73, note 1.

[2] The Society was so completely identified with opposition to the Oath that many seculars used to offer the Oath to new missionaries to find out if they were Jesuits or not (*P.R.O. Rom. Trans.* : Panzani to Barberini, July 25/Aug. 4, 1635).

Archbishop Bancroft maintained, formed the background on which Parliament framed the new Oath.

Roger Widdrington then took upon himself to answer the Pope's two condemnatory Briefs, all the time defending himself vigorously against any charge of heresy and submitting absolutely to the Holy See in a letter addressed to Paul V himself. It was all to small purpose, however, as two of his works, the *Apologia pro jure Principum* and the *Disputatio theologica de Juramento fidelitatis* were placed on the *Index*, the author being called upon " to purge himself. " This he did by sending to Pope Paul his *Purgatio Rogeri Widdringtoni*, professing complete submission and begging the Holy Father to remove the decree of the *Index*. [1]

With the two Papal Briefs and the condemnation of Widdrington to guide them, most English Catholics stood firm and refused the Oath, — an attitude freely stigmatized abroad as sheer obstinacy.[2] In consequence, the minority that favoured it was not inconsiderable ; the latter either took the Oath as it stood, on the ground that the Pope had not actually punished Widdrington, or with the

---

[1] Cf. *passim* the following works of ROGER WIDDRINGTON :

(1) *A Theologicall Disputation concerning the Oath of Allegiance, dedicated to the most Holy Father, Pope Paul the Fifth* (N P., 1613, 8⁰ 422 pp.).

(2) *Rogeri Widdringtoni Catholici Angli ad Sanctissimum Dominum Paulum Quintum, Pontificem Max. humillima Supplicatio* (Albionopoli, 1616, 12⁰, 262 pp.).

(3) *Last Reioynder to Mr. Thomas Fitz-Herbert's Reply concerning the Oath of Allegiance, and the Pope's power to depose Princes* (N. P., 1619, 4⁰, 646 pp.). (Reprint, 1633).

(4) *Strena Catholica seu explicatio breuis et dilucida noui Fidelitatis Iuramenti* (Augustae, 1620, 12⁰).

(5) *A New-Yeares Gift for English Catholikes, or a briefe and cleare Explication of the New Oath of Allegiance* (N. P., 1620, 12⁰).

Also of interest are :

(a) *A Copy of the Decree wherein two books of Roger Widdrington, an English Cathotholick* (sic) *are condemned and the Author commanded to purge himselfe* (N. P., 1614).

(b) *A Copy of the Purgation which the same Roger Widdrington sent to his Holinesse Pope Paul the fifth* (N. P., 1614).

It is noteworthy that all save (2) and (4) are published *permissu superiorum*

[2] B.L. 8618, f. 158 : Toby Mathew to [Card. Barberini ?], Brussels, April 15, 1617 : " Sene truovamolti in tutti le Provincie d'Europa, che credono et dicono sotto mano che li Catt.cl Inglesi che ricusano far il giuramento detto di fedeltà son pur troppo ostinati, et alieni della grandezza del lor Rè."

reservation said to have been made by the King that it was intended to exact nothing but civil obedience. There were even found some Jesuit fathers who allowed this. [1]

Evidence of the pressure maintained by this minority in face of Rome's official frown and the organized opposition of the Society of Jesus, is seen in the reprinting in 1633 (fourteen years after it had been written) of Widdrington's *Last Reioynder*, an affair of 646 quarto pages, while in the following year William Howard, Lord Arundel's son and a future martyr, published by royal licence what appears to be a rehash of all Widdrington's arguments. [2]

Howard made a strong point of the difficulty many Catholics found, and the King made capital of, *viz.* that the Pope could not be drawn to indict any particular clause in the Oath as clearly unlawful. He went on to argue for a *probable* opinion in favour of the Oath and, since to refuse it was unsafe, *pars tutior* might follow when there was a probable opinion to back it. This conclusion he commended to all having the cure of souls, though he submitted his judgment wholeheartedly to the Church, protesting that he " would also have beene willing for peace, and obedience sake, to have lead captive, and blind-fold my will, contrary to my understanding to the observing of his Holinesse Breves, if they had concerned a spirituall, and not a temporall matter. " [3]

---

[1] BRADY, *op. cit.*, p. 88 : *Arch. Prop., Scritt. Ant.* 347, f. 37-48 : *Relata d'In-ghilterra*, 4 Maij, 1626 (*Congr.* 56).

[2] Sir William Howard (1614-1680) was the third surviving son of Thomas Howard, Earl of Arundel and Surrey, and of Aletheia Howard (*née* Talbot), Con's unfailing friend ; created Viscount Stafford, 1640 ; committed to the Tower with four other Catholic noblemen during the Titus Oates Plot, Oct., 1678 ; despite his supposed weakness he defended himself with considerable ability for seven days ; he was nevertheless condemned to be hanged, drawn and quartered — a sentence the King, while avowing belief in his innocence, only commuted to beheading. He died on Tower Hill, Dec. 29, 1680. (Cf. GILLOW, *op. cit.*, vol. V, pp. 522-523.) — Howard had remained staunch to the Faith, despite the fact that he was sent to be tutored by Samuel Harsnett, Bishop of Norwich, who later (1678) became Archbishop of York. A Van Dyck portrait of Howard from the Bute Collection, Cardiff Castle, is reproduced in M. F. S. HERVEY's *Life of Thomas Howard, Earl of Arundel*, facing p. 338.

[3] *A Patterne of Christian Loyaltie* : *whereby any prudent man may clearely perceive, in what manner the New Oath of Allegiance, and every Clause thereof, may in a true and Catholike sense, without danger of Perjury, be taken by Roman Catholikes. Collected out of authours, who have handled the matter more largely*, by WILLIAM HOWARD, an English Catholike, London, 1634, 8°, 61 pp.

Though he had to enforce the Oath for fear of being branded a Papist, King Charles himself was anxious for a settlement of the whole controversy, knowing it would win him the unstinted allegiance of all his Catholic subjects. Father Preston he looked on as his own special champion, while the Jesuits, so hostile to the Oath, he considered the arch-enemies of monarchy. [1] The King was therefore greatly perturbed to hear that Preston's efforts had met with Rome's censure. Fearing the Benedictine had changed his views, Charles summoned him to an audience, during which he gave him a royal command that Father Preston could not be induced to divulge. [2]

The unyielding temper of the Catholics, hardening now, was brought home to the King still more forcibly by the refusal of one of his own household to take the Oath. Sir Richard Lashford was unknown to the Government as a Papist till two of his daughters were found crossing the Channel to enter a nunnery. Cited before the Archbishop of Canterbury, Sir Richard was offered the Oath, which he refused, and in consequence stood in danger of losing both his property and his pension. [3]

Subsequently, the Justices, using some indulgence, submitted the Oath to the man three times, and three times on advice he refused it, losing his office and his pension. The four commissioners declared that neither his Majesty nor they meant to bind him to more than true temporal obedience to the Crown without in any way prejudicing the spiritual authority of the Pope. So after a protest, and with this reservation, Lashford took the Oath publicly and was released, escaping that total loss of his property which he had feared.

The case created a great stir, and its outcome influenced many who had hitherto held out but now were ready to take the Oath with the same reservation rather than lose all they had. [4]

---

[1] *B.L.* 8639, f. 174 : Con to Barberini, Oct. 20/30, 1636. As Fr Blount, the Provincial complained, the fact that some took the Oath made the Jesuits, who refused it, thoroughly odious in the eyes of the Government.

[2] *Arch. Prop., Scritt. Ant.* 134 (1634), f. 218 : Dav. Codnerus (Matteo Selvaggio) to Ingoli, London, April 25, 1634 : " Sua M[ta] gl' hà intimato et commandato espressam[te] un commando il quale in particolare non hà voluto fidarsi meco."

[3] *Arch. Prop., Scritt. Ant.* 134 (1634), f. 218. It was all the more galling to Charles to find that Lashford was a protégé of the Jesuits.

[4] *B.L.* 8619, f. 96 : Dom David to Barberini, London, Sept. 17, 1634.

This incident and the appearance of *A Patterne of Christian Loyaltie*, a copy of which he sent to Rome, induced Dom David Codner, a confrère of Father Preston, to plead for more indulgence by the Holy See in the matter of the Oath.   Slanderous tongues were saying that Rome had no use for heretics save to trample them underfoot. Nevertheless, the King was willing to negotiate, and Dom David advised the sending of a representative to London to discuss the whole business.   Padre Alessandro d'Ales, having been in England on a secret mission to King James, would be *persona grata* to the present Government. [1]

As the Government showed no intention of being indiscriminately severe, several Catholic noblemen thought a compromise could be effected by the removal of certain objectionable words from the Oath.   In this way the King could be given satisfaction, and the Holy See would still be standing firm by its condemnation of the original formula.

Dom David was thereupon approached to put the matter to Rome, which he did in a long letter to Cardinal Barberini.   He related how the late Cardinal Bandini had told him some years before of the desire of the Holy See to give the English King all aid in winning a purely civil obedience from his Catholic subjects and had suggested sending an agent to London ; his Eminence had added that some attempt to have the Oath altered had been made at the time of the French Marriage by de Bérulle and de Béthune in Rome.   Dom David concluded by telling the Cardinal Secretary of the Lashford case as an example of what was happening. [2]

While the Jesuits were ranged unreservedly in the ranks of the opposition, the English Benedictines were becoming identified with the cause of compromise.   The President-General of the restored Congregation, Dom Leander a Sancto Martino, who, it will be recalled, had been sent to survey the religious situation in England prior to Panzani's arrival, immediately appealed to Rome to modify her attitude towards the Oath which he saw as a rock of scandal not only sundering Catholic from Catholic, but weakening the confidence of the King in their loyalty.   To

---

[1] *Arch. Prop., Scritt. Ant.* 134, f. 219 : Matteo Selvaggio to Ingoli, London, July 18/28, 1634.

[2] *B.L.* 8619, f. 96 : Dom David to Barberini, London, Sept. 17, 1634.

alienate his Majesty's natural goodwill could only bring fresh persecution upon the heads of the hapless Catholics and was quite uncalled-for as the King insisted that he required merely civil allegiance and had no desire to usurp the Pope's spiritual juris-diction over the English Catholics. If, therefore, there were any clauses in the Oath offensive to them, his Majesty was quite willing for a subtle interpretation, satisfying to the Catholic conscience, to be placed upon them.

In consequence, pleaded Leander, the Oath took on an entirely different complexion from the attack on Papal rights the canonist Paul V had condemned, and he gave it as his considered opinion as well as that of moderate members of the English Catholic nobility whom he had consulted that the present Pope should suspend his own and his predecessors' declarations against the Oath. To this end the Benedictine submitted a specimen letter that Pope Urban might well send to the King of England. At the same time he forwarded to the Cardinal Secretary an elaborate analysis of the current Oath with his own broad interpretation of it. [1]

Dom Leander also drew up a new oath formula in which, while admitting the Pope's power of excommunicating kings, he denies him any authority binding the consciences of Catholics either to depose princes himself or to empower others, whether subjects or foreign sovereigns, to co-operate in deposing them. The Bene-dictine also condemns as impious and heretical the doctrine of tyrannicide and swears fealty to his sovereign in face of all sentences of excommunication and deposition. The concluding words of this formula were, from Rome's view-point, the most tendentious of all : " I will never demand or accept, of the Pope or of any other person or power, any dispensation, pardon or absolution from this my oath, or any parcel thereof, unless the Holy Catholick Church, in an undoubted lawful general Council, received by my King and country, should in any part thereof decree otherwise. So help me God. Amen. " [2]

---

[1] *Clarendon State Papers*, vol. I, p. 129 : Leander to Cardinal Bentivoglio, July 12/22, 1634 ; p. 185 : Leander to Barberini, Dec. 16, 1634 (corrected Jan. 5, 1635). To this letter is added an elaborate examination of the Oath.

[2] *Ibid.*, vol. I, pp. 210-211 : Leander's Oath, signed under the name John Skidmore. The original is endorsed by Windebank : " Dec. 17th, 1634, Leanders Oath."

Leander submitted his Oath to Windebank and the King. Whether he also forwarded it to Rome is not clear, but he certainly wrote to Barberini in defence of Davenport's book on the *XXXIX Articles* and of William Howard's pamphlet, pleading that as they had been inspired by the best intentions they should not be censured ; there was surely no call for every audacious writing to placed on the *Index*, when Rome discreetly winked at so much that was being written against the Deposing Power in France. Liberal views and probable opinions would have to be tolerated, were the English people to be brought back to union with the Holy See. The principal point of the Oath was tolerated in the whole of France, and the Sacraments were not refused to those who took it. The English Oath should be tolerated in the sense the King said he intended and, to this interpretation, Leander insisted, the Apostolic Briefs already despatched were not prejudicial but only the writings of Cardinal Bellarmine and others of the Society. [1]

The boldness of the Benedictine's pleading and the broadness of his views were looked at askance in England as well as in Rome, and when he set them out for all to see in a pamphlet replying to the twenty arguments which Fr Edward Leedes *alias* Courtenay, S. J., had marshalled against William Howard, he soon found his orthodoxy impugned and abandoned further official intervention in the controversy. [2]

When Gregorio Panzani arrived in England to settle the dissensions that so sharply divided the Catholics among themselves, he was soon interviewed by Mr Secretary Windebank, but stated frankly that he had no express mandate to bargain about the Oath. However, he assured the Secretary of the Pope's and Barberini's earnest desire for the Catholics to show the Crown the utmost loyalty and respect in all civil affairs.

[1] *B.L.* 8620, ff. 31-35 : Leander to Barberini, N.D. [Panzani erat Londini] 1635 (?).

[2] *Ibid.,* HOWARD's *A Patterne of Christian Loyaltie* was answered by *A Discourse against the Oath of Allegiance* by Fr EDWARD LEEDES, *alias* COURTENAY (1634). This treatise supported the Deposing Power, and the Pope's authority to make war and invade countries. It probably circulated only in MS., being written for a conference with Father Preston, who was supposed to have had a hand in Howard's work. The Jesuit's arguments were in turn exposed by Fr Leander's *Remarks upon some passages of Mr Courtenay's book against the Oath of Allegiance* (1635). (Cf. *Clarendon S.P.,* vol. I, p. 258.)

Windebank, in reply, spoke of the King's regard for Pope Urban. Stressing his Majesty's clemency in applying the Penal Laws, the Secretary gave it as his considered opinion that the Pope would be well advised to revise the Briefs of Paul V condemning Catholics who took the Oath. Panzani answered that he feared this could not be done unless the King met his Holiness half-way by making the Oath agreeable to the Holy See.

Windebank then told Panzani of his Majesty's displeasure at the condemnation of Father Preston's book. The Italian professed ignorance of it, but said that it was against the Holy Father's wish that anything had been written on this subject. On Windebank's pointing out that some Catholics took the Oath on the King's proviso that he meant only civil obedience, Panzani replied that these were only a party; in such matters all must act in concert.

Windebank then asked that the Pope should draw up a form of Oath and send it to England. Panzani said he would see what could be done, but all he got for his pains was a rebuke from Barberini for going beyond his instructions : the matter was of too delicate a nature to be dealt with as yet. [1]

When George Con came as accredited Agent from Urban to the Court of the Queen, he forthwith set to work to bring Rome's wishes and the King's into line by getting a Catholic friend to draw up a fresh form of Oath and present it to his Majesty. This course he adopted following Panzani's warning that Cardinal Barberini did not wish the Agent to be looked on as the author of any new formula. [2]

Con made use of the friendship he quickly won with the King to sound him as to his personal view of what should be done in the Oath problem. He found that Charles thought that the Pope should meet him half-way and, that, if he were not able openly to

---

[1] *P.R.O. Rom. Trans.* : Barberini to Panzani, Feb. 28, 1635 : " Cᵃ la matᵃ del giuramᵗᵒ V. S. avverta per l'avvenire di non entrare in modo aᶦcuno in discorso di esso, et molto meno di esser il pᵒ à dar occasione di trattarne." Cf. also BERINGTON, *op. cit.*, pp. 142-146. This uncompromising attitude was also manifested towards the new Oath formula that the King had suggested recently for the Irish Catholics and which Rome still regarded as bearing too hard on the Pope's spiritual power. For this Oath, cf. INGRAM, *op. cit.*, p. 390, note 1 ; also Cox, *History of Ireland*, vol. II, p. 47.

[2] *P.R.O. Rom. Trans.* : Panzani to Barberini, Sept. 13/23, 1636.

approve the Oath, he could at least, by refraining from open disapproval, allow the English Catholics to take it with a quiet conscience. Con promised to put this to the Pope, but pointed out that the Oath contained things which no Catholic could approve without making shipwreck of conscience. Charles suddenly asked if the Sorbonne were Catholic. "Yes," said Con. "Very well, then," the King rejoined, "the Sorbonne holds the Oath to be licit." Con replied that his Majesty must have been misinformed ; some of the French, he had heard, were dubious about the Pope's power to depose princes, but the Oath all held to be unlawful, and as such it been rebutted by the French clergy.

Charles then asked what the Oath contained other than a denial of the power of deposition. "Its offensive character is that it states the opposite opinion to be heretical," answered Con. "But is it not a wicked opinion to subject the royal authority to the whim of a man?" the King retorted. No private person could swear an opinion was heretical, continued Con calmly, until it had been adjudged such by the Church ; as for proving theological or philosophical opinions, that was done by reason not by oaths. This Oath was merely a means used by the ill-disposed for sowing perpetual discord between Rome and England.

Charles insisted that he meant the Oath to bind to nothing more than a loyal obedience, leaving untouched the Pope's spiritual jurisdiction over Roman Catholics.[1] What he wanted was to distinguish the Catholics from Anabaptists and other heretics hostile to monarchy. On hearing this, Con deplored the fact that his Majesty's goodwill had been so ill portrayed in an Oath that appeared to have no other aim that an attack on the Pope's authority. In any matter of purely temporal allegiance he felt sure that the Catholics would be ready to shed their blood in defence of the royal authority.

Charles explained that the real difficulty of the Oath was that it had been confirmed by Parliament. All knew, he said, what a business it would be to summon Parliament and make it change the Oath ; indeed, such a convocation would be a distinct

[1] Hamilton, the Queen's Resident in Rome, had orders to insist with the Pope that the King pretended to no ecclesiastical jurisdiction, but sought only the security of his own person. (*P.R.O. Rom. Trans.* : Panzani to Barberini, Oct. 21/31, 1635.)

danger to the Catholics.   How much easier would it be for the Pope to humour him and tolerate the taking of the Oath by Catholics. The Holy Father could not dissimulate without loss to himself, answered Con.   At this Charles said warmly that, were the Pope to declare *de fide* his power to depose princes, he would find everyone against him.   He would not lack the light of the Holy Ghost in his decisions, retorted Con, though this was hardly the point in question.

Charles then asked why Courtenay's book had not been condemned as scandalous, for he subjected the King not only to the Pope but to his own subjects.   Con agreed that such wicked sentiments should be suppressed, and assured the King of Pope Urban's and Barberini's disapproval.   He further promised his Majesty that no steps would be taken in the matter of the Oath without his being advised of the reason.

A few days after this interview Con and Panzani were asked to dinner by the Earl of Stirling, who was in the King's confidence on the Oath question.   After a long discussion he said that the chief opposition to any change in the formula came from the Archbishop of Canterbury, who, in view of the attitude of Father Preston and the Benedictines in favour of the Oath, was pledged to the King to oblige Catholics to accept it as it stood.   Con protested and begged Stirling to help him disillusion the King, for the Pope neither could nor would ever consent to so impious a procedure.

Stirling then spoke of the need for an Oath omitting all mention of the Pope, and asked Con if he would like to treat of it with the Catholics themselves.   Con said no, refusing even to write to Rome recommending a new formula unless asked to do so by the Catholics. [1]

A month later Stirling came to suggest that denial of the deposing power should be retained, while all offensive reference to the Pope should be deleted.   But Con again emphasized the unlawfulness of Catholics swearing as false what so many of the Church's most eminent members held to be true.   Stirling excused himself, explaining he brought up the question at the King's wish but would not intrigue with it in future. [2]

---

[1] *B.L.* 8639, ff. 75-76, 89 : Con to Barberini, Sept. 6/16, 1636.

[2] *Ibid.*, f. 156 : Con to Barberini, Oct. 13/23, 1636.

Just before this Con had been heartily pressed by the King to speak out his mind on the Oath problem. The Agent, looking a little apprehensive, said that the last time they had discussed the matter he had told his Majesty that the Oath could not be taken without prejudice to the Pope's authority ; he now added that it could not be offered to anyone without frustrating his Majesty's own aims.

Charles looked perturbed and asked why. Excusing his temerity, Con pointed out that those who accepted the Oath would do so either believing the opinions therein condemned to be true or false. If they still held them to be true, they would be swearing against their consciences, and would therefore be the more resentful against the proposers of the Oath. If they genuinely believed them false, they would save themselves from perjury but, as his Majesty must know, the opinion had necessarily conjoined to it a *formidinem oppositi*, as they say in all schools of philosophy, both Catholic and Protestant, and on this score everyone could release himself from the Oath without going to his confessor.

Charles admitted the doctrine but did not see it weakened the Oath, so Con drive his argument to its conclusion. " Supposing, he said, " someone who has taken the Oath to-day goes into the matter more deeply and, after conferring with others, is persuaded in virtue of new and hitherto unthought-of arguments, that the opposite opinion is true, — he is automatically released from the Oath. " " According to that, " said the King, " no Oath would ever bind. " Con replied that the argument would not hold for an Oath that exacted merely a true loyal allegiance to the Sovereign. " In any case, " Charles said, " according to your teaching, any priest can absolve you from your Oath. " At this Con told the King bluntly that he had been misled on many points of Catholic teaching, which held lawful Oaths to be inviolable.

As Charles went on to praise the Oath as a check on the Puritans, Con said sharply that some other means ought to be found to restrain rascals who made sovereigns subject to every popular movement. The King took this in good part, which gave Con courage to tell him that the author of the Oath was a renegade Jesuit, whose aim had been to sow irreconcilable discord between England and Rome, and who to this end had exploited the Gunpowder Plot, a diabolical undertaking, without which the King's father would never have consented to any such Oath.[1]

Charles, admitting the truth of this, said that, if he had the remaking of the Oath, he would willingly remove the Pope's name or any obnoxious phrase; he thought, however, the Pope should declare he had no power to excommunicate — he corrected himself quickly — to *depose* princes.

At this Con asked what compensation the Pope could receive for the loss of such authority recognized by so many Catholic princes. If he were to attempt any such thing, the Holy Father would meet with great opposition as a destroyer of the Pontifical Power. As Charles answered that the Pope would have nothing to fear backed by France and himself, Con hinted that his Holiness would do a great deal for Christendom, were he sure of the King of England.

Charles gave no direct reply but said that if his brother-in-law, Louis, were as absolute a ruler as his father had been, he would make no difficulty in coming out with a declaration that popes could not depose princes. Con begged the King not to listen to the pratings of ambassadors. Henry IV himself had admitted the doctrine, and the present King was too religious ever to advocate the opposite.

Shooting off at a tangent, Charles remarked that in France many opinions were held which tallied with Anglican teaching. Con explained that diversity of opinion was allowed in matters not *de fide* and even in doctrines defined, though not on the particular point defined. Therefore his Majesty might embrace whatever opinion he pleased — within the latitude of the Catholic Church. At this the King said smilingly, " By your good leave, I *am* of the Catholic Church. " Con answered that he wished his Majesty were more so, and a better Catholic than all the Christian princes.

The King moved over to lean on the billiard-table. " George, I tell you in all good part, " he said, " you people hold opinions that cannot be swallowed. You think it a fine thing to write

---

[1] Christopher Perkins, ex-Jesuit, at whose suggestion Archbishop Bancroft had inserted in the Oath, to be passed by both Houses of Parliament, the special clause denying those temporal prerogatives of the Holy See which the Society advocated. For Fr Persons attempt to fix the authorship of the Oath on the Appellant Priests, cf. DODD-TIERNEY, *op. cit.*, vol. V, p. 70, note 1.

books *de non servanda fide hereticis*; you then call us heretics
and are able to break faith with us." To this thrust Con could
only answer that many books were published by Catholics to the
great disgust of the Pope, who could often enough find no adequate
remedy. [1]

The Agent was pleased with this long conversation, as he felt
he had satisfied his conscience and made it clear to the King that
he could hope for nothing from him not in accord with the good
of religion and the wishes of the Pope. [2]

Dread of deposition was an *idée fixe* with Charles for a week
or two later he again broached the subject to Con, who ridiculed
the notion of Pope Urban's wanting to dethrone the King. But
Charles said seriously, " The Pope and I and you will not live
for ever. From this Pope I feel assured of all that is good, but
from the blunders of some of the popes of the past, we may fear
the same for the future. I do not wish my crown to depend on
the courtesy of a capricious or interested man, as many popes
have been." As Con interrupted to deprecate the need of fear,
Charles continued : " You have served Pope Urban from whom I
feel secure of all you tell me ; but if some corrupt Spaniard gets
the tiara, he will declare *ex cathedra* that he can depose a king,
and I may accommodate myself as best I can to the infallibility
of papal decrees." Con replied that even regarding these there
were divers opinions in the Church, one of which his Majesty
could adopt as he wished and still be a Catholic. The King
laughed. " You do not want to accustom yourself to calling
me a Catholic now, " he said. Con murmured he would he could
do so and then die.

The Papal Agent's forthright disillusioning of Charles's unfounded
hopes in the Oath question delighted Cottington, who seemed none
the less relieved that the King had taken all in good part. [3]

Cardinal Barberini, too, was pleased at the way Con had drawn
the King's fire but he had something to say in reply to Charles's
criticism of past popes. Neither Clement VIII nor Paul V nor
Gregory XV had pronounced any deprivation against the King's

[1] *B.L.* 8639, ff. 126-131 : Con to Barberini, Sept. 29/Oct. 9, 1636.
[2] *Ibid.*, f. 174 : Con to Barberini, Oct. 20/30, 1636.
[3] *Ibid.*, ff. 140 seq. : Con to Barberini, Oct. 5/15, 1636.

father. If oaths had in the past been declared null by the Holy
See, it was because they contained condemned matter and as
such stood condemned themselves. The Cardinal was careful
to point out that of all heretic princes separated from the Church,
none thought an Oath of Allegiance needful but the King of England.
The charge that the popes were always jealous of their jurisdiction,
which extended indirectly to temporal affairs, Barberini countered
with the remark that nowadays, by hindering the conferring
of bishoprics and intervening in elections, princes were encroaching
more and more on spirituals. [1]

All this time Sir William Hamilton in Rome had been assuring
Cardinal Barberini that the King of England asked for nothing
but civil obedience from his Catholic subjects, and that therefore
they could take the Oath, or else another could be prepared to
satisfy all consciences. As he said this Hamilton was holding a paper
in his hand, perhaps a copy of the current Oath. This he asked to
be allowed to present it to the Pope, but Barberini put him off,
saying this was choosing a difficult roundabout road to a solution
when the obvious way was to frame a new oath satisfying to
both King and Pope, — the latter would censure nothing unless
his pastoral office was compromised by his silence. In the opinion
of learned and disinterested men, added the Cardinal, the present
Oath could in no way be taken. [2] Con advised that Hamilton
should report this blunt negative to Windebank to forestall false
hopes.

Gregorio Panzani was now on his way back to Rome, taking
with him the draft of a new oath. A copy of this was brought
to Con by Sir Toby Mathew, but he did not attach much practical
importance to it, as he could see no inclination in anyone to change
the terms of the old Oath, save in the King on whose goodwill
he intended working. [3]

Charles showed practical evidence of his good intentions when
one day towards the end of November, 1636, he suddenly pulled
from his pocket an oath formula with marginal notes in his own
hand. This the King showed to Con in all confidence, while

---

[1] *Ibid.*, f. 236 : Barberini to Con, Nov. 28, 1636.
[2] *Ibid.*, f. 182 : Barberini to Con, Nov. 6, 1636.
[3] *Ibid.*, f. 159 : Con to Barberini, Oct. 13/23, 1636.

insisting on his inability to change the current Oath without consent of Parliament.

Con's first criticism in glancing through the King's formula was that it said too openly that the Pope was not to be obeyed on the deposition question. At this Charles said irritably : "You always find something to say. No opinion is sworn to here ; there is only a promise of allegiance in any circumstance whatsoever. Tell me why my Catholic subjects cannot hold opinions held by other Catholics' in France and elsewhere." Con hedged, saying the question of deposition would never arise. Charles agreed as far as Pope Urban was concerned, and the Agent came away with a copy of the King's Oath, which unbeknown to Charles he sent to Cardinal Barberini with the request that it should be kept a secret so as not to compromise him with the King.

In Con's opinion, the words *Deposition* and *Priest* were objectionable in the following extract from the Oath : " I promise and swear that I will defend him and them [*i. e.* Charles and his successors] to the utmost of my power, even with loss of my fortune and life, against all laws, invasions, *depositions*, rebellions, conspiracies, enterprises and undertakings which shall be made against his or their persons, crowns or dignity by whatsoever prince, *priest*, potentate or people, or private person foreign or domestic under pretext of public good, religion or whatsoever colour or cause there be." [1]

Barberini agreed with Con as to the difficulties this clause would be likely to raise. He further objected to the clause : " I likewise promise and swear, as above, that I will not admit any discussion of doctrine that may move me from this my lawful allegiance." This was a delicate matter that would have to be well pondered over, said the Cardinal. The most that could be said for the King's formula was that it was a departure from the old intransigent attitude, and that it was certainly less intolerable than the current Oath as the Pope was not mentioned by name. [2]

The Cardinal Secretary of State quite agreed with what King Charles had said in his long talk with Con the previous September, *viz.* that the excommunication of kings was no safe game for

---

[1] *Ibid.*, ff. 262-265 : Con to Barberini, Dec. 1/11, 1636.
[2] *B.L.* 8640, f. 60 : Barberini to Con, Jan. 22, 1637.

popes inspired by unworthy motives. Nevertheless, the loss of a realm's allegiance or the falling-off of their revenue or reputation was not what popes looked to primarily, but the loss of so many souls — this they must grieve for.

The Cardinal said his Majesty ought not to regard the Pope from the view-point of politics, as politically speaking the affairs of Rome were of no great importance compared to spiritual considerations. The King should therefore look on the Pope as a Father inspired by the law of charity, and with no pretensions in England save as the successor of St Peter.

On the winning of his subject's loyalty Barberini advised Charles to read what Bellarmine had written in reply to King James's book. For the end his Majesty had in view the Cardinal endorsed Con's opinion that the Oath was futile, and in any case the Pope could absolve from it and thus make any Catholic who respected the Holy Father's authority feel safe in conscience.

Touching on the Deposing Power, Barberini said that either the Popes had it from God or not. If not, there was no need to argue about it ; but if they possessed that power, they could not deprive themselves of it at will, otherwise they would cease to be popes. The Holy Father, continued the Cardinal, would never be pressed to make a declaration against this power of deposition,— not by the French King who had the happy prudence of his father Henry IV to guide him, nor by his Majesty of England if he should become a Catholic, for then the Holy Ghost would inspire him to defend the Church as his forebears had done even when other princes abandoned her. It puzzled Cardinal Barberini that Charles was so fearful of the deposing power, for he was not likely to fall into the execrable crimes that deserved deposition, nor was he likely to become a Catholic for other than spiritual motives. [1]

Two or three weeks after he had shown Con his oath formula, Charles again asked the Agent what he thought of it. When Con answered that the two words *Deposition* and *Priest* worried him, the King said he was wrong to take umbrage at the term *Priest*, which was common to both sides; Charles added, with some feeling, that his own priests were just as irritating and impertinent as the Catholics.

---

[1] *Ibid.*, ff. 35 seq. : Barberini to Con, Jan. 8, 1637.

FRANCESCO BARBERINI, CARDINAL SECRETARY OF STATE AND
PROTECTOR OF ENGLAND
(From the Barberini Collection.)

Con told the King it would be better to give restive spirits no chance of resurrecting the odious question of deposition ; the more so as the world could see only too clearly how far the Pope was from doing violence to kings. Back came the old answer, — not all popes had been or would be as Pope Urban. Con agreed, but said his Majesty ought so to arrange matters with the present Pope that no future Pontiff could cause him annoyance. It was possible for him to wield in Rome an influence equal to, if not greater than, that of any other potentate in Europe. Charles smiled at this, saying : " You are not even a Cardinal yet, but you would have to be Pope to make me this offer. " Con's answer was that his Majesty could hope for as much from Urban VIII as from himself or any other of the King's subjects who might wear the tiara. Likewise, from the Cardinals created by Urban he could promise himself as much support as from Cardinal Barberini who in affection for his Majesty surpassed any native of the realm.

Charles allowed all this but slipped into his favourite argument, — what one pope does is undone by another. At this Con walked pleadingly towards the King. " Sire," he said, " let us make a blessed union, and please God the result will be a Concordat with Pope Urban that other popes will be obliged to maintain whether they be French or German. "

Charles looked at him fixedly and then said, " You have a good heart, but tell me why the Pope does not let the Oath stand. If he does, I in return will make a formal declaration that I pretend to nought but civil obedience. " The Agent answered that he had told his Majesty many times the reasons preventing the Pope from doing this. His Majesty should recollect that the Oath had been framed expressly to ferret out the Catholics ; in fact, Con continued vehemently, it was nothing but a tacit accusation that Catholics believed in the assassination of princes, a doctrine detested by the Church as parricide. This was an intolerable slight on the whole Church.

At this Charles tried to maintain that it was the Oath of Supremacy, not of Allegiance, that sought to pick out the Catholics. The latter were not indicted in the Oath of Allegiance, for it did not name them. But Con insisted that the Oath as it stood wronged the name of Catholic ; as he had told Windebank, nothing could be done with it in its present form, despite his desire to do all to give his Majesty satisfaction.

The King then went on to complain of the Jesuits, — a favourite habit of his when he had nothing to add to an argument. First they had approved the Oath, he alleged, and then, out of rivalry with the Benedictines, had set out to oppose it. Con admitted there was too much rivalry among the clergy in England, but told the King, in what amounted to a tacit rebuke, that the Jesuits were like anybody else, there were good and bad among them; but for his part he preferred to remain indifferent to faction and to make enemies not of men but of their vices. Charles protested he wished them no harm, his nature did not incline him to hatred, though many held he had had occasion for it. [1]

All this time the Papal Agent was trying to think out a solution to the King's difficulty that the current Oath, framed and confirmed by Parliament, could not be changed except by Parliament, with the result that any new oath drawn up outside Parliament would carry no sanction against those who refused it, of which the Puritans would be sure to make capital.

It was Con's opinion, however, that if they could only come to terms on a formula lawful for the Catholics, the King, by virtue of the royal prerogative, could dispense with parliamentary decrees, as his sole aim was to assure himself of the loyalty of his Catholic subjects. His Majesty could therefore dispense from taking the current Oath all who accepted the new one; for the Puritans and others he could still abide by the standing laws of Parliament. Unless the difficulty were flanked in this way, Con saw no possibility of introducing negotiations for a new oath.

Reconsidering the King's own formula, Con told Barberini that although not altogether satisfactory, as exacting a *de facto* promise that went too far, at least it attacked no opinions current in the Church.

This was the trouble with a form of oath Windebank had submitted to Con — it asserted points of doctrine backed or denied by such forthright phrases as *I hold, I believe*, which caused the Agent to reject it altogether. Windebank resented this and said rather spitefully that he would not tell the King how the Agent was negotiating, as it would greatly displease him, for at Con's arrival in England, they were nearing a solution of the problem. Con answered coldly that, as nobody before him had had any

[1] *Ibid.*, ff. 13 seq. : Con to Barberini, Jan. 1, 1637.

commission to treat of the Oath, there could never have been any question of a settlement. He added that in this matter he was ready to do all that his conscience and loyalty allowed.

Referring to the King's formula, Windebank promised to try and have the words *Deposition* and *Priest* removed, adding as a parting shot that he had no hope of the King's changing his mind, though doubtless an agreement would mean greater progress than they were making at present. [1]

A week later the Secretary returned in better humour to tell Con that much to his surprise his Majesty had agreed to change the word *Priest* to *Ecclesiastic.* Windebank then asked the Agent why he made so much bones about a word that was common to them both. Con explained that the connotation was different for a Catholic. On the word *Deposition* Windebank said the King stood firm, holding it was a common word sworn to alike by people, clergy and those in authority. Con again stressed the need of removing all chance for idle tongues to raise objections, though he had little hope now of ejecting the offensive word.

In a clumsy effort at baiting Con Windebank then said : " If, as I hope, we reach an agreement on the Oath, you Catholics will multiply like flies." " All the better for his Majesty," retorted the Agent, " as he will be multiplying good subjects. But let us understand each other well : there will be an agreement if you offer the Catholics an Oath they can take in good conscience, in which case the Holy Father will raise no objection. There is no hope otherwise, for if you insert the smallest word touching the Pope or the teaching of the Catholic Church, the same difficulties will crop up as before." All the Secretary could assure Con was that any new proposal would not differ substantially the formula shown him by the King. [2]

A little later Con saw Charles, who told him he had agreed to erase the word *Priest* to please the Pope. " This does not mean I promise to make myself a Papist," he added laughingly. The Agent said he was aware that such a change could not be made in a day without the grace of God.

Though he found the best of dispositions in Charles, Con knew

---

[1] *Ibid.*, ff. 24, 73 : Con to Barberini, Jan. 7, 12/22, 1637.
[2] *Ibid.*, ff. 89-90 : Same to same, Jan. 19/29, 1637.

they could make small advance with the King so dependent on the advice of others. Nevertheless he himself made every effort to discuss the Oath with those he felt might help. A four hours' argument was required to convince his friend Lady Arundel that the Oath could not be taken as it stood. Her husband expressed great surprise that the King had agreed to change the wording of his own formula and, when Con lauded his Majesty's reasonableness, the Earl added they must continue to hope, but as yet hold out little encouragement to the Catholics, who were like the hen who lays an egg and lets all the neighbours know until they come and take it from her. [1]

About this time Con had a visit from the Arundels' son, William Howard, recently knighted by the King. Though a protagonist for the original Oath, before the interview was over Con made him confess that no Catholic ought to swear to an opinion which necessarily carried with it the *formidinem oppositi*, for were he to change his opinion he would still be bound by his Oath. [2] The Agent waxed eloquent in his argument until he finally satisfied himself that Howard would meddle no more in the matter.

Then young Edward Somerset, heir to the Earl of Worcester, a fine Catholic and loyalist, came one day all excited and asked Con if he had discussed the Oath with the King, as his Majesty had veered right round from his former views. Charles, who was very fond of Somerset, had admitted to him in private that the Oath as it stood contained a scandalous proposition, and that he had to sympathize with those who refused it. Somerset said that previously his Majesty had looked upon anyone rejecting the Oath as a bad subject and a traitor. That the Almighty had driven that idea out of the King's head was the greatest boon the Catholics could have hoped for.

The general satisfaction of those around the King at his Majesty's

---

[1] *Ibid.*, ff. 75, 94, 135 : Same to same, 12/22 Jan., 2/12 Feb. 1637 : " Si, disse il Conte, bisogna sperare bene mà dare puoca speranza alli Cattolici, li quali fanno come la gallina, che quando hà fatto un' ovo infetta il vicinato con gridi, finche l'ovo li viene levata."

[2] *Ibid.*, ff. 124, 136 : Con to Barberini, Feb. 2/12, 1637. Con seems here to be having it both ways, as he had previously told the King that conviction of the truth of the opposite would mean *ipso facto* release from the Oath (V. *supra*, p. 261).

consenting to change his oath formula was somewhat damped by the news that Hamilton, when discoursing to that effect to Barberini, had been interrupted by the Cardinal's reminding him of the other objections to the formula still outstanding.

Meeting Con at the Arundels' house, Windebank complained to him of the meagre satisfaction given to Hamilton in Rome, contrasting the condescension of the King in deigning to change his oath. He then went on to speak of a formula submitted by the late Father Leander, in which there had been a promise to resist the Pope and oppose him on the deposition question. Con would neither condemn nor defend the Benedictine — a restraint Barberini commended later — but contented himself with restating the mind of Rome. He added that, if the King resolved to offer an oath acceptable to his subjects, he ought to do so not as a matter of favour but out of sheer justice, and that inspired not by the Law but by his own conscience.

Windebank expostulated that numerous concessions had been made already, — priests and layfolk freed from prison, Pursuivants checked, the Papal Chapel allowed, the Oath changed to suit Con's requirements... Here the Agent pulled him up sharply. While paying full tribute to the Queen's zeal and the King's clemency, he pointed out that his chapel had already been attacked, and the Pursuivants, though they went abroad with more moderation, were still a danger to the general safety. Finally, he said the King's formula was far from satisfactory, for there was still the second clause to which Cardinal Barberini objected, though he personally thought it harmless, considering the whole formula preferable to those submitted to him secretly by the Jesuits and others. [1]

The Cardinal answered Windebank's complaints by saying that the Pope had confided the King's Oath to a junta of theologians under the seal of strict secrecy, not telling them whence the formula came. [2]

While pleased with the efforts Con was making and at his faculty for talking so freely to the King and others, Barberini was still not satisfied with the results obtained. The change from *Priest*

---

[1] *Ibid.*, ff. 178-179 : Con to Barberini, March 2/12 ; f. 117 : Barberini to Con, Feb. 12, 1637.

[2] *B.L.* 8619, f. 170 : Barberini to Con, May, 4, 1637.

to *Ecclesiastic* was trifling ; he thought the King should be content with the phrase *by any prince whatsoever*, as the last word would cover all he meant. If his Majesty would not agree, then the alternative *or* should be placed between *prince* and *ecclesiastic*. Also the word *religion* had better be dropped after the phrase *under pretext of the public good*. The Cardinal finally suggested the omission of the phrases " this being the true duty of a loyal Christian subject... to which by the laws of God and Man, and this my Oath, I confess myself bound."

This was not final, for the Commission to whom the formula had been submitted adjudged it substantially the same as the original, so Barberini still asked time to think over the whole matter (he said a special prayer for England on St Gregory's day), as he was considering sending an old form of Oath of one of the Emperors for Con to submit to the King. [1]

Three weeks later the Cardinal had found several points to add to his letter of March 12. First, he wanted a copy of the King's oath in English (Con had sent an Italian translation, keeping the original given him by Charles) as a word often took on an entirely different significance in translation. Secondly, he objected to the words *I esteem it my duty*, — too decisive and dogmatic a phrase for an Oath, although he could see that *esteem* had in English more the meaning of an *opinion* than of *certain belief* which *stimo* meant in Italian. He therefore suggested *in accord with my duty*. Also the Cardinal preferred *I bind myself* rather than *I confess myself bound*.

Barberini again said he wished to discuss the matter thoroughly and would give no final fiat for the formula, but trusted to Con's prudence to make what progress he could in the meantime. [2]

The Cardinal Secretary's meticulous criticism was embarrassing to Con, who felt, though he dare not say so openly, that the Pope's approval of the formula he had sent to Rome would have

---

[1] *B.L.* 8640, f. 172 : Barberini to Con, March 12 ;   *B.L.* 8645, f. 131 : Ferragalli to Con, March 25, 1637. Barberini was curious to know which were the notes the King had written in it. Con told him they were the words " And truly to testify I esteem it my duty to swear as follows, and as such I swear. " Also the words *deposition* and *priest* (*B.L.* 8640, f. 231 : Con to Barberini, Mar. 30/Apr. 9, 1637).

[2] *Ibid.*, f. 216 : Barberini to Con, April 4, 1637.

brought immeasurable benefit to the Catholics. Con now feared the Court would react unfavourably to all this cool criticism of the King's conciliatory formula. Already the Queen was asking if the Pope knew of all they were doing for the Catholics in England, and if he would know how to exploit such an unhoped-for beginning. [1]

Con's fears were realized after Easter, 1637, when he was summoned to see Windebank who, as Con entered the room, pulled two drafts of an oath from his pocket. One was an exact copy of the King's formula. The other, Con could see at once, had been tampered with on two points so essential that he could not refrain from asking if the offensive words had been inserted expressly to sabotage the negotiations.

As Windebank protested, Con began showing him the absurdity and impossibility of agreeing to such words. After hedging for some time, the Secretary confessed that the King had interpolated them, and urged Con to deal with the matter himself, reminding him of his previous successful bouts with the King, who would listen in patience to no one else.

The changes to which the Agent took such exception were, first, the insertion of *excommunication* between *laws* and *depositions*, (" I promise and swear to defend.. against all the laws, *excommunications, depositions,*" etc.); and secondly, after the promise to reveal all plots, Charles had added the phrase *although known in confession.*

Con now went off, first to the Queen to warn her to be tactful if she was questioned after he had left, and then to Charles. He began by discrediting Windebank's assertion that his Majesty was responsible for such alterations, but Charles said the Secretary had followed his precise instructions. He had made those changes, he said, so as to give the new formula a more advantageous appearance to the Puritans in comparison with the Oath approved by Parliament.

The King enlarged on the difficulties arising from a new oath, while Con stressed its advantages. Charles then told him of the case of a Roman priest he would not name, who, when asked on the King's behalf to take the Oath, refused on the score of the papal prohibition ; the priest then produced a formula of his own quite as much against the Pope and the Bishop of Chalcedon.

[1] *B.L.* 8645, f. 147 : Con to Ferragalli, April 14/24, 1637.

Charles ordered this oath to be shown to Con without its author's name being mentioned, but the Agent had already had it from Windebank that the "Roman priest" was Father Leander, whose simplicity, in Con's opinion, had served only as a stumbling-block to the whole Catholic cause. He did not say this to the King, but merely remarked that his Majesty could take small comfort from an oath backed by one man, when general agreement was vital to his purpose.

Passing on to details, Con pointed out the impossibility of allowing mention of excommunication, — a power of the popes that had never been in question in the Church, and was common to all bishops. Recalling how much the King had conceded on this point in the past, Con said he feared someone with malicious intent had spoiled the royal favour in his regard, so he again protested his utter loyalty and devotion.

Charles, of course, expressed his confidence in Con, and again explained that, though it went against the grain, he had inserted in the oath as a sop to Parliament some defence against the effects of excommunication. But he could say nothing to Con's retort that the effects of excommunication were purely spiritual, and sought refuge in his usual stand-by—the deposition and assassination of kings. Con again told Charles emphatically that the Church condemned the opinion that it was lawful to kill a tyrant, save in a just war. When Charles hastened to say that he was always willing to hear the Catholic position justified, Con said boldly that the men his majesty had around him seemed busier bringing odium on the Catholic Church than in the rational defence of their own dogmas.

Having rid himself of this little spleen that he had had stored up for some time, the Agent passed to the obnoxious clause involving the seal of Confession. After showing the King the importance the Church attached to the inviolability of the *sigillum*, he said it was unseemly to propose the contrary in an oath which, after all, was meant more for layfolk than for priests. To this Charles said simply, "You are right, and Windebank told me he did not know how to answer you; but I do not see why priests should not bind themselves to reveal treason against their sovereign."

After trying various arguments in a vain attempt to convince the King, Con at last burst out laughing. " Sire," he said, " as our reasons do not suffice to move your Majesty, I hope self-interest will do so. Let your Majesty tell me : who would ever come to confess treason to a priest who had sworn he was ready to reveal it ? The Holy Ghost, who guides the Church, has disposed Confession to dissuade men from evil, and a Confessor is bound to pledge himself in every possible way. Believe this, your Majesty, if he who murdered the Duke of Buckingham had gone to confession and been warned that what he was about to do was a great sin, would he not have been deterred, since he said himself he believed he was doing *right* in assassinating the Duke ? In fine, all the resources of secular politics will find no safeguard for the life of princes equal to confession. The prudent confessor will always find means of saving a prince without revealing what is said in confession, which, once the Seal is done away with, itself goes by the board. "

Charles listened patiently, then putting his hands on Con's shoulders, he said, " This argument shows you have a good head and serve the Pope well. " After Con had protested his devotion also to his Majesty, Charles changed the subject and went on to talk about France.

The King had clearly been impressed, for he told Windebank Con had marshalled unanswerable arguments and asked him to see if he could satisfy the Agent. The Secretary, in his turn, called in Cottington to try and persuade Con to make no further difficulty, seeing the King had conceded so much more than had ever been hoped for ; but the Agent answered shortly that others, not he, were to blame for the tediousness of the negotiations.

Con told the Queen of what had passed, but she offered no hope of immediate success ; it would be a lengthy business, causing a great stir in the kingdom. It would be time to look for a settlement when a settlement came. [1]

The Queen was right. Though the Agent's excellent arguments had at the time left Charles with nothing to say, he could not rid himself of that lurking suspicion, ironical in the light of later events, that the Sovereign Pontiff might one day rise up in his wrath and order violent hands to be laid on the heretic King. And, as Con remarked, there was no lack of those whose interest it was to fan the King's suspicion into fear.

[1] *B.L.* 8640, ff. 248-255, 266 ; Con to Barberini, April 14/24, April 21/May 1, 1637.

Thinking to convince Charles once and for all, Con now advised that the Pope should despatch a Brief recalling the various occasions (*e.g.* at the Council of Constance) on which the Church had condemned all violence against princes, even tyrants, showing she detested as parricides the assassins of sovereigns. Such a Brief, Con told Barberini, would be of real service to the Church and gain great praise for the Pope, since it was a common criticism even among Catholics that the Church had never officially disapproved of the Gunpowder Plot. (Cardinal Barberini seems to have ignored Con's request, as he makes no reference to it, and nothing further was heard of the Brief.) The Agent himself had been trying to instruct Charles on these points but, as he said, the King was beset by enemies of the Church telling him Rome had different views now from those she had held in days gone by. [1]

Meanwhile Barberini was awaiting the findings of the theologians who were examining the King's formula. They did not meet until May, 1637, and as they were taking their time, the Cardinal amused himself looking through his *Baronius* for a form of oath used by one of the Emperors. He found one that Louis II had used in 873 to receive the allegiance of his bishops. [2] It was a simple, formula devoid of the rigmarole of safeguards that Charles, perhaps not unnaturally, was demanding. In sending this Oath for consideration, Barberini pleaded for greater trust on the part of the King, who must know Rome sought only his own and his subjects' salvation. Unless his Majesty threw open the door with some show of confidence all their efforts would remain frustrate. [3]

Through all this philandering with formulas neither side was making headway.   Charles was impatient to finish the business and told his wife he was in agreement with Con, though he blamed him for refusing the slightest concession and so being the cause of negotiations dragging on for so long. [4]

---

[1] *Ibid.*, ff. 288-289 ; Con to Barberini, Apr. 28/May 8, 1637.

[2] BARONIUS, *Annales*, vol. XV, p. 269, Anno 873, Ludovico 2⁰ Impʳᵉ : " Quantum sciero, et potuero adiuvante Domino, consilio et auxilio fidelis vobis adiutor ero, ut Regnum quod habetis ad Dei voluntatem, et Sanctae Ecclesiae, et vestrum honorem, atque ad Uestram Saluationem continere possitis et quod Deus vobis adhuc concesserit acquirere, contra omnes homines defendere ualeatis." For an account of this Emperor, v. L. DUCHESNE, *The Beginnings of the Temporal Sovereignty of the Popes*, Chap. XIII : *The Emperor Louis II.*

[3] *B.L.* 8640, ff. 293-294 : Barberini to Con, May 11, 1637.

[4] *Ibid.*, ff. 338-339 ; Con to Barberini, May 19/29, 1637.

The unfortunate Con here, as on the Cardinalate question still to be discussed, fell neatly between two stools. He had worked hard and courageously to win Charles to some concession; he had tried, also, to induce Rome to make some pronouncement that would smooth away the King's fears. But he found all his efforts set at nought by the Roman theologians, who at last lost no time in picking the King's Oath to pieces, so that Barberini wrote gloomily that the formula was now found to be full of difficulties that had not appeared at first sight. He warned the Agent to go very cautiously and " to measure the water well before taking a plunge." Con was to await further instructions before calling the Seculars and Regulars to a conference on the Oath as he had suggested. Above all, neither Father Leander's nor any other formula was to be seriously discussed as this would only provoke the Pope to a Brief condemning the new Oath. [1] The Cardinal had been right in describing the Oath as *materia gelosa,* — with each side jealous of the other's pretensions, it seemed an accord could never be reached.

Seeing that opposition to the King's formula was hardening in Rome, Con now set out details of its origin he had hitherto withheld. He and the King had framed the Oath together, he said, Charles having composed the major portion, while his own part had been confined to blue-pencilling objectionable phrases. All this had been going on for months in complete secrecy, till Con, realizing the matter could not be concluded without the knowledge and assistance of some Minister of State, had suggested telling Windebank as the best-intentioned of them all. The Secretary had made several changes based on his previous dealings with Leander and Panzani, while Con had again retouched the formula several times before despatching it reluctantly, and without pledging himself to it, to the Cardinal Secretary.

Then after Barberini's objection, Con had, at some risk of losing the King's favour, successfully pressed for the removal of the reference to excommunication and confession, assuring his Majesty on the word of the Cardinal Secretary that, whether he became a Catholic or not, he would have nothing to fear from Rome.

After this, Con had forwarded, as Barberini had asked, a copy

---

[1] *Ibid.,* f. 354 : Barberini to Con, June 8, 1637.

of the King's formula in English, [1] in no way attaching himself officially to it, though it had won the approval of Father Edward Knott, *alias* Matthew Wilson, Vice-Provincial of the J esuits, the most learned man in England, said Con, and by no means biassed in the King's favour, and of George Musket representing the Secular clergy. Con had not troubled to consult the Benedictines, as their support, while a foregone conclusion, would be small recommendation of the Oath in Rome.

In the English version the suggested changes had been made. There was only a *de facto* promise and no mention of any doctrine. The word *Deposition* was so placed among the other forms of attack on the King that it had no reference to the Pope rather than to other rulers. *Ecclesiastic* replaced *Priest* and was well separated from *Prince*, as Barberini required. Further, the word *religion* was preceded by *under pretext of* and, as the adjective *Catholic* was omitted, the phrase appeared as directed mainly against the Puritans.

Con's last vain effort to have *Deposition* deleted has its ironical side in view of the King's fate. Charles had justified the inclusion of the word as referring to Parliament as well as to Popes and Princes. When Con assured the King that Parliament would never depose him, Charles answered that since *stantibus sic rebus* neither would the Pope ever attack him, there could be no objection to the word, so the Catholics could lawfully swear to defend him against everybody else and promise allegiance without reserve.

Con was inclined to agree and recommended the Oath, every word of which he had helped to make and which he assured the Cardinal aimed at nothing more than a sincere obedience. The new Oath would carry no penalty for refusing it, while those who took it would be free of the old one. To Barberini's fear of Parliament's attacking the Oath, Con replied that the King would see that next time a Parliament after his own heart would be elected, while in the meantime the Catholics would draw immense benefit from such an Oath.

The Agent admitted that certain specious words had been left in the formula to give it at least the appearance of compensating for

---

[1] Con speaks of enclosing this English version with the necessary changes in his despatch of May 19/29, 1637 (*B.L.* 8640, ff. 334 seq.) It is not there now.

the Parliamentary Oath, but he trusted to Barberini's prudence to answer objections and not to be guided by the metaphysical cases of Suarez, which were to be gone into *pro re nata* and not as an intellectual exercise to fill Christendom with pointless jealousies. [1]

Con's tenacious advocacy of the King's Oath had now spent its force. Barberini's theologians were deducing similarities between the new and the old Oaths, though the differences were in England held to be considerable. As Con said, it was admitted that Suarez, were he writing now, would have less to say on a subject which had to be treated with greater delicacy, — the Jesuits themselves acknowledged that their General had forbidden them to touch the question. [2]

All the Agent's efforts were now rewarded with a mild rap over the knuckles from the Cardinal Secretary who told him not to intrigue himself further in the matter, and when Windebank, the next time he saw Con, began to discourse effusively on the King's Oath, the Agent told him a touch of sarcasm, that it was more than his life was worth to follow his own opinion and push the formula any further. While bowing to his patron's will, Con did not want the English Catholics to blame him for the failure of the negotiations, and could not refrain from a tilt at the Roman theologians for their inability to appreciate the efforts being made to heighten the Pope's reputation in England. They evidently thought, he said, that on the Oath question the English king would veer round from one extreme to the other, — a desirable change but hardly one to be hoped for. [3]

The hold-up in the negotiations was not kept secret for long, and the rumour soon ran round that Con, to ingratiate himself with Rome, had asked the Cardinal Protector (Barberini himself) to

---

[1] *B.L.* 8640, ff. 334 seq. : Con to Barberini, May 19/29, 1637 : " Spero che alla prudenza di V. E. sovveranno risposte à quante obiettioni occorreranno abstrahendo però dalli casi metafisici del Suarez, quali devono esser esaminati pro rè nata, e non per esercitio delli ingegni per empire la Christianità di gelosie superflue." — The views of Suarez on the Oath are to be found in his *Defensio Fidei Catholicae et Apostolicae adversus Anglicanae sectae errores, cum responsione ad Apologiam pro iuramento fidelitatis et Praefationem Serenissimi Iacobi Angliae Regis*, Conimbricae, 1613. Eight of the 12 Chapters of Book VI deal exclusively with the Oath.

[2] *B.L.* 8640, f. 386 : Con to Barberini, June 16/26, 1637.

[3] *B.L.* 8641 f. 16, 25 : Same to same, June 30/July 10, July 7/17, 1637.

appoint a new superior for the English Benedictines and to bind the latter by Oath to oppose the Oath of Allegiance as the Jesuits were doing.[1] Con had this from Lady Arundel and, probing the King on the point, found it to be true.

Some intriguer had been at the King, for he again resurrected his evergreen grievance, — that Rome could easily give him satisfaction on the Oath, as her whole objection to it was dependent on the opposition of the Jesuits. Charles added that he thought Con himself put too much confidence in the latter : they would entice him to their side, he was sure.

The Agent's answer was a spirited one. " Sire, " he said, " I have lived many years in the service of Cardinal Barberini at the Roman Court, where not only the religious orders but the most influential nations of Christendom make their greatest efforts to advance their parties ; but in all my master has ordered me to do, by God's grace, I have shown that impartiality befitting an honourable man. Your Majesty may therefore believe that now, with rigorous orders from the Pope as to impartiality towards the clergy in England, I would not compromise myself with the Jesuits, towards whom I know your Majesty's and the Government's feelings. " Con went on to say that, although he knew Archbishop Laud thought he was too partial to the Jesuits, what Laud thought did not worry him, but that his Majesty should think the same was intolerable. The King knew well enough that he (Con) owed his position and fortune to the Pope and his nephew and the good offices of the Queen, without the slightest reliance on the Jesuits, towards whom he could not act save as the Pope's servant. " I ask your Majesty, am I to declare myself the enemy of the Jesuits to please some monk or friar showing small obedience to the Holy See and, in consequence, a bad servant of your Majesty? I have given your Majesty more trouble on behalf of the Jesuits than others only because they need more help than others. "

Con concluded his defence with the complaint that the King listened to tittle-tattle. Charles ended the interview in his usual manner ; putting his arm round Con's shoulder, he said, " Do not worry. I never have believed anything against you and never will. What I tell you springs from the affection I bear you, — but the Jesuits are as pernicious as the Puritans. "[2]

---

[1] *Ibid.*, f. 51 : Same to same, July 27/Aug. 6, 1637.
[2] *Ibid.*, f. 55 : Same to same, Aug. 4/14, 1637.

Following his orders to the Agent to eschew all official discussion of the Oath, Barberini himself ignored the question for the next six months, apart from a bare mention in November, 1637, that he had not forgotten the matter but that it was beset with difficulties.

For some reason or other the King's composing his own Oath had not been welcomed (it was felt in Rome that it should have come from some well-known English Catholic), so that in the following February (1638), when Barberini took up the question again, it was to ignore all the work Charles and Con had put into their formula and to send an entirely new one.

It was a tactless move likely to antagonize the King, while the formula itself was quite unacceptable from the English point of view as it made not the slightest mention of the Pope and his deposing power.   Also it was colourless, — the only phrase showing it was meant specifically for Catholics was a promise never to ask for absolution or dispensation from the Oath.   It had not, therefore, the slightest change of being passed off on an anti-Catholic Parliament as a substitute for the old one.

Barberini himself may have had some misgivings as to its adequacy, for in sending it he told Con he was doubtful if, in the light of the King's present troubles with the Puritans, it was expedient to take up the negotiations again. Still he could not refrain from expressing the satisfaction it would give if Con could make a final settlement before his return to Rome. [1]

It was more than likely that the Cardinal's excess of caution was due to others besides his Committee of Theologians. Lately a long letter had been written anonymously to London from Rome expounding the pros and cons of the Cardinalate question and violently attacking the Oath. Though Con was not named, he was clearly under criticism. Many among the English Catholics disliked him, and he found enemies even among the members of the Queen's Household. [2]

----

[1] *B.L.* 8642 ff. 81-82 : Barberini to Con, Feb. 6, 1638. For Barberini's Oath formula v. App. VII (b).

[2] *Ibid.*, f. 128 : Con to Barberini, March 9/19, 1638. Con says this letter was written by a *Padre Giovanni*. This was almost certainly Richard Reade *alias* Selbye, professed a Benedictine at Douai, March 21, 1620, as Wilfrid of St. Michael. His pen-name was Joannes Rubeus, and in Rome he was known by

Even Charles, for all his avowed goodwill, was not immune from the baneful influence and turned on Con one day as the Agent was begging him to protect the loyal Catholics against the Scotch rebels. " God forgive you, " he said, " for not having satisfied the Pope that the Oath could be taken by the Catholics, for I would then be obliged to protect them. " Con wearily repeated that he was powerless to urge on the Pope a thing evil in itself and known to be such. As he had so often told his Majesty, there was no lack of Oaths to bind the Catholics to civil obedience without involving their conscience.

At this the King swore by God that Con's obstruction since his arrival in England had increased tenfold the number of Catholics refusing the Oath. " For all that, " he added, with a faint smile, " you will not be a Cardinal yet. " Con hastened to point out that the obstructive arguments he had put to his Majesty had not been communicated by him to others, though he was bound not to hide his opinion of the Oath from any Catholic. It was Laud's malice he blamed for falsifying a thousand things to his Majesty and bringing him into odour, but he again assured the King of his sincerity and loyalty in all that did not prejudice religion. [1]

Con was perhaps magnifying the machinations of Laud, for Charles still spoke well of him privately and in public. Nevertheless he also believed that Sir William Howard, the former champion of the Oath, had tried to turn the King against him.

Primed by all who supported the Oath of Allegiance, Howard came to tell Con he wished for the future to press for an entirely new formula. The Agent, impatient now of the hostility of Catholics and heretics alike, told him bluntly that the service of religion and the King better befitted a Catholic gentleman, such as himself, than association with a pack of quarrelsome monks and priests, who were always trying to swim between two seas and maintain discord among the Catholics. [2] On this point Con's trenchant

the name of Giovanni owing to the difficulty the Italians found in pronouncing Wilfrid. He had kept up a correspondence with Windebank. In Rome he was Procurator of the English Benedictines, 1629-1645, and their President-General, 1645-1649. Cf. GILLOW, op. cit., vol. V, p. 490 ; LEE, Articles of the Anglican Church... explained, p. xiv.

[1] B.L. 8642, f. 139 : Con to Barberini, March 16/26, 1638.

[2] Ibid., f. 171 : Con to Barberini, April 6/16, 1638. The Oath was not the

criticism was mild compared to the personalities indulged in with some exaggeration by Cardinal Barberini, who pointedly blamed the Franciscan, Christopher Davenport, and the Benedictines (all of them dependent, he said, on the pseudo-Archbishop of Canterbury), for the ease with which many Catholics took the Oath of Allegiance. They were heading towards a new schism. [1]

The Papal Agent had not yet heard the last of Howard, who was now to figure in a new and important phase of this tedious affair. Having hitherto expended his energies on the defence of the Oath, he now carried the attack into the camp of the enemy, *i. e.* those who stood out against the Oath in obedience to Rome, and presented to the King a Memorial against priests who refused absolution to those who took the Oath. Laud had a hand in the business and used the occasion to urge Charles to admit to his Privy Council that this was the result of his clemency in tolerating those who refused him due obedience. Luckily Con got to know in time and put the matter in its right perspective, — a quick counter that caused Howard and the Benedictines to deny all knowledge of the document.

Con begged the King not to think ill of those Catholics whom conscience forbade to take the Oath, since his Majesty could see from Howard's Memorial that even those who took it confessed it as a sin. This the King would not have, and said Con was side-tracking the fact that the priests would first ask their penitents if they had taken the Oath and then, if they had, refuse absolution.

As Charles made no attempt to conceal from Con who was the author of the Memorial, Con stressed the unworthiness of the action, adding caustically that, if the man was dissatisfied with the past patience of the Pope, he would soon feel the pinch of the Church's censures to his own and his followers' discomfort.

only question on which the future martyr, Howard, was easy-minded. In June, 1638, much to his shame, he was cited before the Court of High Commission for assisting at a clandestine marriage between George Stuart d'Aubigny, a brother of the Duke of Lennox, and Catherine Howard, a daughter of the Earl of Suffolk. It was performed by a Protestant minister, though both parties were Catholics (v. *supra*, p. 214, note 1). Con's comment is not without its sting : " Questo che pigliano il giuramento non sono m^{to} scrupulosi." (*B.L.* 8643, f. 5 : Con to Barberini, June 22/July 2, 1638.)

[1] *B.L.* 8644, f. 1 : Barberini to Con, Jan. 1, 1639.

In this two and a half hours' audience Con and the King went through all the pros and cons of the Oath again and discussed a new one. It came out that Laud had been telling the King that the present Oath would have been accepted by the Pope but for Con's bad offices. Worse than that, it had been suggested that the Memorial should be sent to Rome and a new Oath negotiated by Hamilton behind Con's back. The Agent could not act as if he knew this, but he wrote off urgently asking Barberini to send him a copy of the Memorial when it arrived, with immediate orders how to proceed — and, above all, not to tell Hamilton he knew of it. But Con found to his chagrin that Barberini already had news of the Memorial and of the relations between Laud and the Benedictines before his despatch reached Rome. The Cardinal, however, praised what he had done and again expressed his anxiety lest the Oath controversy should provoke a schism. [1]

Despite Howard's preliminary success in getting his Memorial presented by Laud to the King and by the King to the Privy Council, his action met with general condemnation. Quick to sense this, he was not above repudiating his creature and was thinking of writing to the Pope to that effect. In Con's eyes he was an intriguer with a passion for meddling in matters with which he was incompetent to deal. [2]

In exposing Howard and his followers the Papal Agent had been at pains to prove that he himself was better acquainted with what the Pope was likely to concede than any of the scoundrels (it was Con's own term) who were ready to compromise and make promises. He could never quite impress this upon Windebank, who was hand-in-glove with one or two clergy who had taken the Oath. His mortification was therefore the greater when he was told that an answer to the Memorial had been received from Rome. [3]

The Papal Agent could hardly blame the English for negotiating over his head while Hamilton was the Queen's accredited agent in Rome. The latter did not hesitate to tell Barberini that, if there

---

[1] *B.L.* 8643, ff. 230, 235 : Con to Barberini, Dec. 7/17, 1638 ; *B. L.* 8644, f. 35 : Barberini to Con, Jan. 22, 1639.

[2] *B.L.* 8643, ff. 247, 255 : Con to Barberini, Dec. 14/24, 21/31, 1638 : " Questo pazzo imbroglione non può vivere senza far negotii de quali egli è incapace."

[3] *B.L.* 8644, ff. 16, 90 : Con to Barberini, Jan. 4/14 ; Feb. 15/25, 1639. This was untrue, as Hamilton had not yet presented the Memorial. V. *infra*, p.285.

had been a bishop in England with whom the Oath could have been adjusted, all would have been well. But as Richard Smith, the Bishop of Chalcedon, had had endless troubles with the Government while in England, Hamilton's remark can hardly have been meant save as a covert attack on Con.

The Scot followed this up with the equally wild statement that the Jesuits wanted a renewal of persecution in England, that the Benedictines were quasi-schismatics, and the Seculars asleep. A new schism, he alleged, was centring round the Oath question, which, but for Con, would have been settled happily. [1]

Two weeks after this outburst Hamilton had to submit Howard's Memorial, which he represented as coming from the Queen. He made a point of the King's displeasure at the priests who refused absolution to those who took the Oath and at others who harassed them : they were rebellious subjects, and his Majesty looked to Rome for a remedy. The King's Oath was only meant for security and the Catholics themselves were complaining of the fastidiousness and restlessness of those who put obstacles in the way of its acceptance.

Barberini answered coolly that the unquiet ones were those who, with memorials such as this, were resurrecting old questions and factions. The Cardinal thought later of telling Hamilton officially that his Holiness could not think of punishing those priests who had refused absolution and that, if he made any pronouncement at all, it would be to commend them as worthy of reward rather than punishment. The King had evidently recognized the malice of the bad Catholics who had drawn up the Memorial, for he had taken no action. Rome was grateful to him for this. [2]

So the document was doomed, and Rome, in the person of Cardinal del Bagno, continued her investigations while awaiting developments from England. These soon materialized when the King, seeing the need, in view of his Scottish expedition, of framing a fresh Oath for the army, conferred at length with Con on the matter. [3]

---

[1] *Ibid.*, f. 44 : Barberini to Con, Jan. 29, 1639.

[2] *Ibid.*, ff. 70, 141 : Barberini to Con, Feb. 12, March 26, 1639.

[3] *Ibid.*, f. 119 : Same to same, March 12 ; f. 169 : Con to Barberini, March 29/ Apr. 8, 1639.

Within a month the Agent was able to write enthusiastically that the King's Oath was ready and surpassed all expectations. No exception could be taken save to the final clause (" from which I hold no power on earth can absolve me *in any part*"). But as Con pointed out to Barberini, that need cause no difficulty once Rome conceded that each individual part of the Oath was lawful beyond doubt. Some attributed the Oath to Laud, which Con denied, though admitting the King had used a recent writing of the Archbishop's.

As a fair augury of the King's desire to push this Army Oath, Con announced the release of four Catholics imprisoned for refusing the the old one ; even Lords Saye and Brooke, who refused it, had been pardoned on the score that it had not been approved by Parliament. [1]

Though Barberini himself, towards the end of 1638, had asked whether the King's expedition would not provide an opportunity for an agreement on the Oath of Allegiance, he could not share Con's enthusiasm for the Army Oath, as his junta of theologians lost no time in condemning the final clause. Reasonably enough they pointed out that it was one thing for something to be *tolerated*, and quite another matter to swear there was no authority to forbid it. The Cardinal regretted that some of the Army had accepted it already, but did not think the majority would. He therefore urged Con to have the clause removed, or else the whole Oath revoked.[2]

Con replied immediately, assuring Barberini that he was not personally pledged to the Oath, but begging him not to make known the difficulties that had arisen in Rome, as Spain, according to a letter he had seen from a Jesuit, approved the Oath and, in consequence, the English Catholics, not examining the matter too closely, would consider themselves happy in being able to follow the new formula. Besides, the old Oath would now become a dead letter. [3]

The Agent accompanied this answer with a covering letter

---

[1] *Ibid.*, ff. 211-215, 242 : Con to Barberini, Apr. 26/May 6, May 13/23, 1639. Cf. *Ibid.*, f. 216 for an Italian translation of the Army Oath. The English version (from f. 217) is printed in App. VII (c).

[2] *B.L.* 8643, f. 213 : Barberini to Con, Dec. 4, 1638. *B.L.* 8644, f. 291 : Same to same, June 25, 1639.

[3] *Ibid.*, ff. 346-347 : Con to Barberini, July 12/22, 1639.

to his friend, Ferragalli, in which he deplored the Cardinal's opposition to the new Oath and to his (Con's) advocacy of it. Far from following Ferragalli's advice and disowning the part he had played in framing the Army Oath, Con claimed full credit for any concessions made so far in a matter hitherto regarded on all sides as unalterable. The Agent insisted, too, on a point on which the cautious Cardinal had repeatedly misunderstood him, *viz.* that in all his negotiations on the Oath in England and in his recommendations to Rome, he had never compromised his position by pledging himself officially without express orders. The only matter on which he had made too confident a promise, and which he now bitterly regretted, was the unfortunate affair of his own promotion to the purple.[1]

[1] *Ibid.*, f. 289: Ferragalli to Con, June 25; *B.L.* 8645, f. 496: Con to Ferragalli, July 12/22, 1639.

CHAPTER XII

NEGOTIATIONS FOR A RED HAT

" It is long since wee have the hopes heir of Sig. Giorgio his aduancement butt I culd wryt nothing, butt nou since our bischop confirmes the same since is cuming frome Rome and our Vicelegat thinkes itt assured I culd nott bott giue you part of my contentment, praying you nottheles to keip all to yourself till wee may wt certaintie publise our Joyis." [1]

It had been a major point of Douglas's mission to Rome in 1633 to petition, in the name of the Queen and with the approval of the King, for the raising of George Con to the Cardinalate on the ground that it would give the English Catholics the leadership and unifying force they so badly needed, and would create in the diplomatic sphere a direct channel of communication between the Courts of England and Rome. [2]

Similarly, part of Panzani's task in England was to test the truth of what Douglas had said, particularly of the alleged desire of Charles to have one of his subjects a member of the Sacred College. Using the Socratic method, Panzani began by casually asking the Queen's Confessor if there was any truth in the rumour that at Court they thought Rome intended making a Cardinal of the Duke of Lennox's brother, a youth of 17 at the Collège de Navarre in Paris, and a heretic, to boot. Father Philip descredited the story and, a match for Panzani in caution, denied that the King and Queen desired any promotion: the question had not been thought of. [3]

---

[1] M.V.HAY, *The Blairs Papers*, p.118: "Laird of Schives to Monsieur Chalmers at the Scots College, Paris, from Vaison the prenult of Februar, 1638."

[2] The point had been mooted as early as 1628, when Padre Alessandro had written to Rome from Munich to stress how great a help towards conversion the creation of an English Cardinal would be. The Pope raised many men to the purple: why not one from England? *B.L.* 7048, f. 48 : Alessandro to *Molto Illmo Sigre* [Barberini?], June 2, 1628.

[3] *P.R.O. Rom. Trans.* : Panzani to Barberini, March 6/16, 1635. **Lennox's**

Henrietta was equally loth to disclose her intentions, but after discreet questioning Panzani came to the conclusion that, when diplomatic relations between the two Courts had been firmly established, the Queen would follow the custom of sovereigns and ask for some such preferment as the Cardinalate to be conferred on a candidate of her choice. Such a request, Barberini told Panzani, would not be welcomed; he must try and shelve the question. [1]

But this task fell to the Cardinal himself. In February, 1636, Walter Montagu, the recent convert, had arrived in Rome to be received with open arms by Pope Urban and his nephew, and lodged in the Chancellery Palace.

Montagu soon spoke of the Queen's desire for Con's promotion,

---

brother the young Abbé Ludovic is probably the boy referred to, though it was George who studied at the Collège de Navarre.

Among the *Clarendon State Papers*, vol. I, pp. 133-137, there is a Memorandum entitled *Reasons for creating an English Cardinal*, drawn up by a Mr Price and enclosed in a letter, both undated, to Mr Secretary Windebank (*ibid.*, pp. 137-138). Mr Price, stressing the political importance of national Cardinals, which he had seen during two years' residence in Rome, talks of the desire of King James to have had a subject of his in the Sacred College and, presuming King Charles is of the same mind, says the advancement of such a man rests ultimately with the resolution of his Majesty, whom both Pope Urban and his nephew were ready to gratify. He then outlines the qualifications necessary from the King's point of view, *viz.* someone truly national, drawing his maintenance from England and from England only ("that, where his obligation is, thither his affection may be wholly carried"), nobly born and possessing at least a capacity for learning, though of more importance was an ability to voice his views in Congregations. Finally, virtue and goodness were of absolute necessity. Price then suggests someone (the document here shows an irritating lacuna) with every qualification and but one fault, his youth, "which he will mend sleeping and waking." Mr Price then says he conceives it his duty to give his own opinion and that of wise and indifferent men whom he has consulted of "the person now most spoken of for this place." It is this : "that they do all conceive that he doth in such a degree want all these requisites for this dignity that his creation would be both a disservice to his Majesty and a dishonour to the Nation." The young nobleman he refers to as "of both the nations" (Scotland and England) seems to indicate the Duke of Lennox's brother Ludovic Stuart who will be noticed more fully in the next Chapter. The person objected to so strongly, though his claims are, commonly spoken of would seem to be George Con.

[1] *P.R.O. Rom. Trans.* : Panzani to Barberini Oct. 14/24 ; Barberini to Panzani, Dec. 5, 1635.

intimating that he had a private commission from the King to put the same request, but Barberini quickly interrupted and begged him not to mention the matter to Urban. Montagu, however, continued to insist and made the alternative suggestion that Con could be sent to England with an episcopal title. This Barberini refused absolutely, but determined to probe deeper into the Cardinalate request. [1]

The Pope's nephew was puzzled by the contention that Charles himself favoured Con, a man he had never seen, spoken to, or tested in any way. The King was evidently going by the report of others, and Barberini was anxious to know on what occasion and apropos of what Con had come under the royal eye. Till he knew this, the Cardinal could form no judgment on the matter and asked Panzani with all due caution to find out for him. [2]

Panzani wrote back that as far as he knew the support for Con came from his fellow-Scots, the Marquis of Hamilton and others, who had been cordially received by him in Rome and whom he had greatly impressed. They had returned loud in his praise, telling the King not only of the favours Con had shown them, but of the loyalty and affection he had professed towards his Majesty. Charles was touched and, always tenacious and constant in his likes and dislikes, had formed an unalterably good opinion of Con, and would naturally think of him if ever he wanted to favour anyone at the Roman Court, where Con was without a rival. [3]

Con had evidence of Charles's regard as soon as he arrived in England, for to his face the King sang his praises to Henrietta, referring to the Cardinalate, and Con had perforce to reply that he had no mandate to treat of such a question. [4]

It was certainly embarrassing for the new Agent to find the King and Queen so enthusiastic about him, thinking his elevation to the purple could be had for the asking. Con tried to appear indifferent, but Henrietta, so Father Philip told Panzani, regarded it as already promised and proposed writing to remind the

---

[1] *Ibid.*: Barberini to Panzani Feb. 5/15 ; March. 17/27, 1636 ; GILLOW, *op. cit.*, vol. V, p. 74, *s.v. Montagu.*

[2] *P.R.O. Rom. Trans.*: Barberini to Panzani, Feb. 17/27, 1636.

[3] *Ibid.* : Panzani to Barberini, March 30/Apr. 9, 1636.

[4] *B.L.* 8639, f. 28 : Con to Barberini, Northampton, Aug. 1/11, 1636.

Pope. Panzani did his best to disillusion her and said he would put the matter to Cardinal Barberini on his return. [1]

Meanwhile Sir William Hamilton had left for Rome to act as Queen's Resident at the Papal Court, where, he arrived in July, 1636. In the personal letters of credence she gave him for Pope Urban and the Cardinal Secretary, Henrietta recalled her former plea for the creation of a native Cardinal, preferably George Con, as a means of improving relations between England and the Holy See. Instancing the affectionate esteem the Agent had so quickly won for himself at Court and the disappearance of the old antipathy towards Catholicism, the Queen maintained her earlier judgment had been correct and that therefore there was all the more reason for granting her request, which she now renewed through Hamilton, begging both Urban and Barberini to listen sympathetically to all he had to say in her name.[2]

Taking his cue from the Queen, Hamilton talked to Barberini of Con's Cardinalate as of something already settled on. He received the same answer as Montagu : the Holy Father would not pledge himself to promote any particular person at any particular time ; his mind was occupied with the Church as a whole, and he would have to take into account the likelihood of other Queens making similar requests. Nevertheless, he had the best of intentions towards the Queen of England, and the welcome shown to Con and his success at the English Court could not but facilitate the affair. These sentiments were repeated to Panzani in the last letter he received from Barberini before leaving England. There was no question of opposition to the King and Queen ; on the contrary, much was expected of them in relieving the Catholics, but in the creation of Cardinals every precaution had to be taken against the pretensions of other queens, and it was neither usual nor fitting for the Pope to tie himself down in any way. [3]

[1] *P.R.O. Rom. Trans.*: Panzani to Barberini, Aug. 8/18 1636. Leaving England on Dec. 15/25, 1636, Panzani took with him from the Queen a peremptory request that was hardly likely to accomplish its purpose :" J'attends l'accomplissement de l'affaire du sieur George Coneus et ay chargé le sieur Grégoire de vous en faire souvenir," (*B.L.* 8615, f. 36 : Henrietta to Barberini, s.d., s.l.)

[2] *B.L.* 8615, f. 40 : Henrietta to Urban, London, March 30, 1636 : f. 42 : Henrietta to Barberini, same date.

[3] *B.L.* 8639, f. 62 : Barberini to Con, Sept. 11, 1636. *P.R.O. Rom. Trans.* : Barberini to Panzani, Oct. 9, 1636,

Con's position at Court now became a delicate one. Against the Queen's support of him, which she considered not only legitimate but laudable, there were his orders from Rome to discountenance the idea that his own advancement to the purple was at the moment a practical proposal to make. Henrietta did not as yet realize this, and it became Con's painful duty, against his own interests and what he evidently thought were the interests of the Catholic cause in England, to enlighten her that her influence with her godfather, the Pope, was not as great as she thought, and that it was futile to continue plaguing Urban and his nephew with petitions for something they had no intention of granting, at least for the time being.

In his failure to impress this upon Charles and the Queen, Con became the innocent cause of the negotiations dragging on interminably and the object of mild recrimination on both sides, — in London he had to face their Majesties' disillusionment, while from Rome came complaints of the Queen's importunity for which he was held to some extent responsible. Unkindest cut of all, — he died with the Red Hat almost within his grasp.

In any conferring of favours Rome clearly wanted a *quid pro quo*, and Con had to talk so plainly to Charles in the cause of the Catholics that he admits that, were not the King so kindly a prince, he would have lost his head rather than won support for his red biretta. [1]

But Con could not stop the Queen from again ordering her Agent to present her petition. With astounding confidence Hamilton went to Barberini and asked that the promotion be made as soon as possible. The Cardinal pointed out that the Pope never made a final declaration till the eve or very morning of a Consistory. He again referred to the claims that other queens would put forward if a Cardinal were created at the request of the wife of a heretic king and without some other justifying cause. To disarm criticism, something striking and definite must be done in England for the Catholics, — the muzzling of the Pursuivants, for example, or concession in the Oath question. This would go down to Con's credit and satisfy the critics.

---

[1] *B.L.* 8639, f. 144 : Con to Barberini, Hampton, Oct. 5/15, 1636 : " Col Rè ho trattato in maniera per servicio della Religⁿᵉ che se egli non forse Principe buono, havrei più presto persa la testa, che guadagnata la buona gratia de S. Mᵗᵃ in ordine ad una beretta rossa."

Hamilton answered that much had already been done for the Catholics and reminded Barberini of the favours the Queen obtained for them with the King's connivance. He then pressed Barberini to put his petition personally to the Pope on St Andrew's Day. The Cardinal did so and brought back the same answer : goodwill but no commitments. In any case, Hamilton was told, preparations for the next Consistory were already too far advanced for Con's case to be discussed now.

It was Antonio Ferragalli, Barberini's secretary, who reported these interviews to Con, his personal friend ; he considered Hamilton's methods of approach all wrong. The Scot took too much for granted ; in pressing for Con's promotion under a threat of his own departure, he had completely misread Barberini's character, for the Cardinal would not be driven and was clearly riled with Hamilton, as he wrote nothing of these conversations to Con.[1]

Montagu, who had written a strong appeal to Barberini in Con's favour, was equally displeased with Hamilton's attitude, and would have urged the Queen to send Sir Kenelm Digby to negotiate the business instead, had not Con and Panzani dissuaded him.[2]

Hamilton had evidently sent home full reports of his talks with Barberini for, when Con came to the Queen to put the Cardinal's argument himself, he found Henrietta ready with a full reply. The Queen was wholly opposed to Rome's policy of awaiting a favourable oportunity for creating an English Cardinal, holding that delay would be detrimental to religion on several counts. She regretted, she said, that his Holiness had not made his decision when Douglas was in Rome. Henrietta was contemptuous of the argument that the Pope would be compromised by the claims of other queens, and refused to admit the parallel. They had Catholic husbands, she declared, to secure preferment for their subjects ; moreover, none was as deserving as she in the cause of the Faith. Compare her with her sister, the Queen of Spain, for example. While she had secured the admission of an Apostolic Minister to England, quite contrary to tradition and the Laws of the realm, her sister

[1] *B.L.* 8639, ff. 252-253 : Barberini to Con, Dec.5, 1636. *B.L.* 8645, ff.60, 93 : Ferragalli to Con, Dec. 5, 1636, Jan. 22 1637. *B.L.* 8619, f. 168 : Ferragalli to Con, Dec. 29, 1636.

[2] *P.R.O. Rom. Trans.* : Panzani to Barberini, Dec. 8/18, 1636.

had been unable to obtain from the Catholic King the continued residence of a Nuncio in Flanders.[1] If, however, these other Queens worked for religion as she did and maintained direct contact with the Holy See, then by all means let them have the reward of their merits.

Henrietta was eloquent, as she could be in a cause that challenged her spirit, but Con, keeping discreetly within the limits of his instructions, made no promises and did his best to pacify her Majesty.[2]

As Panzani was now about to return to Rome, Stirling, the man who had sponsored Douglas's mission, went to Charles with the suggestion that the Italian might take back with him a letter to Cardinal del Bagno, recalling the regard King James had had for him, and asking him again to use his influence in Con's favour. The King consented, saying with a laugh that it was time to give Con's interests a warm recommendation, as for four years they had become rather cold. Stirling made excuses, alleging it was Con himself who always obstructing the affair. This greatly mortified the Agent, who advised against the letter, holding it would be better to leave the matter to Panzani's own sagacity and prudence. But Stirling had his way, at the same time impressing on Panzani that, if he succeeded in pushing Con's case, the whole country would be indebted to him, as all held the Agent in admiration, and despite their differences of belief, all would feel honoured by the creation of a Cardinal.[3]

[1] On the death (in Dec. 1633) of the Infanta Isabella, daughter of Philip II and Regent of the Catholics Low Countries, the Brussels Nuncio, Mgr Fabio de Lagonissa had been replaced by an Internuntio, Richard Paul Stravius, Archdeacon of Cambrai. When later in the year, 1634, a Prince of the Blood! the Cardinal Infante Ferdinand, came to govern the Low Countries, a ful. Nuncio was again appointed, Mgr Lelio Falconieri, Archbishop of Thebes, Regarding Pope Urban as pro-French, the Cardinal Infante did not welcome the appointment and, when Falconieri tactlessly retired to Paris for a while, Ferdinand refused altogether to receive him, and the Nuncio returned home in 1637 without ever entering upon his functions,Stravius continuing in Brussels as Internuncio. (Cf. A. CAUCHIE and R. MAERE, *Recueil des Instructions générales aux Nonces de Flandre* (1596-1635), pp. xxxiv seq.)

[2] *B.L.* 8639, f. 173-174 : Con to Barberini, Hampton, Oct. 20/30, 1636.

[3] *Ibid.*, f. 243 : Con to Barberini, Hampton, Nov. 24/Dec. 4, 1636.*P.R.O. Rom. Trans.* : Panzani to Barberini, Nov. 24/Dec. 4, 1636. Con thought it would make the Anglican clergy talk more freely of reunion if they realized

When Panzani had gone, the King confessed to Con that he also had had doubts as to the opportuneness of the letter, though he had let it go. Yet Rome evidently felt that some positive sign of goodwill must be offered to England, and the Pope made Con a Privy Chamberlain. [1]

The embarrassment Con felt at having to deal diplomatically with a situation in which the favour so eagerly asked for by one side and so consistently shelved by the other was his own preferment naturally restrained the freedom with which he wrote to Barberini. He showed far greater candour in the covering letters he sent to Ferragalli, in whose discretion he had the greatest confidence.

Con told his friend that the Queen was complaining loudly and justly, she thought, of Rome's procrastination and of the ingratitude of Catholics at home. She was doing her best for them, but they did not seem to realize how much of their unprecedented peace they owed her. She felt, therefore, that her efforts should be backed by a mark of special appreciation from the Holy See, and the favour she was asking could only redound to the service of religion and the honour of his Holiness.

Yet, she complained, Montagu and Hamilton had been put off in the same fashion as Douglas three years before, while Panzani's two years in England had seen no advance in the matter, for all the enlightenment he had been able to give the Holy See. The result of such policy could only be that the King's goodwill would wane and the progress of Catholicism in England be indefinitely delayed. Already there was no lack of criticism of the Pope's methods among the ministers at Court. [2]

---

there were honours to be had from Rome. The only ill-effect of his own promotion might be a certain danger to his person at the hands of fanatics (*B.L.* 8645, f. 89 : Con to Ferragalli, Jan. 5/15, 1637.)

[1] *B.L.* 8640, ff. 17-18 : Con to Barberini, Hampton, Dec.22/Jan. 1, 1637/8. *Ibid.*, f. 60 : Barberini to Con, Jan. 22, 1637 : " Sua Sta hà honorato V. S. del titolo di suo Cam^re d'honore." M.V. HAY, however, (*The Blairs Papers*, p.119) says that Con was made a Domestic Prelate.

[2] Barberini was annoyed when he heard of these allegations from Ferragalli. He pointed out that the answers given to Montagu were much less general and limited than those made to Douglas, while now Hamilton was being treated quite openly and sincerely in a way that could only assist matters. The Queen should understand that her request had implications far wider than the good of religion in England. (*B.L.* 8640, f. 234 : Barberini to Con, Apr. 12, 1637.)

In reply, Con thanked her Majesty for helping the Catholics in individual cases, but explained that Rome was awaiting some general concession in law, such as the repression of the Pursuivants or an alteration in the Oath of Allegiance.

The Queen pleaded for patience : a King who had to contend against both the laws of his realm, and his own subjects, was to be pitied ; changes required time, whereas the Pope was temporizing on a point that could be settled any day ; unless the promotion was made immediatly, the whole Catholic cause, — Oath, Pursuivants and the rest — would be ruined.

As Con made as if to reply, the Queen cut him short. " I do not want to listen to you," she said with a smile. " You will only be speaking against your conscience. " " Against my interests," Con interposed a little self-righteously, " but not against my conscience. "

Montagu and Father Philip were all this time assuring the Queen that, with one of his subjects a Cardinal, the King would take heart, while Laud would be held in check. It was a view on which Con preferred not to comment, but Henrietta could see nothing but good in prospect and, persuaded that the promotion was the desire of everyone of influence in the land from Stirling to the King, was quite incapable of appreciating Rome's reasons for delay. [1]

Indeed, Con himself, though always prudently submissive in writing to Barberini, found it hard to see the difficulties Rome found in the way of his promotion. True, the Red Hat was the highest honour the Pope could confer, but every Pope gave a good number. Other Popes had created English Cardinals, and the present Pontiff had already done more than they to earn the praise of posterity by establishing his minister at the English Court and opening a chapel. The English Catholics were jubilant at their unhoped-for tranquillity, while foreign Princes and their ministers were amazed at it. Con was half afraid that after so many changes the time was not yet ripe for greater gains. Perhaps this was Rome's view, too. [2]

Cardinal Barberini was certainly cautious and inclined to be

---

[1] *B.L.* 8645, ff. 96, 102, 110, 147 : Con to Ferragalli, Jan. 12/22, 19/29 ; Feb. 9/19 ; Apr. 14/24, 1637.

[2] *ibid.*, f. 117 : Con to Ferragalli, Feb. 16/26, 1637.

suspicious of the English situation. An impatient expression by Hamilton of desire to leave Rome was interpreted by the Cardinal as arising from fear lest he might suffer the fate of other Catholic diplomats who had been employed by Elizabeth. Con considered this suspicion quite unfounded. Charles had no need of such methods and, if he did stoop to them, it would be better to abandon their diplomatic correspondence altogether.

Pope Urban and his nephew, in Con's view, quite misread the character of Charles. The courtesies shown to Panzani had not been motived by self-interest with a view to obtaining the Red Hat. On the contrary, the matter was not touched on till Panzani made it clear he had come to sound the Queen's mind on the subject. After this admission her Majesty was now quite justifiably asking why Panzani should leave England with a mere recommendation of the English Catholics made to her on Cardinal Barberini's behalf, without any mention of any public declaration against the Pursuivants or the Oath, which was now being put forward by both Con and Hamilton as a necessary condition of Rome's favour. The latter was making no headway and becoming more and more impatient; the fact that he was falling into the same errors as Douglas did not make Con's position any easier. [1]

From the beginning of the negotiation the young Queen's attitude had been that all the difficulties were on her side, while the Pope had only to say the word for an English Cardinal to spring into being.

Barberini now determined to point out what he thought would be realized in England, *viz.* that the obstacles Rome had to overcome were no less difficult than the laws in England against the Catholics. The Pope had to pick his way carefully through an entangled network of diplomacy set up by the German War and the Electorate question, while France and Spain always required tactful handling; the Spanish, as members of the House of Austria, naturally sided with the Emperor, and their minister

---

[1] *B.L.* 8645, f. 117, 126 : Con to Ferragalli, Feb. 16/26, 2/12 March, 1637. Hamilton had made a bad blunder in pushing his way to an audience when Urban went to dine at Monte Cavallo. The Pope soon cut Hamilton short by expressing his wish to return to St Peter's (*Ibid.*, f. 130 : Ferragalli to Con, March 25, 1637).

in Rome was already making trouble over the alleged leanings of the Barberini family towards France. [1]

The latter was now asking for the promotion of Père Joseph, as yet only *éminence grise* to Richelieu, while the Spaniards were running Francesco Peretti,[2] as their candidate for the purple, and had no scruple in accusing the Pope of heading the Franco-Swedish League and in threatening to recall their ambassador from Rome, drive the Nuncio from Madrid and sabotage the Peace Conference at Cologne. If therefore the Red Hat were now awarded to Con at a mere nod from the Queen of England, a French princess, there would be more trouble. Already Barberini's personal regard for England had raised a sneer from the troublesome Spanish Ambassador in Rome, Castelrodrigo, that the Pope's nephew had no friendship but that of a heretic King. [3]

For these reasons was the Pope so insistent that some special mark of favour should be shown to the Catholics by the English Crown, that he might forestall the criticism that the creation of an English Cardinal would be but a faintly disguised favour to France. Unfortunately Henrietta only lent colour to such a view by indiscreetly sponsoring Mazarin's candidature a few months later in an autographed letter to Barberini in which she still pressed Con's claims and thanked the Cardinal for the assurance he had given Hamilton of his good offices on the Agent's behalf. [4]

---

[1] *B.L.* 8640, f. 234 : Barberini to Con, April 12, 1637. Pope Urban, then Maffeo Barberini, had had great success as Paris Nuncio early in the century and Richelieu considered him pro-French, until his election as Pope at all events. Cf. AVENEL, *op. cit.*, vol. II, p. 151, note 1, quoting *Mémoires de Richelieu*, I. XV, p.312: "Jusqu'à son avènement il avoit été de la faction française. C'est un des plus religieux papes qui aient jamais été et des plus grands politiques qui puissent être," — phrases open to a certain ambiguity of meaning that may have been studied.

[2] Francesco Peretti Montalto, scion of the family that had given Sixtus V to the Church was created cardinal at the 8th Promotion held by Urban VIII in Rome, Dec. 10-16, 1641. Cf. CARDELLA, *op. cit.*, vol. VII, s.v. *Montalto*.

[3] *B.L.* 8641, f. 100 : Barberini to Con, Sept. 19, 1637. *B.L.* 8645, f. 199 : Ferragalli to Con, Aug. 29, 1637. *Ibid.*, f. 16 : Same to same, n. d.

[4] *B.L.* 8640, f. 297 : Barberini to Con, May 11, 1637.*B.L.* 8641, f. 185 : Same to same, Nov. 14, 1637. *B.L.* 8615, ff. 44-45 : Henrietta to Barberini. London, Oct. 1637. The following year the Queen wrote to thank the Cardinal Secretary for the sympathetic reception of her recommendation of Mazarin (*Ibid.*, f. 98 : Same to same, s.d. [1638]).

The creation of national Cardinals was, now more than ever, of vital importance to the Powers, for with a Christian Europe in the process of being cleft in twain on the rock of Nationalism, the Papacy was in a strategic position.[1] Some idea of the hopes entertained on the next promotion to the purple and of the consequent mass of intrigue and diplomatic pressure with which the Pope and his harassed nephew had to contend may be gathered from the fact that, although in the first ten years of his Pontificate Urban had held seven Consistories in which Cardinals had been created, there had been none since November 20, 1633 (N.S.), at the time of Douglas's visit to Rome, when eight Red Hats had been conferred.[2]

Then on March 30, 1637 (N. S.) was promulgated the cardinalate of Marcantonio Franciotti, Bishop of Lucca, whose promotion had been reserved in petto since 1633. This caused a good deal of comment in Roman circles, the general opinion being that it would further delay the next Consistory though, as nobody had any positive information to go on, Ferragalli told Con not to presume his own preferment to be indefinitely postponed. He therefore advised that Hamilton, who had lately been worrying Barberini with the case of an Englishman imprisoned in Rome, should drop matters of minor importance for the time being and concentrate on pushing Con's candidature for the next promotion, though it was a mistake to demand, as he had done, antecedent information of Con's success, — an eagerness explainable by the Queen's dissatisfaction with Hamilton's efforts in Rome. Also it was perhaps unwise to insist that provision for the new Cardinal would be made in England, as it might make the Pope suspicious that Con would become too independent of him.[3]

---

[1] Although Protestantism had been in existence for something over a hundred years, it had always been regarded as a revolt against the lawful Leader of the Faith all Europe held. The end of the Thirty Years' War saw the legal status of Protestantism raised from rebel to rival. Henceforth there were two acknowledged religions in Europe with the Pope claiming the right to rule only one. The Peace of Westphalia, 164⁹, is of paramount importance in the religious constitution of Europe.

[2] For a summary of Urban's nominations to the Cardinalate and of the intrigues of the Powers in urging the claims of their candidates, cf. PASTOR, loc. cit., pp. 700-706. For the curriculum vitae of each cardinal, cf. CARDELLA, op. cit., in loco.

[3] B.L. 8645, f. 134 : Ferragalli to Con, April 4, 1637.

With rumour rife at the English Court the wiser heads would not say more than that the Pope had the best of reasons for making the promotion, while Montagu, who professed to be always well primed with Roman news, offered odds at 100 to 1 that Rome would not change its present policy. All seemed to know except himself, Con remarked rather bitterly, when news of Franciotti's elevation dribbled through to him secondhand from Flanders.

But this announcement had given the Queen fresh hope, and impatiently she began to discuss with Con practical issues that would arise with the arrival of the Red Hat. He would stay in England a while to discuss points of religious policy with the King, so as the better to advise the Pope and the Cardinal Secretary on his return to Rome. On the question of maintenance, she had already been told by Barberini through Montagu that she must share this with the Pope, and had promised to give whatever was asked. [1]

Henrietta was not alone in thinking Con's promotion imminent. The Spanish Ambassador talked of it, though his Government's opposition was known. Richelieu had heard that it was likely and had immediately informed the Queen's Almoner, the Bishop of Angoulême. The French Ambassador, anxious for news of when Con would be leaving for Rome, put the question bluntly to the Queen, who dissimulated so well that the Frenchman thought he was the first to tell her of the coming promotion. As he took leave of her Majesty prior to returning to Frence, the Ambassador was at pains to pay special respect to Con and lauded him to the Queen, but Henrietta was astute enough not to be drawn, and changed the conversation.

Con now discovered why the Queen seemed so sure of herself. Hamilton, it appeared, had written to Father Philip giving the impression that the promotion had been decided, and that it would be only a matter of days before the Cardinal Secretary wrote officially informing Con.

The Queen excitedly took the news to Charles, who told her to

---

[1] *Ibid.*, ff. 157-158, 165-166 : Con to Ferragalli, Apr. 21/May ; Apr.28/May 8 ; May 12/22, 1637. At these generous words of the Queen, Montagu had made a modest request for 10,000 crowns to pay his own debts, and 4,000 as allowance ; as he explained naïvely to Father Philip, it was better he should accommodate himself first," as George will never want" !

keep it secret till the Agent's despatch arrived and then to inform him immediately. The days passed, and their Majesties kept impatiently coming to Con for news, but the courier Hamilton had promised did not arrive. [1]

Unhappily, the importunate questioning of the French Ambassador had caused the secret to leak out at Court, and the Queen found herself pestered by the curious. Lord Holland, Lady Carlisle and other ladies all wanted to know if they were to treat Con as a Cardinal already, but Henrietta gave nothing away. The courtiers, not to be denied, now read meaning into every action of the Queen. She knew this and played up to them, treating Con with special deference. [2]

Despite the absence of news from Barberini, Henrietta looked on Con's promotion as certain and even congratulated him. Charles was less optimistic; still, before leaving for the hunt, he told Con to come to him immediately the hoped-for brief arrived. [3] But nothing came, and Con, smarting under the disappointment he shared with the King and Queen, found a vent for his feelings in his letters to Ferragalli.

The Spanish Ambassador in London was saying airily that there would be no creation of Cardinals just yet, as his master had not entirely decided on his own candidates. The boast provoked a smile at first, but as the months passed, and still no news of what seemed once so near, there was exaggerated talk of the power Spain swayed in Rome, despite the trouble she was causing. Was it not her declared policy to hinder Pope Urban from creating more cardinals, that when he should come to die — and his health was not good — Cardinal Barberini and the pro-French party would be a minority in the conclave?

With these remarks Con told Ferragalli to put it plainly to the Cardinal Secretary that delay was only causing hostile critics to laugh up their sleeves. He should carry out what he had a mind to do without heed of princes; doubtful places in the Sacred College could be left vacant, but indefinite postponement on account of one candidate was losing him untold credit, and giving the idea that he was under the influence of Spain.

---

[1] *B.L.* 8645, ff. 167, 177 : Con to Ferragalli, June 16/26 ; June 24/July 4, 1637. *B.L.* 8641, ff. 22, 42 : Con to Barberini, July 7/17, 21/31, 1637.

[2] *B.L.* 8641, f. 30 : Same to same, July 14/24, 1637.

[3] *Ibid.*, ff. 61, 69 : Same to same, Aug. 4/14, 11/21, 1637.

Whether Barberini resented the Agent's outspokenness, or whether he was dissatisfied with Con's failure to get anything but fair words from Charles in the matter of the Oath, the absence of letters from his patron made Con realize he was under a cloud. To Ferragalli he protested his perfect loyalty and desire to serve only his master's interests, yet he felt it his duty to continue reporting fearlessly the criticism Rome's policy was arousing. [1]

Laud had infuriated the Queen by remarking that all that came from Rome was words,—a sneer, she said, he would never have dared to make if the promotion had been settled. Henrietta was contemplating the sending of a special courier to Rome, but Con dissuaded her, though he was convinced, he said with unusual spleen, that the Devil himself could have devised nothing more prejudicial to religion than this policy of postponement.

It was now being freely queried at Court whether there had ever been any truth in the rumour Hamilton had spread. Following the criticism Lady Newport's conversion had raised in the Privy Council, Holland and other Puritan Lords asked the King seriously if Con was to be a Cardinal. " So they give my wife to understand from Rome," Charles answered disdainfully, " but I give their word little credit, though the Pope is a good man." Con had this from a nobleman in his confidence, who added that if his Majesty had been able to say that the Agent was already a Cardinal, he would have had them all afraid.

With the Presbyterians arming in Scotland and their English sympathizers ready to back them, Laud, in a panic, was willing to sacrifice the Papists to their fury (it was the purpose of his Proclamation), but the Queen stayed staunch in opposition, while Con tried to convince the King that by protecting the Catholics he would win the support of Catholic sovereigns. But malicious tongues were telling Charles that the Pope had no confidence in the Catholic powers and would not urge them to support the English King. The Spanish Ambassador was even saying that Urban did not want peace among the Powers, and hinted at dissension in Rome itself, — not a nice thing to hear from a foreign Envoy, Con remarked. He did his best to combat the calumny but, with first-hand evidence of papal procrastination in a matter that seemed so simple, his position was difficult. [2]

---

[1] *B.L.* 8645, ff. 216-217, 224 : Con to Ferragalli,Oct. 6/16, 20/30, 1637.
[2] *Ibid.*, ff. 227, 230 : Con to Ferragalli, Nov. 3/13, 1637.

When at last in November, 1637, Rome's long silence was broken it was only by a letter from Ferragalli to express Barberini's constant goodwill towards their Majesties in the matter of Con's preferment. It was cold comfort but pleasing to the Queen who, hearing that Lord Newport had laid a wager on Con's never becoming a Cardinal, answered with spirit that it was within the power neither of Canterbury nor of all the Puritans in England to make or unmake a Cardinal, and his Lordship would do better to make his bets on matters within his competence. [1]

Con was disappointed that Barberini had not written, and again stressed the Queen's impatience and his own embarrassing position. If he had known he was going to be treated like this, he told Ferragalli, he would have walked barefoot to Constantinople rather than have come to England. [2] He said frankly that in the last few months great opportunities had been lost of presenting a bold front to the Puritans. It was not a game they were playing in England that it could be treated so lightly; there was revolution in the air.

The Queen now saw the mistake she had made in speaking of the promotion before it had taken place; so much talk had stirred up jealousy. She told Con that Laud was doing all he could to harm his cause and make him break with the King, and in this interminable delay he saw his chance. [3]

At Christmas came a courier with the news that the promotion had definitely not taken place and Con, while always professing loyalty and affection to the Pope and his nephew, again allowed his disappointment a vent. Aware that self-interest might deceive him, he still felt sure that had Urban and Barberini any real idea of the state of opinion at the English Court, there would never have been this tedious delay.

Con's position was certainly not to be envied. Added to the

---

[1] *B.L.* 8645, ff. 236-237 : Con to Barberini, Nov. 10/20, 1637. *B.L.* 8641, f. 206 : Con to Barberini, Nov. 17/27, 1637.

[2] *B.L.* 8645 f. 239 : Con to Ferragalli, Nov. 17/27, 1637 : " Si V. S. vedesse con qual impatienza la regina aspetta questa nuova della Promot.ne restarebbe attonita. E possibile che 'l Demonio habbia potuto prevalere. V. S. mi creda che se io havessi creduto questo, sarei andato primo à Costantinopoli scalzo che in Inghilterra come son venutoe, mi affliggo invedere che non è stato appresso il pregiudicio."

[3] *Ibid.*, f. 250 : Same to same, Dec. 8/18, 1637.

anxieties of the negotiations, his health, which had never been good, was slowly failing, for he suffered badly from headaches and the cold; worse still, he had the mortification of hearing his low state of health put down by unkind tongues to personal chagrin at his lack of preferment: the kind souls who had slandered him on his arrival, he says, were doing their best to cast a cloud over his departure. [1] Nor did he find any solid support among the Catholics. Several of the clergy attributed the delay in promotion to Con's negligence and the publicity allowed the activities of the Duchess of Buckingham, Mrs Porter and other lady penitents of the Jesuits. Others freely criticized the Pope's lack of interest in England and her affairs. The Puritans, they said, were gloating over it and gaining credit by the fulfilment of what they had always foretold. [2]

Other tales spread by the Catholics were that Con, not Laud, had dictated the Proclamation against them, and that he had been ordered from the country by the King. Such irresponsible chatter at length forced Con to ask the Jesuits and other confessors to stop their penitents talking so much.

Opposition to Con's advancement now united men of all parties, — Sir Toby Matthew, an extreme partisan of Spain, and an interminable talker; Duperron, Bishop of Angoulême, the Queen's Almoner, who suggested it would be more to her Majesty's honour to have a servant of her own than one of the Pope's.

Holland, who politically at least was a Puritan, was already advising the King to break off negotiating on Con's behalf, not that he did not deserve the Red Biretta, but that its effect could only be to give the Papists a leader and magnify their importance; he was sure, he went on, that Con had always been more the Pope's man than the King's, etc. etc. Charles answered shortly but with some feeling that he did not intrigue in such matters nor pretend with the Pope to make or unmake Cardinals. [3]

Anxious about the situation nevertheless, Charles asked Con early in the New Year to tell him in confidence why the promotion had not been made. As much in the dark as the King, Con could

[1] *Ibid.*, f. 254 : Same to same, Dec. 29/Jan. 8, 1637/8.

[2] *B.L.* 8645, f. 286 : Same to same, March 9/19, 1638. *B.L.* 8642, f. 127 : Con to Barberini, March 9/19, 1638.

[3] *B.L.* 8642, ff. 15-16 : Con to Barberini, Dec. 29/Jan. 8, 1637/8.

only reply vaguely that it was not the psychological moment, and that there was nothing forcing his Holiness to it ; on the contrary, the impertinence of certain ministers had caused him to defer it beyond his original intention. Charles then asked the Papal Agent if he were sure of ever becoming a Cardinal.   Again Con hedged and referred him to the Queen, if he would know the mind of the Pope and his nephew.   To this the King replied that her Majesty had often spoken of her hopes, but lately she seemed doubtful of success.   When Con pointed out that no precise time had been given, Charles asked him to try and push the business through as soon as possible, as postponement was only prejudicing the negotiations and causing him considerable annoyance, which the promotion could remove. [1]

It was the fraternizing between English Puritans and Scotch Presbyterians that was causing the King such anxiety at the moment, and Con used this as a motive for urging Charles to put his confidence in the Catholics, assuring him of help from the Pope and Barberini in case of need.   The King thanked Con and expressed his regard for Urban, only regretting two things, — that the Pope was being forced by secular princes to adopt resolutions alien to his mind and, secondly, that he was dying.   Con protested that no Pontiff had ever opposed so strongly the importunities of princes. He added that although the Pope's health was not good, he might live for years. [2]

In reporting these conversations to Barberini, Con urged more than ever the necessity for a prompt decision on his advancement, as things were rapidly approaching a crisis for the English Catholics : they would either be completely wiped out by the violent jealousy of their enemies or else receive vigorous protection from the King, — there would be no half-measures. Con emphasized the anomaly of his own position : he was meeting with opposition on all sides on the score of his coming promotion, and yet he had not the protection this would afford him.[3]   To confer the Red Biretta a

---

[1] *Ibid.*, f. 34 : Same to same, Jan. 5/15, 1638.

[2] Con said he had discovered that stories of Urban's grave illness and of the scurry of Cardinals to Rome had been brought back along with other gossip by an Englishman, Melmy (?), who sold them to Laud as state secrets. (*B. L.* 8642, f. 47 : Con to Barberini, Jan. 12/12, 1638.)

[3] Though Laud was outwardly polite to the Papal Agent and, on the rare

month or two before he intended could make no difference to his Holiness, Con argued, whereas it would mean a good deal to the pretensions of the English Catholics in view of the clash ahead. If, as he suspected, the Pope was awaiting the end of the German war to make his choice of new cardinals less controversial, the policy was faulty where England's candidate was concerned, for with the continent once more at peace, the English King would find it necessary to increase his prestige by the settlement of his differences at home, and this would only be at the expense of the Catholics. On the other hand, while the continental war still raged, Charles could oppose the Puritans, undertake the reform of Scotland and still favour the Catholics.

But however hard Con pleaded, he felt his arguments did not appeal to Rome, otherwise the loss of so much time was inexplicable.[1]

At Con's departure from Rome, the Pope had seemed well-disposed towards his promotion, but evidently he had now swung round completely, as Barberini disclaimed all responsibility for the delay and even supported the impulsive Hamilton's request at an audience for leave to dispatch a courier post-haste to England announcing the desired promotion. This was of course refused and Hamilton, to the great annoyance of the King and Queen, wrote home for leave to retire for a few months to a distance from Rome, where he felt his presence was no longer of use. [2]

Barberini was once again writing regularly to Con every week, and his silence on the Cardinalate question was therefore the more pronounced. The Queen was indignant and asked petulantly if Rome realized the annoyance that the premature announcement, then the postponement of the promotion had caused the King, who was being forced to make continual statements that he had no wish to change his realm's religion, in order to counter the efforts of opponents of Con who were pressing Charles to break off correspondence with Rome.

occasions they met, doffed his cap to him, Con was convinced that the Archbishop alarmed at the prospect of having a Cardinal in the country, was doing all he could to discredit him. The Agent blamed all his daily worries on to the madness of Laud excited by the malice of the Puritans. *B.L.* 8642, ff. 68, 76 : Con to Barberini, Jan. 19/29 ; Jan. 26/Feb. 5, 1638.

[1] *B.L.* 8645, ff. 264, 267 : Con to Ferragalli, Jan. 19/29, 1638.

[2] *B.L.* 8642, f. 57 : Barberini to Con, Jan. 23, 1638. *Ibid.*, ff. 67, 72 : Con to Barberini, Jan. 19/29, Jan. 26/Feb. 5, 1638.

Con replied wearily that he had made everything known. When he attempted to blame all the troubles of the Catholics on to Laud's pandering to the Puritans, the Queen pointed out that this had only happened *after* the circulation of the Cardinalate rumour. Suspecting the King of being privy to the business, Laud had tried to discover his mind and had even sounded her Majesty, but without success.

Henrietta again suggested the sending of a special courier to Rome, but only if success were certain — she had no wish to be laughed at by her husband. Con again turned down the proposal, so the Queen asked him to put the request to Cardinal Barberini in her name, pointing out the ground they were losing daily. [1]

Near the end of February, 1638, the Cardinal Secretary began at last to acknowledge the constant appeals to him. He protested again that he personally was in favour of Con's promotion. The general promotion could not be any longer postponed, in his opinion, as the Powers were putting forward their candidates with unusual energy and taking it for granted that the Pope would give them satisfaction as soon as possible ; and the Holy Father, desirous of peace and the good of Christendom, would require the greatest delicacy and tact to counter private interests among the princes. Things were coming to a crisis.

Barberini said he felt the greatest sympathy for Con's troubles and the distrust shown by the King. He continued to plead his cause, but difficulties kept cropping up. The Pope had expressed the fear that, once Con was raised to the purple, no one else from England would be allowed to enter the Papal service. Barberini told his uncle the Queen would see to this, and it could be arranged for Con to nominate his successor before he left England. But Urban was no longer really interested in the matter, despite the efforts of Barberini and Hamilton. [2]

Ferragalli confirmed these signs of the Cardinal Secretary's own interest in Con's promotion, which he hoped to get through by June, as even if peace was not made by then, he did not expect the general creation of Cardinals to be delayed beyond the summer. [3]

---

[1] *Ibid.*, f. 67 : Con to Barberini, Jan. 26/Feb. 5, 1638.
[2] *Ibid.*, ff. 108, 116, 148 : Barberini to Con, Feb. 27 ; March 6, 27, 1638.
[3] *B.L.* 8645, f. 299 : Ferragalli to Con, April 24, 1638.

Meanwhile, in England Con had to face a barrage of attacks on the Pope's policy even from the staunchest Catholics, and he found himself making the lamest excuses for the delay, — he told Lady Arundel the Pope was not in the habit of creating cardinals in ones ; [1] he even took the blame on himself, saying he had written to Rome that there was no immediate call for his advancement. [2]

To the Queen he spoke more openly : the next promotion of Cardinals depended on Rome's decision to await the end of the war or not. It would therefore be soon, said Henrietta shortly, as the Pope could not be blind to the impracticability of a treaty of peace at the moment. In more conciliatory tones she added that she regretted this decision as peace was unlikely for months ahead, so that even if the obstacles to it began to be removed immediately, the Consistory must be delayed for some time. As for the other alternative, *viz.* that Rome would proceed with the election of Cardinals on the idea that there was little prospect of the war ending, the Queen said logically enough that she could not see at what point one could say that the idea of peace had been abandoned, for, although the wintry season and the tardiness with which the Plenipotentiaries met might prolong hostilities, yet each side would continue at least to express a desire for peace, so that the Papal Envoys could still not exclude the possibility of making a Treaty at Cologne, and the Legate would be persuaded to stay on. Her Majesty therefore came to the sad conclusion that Con's Red Hat was still afar off, much to her mortification as she had pledged herself to the King to obtain it. [3]

In their undisguised opposition to the Barberini, the Spaniards were exploiting with all their cunning the Pope's waiting policy. Their Ambassador in London tried to put the whole blame of delay on Père Joseph, till Con cut him short with the remark that

---

[1] Urban's first two promotions had, however, been single ones, *viz.* that of his nephew, Francesco, in 1623, and of his brother, Antonio, the Capuchin Cardinal di Sant' Onofrio on Oct. 7, 1624 (Cf. CARDELLA, *op. cit.*, vol. VI, p. 243).

[2] *B.L.* 8642, ff. 85-86 : Con to Barberini, Feb. 2/12, 1638. Lady Arundel offered to get the Queen's Secretary, Sir John Winter, to send a special courier to petition the Pope, but Con begged her not to meddle. The same well-intentioned lady had somewhat tactlessly given Con a length of scarlet cloth for Christmas, but the Papal Agent excused himself from accepting what he did not yet need.

[3] *Ibid.*, f. 127 : Con to Barberini, March 9/19, 1638.

if both Spain and France showed less eagerness in pushing candidates for their own ends, the Pope would be obliged neither to defer the Consistory, nor to promote men whose choice would meet with opposition. [1]

The Ambassador tried again, hinting that the differences between Cardinal Francesco and Cardinal Antonio Barberini [2] were at the bottom of all the Pope's troubles. Con retorted that this was pure guesswork on the part of Castelrodrigo, the troublesome Spanish Ambassador in Rome. The Ambassador then confessed to Con that the difficulties between Spain and the Holy See were the work of Olivares, and said that his government would be content not to press the candidature of Peretti for membership of the Sacred College, if by holding back they could further delay the general promotion and prevent it ever taking place during Urban's lifetime.

The ill-health of the Pope for the past year had made it seem unlikely that he would live long ; in consequence, scope for intrigue and opposition to the Cardinal Nephew had increased. Now news came through the French and Spanish Embassies that the Pope was critically ill, and Con was told by the sarcastic Ambassador that even if he did not get his Red Hat from Urban, he could surely rely on any future pope for it. [3]

It was particularly trying for the Papal Agent to hear such news from such a source (he had had no intimation from Rome) and he began to despair of doing any further good in his present position and to talk of returning to Rome. He felt like one in a trance, he wrote to Ferragalli, not knowing which way to turn.

Hamilton was of like mind and had recently left Rome for Tivoli, much to Charles's annoyance. Moreover Stirling, who had originated the idea of a correspondence between England and the Holy See, was now out of favour over the Scottish troubles, for which, as Secretary, he was held to some extent responsible. He had, besides, received no reply to his letter to Cardinal del Bagno.

---

[1] *Ibid.*, f. 90 : Same to same, Feb. 2/12, 1638. *B.L.* 8645, f. 285 : Con to Ferragalli, March 9/19, 1638.

[2] Whether the uncle or the younger brother is not clear ; the latter is more likely as the elder Antonio Barberini normally went by the title Cardinal di Sant' Onofrio.

[3] *B.L.* 8642, f. 188, 222 : Con to Barberini, April 20/30, May 18/28, 1638.

This irritated Charles the more, as he had given leave for the letter against his will. The King seemed now to be cooling considerably towards Rome. [1]

These were a succession of cruel disappointments for Henrietta, and to cap all, there was the fear that any day might bring the news of the demise of her godfather the Pope, whose passing would ring the death-knell of all her hopes for the Catholic cause in England. [2]

Whether or no Con's threat of resigning was made simply to relieve his feelings, it was taken seriously by his Roman friends. Barberini sent a conciliatory message, explaining that his own difficulties were mounting daily before his eyes and begging Con to do nothing more drastic than retire to some place out of town, if he felt so inclined, as the question of his successor must be considered before he could leave. Ferragalli, showing more anxiety, gave the same advice, appealing to his friend's prudence to remain in England. He insisted that Cardinal del Bagno, Mgr Boccabella, and the Conte di Carpegna were most friendly disposed towards him, and would scarcely credit Con's suggestion of leaving and abandoning all he had so far accomplished for the stabilization of diplomatic relations between England and the Holy See.

Ferragalli, apologizing for his former promise that the Consistory and Con's affair would both be over by June, said he could not have foreseen the upsets caused by the unexpected arrival in Rome of an Ambassador Extraordinary from the Emperor, Prince von Eggenberg. Barberini, in particular, had been occupied with consultations and other worries with which Con would have been the first to sympathize had he known. [3]

---

[1] *Ibid.*, ff. 176, 188, 208, 253 : Con to Barberini, Apr. 13/23, 20/30 ; May 4/14 ; June 15/25, 1638. In discussing the Oath with the Agent in March, Charles had said somewhat mysteriously that, despite all Con's efforts, he would not be a cardinal (cf. Chap. XI, p.282 ; also the anonymous document in App. VIII).

[2] *Ibid.*, f. 157 : Same to same, March 23/Apr. 2, 1638. *B.L.* 8645, ff. 322-323, Con to Ferragalli, May 18/28, 1638.

[3] *B.L.* 8645, f. 336 : Ferragalli to Con, July 10, 1638. Johann Anton von Eggenberg arrived in Rome, June 8, 1638, to announce the election and coronation of Ferdinand III. Owing to a dispute over procedure lasting several months, the Ambassador could not make his " solemn entry" till November 7. Cf. PASTOR, *op. cit.*, vol. XIII, 1. Abteilung, p. 487.

The Cardinal, who had Con's promotion genuinely at heart, as a letter to Montagu in October shows, was disappointed at receiving no support from Eggenberg, who although sympathetic towards Con's candidature was creating fresh difficulties by demanding the Red Biretta for the Prince-Bishop of Vienna as the price of the Emperor's patronage of the Co'ogne Conference. [1]

Hamilton's hastiness was as usual not helping matters. He gave it out that Con was already selling off his goods prior to his return, and told Barberini bluntly that, if Rome intended favouring the King of England, this delay was small help. Barberini retorted tartly that they had never meant to make a Cardinal at the instance of a heretic king ; even the agreement to do so at the request of the Queen was only a tacit one and would only become operative when something definite had been done for the cause of Catholicism in England. [2]

However tortuous the tangle of intrigue forcing the Pope to defer appointments to the Sacred College, there was little doubt that this shelving of the English candidate brought disillusionment to those privy to the proposal, and disillusionment soon deepened into distrust of Rome. Barberini seemed sensible of this and, in December, 1638, wrote anxiously to ask if the King and Queen were growing tired of the Agency. While reassuring him that this was not true, Con admitted there were whisperings in England that Rome was using the Agency for her own ends, to gather State news and, through Con's friendship with the King, to excite the jealousy of other princes. [3]

The high hopes raised by Hamilton in September, 1637, had certainly been given a backing by the unique position the Papal Agent had fashioned for himself at the English Court. Con was popular with all and had the King for his firm friend. The result was a period of unparalleled quiet for the Catholics, — a miracle in face of the ever-growing bitterness of the Puritans. The attacks

[1] *B.L.* 8645, ff. 402-404 : Ferragalli to Con, Jan. 1, 1639. *B.L.*8632, N° 26 : Barberini to Montagu, Oct. 23, 1638. PASTOR, *loc. cit.*, p. 484 : " Der Kaiser liess am 6. September als Entgelt für seine Nachgiebigkeit betreffs Köln den roten Hut für den Wiener Fürstbischof Wolfradt fordern."

[2] *B.L.* 8645, f. 388 : Ferragalli to Con, Nov. 10/20, 1638.

[3] *B.L.* 8643, f. 212 : Barberini to Con, Dec. 4, 1638. *B.L.* 8644, f. 22 : Con to Barberini, Jan. 4/14, 1639.

the Scots were making on Episcopacy, said Con, made Charles regret more than ever that he had not the presence of a Scottish Cardinal to give prestige to his cause. But Con had been two years in England, and they were no nearer the goal. Even Windebank and others in sympathy with the Catholics were now telling the King that Con would never be made a Cardinal, while Henrietta admitted that, if Urban was waiting for peace first, the promotion would not come in their day. [1] She was the more despondent as Hamilton clamoured to come home, and there was talk of Count Carlo Rossetti's replacing Con, but no mention of the latter's preferment. "They have certainly humiliated me," she exclaimed bitterly. [2]

While always professing interest in the English situation, the Cardinal Secretary was immersed in the problems that made the choice of new Cardinals an affair of international importance. The death in December, 1638, of Père Joseph, who himself had had his eye on the purple, had simplified matters a little, but there was always Spain to be dealt with, and with regard to England Barberini would not commit himself to more than saying how satisfied the Pope was with Con's work there. [3]

But this was nearly the end. Con's doctors told him he could never stand another English winter; in any case his *triennium* was nearly completed and, at the prospect of an early return, he emphasized for the hundredth time the advantages of immediate concession to the petition of the Queen who had justifiably looked for support for so long. Con insisted now as always that the request was not at all a personal one to satisfy either the Queen's

---

[1] *B.L.* 8643, f. 222 : Con to Barberini, Nov. 30/ Dec. 10, 1638 : " Mi hà replicato più volte la Regina che non sarà a' nostri giorni, sè si vuole aspettar la pace," — a prophetic remark for, when the Thirty Years' War ended in 1648," not only was there still no Red Hat for England, but the fortunes of those favouring it had suffered complete eclipse. Pope Urban was dead, and the Barberini family largely out of favour. Con, the only candidate ever really considered by Rome, was dead. Henrietta, Father Philip, Montagu, Windebank — all were in exile, while Charles was rapidly approaching his own consummation, which was to bring in its train the ruin of the Catholic cause in England for a period of years.

[2] *Ibid.*, ff. 121, 153, 156, 199 : Same to same, Sept. 28/Oct. 8 ; Oct. 19/29 ; Nov. 16/26, 1638. *B.L.* 8644, f. 22 : Same to same, Jan. 4/14, 1639 :" E quando la Regina sentì nuova del successore senza intendere della Promot^{ne}, disse : *Al certo mi hanno abbassata.*"

[3] *B.L.* 8644, ff. 25, 206 : Barberini to Con, Jan. 15, Apr. 30, 1639.

vanity or his own ambition. All concerned in it had the real interests of religion at heart, which they considered the creation of a cardinal a unique means of furthering ; a quick decision in the matter would put a check on opposing forces that were now so rapidly gathering strength. [1]

Con's importunity brought a mild rebuke from Ferragalli, who told him not to write so often on a matter in which the Cardinal Secretary, with the best will in the world, was heavily handicapped. Con took the rebuff much to heart, and his friend apologized, while Barberini declared that the postponement of the Consistory was more prejudicial to him than to anyone else. [2]

Barberini's assertion that the Pope was hampered by consideration of the Catholic powers always exasperated Con, who had some straight things to say of the princes and their claims. No European power, he declared, liked the good understanding that had sprung up between Urban and Charles and, although the Catholic Kings for very shame made a show of applause, in reality they were doing all in their power to ruin it, while Rome's dilly-dallying was playing straight into their hands. Instead of setting this correspondence with England on a sound foundation, the Pope was trying to reconcile the punctilios of France, Spain, Germany and Venice, — the very countries which, while loudly praising the Anglo-Roman Agency and denouncing the postponement of the next Consistory, were working secretly against the one and for the other, so as to shoulder the evil consequences on to the Pope himself. Rome was losing all along the line, Con added ; it made him feel he was dreaming to see the Pope allow himself to be so abused. [3]

After Hamilton's unfortunate dispatch of two years before, Con had advised Barberini to choose one of two alternatives, — either to hold the General Consistory and include all the candidates sponsored by the Catholic princes ; or to leave the latter unsatisfied, while conferring one Red Hat at the request of the Queen of England. He had understood that the latter course would be followed and had prepared the Queen for it. She could

---

[1] *Ibid.*, f. 48 : Con to Barberini, Jan. 25/Feb. 4, 1639. Charles said he was the more mystified at Rome's inaction as the matter clearly concerned the Pope's interests more than his own or his wife's.

[2] *B.L.* 8645, ff. 414, 419 : Ferragalli to Con, Jan. 22, 29, 1639.

[3] *Ibid.*, f. 420 : Con to Ferraggalli, Jan. 25/Feb. 4, 1639. *B.L.* 8644, f. 53, 168 : Con to Barberini, Jan. 25/Feb. 4 ; March 29/April 8, 1639.

easily have persuaded the Powers not to oppose her demand ; several foreign Ministers in London had actually assured Con of their support ; his particular nomination they would not oppose, they declared, though all showed they wanted to involve the Pope in an indefinite postponement of the general promotion by pushing their own nominees and cramping the Pope's choice of men who would serve him disinterestedly and without danger of corruption. Before all this potential support was lost, still more, before the King set out on his Scottish campaign, the English promotion should be made. [1]

The incessant advocacy of Con's advancement by the Queen, Douglas, Hamilton, Montagu and the rest, coupled with his own pleadings, must have made the Papal Agent feel that he lay open to the charge of intriguing on his own behalf, despite his constant protestation that he sought only the good of religion, which Barberini assured him that he believed. [2]

He now heard that the Jesuits had made representations to Rome in his favour, and he hastened to protect himself from his friends, assuring the Cardinal Secretary that he had neither asked their help nor flattered them in any way. Barberini wrote back reassuringly : he had not heard of any such petition, nor, if one were made, could it harm Con's cause. He needed no advocate. [3]

The ironical ambiguity of the remark stung Con to a further outburst to Ferragalli. It was three years since he had come to England, and he was still as far as ever from the purple ; three years before that Douglas had broached the subject — six years and still at the starting-point ! There was not a pope from Clement VII downwards — and he hoped there were never to be such another in the Church of God—who would not have seized the opportunity of honouring a Queen so deserving of religion as the Queen of England. What would Clement VIII and Bellarmine have said of such a chance lost ? But times and circumstances had changed, Con said sadly. As an English Catholic had told him a year ago " non sumus ex semine eorum per quos salus facienda est in Israel." [4]

---

[1] *B.L.* 8644, ff. 61, 167 : Con to Barberini, Feb. 1/11 ; Mar. 29/Apr. 8, 1639.

[2] *B.L.* 8645, f.463 : Con to Ferragalli, May 3/13,1639 : " Quello che m'afflige è che non sarà possibile di credere quello che Dio sà d'essere verissimo, cio è che la mia inquietudine sia nata non per interesse proprio, mà per zelo del servitio di Dio, e delli padroni."

[3] *B.L.* 8644, f. 177 : Con to Barberini, April 12/22, 1639.

[4] *B.L.* 8645, ff. 463, 488 : Con to Ferragalli, May 3/13 ; June 12/July 1, 1639.

TOMB OF MGR. GEORGE CON, PAPAL AGENT TO QUEEN
HENRIETTA MARIA
From the church of San Lorenzo in Damaso, Rome.

The keenest mortification of all for Con was the thought that in his diplomatic dealings with the King — Oath Formula, Palatinate, Jesuits and the rest — he had committed himself in nothing except the likelihood of his own preferment. Before he had left Rome all had seemed favourable, and his early despatches from Barberini had confirmed the hope. Their Majesties had taken it for granted, and he had found himself responding to their kindness and buoying up their hopes. It became all the more humiliating for him, therefore, to be himself the instrument destroying their illusions as he had continually to report unsatisfactory news from Rome. Now his term of office was completed and, soured in mind and sick in body, he prepared for his journey home. [1]

It was typical of this tedious business that at this stage the Pope's intentions in regard to Con became more explicit. At an audience with his uncle in August, Barberini made a stand for Con's promotion, telling the Pope how annoyed the Queen was that Rossetti, Con's successor, had left Rome without it. But although Urban would not be hurried, he suggested that an allowance be paid to Con to enable him to stay on in England and await his Red Hat. Barberini discussed this with Ferragalli who, however, told his Eminence that another winter in England would be fatal to Con. Barberini spoke regretfully of this and said more than once how sorry he was that Cardinal Franciotti's place reserved *in petto* had not been kept for Con. [2] He then suggested a French spa where the Agent could look after his health and still be within easy reach of England, so that when the news of his preferment arrived he could cross the Channel again to pay his respects to their Majesties as a Prince of the Church.

Ferragalli was enthusiastic for the plan, and wrote delightedly to Con of the nearness of what he had awaited so long.[3] Two or three months in France, and then... But perhaps Con had a premonition of something else that awaited him. In two or three months he was back in Rome, and early in the New Year was dead.

[1] *Ibid.*, f. 496 : Same to same, July 12/22, 1639.
[2] *Ibid.*, f. 509 : Ferragalli to Con, Aug. 6, 1639 : " Giuro à V.S. che gli viddi cader le lagrime, e sospiro più d'una volta il capello dato al Card^{le} Franciotti non perche non habbiamo volentieri esaltato quel Sig^{re}, mà perche quel luogo già riservato in petto havrebbe puotuto servire per costà."
[3] *B.L.* 8644, ff. 392, 402 : Barberini to Con, Aug. 27, Sept. 3, 1639. *B.L.* 8645, ff. 516, 533 : Ferragalli to Con, Aug. 20, Sept. 17, 1639.

CHAPTER XIII

MORE CANDIDATES FOR THE PURPLE

" ... *je vous ay toujours recongnu tres porte a mobliger pour*
doubter en sette occation (i.e. the death of Con) *de vos bons*
offises vers sa sa[inte]té pour me conserver la grace quil mavoit
acordee par la nomination dun cardinal ; les mesmes raisons
pour quoy il me lavoit acordee sont aussy fortes que jamais qui
est le bien de la religion catolique en se peis : et aussy une
aprobation que sa sa[in]tete fait de mes soings pour sest effect
dont cest grace me sera une marque particuliere. Je tacheray
de choisir une personne propre pour sest effect... " [1]

A few days before George Con left London, a sick, disillusioned
man, Mgr Carlo Rossetti arrived from Rome to replace him. Met
by Con and Fr Philip a few miles outside London, the new Agent
was immediately shown the Papal and the Queen's Chapels,
appearing immensely impressed. He was greatly gratified, too,
by the courtesy visits paid him by the Venetian Ambassador and
the Residents of Spain and Florence, all of whom Con had warned
of his coming. Walter Montagu, the recent convert, called on his
own account the very day of Rossetti's arrival.

More overwhelming still was the welcome accorded him by the
King and Queen. Prior to landing in England, Rossetti had been
careful to discard his Monsignor's title with his soutane (he was a
Privy Chamberlain but not yet a priest), and he was introduced by
Con under his hereditary title of Count. Their Majesties were
delighted with the courtliness of the Italian noble as he presented
his letters of credence from the Pope to the Queen. Charles read
the document with great interest, but her Majesty was more curious
to know the young Count's age, which a surreptitious questioning

---

[1] *B.L.* 8615, f. 68 : Queen Henrietta to the Cardinal Secretary, N.D., but
arrived in Rome, May 4, 1640.

of Con revealed to be twenty-eight, three years less than her own [1].

The most devoted of wives, Henrietta was none the less ready to welcome witty, congenial companions around her, and Rossetti soon learnt to turn to good use in the cause of the Catholics the frequent conversations, half-French, half-Italian, that he had with the Queen. He struck up a quick friendship, too, with Windebank, the Secretary finding in the Italian another Panzani, ready to be impressed, and sympathetic to his views on reunion. [2]

The privileged position that the Agent gained with persons of such influence enabled him to be of the utmost assistance to Catholics in distress, in whom he showed the greatest interest, particularly in cases brought to his notice of hardship and persecution in the Counties, notably in Norfolk, Suffolk, Cornwall and York, where the lot of Papists was anything but enviable. But devoted though he was to the harassed Catholics, Rossetti soon found himself embroiled in a delicate exercise of diplomacy which, like so much that was talked of in these years, occupied a great deal of time, offered varying hope of success and in the upshot led nowhere. [3]

The deep disappointment that the Queen had suffered over George Con was soon crowned by the news of his death, and she might have felt inclined to abandon her cherished ambition of a Cardinal's Hat for England, had not the hopefulness of the last letters Con received spurred her to fresh effort. Looking round for a new candidate worthy of her support, her eye soon lighted on Walter Montagu. [4]

---

[1] *B.L.* 8644, f. 394 : Con to Barberini, Aug. 23/Sept. 2, 1639. *P.R.O. Rom. Trans.*, Rossetti Corr., vol. I, ff. 1-2 : Rossetti to Barberini, Aug. 23/Sept. 2, 1639. *Arch. Secr. Vat., Nunz. d'Inghilterra* 4 : *Maneggi di Mons^re Rossetti in Inghilterra*, f. 18 *verso. Ibid., Epist. ad Principes*, vol. LI, N° 133 : Urban to Henrietta, Apr. 16, 1639.

[2] *P.R.O. Rom.Trans., Rossetti Corr.*, vol. I, ff. 10, 20 : Rossetti to Barberini, Sept. 16, 29, 1639.

[3] *Ibid.*, ff. 28, 64, 169 : Same to same, Oct. 7 ; Nov. 18, 1639 ; March 30, 1640.

[4] The Queen put Montagu to the fore in the letters of condolence (other than the one cited above) she wrote to the Pope and Barberini on the death of Con. In these letters she seems to take it for granted that Con was about to be made a Cardinal at the time of his death. (*B.L.* 8615, f. 51 : Henrietta to Urban, N.D., N.P. ; f.53 : Henrietta to Barberini, N.D., N.P.) In the *curriculum vitae* attached to Con's name in the *Nomina Alumnorum* of the Scots College, Rome, are found the words " *Cardinalis designatus* sed mors praevenit."

Mary Ward, foundress of the English Ladies, was in London when news of Con's death arrived, and immediately wrote to the Cardinal Secretary recommending Walter Montagu to replace the late Papal Agent as a candidate for the cardinalate. Whether her letter was inspired by the Queen is not clear, but her standing with Pope Urban and his nephew was known, and it is likely her good offices had been canvassed in the cause. She professed, at all events, to speak in the name of the nobility in preferring Montagu's claims to the honour that had been destined for Con. He was of good birth and excellent parts, she said, and had conducted himself singularly well since becoming a Catholic, being distinguished by a profound respect for the Holy See and the persons of the Pontiff and the Cardinal Secretary. [1]

But naturally it fell to Rossetti to discover who was likely to receive the Queen's support and to present her recommendations officially. This he was asked to do by Henrietta herself and by Montagu. The Agent could see at once that there was no lack of aspirants to Con's frustrated honours, and that all were setting to work in various ways to procure the due presentation of their claims. [2]

Presumably Major Hay is interpreting this phrase when he calls Con a cardinal *in petto* (Cf. *The Blair's Papers, loc. cit.*). I have found no other evidence of this,—there is none in the inscription on his tomb in San Lorenzo in Damaso, —nor can there be from the very nature of a reservation *in petto*. The impossibility of arriving at a satisfactory conclusion in such cases was seen in the acrimonious controversy over Lingard between Cardinal Wiseman and Tierney the historian and Southwark Canon.

In the letters he sent to the Queen recalling Con, and again after the latter's death, Pope Urban spoke in terms of the greatest praise of the Scot, yet made no allusion to any intention of giving him a Cardinal's Hat. Silence on such an occasion is of the greatest significance. Cf. *Arch. Secr. Vat., Epist. ad Principes*, vol. LII, No 87 : Urban to Henrietta, Dec. 3, 1639 ; No 159 : Same to same, May 12, 1640.

Again, the Cardinal Secretary, who of all people knew his uncle's mind, is emphatic that Urban never went beyond a vague intention of promoting Con, provided that his English mission were a success, which it was not. " ... S. Sta non hà mai passato il termine che d'intentione... il Sr Coneo... fu inviato in Inghilterra accio tanto piu meritasse la Religione Cattolica, et si venisse a facilitare la sud^a dimostratione." (*B.L.* 8650, f. 352 : Barberini to Rossetti, Nov. 30, 1641.)

[1] *B.L.* 8620, ff. 54-55 : Mary Ward to Barberini, London, Feb. 14, 1640.

[2] *P.R.O. Rom. Trans., Rossetti Corr.*, vol. I, f. 125 : Rossetti to Barberini, Feb. 10, 1640.

Within a few days Rossetti was able to report on the qualifications of at least four serious candidates, namely, the Abbé Ludovic
Stuart d'Aubigny, Walter Montagu, Mgr Duperron, Bishop of
Angoulême, and Father Robert Philip, — the last three all in the
service of the Queen.

The Duke of Lennox had already in the previous year pleaded
for the Queen's patronage of his young brother, Ludovic, but
her Majesty had then been pledged to support Con. When the Duke,
imagining perhaps that Red Hats were to be had for the asking,
requested that his brother be considered at the next opportunity,
Henrietta pointed out that he must merit the honour over long
years ; she also suggested cuttingly that it would be helpful if the
Duke bore himself better towards the Catholics than he had done
hitherto. [1]

With Con's death, the Abbé Ludovic, cousin to the King, was
claiming more serious attention. He was eighteen years of age,
Rossetti reported, of irreproachable habits, possessed of more
than the rudiments of learning and, although not a born Catholic,
had embraced the Faith some five or six years previously. [2] The
boy had little personal fortune, but his eldest brother, James,
Duke of Lennox, was immensely rich. The whole family had the
favour of the king, and Rossetti was of opinion that Charles would
ask his wife to support Ludovic, but that, if she did so, it would
be purely to please her husband, as she disliked Lennox.

Montagu was well enough known to Barberini, but Rossetti
added some practical considerations. He had no income other
than a pension from the Queen, was not a man of learning,
while his parents and relatives were all Puritans. This last
circumstance caused the Catholics to look at him askance,
besides which the King regarded his candidature with the
greatest displeasure. The Queen's favour, however, Montagu had
won through the Duchesse de Chevreuse and Henry Jermyn, a
Protestant. The latter, the Queen's Vice-Chamberlain and high
in the esteem and confidence of her Majesty, was pushing his
friend for his own ends, urging Henrietta to nominate Montagu
exclusively. They were working with great secrecy so as to present

[1] *B.L.* 8644, f. 125 : Con to Barberini, March 18/18, 1639.
[2] This is too conservative an estimate — V. *supra*, p. 214, note 1, where a
notice of Ludovic and his family is given.

their case as well as possible to the Cardinal Secretary, and Montagu was getting Sir Kenelm Digby to go to Rome on his behalf.

Next came the Bishop of Angoulême, the Queen's Almoner and a nephew of the great Cardinal Duperron, — a good and virtuous man, aged thirty-two, and well-liked at Court. Little hope was placed in him, however, as he was French.

Lastly there was Father Robert Philip, the Queen's Oratorian Confessor. He was a Scotsman, aged fifty-five, of excellent conduct and great virtue, but with no ambition for the part. [1]

While Rossetti was gathering details of those likely to receive support in England, Cardinal Barberini had written to specify the qualifications that Rome would require in any candidate seriously suggested for the purple. These the Agent put tactfully to the Queen by way of an allusion to Con, whom he spoke of as a theologian of great merit, of exemplary conduct, and, moreover, a subject of the King. Although possessed of no fortune, he would have had enough from his services to Barberini to suffice for so moderate a man. Such were the qualities demanded in any candidate. Seeing that Rossetti was talking to orders, the Queen agreed. The Agent then suggested that before her Majesty made up her mind to adopt any particular candidate, it would be wise to submit several names to his Eminence. The Queen said she would do this and send a letter to the Pope by Peter Fytton, who was going to Rome to prepare for the arrival of Sir Kenelm Digby. [2]

Though they never came down to particulars, Rossetti was of the opinion that Henrietta would nominate Ludovic Stuart and Walter Montagu jointly, — the former to please her husband, the latter as the candidate she preferred to all others. [3]

---

[1] *P.R.O. Rom. Trans.*, *Rossetti Corr.*, vol. I, ff. 130-131 : Rossetti to Barberini, Feb. 17, 1640.

[2] Peter Fytton, *alias* Biddulph, later Dean of the English Chapter (1643-1650) had been a successful Agent in Rome for the English Clergy from 1631-1637, a post he again held from 1650-1655. He appears to have been in Roma also from 1640-1643 preparing for Kenelm Digby who was now (1640) awaiting orders to replace Hamilton, as Queen's Resident in Rome. Rossetti had heard that Digby had aspirations to the purple himself though his ambition was a secret little known as he did not wish to incur Montagu's jealousy. (*P.R.O. Rom. Trans. Rossetti Corr.*, vol. I, f. 143 : Rossetti to Barberini, March 2, 1640.) Cf. GILLOW, *op. cit.*, vol. II, s.v. *Peter Fytton*.

[3] *P.R.O. Rom. Trans.*, *Rossetti Corr.*, vol. I, f. 134 : Rossetti to Barberini, Feb. 24, 1640.

The information Rossetti had gleaned was confirmed by Secretary Windebank, who told him the King was greatly displeased at the suggestion of Montagu's name.   His promotion would be fraught with pernicious consequences for the Catholic religion in his realms — Windebank laid special stress on this point, probably at the King's behest as he had just left his Majesty.   He then went on to put the case of Ludovic Stuart, a young man of most princely and remarkable family, and of some expectations.   The Secretary asked that this be pointed out to Cardinal Barberini.   Rossetti was non-committal.   It was not his task, he said, to sponsor such recommendations to Rome, but to serve the English Catholics, fulfil the Cardinal Secretary's orders and receive those of the Queen, but of no one else. He was only too anxious to serve his Majesty in all that did not prejudice religion, but could do nothing without the Queen's orders.

The situation was interesting.   Charles was showing the greatest anxiety to exclude Montagu and have his cousin elected, Henrietta wanted just the contrary ; while both seemed keener on the rejection of those they disliked than on the acceptance of their own choice. [1]

The Queen tried many times to move Charles to favour Montagu's candidature, but the King was inexorable, and it may well have been at his instance that the Paris Nuncio wrote to Rome on Ludovic Stuart's behalf, despite the latter's close friendship with Richelieu.   When news of this letter reached London, the Queen questioned Rossetti, but he was able to declare complete ignorance of it.   Henrietta thereupon sent Fytton straight off to Paris to treat with Mazarin on Montagu's behalf and to angle for letters from Louis, her brother, to Cardinal Antonio Barberini, the Pope's younger nephew.

Fytton's ultimate objective was Rome, whither he was bearing letters for Urban and his two nephews, — all with recommendations for the purple.   He had orders from the Queen to treat with the Cardinal Secretary, first of all in general terms, and then to narrow down the discussion to the person of Montagu.   The latter, who doubtless was the real author of these instructions, had himself written to Cardinals del Bagno, Spada and Bichi, all of whom in their Nuncio days had been in touch with English affairs and were

---

[1] *Ibid.*, f. 139 : Rossetti to Barberini, March 2, 1640.

therefore likely to be called upon for advice on anything that
concerned England.   These letters, which Fytton was also carrying,
ostensibly only complimentary, were nothing less than a plea by
Montagu in his own behalf ; Fytton was told to deal principally
with del Bagno and to make him understand clearly that although
the Queen was presenting Ludovic Stuart's name to please the
King, she was in reality highly desirous of excluding him. [1]

All this showed excellent generalship on the part of Montagu
in preparing his plan of campaign, but it was rather spoilt by the
fact that Rossetti, piecing it together from information let drop
by Montagu, Windebank and the Queen, immediately retailed it to
Rome, where Barberini had it all before ever Fytton arrived.

Meanwhile, Sir William Hamilton, who was still Queen's Resident
in Rome, had busied himself in obtaining reassurances of the Holy
Father's continued goodwill towards the Queen in the cardinalate
business.   Barberini even promised to leave a place open among
the nominees for the approaching promotion, until her Majesty
had had time to make her mind known.

This was the last piece of diplomatic work Hamilton performed.
His impulsiveness and impatience had never dovetailed in with
Roman methods of negotiation, and he had been a constant source
of irritation to both Charles and Barberini, though the latter
could not help liking him.   Hamilton had so often asked for leave
to return that now his recall involved no embarrassment.   Actually
Montagu had engineered it, as the Scot happened to be a relative
of Ludovic Stuart, Montagu's rival, and would therefore be interested
in his pretensions to the purple. [2]

Rossetti's personal preferences were for young Stuart, whose
virtue, birth and expectations gave the greatest hope for the
cause of Catholicism in England.   The Agent approached the
Queen Mother to ask her to impress upon her daughter that such
qualities were of prime necessity in a future Cardinal ; but he found
Marie de' Medici not at all inclined to favour Ludovic Stuart,
because of his friendship with Richelieu who had wrought her
downfall.   She was quite willing, however, to tell Henrietta that
Montagu had not the necessary qualifications.

Rossetti then went on a similar errand to Father Philip, telling

[1] *Ibid.*, ff. 150, 157 : Rossetti to Barberini, March 16, 23, 1640.
[2] *Ibid.*, ff. 182, 195 : Rossetti to Barberini, Apr. 28, May 11, 1640.

him that news of the Queen's favouring Montagu had leaked out in Italy and had raised opposition among the zealots, who were commenting unfavourably on his lack of learning and his all too recent conversion from heresy.

Evidently acting on orders, the Papal Agent was carefully " planting" the objections to Montagu, so that the Queen would hear them voiced on all sides. This was the more necessary, as Fytton had now written to say the Pope had again expressed his wish to create an English Cardinal and had spoken very favourably of Montagu. The message was not slow in being flaunted, till it was discovered that Fytton had written at the same time to an English lady, telling her that Urban wanted to promote Ludovic Stuart. This was immediately taken by Montagu to the Queen, who was greatly annoyed. [2]

Cardinal Barberini himself thought Ludovic had nothing but his nobility to recommend him, and was at first inclined to favour Montagu, whom he had known personally and admired. He had to admit, however, that practically all the Sacred College were against the man, and he asked Rossetti to get the King to show him more favour. [2]

But Rossetti was pursuing his mild campaign against Montagu's claims and asked Father Philip to do the same. Scenting something in the wind, Montagu walked straight in to sound the Queen as Rossetti left, but Henrietta divulged nothing, and Montagu had to rest content with an appeal to her to direct the Papal Agent to write to Barberini on his behalf. The Queen immediately sent for Rossetti and, after telling him what had occurred, explained that she did not wish Montagu to know the true source of the opposition to him, but wanted to make him think the difficulties arose chiefly from the King.

In view of the religious unrest in the country and the accusations levelled at the King of being a Papist at heart, opinion was hardening at Court that it was not the psychological moment for the creation of an English Cardinal. The next best thing would be the advancement of the Bishop of Angoulême. Rossetti could see that, with Montagu ruled out, the Queen inclined to this solution, and he

[1] *Ibid.*, ff.200 seq., 216, 220 : Rossetti to Barberini, May 18, June, 1, 8, 1640.
[2] *Ibid.*, f. 226 : Barberini to Rossetti, June 9, 1640.

hastened to insist that Rome would consider only one of the King's subjects. [1]

The Agent seemed to have persuaded the Queen of the futility of supporting Montagu (though she would not as yet declare herself openly against him), when Fytton wrote from Rome to Montagu himself, recounting an audience in which he said Barberini had put the difficulty of Montagu's recent conversion, which time would, however, gradually overcome.

The Cardinal's own account of the interview is enlightening. He said he had turned down Fytton's petition for his friend as gently as possible, but that it had been taken very badly. He had, therefore, again stressed his personal appreciation of Montagu, while making it clear that he not only lacked all the qualities necessary for the Cardinalate, but that there was also strong opposition to him by many versed in foreign affairs.

Though Hamilton had previously written assuring the Queen that the candidate she supported would ultimately be elected, Henrietta now began to have some misgivings and tried without success to sound Rossetti on the point. She was now quite convinced of the uselessness of sponsoring Montagu and, although Fytton might still have plenty to say his behalf, there was no vestige of authority behind him but that of Montagu himself.

The Queen had also seriously considered Father Philip. He was a splendid man, worthily fulfilling his office and setting a fine example, but as he had absolutely no fortune, he would have to be provided with everything, — far too expensive a project. So her Majesty persisted in favouring her Almoner, Angoulême, though Rossetti insisted, besides other objections, that only the creation of a native Cardinal would have the hoped-for effect in the realm. For this reason the Agent continued to stress Ludovic Stuart's good qualities, though he realized the power of the Queen's opposition to his brother, Lennox. [2]

As soon as Rossetti received the correct version of Barberini's interview with Fytton, he left for Oatlands to talk the matter over with the Queen, but found Montagu still pleading for her patronage with greater energy than ever. At last he over-reached himself,

---

[1] *Ibid.*, f. 239 : Rossetti to Barberini, June 22, 1640.
[2] *Ibid.*, f. 246 : Rossetti to Barberini, June 24, 1640. Deciphered Aug. 1, with an *Apostilla del Cardinale* added.

blurting out that her Majesty ought to show more determination in the matter and insist on him alone. He also accused Rossetti of voicing his own whim and fancy rather than the mind of the Cardinal Secretary, which he (Montagu) knew only too well from Fytton. This rash statement, as impertinent as it was imprudent, caused the Queen for the first time to come out openly against Montagu. He continued to argue but met only with rebuffs.

Rossetti, who heard all from Father Philip, showed considerable restraint in telling the Queen what he had previously told her Confessor, *viz.* that although the Cardinal Secretary liked Montagu personally, there was a strong body of opposition in certain quarters, which would regard the promotion of a recent convert, whose father was still a prominent anti-Catholic Calvinist, as unprecedented, maladroit and likely to scandalize. In addition, the Sacred College would be disgusted at the promotion of a person having neither learning to recommend him nor nobility, for his father, the Earl of Manchester, had begun as a lawyer.

As Rossetti suggested that Fytton, in mistaken zeal, might still continue presenting Montagu's case, the Queen consented to his writing to the Cardinal Secretary, disavowing in her name anything Fytton might say other than in the interests of Sir Kenelm Digby, for whose coming he was to prepare.[1]

This precaution of Rossetti's showed foresight, for a few days later he heard that Montagu and Digby had sent instructions to Fytton to make fresh efforts with Barberini, using these arguments : first, that the Queen still strongly recommended Montagu, and thought the Pope and Cardinal Secretary, in considering any names she put forward, would need information which none could supply better than she. Her Majesty, therefore, thought it superfluous to nominate two or three condidates (besides the difficulty of finding that number of fitting subjects in England), when the ultimate choice would be made on her advice, and none knew better than she the outstanding merit of Montagu. Secondly, the King had nothing against the man. Thirdly, the newness of Montagu's conversion was not to the point. One could cite as precedents the rapid change-over of St Paul from persecutor to Apostle, or of St Ambrose from pagan to Archbishop in a week.

---

[1] *Ibid.*, f. 262 : Rossetti to Barberini, July 6, 1640.

There were many such examples in the Early Church, and more recently the striking conversion and subsequent preferment of the French Cardinal, Duperron. [1]

Fourthly, most curious of all arguments and one in which Montagu seems to be making a bold bid to " jump" the objection that he had no theology, Fytton was to point out (and to a Cardinal Secretary!) that, theologically speaking, an heroic act of virtue alone sufficed to awake in the soul immediately the habit of those virtues which by ordinary acts would take years to form. The minor of the syllogism was that Montagu from the time he had declared himself a Catholic had shown the utmost steadfastness. *Ergo...* The conclusion was left to the Cardinal.

Lesser arguments were added, but none was likely to sway Barberini with Rossetti to tell him the true mind of the King and Queen. Montagu was still trying to persuade Henrietta to write to Rome in his favour and to break off negotiations if her choice was not accepted. Some said that he wanted to go to Rome himself to plead his own cause and was delaying Digby's departure for that reason. But none of the cards were falling right for Montagu now; even when the Queen tried to get him the consolation prize of a Vice-Chamberlaincy, the King refused to have him.

While Montagu was making more feverish efforts with less and less effect, Rossetti, in quiet opposition, was fostering the claims of Ludovic Stuart who, he told Windebank, was looked on favourably in Rome. Taking the hint, the Secretary reported to the King that Montagu's star was falling rapidly and said his Majesty should try to persuade his wife to transfer her support to Ludovic whom the Papal Agent was praising so much.

This Charles did, but Montagu soon worried it out, and accused Rossetti to the Queen of working secretly against him for Lennox's

---

[1] Jacques Davy Duperron (1556-1618), after precocious classical and Hebrew studies, was urged by the poet Philippe Desportes to abandon Calvinism. After a profound study of the Fathers, he did so at the age of twenty. Presented by the poet to Henry III, he was appointed *Lecteur du roi* and, in 1591, Bishop of Évreux, where he showed great zeal for conversions. He influenced the conversion of Henry IV in 1593. Made a Cardinal by Clement VIII in 1605. A skilled controversialist, Duperron was distinguished by a deep erudition and a compelling eloquence.

brother. When Henrietta taxed the Agent with this, he told her plainly that anything he had said to Windebank was no more than the truth and in no way a slight upon her Majesty, whom he begged to suspend judgment till she received more certain information from Rome.

Anxious for the whole business to be settled, and thoroughly tired of Montagu's importunities, the Queen tried to shake him off by sending him to interview Rossetti. The Agent coolly put Rome's objections to Montagu once more, always assuring him of Cardinal Barberini's personal regard. [1]

But Montagu was not finished yet, and with his usual ardour threw himself into what was resolving itself into a duel with Rossetti for the Queen's favour. He tried to impress upon her Majesty that her honour was at stake in her demand that he should be a Cardinal, but Rossetti, hearing this, made it quite clear that the Queen was in no way pledged to continue her support, which had only been an act of grace on her part and had never been looked on in Rome as anything else.

This passage of arms had taken place at Oatlands, where Montagu now took advantage of Rossetti's absence in town on business to attempt to win the King's consent to his candidature, telling the Queen that this was all Rome was waiting for and that it would be to her honour to obtain it. But the Papal Agent soon gave Montagu the lie when he returned, repeating the old objections to him and insisting that the King's opposition was so secondary a consideration with Rome that, were it removed, Montagu would not be better placed. [2]

Soon afterwards Montagu came to tell Rossetti that he had instructed Peter Fytton to drop all negotiations with Cardinal Barberini (the latter was amazed that Montagu should ever even have tried anything so artless) in view of the projected departure of Digby for Rome. Sir Kenelm seemed in no hurry, however, and was contemplating a cure at Tunbridge Wells. [3]

---

[1] *P.R.O. Rom. Trans., Rossetti Corr.*, vol. I, ff., 270-271 : Rossetti to Barberini, July 13, 1640.

[2] *Ibid.*, ff. 276, 296 : Rossetti to Barberini, July 20, 27, 1640.

[3] Actually he did not go to Rome till 1645, when Innocent X was Pope, returning the following year, and undertaking a second mission to the Pope in 1647.

But Montagu's apparent admission of the hopelessness of his chances was a feint before he returned with a subtle flank attack. He told Rossetti that the Queen deserved some mark of the Pope's favour after all she had done for religion and that, although Cardinal Barberini was ready with expressions of regard for her Majesty, he seemed less eager in doing anything positive to show it.

Montagu then proposed that Father Philip be put forward as the Queen's candidate for the cardinalate, and that he (Montagu) be sent to Rome to do it. The plan was a cunning one. Father Philip was nearly sixty and did not enjoy good health. Montagu's moment would come at the Oratorian's death; in the meantime, as a Cardinal, the Scot's influence could be used to improve his chances.

Rossetti appeared to take all this in, then immediately went off to urge the Queen Mother and Windebank to support Ludovic Stuart. [1]

But Montagu had gone with his new plan to the Queen and had again tried to persuade her that there was nothing against him in Rome but the King's known dislike of him, which her Majesty could remove if she would. He was astute enough to put this plea at the moment of the Queen's confinement (Prince Henry was born July 8, 1640) when she would feel least capable of opposing him, while the King would be most inclined, as he always was at such times, to grant her all she cared to ask.

Montagu therefore begged her Majesty to win her husband's consent to his co-nomination with Ludovic Stuart, to write with her own hand to the Pope and, in addition, to give him a letter

[1] *P.R.O. Rom. Trans., Rossetti Corr.,* vol. I, f. 304 : Rossetti to Barberini. Aug. 3, 1640. As a matter of fact Rome would have accepted Father Philip's candidature in the last resort, despite his lack of both blue blood and fortune, What told against him more than this was his partisanship with the English Clergy and with their desire to set their Chapter on a permanent basis. (*Ibid., Rossetti Corr.,* vol. II, f. 15 : Barberini to Rossetti, Sept. 8, 1640). INGOLD, *op. cit.,* vol. I, p. 230, refers to a letter from Urban, of which I can find no trace, offering a Red Hat to Fr Philip if the Queen would nominate him. This letter, so the story goes, fell into Fr Philip's hands, and he was so little moved at the prospect of the purple " qu'il dissimula humblement l'estime que le Pape faisait de lui, et ne rendit jamais cette lettre à la reine." So facile an escape from the honour would have been impossible with the Papal Agent at Court to inform the Queen of the Pope's intentions.

of recommendation to allow him to continue to work in his own interests.

Despite Montagu's choice of the psychological moment, Windebank and Father Philip were of opinion that Charles, who had never liked Montagu even before his conversion, would never yield to his wife in the matter. But, as a precaution, Rossetti told the Confessor to dissuade the Queen from asking. This order the Agent had from Barberini who had now become genuinely angry with the new convert's lordly attitude in the Cardinalate affair, as if he had a *jus ad rem*. [1]

It happened as Rossetti had feared, — like the man in the Gospel, Montagu was heard for his very importunity, and the Queen began wearily to discuss his case again with the Papal Agent who, however, did not hesitate to tell her Majesty that to persist in face of objections which were insuperable was likely to wreck all chance of a Red Hat for England.

Nevertheless, while avowing that she had no wish to run counter to the Cardinal Secretary, the Queen insisted that there was something to be said for Montagu. The objection that he lacked theology was not altogether true, — he had what might be counted a sufficiency of knowledge. As to his father's being a Calvinist, it was hardly fair to saddle him with that.

In reply Rossetti made it clear that Rome's objections were not to be looked upon as personal defects in Montagu, but that she had to regard them in the light of the general good of religion, always so jealously guarded by the Popes. It was not so many years since an Englishman had been raised to the purple and, in the event of the honour being repeated, all eyes would be turned on the new Cardinal, to compare and constrast him with the old. It was not considered that Montagu was sufficiently grounded in ecclesiastical lore, an absolute necessity and the only excuse for promoting any convert from heresy to the cardinalate. Besides this, neither common opinion nor the College of Cardinals favoured him, and there were those who prophesied evil consequences from his preferment. [2]

---

[1] *P.R.O. Rom. Trans.*, *Rossetti Corr.*, vol. I, p. 314, Rossetti to Barberini, Aug. 10, 1640, with an *Apostilla del Cardinale.*

[2] *Ibid.*, f. 337 : Rossetti to Barberini, Aug. 17, 1640— a gloss of Barberini's says :" I Card[ll] Inglesi son stati Roffense, Pole et Alano, egli (*i.e.* Montagu) non è simile ad alcuno di qti et massime ai due primi quali furono grandissimi."

Peter Fytton, it appeared, was as slow to take a hint in Rome as Montagu in England. Ignoring the polite negative Barberini had handed him, he wrote home a glowing account of the personal esteem the Cardinal had showed for Montagu, interpreting this as still leaving the door open, if the Queen would only persist in her earlier request. [1]

Despite all the goodwill in the world the Roman authorities and the Queen of England had been set at such cross-purposes by the machinations of Montagu that Rossetti despaired of reaching any result on the lines they were pursuing, and began to look round for new names not yet considered.

At Barberini's request he ransacked the list of English Benedictines, and put forward the name of Father Barlow, superior at Douai, a man of fifty-five, of excellent life, good family and deeply read in theology. He was well enough liked by the Court, but Barberini would make no comment till he knew the general opinion of the man in England. [2]

Laymen with the necessary qualifications were hard to find, though Rossetti suggested the third son of Henry Somerset, Earl (soon to be Marquis) of Worcester, a splendid convert and an ardent royalist, who led the life of a *grand seigneur* away on his Monmouthshire estates. [3] The nobility of the family was unquestioned ; they were, besides, on excellent terms with the King. Against this, the boy in question, being third son, had no fortune nor had he any theological training, though he had studied philosophy. He was a great friend of the Jesuits, and had called on the Papal Agent

---

[1] *Ibid.*, vol. II, ff. 3 seq. : Rossetti to Barberini, Sept. 7, 1640.

[2] William Rudesind Barlow, O.S.B., S.T.D. (1584-1656) was Prior of St Gregory's, Douai, 1614-1621 ; President-General of the English Congregation, 1621-1629 ; Prof. of Theology at the College of St Vedast for 40 years, he was regarded as one of the outstanding divines and canonists of his time. His brother, Edward Ambrose Barlow, O.S.B. (1584-1641) was ordained at Douai 1616 and worked on the English Mission, chiefly in Lancaster, till his martyrdom in 1641. Their father was Sir Alexander Barlow of Barlow Hall, near Manchester, — an ancient family. Cf. GILLOW, *op. cit.*, vol. I, pp. 134-136.

[3] Rossetti had spoken of the *Worcester* family, and it is evidence of the sharpness of Barberini, whom nothing escaped, that he was able to correct the Agent by a reference to his *Catalogo dei Rè, Duchi et Conti*, telling him *Worcester* was the title and the family name, *Somerset*. (*P. R.O. Rom.Trans., Rossetti Corr.,* vol. II, f. 103 : Barberini to Rossetti, Oct. 27, 1640.)

to tell him he wanted to go and live in Rome, — a hint that he had ambitions, though he made no open allusion to them.

That any prospective candidate for the purple should come to Rome at this ill-chosen moment was the last thing the Cardinal desired, lest the new and notoriously anti-Catholic Parliament (Barberini was writing during the few months that separated *Short* and *Long* Parliaments) should make any onslaught on Englishmen visiting the headquarters of Popery. Rossetti was therefore told to divert likely tourists to Florence or Venice. [1]

Whether, as was said, Sir Kenelm Digby ("the leading amateur of his period.. perhaps the arch-amateur of all history") seriously hoped to add the Red Biretta to the other achievements of a most versatile career, Cardinal Barberini showed greater interest in his young brother, Sir John, who had studied in the English College, Rome, (1624-1627) under the *alias* Salisbury. But his bent was for soldiering. Although his mother never wished him to use his sword in foreign wars, he served the King as a Cavalry Colonel in the Scottish trouble, and was badly wounded and captured by the Scots at Newcastle in September 1640. While under threat of death for his Catholicism, he showed intrepid constancy and, in speaking of him, Barberini was possibly moved more by admiration than by any serious intention of advancing him to the purple. Not that young Digby's military exploits need prove a hindrance, where there was the outstanding precedent of Barberini's own brother, the younger Cardinal Antonio, who contrived to reconcile the wearing of a captain's visor with that of the Red Biretta. [2]

It seems incredible after the rebuffs he had met with on all sides, that Walter Montagu should still think his chances worth pursuing and his ultimate success only postponed. Even his friend Fytton tried to persuade him of the utter groundlessness of his hopes, while Rossetti told him again that time could make no difference : the work he had done for Catholics in England was much appreciated, and would no doubt gain him great merit for the next world, but it could never win him a Cardinal's Hat in this. [3]

Barberini was equally blunt. Robert Pendrick, Hamilton's

---

[1] *Ibid.*, vol. I, ff. 272, 298 : Rossetti to Barberini, July 13, 27, 1640.

[2] *Ibid.*, vol. II, ff. 20, 52 : Rossetti to Barberini, Sept.14, Oct. 5, 1640. (Cf. CARDELLA, *op. cit.*, vol. VI, p. 278 ; GILLOW, *op. cit.*, vol. II, p. 70.)

[3] *Ibid.*, ff. 114, 277 : Rossetti to Barberini, Nov. 2, 1640, Jan. 11, 1641.

secretary, had tried to open the case again, alleging that Montagu was the only fitting candidate available, and that the King had withdrawn all objection to him. The Cardinal's reply was brief: the Pope wished to have no more to do with the matter. [1]

Although the Cardinal Secretary still seemed to favour Ludovic Stuart for promotion, and Rossetti continued to speak of him to the Queen, it was becoming clear that, as Rome neared the end of the eight years delay that had become so wearisome to the flesh of the Catholic powers, [2] the situation in England would make the promotion of an English candidate more impolitic than ever and, in fact, the tedious negotiations begun with the despatch of Douglas to Rome in 1633 received their final *coup de grâce* from the anti-Catholic Parliament.

The negotiations between England and Rome, officially secret, had long been suspect, but there was no further secret to keep when Parliament intercepted letters from Fytton to Montagu. The Queen immediately decided to defer indefinitely her petition for an English Cardinal. She still had some vague hope that her desires would be met by the promotion at her request of one of her own countrymen and again suggested Angoulême, though she could not resist adding a good word for Montagu. [3]

This last imprudence made Barberini lose all patience. He wrote to say that the Queen was wasting her time in presenting either Montagu, rejected so often and with such emphasis, or Angoulême whose promotion could do no good to the cause of Catholicism in England, which must ultimately be the criterion by which the Pope would act. Her Majesty must no longer be deceived on the point, — the Red Biretta would never be conferred merely to please her. [4]

---

[1] *Ibid.*, vol. III, f. 218 : Barberini to Rossetti, May 25, 1641.

[2] Richelieu voiced his disgust at Rome's delay with his usual vigour : " Les longueurs insupportables de la promotion m'ont fait résoudre d'escrire à M. le Card. Barberini... s'il la reçoit selon l'intention de l'autheur, il en tirera du profit." (Avenel, *op. cit.*, vol. VII, p. 853 : Richelieu à Mons. Mazarin à Thurin. De Paris, 27 fév. 1641.)

[3] *P.R.O. Rom. Trans.*, *Rossetti Corr.*, vol. III, ff. 230, 251 : Rossetti to Barberini, June, 7, 21, 1641. *Ibid.*, vol. IV, f. 4 : Same to same, Sept. 7, 1641.

[4] *B.L.* 8650, f. 331 : Barberini to Rossetti, Nov. 23, 1641. Rossetti sent Barberini from Cologne a summary of the Cardinalate affair since the death of Con. (*B.L.* 8650, ff. 448-457 : Rossetti to Barberini, Cologne, Dec. 29, 1641.)

The storm that now broke over England, after a decade of unprecedented calm for the Catholics, settled the matter, — there was no Englishman among the royal nominations when, on the December 16, 1641 (N. s.), Pope Urban created thirteen Cardinals in the first promotion he had made since 1633. [1]

[1] DENIS, *Nouvelles de Rome*, N° 7, p. 14 : *Extrait d'une lettre escrite de Rome, le* 17 déc. 1641, gives the following candidates accepted at royal petition (the first since 1629) :

    Jules Mazarin nominated by the Most Christian King.
    Rinaldo d'Este   "   "   King of Hungary.
    Francesco Peretti Montalto"   King of Spain.
    Marcantonio Bragadino   "   Republic of Venice.

This was Urban's 8th Promotion of Cardinals ; the 7th had taken place on, Nov. 28, 1633 (N.s.) when nine Cardinals had been created, one of whom, Franciotti, had been reserved *in petto*. Urban was to hold yet one more Promotion before his death, *viz.* on Dec. 14, 1643 (N.s.) when two interesting recipients of the Red Hat were Juan De Lugo, the Jesuit theologian, who popularized the use of quinine, and Carlo Rossetti, who had moved hurriedly from London to become Nuncio at the Cologne Peace Conference. The English Catholics were delighted at Rossetti's promotion, and the fact that they took some of the honour on themselves bears pathetic witness to the hopes they had had of a Cardinal of their own. Among the Barberini MSS. (*B.L.* 8620, ff. 75-88) are eight letters of congratulation, two signed by a number of clergy, secular and regular, and bearing the ominous address *ex carcere Nouae Portae.*

CHAPTER XIV

LONG PARLIAMENT AND POPERY

> " Very sicke
> Is Catholike,
>   Alas! Alas!
> The Parliament
> Is fully bent
>   To put down Masse.
> Jesuit and Frier
> Hand in the brier
> Like Dun in the Mire,
>   Well-a-day!
> And those that were my stay
> Must hang or runne away
>   O hone! O hone!
>   Is't not well, sir?" [1]

With the troubles in Scotland consequent on the revival in March, 1638, of the National Covenant that had been drawn up in 1580 against Rome, Charles proposed undertaking a punitive expedition against the Presbyterians of his native land, and to forestall the necessity for convoking a Parliament with which he had now dispensed of so long, he began to look elsewhere for funds. It was a chance for the English Catholics to prove their loyalty and Cardinal Barberini, regarding the expedition in the light of a crusade against Calvinism, was not only anxious for the Catholic gentry to flock to the royal standard but urged the Papal Agent (Con had not then left) to organize a substantial monetary contribution from the Catholics to the King. [2]

---

[1] From *The Masse-Priest's Lamentation for the strange Altercation begun in this Nation*. Rous's *Diary*, pp. 118-119.

[2] *B.L.* 8644, f. 150 : Barberini to Con, March (?), 1639.

So on April 4, 1639 (o.s.), at the express wish of the Queen a meeting of leading Catholic priests and laymen was held at the Agent's house and, after considerable debate, a list of collectors was drawn up, so many for each county and fifty Catholic gentlemen in all. Two letters urging the collection on the Catholics were then drafted, one signed by the heads of the clergy, secular and regular, the other by the laity. A third letter, purporting to speak in the name of the Queen, was signed by Sir Kenelm Digby and Walter Montagu. A fortnight later Henrietta herself penned a personal appeal to the gratitude the Catholics owed the King ; she authorized the collectors to distribute copies of her letter. [1] At the same time the Queen and her mother begged the Catholics, with Holy Week at hand, to join in their prayers for the King's success and to that end also proposed a day's fast, which was readily agreed to. [2] To Papists already heavily overburdened praying, however, came easier than paying and, with the collectors somewhat overbearing in their assumption of authority, Popish purse-strings stayed untied and Con became impatient.

At the end of May the Committee held three meetings, giving 50,000 crowns as the rosiest estimate of the collection. " Difficulties always crop up where money is concerned," Con wrote drearily. Barberini, too, was disappointed but hoped the King would pity

---

[1] The letter signed by the clergy is printed from *B.L.* 8644, f. 176 in App. IX. The other letters, together with the list of collectors for each county and the Queen's message to the Commons referred to later, were published in 1641 in pamphlet-form, presumably by order of Parliament. (Cf. Bibliography B., Literary Sources, *Anon.* : *A Coppy*, etc.). This meeting was, seemingly, intolerably long-winded and Con, viewing the proceedings with eyes italianized by twenty years residence abroad was scathing in his criticism of the English love of harangue :" Non mi meraviglio che questa natione brama tanto Parlam[t1] attesa l'infinita inclinatione che hanno di fare li savii discorsi, censuare, riformare, e votare con libertà, e contradittione delli compagni, volendo ognuno le cose à modo suo, e tutto questo apparisce in questo piccolo congresso, havendo bisognato le forze d'Hercole per ridurre le cose à qualche ordine." (*B.L.* 8644, f. 181 : Con to Barberini, April 5/15, 1639.)

[2] *B.L.* 8644, f. 177 : Con to Barberini, April 5/15, April 1639. Always thoroughgoing in her enthusiasms, Henrietta suggested a special gift from the ladies of the realm, and actually appointed Lady Carlisle and Lady Denbigh as collectors, but the project came to nothing. (*Ibid.*, ff. 201, 245 : Same to same, April 19/29 ; May 13/23, 1639.)

rather than condemn the poverty of the Catholics, bled as they were by pursuivants serving the crown to their own profit. [1]

Fully cognizant of the effort being made to raise money among the Catholics, the Government was showing them singular favour. The Agent was therefore fearful lest their lack of response in hard cash might provoke the re-enforcement of fines that would mulct them of more than even a generous voluntary contribution would have done. But it was impossible to make them see wisdom, he said impatiently.

Some Catholics tried to avoid subscribing on the specious plea that, as at the moment the King was at peace,he had no more need of money. It irritated the Agent in the extreme that Catholics, who,he said,would not be suffered to breathe but for royal protection from the penal laws, were short-sighted enough to make a statement so offensive to the King.

The collectors went on with their work, however, and by mid-July had 40,000 crowns ready for the King who requested them to pay it to the Lord Treasurer. Charles was at that moment urgently in need of ready cash (he was to set out for Scotland in August), and it was a rare stroke of fortune that the Catholics' £10,000 had come in so opportunely : it pleased and impressed Charles the more. [2]

The collectors held out hope of a like sum by Michaelmas. Con, too, thought this possible, provided things were managed properly ; but he could not help adding that he sincerely hoped he would be gone by that time. In organizing the contribution he had had to contend not merely with the reluctance of the Catholics themselves. There were also enemies without, trying to persuade the Papists to subscribe to other collections and thus spoil the total of their collective effort as Catholics. Another attempt to sabotage the contribution was the distribution of a patent forgery purporting to be a letter from the Pope ordering Con to stop the collection. [3]

---

[1] *Ibid.*, ff. 226, 245, 256 : Same to same, May 3/13, 10/20 ; May 24/June 3 ; ff. 322, 356 : Barberini to Con, July 9, 30, 1639.

[2] *Ibid.*, f. 299, 318, 328, 351 : Con to Barberini, June 21/July 1 ; June 28/July 8 ; July 5/15, 19/29, 1639.

[3] *Ibid.*, f. 340 : Con to Barberini, July 12/22, 1639. Con enclosed a copy of the forgery with his letter of July 5/15 (*Ibid.*, f. 326). Its falseness is evident from the awkwardness of many of the ecclesiastical expressions used ; also it

The Puritan opposition was now quickly gathering strength and preparing to attack the Roman Agency at the psychological moment when the departure of Con (he had gone, as he had hoped, by the end of August) would find his successor, Rossetti, strange to the task and unsettled. Appeals were soon made to the King to stop certain meetings held at the Agent's house, but Rossetti was able to tell Charles that their chief concern was with the second half of the Catholic contribution to his Majesty. The first attack had failed. [1]

Talk against the Agency and the Papists in general was a common topic now and, anticipating trouble, Rossetti warned all heads of orders, as well as the laity, to use the utmost circumspection. He used greater caution and secrecy in the conduct of his own chapel, and, as there were necessarily large crowds coming at Christmastide (1639), he did away with the afternoon hour's Catechism customary on Feast Days. [2]

The Papal Agent was well aware the clash would come with the calling of Parliament, and urged both Queen and courtiers to stay the King from yielding to constant clamours for convocation. [3] When it became certain that a Parliament would be called, voices were raised against the Papists all over the realm ; there were gloating jeers that they were going to get the fright of their lives, they who had been so sure of themselves would soon be shouldering their meed of woe. Remarks were made openly at Lady Holland's (she and her husband were, politically speaking, Puritans) that the English religion would at last win weight in the kingdom, and Romanism be utterly destroyed. The correspondence with Rome was declaimed against as particularly prejudicial to their " English ". religion, and a Parliament, it was considered, would be worth while if it did nought else than wreck it.

All this terrified the Catholics, especially the priests, who began talking of flight. While Windebank warned all to lie low, Rossetti

is clear that the Pope would not prohibit an enterprise that had the Cardinal Secretary's full and repeated approval (*B.L.* 8644, ff. 322, 365, 382, 391 : Barberini to Con, July 30, Aug. 20, 27, 1639).

[1] *P.R.O. Rom. Trans., Rossetti Corr.*, vol. I, f. 53 : Rossetti to Barberini, Nov. 4, 1639.

[2] *Ibid., Rossetti Corr.*, vol. I, ff. 89, 94 : Rossetti to Barberini Dec. 23, 30, 1639.

[3] *Arch. Secr. Vat., Nunziatura d'Inghilterra 4, Maneggi ecc.*, f. 20 v.

calmed them as best he could, promising to appeal to the Queen and to Charles himself as the need arose. He now decided to have Mass in a private room that the Catholics attending might not be noticed.

Feeling grew fiercer as the opening of Parliament approached, the more so, as it was the general opinion as early as February that there would be a quick dissolution, and the Puritans knew it would be now or never to enforce the Penal Laws and rid themselves, at a swoop, of the Papal Agent and the Capuchins, for with them would go the two best Public Chapels in London.

Monday, April 13, 1640, saw less than the traditional royal pageantry at the opening of Parliament, as Charles went to Westminster by water, but hope ran high when the King allowed the Catholic peers to take their seats without being troubled with the Oath, a thing unheard of since the days of Elizabeth. Yet the Commons lost no time in attacking the Royal Prerogative, while demands were made for the abolition of the Star Chamber and for the enforcement of the laws against the Catholics. Questions were put against all the London Catholic Chapels, threats were heard of burning Rossetti's house. [1]

Luckily the Catholics did not suffer as they had feared, for May 4 brought the session to an end, — a three weeks' affair. Yet the dissolution brought in its train armed riots in the City with bills posted on the Palace at Whitehall, attacking Laud and calling on patriots to save liberty. Leaflets with the names and addresses of priests were distributed in the streets ; Rossetti's house was again threatened, but he refused to budge, though he had the Blessed Sacrament moved to safety. Then squibs and broadsides were found calling on the defenders of the purity of the Gospel to meet at a certain place to go to the house of the Pope's minister, raze it to the ground and murder him : that night Rossetti retired to Marie de' Medici's house. Troops were ordered out to guard the two Queens, but the houses of Catholics were freely looted : it was one way at least, albeit a costly one, of convincing Charles that they were no traitors to the Crown.

There seemed no limit to the insolence of the Puritans, for on the

---

[1] *P. R.O. Rom. Trans., Rossetti Corr.*, vol. I, ff. 96, 147, 155, 181, 204 : Rossetti to Barberini, Jan. 6 ; March 9, 23 ; Apr. 28 ; May 18, 1640.

window of the King's antechamber had been scratched with a diamond : " God save the King. God confound the Queen with all her offspring. God grant the Palatine to reign in this realm. " [1]

Now came news of a secret understanding between English Puritans and Scotch Covenanters to fight Popery no less than Episcopacy and Kingship. This alarmed Laud who, still pitifully anxious to disavow all connection with Rome, burnt more Catholic books and on Whitsun Eve, 1640, actually went down on his knees to Charles, imploring him to persecute the Catholics as a matter of sheer political expediency. Another of the Archbishop's less worthy suggestions (this time to get money) was the arrest of priests and of all Catholics known to attend the Chapels. To this end he issued a proclamation against forty-seven priests, many of whom appealed straightway to Rossetti. The Agent interviewed the Queen, instancing a number of arrests where fines paid had gone no farther than the pockets of the informers. He stressed the fact that to put Catholics in prison would only alienate them from their present loyalty : the King stood to lose. Rossetti added that, if the King needed money, he was agreeable to another unostentatious levy on the Catholics by authorized persons. This the Queen told Charles, and he accepted. So neither priests nor laymen suffered further molestation under the proclamation. [2]

During all this period of anxious activity Rossetti had taken a house at Oatlands to be near the Queen in case appeal were needful. At Oatlands on July 8, 1640, Henrietta gave birth to a boy, [3] and it was characteristic of Charles that, in face of Laud's activities and an unpromising future, he gave orders for the release of all Catholic priests and layfolk, with a guarantee that they would be no further molested while the Queen was abed. Again the Catholics could go quietly to the Chapels, though Rossetti felt ever apprehensive of Laud, who would issue

---

[1] *Ibid., Rossetti Corr.*, vol. I, ff. 206 seq., 213, 221-223 : Rossetti to Barberini, May 25 ; June 1 and 8, 1640.

[2] *Ibid., Rossetti Corr.*, vol. I, ff. 222, 242, 249 : Rossetti to Barberini, June 8, 22, 29, 1640.

[3] Prince Henry, Duke of Gloucester, whom, during the Commonwealth, his mother tried to convert. She failed through the exiled Charles II's intervention. The boy died of smallpox soon after the Restoration, September, 1660.

edicts on the slightest provocation, as he did when a man from the Spanish Embassy boxed the ears of a Puritan. [1]

Prince Henry's birth was the last respite the Catholics were to enjoy. Soon it was blowing up again for the storm to break in November with the calling of a Parliament that would never end. [2] In August Windebank came running to Rossetti with a squib he had found in the King's antechamber, containing a blustering threat to fire the Capuchins' chapel and prophesying but a short span of life for the Papal Agent. [3]

The Puritans were handing out their threats with some prodigality now, — the royal authority, bishops, papists, all came under the lash. Most of all were they determined in the coming Parliament to stop the King from corresponding with the Pope. Father Philip now spoke to Rossetti of his fears for him and for the Agency itself ; the Italian, while determined to stand at his post by the Queen as long as was reasonably safe, could see that his presence might do more harm than good to the Catholics by provoking the Puritans. He therefore placed himself at the Queen's orders. Henrietta was resolved to keep up the Agency as long as possible as a guarantee of the rest — the Chapel and Almoner she was allowed under her Marriage Contract. [4]

---

[1] *P.R.O. Rom. Trans., Rossetti Corr.*, vol. I, f. 281 : Rossetti to Barberini, July 20, 1640. Rossetti sent Barberini a copy of one of Laud's warrants. (Cf. *B.L.* 8647, ff. 430-431 ; Italian translation, ff. 432-434). It was to one Thomas Thrasher,Gent., Sworn Messenger of the King's Chamber, and given at Lambeth, July 2, 1640, signed by Laud and the Bishop of Rochester. It was a warrant allowing Thrasher to search any houses he held under suspicion of concealing suspect persons, books, writings or letters, seditious, dangerous, schismatic, heretical or Popish, or whatsoever thing relating to seditious or Popish use or printing machines, etc. He was also empowered to imprison inventor, writer, printer, publisher or seller of these books, or of relics or other monuments of Popery. Also all refusing to leave their children to be lawfully baptized, or who procure or allow them to be superstitiously baptized by a priest, and so on.

[2] As soon as he heard Parliament had met, Cardinal Barberini predicted the probability of its proving a permanent one : "Sento che potrebbe il parlamento durar lungo tempo, et quel che è peggio puotrebbe volersi stabilire un parlamento perpetuo." (*P.R.O., Rom. Trans., Rossetti Corr.*, vol. II, f. 183 : Barberini to Rossetti, Dec. 1, 1640.)

[3] *Ibid.*, f. 364 : Same to same, Aug. 31, 1640.

[4] *Ibid., Rossetti Corr.*, vol. II, ff. 68, 79, 118, 136 : Rossetti to Barberini, Oct. 12, 19 ; Nov. 2, 9, 1640.

The new Parliament, the *Long*, had scarce met before a descent
was made on Rossetti's house.   It was at dead of night, 1 a.m., that
they came, a hundred armed men led by three Parliamentarians
and Justices of the Peace, who banged at the door, shouting that
they had a warrant to search for arms.   George Gage [1] who lived
next door, was called from his bed to interpret, and explained that
Count Rossetti was not English and so not subject to this law.
Thereat the intruders grew angry, threatening to force a way through.
Gage retorted that to bluster in such fashion without showing their
warrant was no way to treat the meanest subject, still less a foreign
noble.   For half an hour they wrangled in the rain, till it was
agreed to send to Mr Secretary Windebank for advice.   The
Justices now asked if they might wait inside in the dry.   Once
away from the mob they changed their tune and mutual courtesies
were exchanged.   Soon word came from Windebank that he knew
nothing of the warrant which had probably been given by the
other Secretary, suave Sir Harry Vane.

Rossetti's private opinion was that the men had come to see
if they could discover any trace of the Papal Agent's relations
with the King.   To avoid visits from worse people, he decided
to give the Justices the satisfaction of seeing nothing and led them
personally through his house.   Completely disarmed by the
courtesy of the Count, they stopped to admire his pictures, doffed
their hats as they entered the chapel, even making a reverence
towards the altar.   They then left, a little sheepishly perhaps,
begging the Agent's pardon for putting him out.   The Queen was
furious, Vane apologized and there the matter ended. [2]

Now fully launched on its career of destruction, Parliament
lost no time in tilting at its favourite targets.   John Pym, voicing
the general suspicion of changes in religion and government, brought
the following points to the notice of the House: " The Papists

---

[1] There were two well-known secular priests of this name. The first, son of
Edward Gage, was a friend of Toby Mathew and had been held in great esteem
by King James, who had employed him in Rome during the Spanish Marriage
negotiations (v. *supra*, p.29). The second George Gage, the son of John Gage,
became in 1640 Secretary to the English Chapter, and was later appointed
by the Holy See Protonotary for England (Cf. GILLOW, *op. cit.*, vol. II, pp.
356-357).   The latter is probably in question here.

[2] *B.L.* 8620, ff. 11-12 : G. Gage to *Admodum R.Dne* [Barberini's Secretary ?],
London, Nov. 6, 1640.

partie alter Religion and this is by setting difference betweene the King and his subiects, and Tenetts of Papists undermine our Religion. 2 pt. The corrupt parte of our clergie [he meant Laud's reformers] that make things for their owne ends and will an union betweene us and Rome. 3 pte. Agents for Spaine and other Kingdomes by pensions to alter Religion and gover[n]ment. 4. Those that are for their owne preferments and further all badd things are worse than papists, those are willing to runne into Popery." Pym then went on to attack the Laudian reform on four heads : "1. Ecclesiastical Courts. 2. Discountenancing of forward men in our Religion. 3. Countenancing their owne partie or else noe promotion. 4. By negociating Agents from hence to Rome and from Rome to this place to extirpate our Religion, proofe will appeare." [1]

After Pym's summing-up of the common religious grievances, an alarmist note could be heard in nearly every speech. Four days later Mr Rigby, the member for Lancashire, who had wind of a letter sent by Rossetti to various priests asking the faithful to fast on Saturdays for the Queen's special intention (the safety of the King), felt he could talk of " a Popish Ecclesiasticall Hierarchie and Governement over the whole government of this Kingdome." At this Pym regaled the House with a tale of an Irish priest, one William O'Connor, who had confided to a Mrs Anne Hussey that " many thousands were in pay to be ready to cut all the Protestant throats." Asked how that could be, he said by killing the King first, and his own hand would do it. Mistress Anne had been brought before Windebank, who took no notice of the woman, however, referring her to his secretary. He was censured by the House for his negligence. [2]

This gave a Mr Thomas Cooke the chance to tell of several priests whom Windebank had discharged in writing. The Secretary's defence was that his acts had been purely official ; if he had done anything from personal motives, he was ready to answer for it to the House. Consequently, the next day, November 12, one Weekes, Keeper of the Gatehouse, was examined and gave the Commons the following items of information : " Preist Fisher committed by the Lordes and discharged by Secretarie Windebanke.

---

[1] SIR SIMONDS D'EWES, *Journal*, p. 8.
[2] *Ibid.*, p. 25 and note.

John Goodman was committed and discharged by Mr Secretarie. Thomas Reynolds was convicted and committed and discharged by the same : And warants were produced under the Secretaries hand to the same effect." Windebank was then asked would he avow his hand to the warrants or releasements of Jesuits and Priests. " Hee did and was bid withdrawe." Sir Thomas Jermyn then told the House in the King's name that his Majesty " having taken notice of the accusation laide against his secretary.. did command him to signify to the house, That hee had command his Secretary to give warrants of releasements for sundry Jesuites and Priestes."[1] So Charles had shouldered the responsibility, but Windebank's sentiments were well-known and the respite he won was short-lived.

Rumours were soon rife of a " grand conspiracy of the Pope and his Iesuited Instruments, to extirpate the Protestant Religion, re-establish Popery, subvert Lawes, Liberties, Peace, Parliaments, by Kindling a Civill War in Scotland, and all his Majesties Realms, and to poyson the King himselfe in case hee comply not with them in these their execrable Designes."

Accusations were freely made against prominent Catholics, among others, Lady Arundel and Sir Toby Mathew, the latter being described, not without imagination, as " a Jesuited Priest of the Order of Politicians, a most vigilant man of the chief heads, a man principally noxious, and himself the plague of the King and Kingdom of England : a most impudent man who flies to all banquets and feasts, called or not called, never quiet, always in action, a perpetual motion, thrusting himself into all conversations of Superiors, he urgeth Conferences familiarly that he may fish out the minds of men." [2]

A Mr Glynne told the House that " the papists doe generallie

---

[1] D'EWES, op. cit., pp. 25 and note ; 31 and note 8 ; 32 and note. Three years later this clemency of the King towards priests was pilloried in print, when Prynne the Puritan published The Popish Royall Favourite ; or a full discovery of his Majesties extraordinary favours to and protections of notorious Papists, Priests, Jesuits, manifested by sundry letters of grace, warrants, etc. (London, 1643).

[2] A. H. MATTHEW, Life of Sir Tobie Mathew, p. 308 citing RUSHWORTH on the Discovery relating to the Plot. Rec. Oct. 15, 1640, from PRYNNE'S Romes Master-Peece.

flocke to Denmarke (*i.e.* Somerset) Howse with as much boldness as anie protestants doe to the Church." He then reported that there were nineteen Peers of the Realm and two Countesses that were Papists, though the general run of the latter were "meane men and few of any note." [1]

Parliament now issued warrants for the houses of Papists to be searched for gunpowder and muskets. Soon a proclamation was made, under a law of Elizabeth long fallen into desuetude, ordering convicted Papists under pain of death to withdraw ten miles from London within fifteen days. But as Charles would only allow the decree to be enforced against Catholics owning a country house, it was not only no hardship but many were only too glad to slip away from the perils of London. In any case, wrote Rossetti cynically, he felt sure a little largesse would soon buy back entry to Town. In fact, the Catholics were more fearful for the future than the present. [2]

Parliament had not only cleverly linked up Popery with its attack on Laud's reform and the kingly power, it even pretended to see the price of blood in the hated Ship Money demanded by the King: pamphlets were distributed alleging against the grant of Ship and Conduct Money "that the money is used for setting up idolatry, and that large sums are sent to the Pope in exchange for relics sent over by him." [3]

Though Charles had saved Windebank from the recent charges brought against him, Parliament was determined that the Secretary should not escape, and on Tuesday, December 1, Mr Glynne gave the House fresh information of priests released by warrant of the Privy Council or personal order of Windebank; over three score letters of grace he spoke of, twenty-nine under Windebank's hand alone. The Council's warrants were signed by the two Archbishops and all saw the recipients safe across the sea. Mr Glynne then told of the case of a Mr Carrell, a secular priest, who had been committed by the King's sign manual and yet discharged at a word from Windebank to the Keeper of the Clink. To other priests (one Gunpowder Smith among the rest) Windebank had given letters of protection

[1] D'EWES, *op. cit.*, p. 90.

[2] *P.R..O. Rom. Trans., Rossetti Corr.*, vol. II, ff. 148, 158, 161, 179 : Rossetti to Barberini, Nov. 16, 23, 30, 1640.

[3] MATHEW, *op. cit.*, p. 305.

that none should molest them, while "divers that were diligent in the discoverie of priests were discouraged and threatened by Secretarie Windebank." Not one of forty-seven letters of grace had been entered in the Signet Office and, since Mr Secretary Coke's departure, priests and Jesuits flocked to Windebank's house "as the irone to the loadstone." In forbidding judgment to be executed on men convicted of treason, the Secretary was freely charged with arrogating to himself a more than royal prerogative. [1]

A few days after this long indictment Parliament sent for Windebank, but he was not to be found. Though Charles had signed with his own hands the offending favours the Secretary had dispensed to priests, Windebank knew it was not enough to save him and, yielding to the inevitable, he slipped across the sea, armed with a letter from Henrietta to Louis, asserting that he went to exile for nought but loyalty to his King. Rossetti wrote to Rome in generous praise of the ex-Secretary who had deserved so well of the Catholics. The Count offered him his house in Italy. [2]

On the day Mr Glynne had brought his charges against Windebank, Sir John Culpepper had also spoken against the Secretary, and had further moved " an humble remonstrance to the King about the growing of poperie ; that an act bee drawen against the growth of poperie ; and that the committee enquire what the person is that is called the Pope's nuntio ; and what authoritie hee hath." [3] The net was drawing closer.

The law of Elizabeth that made the priesthood a capital crime Charles had long left idle, releasing condemned priests on the legal fiction that they would submit to the penalty when called upon. Parliament now proposed turning fiction into fact by re-calling these " condemned " men. Rossetti stood ready to appeal to Henrietta, but he had to confess, instancing the Strafford affair, that neither King nor Queen held any real power.

Their helplessness was evident in the insolent way Parliament discussed their private affairs. There was frequent mention of the Papal Agency, and talk of tampering with the Queen's Marriage Pact by proposing that she should send away her Catholic servants.

---

[1] D'EWES, *op. cit.*, p. 89.

[2] *P.R.O. Rom. Trans., Rossetti Corr.*, vol. II, ff. 177, 219 : Rossetti to Barberini, Nov. 30, Dec. 21, 1640.

[3] D'EWES. *op. cit.*, p. 91.

Henrietta replied spiritedly that all her Protestant ones would be sent packing too and fresh Catholics be brought to serve her. Louis, her brother, soon got wind of the project, and on meeting the English Ambassador's wife said, " Tell your husband I do not want to meddle in Parliament's affairs, so let them keep off my sister's Marriage Articles, otherwise I know well what I shall have to do." [1]

Eager to vent its spleen on the Catholics, Parliament was given an excellent opportunity when a Member (one of the Justices who had searched Rossetti's house) was attacked and wounded while carrying in his hand a list of Catholic names. It turned out that the attacker was not only a lapsed Catholic who attended the Protestant Church and had not frequented the Sacraments for ten years, he was also a maniac, whose father and sister had been mad and who had already manifested throat-cutting proclivities towards his own wife. However, it was soon blazed about Town that a member of Parliament had been murdered by a Papist and that something would have to be done about the Catholics or all would be exposed to the same danger. As a precaution a guard of 400 men was set at Westminster.

The obvious effect of such an act at such a time, and of the embellished accounts of it told in tavern and alehouse (where, as Laud said bitterly, "too many were as Drunk with Malice, as with the Liquor they sucked in "), was to make the streets thoroughly dangerous for Catholics, who soon found themselves baited by strolling gangs of that type of looter who emerges unfailingly in troublous times ready to vaunt a violent patriotism — and incidentally to fill his pockets — at the expense of the unfortunate alien. To put some show of legality on the persecution, Parliament issued orders for all Catholics not yet convicted to be brought before the Law and their goods confiscated. At the same time the House was confronted with a monster delegation of 3,000 persons bearing with great solemnity a Petition of 20,000 Puritans that the Church of England might be restored to the primitive purity of the Gospel by the rejection of such Romish accretions as bishops, preaching-surplices, the sign of the Cross at christenings,

---

[1] *P.R.O. Rom. Trans., Rossetti Corr.*, vol. II, ff. 176, 205 : Rossetti to Barberini, Nov. 30 ; Dec. 14, 1640.

and reverence at the Holy Name. It was further asked that the altar be reduced to its normal function as a table, and that the " Supper" be received sitting according to Calvinist custom. [1]

It was a time of great anxiety for Rossetti. He sent all his papers for safety to the Queen Mother's house, though he himself still refused to budge, an intrepid courage praised by both the Pope and his nephew. But the question of the Agent's departure had to be faced, and Barberini left it to Rossetti's judgment to choose the right moment. To avoid the impression that fear of Parliament was driving the Papal Agent to safety and to leave the door open for a possible return, the Cardinal suggested various official reasons Rossetti could give for his going, *e.g.* to help the Paris Nuncio, to take a cure at Spa, to assist Mgr Macchiavelli, the new Nuncio Extraordinary at Cologne. [2] Though this last would appear the most plausible, there were two objections : first, the Cologne road was none too safe for the traveller ; secondly, Parliament might suspect him of going there to oppose the Palatine. Perhaps it would be best for the Agent to lie hid in the Low Countries — Bruges, Malines, best of all Louvain, — ready to return if occasion offered. These suggestions of the Cardinal Secretary were, as he said, only tentative, and he told Rossetti to await further orders, and meanwhile to consult with the two Queens. [3]

Henrietta and her mother talked the matter over and decided the Count should leave, especially as he could keep up the Agency correspondence from Flanders or Cologne. The Queen had spoken to Charles about it, and neither could see any other way of appeasing the Puritan hatred of the Agency. Both feared for the Agent's personal safety and though Rossetti thought there was no reason to make a move till Parliament did so, he yielded to the Queen's wishes and now went every night to her mother's house. [4]

[1] *Ibid.*, ff. 193, 220, 231 : Rossetti to Barberini, Dec. 7, 21, 28, 1640.

[2] On Sept. 10, 1640 (N.S.) the Pope had announced in Consistory the recall of Card. Ginetti after four years at Cologne as Legate *a latere* in a fruitless pursuit of peace. To replace him the Pope appointed Mgr Francesco Maria Machiavelli with the title of Nuncio Extraordinary. He was raised to the purple, Dec. 16, 1641 (Cf. PASTOR, *op. cit.*, vol. XIII, 1ᵉ Abteilung, pp. 493, 704).

[3] *P.R.O. Rom. Trans., Rossetti Corr.*, vol. II, ff. 107 seq., 172 : Barberini to Rossetti, Oct. 27 ; Nov. 24, 1640.

[4] *Ibid.*, ff. 214, 235 : Rossetti to Barberini, Dec. 21, 28, 1640.

With the New Year, 1641, the outlook for Rossetti and the Catholics, though the opposite of bright, seemed as if it might be brought on to a bargaining basis. The Puritan Parliament, in which the extremists clamoured for a republic, did not like the Queen, but feared France, and Henrietta hoped that this would prevent any overt attack on the concessions granted in her Marriage Contract. The Papal Agency was not among these, however, and the Queen found bitter hostility to it among Members with whom she conferred. On the other hand, the Catholics looked on the Agent's presence as a safeguard, and Henrietta was determined to hold out for it as long as possible. [1]

There were other Catholic powers besides France to be feared (it had even been suggested Rossetti could stay on in the service of one of them), and the situation looked more hopeful when this was pointed out, together with its corollary of avoiding molestation of the Catholics, in several speeches in the Commons, particularly by the mercurial Lord George Digby, a convert who later became one of the King's most brilliant and dangerous advisers. In consequence, the House seemed in favour of deferring any onslaught on Rossetti's status till the French Ambassador arrived and they could drive home their position to advantage. [2]

Unhappily, at this moment the issue between King and Parliament was brought to a head over a Popish priest. John Goodman, a convert parson, had already served terms in Newgate (1635) and the Gatehouse (1637), from which he was released by a warrant from Windebank in September, 1639. Soon he was again committed to Newgate, betrayed by a fellow-priest, and condemned to death. The Queen pleaded for him with Charles, who assured her that if there was nought but his priesthood against the man he would not die ; he thereupon wrote out an order with his own hand suspending the execution fixed for January 22, a Friday. Mr Secretary Vane announced this to the House the next day. Mr Glynne therewith rose to protest against this affront to Parliament, which " when so many Preists and Jesuites swarmed heere in the city was a great dishartening to those whoe were good, and an encourage-

[1] *Ibid.*, ff. 279, 295 : Rossetti to Barberini, Jan. 11, 18, 1641.
[2] *Ibid.*, ff. 284, 296, 313 : Same to same, Jan. 11, 18, 25, 1641.

ment to them whoe were evill. " The Commons thereupon decided
to bring the matter before the Lords. [1]

The following Wednesday the inevitable Mr Glynne, reporting for
a Committee appointed the day before to discuss this and similar
cases, gave reasons why Goodman should be executed. He then
went on to declaim against " the boldnes and impudencie of preists,
friers and Jesuits (besides such as attended the Queenes Majestie)
walking at noone day. That within a shorte time ther had been
above fourescore preists and Jesuites delivered out of prison and
sett at large, some after they had been condemned of high Treason
and some before. That ther was resident heere a " Nuntio" or agent
from the Pope. That divers went as ordinarilie and frequentlie to
masse to Denmark house and S. James and to the Chappels of
forraigne Ambassadors as to any Church in London. That the
60,000 £ promised to have been lent by the citie of London,
for the paiment of the Kings armie and the rileife of the Northern
counties had been staied because of the saied Goodman's Reprive...
For all which they should desire the Lordes of the Upper Howse
as before to intercede with his Majestie that the saied preist or
Jesuite might bee executed and that some speddie course might
bee used for clearing the Kingdome of the residue of that brood. " [2]

But Charles, in face of the loss of £60,000, was obstinate in
well-doing : he did not sell men's lives, he said. He had freed the
man at the instance of the Queen, and would stand by his word.
The answer pleased Parliament ill, but Henrietta was fighting
this as a test case, not only of the condemnation of priests but of the
royal authority itself. Rossetti put the issue clearly to the Cardinal
Secretary :" If Goodman lives, the King holds on to his authority ; if
he dies, Parliament will be free to proceed against anyone with
impunity. " [3]

The Londoners took up the case, pillorying the priest in caricature

---

[1] *Ibid.*, f. 337 : Rossetti to Barberini, Feb. 1, 1641 : D'EWES, *op. cit.*,
pp. 278-279. GARDINER S.R., *History*, vol. IX, p. 264 ; GILLOW, *op. cit.*, vol.
II, pp. 530-533.

[2] D'EWES, *op. cit.*, p. 290.

[3] *P.R.O. Rom. Trans., Rossetti Corr.*, vol. II, f. 359 : Rossetti to Barberini,
Feb. 8, 1641 : " Le cose però si trovano a stretti termini, poiche se vive, resta
il Rè con l'autorità ; se muore, il Parl° rimane in libertà di operar' senza regola,
e ragione, con discapito di qualunque persona."

and catch. On January 29, Lords and Commons waited at Whitehall with a threefold petition, — against Rossetti, for the execution of all Elizabeth's laws against the Papists, and for Goodman's death. Realizing all that was at stake, the priest offered himself to Charles as a token of peace between King and Parliament, asking his Majesty to throw him on the mercy of Parliament. Charles did so, at the same time solemnly warning the two Houses that to put the priest to death would not only insult his Majesty but antagonize Catholic kings. On the other points of Parliament's petition he said that Rossetti was here to deal with such correspondence as was necessary for the Queen's free practice of her Faith, as provided for in the Marriage Treaty. He was content for the Penal Laws to be enforced, he added, but made a plea for moderation, in view of the irritation they would cause on the Continent. [1]

Fearful of their responsibility, Parliament desisted, and the reprieve for Goodman stood. But the damage was done, and the Commons became increasingly curious of the Queen's dealings with the Pope and all that had been going on behind the scenes during these years. As Rossetti wrote ruefully to Rome : " This affair of the priest has upset everything. "

Walter Montagu and Sir Kenelm Digby were called to the Bar of the House and closely questioned of what they knew of " Seignior Con " and " Councellor Rosetto, " whether they were the Pope's Nuncios, what they did in England and so on. Particularly pointed questions were put as to the Catholic contributions Con had organized for the King, and it was again Mr Glynne who brought the matter to the Members' notice, saying " that the sum of it all was that the Superior of the priests or Jesuites of England (meaning Con, presumably) tooke upon him, as a Father of the Church to perswade the papists of England, whome he cals ther Catholikes, to contribute at least the tenth parte of ther estate. " The two Catholics, taking their cue from Charles, replied as non-committally as they could, but " divers moved about ther relation that ther was enough in it to discover great machinations against religion. " [2]

---

[1] *Ibid.,, Rossetti Corr.*, vol. II, f. 375 : Rossetti to Barberni, Feb. 15, 1641.
[2] *Ibid.*, f. 357 : Rossetti to Barberini, Feb. 8, 1641 ; D'EWES, *op.cit.*, pp. 290 seq., 302, note 6. D'Ewes says specifically that Montagu did not betray Con's

Henrietta then tried to calm the Commons with a message of goodwill and a promise to check the great resort to her chapel. It was rudely received. " After the Comptroller had ended the reading of the same paper ther was a general silence. Then some called to proceede to the busines of the day.. Then Sir Hugh Cholmelie moved that wee might returne our thankes to the Queene by that honourable person that brought us the message ; but none saied well moved or gave anie great approbation of it." [1]

The Commons were now in an inflammable condition and soon sniffing the powder of another Popish Plot. Committees were formed to investigate the " Welch popish armie and the popish Hierarchie," — the former a force raised in Ireland for the King's service by the Earl of Worcester and his son Lord Herbert, Catholics both. Someone in the House produced letters of Windebank's dated the previous August ordering the Earl of Pembroke to obey Worcester in everything. Another then reported that Sir Percy Herbert, a staunch Papist with wide sway in Monmouthshire, had taken arms from the County Magazine to his house. Further uneasiness was felt at the appointment of Lord Arundel as Earl Marshal, and of Lord Cottington as Constable of the Tower, posts of authority in the hands of two pro-Papists. [2]

Parliament now decided to investigate the reference the member for Lancashire had made to a letter sent the previous November by Rossetti to (among others) a Father Sands, a Lancashire priest, ordering a weekly fast for the Queen's intentions. Sir Harry Vane came to question the Agent, saying that the Commons deduced from the letter, first, that Rossetti exercised jurisdiction in England ; secondly, that the Queen had some secret plan ; and lastly, that some spiritual direction seemed indicated.

Rossetti replied that the letter clearly showed that he had written at the Queen's command, and was therefore not exercising a personal jurisdiction. Next, her Majesty's intention was open to all, and could have been heard from her chapel pulpit, — it was for her

---

part in the contribution (op. cit., p. 295) and his first-hand evidence would appear to be of more value than that of Rushworth who maintains that both Digby and Montagu told of the late Agent's activities (RUSHWORTH, op. cit., vol. IV, p. 164).

[1] D'EWES, op. cit., p. 324.

[2] Ibid., p. 349.

husband's happy home-coming from Scotland. On the point of spiritual direction the letter clearly showed, the Agent repeated, that he had acted in the service of the Queen.

Both Charles and Henrietta were pleased at Rossetti's reply, but Vane hinted that Parliament was anxious to cite the Agent before them, and was also debating the removal from her Majesty's household of such doughty champions of Popery as Wat Montagu Sir Kenelm Digby, Sir Toby Mathew, and Sir John Winter, the Queen's Secretary. [1] All had appeared before Parliament, and Rossetti was to face the same charge,— lese-majesty in collecting the Catholic contribution set on foot by Con.

Some members murmured that Rossetti stood condemned under the Law of the land as a servant of the Pope ; they called him, among other things, an " incendiary of the realm." However, there was no real charge they could fasten on him, and, deciding to act with caution, the Commons complained to the Peers of the presence of a Papal Nuncio likely to upset the nation, and asked them to take some action in the matter.

The Queen was now thoroughly alarmed for the Agent's safety and talked of taking him to France with her in six weeks' time, a plan Barberini approved. Meanwhile she tried to persuade some of the Peers not to allow Rossetti to be brought before the Bar of the House. When the Lords approached the King on the matter, they received the same reply as before : the Queen's correspondence with the Pope was necessary for the free exercise of her religion. Charles added, however, that as to the person of Rossetti he would give Parliament every satisfaction. It seemed a clever compromise — indeed the only one — to save the substance of the Agency at the sacrifice of the particular Agent. As the Queen wrote to Barberini, Parliament would not be satisfied till they saw the back of Rossetti, — they knew him ; but some minor official unknown to the Commons could still stay on to conduct the correspondence with Rome. [2]

---

[1] *Ibid.*, p. 488 ; *P.R.O. Rom. Trans., Rossetti Corr.*, vol. II, f. 361 seq. : Rossetti to Barberini, Feb. 8, 1641. *Ibid., Rossetti Corr.*, vol. III, f. 3 : Same to same, March 1, 1641.

[2] *P.R.O. Rom. Trans., Rossetti Corr.*, vol. II, ff. 364, 371 ; *Ibid.*, vol. III, f. 69 ; Rossetti to Barberini, Feb. 8, 15 ; March 23, 1641.

Arrogant speeches against the Faith were now heard everywhere, and Catholics were ridiculed in the streets in broadside and ballad :

" The Papist pore,
Turnde out of dore,
Alas ! Alas !
And holy Frier
Is in the Mire,
Farewell deere Masse !
For now all priests
Banished thou seest. " [1]

Rossetti's departure was now only a matter of time. Already Father Philip had suggested his secretary's staying on in his stead. This was Girolamo Piombini, a Canon, who in England kept to his lay title, Cavaliere. He did not relish the post but was ready to obey orders. Though Barberini was willing enough for him to stay, providing he did not touch on the Cardinalate question, he did not welcome this talk of Rossetti's leaving the country, and thought it would be more to the interest of the Catholics if he merely slipped into hiding somewhere in the country.

The Cardinal was suspicious, too, that the Agency was being not only attacked by the Puritans but sabotaged by certain friends of the Queen (Montagu the chief) who were interested in the promotion of an English Cardinal and irritated at the long postponement. But on hearing from Rossetti, Barberini changed his opinion and apologized for thinking this. However, he did consider that the Queen was banking too much on French aid, and felt sure that through her servants her views were an open book to Richelieu. [2]

Writing in April, Rossetti said he was resolved to leave with the Queen Mother in three months' time. He was safe enough until his case was brought before Parliament, and the Queen forced to take action ; he even hoped that before the summer came Parliament would be prorogued, and he stay on, for there were rumours of an imminent rupture between King and Commons, due to the latter's

[1] Rous's *Diary*, pp. 118-119.
[2] *P.R.O. Rom. Trans., Rosetti Corr.*, vol. II, ff. 343 seq. ; *Ibid.*, vol. III, ff. 35, 52 ; Barberini to Rossetti, Feb. 2 ; March 2 and 9, 1641. *Ibid., Rossetti Corr.*, vol. III, ff. 1, 19 : Rossetti to Barberini, March 1, 8, 1641.

onslaught on the royal authority. Now, said Father Philip with the most grandiose optimism, would be the psychological moment for Charles to sever all ties with Parliament and Puritans, couple his cause with that of the Catholics and, by proclaiming his own conversion or at least liberty of conscience, put in a claim to material aid from the Pope. [1]

Rossetti had word that the whole status of the Agency would come up before the House in May, when the charges against Laud were to be dealt with. Already in March the Archbishop had been brought to London —he was mobbed on the way – and accused by the Lower House to the Peers on twelve heads, reducible to desiring the subversion of Law and Government by subordinating all to the will of the King ; wishing to establish a new religion ; corresponding with Rome (incriminating autographs of his were alleged to have been found — a pure invention), and treating with the Pope's man in England. [2]

With Laud on the point of impeachment, the mob might well chant in the streets :

> " *U R I C , pore Canterburie, in a tottering state,*
> *P O P E some say youde be, but now t's too late,*
> *R U 2 Y Y for all those eyes are now upon you?*
> *U R A K if that you say that they will wrong you.* "[3]

Towards, the end of April the Commons found the weapon they sought to strike Rossetti and the Papists, — a priest turned false witness. One Bruno, a Friar Minim who had once stayed with Con, let himself be arrested and taken before Parliament. He received gentle treatment, was sent to Prison and began to write — ten pages of diabolical fabrication. He was a famous preacher in high credit with the Catholics, he alleged, and knew all that went on in Rome, France and Spain. Plying a virulent pen against the Jesuits and the Court of Rome, he attacked George Con and Father Philip in particular, and spoke bitterly of the reciprocal Agency, revealing that Hamilton had left his secretary, Pendrick, in Rome. Rossetti, a man who might do much harm, would probably also leave someone

---

[1] *Ibid., Rossetti Corr.*, vol.III, ff. 101,121 : Rossetti to Barberini, April 12, 19, 1641.

[2] *Ibid.*, ff. 39, 140 : Rossetti to Barberini, March 15 ; April 26, 1641.

[3] Rous' *Diary* p. 109 : The K in the last line stands for Knave.

to carry on his evil work ; it was therefore necessary to cut out the whole canker. The Friar conclu ded with a list of the names of orders and heads of orders in England.

This document, calculated utterly to prejudice the cause of the Catholics, was then put into the hands of Parliament. The writer soon tried to forswear what he had written, but his hand betrayed him and, at the time of Rossetti's writing to Rome, he was expected to preach against the Church from the pulpit of St Giles, Sunday, April 25, 1641 (o.s.). [1]

In an effort to be as fair as he could to the harrassed Catholics, the King only succeded in adding fuel to the flames when Parliamentarians waited on him at Whitehall for an answer to their petition of three weeks before that all Catholics be dismissed their Majesties' service, the Irish Army disbanded and the Papists disarmed. Charles replied firmly : the first point was his own affair ; as to the second, he was willing enough for all to go quietly to their homes — but not until everything was peaceful in England and Scotland. The third point he agreed to, provided the Law was abided by and no force used save against Catholics convicted of holding offensive weapons.

It was the most solid stand yet made against Parliament, but when the deputation made as if to reply, Charles spoilt all by refusing to listen and stalking off. It was a lack of tact typical of the King, and Parliament showed its resentful mood in an order confining their Majesties to Whitehall. All now counselled Rossetti to go, though Henrietta asked him to wait till the Strafford case was settled. He could then leave Piombini behind and himself await Barberini's orders in Ghent. [2]

At Charles's refusal to sign Strafford's death-warrant, Parliament threatened to clap King and Queen into the Tower. They thought of flight, their carriages were ready (the Louis XVI parallel springs to mind), but an armed band of 2,000 was posted around the Palace. Within all was confusion, men and women confessing their sins, standing or on their knees, for rumour ran round of a popular rising to massacre the Catholics. The Capuchins scattered like sheep to friendly houses, and Rossetti kept his doors bolted

[1] *P.R.O. Rom. Trans.*, *Rossetti Corr.*, vol. III, ff. 154 seq. : Rossetti to Barberini, May 3, 1641.

[2] *Ibid.*, ff. 172, 184 : Rossetti to Barberini, May 10, 17, 1641.

for six days. Small wonder that the King, the wracked with visions of his wife and children at the mercy of the mob, torn between loyalty and love, sacrificed his friend and servant, and reluctantly put his name to the deed that sent Strafford to the block. For that act " Charles bled inward tears of blood to the day of his own death by the same violence. " [1]

All letters from abroad were opened now, but by a stroke of luck one from Mgr Scotti, the Paris Nuncio, to Rossetti advised the latter's return to Rome, which inclined Parliament to deal leniently with the Agent and offer him every facility for his departure, — a passport signed by the King protecting Rossetti and his suite on their passage out of England, together with security should they wish to return. Charles made a personal offer of a royal vessel as far as Dunkirk.

It was now nearly June and, with the warmth of the weather increasing danger from plague, Rossetti hoped Parliament would rise earlier than usual for the summer recess. He informed the Commons that he would like to leave with the Queen Mother, who was now awaiting her passport. While tilting at the Papists and the Queen, a French princess, Parliament was trying desperately to keep friendly with France, and was therefore only too eager to set poor Marie de' Medici on her travels again, this time to her death. Maintaining a chapel of her own, she had served the Catholics only too well while in England, but the antagonism of her former protégé, Richelieu, was well-known. He had driven her to the English Court to embarass Charles and mortify Henrietta; having succeeded, he would be further gratified now to see her hounded from the realm. [2]

Prominent Protestants, as well as Catholics, among the nobility came to pay their respects to Count Rossetti as the day of departure drew near. On June 19 he had a farewell audience of the Queen, presenting Piombini. When the latter withdrew, Henrietta told

---

[1] BELLOC, *King Charles I*, p. 251 ; *P.R.O. Rom. Trans., Rossetti Corr.*, vol. III, f. 194 : Rossetti to Barberini, May 24, 1641.

[2] It was a sad fate for the mother of Louis of France, of the Queens of England and Spain, of the Duchess of Savoy, whom only a short time before, Edmund Waller had hailed as :

> " *Great Queen of Europe ! where thy offspring wears*
> *All the chief crowns ; whose Princes are thy heirs.*"

Rossetti that, with Parliament saying that anyone representing the Pope in the country stood guilty of lese-majesty, it would be wiser for Piombini to retire with Rossetti to Flanders and watch the situation from there. The Queen added that Duperron was to go ; she was struggling now to keep at least her Confessor and Capuchins. [1]

As Rossetti was on the point of departure, two members called at his house to request him in the name of Parliament to appear before the Bar of the House. Rossetti sent to say he was " not at home, " and feft straightway for the Venetian Ambassador's ; at the same time he sent word of the situation to the Queen, who let Charles know. The King dispatched Lord Dorset (Edward Sackville, a Catholic) to calm the Commons who still clamoured to interview the Papal Agent, though they sent him their respects, which Rossetti, with mixed feelings perhaps, reciprocated. They wanted him on a charge of giving asylum to priests, and also for delaying his departure. For the latter fault he soon found a remedy, andon July 8 crossed to Dunkirk *en route* for Ghent. [2]

---

[1] *P.R.O. Rom. Trans., Rossetti Corr.*, vol. III, ff. 222, 229, 267, 278 :Rossetti to Barberini, May 31 ; June 7, 21 28 ; July 5, 1641.

[2] *Ibid.*, ff. 275, 297 : Rossetti to Barberini, July 5, 19, 1641.

CHAPTER XV

ROME AND A LOAN

" And though likewayes it were almost as easie to blow up the whole Ile of Brittaine to the Moone with a Powder Traine, as to divorce the Princes abused soul from those inward and malignant Heresies which have been propagate to him from his Uncatholicall Ancestors ;.. but, like an Adder, he still stops his Eare at the voice of the charmer... Though (my dearely beloved) all these heavie Verities discover to Us many and huge mountaines of Impediments, which will be hard to remove, let us gird up our loynes notwithstanding." [1]

While all knew from the first assembly of Parliament that a crisis was coming which would decide the fate of English Catholicism as well as of Kingship and the Laudian Church, it was the hope of those around the King that gold might resolve the situation in his favour, enabling him to buy off his chief opponents, or putting into his hands the power of fighting them to the end : victory was morally certain for the side with the longest purse.

If such was the solution, it surely lay in the hands of the Queen, with all her Catholic connections, to plead for financial help for her husband and, as it was increasingly evident that the Catholics must stand or fall by the banner of the King, the Pope seemed the most likely source of assistance. It therefore became Rossetti's chief task before he left England, and again while he was at Cologne, to negotiate a loan from the Pope to the English King.

The question had come up in Con's time. During the previous summer Windebank had one day recalled a remark of Urban's to Sir

---

[1] *The Passionate Remonstrance made by his Holinesse in the Conclave at Rome upon the late proceedings, and great Covenant of Scotland,* etc., published in Edinburgh in 1641. This scurrilous lampoon reveals the confidence of even the most Calvinistic of the King's opponents that, no matter how hard pressed he might be, he would never yield to Rome.

William Hamilton that he would be ready to help the English King out of financial difficulty. The Secretary said he thought the Pope ought to send them a substantial sum of money. With somewhat heavy humour the Agent asked what amount would turn the Government into honest men. Windebank replied that £100,000 sterling at least should make a nice present. Bitingly sarcastic this time, Con asked how many parish churches and cathedrals the Catholics could have back for such a sum. Windebank allowed that the Agent had scored with a touch on the quick and, suddenly serious, began talking of the peace and quiet that the Catholics had enjoyed from the King's clemency. Con countered by emphasizing the extensive drain on the Papal Treasury, and suggested that if any help at all were given it should be laid out in maintaining a company of troopers in the service of the Queen. To this Windebank objected that unless the aid given was quite general it would be of little use. They were thus at cross-purposes, and Con had nothing more to do with the question. [1]

Barberini commented on Windebank's big ideas — English generosity, he called it — in asking for £100,000, and said that although he had hopes of getting more money, he would have to have a good deal in hand to be in a position to assist the Queen of England. [2]

When the question was raised again during the interim between the Short and Long Parliaments, the Cardinal Secretary put the issue bluntly : the Holy See could not be expected to aid a heretic King in what was not the direct defence of the Faith. [3] Were Charles to declare himself a Catholic, the Pope would be able and ready to send him money and men ; on ships ostensibly carrying

---

[1] *B. L.* 8644, f. 255 : Con to Barberini, May 24,/June 3, 1639.

[2] *Ibid.*, f. 322 : Barberini to Con, July 9, 1639.

[3] The eternal crusade against the Turk and the defence of Papal territory were two of the cases of extreme urgency required for the use of the 3,000,000 scudi deposited as a reserve by Sixtus V (1585-1590) in Castel Sant'Angelo to prevent the utter depletion of the Treasury. By May, 1591, 400,000 scudi had already been withdrawn for the defence of Avignon against the Huguenots. During Urban VIII's pontificate lavish expenditure on troops, galleys and fortresses, together with the heavy costs of the wars of Mantua and Castro, meant a continual cry for ready money, which the Pope met constantly by melting down and reminting old coins and foreign specie. Cf. E. RODOCANACHI, *Le. Château Saint-Ange*, pp. 180 seq., 205.

a cargo of alum from 6,000 to 8,000 men might be taken gradually to foregather at Liége, where Barberini had many friends, there to await transport to England. [1]

Parliament had not been long in session before the Queen sent the Cardinal Secretary via the Paris Nuncio an urgent plea for a substantial loan. Appealing to Pope Urban's zeal and interest in the English Catholics, Henrietta described the straits in which Charles found himself and the onslaught Parliament was making against the Catholics, banishing them ten miles from London and threatening full enforcement of the Penal Laws ; her own Marriage Contract again stood in danger of violation by the expulsion of the Capuchins. If the King was now hard pressed, the Queen pleaded, it was largely on account of his clemency to the Catholics. The only way out for both King and Catholics, who had everything to gain, was the bribing of the Puritan leaders, but as the disorders in England made the raising of a large sum impossible, she appealed to his Holiness for a loan, on security, of half a million crowns (£125,000). The Queen begged the Pope and his nephew to let the scheme go no farther (only they three knew) but to answer as soon as possible and, if they agreed, to send her the money in small quantities by bills of exchange. [2]

---

[1] *P.R.O. Rom. Trans., Rossetti Corr.* vol. I, f. 326 : Rossetti to Barberini, Aug. 10, 1640. *Ibid.*, f. 255 : Barberini to Rossetti, June 30, 1640 : " ..quando si trattassi di sostenere un Re dichiarato Catt^{co}, e della difesa della nostra Santa Religione che puo quando S. M^{ta} dichiarasse tale di quà non si guardarebbe a mandarli danari, et armarsi con inviare soldatesca sopra i Vascelli che fingessero venir qua per caricare allumi, et costà riportassero sei, o otto mila persone che sin' all' ultimo spiro servissero S. M^{ta}..." *Apostilla del Card^{le}*, 12 Sett^{re} : " quando si volesse valere della gente di quà e bene avvisare con mandar le navi accio la gente che fusse arrolata vi potesse imbarcare oltre a qualche numero che si potrebbe veder sotto altri pretesti d'unire nel paese di Liegi ; ma a tutto vi vuole del tempo."

[2] *Ibid.*, vol. II, f. 187 : Rossetti to Barberini, Dec. 7, 1640. *B.L.* 8615, ff. 84-86 : Henrietta to Barberini, — 1641 (venuta con l^{re} di Mon^{re} Nun^o in Francia di Gen^o) : " ..les desorderes de se peis sy randent impossible de trouver ysy une belle somme dargent quil faudroit a cause *de lesclat que sela seroit* se qui pourroit aussy frustrer le sucses : sest pour quoy jay cru en premier lieu esttre obligee davoir recours a sa saintete pour luy demander son assistance en une occation sy presante et (dans) le danger sy inevitable sans se remede a fin quil voye quil nia rien que je ne desire exposer en sette cause je mofre a donne telle caution qui sera valable pour la somme de cinc cent mil escus : car les catholiques estant une fois eschaper de se parlement present il ne avoit que a esperer et rien a

Barberini sent his reply through the same medium, the Paris Nunciature, but he gave no decision as to the loan, simply declaring his willingness to help, despite his own difficulties, and asking for more detail of her Majesty's plans. [1] At the same time he wrote to Rossetti expressing surprise that the Queen had not worked through him, and ordering the Agent, while professing ignorance of the request, to lead her Majesty and Father Philip to talk of the desired loan. He added that meanwhile he would think over the whole matter, though he did not consider the Queen's request practicable save on the condition he had already given : the King's conversion. This stipulation the Cardinal repeated the following week. [2]

In the meantime Father Philip had of his own accord approached Rossetti, remarking that the Pope had helped the Emperor, hard-pressed by heretics in Germany, and that the Queen was of opinion he might do the same for her husband in similar straits in England. When the Agent pointed out the difference made by the Emperor's religion, the Queen's Confessor, seeing the hint, declared that for the King to become a Catholic in his present helpless position would mean the loss of his throne. He added that the Queen promised that her husband would grant liberty of conscience in all his realms once he won back the power to do so, provided the Pope helped him with money now, if not directly, at least through the King of France. Rossetti made no comment, save a promise to put the matter to Rome. [3]

A fortnight later Father Philip brought up the subject again in similar terms, adding that the King knew now what he had been unwilling to admit before, *viz.* that the Puritans were out to destroy Kingship, while the Catholics were loyal to it. It was therefore to be hoped that his Majesty would take his stand by them, grant liberty of conscience and himself become a Catholic,

craindre dhors en avant : et le seul moyent est seluy que je propose : sest pour quoy je vous prie de communiquer se sy a sa saintete a qui je suplie tres hum-blemant de ne le consulter quavec vous car sy sela venoit a esttre seu je serois perduee.."

[1] *B.L.* 8632, N° 40 : Barberini to Henrietta, Feb. 18, 1641.

[2] *P.R.O. Rom. Trans., Rossetti Corr.,* vol II, ff. 319, 350 : Barberini to Rossetti, Jan. 26, ; Feb. 2 1641.

[3] *Ibid,* f. 263 : Rossetti to Barberini, Jan. 4, 1641.

though this he would only do of his own free will, never under pressure from the Queen. [1]

Charles was now in sore financial straits, unable to subsidize his mother-in-law any longer, forced even to reduce his table.

Early in February, Cardinal Barberini, repeating that the King's conversion could alone unbolt the bars of the Papal Treasury, denied Father Philip's assertion that this would mean the loss of the throne, and instanced the case of the Duc de Bouillon, [2] who had been a Catholic many months before the fact was known. In any case, the Cardinal added bluntly, for a king the loss of a kingdom meant in actual fact the loss of his authority, and this had gone from Charles already. He therefore advised him to fortify some retreat for his family and hold all the ports with men he could trust.

Barberini told Rossetti that, in the event of the King's conversion, he would like to know in good time exactly what help would be needed that he might get into touch with the Duc de Bouillon, a friend of the Pope's, and with his adherents in Flanders, Liége and the neighbouring districts of Germany. Also, help could be called from Spain and France, and sent over to England through French, Dutch or Flemish ports. The Cardinal said he thought London could be taken and occupied with a large force, and the King might then make what laws he pleased, as with London went the whole nation.[3] Further, Barberini added naïvely that, although

---

[1] *Ibid.*, ff. 289 seq. : Same to same, Jan. 18, 1641.

[2] Frédéric-Maurice de la Tour d'Auvergne, Duc de Bouillon, born 1605, elder brother of the great Turenne. His conversion was welcomed by a brief from Urban, July 20, 1635 (N.S.). Served in Holland and Italy, 1642 ; accused of complicity in the *Cinq-Mars* plot against Richelieu ; released from prison but driven from France and took over command of Papal troops in Italy, 1644. On his conversion cf. PASTOR, *op. cit.*, vol. XIII, 1. Abteilung, p. 556.

[3] Barberini's estimate of the situation was a correct one. The population and wealth of the City of London stood relatively higher than at the present day, while its organization assumed a paramount importance in the absence of a standing national army. Moreover, in 1641 before the issue had become clear, the capital inclined to the King (the Lord Mayor and most of the Aldermen were royalists), for the wealthier citizens had that distrust of national disturbance which is the natural attitude of the merchant of large commitments ; and in addition they despised the petty tradesmen and apprentices who flocked to hear the incoherent preachings of fanatical Puritans. (Cf. GARDINER, *History*, vol. X, pp. 82-83.)

Puritanism might be deeply rooted in England, he thought Calvinists would turn more readily to Catholicism than to Anglicanism.

Discussing the willingness of the King to promise liberty of conscience, while still refusing to become a Catholic himself, the Cardinal said there would not only be the difficulty of helping a heretic, but there would still be no guarantee that Parliament might not at any time revoke the grant. In other words, while the King would be receiving hard cash, he would be giving in return a promise the actual fulfilment of which was an uncertain affair of the future : altogether bad business. Another point,—"toleration" might be variously interpreted ; in its fullest connotation it would include all sects, whereas Rome only wanted it for the Catholics. [1]

This question of liberty of conscience was put to a special congregation of Cardinals who, lawyer-like, remembered it had been granted implicitly in the *Article Secret* of the Queen's Marriage Contract and in a greater degree than in the Spanish Articles. Their Eminences naturally concluded that if this had not been enough to win toleration, another promise would not help. In any case, some security would have to be given against the future machinations of Parliament. Also it should be stated clearly if public churches were to be permitted. Rossetti was therefore to find this out and also to stress the Pope's powers of persuasion with Catholic princes as well as with the English Catholics themselves. These powers would be at the King of England's service — when he became a Catholic. [2]

Barberini was of opinion that if the Pope came to Charles's aid at all, it should be in conjunction with the King of France, — yet how could this be when the latter was in league with the Dutch, the Swedes and other heretics? Again stressing the poverty of the Church, the Cardinal offered Henrietta 15,000 crowns on his own account : it was all he could afford. At the same time he expressed the fear that the Queen's request as put to him was already known to Richelieu, seeing that her letter had passed through France. [3]

When in obedience to the Cardinal's orders Rossetti pursued

---

[1] *P.R.O. Rom. Trans., Rossetti Corr.*, vol. II, f. 367 : Barberini to Rossetti, Feb. 9. 1641,

[2] *Ibid.*, f. 381 : Barberini to Rossetti, Feb. 16, 1641.

[3] *Ibid.*, f. 395 : Same to same, Feb. 23, 1641,

his discreet inquiry into this plan of the Queen's for buying off the Puritans, he was told by Father Philip that in his opinion the scheme would have little lasting effect, as the Puritans, once they had pocketed their bribes, would only reopen persecution, so deep-rooted was their hatred of Popery. Walter Montagu, on the other hand, thought bribery would effect its purpose, so Rossetti told him of the objection Father Philip had raised, adding for himself that he could not see how the money could ever be distributed for such a contingency as the buying off of persecutors; in any case the sum would need to be a substantial one if it were to be at all effective, and that would necessitate its passing through the English merchants, all of whom were Puritans. The plan would thus soon be revealed to the great prejudice of the Catholics. [1]

Rossetti told Father Philip what Barberini had said of the King's conversion and the case of Bouillon. The Queen, when told, said she had had the parallel in mind. She added that she was keenly desirous of her husband's becoming a Catholic, but could not say whether he would take the step. At least he would grant toleration, by which he meant to allow public churches and the practice of the Faith without let. As Father Philip explained to the Papal Agent, the King was hoping to triumph by means of Catholic help, but he was personally timorous and slow of resolution. Rossetti replied that the Queen must make it her task to spur him on to action, pointing out how her own father's conversion had helped to stabilize affairs in France. [2]

A little later the Papal Agent again saw Father Philip, so as further to clarify the position. If the King would go no farther than a promise of liberty of conscience, then the Holy See, alone and poor, could offer little help. Were the King to become a Catholic, then the many other before-mentioned sources could be tapped.

When she heard the report of the Roman Cardinals, the Queen quite agreed that toleration was implicit in her Marriage Articles and that Rome would want something much more definitive now. She therefore made up her mind to go over the whole question thoroughly with the Papal Agent. [3] First of all she sent Montagu

[1] *Ibid.*, vol. III, f. 23 : Rossetti to Barberini, Mar. 8, 1641.
[2] *Ibid.*, f. 61 : Same to same, Mar. 22, 1641.
[3] *Ibid.*, ff. 91 seq. : Same to same, April 5, 1641.

to tell Rossetti what he knew already, that she had asked Cardinal Barberini for half a million crowns, with the promise that, once Charles was master of the situation, liberty of conscience would follow for the Catholics. The question of his personal conversion was an exceedingly difficult one, and not even toleration would be granted unless the King could crush the Puritans, at present a superior force. The Queen said she hoped this would come about through the help of the Irish Catholics, the English Protestants and her brother, Louis. [1]

All this from Montagu. Early in May, 1641, Henrietta gave Rossetti an hour's audience, during which they discussed three important questions, — the likelihood of a place in the Sacred College being kept for an English Cardinal; the question of Rossetti's staying on in face of Parliamentary pressure for his departure; thirdly, the exact *quid pro quo* that would be made for a Papal loan, — Charles's conversion, or a mere promise of toleration.

On the last point Rossetti emphasized the difficulty the Pope would have in raising money to lend to a heretic king for so uncertain a prize as this promise. The difficulty could be solved in two ways, — by the free exercise of the Faith becoming an established fact in England, that is, at some remote future date, or *hic et nunc* by the King's conversion. It was then the Queen's turn to outline Charles's difficulties: he had men enough, it was money he needed, yet in return he was not in a position actually to grant liberty of conscience but only to promise it. If Rome could suggest a way of persuading Parliament to grant toleration immediately, the King would be only too glad to accept that way out, as he could not see his way to becoming a Catholic as yet. The other solution, the Queen concluded, was for the King to win his way back to power with the aid of English, Dutch and French troops, *and* a loan from the Pope. If this plan were pursued and successful, the Catholics would have nothing further to suffer from the laws of the realm. [2]

When in the early summer of 1641 the violent enactments of Parliament promised to plunge both Charles and the Catholics into more certain ruin, Rossetti again urged the King's conversion and an immediate grant of toleration, as the solution of the

[1] *Ibid.*, ff. 103 seq.: Same to same, April 12, 1641.
[2] *Ibid.*, f. 165: Same to same, May 10, 1641.

situation. The Queen put the problem before Charles who, while refusing to become a Catholic, made a definite offer, in return for the Pope's aid, of full liberty of conscience in Ireland with permission for the English Catholics to frequent unmolested the Queen's and the Embassy Chapels, and to practise their Faith freely in the privacy of their homes. When he regained his authority he would allow them to open public churches as well. The King added that he wished to stamp out all religions but the Protestant and the Catholic.

Here at least was a clear-cut offer, and Rossetti asked the Queen to write it in her own hand to the Cardinal Secretary, first asking the King to sign it for security's sake. The Agent now found out (the Queen would not tell him before) that their Majesties would ask the Pope for 600,000 crowns to be drawn on Cologne banks. He thought, however, they would be satisfied with 400,000. [1]

In June, 1641, Cardinal Barberini, replying to the Queen's request for ‘suggestions,’ urged the King's conversion as the solution to his troubles; it might seem the harder way, he would have to brave opposition and human respect, but it was surely the way inspired of God. The Queen should therefore aim at this, however difficult or distant it might seem. The Cardinal agreed with the King's own plan of building up a powerful army; for this reinforcements would be needed, and these he could have by giving some sign, certain even though secret, of his intention of becoming a Catholic. A mere promise of toleration would not be enough, for it was the English King's personal attachment to the Faith that the Pope and the Catholic princes so desired to see; when they saw it, then Pope and princes could decide on ways and means of sending him help. [2]

A temporary break occurred in the incessant stream of the Queen's demands and of the Cardinal's equally insistent answers when in July Rossetti left London for Flanders. He had given out as his

---

[1] *Ibid.*, f. 237 : Same to same, June 14, 1641.

[2] *Ibid.*, f. 241 : Barberini to Rossetti, June 15, 1641 : “ .. ma maggior nervo d'Armi ausiliari oltre le proprie havrà dando secreto cenno, ma con sicurezza di volersi far Catto^co, che ristringendosi al sol partito di dar la sola liberta di conscienza... E. S. Sta certiorata con mezzi sicuri di tal disp^ne del Rè potrebbe offerirsi di trattar con ogni possibile secretezza e efficacia con le Corone del modo e quantita con che potrebbero contribuire le lor aiuti” .

reason for leaving the realm a call to assist Mgr Machiavelli in Cologne. Pretext became prophecy when in September, while at Ghent, he heard of his nomination as Archbishop of Tarsus and Nuncio Extraordinary to the Peace Conference at Cologne in succession to Mgr Machiavelli. This appointment meant the abandonment of the somewhat vain hopes entertained by Rossetti and Barberini of maintaining the Agency in England that had promised so much five years before. [1]

Nevertheless, despite his numerous new tasks (he had to prepare for ordination and consecration, besides his diplomatic work) the new Nuncio still kept in close touch with England, and continued to negotiate the long-awaited loan. Indeed, if this were ever to materialize, Rossetti at Cologne would be in a most central and favourable spot for the remittance of large sums of money. There were, however, new difficulties now on the side of the Holy See for in the summer of 1641 the Papal forces had been fully occupied with the Duke of Parma. Then in October Barberini asked Rossetti to try and find out if it was true that the Grand Duke was sending 100,000 crowns to England, and if so, why — to levy troops or to assist the Queen? [2]

The possibility of French and Spanish help, which Barberini had envisaged in the event of Charles's conversion, came up again at the end of the year 1641. The French Ambassador, whose arrival Henrietta had been awaiting so anxiously before Rossetti left, was now in England and had made a declaration in which he

---

[1] *Ibid.*, ff. 368, 398 : Rossetti to Barberini, Aug. 17 ; Barberini to Rossetti, Aug. 31, 1641. *Ibid.*, vol. IV, ff. 3, 40, 42, 62 : Rossetti to Barberini Sept. 7, 25, 28 ; Barberini to Rossetti, Oct. 19, 1641.

[2] *Ibid.*, vol. IV, f. 54 : Barberini to Rossetti, Oct. 5, 1641. *B.L.* 8650, ff. 252, 255, 263, 315 : Rossetti to Barberini, Oct. 27, Nov. 3, 16, 1641. Barberini's anxiety was due to the fact that his family's notorious quarrel with the Duke of Parma had now involved the Holy See in a war over the Duchy of Castro. The combined forces of Parma, Tuscany, Venice and Modena were ranged against the Papal troops led by Cardinal Antonio and Don Taddeo, the Pope's nephews. To relieve the drain on Papal funds, the City of Rome made in 1641 an extraordinary grant of 150,000 scudi. Between 1584 and 1641 only eleven such grants had been made, of which this was the second large stand the only one for armaments. Cf. A. COPPI, *Discorso sul Consiglio e Senato di Roma*, p. 61 ; PIO PAGLIUCCHI, *I Castellani del Castel Sant'Angelo*, vol. II, pp. 65 seq. ; RODOCANACHI, *op. cit.*, p. 209.

demanded strict observance of the terms of the Queen's Marriage Articles ; as this was hardly likely to happen, French intervention seemed to be threatened. This would offer an opportunity not only of restoring the King to his position of authority, but of rooting out all sects with the combined forces of the Irish and of English Catholics and Protestants. With the King fully appreciating the loyalty of the Catholics, and the Queen ready to fight against his timidity and irresolution, many good judges thought the Catholic cause now stood a good chance of success. [1]

Such optimism was hardly born out by the misfortunes that had befallen English Catholicism in the last few months. Almost simultaneously with the departure of the Papal Agent a quick rot had set in which was to see the final disintegration of all that the Catholics had built their hopes upon in the last few years. Even as Rossetti was leaving, Father Philip was cited by Parliament concerning a letter he had written to Wat Montagu discussing the possibility of Papal aid for the Queen. He did not answer the summons, and a warrant was issued for his arrest, whereupon Charles advised him to comply. He did so, admitting the authenticity of the letter, which Parliament had printed and put into circulation.

Later, articles of impeachments were issued against the Queen's Confessor, embodying such highly diverse charges as stirring up the Pope to issue briefs against the Oaths of Supremacy and Allegiance ; teaching the damnable doctrine of King-killing ; being the cause of the monopolies projected against the Forest of Dean, the soap trade and the making of buttercasks ; allowing himself to be ruled by Sir Toby Mathew, Wat Montagu and others, and traducing the tender years of the Prince to Popery. At the same time was published *A perfect coppy of the Popes breve sent from Rome to Fr Philips by Seignior Giorgio* — a clumsy forgery of some three or four lines long. At last the Commons went too far, printing a libel against the French Ambassador and, when Richelieu's name was mentioned in the proceedings against Father Philip, they were given the hint that they were on dangerous ground, and let the matter drop.

In November the Queen's Confessor, when questioned again by a

---

[1] B.L. 8650, ff. 252, 316 : Rossetti to Barberini, Cologne, Oct. 27 ; Nov. 16, 1641.

committee of Peers on secret plottings in Ireland implicating her Majesty, wriggled out of a compromising position by refusing to swear on an English Bible. He was committed to the Tower, but later sent for custody to Somerset House. In the following February he left with the Queen for the Hague. [1]

Parliament was systematic. After dealing with the Queen's Confessor, they bore down upon her Capuchins, a Pursuivant apprehending their Superior at the very door of Whitehall Palace. The protests of the French Ambassador and the Queen were ignored, the latter's helplessness being emphasized when another priest was taken by a Pursuivant in Somerset House without resistance. [2]

Parliament was wielding an absolute power against Popery. In January, 1641, an edict had been issued ordering all priests, under pain of death, to quit the country by the following April 7. They scattered on all sides, some across the seas, some slipped to hiding in the country, some retired behind the barred doors of their town dwellings, some fled for sanctuary to the Embassies, to the Spanish in particular. Even diplomatic immunity went by the board when the Venetian Ambassador's own chaplain was condemned to death. Not a week passed but that two or three priests were caught, and layfolk were forced before Parliament to take the Oath.

On July 26, the Feast of St Anne on which George Con had crossed the channel so auspiciously five years before, there began that butchery which Charles had striven so conscientiously to avoid while he held the power. On that day died Father William Ward, a venerable Franciscan of seventy-six. [3] A few weeks later, in September, Dom Edward Ambrose Barlow, O. S. B. (brother of

---

[1] *P.R.O. Rom Trans.*: *Rossetti Corr.*, vol. III, ff. 297, 323, 340 : Rossetti to Barberini, July 19, 27 ; Aug. 3, 1641. INGOLD, *op. cit.*, vol. I, p. 228 ; GILLOW, *op. cit.*, vol. V, pp. 304-305 ; FOLEY, *op. cit.*, vol. V, pp. 1013-1014. (Also cf. *Impeachment and Articles of Complaint against Father Philips, the Queen's Confessor*, 1641.)

[2] *P.R.O. Rom. Trans.*, *Rossetti Corr.*, vol. III, f. 385 ; vol IV, f. 22. Rossetti to Barberini, Aug. 31, Sept. 14, 1641.

[3] *Arch. Prop.*, *Scritture Antiche* 84, f. 122 : Theodoro della Pietà to Ingoli, London, Aug. 7, 1641. *P.R.O. Rom. Trans.*, *Rossetti Corr.*, vol. III, ff. 318 seq : *Narratio eorum quae gesta sunt in morte D[n1] Gulielmi Wardi Sacerdotis Angli* ; *Ibid.*, f. 348 : *Inghilterra, Avvisi* ; *Ibid.*, f. 371 : Rossetti to Barberini, Aug. 17, 1641.

Dom William Rudesind Barlow mentioned for the Cardinalate) was hanged, drawn and quartered at Lancaster. [1]

In early August the King was expected to leave any day for Scotland — he cherished vain hopes of a reaction in his favour — and many Catholics stood in dire dread of a general massacre. Others were reassured by Charles's command that nothing further was to be done in the matter of religion during his absence, and by his ordering, before he left, the release from prison of a Franciscan, Father Wilton, much against Parliament's wish. [2]

Meanwhile, anti-Catholic opinion in England had been further incensed by the sporadic but fierce revolt in Ireland where Charles had been forced to disband the army. The dispossessed Irish turned on the alien usurper of lands that many still remembered as their own and, in the white heat of desperation, outrage, cruelties and murders were committed, in which several thousand Protestants met their deaths. Of the exact number the wildest rumours reached London, the highest flight of imagination putting the figure at 300,000. [3] The insurrection was a bid for religious as well as political freedom, and the Privy Seal interpreted it to the Commons as a horrid, infernal plot by Jesuits and Papist priests to massacre the two chief justices with all the Privy Council and Protestants in Ireland. [4]

This had followed on a bitter protest by the Archbishops and Bishops of Ireland against toleration of Popery, which they stigmatized as superstitious and idolatrous. The Papists' teaching being erroneous and heretical, and their Church apostate, to allow them any freedom in the practice of their religion was a grave sin, implicating the tolerant in the guilt of superstition and idolatry;

---

[1] *B.L.* 8650, f. 262 : Barberini to Rossetti, Nov. 2, 1641 ; GILLOW, *op. cit.*, vol. I, p. 135.

[2] *P. R. O. Rom. Trans., Rossetti Corr.*, vol. III, f. 389 : Rossetti to Barberini, Aug. 31, 1641.

[3] H. BELLOC, *Charles the First*, pp. 253-254. Here the variations on the number massacred are given according to the mentality of those concerned. Apologists for the rising put the figure as low as 2,000 ; even modern anti-Irish historians cannot in fairness go beyond 5,000, yet contemporary tales varied from anything between 100,000 and 300,000.

[4] *B.L.* 8650, f. 364 : An Italian translation of the Lord Privy Seal's relation of the horrid and infernal plot in the Commons, Nov. 1, 1641. It was printed and sold by Thomas Bankes of Blackfriars.

while to show toleration even after the payment of fines was to sell religion and souls. Their lordships concluded with a prayer that the authorities might be inspired to zeal for the spread of religion against the superstition and idolatry of popery. [1]

At the end of November the King was back from Scotland, gratefully surprised at his reception and the cheers of the Londoners, though it merely meant that his supporters took to the streets for the occasion. Barberini warned the King to beware of the fickle applause of a crowd that had treated him so shabbily before, — a contrast to the loyalty of the English and Irish Catholics, the latter of whom had taken up arms for him. [2] There were others more numerous ready to shout him down when the time came. That moment was fast approaching, for after Parliament's *Grand Remonstrance* of November, there were dark hints at an impeachment of the Queen, and Charles, after long hesitation and discussion with his wife and friends, screwed up his courage to one of those bold steps he made so often in his life, and as often failed to push to a successful conclusion, — it was only in the drama surrounding his death that the King made no mistake.

On Monday, January, 1642, at three in the afternoon the King strode from Whitehall to Westminster, determined on impeaching the impeachers, the Five Members. But the warnings of Lady Carlisle and the French Ambassador had travelled faster. After a quick glance round the House, with the Speaker refusing all information, Charles remarked ruefully, " I see the birds have flown," adding, " I assure you I did never intend any force." It was a naïvely honest remark. He would have proceeded legally against the members, but what chance had he of being believed when he had come with a band of 400 men? The House was in an ugly mood, and voted the King's action illegal. [3]

On the following Saturday Charles and his family left London for the safety of Hampton Court, and he was only to return to die. The absence of the King was signalized a fortnight later by the killing of two priests. On January 21, after a trial at the

---

[1] *P.R.O. Rom. Trans., Rossetti Corr.*, vol. III, f. 365 : Rossetti to Barberini, Aug. 10, 1641, enclosing *Protestatio Archiepiscoporum et Episcoporum Hyberniae adversus Tolerationem Papismi.*

[2] *B.L.* 8651, f. 5 : Barberini to Rossetti, Jan. 4, 1642.

[3] BELLOC, *op. cit.*, pp. 253 seq. ; GARDINER, *History*, vol. X, pp. 128-129.

Old Bailey, a Benedictine convert, Bartholomew Alban Roe, was dragged to Tyburn on a hurdle with Mr Thomas Greene, *alias* Reynolds, a secular priest eighty years of age. After each had addressed the crowd, they were hanged, and as a concession, allowed to hang till dead. They were then drawn and quartered in the usual way, their quarters being placed on the principal gates of London, their heads on London Bridge. Their companions in death were three thieves. [1]

Later in the year, after the Queen had crossed to Holland, (Charles saw her off at Dover on February 23), a convert secular priest Hugh Green was hanged, drawn and quartered at Dorchester, while Tyburn witnessed the deaths of Thomas Bullaker, a Franciscan, of Thomas Holland, a Jesuit, and of Mr Edward Morgan, a secular. At York two more priests suffered, one young, one aged, — Edward Catherick, and John Lockwood or Lascelles. Their heads were fixed on poles at the Bars of the city.

Each execution now was a fresh flaunting of power by Parliament in the face of the helpless Charles. In April, 1643, the convert Henry Heath died at Tyburn, to be followed in December by Arthur Bell, Franciscans both. Next year, 1644, after the fall of Lincoln, the Parliamentarians shot a layman, Robert Price, without the semblance of a trial, on the mere confession that he was a Catholic, and in September, Ralph Corby, a Jesuit, and John Duckett, a secular, died for their priesthood. The following February, Henry Morse, S. J., was executed at Tyburn. In 1646 four priests were hanged, drawn and quartered, Philip Powel a Benedictine, John Woodcock a Franciscan, and Edward Bamber and Thomas Whitaker, two seculars. Father Powel died at Tyburn, the rest at Lancaster. [2]

There can be no complete record of the numbers left to die like rats in their dungeons during the period of Parliament's increasing power. In the eyes of the Puritan the cause of the Papists had long been intertwined with the cause of the King. Catholic and Cavalier were synonymous terms.

While the edifice of Catholicism in England was quickly crumbling, the Cardinal Secretary turned his attention to Ireland. He was at

[1] *B.L.* 8623, f. 46 : George Musket to Barberini, Douai, Feb. 10, 1642. GILLOW, *op. cit.*, vol. III, p. 38 ; vol. V, p. 438.

[2] GEORGE STEBBING, *The Church in England*, pp. 438 seq.

first not clear as to whether the rising was directed against Parliament or the Crown, but he expressed his hope that the Catholic
nobility would throw in their lot with the rebels, and that all
would then make common cause with the King. [1]

It seemed that his wish would be realized, for in December,
1641, Lord Dillon crossed from Ireland to inform Charles that the
Catholic lords were ready to rally to him in return for complete
liberty of conscience and an independent Irish Parliament. Pym
had Dillon arrested, however, and quickly brought in a motion,
which the Commons passed, to provide funds for hurrying troops
over to Ireland to crush the rebels. [2]

Watching affairs closely from Cologne, Rossetti could appreciate the
King's dilemma, for in the present temper of the nation any major
concession to the rebellious Irish must prejudice his cause in
England. He considered, however, that the King would be helped
indirectly, if the Catholic powers could be induced to support the
Irish revolt. [3]

Cardinal Barberini had the same idea and instructed the Nuncio
in Madrid to approach Olivares. The Spanish minister's reply
was discouraging. He said that the unrest in his Catholic Majesty's
own dominions precluded any intervention on his part. Indeed,
he had had to ask the English Parliament's leave to levy 10,000
Irish for the Spanish army, — a permit readily granted, as it meant
that the English King would thereby be prevented from pressing
them for service in England.

In Cologne, Rossetti was hearing similar excuses from Count Walter
Zapata, the Spanish minister there : the King of Spain would be
willing enough to help the Irish, were he not otherwise occupied.[4]

The early success of the rising and the slowness with which
troops were sent from England to quell it, owing to difficulties of
transport across the choppy St George's Channel, made Barberini
realize the advantage of immediate assistance, and he ordered
Rossetti to persevere in persuading Zapata to ask his government to
allow their ministers in Flanders to send help to Ireland : a sum of

---

[1] *B.L.* 8651, ff. 2-3 : Barberini to Rossetti, Jan, 4, 1642.

[2] GARDINER, *History*, vol. X, pp. 96, 113.

[3] *B.L.* 8651, ff. 140, 168 : Rossetti to Barberini, Feb. 2, 9, 1642.

[4] *B.L.* 8650, f.368 : Barberini to Rossetti, Dec. 7, 1641. *B.L.* 8651, ff. 2-3 :
Same to same, Jan. 4, 1642.

100,000 crowns could not hurt the King of Spain, despite all his troubles. With a view to obtaining this money, Rossetti was told to discover how much authority the Brussels ministers really possessed.[1] At the same time Barberini himself wrote to Don Francisco de Melo, who had recently succeeded Don Fernando, the Cardinal Infante, as Governor of the Catholic Low Countries. The letter gave a general recommendation of the cause of the English Queen as that of the Church, at the same time hinting that, as success depended on the energy of the English and Irish Catholics in not downing arms, a small subsidy would be very welcome. [2]

In writing to Rossetti, the Cardinal had also suggested that it would pay the Duke of Bavaria and the Archbishop-Elector of Cologne to support the Irish revolt in order to keep the English occupied and prevent their meddling in the Palatinate. The Nuncio brought the point to the notice of the Imperial leaders in Cologne and found the situation fully appreciated, but the answer was always the same : the Emperor had no money. [3]

Rossetti then made an effort to move Zapata by recalling the devotion of the Irish to Spain, and the support the latter had given to former risings. The two countries were near, and what had been done before could be repeated. [4] The Count tried to shelve the question by saying that the great need of the Irish was for muskets, which could best be had in Hamburg. At length he promised to write to the Spanish Governor in Flanders, though he did not hold out much hope of his acting without consulting Madrid. Thereupon Rossetti resolved to write too. [5]

Towards the end of February, 1642, the Nuncio again approached Zapata, but the Spaniard would not reveal whether he was in communication with Madrid and Brussels, merely suggesting that, if Spain gave help to the Irish, the Duke of Bavaria should do the same. The answer Rossetti received to his own letter was more

[1] B.L.. 8651, ff. 21, 98 : Same to same, Jan. 11 ; Feb. 1, 1642.

[2] Ibid., f. 186 : Same to same, Feb. 22, 1642.

[3] Ibid., f. 23 : Same to same, Jan. 11, 1642. Ibid., ff. 221 seq., 239 : Rossetti to Barberini, Mar. 2, 9, 1642.

[4] Ibid., f. 117 : Same to same, Feb. 2, 1642. Nevertheless, the Nuncio counselled caution to Barberini in view of the disastrous effects of Spanish interference in previous Irish rebellions. He is referring to the abortive efforts of Hugh O'Neill, Earl of Tyrone, to free his country in 1579 and 1601.

[5] B.L.. 8651, ff. 140, 168 : Rossetti to Barberini, Feb. 2, 9, 1642.

satisfactory.   He was told that Don Francisco de Melo was sending a cargo of 3,000 muskets to Ireland on Dutch boats bound ostensibly for Spain.   A week later came news of a similar cargo that had been driven by storms on to the Irish coast, — a blind to deceive the Parliamentarians.   The Spanish ministers in Flanders seemed willing enough to assist the Irish, but insisted on the greatest caution and secrecy. [1]

On the practical point of sending arms to Ireland in safety, Cardinal Barberini had great hopes of France, as the nearest and most powerful ally.   He therefore wrote to Richelieu, begging him to further the cause of religion and of his master's sister, as the Holy See was in no position to give substantial aid to anyone, least of all to a non-Catholic king.   The Cardinal added, however, that on his own personal account he was ready to send a present of between 30,000 and 40,000 crowns to Queen. [2]

Richelieu's reply was evasive.   He remarked testily that the Queen of England could be helped first by advice, but that she refused to listen save to those who pleased her.   Secondly, she might be helped by force of arms, though this was hardly practicable in the actual state of Christendom, where every nation had troubles of its own to cope with.   The only way to benefit England was to put Spain as low as possible to prevent her siding with the enemies both of the English King and of Catholicism.   The Pope and the Cardinal Secretary could further this end, first by a bold resolution to win back Papal territory lost in Italy, and secondly, by a judicious selection of new cardinals, who would render Barberini himself absolute master in the next conclave, and secure the election of a pope who would pursue the same policy as his predecessor.   If his Holiness was prepared to take action in Italy, France would place at his disposal a fleet of seventy-five ships. [3]

Henrietta wrote to her native land on her own behalf, and receiving as little satisfaction as Barberini, she sent over Walter Montagu,— not a happy choice in view of his earlier diplomatic

---

[1] *Ibid.*, f. 239 : Same to same, Mar. 9, 1642.

[2] *Ibid.*, ff. 2-3 : Barberini to Rossetti, Jan. 4, 1642.

[3] AVENEL, *op. cit.*, vol. VI, pp. 894-896 : *Mémoire dresssé pour respondre à ce que M. le Cardinal Barberin a mandé par le Sieur de Monteuil, touchant l'Angleterre duquel M. de Fontenay se servira selon qu'il jugera de devoir faire. Ibid.*, vol. VII, p. 301 : Richelieu to Barberini, Jan. 27, (1642).

failures and the poor opinion Richelieu had of him. In effect, Montagu returned with profuse expressions of goodwill and nothing more. [1] Charles and Henrietta could, indeed, hardly hope for much practical sympathy from the man whose government of France they so distrusted. The Queen had inherited her dislike of Richelieu from her mother, and Barberini, seeing the game the Frenchman was playing, said he could hardly blame her. In his opinion, Richelieu did not estimate the danger in England at its real value. Moreover, he heard from the Paris Nuncio that France was trying to treat in friendly fashion with Parliament. It was hopeless, therefore, to expect help from that quarter. [2]

After the disappointing answers of the Spaniards and the French, Barberini was at last able to record a subsidy he had won for the Queen. It was from the Catholic Earl of Worcester, who offered the Cardinal 30,000 crowns for the cause of the Queen and the Catholics. He insisted, however, on the strictest secrecy, asking Barberini to give the money in his own name. [3]

On the question of payment, Rossetti advised the Cardinal Secretary to await the moment when it would be most appreciated. Meanwhile the money could be remitted to Cologne, where he would watch the march of events. The Nuncio's point was that the situation in Great Britain was changing rapidly ; moreover, sterling stood high and what might appear a considerable sum in Italy could effect little in England. The best policy was to hold the money over till other sources had been exhausted and, in the meantime, to keep the Irish devoted to the Holy See by sending help in kind,—muskets, powder and shot, —which would cost less and make a better impression that a small subsidy in sterling. [4]

Rossetti soon added another reason for caution, for he heard in March that Mr Secretary Nicholas had told the House of Commons that the Pope was greatly offended at the persecution of the English Catholics and intended subsidizing the Irish rebels if it continued. The House was in high dudgeon, clamouring for increased severity against the Papists. Rossetti pointed to the

---

[1] *B.L.* 8650, f. 363 : Rossetti to Barberini, Dec. 1, 1641.

[2] *B.L.* 8651, ff. 91, 243 : Rossetti to Barberini, Jan. 26 ; Mar. 9. *Ibid.*, ff. 98, 248 : Barberini to Rossetti, Feb. 1 ; Mar. 15, 1642.

[3] *Ibid.*, ff. 174-176 : Barberini to Rossetti, Feb. 15, 1642.

[4] *Ibid.*, f. 200 : Rossetti to Barberini, Feb. 23, 1642.

moral : the Holy See must be circumspect in giving help if the cause of the Catholics was not to be prejudiced utterly. [1]

The following month, therefore, when the 30,000 crowns were paid over to the Queen at the Hague, the Cardinal Secretary insisted on his name being kept out of the transaction. A little later Henrietta asked him to continue his good offices with France and also to persuade the Pope to help her if he could. [2]

Following the other point of Rossetti's advice, Barberini began questioning Irishmen in Rome on the practical needs of the insurgents. The answer was money, arms, ships, pioneers, sappers and captains. Analysing this comprehensive list, the Cardinal voiced his opinion that captains would volunteer from France and Flanders ; there were many Irishmen in both countries, and those from Flanders would take engineers and miners with them. Ships, on the other hand, were an expensive item. The person best qualified to supply them was the Prince of Orange, whose son had recently married Charles's daughter, Mary. Barberini therefore ordered Rossetti to urge the Queen Mother, Marie de' Medici, to use her influence with Orange. Henrietta, however, was already at the Hague on the same errand. The Cardinal Secretary considered ships of paramount importance to the King, if he was to maintain contact with Ireland. To the same end he advised Charles to make sure of some port, the more so as he had now left London.

Barberini's calculations had all along been made on the understanding that not only would the English Catholics rally in a body to the King, which could in fact be counted on, but that the Irish rebels would also declare for him, — a more doubtful issue. At the Paris Nuncio's suggestion, it seems that a priest had already been sent secretly to Ireland, bearing letters from the Pope and Barberini to spur on the Irish in their fight for the Faith. When the news leaked out, Charles was straightway suspicious, and a complaint was lodged through Robert Pendrick, Sir William Hamilton's secretary, who had remained in Rome in charge of the Queen's affairs. Barberini at once hastened to explain that the

---

[1] *Ibid.*, ff. 37, 314 : Same to same, Jan. 12 ; Mar. 30, 1642. Also *ibid.*, f. 270 : *Avvisi di Londra*, Feb. 14, 1642. GARDINER, *History*, vol. X, p. 100.

[2] *Gradwell MSS.*, NICOLETTI's *Vita manuscritta d' Urbano VIII*, pp. 279-280. *B.L.* 8615, ff. 91-92 : Henrietta to Barberini, July 8, 1642.

Holy See had no designs on Ireland but was only anxious for the Royal authority upon which the cause of Catholicism in the British Isles depended. [1]

The question of a *rapprochement* between the Irish and the King was soon to be debated, for on October 24, 1642, two months after Charles had raised his standard at Nottingham and the morning after his victory at Edge Hill, the General Assembly of Confederated Catholics gathered at Kilkenny in what was virtually a Parliament of the Irish nation. Their purpose was to create a provisional body for their own protection, pending the time when the King could undertake it himself.

Early in the New Year, 1643, Charles authorized James Butler, Earl of Ormonde and commander of the Royalist troops in Ireland, to sound the Confederates on the exact nature of their demands. While warning Ormonde that he could on no account agree to public toleration of Catholicism in law, the King urged him to procure a cessation of hostilities as best he could to enable troops to be withdrawn to England.

The importance of the Confederation was fully realized by Pope Urban, who on April 18, 1643, appointed Pier Francesco Scarampi, priest of the Roman Oratory, to report on the Irish situation. The new Agent landed at Wexford in July, 1643, bringing with him Briefs and Indulgences for the supporters of the rising, as well as ammunition and 30,000 crowns collected in Rome by the Irish Franciscan, Luke Wadding. At the same time Barberini was again able to send the Queen through Lord Herbert, son of the Earl of Worcester, a donation of 25,000. [2]

Scarampi soon saw that the Anglo-Irish Catholics of the Pale, weary of war, were eager to come to terms with the King even for so small a prize as the private practice of their Faith in the privacy of their homes. The "old" Irish and the clergy, on the other hand, were resolved on complete liberty of conscience, and the Agent urged them to pursue the war. On September 15, however, after a fifth appeal from Charles, Ormonde succeeded in making a truce

---

[1] *B.L.* 8651, ff. 174-176, 187 : Barberini to Rossetti, Feb. 15, 1642.

[2] E.D'ALTON, *History of Ireland*, vol. II, p. 276. *B.L.* 8615, f. 94 : Henrietta to Barberini, Oxford, Sept. 28, 1643. Worcester had already given £200,000 to the King.

for a year. The King thereupon withdrew four regiments, as well as 2,000 Irish, for action against the Parliamentarians. At the same time he rewarded Ormonde with the title of Viceroy, telling him to offer the Confederates still better terms.

With this hope the latter sent a delegation to Oxford in March, 1644, to confer with the King. Their demands, in return for their own devoted service and a body of 10,000 men, were for a general Act of Oblivion, a freely-elected Parliament and the repeal of the Penal Laws. Fearful of the effect of such concessions in England, Charles tried to elude the dilemma by referring the Confederates back to Ormonde. The Viceroy, however, by demanding the dissolution of the Confederation and refusing any greater toleration than that granted by Elizabeth, only succeeding in effecting a deadlock. [1]

In July, 1644, Pope Urban VIII died, and with the election of the pro-Spanish Cardinal Giambattista Pamfili as Innocent X, the fortunes of the Barberini family, whose leanings towards France had long been suspect, suffered eclipse ; none more so than those of Cardinal Francesco, in whom Charles and Henrietta had placed such hopes. [2]

At once the Confederates sent their secretary, Sir Richard Bellings

---

[1] M. J. HYNES, *The Mission of Rinuccuni, Nuncio Extraodinary to Ireland*, 1645-1649, pp. 11 seq.

[2] The Barberini lay under a cloud during the whole of 1645, while investigations were made into their maladministration of Church funds. Pope Urban had exempted them from keeping set accounts ; this, together with the enormous increase in the family's annual income during the late Pontificate (from 20,000 to 400,000 crowns), laid them open to exaggerated charges of misappropriation, Pope Innocent alleging that they owed the *Camera Apostolica* 10,000,000 crowns. Threatened with imprisonment in Castel Sant' Angelo, the family took to flight between 1 and 2 a. m. one Tuesday night in January, 1646, leaving Rome by the Porta delle Fornacei. Mazarin, who, recalling his own sufferings at the hands of the Barberini, professes to speak impartially, declares that their chief crime in the eyes of Innocent was their sympathy with France as against the House of Austria in the German War. For this reason France gave them asylum, and later in the year even threatened Italy with her fleet till the Pope restored to the Barberini the dignities of which they had been deprived. Cf. DENIS, *op. cit.*, pp. 21-22, 111-113, 118 ; A. CHÉRUEL, *Lettres du Cardinal Mazarin*, vol. II, p. 103 : Mazarin to Padre Mazarini, Maestro del Sacro Palazzo, Nov. 25, 1644 ; p. 276 : Mazarin to Duc de Longueville, Jan. 13, 1646 ; p. 281 : Mazarin to Brasset, Feb. 3, 1646 ; p. 326 : Mazarin to M. le Prince, Oct. 4, 1646.

to seek the favour of the new Pope. To the Irishman's surprise he
found Pope Innocent already resolved upon sending the Prince-
Archbishop of Fermo, Giovanni Battista Rinuccini, as Nuncio to
Ireland with extensive powers of canonical visitation and reform in
applying the disciplinary decrees of Trent, and with instructions
to urge the Irish people to be content with nothing less than
public toleration of their Faith in a permanent treaty. On this
point the Nuncio was warned against Ormonde's likely attempt at
damping the ardour of the Irish by a series of petty concessions.
On his way through France Rinuccini was to reassure the English
Queen, who was now in exile, that his mission was in no way
prejudicial to the English Crown, and that once the common
enemy was beaten the Irish would flock to the aid of the King and
of their fellow-Catholics in England. [1]

Meanwhile Charles, in urgent need of Irish troops, had appointed
an Ambassador of his own to confer with the Confederates. The
devout Catholic Lord Herbert was created Earl of Glamorgan and
invested with extraordinary powers to grant such concessions " as
it were not prudent for the King or his Viceroy to make public, "
but which would be pledged " on the word of a King and Christian "
just as if they had been granted under the Great Seal.   Even were
Glamorgan to go beyond what the Law would warrant or the King
could grant, Charles promised " to maintain the same with all
his might and power. " Any religious concessions, however, were
to be granted under the strictest secrecy.

Reaching Kilkenny in August, 1645, Glamorgan at once concluded
a treaty with the Confederates, despite the opposition of Scarampi,
who protested at the religious articles being kept secret.   In these
public liberty of conscience was granted to the Irish, together with
the possession of all ecclesiastical buildings not at the time in the

---

[1] HYNES, *op. cit.*, pp. 15 seq.   Citing a Venetian despatch, Hynes maintains
(p. 23) that the Queen refused to received Rinuccini in Paris " on the ground
that his title inferred sovereignty over the subjects of her husband." Digby,
on the other hand, during his second visit to Rome in 1648, protested vigorously that, despite a stay of several months in Paris, Rinuccini deigned neither
to discuss his mission with her Majesty nor even to pay her his respects, as if
he were being sent to her mortal enemies rather than to her subjects. Cf. *Bibl.
Vat., Cod. Chigiani* N. III, 69 : *Discorsi politici, Relationi ecc.*, ff. 176-198 :
*Scrittura data à Nro Sre Papa Innocenzo Xmo dal Sig^r d'Igby, Residente della
Regina d'Inghilterra*, 1648.

hands of Protestants. Such privileges were to be confirmed in the next Parliament, though the Viceroy was not to interfere with the immediate enjoyment of them. In return, 10,000 men were to be sent to the King. At the same time Glamorgan drew up a defeasance whereby the King would be bound by the treaty only in so far as it pleased him. [1]

All seemed well until on October 17, a copy of this Secret Treaty was found in the pocket of the warlike Archbishop of Tuam, slain on the field of Sligo. The subsequent publication of the document by Parliament ruined the Royalist cause. But Glamorgan was already face to face with further difficulty. On October 21 Rinuccini had landed at Kenmare with money and munitions for the Confederates. Arriving in Kilkenny on November 12, the Nuncio made no secret of his opposition to Glamorgan's Treaty, until at an interview on December 20 the Earl succeeded in winning his reluctant assent by further pledging the King's conditional consent to the appointment of a Catholic Viceroy and to Catholic bishops sitting in Parliament. [2]

The confusion of authority caused by Glamorgan's secret powers was now seen, for on arriving in Dublin the Earl found himself under arrest. The consternation of the Confederates was great enough for Ormonde to release him on January 21, 1646 and Glamorgan again tried to bring the Treaty to a conclusion, but by this time the King's disavowal of him was known. Rinuccini refused to proceed without confirmation, at the same time confiding to the Confederates that he had advance news of a more favourable treaty that the Pope had made in Rome.

This was the result of the arrival in Rome several months before of the Queen's new Agent, Sir Kenelm Digby, handsome and gigantic, the Compleat Chevalier. Ordered by the Pope to present his case in writing, Digby drew up a characteristic memorandum in which he stressed the loyalty of English Catholics and all that the Queen had done for the Faith. With the help of his Holiness she hoped to do still more by drawing the King and the Irish Confederates

---

[1] HYNES, *op. cit.*, p. 14.

[2] That Glamorgan was justified in going to such lengths with Rinuccini, cf. the extraordinary letters of credence that Charles sent to the Pope and Cardinal Spada. The copies printed in App. X were taken from the originals in the Vatican Archives kindly pointed out to me by the Prefect, Mgr Angelo Mercati.

together against the common enemy, Parliament, which had attacked the King for secretly favouring the return of his realms to Catholicism and subjection to the Holy See.

To show the Pope how easy such reunion would be once the King was inspired to it, Digby pointed out that the English Reformation had left untouched the framework of the old Church, Bishoprics with their revenues, Cathedral Chapters, Parishes and the rest. While the King's authority was maintained, these would remain inviolate ; if he failed, they too would disappear. It had always been the way of Parliaments to aggravate the laws against Catholics, and the present Parliament was more determined on the extinction of the Faith than ever any King had been. In Ireland, especially, did Catholicism depend on the preservation of the monarchy.

This being so, help given to the King could in no way be criticized as the sustaining of heresy, but must go to the credit of the Holy See. The Queen of England, therefore, asked assistance in the stabilization of what had been attained so far in Ireland, and in winning security for the Catholics of England. The two causes were complementary, for once the Irish were rid of Parliamentarians and Scots their swords could be turned against heresy in England to open up the road to the conversion of the whole kingdom.

Digby then drew a colourful picture, reminiscent of Gondomar's dream of more than twenty years before, of the consequences of England's uniting with Rome under a Catholic government : Holland would be forced to follow, the Huguenots of France could no longer keep their independence, while the Hanse Towns of Germany would be obliged to grant liberty of conscience, if they would preserve their trade connections, — all the North would thus swing back to the Roman obedience. Finally, the Turk, a constant menace to the Italian sea-board, could in his turn be threatened with the English fleet. In short, a Catholic England would give the Holy See immeasurable support in maintaining the equilibrium of Christendom and in crushing the monster then menacing it.

Returning from fancy to fact, Digby told how Charles, under a charge of romanizing and favouring the ministers of the Pope, was being refused succour and obedience by his own people. He had lost his ships, and London had declared against him, yet a well-managed campaign would turn the scales in his favour, if only he had the wherewithal. The Agent therefore appealed to his

Holiness to offer the King, not indeed the spoils of the Church's treasury, but a sum of money, which could easily be found for so glorious an enterprise. [1]

Undoubtedly Digby had set out to impress upon the Pope the necessity of regarding Charles as the champion of the Faith, in order to divert into the King's hands the subsidies destined for Ireland. His pleading was sympathetically received and he wrote full of hope to his friends. [2] He was given a present of 20,000 crowns for the Queen together with certain arms and ammunition, but there his success seems to have ended, for Rinuccini wrote from Ireland to protest against any partition of subsidies between the English King and the Irish Confederates. The Cardinal Secretary, Pamfili, thereupon reassured the Nuncio that whatever Digby received would in no way prejudice the help to be given to Ireland. [3]

The Agent stayed on in Rome but his assurances of the goodwill of Charles and Henrietta had been largely discounted by Rinuccini, and Digby found the Pope prepared to grant a substantial loan only on the strictest security. On November 30, 1645, however, articles were drawn up by the Cardinal Secretary, to which Digby gave assent in the Queen's name. The conditions were these: that the King should grant the Irish entire liberty of worship with a completely independent Parliament; that he would place Dublin and all other Irish strongholds in the hands of Irish or, at least, of English Catholics; lastly, that the King's forces should join the Confederates in expelling Scots and Parliamentarians from Ireland.

---

[1] *B.L.* 8616, ff. 115-122: *Digby's Memorandum*, N. D., but probably in the late spring of 1645.

[2] *Calendar of State Papers*, 1644-1645, p. 546: Henry Jermyn to Lord George Digby, Paris, May 30/June 9, 1645: " Sir Kenelm Digby is arrived at Rome, and has had audience with the Pope, who has given him the best reception that the first visit was capable of, that is, the fairest promises in general that can be wished; if he may be relied on there are good hopes of money there, but you know he is of a sanguine family, and himself yet the melancholiest of it; he has visited some other of the petty princes of Italy, but they are a frugal generation."

[3] HYNES, *op. cit.*, p. 26. *Arch. Vat., Nunz. di Francia* 89, f. 159: Henrietta to Innocent, St-Germain-en-Laye, Sept. 15, 1645. The Queen here thanks the Pope for the arms and ammunition he has given her, and for a further promise of money.

When this was accomplished, the Pope promised to send the Queen 100,000 Roman crowns. Furthermore, his Holiness required the King to revoke all laws against Catholics in England and to place them on an equality with Anglicans : this was to be confirmed by the next Parliament. Meanwhile, the Supreme Council in Ireland was to send to England 1200 foot under Irish officers, who were to be supported on landing by between 2500 and 3000 English horse under Catholic command. Thereupon a further 100,000 crowns would forthcoming from Rome, and similar payments would be made for the following two years in accordance with the Pope's means and the advantages gained.

Realizing to some extent the difficulty that Charles would find in giving immediate effect to these conditions, the Pope allowed him ten month' grace, after which the agreement would fall through. But the King was already helpless, for the brilliant victory of Cromwell at Naseby in the previous June had completely disintegrated the Royalist military organization. In England the war was virtually at an end. [1]

At the end of the year Digby left Rome with the treaty, a copy of which had been forwarded to Rinuccini, who was given *carte blanche* to make what modifications in the articles he thought advisable. Addressing the General Assembly of Confederates on February 7 and 9, 1646, the Nuncio told them of the Roman treaty, appealing to them to await the arrival of Digby with the original text, as it offered greater advantages than the terms of Glamorgan's peace. After certain opposition Rinuccini won his point, and on February 16 an accord was signed for a truce until May 1 to await the coming of Digby.

The Queen's Agent, however, had no intention of going to Ireland, and was waiting with the Queen in Paris for the King's approval of the Roman Articles before returning to collect the money the Pope had promised. He waited in vain. In March Charles wrote from Oxford directing his wife to treat directly with Rome, and asking naïvely that " the Pope and the English Catholics will visibly and heartily engage themselves for the re-establishment of the Church of England and my crown.. against all opposers

---

[1] HYNES, *op. cit.*, pp. 50-55 ; GARDINER, *History of the Great Civil War*, vol. III, pp. 49-57.

whatsoever." In return the King promised the removal of all Penal Laws oppressing the Catholics, " as soon as God shall enable me to do it. " [1]

Such an offer despite its vagueness might have been regarded as an acceptance of Digby's Articles ; but a few weeks after making it, Charles left Oxford in disguise and, wandering uncertainly towards the north, gave himself up to the Scots at Newark on May 6, 1646. Then,in order not to prejudice his negotiations with the Presbyterians, he definitely turned down the Roman Treaty, a procedure not altogether unexpected for, although Innocent had replied favourably to Henrietta's fresh plea for assistance, [2] the Cardinal Secretary, Pamfili, had already remarked on the helpessness of the King.

The King was now no more than a chattel, bartered by the Scots to the Parliamantarians, stolen from the latter by the Army.

Charles continued to offer toleration to such Catholics as would take a modified Oath, and a proposal of the sort was actually submitted by certain Catholic divines to Rome, but nothing came of the scheme. [3]

Returning to Rome, Sir Kenelm Digby tried repeatedly during the late summer of 1647 and again in 1648 to win support for Charles by holding out specious hopes of toleration for the English Catholics, but the Pope realized the uselessness of treating with a King who was sovereign in name alone. With the final triumph of the anti-Catholic forces culminating in the King's death, all hope of benefit for the Faith both in England and Ireland had to be indefinitely abandoned. [4]

For the shortest of respites the proscribed Papist had been allowed the light of day, but from the first the sky had been anxious and troubled. The clouds had gathered quickly and, with the breaking of the storm, the Catholics crept back to the Catacombs.

---

[1] *Charles I in* 1646 : *Letters of Charles I to Queen Henrietta Maria, Camden Society*, N° 63, pp. 24-25 : Charles to Henrietta, Oxford, March 12, 1645/6.

[2] *Arch. Vat., Epistolae ad Principes*, vol. LV, f. 446 : Innocent to Henrietta, Nov. 6, 1646.

[3] GARDINER, *op. cit.*, vol. III, p. 354.

[4] HYNES, *op. cit.*, pp. 70-71, 159 note 3, 175-176. The reasons for the failure of the Rinuccini mission are here described in detail. For the Queen's complaints of lack of support cf. The Digby report cited *supra* p. 380, note 1 ; also her letter to Pope Innocent dated from St-Germain-en-Laye, Sept. 17, 1467 in *Arch. Vat., Nunz. di Francia* 89, f. 190.

CHARLES I

Engraving of a marble bust by Bernini. Reproduced by courtesy of the
Trustees of British Museum.

(For a notice of this engraving and of the original bust, see Appendix I.)

EPILOGUE [1]

" I die in the Christian faith, according to the profession of the Church of England, as the same was left me by my Father of most blessed memory." Even to the scaffold the King stood steadfast in the Anglicanism, which to the amazement of Popes, Cardinals and Roman Agents had always satisfied him. The logical Latin never understood how Charles could be deceived by the specious argument that 'Roman' and 'Catholic' were a contradiction in terms, when his own form of Catholicity was followed by only a small minority even of his subjects.

Although the King's religious views presented Rome with a problem that she never solved, there still remained the greatest hope of appealing to the King's natural goodness to grant open toleration for the English Catholics, even after his first Parliament had **forced him to break the promises he had made in his Marriage Treaty.**

Having taken the decision to rule alone, Charles allowed his ever-deepening love for his wife to dictate a policy that a formal treaty had failed to win. As the relief of the Catholics depended so much on his personal favour, it was only natural that Charles should endeavour to capitalize his clemency by demanding in return the Pope's good offices on behalf of his exiled sister and nephews, and in the matter of the Oath.

On the first point the pro-French Urban had neither the influence nor perhaps the inclination that Charles had counted on. The second point was of greater importance and complexity. While it must remain a matter of regret that so chimerical a claim as the power of the Popes to depose princes should have stood in the way

1 For a criticism of much that is recounted in this book, cf. App. XI.

of an agreement that might have considerably improved the status of the English Catholics, it is difficult to see how a compromise could have been reached, for Charles, unable to abolish an Oath passed by Parliament, was asking the Pope not only to wink at the rejection of what was considered an unalienable part of the pontifical authority, but to allow Catholics to swear such a claim to be damnable, impious and heretical. It was altogether too strong a demand.

Nevertheless, Charles was led to believe that he could win his point by a voluble minority of English Catholics in favour of the Oath. On this as on other matters the deplorable divisions among the English Catholics made it extremely difficult for either Rome or the King to deal with them. Moreover, they failed to realize that the relative tranquillity they enjoyed was dependent on a contingent cause, — the personal goodwill of Charles and his ministers, who, as it happened, were for the most part Catholic at heart. By indiscreet use of their privileges the Catholics, in London at least, provoked the hostility of the Puritans, and at the same time alienated the sympathies of those on whose favour their liberties depended.

The creation of a native Cardinal as a solution to the difficulties of the English Catholics was sponsored enthusiastically by the Queen and, at first welcomed by Charles as a possible means of bringing direct influence to bear on the Pope and the Catholic powers in behalf on his sister; later, when this seemed doubtful and when the growing influence of Laud was opposed to the rival dignity, the King became indifferent and possibly hostile to the project, fearful perhaps of the effect on the Puritans, whose power was increasing daily towards the end of Con's stay in England.

Pope Urban's attitude towards the promotion seems to have been one of indifference, while Barberini, although favouring his friend's advancement, did not hesitate to play off the difficulties which at the time beset the promotion of Cardinals as a means of shelving the Queen's request. That the latter and George Con should have emphasized the paramount importance of having an English Cardinal was only natural; it is more than doubtful if it would have had all the advantages they claimed for it.

On the question of Reunion several points stand out clearly. One can see Rome's reluctance to discuss the matter with men backed by no authority but their own, and who sought a compromise she was not prepared to make. The efforts of such men as Davenport and Leander only served to buoy up the hopes of concession held by Anglican divines, while Panzani seems to have been completely deceived by the sighs for reunion that he heard from Windebank and Cottington, two men whose faith was not robust enough to incline them to practise it at a sacrifice.

That Corporate Reunion was impossible without a lead from Laud, which was anything but likely, was clearly seen by Con. It was the latter's turn to be led astray, however, on the convert question. As most of the courtiers who came into the Church were his personal friends one may forgive the lyrical enthusiasm of his despatches ; he was, none the less, giving Rome a false impression of the importance of the movement towards the Church, which, however laudable in itself, was confined within the narrow limits of Court circles. A similar charge of over-emphasis may be brought against Con for the colourful reports he gives of his conversations with Charles, the dilettante theologian and art-lover. Although the Agent was honest enough to admit that he never saw any likelihood of the King's conversion, he certainly sought to impress Rome with Charles's nearness to the Church's doctrines and with his own influence over the King, in the hope that the much-discussed Red Hat might become a reality.

Of the three Agents Rossetti was possibly the most astute diplomat. Although inclined to be unduly impressed by Windebank on the Reunion question, he dealt skilfully with the second stage of the Cardinalate affair, and showed to advantage in the difficult situation created for him by the anti-Catholic hostility of Parliament.

When in 1640 the rich squires and lawyers assembled at Westminster, they came with a long-standing grievance : the King had seen fit to rule and tax the country without consulting them. The reforms of Laud and the privileges accorded to the Papists were also a source of irritation, but it was absolute kingship that they were bent on destroying. The religious question, however, gave them a chance to raise a popular scare that the King meant to subject his realm to Rome. The cry was taken up, by the Scotch Covenanters particularly, and led perhaps more than anything else to the King's ultimate defeat. " It seems that the opinion is grown general, " says a contemporary letter, " that whoever is not Scottishly must be Popishly affected. "

But despite the rumours spread round, to which Charles's conduct often lent colour, despite the bait held out to him, one can say with some certainty that the King was too convinced an Anglican ever to have contemplated conversion either to Catholicism or to Presbyterianism. "Albeit we differ in matter of religion," he wrote to his wife in March, 1646, just before yielding to the Scots, "yet thou must esteem me for having care of my conscience."

That he intended granting a greater measure of toleration to the Catholics seems more probable. From what he had seen of them they were well-disposed subjects, occasionally embarrassing to him at Court and in Town, but in the country leading harmless retired lives, while all of them, despite a theoretical quarrel with the Royal Supremacy, were thoroughly loyal to the monarchy. To rally such men to his standard it was worth while promising a toleration in law which they had enjoyed in practice since the dissolution of Parliament of 1629.

With a lack of realism typical of him, Charles did not see until it was too late that a hint of such concessions was the most powerful weapon that he could place in the hands of his enemies, enabling them to gather against him all whom a cry that the King was betraying the country to Rome would arouse to indignant revolt. The knowledge that the King intended using Irish Papists against them only aggravated his crime in their eyes. The moment he realized this, Charles repudiated the powers that he had given to Glamorgan and declined the treaty with the Pope, thus laying himself open to the gravest charges of duplicity.

Charles I possessed to a greater degree than most of his family that infinite capacity for taking the wrong step, a characteristic that has always entwined itself around the strange romance of the Stuarts. One might say almost the same of the Barberini. In face of the momentous happenings that swept across Europe with the wave of revolt against legitimate Kingship in the second quarter of the 17th century, the friendly relations that passed between the Courts of England and Rome must have seemed to both parties of but minor importance, however pleasant. The fact that at both Courts there were rulers and ministers of only mediocre capabilities, who were themselves plunged into the maelstrom of events they sought in vain to control, explains why no practical result was forthcoming, when there was so much that might have been done.

APPENDIX I

ROME, CHARLES I AND ART

" A refined, conscientious, kind-hearted gentleman, with a taste for theology and a passion for art." [1]

Now that the " vindication" of Charles I has becoming so popular an exercise with historians, his patronage of the arts will be perhaps more widely appreciated. Where Elizabeth had shown the poorest taste in her collections of frivolous curiosities and elaborate nick-nacks, Charles brought to his collector's urge the devotion of a votary and the critical ability of an artist. He was the first English sovereign to open galleries of paintings and sculpture, he was the first to give Italian Renaissance architecture a somewhat tardy welcome to England. His taste as a connoisseur was excellent, his diligence as a collector untiring, though he had neither the wealth nor the opportunity for that personal ransacking of the galleries and studios of the Continent and particularly of Italy, which gave Thomas Howard, Earl of Arundel, a unique position among art-loving Englishmen of his day. The latter's collection preceded the King's, and his famous marbles still perpetuate his name. [2]

With the exception of Lord Arundel, Charles was as far in advance of his subjects in esthetic sense as he was in his ideas of religious toleration. He purchased for his gallery at Whitehall

---

[1] EVAN JOHN, *King Charles I*, p. 76.

[2] Cf. *passim* M. F. S. HERVEY, *The Life, Correspondence and Collections of Thomas Howard, Earl of Arundel*. In particular cf. pp. 473-500, where *The Arundel Inventory of Pictures etc. of* 1655 is to be found. It was drawn up in Amsterdam the year following the death of Lady Aletheia Arundel, George Con's friend, as the larger part of the Arundel collection of pictures, drawings and *objets de vertu* had followed the Arundels to the Low Countries in 1641. This list of 799 pieces was hastily put together and is not exhaustive. For further notes on Arundel's German and Flemish portraits, and the influence of his Italian pictures on Van Dyck, cf. M. VAES, *Le séjour d'Antoine Van Dyck en Italie*, in the *Bulletin de l'Institut historique belge de Rome*, 4º fascicule (1924), pp. 189 seq.

the entire collection of the Duke of Mantua, one of the finest in Europe, and it is said that the keen competition between himself and Philip IV of Spain doubled the price of any work of genuine merit. [1]

Monarchs have so often played Maecenas as a means of purchasing a vicarious immortality for themselves and, while many a master's name has been lost to posterity, his *chefs-d'œuvre* are referred to as a Louis Quinze time-piece, a Queen Anne cabinet, or a Regency sconce. But Charles I has left his name to no outstanding style of architecture, painting or sculpture, yet his interest in the art of his day was a deep and catholic one. " He himself had singular skill in Limning and Pictures... nor unskilful in Musick.. had a quick and sharp conception, would write his mind singularly well, in good language and style. " [2] For all that he never pretended to personal merit as painter or writer ; it is as critic, friend and adviser of artists that he deserves a credit not yet fully accorded him. He could suggest subjects to his two great contemporaries, Van Dyck and Peter Paul Rubens, both of whom he knighted ; similar advice he gave to his architect, Inigo Jones, the deviser of those curious mechanical elaborations that were such a popular attraction at the Court Masques. The King's superb gallery of statues, paintings and antiquities went mainly to the embellishment of his twenty-four palaces all of which were furnished with complete elegance.

Charles's contemporary on the Papal throne, Urban VIII, poet and *littérateur*, was himself the patron of artists, Guido Reni and Bernini the most prominent, for the Barberini, despite the gibe at their habit of breaking up old monuments of art to provide material for new (" quod non fecerunt barbari, fecerunt Barberini ") were the recognized art patrons of Rome.

With the exchange of courtesies between the English and Papal Courts, both parties, Charles no less than the Pope, realized the value of their mutual interest in art as neutral ground on which they could consolidate their new-found friendship and, as has been seen from Con's despatches, the subject provided the King with

---

[2] ADAMS, *op. cit.*, vol. I, pp. 134-135 ; The Mantua collection arrived in England in 1628 (Cf. VAES, *loc. cit.*, p. 189 note 3).

[3] LILLY-MASERES, *op. cit.*, p. 138.

an excellent blind to hide from his less sympathetic subjects the religious matters he so often discussed with the Papal Agent.

Though Charles had little to do with Panzani, he soon found that Cardinal Barberini was willing to send the Queen pictures through the Agent, and Panzani wrote for Barberini to send over an *Eve* by a young Roman artist and also several pictures by Francesco Albani, the friend of Guido Reni, by Alessandro (Turchi) Veronese also called L'Orbetto, and by Stella, or Jakob Van der Star, the young Fleming who migrated to Rome in 1623 and later came under the protection of Richelieu, who appointed him *peintre du roi.* [1]

In the spring of 1635 the body of the Virgin Martyr, St Martina, had been discovered in Rome, and Barberini sent the Queen a relic which Panzani took to Theobalds in July. Charles was more interested in the reliquary, which was beautifully chased and set with rare crystals. In the following January, 1636, Panzani again brought the Queen a *Da Vinci* and a *Del Sarto*, which he says Charles and Inigo Jones examined most carefully. [2]

These gifts were no secret, and the arrival at Court of George Con was a cause of great uneasiness to the Puritans who thought he was deceiving the King " with gifts of pictures, antique idols and suchlike trumperies brought from Rome, " [3] — an allusion, perhaps, to the variegated array of smaller gifts (the usual weapons in the armoury of an ambassador) that Con brought with him to England. [4]

The quick friendship formed between Charles and the Agent was no doubt helped considerably by Con's diplomatic generosity. As they walked or talked, Con would show the King certain gems he had— a cameo *Head of Medusa*, a *Giordano Pio* (Hans Jordaens, the Potlepel?) cut in amethyst, a tiny cameo *Hercules and Diana*,

---

[1] For details of these and other artists mentioned cf. A. SIRET, *Dictionnaire des peintres* and the *Allgemeines Lexikon der bildenden Künstler,* in loc.

[2] *P.R.O. Rom. Trans.*: Panzani to Barberini, March 13/23 ; July 1/11, 1635 ; Jan. 20/30, 1636 ; Barberini to Panzani, April 11, 1635. *B.L.* 8632, No 5 : Barberini to the Queen, Mar. 11, 1635.

[3] D'ISRAELI, *op. cit.*, vol. III, p. 108.

[4] *B.L.* 8639, ff. 1-3 : *Nota di robbe consegnata al Sig^r Giorgio Coneo per portarle in Inghilterra.*

and a miniature by the Paduanino, Ottavio, son of Ludovico Leoni called the Paduano.   When the King expressed his delighted admiration of the jewels, Con offered them to him, deprecating the Marquis of Hamilton's protest that he was too generous. About the same time the Agent records the safe arrival of an agate vase, presumably for the King or Queen. [1]

In February, 1637, Con presented the Queen with a crucifix and a picture of St Michael on behalf of the Cardinal di Sant' Onofrio, the Pope's Capuchin brother. A few months later her Majesty held a private 'view' of all the pictures sent her by Cardinal Barberini, exhibiting them in her chapel at Somerset House for the benefit of the Catholics. [2]

The King did not merely wait for chance gifts to add to his collection ; he knew what he wanted and made use of Sir William Hamilton's residence in Rome to get it.   The latter was at one time negotiating for a statue of *Adonis and Meleagro*— probably the *Adonis* in the Villa Ludovisi of which Charles was particularly covetous ; but not even the influence of Cardinal Barberini could persuade the Duchess of Fiano to part with it. [3]

Of all the royal palaces perhaps Greenwich was the best.   It had been the delight of Henry VIII, Elizabeth and Anne of Denmark, and Charles's Queen took no less an interest in it. It was completed in 1635 under the direction of Inigo Jones, its ceilings adorned with frescoes by Orazio Lomi, the Gentileschi, who did a good deal of work for Charles in England, and probably died there. [4] Henrietta was eager for Guido Reni to paint something specially for her own apartment, and in March, 1637, Con forwarded the measurements of the room to Rome.   Cardinal Barberini personally superintended the work, asking Con for details on the exact position the picture would have, where the windows would be in relation to it and at what angle the light would enter the room. The size required was so large that a single canvas was not possible, but Barberini promised to see that no figures were

[1] *P.R.O. Rom. Trans* : Con to Barberini, Sept. 29/Oct. 9, 1636.

[2] *B.L.* 8640, f. 139 : Same to same, Feb. 16/26, 1637.

  B.L. 8641, f. 126 : Same to same, Sept. 29/Oct. 9, 1637.

[3] *B.L.* 8640, f. 75 : Same to same, Jan. 12/22, 1637.

[4] ADAMS, *op. cit.*, vol. I, p. 135. *B.L.* 8640, f.176 : Con to Barberini, March 2/12, 1637.

painted over the joins. The subject suggested to the Cardinal as giving full scope to Reni's genius was the *Rape of Aurora by Cephalus,* the fable as told by the poet. This Barberini objected to for several reasons, and at his own discretion changed the theme to *Bacchus finding Ariadne.* Evidently some attempt had been made to keep to the former subject, for a month later (Feb. 20, 1638) the Cardinal wrote to say it would not be possible to change now as Guido had taken up the new subject with enthusiasm, and he did not think it good to thwart the genius of an artist![1]

The keenness of which Barberini spoke did little to hurry the painter, although, once it was finished, the Cardinal declared that Reni had never painted a better picture. In October, 1640, the Queen intimated to his Eminence that she would be pleased to accept the work and in the following spring spoke of sending Fairfax for it to Leghorn. The Cardinal directed it to be taken *via* Marseilles, the Rhône and Lyons.[2] Possibly to compensate the Queen for the delay, Rossetti presented her Majesty with a large *Nativity* by Titian for Christmas, 1640. Charles was particularly delighted with this picture.[3]

Undoubtedly the most interesting of all the artistic transactions between Charles and Urban was the Bernini Bust of the English King. Charles had long been eager for a bust of himself from the scalpel of the Italian master who had already attained to European fame, and who was to leave so many marks of his genius within and without St Peter's and in the piazzas of Rome.

Charles was greatly gratified when the Pope, Bernini's patron, gave leave for the bust to be made, and the impossibility of his giving the artist a personal sitting was a difficulty ideally overcome by Van Dyck's painting the head of the King in three positions for the sculptor to copy. This portrait was taken to Rome by

---

[1] *B.L.* 8641, f. 200 : Barberini to Con, Nov. 21, 1637. *B.L.* 8642, ff. 29, 92 : Same to same, Jan. 9 ; Feb. 20, 1638. There are two pictures of Bacchus and Ariadne by Reni known at present, — in the Galleria San Luca, and in the Galleria Albani, both in Rome. Cf. *Allgemeines Lexikon der bildenden Künstler, s. v. Reni.*

[2] *P.R.O. Rom. Trans : Rossetti Corr.,* vol. II, f. 74 : Rossetti to Barberini, Oct. 9/19, 1640. *Ibid.,* vol. III, ff. 129, 139 : Same to same, April 19, 1641 ; Barberini to Rossetti, April 20, 1641.

[3] *Ibid.,* vol. II, f. 237 : Rossetti to Barberini, Dec. 28, 1640.

a Mr Baker, and the work was begun. [1]   In August, 1636, it was reported as nearly finished, but it was not until April of the following year that Barberini wrote to say he had seen the bust, to which Bernini had given of his best, though under the circumstances it was impossible to expect a perfect likeness. [2] In fact Bernini declared next year to Nicholas Stone, a young English sculptor working in his studio in Rome : " I conclude that itt is the impossiblest thinge in the world to make a picture in stone naturally to resemble any person. " [3]

The work caused great interest in Rome, Cardinals, Ambassadors and all persons of quality flocking to see it before it was sent to England.   There were a few stains in the marble on the forehead, but, as one wag suggested, these would quickly disappear once the King became a Catholic ! [4]

Cardinal Barberini took infinite precautions over the transport of so precious a work of art to London. He appointed Thomas Chambers, a kinsman of Con's, to take charge of it, giving him minute instructions covering every phase of the journey, the people he was to meet, the type of boat to take, and the manner in which the bust was to be packed and guarded. There was

[1] The triple portrait remained in the possession of the sculptor's family at the Palazzo Bernini till 1796 when it was bought by Mr Irvine, a dealer, and from him passed through several dealers' hands till it was bought in 1822 by George IV, who placed it in the Picture Gallery at Windsor Castle, where it now hangs. (Cf. *Burlington Magazine*, vol. XIV, p. 338.)

[2] A. RIEGL, *Filippo Baldinucci's Vita des Gio. Lorenzo Bernini*, p. 116. *P.R.O. Rom. Trans.* : Panzani to Barberini, June 3/13, 1635 ; Aug. 15/25, 1636. *B.L.* 8640, f. 261 : Barberini to Con, April 27, 1637.

To demonstrate the difference between a bust taken from life and one made from a painting, Bernini was only too ready to accede to Mr Baker's request for one of himself and, although Urban vetoed the work when it was still only in mould, forbidding any bust but that of Charles to be sent to England, Bernini eventually finished it. After going through various hands, including those of Sir Peter Lely, Henry Grey, Duke of Kent, and Philip Yorke, 2nd Earl of Handwicke, this bust passed into the possession of the Marquess of Anglesey. (Cf. *Burlington Mazagine, loc. cit.*)

[3] *Burlington Magazine, loc. cit.* In Oct., 1638, Nicholas Stone the younger, son of the well-known London sculptor and tomb-maker, worked in Bernini's studio and kept a diary of his conversations with the sculptor on the subject of the King's bust. This document is in the British Museum, *Harl. MSS.* 4049.

[4] *B.L.* 8645, f. 152 : Ferragalli to Con, April 27, 1637,

is dated 1635, he did not die until 1669 and this may well be his work. [1]

A large part of Charles's collections of art treasures soon came under the auctioneer's mallet and found eager buyers in Queen Christina of Sweden, the Duc d'Orléans and other European royalties. In March, 1649, Parliament appointed a commission to draw up an inventory of the personal effects of the late King, of the Queen and of Prince Charles. The complete catalogue was " a magnificent folio of near 1,000 pages, of an extraordinary dimension, bound in crimson velvet and richly gilt, written in a fair large hand, but with little knowledge of the objects which the inventory writer describes. " The sale spread over the years 1649-1652 and some of the prices fetched are illuminating. A Raphael *Madonna* brought in £1,000 ; a *Nativity* by Giulio (Pippi) Romano, the pupil and companion of Raphael, £500 ; a small *Madonna and Child* by Raphael, £800 ; several *Titians* made about £100 apiece, while a small equestrian portrait of Charles by Van Dyck was bought for £20 by Sir Balthazar Gerbier, the Court painter and diplomat, whom Van Dyck had superseded. [2]

---

[1] Cf. *Bryan's Dictionary of Painters and Engravers*, s. v. *Robert Van Voerst*.

[2] G. S. Stevenson, *Charles I in Captivity, Introduction*, p. 30 ; Adams, *op. cit.*, pp. 137-139.

APPENDIX II

No Bishop, No King   (King James's slogan
at Hampton Court Conference, 1604.)

It was evident to all that one of the major issues in the war
between Charles I and his subjects, English and Scottish, was
the position of the episcopate in the government of the Church.
As old Sir Edmund Verney grumbled on the morning of Edge Hill
(Oct. 23, 1642), the war was all about bishops, and he detested
bishops. [1]

In the light of this it is interesting to watch the evolution of
Charles's mind on the status of the episcopate, for the opportunities he had at Court of finding out the Catholic view in talking
with the Queen's confessor and the Papal Agent undoubtedly
influenced him.

In April, 1635, Panzani records a conversation at table in which
the King started to argue whether the Catholic view really was
that bishops were *de jure divino*. A Scottish Catholic present
maintained that it was, which the King denied and took a wager
on it. The question was referred to Fr Philip, who decided in
favour of the Scot, but Charles would have none of it and said
he wanted to consult others on the point. [2]

Subsequently, the King had a number of discussions with
Fr Philip on the subject. He was still not convinced of the
Catholic view, when Con arrived to be confronted with the same
question. The Agent assured Charles that the Council of Trent
held that Bishops were *de jure divino* in the Church. The King
said he would give anything to see an autograph of the Pope
subscribing to the same opinion. Con told him that his Holiness
was not in the habit of putting his signature to anything so easily,
but said there were many ways of assuring his Majesty of the
mind of the Pope on this truth. Fr Philip asked Con to have

---

[1] Evan John, *op. cit.,* p. 246.
[2] *P.R.O. Rom. Trans.* : Panzani to Barberini, April 17/27 1635.

sent from Rome some testimonial that the Pope did hold this doctrine, as it would be a good thing for the King to be enlightened for once on a dogma of the Church, and would show up the malice of those who misinterpreted her. Con made some excuse and changed the conversation, but in his next despatch he mentioned it to the Cardinal Secretary, leaving the matter entirely at his discretion while suggesting that the subject could be introduced in a letter sent to him to the effect that his Holiness, wishing to clear up any misunderstanding there might be as to the divine origin of the episcopate, would not promulgate any new definition but simply insist on making known the received teaching of the Church. [1]

Barberini evidently thought the matter important as he wrote back to say that the advisability of writing in the way Con suggested had been discussed on Saturday, March 7 (N. S.), by a congregation of Cardinals presided over by the Cardinal di Sant' Onofrio (Antonio Barberini, Senior, the Pope's Capuchin brother). Their Eminences asked the Secretary, Mgr Boccabella, to appoint as soon as possible a committee of theologians to draw up their opinion. [2]

As far as Rome was concerned, the matter was in safe hands and there it was to stay for some time ; Charles, however, was restless and had the question constantly in mind.

A month or two earlier he had discussed royal appointments to bishoprics with Con and the Ambassador of Parma. Charles said that the Kings of France and Spain conferred bishoprics just as freely as the King of England. This the Ambassador denied, saying that the Pope made the decision. Con then reconciled the divergent views by explaining that the King often recommended a candidate, though the Pope actually conferred the See. Charles said that these were recommendations the Pope could not reject. Con denied this but agreed that generally the Pope was pleased to accept the King's candidates when they were worthy. [3] Commenting on Con's report, Barberini challenged the King to cite any particular case : there were many complaints, on the contrary, that the Pope wished to be independent of princes. [4]

---

[1] *B.L.* 8640, ff. 52-53 : Con to Barberini, Hampton, Jan. 5/15, 1637.
[2] *B.L.* 8640, f. 170 : Barberini to Con, March 12, 1637.
[3] *Ibid.*, f. 12 : Con to Barberini, Hampton, Dec. 22/Jan. 1, 1636/7.
[4] *B.L.* 8642, f. 117 : Barberini to Con, March 6, 1638.

A year and more had passed and still no reply from Rome, when Charles again broached the subject that worried him, reproaching Con for never having let him know the Pope's opinion. The Agent answered that his Holiness's views were known to the whole world and, as he was his representative in England, his Majesty might well believe him on such matters. At this Charles said in triumph : " Did I not tell you more than a year ago that you would never show me the Pope's opinion in writing?" This, Con said, he had never promised to do. " Yes, that is true," rejoined the King smartly, " because you did not wish to pledge yourself to anything that would not succeed. I tell you I have again had information how they negotiate in Rome." [1] " God grant your Majesty's information is good and true," the Agent replied with a touch of sarcasm, and changed the conversation.

He immediately wrote off to Barberini complaining of the mortification he felt at the non-arrival of Rome's answer to the King's persistent questioning. The Cardinal Secretary replied by return that the tradition in the Roman Church, from St Peter to Pope Urban, clearly showed the opinion of the Apostolic See on the ordination of bishops, a view that the Pope would very much like to put into practice by placing a bishop in England, were he not held back by fear of harming the cause of the Catholics in that country. Session XXIII, Cap. 4, of the Council of Trent gave the mind of the Holy See regarding the ecclesiastical hierarchy. The Cardinal added that he was exceedingly pleased the King was not afraid of discussing these questions with the Pope's Agent. [2]

---

[1] *B.L.* 8643, ff. 77, 80 : Con to Barberini, London, Aug. 24/ Sept. 3, 1638.

[2] *B.L.* 8640, f. 123 : Barberini to Con, Oct.9,1638. The theologians of Trent appear to have been as wary of committing themselves as Barberini was now. After the question of the divine origin of the episcopate had provoked heated debate, the Council was content simply to declare bishops to be the successors of the Apostles and higher in the hierarchy than priests ; as such they reserved to themselves the administration of some sacraments and certain other functions. But there is no pronouncement on the superiority of the episcopate over the priesthood as of divine right. In Canon 6, which defines the composition of the Sacred Hierarchy and the position of bishops appointed by the Holy Ghost as the rulers of the Church, there is not the slightest mention of the immediate or mediate origin of their jurisdiction. Cf. A. MICHEL, *Ordre, Concile de Trent,* in the *Dictionnaire de theologie catholique,* col. 1358-1359. For the actual text of Trent, cf. DENZINGER-BANNWART, N. 960 (ed. 1928).

To Con this reply was not very satisfactory; he had all along been pressed by the King for a signed statement of the Pope rather than a reference to former canons. He suspected, as he bluntly told Barberini, that someone who knew the King better than he had advised the Cardinal over his (Con's) head not to give the desired declaration.

Meanwhile the Agent had discovered the reason for the King's persistent demands: someone had put it into his head that the Jesuits held, as the Puritans did, that episcopacy was not *de jure divino*, and that the Pope was unwilling to go against the opinions of the Society. [1] Barberini, on the other hand, suspected that Charles's interest in the matter was centred on its being shown that, as both popes and bishops received the same ordination from God, all enjoyed equal authority and that therefore the Roman Pontiff enjoyed no primacy of jurisdiction. [2]

The truth of the matter seems to have been that Charles's keenness for an authoritative statement by the Pope was simply that he might find a confirmation of what was now becoming his own view, as against that of the Puritans, who argued that episcopacy was simply a system of government that had been set up by the papal power and since rejected by all the reformed churches as injurious to the Church of Christ and the Civil State. " This is not to be found in the Apostles' writings, nor doth the Holy Ghost vouchsafe to name it, as being an overtopping title which Christ approves not of. " [3]   The Puritans were therefore attempting to carry the notion: *Prelacy equals Popery*, though many of their less extreme opponents, pleading for prelacy not as a divine institution but as necessary for the discipline and government of the Church, were trying to prove the opposite. Appealing to history, these latter claimed that " the abusing of episcopacie has beene a great and constant designe of the Papacie; and that it was so in the Trent Councell: no one thing having more exalted that Mother of Abominations, the See of Rome, than the exempting of Presbyters, as Jesuits and others, from the power and government of Bishops. " [4]

---

[1] *Ibid.*, f. 219 : Con to Barberini, Nov. 30/ Dec 10, 1638.

[2] *Ibid.*, f. 174 : Barberini to Con, Nov. 6, 1638.

[3] *An appeal... to every impartiall, iudicious and Godly Reader, whether the Presbyterie or Prelacie be the better Church-Government*, p. 12.

[4] *A modern Advertisement concerning the present Controversie about Church Government*, pp. 7, 9.

When the Puritans decided to attack on historical grounds, they used the argument, later to become so popular with the German higher critics of the history of religions, *viz.* that episcopacy was one of the many pagan institutions adopted and baptized by Christianity. The heathen Britons, they said, had their Archflamins and their Flamins ; the Archflamins of London, York and Chester became Archbishops ; the Flamins, Bishops. [1]

It was no secret that the attack on Prelacy in the Anglican Church was a means of delivering a back-handed blow at the encroachments of Popery and all that smacked thereof in Court circles. The Scottish Covenanters showed they realized this two-fold significance of the struggle by printing an amusing lampoon purporting to be a letter from Rossetti to Urban VIII, in which the Papal Agent predicts with the fall of episcopacy the ruin of the whole Catholic cause in England. " Oh the cunning Hereticks the Scots ! they have besieged us most subtilly and sprung a mine as it were under your Holinesse owne throne. Amongst other inveagling devices, they have coined such a blasphemous way of argumenting against Venerable Episcopacy, that it will prove most destructive of that heavenly Hierarchy, by which your Holinesse had anchored on the beauty of this Church. As to the Assembly of the high Court of Parliament here .. 'tis more terrible then many Armies with bannies, and by unmercifull wayes intends a mighty vengeance against the Romish and Prelate faction. Your Holinesse had wisely, and effectually too, established your right, and continued your possession in those parts, by that Hierarchy : But now the glory is departed from those mighty Champions." [2]

From this triumphantly ironical little forgery it will be seen there was no doubt in the minds of Charles's opponents as to the significance of the " Bishops Wars." Laud's regulations for the reform of discipline within the Church, the encroachment of authority by the Ecclesiastical Courts,— all this they mistakenly coupled with the known conversion movement towards Rome, and the improved status of the Catholics due to Charles's personal views on toleration and his regard for the Papal Agent. To the

---

[1] *The Petition for the Prelates briefly examined,* p. 10.
[2] *The Passionate Remonstrance, Rozzetti's Letter* (no pagination).

Calvinist, whether English Puritan or Scottish Presbyterian, Prelacy meant a stepping-stone to Popery and insistence on it by the King and the Archbishop was a warranty of their ultimate aims.

The Puritans attacked the Ecclesiastical Courts not only in the exercise of their jurisdiction, but still more did they call in question the source from which it was derived. In a speech to the House on the national grievances, John Pym made as if to uphold the prerogatives of the Crown against these Courts, which claimed their jurisdiction as of divine right and not through the King.[1] The anti-royalist leader probably knew well enough that he would only be embarrassing the King by pleading a prerogative of the Crown to which Charles no longer laid claim. Several years earlier the King had issued an edict renouncing all spiritual jurisdiction in favour of the Ecclesiastical Courts,[2] and even before that he had caused a considerable discussion at Court by denying in the presence of his courtiers that he was head of the Church.[3]

Later, by the time the practical issue between the two parties had been joined, Charles had become convinced in his own mind. Taking his stand on the unanimous consent of the Fathers and the teaching of the early Church, he saw that episcopacy had clearly been the primitive form of Church Government and that the distinction between a *presbyteros* and an *episcopos* had been quite definitely held, since the former could not lawfully ordain.[4] He was therefore convinced that his fight for episcopacy was a fight for an article of faith in which his conscience would not allow him to yield one jot. " I believe," he wrote to his wife

[1] *Calendar of State Papers* (1640), p. 46 : *Minute of John Pym's Speech*, April 17, 1640.

[2] *B.L.* 8641, f. 93 : Con to Barberini, London, Sept. 1/11, 1637 : " è uscito un' editto nel quale il Rè rinuncia alla giurisditt^{ne} spirituale rimettendola alla Corte Ecc^{ca}."

[3] *B.L.* 8640, f. 194 : Con to Barberini, London, 9/19 March, 1637. This disavowal was occasioned by the publication in Passau of a book which declared that the Kings of England were so many Antichrists as they claimed the headship of the Church. Charles said he made light of the book, as he was not head of the Church.

[4] *The Papers which passed at Newcastle betwixt his Sacred Majestie and Mr Al. Henderson : concerning the Change of Church Government. Anno Dom.* 1646 (London 1649).

in 1646, " the bishops are *jure divino*, because I find as much authority for them as for some articles of the creed ; and for the Presbyterian Government, I hold it absolutely unlawful, one chief (among many) argument being, that it never came into any country but by rebellion." [1]

---

[1] *Charles in* 1646, p. 26 : Charles to Henrietta, Oxford, March 16, 1645/6.

APPENDIX III

Memorandum on the Franco-Spanish league against England

(Cf. Chap. III)

Copia della memoria data dall' Amb[re] di Spagna al P[re] Berullo nell' affare d'Inghilterra. (*B.L.* 8065, ff. 360-361 : Sent by Spada, Oct. 23, deciphered Nov. 4, 1626.)

N. B. Certain italianisms introduced here by the copyist have been replaced by the original Spanish words.

Que la Francia approvaba el designio que el Rey de España tenia de resentirse del mal proceder de los Ingleses, que dezian que él queria hazer una entrada en Irlanda por el interés de la Religión, sobre lo qual el S[nr] Card[l] dixo que no podria bastantemente alabar este buen zelo, que creya que Dios pedia alguna de estas dos Coronas en un tal sujeto, y podria asegurar que el Rey su' Amo escucharia esto con mucho gusto, y que le pareze que los Ingleses querian forzar la Francia y la España, que si el Rey tuviera Vaxelles pudieran hazer con puntamiento una buena entrada, y que al mismo tiempo que la España emprenderia la Irlanda, la Francia emprenderá asi la Isla Aouic (sic - *i.e.* Wight), por lo qual obligava después a la Englatera a establecer y asegurar la Religión... Que si se haze un tratado entre las dos coronas para unirse en un mayor designio, la primera cosa que será menester hazer, es obligarse á no hazer ningún accuerdo con los Ingleses sin el consentimiento de uno y del otro.

Que desde luego se dava palabra, que quando este tratado no se hiciese (?), y quando asi mismo la Englaterra diese satisfacción a la Francia en lo presente, no por eso se hará oposición a la entrepresa dispuesta por la España, y que hallará S. M[d] Chss[a]. la asistencia de Vituallas y otras cosas como estado arriba.

APPENDIX IV

MEMORANDUM, WITH QUESTIONS AND ANSWERS,
SUBMITTED BY SIR ROBERT DOUGLAS TO POPE URBAN VIII,
LATER SENT BY BARBERINI TO CARDINAL DEL BAGNO,
Feb. 11, 1634.

(Cf. Chap. V).

A. (*B.L.* 8656, f. 175.)

Douglas's Request.

P^{mo} che cosa possono sperar i Cattolici, quando venisse qualche persecutione.

2. Che aiuto sì darebbe alla Regina per avanzamento della Relig^{ne} Catt^{ca}, e stabilimento del suo stato, quando il Rè venisse à morir prima di Lei.

3. Sì piacesse à N. S^{re}, et à S. Em^{za} di mandar un' confidente in Germania che indirettamente potesse avanzar le cose desiderate da Rè.

4. Che N. S^{re} prometta al Sr Roberto di realmente dare ogni assistenza alla pacifica restitutione del Palatino, secluso però il pregiudicio della Relig^{ne} Catt^{ca}.

5. Che S. Em^{za} scrive al Sr Card^{le} di Bagno di trattar liberam^{te} co'l Sr Roberto sopra questo punto del Palatino. E che gli dica il suo parere. E in che può aiutere il Rè. E che S. Em^{za} scrivi al Segretario pienam^{te} lo stato del negocio, e come hà procedute il Sr Roberto.

Urban's Answer.

Che S.S^{tà} sempre gli abbraccerà. e che n'hà data però la protettione à suo Nipote.

Che proponga i remedii per questo mentre che così in generale non sì può antivedere in che disposit^{ne} starà il mondo.

Che bisogna sempre presupporre il bene della Relig^{ne} Catt^{ca} del resto che potrà trattar co'l Card^{le} Barberino e se li pare potrà accennar del Card^{le} di Bagni.

Il simile al 4º e con parole generali.

Al 5º parimente.

Douglas's Request (contd)

6. Che'l P. Alessandro habbi licenza di scrivere al Segretario.

7. Che N. S^re dia ordini al Sr Roberto d'informar il Rè del danno che può arrivar alli Regni di S. M^ta, sè non permette liberam^te che s'accommodino le differenze trà li Missionarii.

Urban's Answer (contd)

Che S. Sta ne parlerà al Card^le Barberino.

Si può discorrere più in generale parendo le particolarità, come riguardano cose politiche, forse minori all' autorità di S. Sta nondimeno quando li paia, accennarli e il mantener dua partiti per Principi forastieri in Inghilterra, e cosi per q'sta via si sappia tutto quello si fà nella Corte.

B. (*B. L.* 8656, f. 177.)

Alcuni considerationi per S. Em^za (*i. e.* from Barberini to Bagno) Alcuni punti che egli (Douglas) hà desiderato, che sè gli incarichino in nome di S. B^ne. (Enclosed, Barberini to Bagno, Feb. 11, 1634.)

Sarebbe bene che'l Sr Roberto Duglasio fosse incaricato da N. S^re e da V. Em^za delli sequenti punti ; et il med^mo Sr Roberto lo desidera, e stima necessario.

P^mo che S. M^ta Rè della Gran' Bretagna non permetta in modo alcuno, che li Cattolici siano molestati da quelli Persuivant, come si chiamano ; S. M^ta non ne riceve utile alcuno, mà si bene alienatione de Catt^cl.

2°. che S. M^ta vogli moderare le contributioni et esattione de danari cavati da Catt^cl, ecc.

3°. che S. M^ta dichiari la sua mente, se gli aggradisce d'haver per li Catt^cl sudditi suoi uno, o più Vescovi.

4°. che S. M^ta voglia mandar quî un confidente, che risieda presso N. S^re in nome della Regina e prometta che un' altra persona stia à Londra segretam^te sotto la protettione della Regina ; per il cui mezo si possi trattare di aggiustar ogni accidente et intentione.

APPENDIX V

PANZANI'S ACCOUNT OF THE ANGLICAN BISHOPS

(Cf. Chap. VII)

(*P.R.O. Rom. Trans.*: Panzani to Barberini, Apr. 27/ May 7, 1636.)
(*N.B.* To facilitate identification, proper names have been translated.)

1. CANTERBURY (William Laud): huomo dotto e prudente, è stato Vicecancellario nell'Univ. d'Oxford. Dopoi è stato fatto Vescovo di Londra, e poi Arcivescovo di Cantuaria. E celibe, hà circa 60 anni; è piccolo di statua; è il primo del Consiglio del Rè; è d'animo moderato, e non alieno dalla Religione Cattolica; con tutto il suo sforzo attende all'utile del Rè, et ad accrescer l'entrate Regie, e forsi per questa ragione è più grato al Rè di qualsivoglia Consigliere. E pronto à tutti li Consegli di qualsivoglia affare, e le cose Ecclesiastiche di questo Rè in tutto, e per tutto sono regolate da lui. E tenuto Arminiano e quasi in tutti li Dogmi s'accosta molto alla Chiesa Romana. Onde dopo che hà acquistata la gratia del Rè hà innovato circa la Religione tanto nella Chiesa d'Inghilterra quanto di Scotia. Hà fatto erigger Altari e metter imagini sacre in molti luoghi. Hà molto à cuore l'honore e gloria del Clero. Molti pensano che habbia in animo di riconciliare questa Chiesa con Roma; altri credono il contrario; e gli uni, et gli altri hanno le sue ragioni, perche da una parte si vede che affetta d'accommodarsi alli riti Cattolici in diverse cose, ne' pare habbia in odio la Religion Cattolica ô li Cattolici. Dall' altra parte alcune volte si mostra rigidissimo contra li Cattolici, mà questo da alcuni è interpretato che lo faccia non per odio della Religione, mà per una certa prudenza per meglio sfuggire li rumori, e querele de Puritani. Favorisce in estremo il Giuramento di fedeltà; et in questo è inessorabile contro Cattolici

2. LONDON (William Juxon): nato in Cicestria del Contado di Sussexia di parenti assai mediocri, hà 48 anni, alto di corpo e magro, è assai sano, hà studiato in Oxford; è stato fatto Vescovo di Londra e Decano delle Cappella Regia per opera del Cantuariense, e dall'istesso ultimamente è stato fatto Tesoriere. E molto

dedito alla caccia, è celibe, molte moderato, si crede Arminiano
odia molto li Puritani e li Giesuiti, depende in tutto dall'
Arcivescovo, ancorche prima d'esser Tesoriere mostrasse amicitia
col Sr Cottington, et adesso per esser novo nell'Officio, tuttavia
spesso tratta coll'istesso Cottington. E poco versato nelle cose
politiche ; professa di non haver altra mira che all'utile del Rè,
e però voler attendere al Tesoriato con le mani nette, il che anche
disse al Rè, quando gli diede detto Officio. E molto moderato
nelli suoi affetti. E lontano da ogni sorte di fasto et ambitione.

3. YORK (Richard Neyle) : coniugato ; del consiglio del Rè ;
assai moderato.

4. DURHAM (Thomas Morton) : celibe, violente Puritanissimo,
molto dotto, e nostro nemicissimo.

5. WINCHESTER (Walter Curle) : dotto, coniugato, moderato.

6. WORCESTER (John Thornborough) : decrepito, dotto, moderato, coniugato.

7. CHESTER (John Bridgeman) : doto, coniugato, moderato.

8. St DAVID's (Theophilus Field) : molto moderato e faceto.

9. LINCOLN (John Williams) : molto nobile, celibe, dotto,
moderatissimo, inimico del Cantuariense, e seconde alcuni amico
de Giesuiti, si non per altro per valersi de loro amici.

10. SALISBURY (John Davenant) : dotto, celibe, vecchio, nemicissimo nostro.

11. COVENTRY (Robert Wright) : coniugato, quasi Cattolico.

12. GLOUCESTER (Godfrey Goodman) : celibe, moderatissimo
e vorrebbe haver un Sacerdote in casa Cattolico.

13. ELY (Francis White) : coniugato, dotto, già era molto
nemico, adesso s'è aliquanto moderato.

14. EXETER (Joseph Hall) : dotto, coniugato ; hà stampato
Puritanissimo.

15. LLANDAFF (William Murray) : molto moderato.

16. CHICHESTER (Richard Montague) : dotto, coniugato, hà
stampato molto, adesso stampa le historie Ecclesiastiche, e professa
d'andar per il meza poiche, come esso dice, le Centuriatori Magde-
burgensi hanno dato troppo contro la chiesa Romana et il Baronio
gli è stato troppo favorevole ; è moderatissimo, di circa 60 anni,
mà secco, e però si crede sia per viver molto se il mal di pietra
non l'uccide. Un' suo figlio vuol venire a Roma. Sarebbe bene
che qualche Cattolico non Giesuita, di dottrina insigne, e prattico
delle lingue pigliasse amicitia seco almeno con lettere, e studiasse

il suo apparato all' historia ecclesiastica, e vedesse di mostrargli dolcemente li suoi errori accio li possa corregere con honor suo, che, se si và per via [di] correttioni, e prohibitioni publiche, saremo ruinate, e questo punto è molto considerabile, perche essendo egli dottissimo, e versatissimo in tutte le lingue, e rimaneggiando li principali della nostra Religione, può far incredibile danno et utile.

17. NORWICH (Richard Corbet): coniugato, non male affetto alla nostra religione. (N. B. Panzani gives the name RICHARD BENE. He is confusing two names, *viz.* Richard Corbet, Bishop of Norwich, 1632-1635, and Matthew Wren, who held the see from 1625-1638. Panzani, using an old list, gives Wren under Hereford. Cf. LE NEVE, *Fasti Ecclesiae Anglicanae, in loco.*)

18. CARLISLE (Barnaby Potter): coniugato, non è cattivo.

19. St ASAPH (John Owen): assai buono.

20. ROCHESTER (John Bowle): puritanissimo.

21. BATH & WELLS (William Price): coniugato, non molto cattivo.

22. OXFORD (John Bancroft): celibe, molto versato nella politica ecclesiastica, et è molto nostro amico.

23. BRISTOL (George Coke): vive molto cauto, e però non si conosce la sua natura.

24. BANGOR (Edmund Griffith): moderatissimo.

25. PETERBOROUGH (Francis Dee): non cattivo.

26. HEREFORD (Matthew Wren) molto moderato.

27. Il vescovo dell'ISOLA DI MONA non è cattivo mà non è Barone, onde non entra nel Parlemento.

APPENDIX VI

(Cf. Chap. IX)

(*B.L.* 8641, f. 146 : enclosure from Con to Barberini, London, Dec. 20, 1637,
reached Rome, Jan. 8, 1638).

The Kings Majesty finding of late that some of His Majesties naturall born Subjects have abused His Majesties Princely goodnesse and the ease which they enjoy under His gracious and milde Government by withdrawing sundry His subjects to the Romaine superstition, and to forsake the Church of England ; and likewise by resorting to Masses, and service celebrated according to the Rites of the Church of Rome, expresly contrary to the Lawes of this Realm, and in contempt of sundry Acts of Parliament, Proclamations, and Orders of the Privie Councell, and to the great scandall of His Majesties Government both in Church and State ; For prevention whereof for the time to come, and for the preservation of Religion, as it stands established in the Church of England, which His Majestie is resolved constantly to maintain ; His Majestie in His Princely Wisdome, hath thought fit to set forth this declaration of His Roayall Will and Pleasure ; whereby He doth not only straightly charge and command all and every His subjects to take notice, that the former Statutes, Proclamations and Orders of the Privie Councell, published and made for reformation of the like misdemeanors, are still in full force, but expresly wills and commands all and every person and persons, Clerks and Lay, that they from henceforth forbear to attempt or endeavour to withdraw any of His Majesties subjects from Religion, as it is now professed in the Church of England, or by perswasions or any other means to distract them in the same, or to sollicite them to adhere to the Church of Rome ; under pain of the severest punishments which by the Lawes and Statutes in such case are provided. And His Majestie doth hereby further declare, that if any of the Romane party shall from henceforth, in contempt of this His Majesties Admonition, and of the Statutes, Proclamations, and Orders abovesaid, give scandall by celebrating or hearing of any Masse or Masses, or any other Service which shall be celebrated after the Rites of the Church of Rome, That then His Majestie will cause to be put in execution against such contumacious persons, those penalties which by the Lawes and Statutes are to be inflicted upon all those that wilfully and scandalously transgresse the same. And of this His Majestie will expect a better accompt of His Officers and Ministers whom it shall concern, then heretofore they have made.

Given at the Court of Whitehall, the twentieth day of December, in the thirteenth yeare of His Majesties Reign.

GOD SAVE THE KING

Imprinted at London by Robert Barker, Printer to the Kings most excellent Majestie: And by the Assignes of John Bill 1637.

APPENDIX VII

(a) ITALIAN TRANSLATION OF THE OATH
COMPOSED BY CHARLES WITH CON'S ASSISTANCE
(English version not to be found)

(Cf. Chap. XI)

(*B.L.* 8639, f. 265 : Con to Barberini, Dec. 1/11, 1636.)

Io prometto e giuro avanti Dio onnipotente nella più stretto et obligatoria forma che quasivoglia giuram^{to} può esser preso da un christiano, che io per sempre conserverò al nostro gratioso e legitimo Rè, e naturale sovrano il Rè Carlo e suoi heredi e successori vera fedeltà et allegantia (*sic*) in quella più ampia maniera che un suddito christiano deve far al suo Rè, e sovrano Principe, e per testificar questo veram^{te} *stimo mio debito* di giurar come segue e per tanto : Prometto e giuro che defenderò esso e loro fin'all'ultimo del mio puotere, anzi con perdita delle mie fortune e vita contro tutte le leghe, invasioni, *depositioni*, ribellioni, cospirationi, imprese et assumpti che saranno fatti contro la sua ò loro persone, corone ò dignità da qualsivoglia Principe, *Sacerdote* ò Potentato, Popolo ò persona particolare, domestica ò forestiera, sotto pretesto di ben publico, *Religione*, ò qualsivoglia colore ò causa che vi sia.   Parimente prometto e giuro che in qualsivoglia tempo verrò à sapere à casa à fuori di qualche trattato, cospiratt^{ne}, tradimento, lega, segreta machinat^{ne} ò attentato spettante all' invasione, danno ò pregiudicio della sua ò loro persone, stati ò dominii, ò per terra, ò per mare, di opporre me stesso, et impedirli conforme al mio potere, et a scuoprire à Lui ò Loro, quello che verrò a sapere con ogni diligenza possibile e fretta, *essendo questo il mio debito d'un christiano, e fedel suddito* Parimente prometto e giuro come sopra che non ammetterò alcuna conferenza di dottrina che mi possa rimuovere da questa mia legitima fedeltà e giuram^{to}, mà scuoprirò quelli che procureranno di sedurmi dall' effettuat^{te} di quello, al quale, *per leggi di Dio et huomini, e questo mio giuramento* mi confesso obligato.   Parimente giuro e prometto come sopra, che io nè procurerò da per me stesso ne essendo procurato da altri nemici e malevoli del mio Sovrano, accettar nessuna rilassatione da questo mio giuram^{to} e fedeltà, e contravenendo à qualsivoglia punto di ciò, sarò colpevole di spergiuro, e sommo tradimento contro Dio et il mio Principe. E tutto questo sopra detto, con ciascheduna parte di esso, prometto e giuro fedeltà certam^te conforme al senso litterale delle parole senza equivocatione ò riservatione mentale renuntiando avanti Dio e gli huomini à tutte le espositioni, quali possono pervertere in qualsivoglia modo questa mia dovuta a sincera fedeltà.

(b) THE KING'S ARMY OATH.

(B.L. 8644, f. 217: Con to Barberini, Apr. 26/May 6, 1639.) (Ital. copy, *ibid.,* f. 216).

I, *A.B.,* doe sweare before the Almightie, and everliving God, that I will beare all faithfull alleageance to my true, and undoubted Souraigne lord King Charles, who is lawfull King of this Iland, and all other his kingdomes, and Dominions, both by sea, and land, by the lawes of God, and Man, and by lawfull Succession. And that I will most constantly, and cherefullie, even to the uttermost hazard of my life and fortunes oppose all Seditions, Rebellions, Conspiracies, Couenants, Coniurations and Treasons whatsoever against his Royall dignitie, Crowne, or Person raised, or sett up under what pretence, or colour whatsoever. And if it shall come wailed under pretence of Religion, I hold it more abominable before God, and Man : And this Oath I take uoluntarilie in the true faith of a Good Christian, and most loyall subiect, without any equiuocation, or mentall reseruation whatsoeuer, from which I hold no power on earth can absolue me in any part.

(c) FORMULA SUGGESTED BY CARDINAL BARBERINI.

(B.L. 8642, ff. 81-82 : Barberini to Con, Feb. 6, 1638.)

Ego *N.* uerè et sincere agnosco in conscientia mea coram Deo et Mundo, sereniss^m D.N. pro legitimo ueroq. huius Regni et aliorum M^tis Suae Dominiorum et Regnorum Rege, et eidem tanquam supremo Dn̄o et uero Principi super me immediate post Deum in temporalibus constituto, honorem exhibebo, seruiam atq. obediam. Iuro preterea me pro uirili cum omnibus bonis, corpore, et uita, M^tis

suae personam, coronam, et dignitatem et legitimos similiter heredes,
et successores illius contra quoscumq. conatus, qui iniustè in eum,
uel eorum aliquem quomodolibet fient siuè domi intra Regnum,
siuè foris, per conspirationes, rebelliones, proditiones, machinationes
ac seditiones defensurum.   Et iurabo quantum in me est, ut Conatus
ac alia prodita M^{tis} suae, seu heredibus et successoribus eius dete-
gantur, et patefiant. Deniq. iuro, me numquam absolutionem
aliquam ac dispensationem procuraturum, cum mea deliberata
uoluntas sit, omnia et singula supra expressa firmiter et inuiolabiliter,
semper, et ubiq. seruare, et hoc sincère iuxta co[mmun]em sensum,
et intellectum uerborum, absq. omni equiuocatione, mentali eua-
tione, uel secreta quacumq. reseruatione, sic me Deus adiuvet, etc.

APPENDIX VIII

AN ANONYMOUS DOCUMENT
PURPORTING TO BE WRITTEN IN THE KING'S NAME,
AND REQUESTING THAT
GEORGE CON SHOULD NOT BE ADVANCED TO THE PURPLE,
MARCH, 1638/9?

(Cf. Chap. XII)

(*B.L.* 8615, f. 64.)

Londini 22 Martij stylo veteri.

Dnus secretarius habet a Rege mandatū scribendi vobis vt cure-
tis significari S^mo et Em^mo Barberino, tantū ab esse vt sit desideriis maiestatis suae, vt promoveatur Dnus Georgius Conaeus, quod
potius existimabit praeiudiciū sibi factum ; hoc presertim tempore,
quo status Rerum talem promotionem non fert. Haec est vera et
substantialis ratio, et debetis eam urgere.

Recipietis literas a dno Secret : hodie vel cras circa promotionem
D. Georgij, debebant simul cū his mitti, sed iā mittentur via ordinaria. ex his videbitis clare quae sit mens Maiestatis suae circa eam
promotionē, et simili tenore debetis procedere.

This document asking, in the King's name, for the Red Hat *not*
to be conferred on Con may clearly have an important bearing on
the long postponement according to the year to which it is assigned ;
unfortunately only the month is given.

If it had been sent in March, 1637 or 1638, it would go far to
explain Rome's persistent delay. This seems hardly likely, however,
as up to as late as Jan. 1639, Charles was talking as if he still wanted
Con's promotion (cf.p. 313 n. 1). Also, about the same date Hamilton,
to whom this dispatch was in all probability sent, was still advocating Con's cause. Nevertheless in the light of Charles's cryptic
remark to Con in *March*, 1638, (cf. p. 282) this letter must be
given full significance.

APPENDIX IX

LETTER FROM SUPERIOR OF MISSIONARIES TO THEIR SUBORDINATES
URGING CATHOLIC CONTRIBUTION

(Cf. Chap. XIV)

(*B.L.* 8644, f. 176.   Sent with Con's despatch of April 5/15, 1639.)

The enclosed Aduises and Motiues, being so ample, as you will perceaue by perusing them, it will not be needfull that we enlarge ourselves upon anie Particulars, concerning the conduct of the Business, w^hc they direct the way in.   This therefore serueth only to conuey them to you, as we are entreated by those that have mett heer, and haue undertaken to doo ; and to desire you to repaire immediately unto ye Collectour, to whome ye enclosed Motiues are diuerted, and to deliuer the same unto him, in the name of all the Noblemen, and Gentlemen, togeather with ourselves assembled heer at London, by the Queenes comandment, to sett forward the worke.   And we pray you, assure him in the most efficacious manner you can (engaging all our creditts for the Truthe thereof) that it is the sense of us all, both Eccleciasticall and lay persons ; that besides the discharging of their, and our duties, to God, and the King, it mainly importeth the good of Catholicks, to haue this busines to be good successe.   Therefore entreate him to deale actiuely, and efficaciously, and speedily, according to those Aduises and Motiues.   We are so wel perswaded of his deuotion, to putt forward so pious a werke, as that we doubt not, but he will be as wel satisfyed in the needfulnes of the thing, and be readie to employ himself in it (receauing the assurances thereof, and perswasions thereunto, only from our hands) as if they came by all the most formall wayes, that can be imagined ; which, in a busines of this nature, can not be expected.   And although the Aduises and Motiues be diuerted only to Lay Gentlemen, yet we desire you (and we haue answered for you, y^t you will) employ yourself, and tell those that depend on you, sincerely to sollicite and dispose all their mindes, whome you haue relation unto as powerfully as you can, to contribute chearfully, and Bountifully upon this occasion : which, as it is the first that euer we laboured in, of this kinde ; so

we hope in God, it will be the last ; there being no probabilitie of
so pressing and so urgent a necessitie to occurre anie more.

Yours

Ant : Champney

William Price

Thomas Dede

ffrancis Dauenport

Henry More

London this 4th
of Aprill 1639

     * This letter was to authorize other letters to be sent out. (The Superior
of the Carmelites was absent, and did not sign.)

APPENDIX X

AUTOGRAPH LETTERS OF CHARLES I
TO INNOCENT X AND CARDINAL SPADA
PROMISING TO FULFIL WHATEVER ARRANGEMENT GLAMORGAN
MIGHT MAKE IN HIS NAME
i. e., WITH RINUCCINI AND THE IRISH CONFEDERATES

(*Arch. Vat., Instrumenta Miscellanea,* N° 6635.)

Beatissime Pater,

Tot tantaque testimonia fidelitatis et affectus consanguinei nostri Comitis Glamorganiae iamdudum accipimus, eamque in illo fiduciam, meritò reponimus, ut Sanctitas Vestra ei fidem meritò praebere possit, in quacunque re, de qua vel per se, vel per alium nostro nomine cum Sant^a Vestra tractaturus sit. Quaecunque verò ab ipso certò statuta fuerint, ea munire et confirmare pollicemur. In cujus rei testimonium brevissimas has scripsimus manu et sigillo nostro munitas, qui nihil magis habemus in votis, quam ut favore vestro in eum statum redigamur, quo palam profiteamur nos,

Sanctitatis Vestrae
Humillimum et obedientissimum
servum

Apud Curiam nostram
Oxoniae Octob : 20. 1645

CHARLES R.

(size, 17 × 10.7 cm.)

Eminentisseme Domine. Pauca scripsimus B^{mo} Patri de fide adhibenda consanguineo nostro Comiti Glamorganiae, vel cuilibet ab eo delegato : quem ut Emin^a V^a pariter omni favore prosequatur, rogamus : certoque credat nos ratum habituros, quicquid a praedicto Comite, vel suo Delegato cum Sanct^{mo} Patre, vel Eminentia Vestra transactum fuerit.

Emin^{ae} V^{ae}
Fidelissimus Amicus

CHARLES R.

Apud Curiam
nostram Oxoniae
Octob : 20 1645.

(size, 9.5 × 8.5 cm. with the seals intact.)

APPENDIX XI

(*Southwark Diocesan Archives*: *Gradwell MSS.*, vol. I, p. 287.)

Corby Castle, 2d August, 1839.

Dear Sir,

I fear that Mr Tierney will not receive from the transcripts in the *State Paper Office*, as to the times of James I and Charles I, anything like what may be gathered in your three volumes, they

---

[1] Henry Howard (1757-1842), the eldest son of Philip Howard of Corby, was an English Catholic of wide culture and of the staunchest loyalties to both Church and State. After early studies at Douai with the English Benedictines and at the University of Paris, he entered the Theresian Military Academy at Vienna, being baulked by his religion from all chance of promotion in the British Army. Brilliant success at Vienna and again at Strassburg still brought him no encouragement from the British Government, despite his offer to go as a volunteer to America. He therefore continued his educational studies, returning in 1784 to Corby, where he soon manifested a strong interest in English and European politics, joining the society of *Friends of the People* for parliamentary reform. The Penal Laws still forced him to refuse the offer of a seat in Parliament, but their partial relaxation in 1795 enabled him to obtain a captaincy in the York Militia. As a result, when the Napoleonic Invasion theatened seven years later, he raised the Edenside Rangers and later organized the Cumberland Rangers.

All this time Howard was engaged in literary pursuits, while his interest in politics increased. His views on the Oath of Allegiance demanded of Catholics were elicited by an article in *The Times* of Nov. 20, 1827. As *The Times* ignored his reply, he published it in the *Dublin Review*, vol. II, p. 583.

Playing a leading part in the efforts being made for Catholic Emancipation, Henry Howard, while firm in his Faith, sought by his writings and personal contacts to conciliate his opponents, publishing in 1824-1825 *Remarks on the Erroneous opinions entertained respecting the Catholic Religion*, and in 1827 *Historical References*, a collection of notes on his previous pamphlets : his aim here as elsewhere being always to conciliate as well as to convince.

Howard was highly respected as a country squire of considerable literary

may however serve as vouchers to them.   I am glad you do not want them, as I have only just got through the 1st volume, to which the 2d appears   rather a repetition — I have,   properly, only done with Panzani and Coneò.

It is, from these two Memorials, impossible not [to] commiserate the State of Catholics during those days ; when the dissensions among their own Clergy, and their own opinions on the validity of the ecclesiastical authorities set over them, the uncertainty in which these matters were even left by the Court of Rome, and as to their civil existence ; the different opinions in what related to the oath of allegiance proposed by James I — the result of all of which discrepancies is in my mind, that the Catholic Body, and possibly the Return of the whole Kingdom, to unity with the Head [of] our Church, was in the event sacrificed, to the undue claim of the Popes to depose Princes, and absolve subjects from their allegiance ; being impolitically, uselessly and in my opinion unjustifiably, maintained.

The letters from and to Panzani shew, perspicuously,the untoward state the Catholics of our Country were placed in, as I have said, both as to conscientious fulfillment of their duties in religion, both as to their spiritual superiors, and the exercise of their worship *in foro conscientiae*, and as to what related to the political and civil existence and duties as subjects, whilst they were subjected to the most severe sufferings.

It appears to me from the Documents relating to Panzani's Mission, that had he been continued, and not received the positive prohibition from Rome, even to mention the oath ; and from the opinion he gives of the King's mind, of his ministry, and even of Laud, Montague and other Bishops, and many of the Anglican Clergy, that with prudent management, and on principles now admitted, giving up the dire claim, that it is possible, (I am in-

and scientific attainments, the breadth of whose interests may be measured by the variety and eminence of his friends and correspondents, among whom were Charles X, Louis-Philippe, Henry Bathurst, Bishop of Norwich, Sidney Smith (these last two strong supporters of Catholic claims), Walter Scott, Giuseppe Mezzofanti, Lingard, Sir Cuthbert Sharpe, P. Fraser Tytler, Canon Tierney, Miss Agnes Strickland and Sir Humphrey Davy.

A complete list of Howard's works will be found in GILLOW, *op. cit.*, s. v. *Henry Howard of Corby.*

clined to think probable) that the Union might have been brought about.

Panzani gives a most interesting account, in the last part of his Dispatches, of the Private Character, moral conduct and feeling [of] both King and Queen and their Court, and of the disposition of the Governing Powers of the Country, to favour the accomplishment of his wishes.

The subsequent legation of Conn, gives to me the impression that the King's mind, proved by his conferences with Conn and others, shewed a disposition on his part to become a Catholic, and support an union with the Holy See : but which the Pope, the Cardinal and Conn, put down entirely by their persevering in all ways, to maintain the *Deposing Power*.

You see the workings of the Kings mind on the subject, till it is entirely scotched (?) and become alienated, and that the same effect is produced on his ministers and Government and on the leaders of the clergy who coincided in his views. — He frequently tells Conn that he will repent of the obstinate resistance which is made to his obtaining the entire, and in his mind requisite allegiance of His subjects, and then only, when so pushed he decides on the Proclamation, declaring that he remains fixed to the Church of England Dogmas and Establishment. — It is inferred that Hamilton's Reports from Rome, (which I suppose may be in the State Paper Office) must have, from the manner his negociations were treated at Rome, contributed to bring the King's mind to this adverse opinion and conduct towards the Catholics, in the Report of February 7, 1639, — the measures of Paul V were even hinted at to Hamilton. Conn in my mind should have been sent away long before he went— the King shewd great and persevering patience with him. —Rome it is clear supported all who held the deposing doctrine, and would not agree to any thing like prohibiting their works — whilst it condemned Preston,the Benedictines and the clergy who took the other side. —But it is remarkable that in the meeting of Cardinals the Sacred College held on English Affairs, as reported by Barberini (March 1637) that though the[y] cavill'd at some words of the oath, merely *recommending* omission, they did not touch on, or object to the main article, as *declaring* against the power of Deposition etc. — The King had, I doubt not, conceived from History, from the conduct of Paul V and Pius to Elizabeth, Clement VIII to his father, and the principles so obstinately persisted in by Urban IV (*sic*), Barberini and Con bent his mind that it was requisite that the Oath of fidelity should be formal and comprehensive for the Catholics ; without which, if he adopted the Catholic Religion or attempted the Union, he must positively submit himself and his Kingdom to the deposing power, and to this his mind revolting, he gave up all thoughts to the communion. When driven [to] further straits, during Rossetti's time, both he and all who sided with him, though they might make another shew to get money, had become more inimical to Catholics, whom they cons[idered a]s subjects, unsettled as to the principle of civil allegiance. [1]

I remain Dear Sir I fear after illegible statement done in haste

Very truly yours,

H. Howard.

---

[1] The rest of the letter refers to transcripts from the State Paper Office, but of another period.

INDEX OF NAMES AND PLACES

signs promise of relief for
Catholics 63; keeps promises
to Catholics 76; early quarrels
with Henrietta 79 seq.; forced
by Parliament to measures
against Catholics 79; resents
interference of French 81; ex-
pells French 85; dissolves
Parliament and is reconciled
to Henrietta 104; conversion
discussed in Rome 105 n. 4;
refuses Catholic baptism for the
Prince 107; allows his wife a
bishop 108; kind to Catholics
112; desire to help his sister
126; supports Douglas's plea for
a Cardinal 128; asks purely
civil allegiance in Oath - feels
strongly thereon 146; warns
Papal Agent 149; agrees to
exchange of agents, hopes to
influence the Pope 155 seq.;
friendship with Papal Agent
159; intervenes for Catholics
164 seq.; deplores Reformation
173; on Confession 174; reunion rather than polemics 187;
prefers Pope to Puritans 190;
sensitive to romanizing because of gossip 198 seq.;
grants composition of fines 217;
annoyed at indiscretion of Catholics 225; mitigates Proclamation 226; warns agent 227-
228; interest in theological
discussion 232 seq.; his memories of Catholic Spain 233;
disputes Trent 234; insists he
is Catholic 235 seq.; criticizes
fables in Saints' lives 236;
and Clement VIII 237; wants
Powder Plot condemned 238;
knows the Fathers 239; on
cultus to Fr Garnet 340; criticizes Catholic Kings 241; thinks
Jesuits pernicious 243; saves
Jesuit from execution 244 seq.;

fear of sharing Elizabeth's fate
247; eager for compromise on
Oath 254 seq.; discusses Oath
261 seq.; cannot stomach all
Rome's teaching 262; dread of
deposition 263; friendship with
Papal Agent 232 seq.; devout
to Our Lady 234; appeals to
Early Church 239; anti-Jesuit
prejudice 243, 268; and Pursuivants 244; anti-Richelieu
247; fears excommunication
and deposition 263, 274; a
satisfied Anglican XII, 248;
drafts new Oath 265, 417;
fears change of policy in Popes
267 seq.; complains of Jesuits
268; agrees to change his
Oath 269 seq.; tells of Leander's Oath 273; thinks Confessors should reveal plots 274;
blames Con's intransigence
276-282; blames Jesuits for
Rome's opposition to Oath
280; re-discusses Oath question
284; pushes Army Oath 286;
favours Con for Red Hat 290;
disillusioned 292; agrees to
letter of recommendation 294;
anxious for promotion 301, 305;
mistrusts Rome 302; rebukes
Holland 304; annoyed with
Hamilton 306, 309; welcomes
Rossetti 316; favours his cousin
Ludovic and opposes Walter
Montagu for the purple 321 seq.;
accused of being Papist 323,
389; expedition against Scotland 334; takes on himself
relief of Catholics and priests
339, 343 n. 1; solicitous for
Papal Agent 347, 350; and
Goodman Case 349; stand
against Parliament 355; signs
Strafford's death-warrant 356;
suffers for Catholics 361; conversion urged 361, 362 seq.,

IMPRIMATUR

de mandato

Lovanii, die 25ª martii 1935

† P. Ladeuze, *Rect. Univ.*